*The Paraguayan War*

# THE Paraguayan War

CAUSES AND EARLY CONDUCT

2ND EDITION

Thomas L. Whigham

UNIVERSITY OF CALGARY Press

© 2002, 2018 Thomas L. Whigham
First edition 2002
Second edition 2018

University of Calgary Press
2500 University Drive NW
Calgary, Alberta
Canada T2N 1N4
press.ucalgary.ca

This book is available as an ebook which is licensed under a Creative Commons license. The publisher should be contacted for any commercial use which falls outside the terms of that license.

Library and Archives Canada Cataloguing in Publication

Whigham, Thomas, 1955-, author
    The Paraguayan War : causes and early conduct / Thomas L. Whigham. — 2nd edition.

Previously published: Lincoln, Neb. : University of Nebraska Press, 2002.
Includes bibliographical references and index.
Issued in print and electronic formats.
ISBN 978-1-55238-996-6 (softcover).—ISBN 978-1-55238-994-2 (open access PDF).—ISBN 978-1-55238-995-9 (PDF)

    1. Paraguayan War, 1865-1870. I. Title.

F2687.W54 2018               989.2'05              C2018-901554-3
                                                   C2018-901555-1

The University of Calgary Press acknowledges the support of the Government of Alberta through the Alberta Media Fund for our publications. We acknowledge the financial support of the Government of Canada. We acknowledge the financial support of the Canada Council for the Arts for our publishing program.

  Canada Council for the Arts  Conseil des Arts du Canada

Copyediting of second edition introduction by Ryan Perks
Cover image: Detail from *Crossing of the Arroyo San Joaquin* by Candido López (Museó Historicó Nacional, Buenos Aires)
Page design and typesetting of second edition introduction and cover design by Melina Cusano

For Ilse Hanning,
who opened the door
for a little boy

# Preface to the 2018 Edition

When the first edition of this work appeared with the University of Nebraska Press in 2002, it was safe to assume that the 1864–1870 Paraguayan (or Triple Alliance) War was little known outside of Paraguay, and in that country it tended to be treated as the stuff of legend rather than as a key subject for scholarly research and debate. A few historians in Europe, South America, and the United States had touched on the war in the course of their studies, but they were mostly working in isolation from each other. More than a few had given up hope that the topic would ever get the attention that it deserved. They observed that a full and synthetic treatment of the Paraguayan War required research in archives and libraries in a half-dozen countries, and none had the energy, the time, or the resources to undertake such an investigation. I had already been thinking of making a stab at providing just such a synthesis, but I, too, was under no illusion that the full story would be easy to understand or analyze. Any effort to do this would require many years of work, probably upwards of a decade.

Little did I know at the time that many other scholars had either started their own exciting research on the war or were soon to be pulled into its vortex. As many have pointed out, such investigations can assume the proportions of an obsession, for the Paraguayan War tells so much about society, conflict, and identity in South America and yet keeps begging more questions. Indeed, the torrent of new studies that have appeared since 2002 has, I think, confirmed my initial thesis that the Paraguayan War was a catalyst to change historical patterns and politics in the southern continent in an unmistakable way. This made it broadly appealing to scholars and readers. All that really remained was to get the books published and the debates rolling.

When Paraguayan president Francisco Solano López seized the Brazilian steamer *Marqués de Olinda* in November 1864, few could have foreseen the devastating conflict that he had unleashed. Little more than five years later, President López, along with most of his fellow Paraguayans, and tens of thousands of Brazilian, Argentine, and Uruguayan soldiers, was dead. Many others had been evacuated from the battlefields and now lay broken and maimed in military hospitals from Asunción to Buenos Aires, Montevideo, and beyond. Paraguay's civilian population had shrunk to less than half of its prewar total and the country's economy had largely ceased to function. In Brazil, the army gained a measure of political clout that it had never previously enjoyed and which it did not fail to use in future years, often against the emperor whose honor the soldiers had so vigorously defended in Paraguay. The Brazilian Empire's inability to win a quick victory sharply revealed the monarchical regime's many weaknesses. In Argentina, the national government used the conflict to settle its domestic political agenda by crushing its provincial rivals, setting up a pattern of economic development that favored the great landowners of Buenos Aires, and assuring that future struggles in the region would likely center on questions of class rather than provincial disputes. In sum, the Triple Alliance War was a crucible that permanently changed political parameters in South America.

All the scholars who have worked on the war since 2002 argued for its centrality and wished to see it accorded a more prominent place in the historiography of nations and society. Their concern was in part political. The war's sesquicentennial was due to begin in 2014 and various governments in South America were allocating funds to commemorate the struggle. Grade-school textbooks in each country attested to the war's importance, but few scholarly works had been written in recent years, so government ministers in charge of cultural matters were actively searching for new faces and new work to sponsor. Many of the younger scholars eventually put in an appearance as talking heads in television documentaries.[1] And a great many more took the opportunity to reacquaint themselves with the classic works and make the effort, finally, to talk with each other about what the war meant.

Not surprisingly, major academic conferences were now regularly being held to address this new scholarship; many people were excited about future possibilities. Several conferences held outside South America actually got the ball rolling. As early as 2001, a panel at the Society for Military History's Calgary conference was devoted to research on the Paraguayan War.[2] Then, in 2005, a three-day conference was held at the École des Hautes Études de Sciences Sociales in Paris under the name "Le Paraguay a l'Ombre de ses Guerres." Finally, in 2008, a series of major conferences was inaugurated at the University of Montevideo with the convocation of the Jornadas Internacionales de la Historia del Paraguay, which has met in the city biennially ever since. Although the *jornadas* cover a wider scope of Paraguayan history than just the 1864–1870 conflict, they clearly offer a venue for an international audience to discuss the war. A number of the scholars who had participated in the Calgary and Paris conferences attended the Montevideo *jornadas* and saw their contributions published in conference proceedings.[3]

The Jornadas Internacionales de la Historia del Paraguay were not the only academic conferences that were held during these years. A major conference touching on various aspects of the war was also held at Argentina's Museo Histórico Nacional in 2008.[4] The armed forces of the Platine countries and Brazil, which have their own historical institutes, have also held meetings focusing on the scholarship of the war. A good example of this latter sort of organization is the Encuentro Internacional de Historia of the Uruguayan Army, which regularly addresses the "Operaciones Bélicas de la Guerra de la Triple Alianza."[5] There have also been regional academic conferences, often hosted by state universities in both the Argentine Northeast and Brazil, that deal extensively or partially with the war. There are other examples, but the main point is that what was once a relatively limited scholarly endeavor has grown dramatically in scope and ambition.

The conversations that have unfolded at these conferences have been generally healthy, though in some quarters they inspired a reaction that confirmed, rather than challenged, the old dichotomies that had defined the analysis of the war. One might have thought that the traditional Lopista versus anti-Lopista interpretations would have already spent themselves by the 1970s.[6] The adherents of both camps proved surprisingly resilient, however, and relatively immune to the new scholarship, much of which they refused to read. The Lopistas gained some ground through the internet, which, as everyone knows, has given a venue to some good work but has also highlighted some of the most ahistorical approaches.

Revisionists of both the Left and the Right also got a curious new lease on life in 2012, when the Paraguayan legislature abruptly passed an impeachment measure to depose Fernando Lugo, the country's populist left-wing president. Though this action was, strictly speaking, legal, it brought the immediate condemnation of the governments of Uruguay, Brazil, and Argentina, which moved to enact provisions within the MERCOSUR agreement to diplomatically isolate Paraguay. The reaction to this censure in Paraguay was entirely predictable—even left-wing activists denounced the neighboring countries as a new Triple Alliance engaged in an undeclared war against Paraguay reminiscent of what the country faced in the 1860s. As one newspaper put it, the "malignant spirit of the Alliance has been reincarnated among those who govern the neighboring countries."[7]

Although the formal actions of the three countries (along, it should be noted, with Chavez's Venezuela) were of short duration and had a limited effect in a Paraguay that was experiencing an economic boom, the reference to the Triple Alliance certainly stirred historical memories among people who saw themselves as perennial victims. Rightly or wrongly, it offered them a new chance to grapple with the legacies of the 1860s. And those readers of Paraguayan national newspapers who stretched their imaginations far enough even found in Venezuela's unmistakable machinations a useful—or insidious—analogue to the "Perfidious Albion" of the 1864–1870 struggle.

Outside critics who normally would never have found much to endorse in a Colorado-dominated Paraguay were made nervous by these references to the Triple Alliance War, and those commentators on the right who dissented from their countries' policies vis-à-vis Paraguay began in 2012 to find a reason to praise the ghost of Francisco Solano López. Politicians throughout South America who perceived little need to back up their arguments with rational historical proof nonetheless gave the green light to scholars to start afresh their more serious investigations. All of this gave far greater immediacy to the Triple Alliance struggle as a subject for research.

The reaction to Lugo's 2012 impeachment made evident something that should have been clear from much earlier: the war really had sunk deep roots not only among the Paraguayans, but also among Brazilians, Argentines, and Uruguayans who felt a common sense of guilt in their appraisal of regional imperialism. Anthropological research on collective memory in rural Paraguay has revealed the war's continued pull in the countryside.[8] And in the cities, where television, radio, and print media play an active role in shaping public perceptions, rarely a day goes by without some explicit reference to the war and what it might mean for today's world.

So many books and scholarly articles on the Triple Alliance War have appeared since 2002 that I hesitate to mention more than a few of the more interesting works and themes. When I first started researching the conflict in the early 1990s, for example, I was told by more than one South American historian that photographs and images of the war were so rare as to not be worth searching for. Now, I can happily report that

*The Paraguayan War*

more than a few volumes of images have been published that reproduce a substantial corpus of the war's photographic and lithographic record.[9] Similarly, the publication of hitherto little-known or difficult-to-access primary sources has made possible new insights into the war's effects on society. These elements are only now being explored, but the prospect of unexpected discoveries is very solid indeed.[10] The themes that Hendrik Kraay and I sought to address in our 2005 compilation, *I Die with My Country*—notably the war's social impact and its relation to race, gender, and nationalism—continues to attract attention from Latin Americanists. The "war and society" approach pioneered by military historians has also sown some exciting crops and, in the case of the Paraguayan War, the harvest promises to be plentiful. The concomitant effect on how military historians and social scientists conduct their work in South America has likewise been noteworthy.[11]

Several broad overviews of the war have appeared in recent years. One was Chris Leuchars's *To the Bitter End*, which appeared early in 2002. Though it focused narrowly on the military dynamics of the war, and did so using only secondary materials, it offered some of the most suggestive insights in this area since the publication of General Augusto Tasso Fragoso's opus in 1957.[12] Four other studies appeared afterwards, all building upon previous military and diplomatic histories (most notably the Spanish edition of Francisco Doratioto's landmark study, *Maldita Guerra*, which was first published in Portuguese in 2002).[13]

The problem these authors faced is that they required extensive research in archives in many countries and a solid understanding, if not a mastery, of at least four different historiographical traditions (not counting the many variants of revisionism). Even in an age of internet communication and competent inter-library loan services, this represented no small challenge for the scholar. And yet there has been significant progress. Luc Capdevila's *Une guerre totale* provides a fascinating "archaeology" of the war, one based on extensive archival research and a thorough analysis of French consular records. Marco Fano's *Il Rombo del Cannone Liberale* does something similar (and with a similar enthusiasm) with the Italian documentation, covering the war battle by battle and providing an analytic model that finds inspiration in broader Platine themes. Published by Santillana-Taurus in Paraguay, my own three-volume *La guerra de la Triple Alianza* attempted to provide a balanced analysis with attention given to all four countries. Ana Squinelo's two-volume *150 Anos Depois*, a focused compilation of articles, principally by Brazilian authors, has stimulated comment for its handling of a variety of topics connected with the war. Finally, another compilation, this one entitled *Uma Tragédia Americana*, and edited by Fernando da Silva Rodrigues and Fernando Velozo Gomes Pedrosa, appeared in 2015 and, in general, can boast the same strengths and weaknesses as that published by Squinelo.[14]

It may be somewhat early to judge the impact of these recent studies of the war and the various congresses and scholarly conferences called to discuss the conflict, but no one can doubt that the old times of very limited production are over. There certainly has been no dearth of works on more specific topics touching on the Triple Alliance conflict. Brazilian scholars, for instance, have developed an interesting subfield examining recruitment for the war effort, the principal way in which the conflict stretched its tendrils deep into Brazilian society. Literally dozens of studies trace the economic, political, and social impact of wartime demands for manpower in the empire's far-flung provinces; all underscore the severe social tensions and limited state capacity that wartime recruitment threw into sharp relief.[15]

We have also seen published several traditional biographies of figures who were instrumental in shaping the history of their respective countries and who initially gained fame on the battlefields of Paraguay.[16] The role of women, both on the home front and in support of the armies in the field, has increasingly been recognized.[17] So has the role of journalists during the conflict, on the Allied side, where we see efforts both in support and in opposition to the war effort, as well as on the Paraguayan side, where journalism served to inflame a Guaraní-language nationalism.[18] The elaborate victory celebrations in

Brazil, amply covered in the press, have also drawn some attention from historians who are opening a cultural history of the war.[19] And there are also a few new contributions to add to the already ample corpus of work on the diplomatic history of the war.[20]

The literature on the war's Spanish-speaking belligerents has expanded in many different directions over the last decade. While there is still circulating a variety of shoddy polemical work that fails to meet the standards of rigorous scholarship (such works also appear in Brazil), some excellent publications have recently appeared. These include works on little-known aspects of military organization and analyses of atrocities.[21] Resistance to the Allied war was particularly noteworthy in Entre Ríos, Corrientes, and the provinces of western Argentina, and that theme also continues to inspire attention from scholars.[22] There is even an unusual article that examines the war's effects on the establishment and operation of psychology as a discipline and profession in South America.[23] Clearly, these are halcyon times for the study of the Triple Alliance War, with the new work laying the foundation for future syntheses of the conflict and its multiple impacts on the countries and societies torn by the many years of fighting.

It has been a rewarding business for me to see this transformation in the scholarly literature and to feel that my hunches about the war's significance have been confirmed in the quantity and quality of new works coming to the fore. This year, with the publication of *The Road to Armageddon: Paraguay Versus the Triple Alliance, 1866–1870*,[24] I finally bring my major studies of the Paraguayan conflict to a conclusion. It has indeed been a long road, and perhaps it is in order here to explain why it has taken so long and to emphasize once again how much of a debt I owe to other people. I finished much of the research and writing for my study of the last four years of the war back in 2013, when there was considerable pressure for me to bring out a second volume with Nebraska to complete the story. But since the appearance of the first volume, the editors who had promoted its publication had moved on, and their replacements at Nebraska were less interested in a second volume, which they thought a risky venture in economically tight times in the United States.

Since it was irrational to suppose that another American academic press would publish a second volume when it did not have the first in hand, I endeavored to reconfigure the materials for 1866–1870 in a new and separate study that did not necessarily rely on that first volume. This work, which benefited from much of the new scholarship listed above, also had a difficult time finding a home. One press, reflecting a short-sightedness that was typical of that moment, insisted that I cut another two hundred and fifty pages of text, and when I responded that this would ruin the content and turn the book into just another summary treatment, the press cut me loose. It was a low moment for me, knowing in my gut how important this subject was yet not being able to convince anyone to publish my "big book"—and this in spite of the ongoing praise that it had engendered from its readers. It was an upsetting business, feeling that in my own country I was talking to flat-earthers.

But as it turns out, I was no Sisyphus pushing an impossibly heavy stone up an embankment. I kept looking, and then, eureka! I found the University of Calgary Press. I cannot express with sufficient energy the gratitude I feel for the serious treatment that people at the press gave me throughout the process of getting *The Road to Armageddon* into print. They never insisted that I take a chainsaw to my text. Instead, they offered helpful suggestions and support at every juncture. They learned to appreciate the war in much the same way I had. They also put me together with a talented copy editor, with whom I had many fruitful discussions about elegant writing and how standards can be maintained when people no longer seem to know the difference between "who" and "whom." Above all, the staff at Calgary has been flexible, and this has made all the difference for me. One proof of that flexibility is seen here in their willingness to reissue the earlier volume that had previously appeared with Nebraska (whose staff also deserves my thanks for having facilitated the reversion of rights to me). Now, with both books being given as broad an audience as possible thanks to the University of

Calgary Press, I look forward to an even greater expression of interest on the part of the English-language world in a topic that has defined my career. I still say that the Paraguayan War was a catalytic phenomenon that made possible myriad changes in South America. It has also been catalytic for me, personally. For all of the feelings of sadness and tragedy that it summons up, it has helped me see people in a new light, as survivors, and as creative participants in their own destiny.

Thomas Whigham<br>
Watkinsville, Georgia<br>
November 2017

## Notes to Preface

1   I have participated in the production of two such television documentaries, *Guerra do Paraguai. A Guerra esquecida*, directed by Denis Wright (Raccord & Baderna Producções, 2005) and *A Ultima Guerra do Prata*, directed by Alan Arrais (TV Escola, 2014). Other similar films have been produced, including *Cándido López y los campos de batalla*, directed by José Luis García (Aizenberg Producciones, 2005); *Eliza Lynch, Queen of Paraguay*, directed by Alan Gilsenan (Coco Television, 2013); and *Guerra do Paraguai—A Nossa Grande Guerra* (History Channel-Latin America, 2015).

2   The participants in the Calgary panel agreed to pool their efforts in the subsequent release of a published compilation of their work. See Hendrik Kraay and Thomas L. Whigham, eds., *I Die with My Country. Perspectives on the Paraguayan War, 1864–1870* (Lincoln: University of Nebraska Press, 2004). An updated edition of this work has only recently been published in Spanish as *Muero con mi Patria. Guerra, Estado y sociedad. Paraguay y la Triple Alianza* (Asunción: Tiempo de Historia, 2017).

3   See Juan Manuel Casal and Thomas L. Whigham, eds., *Paraguay: El nacionalismo y la guerra: Actas de las Primeras Jornadas Internacionales de Historia del Paraguay en la Universidad de Montevideo* (Asunción: Servilibro y Universidad de Montevideo, 2009); Casal and Whigham, eds., *Paraguay en la historia, la literatura, y la memoria: Actas de las II Jornadas Internacionales de Historia del Paraguay en la Universidad de Montevideo* (Asunción: Tiempo de Historia y Universidad de Montevideo, 2011); Casal and Whigham, eds. *Paraguay: Investigaciones de historia social y política. III Jornadas Internacionales de Historia del Paraguay en la Universidad de Montevideo* (Asunción: Tiempo de Historia, 2013); Casal and Whigham, eds. *Paraguay. Investigaciones de historia social y política. II: Estudios en homenaje de Jerry W. Cooney* (Asunción: Tiempo de Historia, 2016).

4   "La Guerra del Paraguay: Historiografía, representaciones, contextos," whose proceedings appeared in *Nuevo Mundo/Mundos Nuevos* in 2009, http://nuevomundo.revues.org.

5   See https://www.estudioshistoricos-en.edu.uy/ixencuentroguerratriplealianza.html.

6   Revisionists of the extreme right and left (who have far more in common with each other than the empiricists they tend to condemn) continue to churn out studies and polemics that repeat the "populist" interpretations of the war's causes and conduct. The only real difference with the earlier works is that the newcomers find it harder to distinguish between assertions and facts and display little interest in documentary evidence. See, for instance, Luis Agüero Wagner, *La guerra del Paraguay (análisis breve de la historia real)* (Asunción: Editorial F17, 2006); Felipe E. Bengoechea Rolón, *Humaitá. Estampas de epopeya* (Asunción: Don Bosco, 2008); Leonardo Costagnino, *La Triple Alianza contra los países del Plata* (Buenos Aires: Gazeta Federal, 2011); and Daniel Pelúas and Enrique Piqué, *Crónicas. Guerra de la Triple Alianza y el genocidio paraguayo* (Montevideo: Arca Editorial, 2017).

7   "Ñe'émbeweb," *ABC Color* (Asunción), 13 July 2013.

8   Capucine Boidin, "Pour une anthropologie et une histoire regressive de la Guerra de la Triple Alliance (2000–1870)," *Diálogos* 10, no. 1 (2006): 65–87; and, more broadly, see Boidin, *Guerre et métissage au Paraguay, 2001–1767* (Rennes: Presses Universitaires de Rennes, 2011).

9   Ricardo Salles, *Guerra do Paraguai: Memórias e imagens* (Rio de Janeiro: Edições Biblioteca Nacional, 2003); Pedro Paulo Soares, "A Guerra da Imagem: Iconografia da Guerra do Paraguai na Imprensa Ilustrada Fluminense" (master's thesis, Universidade Federal do Rio de Janeiro, 2003); Miguel Ángel Cuarterolo, "Images of War. Photographers and Sketch Artists of the Triple Alliance Conflict," in Kraay and Whigham, eds., *I Die with My Country*, 154–178; Mercedes Vigil y Raúl Vallarino, *La triple alianza: La guerra contra el Paraguay en imágenes* (Montevideo: Planeta, 2007); Augusto Roa Bastos, *Memorias de la guerra del Paraguay: La transmigración de Cándido López, frente a frente, el sonámbulo* (Asunción: Servilibro, 2009); Antonio María Boero y Ramiro Antonio Boero Ruiz, *La guerra del Paraguay: La historia a través de la imágen* (Rivera, UY: Museo sin Fronteras, 2005); José Ignacio Garmendia y Miguel Angel de Marco, *José Ignacio Garmendia: Crónica en imágenes de la guerra del Paraguay* (Buenos Aires: Fundación Universitaria Católica Argentina, 2005); Alberto del Pino Menck, *La guerra del Paraguay en fotografías* (Montevideo: Biblioteca Nacional, 2008); and Javier Yubi, *La Guerra grande: Imágenes de una epopeya* (Asunción: El Lector, 2010).

10  For examples, see Joaquim Cavalcanti d'Albuquerque Bello, "Diário do Tenente-Coronel Albuquerque Bello: Notas extraídas do caderno de lembranças do autor sobre sua passagem na Guerra do Paraguai," *Documentos Históricos* 112 (2011); Thomas Whigham and Juan Manuel Casal, *La diplomacia estadounidense durante la Guerra de la Triple Alianza: Escritos escogidos de Charles Ames Washburn sobre el Paraguay, 1861–1871* (Asunción: Servilibro, 2008); Whigham and Casal, "El ministro Washburn habla del caudillismo rioplatense," *Estudios Paraguayos* 34, no. 1 (Dec. 2016): 139–151; Agustín Angel Olmedo, *Guerra del Paraguay: Cuadernos de campaña* (Buenos Aires:

Academia Nacional de la Historia, 2008); Thomas Whigham and Ricardo Scavone Yegros, eds., *José Falcón, Escritos históricos* (Asunción: Servilibro, 2006); Marco Fano, *El Cónsul, la guerra y la muerte* (Rome, 2011); Guilherme de Andréa Frota, ed., *Diário Pessoal do Almirante Visconde de Inhaúma durante a Guerra da Tríplice Aliança (Dezembro 1866 a Janeiro de 1869)* (Rio de Janeiro: IHGB, 2008); Carlos Heyn Schupp, ed., *Escritos del Padre Fidel Maíz, I. Autobiografía y cartas* (Asunción: Unión Académique Internationale y Academia Paraguaya de la Historia, 2010); Dardo Ramírez Braschi, "Registros y apuntes de Tomás Mazzanti sobre la guerra contra el Paraguay (1865)," *Anales de la Junta de Historia de Corrientes* 8 (2006); and Renato Lemos, "Benjamin Constant: the 'Truth' behind the Paraguayan War," in Kraay and Whigham, eds., *I Die with My Country*, 81–104.

11  For examples, see Pedro Santoni, ed., *Daily Lives of Civilians in Wartime Latin America: From the Wars of Independence to the Central American Civil Wars* (Westport, CT: Greenwood, 2008); Celso Castro, Vitor Izecksohn, and Hendrik Kraay, eds., *Nova história militar brasileira* (Rio de Janeiro: Editora FGV and Editora Bom Texto, 2004); Nicola Foote and René D. Harder Horst, eds., *Military Struggle and Identity Formation in Latin America: Race, Nation, and Community during the Liberal Period* (Gainesville: University Press of Florida, 2010); Jerry W. Cooney, "Economy and Manpower. Paraguay at War, 1864–1869," in Kraay and Whigham, eds., *I Die with My Country*, 23–43; Matthew M. Barton, "The Military's Bread and Butter: Food Production in Minas Gerais, Brazil, during the Paraguayan War" (paper presented at the Latin American Labor History Conference, Duke University, Durham, NC, 1 April 2011).

12  Chris Leuchars, *To the Bitter End: Paraguay and the War of the Triple Alliance* (Westport, CT: Greenwood, 2002). Augusto Tasso Fragoso's five-volume *História da Guerra entre a Tríplice Aliança e o Paraguay* (Rio de Janeiro: Biblioteca do Exército, 1957) still has much to teach us today. See also Thomas L. Whigham, "La guerre détruit, la guerre construit. Essai sur le developpement du nationalisme en Amérique du Sud," in *Les guerres du Paraguay aux XIXe et XXe siècles*, ed. Nicolas Richard et al. (Paris: CoLibris, 2007), 23–32.

13  Francisco Doratioto, *Maldita Guerra: Nueva historia de la Guerra del Paraguay* (Buenos Aires: Emecé, 2004).

14  Luc Capdevila, *Une guerre totale: Paraguay 1864–1870, Essai d'histoire du temps présent* (Rennes: Presses Universitaires de Rennes, 2007); Marco Fano, *Il Rombo del Cannone Liberale*, vol. 1, *Il Paraguay prima della guerra* and vol. 2, *La guerra del Paraguay (1864–1870)* (Rome, 2008); Thomas L. Whigham, *La guerra de la Triple Alianza*, 3 vols. (Asunción: Santillana Taurus, 2010–2012); Ana Paula Squinelo, *150 Anos Depois. A Guerra do Paraguai: Entreolhos do Brasil, Paraguai, Argentina, e Uruguai* (Campo Grande, BR: UFMS, 2016); and Fernando da Silva Rodrigues and Fernando Velozo Gomes Pedrosa, *Uma tragedia Americana. A Guerra do Paraguai sob novos olhares* (Curitiba, BR: Ed. Prismas, 2015).

15  For a few examples, see Vitor Izecksohn, "Recrutamento militar no Rio de Janeiro durante a Guerra do Paraguai," in Castro, Izekcsohn, and Kraay, eds., *Nova história militar brasileira*, 179–208; Miquéias Mugge and Adriano Comissoli, eds., *Homens e*

*armas: Recrutamento militar no Brasil, século XIX* (São Leopoldo: Oikos, 2011); Johny Santana de Araújo, *"Um grande dever nos chama": A arregimentação de voluntários para a Guerra do Paraguai no Maranhão, 1865-1866* (Imperatriz, BR: Ética, 2008); Vitor Izecksohn and Peter M. Beattie, "The Brazilian Home Front during the War of the Triple Alliance, 1864-1870," in Santoni, ed., *Daily Lives*, 124-145. For an Argentine interpretation of similar themes, see Miguel Ángel de Marco, *La guerra del Paraguay* (Buenos Aires: Planeta, 2003).

16  See Alfredo Boccia Romañach, "El caso de Rafaela López y el Bachiller Pedra," *Revista de la Sociedad Científica del Paraguay* 7, no. 12-13 (2002): 89-96; Catalo Bogado Bordón, *Natalicio de María Talavera. Primer poeta y escritor paraguayo* (Asunción: Casa de la Poesía, 2003); Siân Rees, *The Shadows of Elisa Lynch. How a Nineteenth-century Irish Courtesan Became the Most Powerful Woman in Paraguay* (London: Review, 2003); Lilia Moritz Schwarcz and John Gledson, *The Emperor's Beard: Dom Pedro II and his Tropical Monarchy in Brazil* (New York: Hill and Wang, 2004); Miguel Ángel de Marco, *Bartolomé Mitre* (Buenos Aires: Emecé, 2004); Liliana Brezzo, "Tan sincero y leal amigo, tan ilustre benefactor, tan noble y desinteresado escritor: los mecanismos de exaltación de Juan Bautista Alberdi en Paraguay, 1889-1910" (paper presented at the XXVII Encuentro de Geohistoria Regional, Asunción, 17 August 2007); José Murilo de Carvalho, *D. Pedro II* (São Paulo: Companhia das Letras, 2007); James Schofield Saeger, *Francisco Solano López and the Ruination of Paraguay. Honor and Egocentrism* (Lanham, MD: Rowman & Littlefield, 2007); Adriana Barreto de Souza, *Duque de Caxias. O Homen por Tras do Monumento* (Rio de Janeiro: Civilização Brasileira, 2008); Francisco Doratioto, *O General Osório. A Espada Liberal do Império* (São Paulo: Companhia das Letras, 2008); Kerck Kelsey, *Remarkable Americans. The Washburn Family* (Gardiner, ME: Tilbury House, 2008); Michael Lillis and Ronan Fanning, *The Lives of Eliza Lynch. Scandal and Courage* (Dublin: Gill & Macmillan, 2009); Alberto del Pino Menck, "Armas y letras: León de Palleja y su contribución a la historiografía nacional" (master's thesis, Universidad Católica del Uruguay, 1998; revised version read before the Segundas Jornadas Internacionales de Historia del Paraguay, Universidad de Montevideo, 15 June 2010); and John H. Tuohy, *Biographical Sketches from the Paraguayan War, 1864-1870* (Charleston, SC: Createspace, 2011).

17  Maria Teresa Garritano Dourado, *Mulheres comuns, senhoras respeitáveis: A presença feminina na Guerra do Paraguai* (Campo Grande, BR: Editora UFMS, 2005); Hilda Agnes Hübner Flores, *Mulheres na Guerra do Paraguai* (Porto Alegre, BR: EDIPUCRS, 2010); Barbara Potthast, "Protagonists, Victims, and Heroes: Paraguayan Women in the 'Great War,'" in Kraay and Whigham, eds., *I Die with My Country*, 48-52; Potthast, "Algo más que heroínas: Varias roles y memorias de la guerra de la Triple Alianza," *Diálogos* 10, no. 1 (2006): 89-104; Eduardo Rial Seijo y Miguel Fernando González Azcoaga, *Las cautivas correntinas de la guerra del Paraguay, 1865-1869* (Corrientes, AR: Editorial Amerindia, 2007); and Ana Maria Colling, "Os silencios da Guerra do Paraguai—a invisibilidade do feminino," in Squinelo, ed., *150 Anos Após*, 233-250.

18  Aníbal Orué Pozzo, *Periodismo en Paraguay. Estudios e interpretaciones* (Asunción: Arandurā Editorial, 2007); María José Navajas, "Polémicas y conflictos en torno a la

guerra del Paraguay: los discursos de la prensa en Tucumán, Argentina (1864–1869)" (paper presented at V Encuentro Anual del CEL, Buenos Aires, 5 November 2008); Hérib Caballero Campos y Cayetano Ferreira Segovia, "El periodismo de guerra en el Paraguay," *Nuevo Mundo/Mundos Nuevos* (2006), http://nuevomundo.revues.org/; Michael Kenneth Huner, "Cantando la república: La movilización escrita del lenguaje popular en las trincheras del Paraguay, 1867–1868," *Páginas de Guarda* (Spring 2007): 115–134; María Lucrecia Johansson, "Paraguay contra el monstruo anti-republicano: El discurso periodístico paraguayo durante la Guerra de la Triple Alianza (1864–1870)," *Revista Historia Crítica* 47 (2012): 71–92; Johansson, *Soldados de Papel. La propaganda en la prensa paraguaya durante la Guerra de la Triple Alianza (1864–1870)* (Cádiz, ES: Ayuntamiento de Cádiz, 2014); Thomas Whigham, "Building the Nation While Destroying the Land: Paraguayan Journalism during the Triple Alliance War, 1864–1870," *Jahrbuch für Geschichte Lateinamerikas* 49 (2012): 157–180; Wolf Lustig, "¿El guaraní lengua de guerreros? La 'raza guaraní' y el avañe'e en el discurso bélico-nacionalista del Paraguay," in Richard et al., eds., *Les guerres du Paraguay*, 525–540; Alicia G. Rubio, "El teatro y la guerra del Paraguay: ¿Forjando la identidad nacional?" *Nuevo Mundo/Mundos Nuevos* (2009), http://nuevomundo.revues.org; Liliana Brezzo, " 'Reparar la nación': Discursos históricos y responsabilidades nacionales en Paraguay," *Historia Mexicana* 60, no. 1 (2010): 197–242; Luc Capdevila, "El macizo de la guerra de la Triple Alianza como substrato de la identidad paraguaya," *Nuevo Mundo/Mundos Nuevos* (2009), http://nuevomundo.revues.org; Capdevila, "O gênero da nação nas gravuras. *Cabichuí e El Centinela*, 1867–1868," *ArtCultura* 9, no. 14 (2007): 55–69; Victoria Baratta, "La guerra de la Triple Alianza y las representaciones de la nación argentina: un análisis del periódico *La América* (1866)," in *Memoria del Segundo Encuentro Internacional de Historia sobre las Operaciones Bélicas durante la Guerra de la Triple Alianza* (Asunción: Ñeembucú, 2010), 13–30; Ticio Escobar, "L'art de la guerre. Les dessins de presse pendent la Guerra Guasú," in Richard et al., eds., *Les guerres du Paraguay*, 509–523; and Ignacio Telesca, "Paraguay en el centenario: La creación de la nación mestiza," *Historia Mexicana* 60, no. 1 (2010): 137–195.

19   Marcelo Santos Rodrigues, "Guerra do Paraguai: Os caminhos da memória entre a comemoração e o esquecimento" (Ph.D. diss., Universidade de São Paulo, 2009); Wiebke Ipsen, "*Patrícias*, Patriarchy, and Popular Demobilization: Gender and Elite Hegemony at the End of the Paraguayan War," *Hispanic American Historical Review* 92, no. 2 (2012): 303–330; Hendrik Kraay, *Days of National Festivity in Rio de Janeiro, Brazil, 1823–1889* (Stanford: Stanford University Press, 2013), 240–69.

20   See Cristóbal Aljovín, "Observaciones peruanas en torno a la guerra de la Triple Alianza" (paper presented at V Encuentro Anual del CEL, Buenos Aires, 5 November 2008); Fernando Cajías, "Bolivia y la guerra de la Triple Alianza" (paper presented at V Encuentro Anual del CEL, Buenos Aires, 5 November 2008); Francisco Doratioto, "La política del Imperio del Brasil en relación al Paraguay, 1864–72," in Richard et al., eds., *Les guerres du Paraguay aux XIXe et XXe Siècles*, 33–48; Ori Preuss, *Bridging the Island. Brazilians' Views of Spanish America and Themselves, 1865–1912* (Madrid: Vervuert, 2011); and Thomas L. Whigham, "Silva Paranhos e as Origens dum Paraguai Pos-Lopes (1869)," *Revista Diálogos* (Universidade Estadual de Maringá) 19, no. 3 (2015):

1085–1119 (English version: "Silva Paranhos and the Construction of a Post-Lopista Paraguay," *Tesserae. Journal of Iberian and Latin American Studies* 21, no. 3 [2015]: 221–241).

21  Ricardo Pavetti, "La ocupación de Mato Grosso através de fuentes paraguayas," *Diálogos* 9, no. 2 (mayo 2005): 11–35; Dante Aníbal Giorgio, "Yatay, la primera sangre: El primer hecho de armas de importancia en la guerra de la Triple Alianza," *Todo es Historia* 445 (ago. 2004): 48–60; Fernando Cesaretti and Florencia Pagni, "El frente olvidado de la guerra del Paraguay: Mato Grosso, el problema limitrofe brasileño-paraguayo," *Todo es Historia* 481 (ago. 2007): 6–22; Orlando de Miranda Filho, "Depois da queda: a provincia de Mato Grosso após a derrocada do forte de Coimbra durante a Guerra do Paraguai (1864–1868)," in Squinelo, ed., *150 Anos Após*, 2: 203–222; Nidia R. Areces, "Terror y violencia durante la guerra del Paraguay: 'La massacre de 1869' y las familias de Concepción," *Revista Paraguaya de Sociología* 41, nos. 119–121 (2004): 379–404; Juan Manuel Casal, "Uruguay and the Paraguayan War: The Military Dimension," in Kraay and Whigham, eds., *I Die with My Country*, 119–139; Thomas L. Whigham, "Aspectos claves de la larga resistencia paraguaya: disciplina militar, cohesión burocrática y la egomanía indomada del Mariscal López," in *A 150 años de la Guerra de la Triple Alianza contra el Paraguay*, ed. Juan Carlos Garavaglia and Raúl Fradkin (Buenos Aires: Prometeo Libros, 2017), 11–52; Whigham, "Brazil's 'Balloon Corps': Pride, Desperation, and the Limits of Military Intelligence in the Triple Alliance War," *Luso-Brazilian Review* 52, no. 2 (2015): 1–18; and Whigham, "Comentario sobre la guerra del Paraguay en la provincia de Corrientes. Impactos politicos, daños, y consecuencias en la población civil," *Universidad Nacional de Nordeste. Revista de la Facultad de Derecho y Ciencias Sociales y Políticas* 9, no. 16 (2015): 237–242.

22  Pablo Buchbinder, "Estado, caudillismo y organización miliciana en la provincia de Corrientes en el siglo XIX: el caso de Nicanor Cáceres," *Revista de Historia de América* (Instituto Panamericano de Geografía e Historia, Costa Rica) 136 (2005): 37–64; Buchbinder, "Gente decente y 'paysanos' contra la guerra: Dimensiones de la resistencia a la Triple Alianza en la provincia de Corrientes," *Iberoamericana* 47 (2012): 29–48; Dardo Ramírez Braschi, *La guerra de la Triple Alianza a través de los periódicos correntinos (1865-1870)* (Corrientes, AR: Moglia, 2004); Ramírez Braschi with José Luis Caño Ortigosa,"La influencia de la presencia militar brasileña en Corrientes durante la guerra de la Triple Alianza," *Anuario de Estudios Americanos* 70, 1 (ene.-jun. 2013): 249–271; Ramírez Braschi, "Daños y saqueos durante la Guerra de la Triple Alianza. El poblado de Bella Vista ante la ocupación paraguaya de 1865,"

*Folia Histórica del Nordeste* 21 (2013); Braschi, "Corrientes ante la invasión paraguaya de 1865," *Revista de Historia Militar* 3 (2014): 97–123; Braschi, *La guerra del Paraguay en la provincia de Corrientes. Impactos politicos, daños y consecuencia en la población civil* (Corrientes, AR: Moglia, 2014); Braschi, *Política correntina en tiempos de guerra 1865-1870* (Corrientes, AR: Moglia, 2016).

23  José E. García, "La guerra contra la Triple Alianza y su efecto retardario para la psicología paraguaya," *Procesos Históricos* 11, no. 21 (ene.-jun. 2012): 26–75.

24  Calgary: University of Calgary Press, 2017.

# Contents

| | |
|---|---|
| *List of Illustrations* | ix |
| *List of Maps* | ix |
| *Acknowledgments* | xi |
| *Introduction* | xiii |

PART I: THE DAWN OF NATIONHOOD
- 1. Environment and Society — 3
- 2. The Rise of Politics — 21
- 3. War and Nation Building — 48

PART II: UNEASY NEIGHBORS
- 4. Paraguay Faces the Empire — 77
- 5. The Misiones and Chaco Disputes — 93
- 6. The Uruguayan Imbroglio — 118

PART III: THE WAR BEGINS
- 7. Military Preparedness — 165
- 8. The Mato Grosso Campaign — 192
- 9. Neutrality Tested — 217

PART IV: THE PARAGUAYAN OFFENSIVE
- 10. Corrientes under the Gun — 257
- 11. The Battle of the Riachuelo — 308
- 12. The March into Rio Grande — 328

PART V: THE TIDE TURNS

    13. Missteps in the South     351
    14. The Siege of Uruguaiana     374
    15. Retreat to Paso de la Patria     391

Conclusion: The End of the Beginning     416

    *Notes*     423
    *Index*     505

ILLUSTRATIONS

*following page 254*

1. José Gaspar de Francia
2. Carlos Antonio López
3. Emperor Dom Pedro II
4. Justo José de Urquiza
5. Bartolomé Mitre
6. Venancio Flores
7. Marshal Francisco Solano López
8. Eliza Lynch
9. Joaquim Marques Lisboa, baron of Tamandaré
10. Charles Ames Washburn
11. Paraguayan army assembled at Asunción
12. Fort at Nova Coimbra
13. Battle of the Riachuelo
14. Adm. Francisco Manoel Barroso
15. Battle of Yataí
16. Argentine encampment near Uruguaiana
17. Lt. Col. Antonio Estigarribia
18. Allies land at Corrientes

MAPS

| | | |
|---|---|---|
| 1. | South America, circa 1850 | 26 |
| 2. | Disputes with Brazil | 79 |
| 3. | Chaco and Misiones Disputes | 99 |
| 4. | The Banda Oriental, 1864–65 | 133 |
| 5. | The Mato Grosso Campaign, 1864–65 | 195 |
| 6. | The Corrientes Campaign, 1865 | 263 |
| 7. | Battle of the Riachuelo, 11 June 1865 | 310 |
| 8. | The Advance into Rio Grande | 331 |
| 9. | Battle of Yataí, 17 August 1865 | 368 |

# Acknowledgments

The inclination to give heavy weight to individual scholarship is well known in academic circles. The truth, of course, is that anyone embarking on a major study accumulates many scholarly and personal debts. My case is no different. I can hardly begin to thank all those friends and colleagues who have given me their encouragement and advice since I began this project some years ago. Most of what is good in the following volume comes as a direct result of their help.

Research in South America and the United States was made possible by grants from the Fulbright-Hays Program, the American Philosophical Society, and the University of Georgia Faculty Research Program.

I am grateful to the directors and staffs of various archives and libraries, including Asunción's Archivo Nacional, Biblioteca Nacional, Centro Paraguayo de Estudios Sociológicos, and Museo Histórico Militar; the Archivo General de la Nación (Buenos Aires), Archivo del Banco de la Provincia de Buenos Aires, Museo Mitre, Archivo General de la Provincia (Corrientes), Instituto de Investigaciones Geo-históricas (Resistencia), Archivo Histórico y Administrativo de Entre Ríos (Paraná); Instituto Histórico y Geográfico Brasileiro (Rio de Janeiro), Biblioteca Nacional (Rio), Biblioteca e Arquivo do Exército (Rio), Serviço Documental Geral da Marinha (Rio), Arquivo Histórico do Rio Grande do Sul (Pôrto Alegre); Biblioteca Nacional (Montevideo); Oliveira Lima Library (Washington), Nettie Lee Benson Library (University of Texas at Austin),

Spencer Library (University of Kansas), and Tomás Rivera Library (University of California, Riverside).

Scholars in several countries lent me critical counsel. Canadians Roderick J. Barman, Robert Wilcox, Stephen Bell, and Hendrik Kraay were especially helpful, as were Brazilians Heraldo Makrakis, Eliane Pérez, and Eduardo Italo Pesce. Uruguayans Alicia Barán, Luis Rodolfo González Rissotto, and particularly Juan Manuel Casal alerted me to some unusual sources and corrected some errors and weaknesses in the manuscript. I received other useful criticisms and advice from Argentines Tulio Halperín Donghi, Ariel de la Fuente, Dardo Ramírez Braschi, Alberto Rivera, and Miguel Agustín Medrano. And I owe an equal debt to Paraguayans Milda Rivarola and Arnaldo Fernández, Germans Wolf Lustig and Barbara Potthast, and Russian Moises Al'perovich.

In the United States, I benefited from the valuable suggestions of Richard Graham, Carol Reardon, William McFeely, Erick Langer, Peter Hoffer, Amber Smock, John Chasteen, Jeffrey Needell, Bryce Jaeck, and Shawn Lay. Theodore Webb, Billie Gammon, and Joseph Howell shared some fascinating documents with me. My greatest appreciation of all goes to Tom Davies, J. T. LaSaine Jr., Loren "Pat" Patterson, and Jerry W. Cooney, each of whom contributed immeasurably to the realization of this project.

Finally, I am grateful to my family and to many friends whose personal support was so very important to me during difficult times. My wife, Marta, had to tolerate a crotchety husband and an avalanche of dusty papers coming at her and our two sons from seemingly every direction. The following study is, as much as anything, a tribute to their patience and love.

# Introduction

Axioms about the nature of war are as old as war itself. Thucydides said that men go to war out of fear, interest, or honor. Centuries later, Carl von Clausewitz argued that war is politics expressed through other means. And William Tecumseh Sherman succinctly and memorably noted that war is "all hell." None had Paraguay in mind, but the lessons of Syracuse, Austerlitz, and Kennesaw Mountain were also applicable to that South American republic and its neighbors between 1864 and 1870. War can breathe new life into moribund political systems. It can push humble figures into positions of prominence. It can redefine nations. But it also kills comprehensively, often cutting down the innocent with the culpable and leaving devastation in its wake. The Paraguayan War, in all these ways, was no different than all the conflicts that preceded it.

Yet the Paraguayan (or Triple Alliance) War was unlike anything that had been seen in that part of the world. It presented a striking blend of the modern and the antique, with ironclad warships and observation balloons sharing the stage with battalions of barefoot soldiers carrying bamboo lances.

The war also had wide-ranging political effects; it made possible the final consolidation of Argentina into a single nation-state and opened a new chapter in the struggle between the Blanco and Colorado Parties in Uruguay. It cast the military into the forefront of Brazilian politics, a trend that ultimately led to the overthrow of the empire. And it crushed

Paraguay, wrecking its economy and social institutions, and causing its population of 450,000 to shrink by nearly 70 percent.

The Paraguayan War bears the same relation to the history of South America that the American Civil War does to that of North America. Yet despite the centrality of the war in the experience of four countries, relatively few scholars have examined it. This is due in part to difficulties in the documentation, which is found dispersed in a score of different archives, libraries, and private collections in nearly as many countries. Consulting even a portion of this material constitutes such a formidable task that most scholars have limited their investigations to secondary accounts.

Another problem facing researchers concerns the heated polemics that erupted during the war and continued for at least a generation thereafter. Political agendas and philosophical inflexibility clouded the issues, and few attempts were made to understand what actually occurred. No interpretation has been wholly satisfactory, and this has led to many fruitless arguments about initial causes and motivations. Meanwhile, scholars have attempted little real analysis of the war itself. In offering this first of two volumes on the topic, I hope to relate a complicated tale as clearly and as thoroughly as possible.

I believe that the best explanation of the war's origins and progress lies within a narrow realm of politics. Specifically, the war can be traced to political ambitions and how those ambitions expressed themselves in the construction of new nations. The dictionary defines "nation" as a community of people comprising one or more nationalities with its own territory and government. The average inhabitant of the southern continent, however, had a myriad of daily problems to overcome and therefore little interest in any "nation" that he could not see with his own eyes. He had minimal regard for other "citizens" he neither knew nor understood. What could they do for him in practical terms? If they had different customs, a different language, and a different view of the world, then how could they be part of *his* polity?

Paraguay was the only "nation" or "near-nation" in the region, based as it was on narrow traditions of paternalism and community solidarity within a unique cultural environment. This environment was, in some ways, more Indian than Spanish in character. It provided Paraguayans with their own language, Guaraní, and with an identity that seemed broadly "national" even during the colonial era. Perhaps Chile had a measure of such national sentiment during the same period, but neither Argentina nor Brazil could claim anything like it.

"Argentina" was essentially a city—Buenos Aires—with a typically urban political culture and a modernizing "liberal" elite that sought to project its image of the nation on a backward and recalcitrant countryside. The people of the countryside (or *campo*) had little love for the *porteños*, as the inhabitants of Buenos Aires were called, and certainly no interest in living in their shadow. For the country people *(provincianos)* to accept a united Argentina under *porteño* rule, they needed to conceive of themselves as "Argentines" rather than Riojanos, Entrerrianos, or Salteños. They had no historical preparation for this perspective, just as Venetians and Bavarians found it difficult to think of themselves as Italians and Germans. Unlike the people of Paraguay, the Argentines had to have their national identity created for them. This was a most uneven process, for if the provinces rejected any aspect of that depiction, then the *porteños* were bound to force it upon them.

Brazil was a huge country with complex social divisions. In cultural terms, the north and northeastern regions were very different from the cities of Rio de Janeiro and São Paulo and from the broad plains of Rio Grande do Sul. True, the Portuguese language and a shared corpus of Old World traditions knitted Brazil together after a fashion. Certain regions drew far more upon these traditions than others, however, and one important social group—African slaves—adapted to the cultural milieu only through coercion. As for language, the Carioca, Paulista, Gaúcho, and Sertanejo variants of Portuguese, though mutually intelligible, differed substantially in vocabulary and accent. Above all, the provinces of the new Brazilian Empire suffered from their isolation, a circumstance that was as crushing as it was unavoidable.

What Brazil lacked in social unity it partly made up through the tenacity of its ruling elites in their dedication to the institutions of slavery and the Bragança monarchy. The Brazilian "nation" reflected elite interests. These elites were great merchants, bureaucrats, ranchers, and planters—well-placed persons who married among themselves. Many had earned legal or medical degrees at European universities. They dressed alike and had the same habits. They shared jokes and profundities with each other in Latin, a practice that helped define them as a group by setting them apart from other Brazilians (the majority of clerics not excluded).

The elites considered politics their natural preserve. At the same time, though, they acknowledged an exalted position for the emperor. They left it to him to protect the masses, whom they thought incapable of self-government and unworthy of much attention in any case. The Brazil that the elites wished to create explicitly conflated the role of monarch and nation, the better to defend their traditional privileges while moving the country forward economically. They argued that the monarch prevented social breakdown, while the nominal republicanism of the Spanish American states yielded nothing but strife. The emperor ought to be at the center of any modern political system, they maintained, for he symbolized all that was civilized, all that the country should aspire to.

Each of the countries that participated in the Paraguayan War offered its own solution to the challenges of independence. Paraguayan leadership was outwardly more persuasive in convincing the population to accept its definition of "nation." This was partly a matter of scale. Paraguay was a small country, easier to control, and possessed of a strong sense of community. Yet both Argentine and Brazilian elites felt certain of their own interpretations of nationhood. Which model was to be more sustainable, that of a small nation with clearly defined politics and culture or that of a large nation with imported or artificial politics and civic culture? This question was not framed as a simple matter of ideas and words but of actions. And these actions tended to be bloody.

The struggle over the specifics of nationhood was obvious in the case of Uruguay, the fourth country involved in the Paraguayan War. The Banda Oriental, as it was commonly called, had seen great competition between the Spaniards and Portuguese during the colonial period. Even after independence was gained, foreign intervention and partisan struggle between Colorados and Blancos kept Uruguay in near chaos through the mid-1860s. Under such circumstances, its people could not decide which national path to choose. Therein lay their tragedy and that of the region as a whole.

The clashes that erupted between the partisans of these various approaches ranged from simplistic efforts to sway the opinions of the poor to intermittent confrontations over disputed territories and access to rivers. These inevitably led to full-scale conflict that involved hundreds of thousands of people. The Paraguayan War was the bloodiest and most profound result of a process that spanned generations.

Four interlocking historical patterns are discernible throughout. First, borders—national and otherwise—were unstable, even when treaties carefully defined them. Second, economic rationale impelled violent encounters across these frontiers, as efforts to control resources and trade routes outweighed respect for formal sovereignty. Third, politics were confused and divisive, with the writ of central authority extending only tentatively into the interior. Finally, and ironically, the feature that did hold people together was a martial tradition of some antiquity. People accustomed to fighting little wars were ready to fight a great one. When it came, it was terrible.

The Paraguayan War was a conflict of common men—farmers, ranch hands, shoemakers, peddlers, and many others—men who came together, spent many sleepless nights, celebrated, starved, drank themselves into stupors, grieved, and suffered every imaginable tribulation. To such men, the war had nothing to do with the construction of a more-perfect human community. They would flinch at the suggestion that their efforts fit some Whiggish model of events. After all, it was their blood that covered the fields of Paraguay, their lives that would never be the same. To them, the war was not political but personal, horrible evidence of the price that some men pay for other men's dreams.

*The Paraguayan War*

# I

# The Dawn of Nationhood

# Environment and Society

## 1

The Paraguayan War had many causes. Some were particular to the 1860s, whereas others date back to the late colonial and early independence periods when certain political parameters first began to take shape. And some of the causes of the war, and especially the reasons for its ferocity and duration, can be understood only by delving far back into the Platine past and taking the measure of people as they adapted to a radically changing environment.

Thousands of years ago, when human beings first wandered into the southern reaches of South America, their needs were of the most immediate sort. Simple survival concerned them most. In this they had some luck, for nature had filled the waterways of the Platine interior with many species of fish. Likewise, the forests and plains held all manner of game, from the rabbitlike *vizcacha* to the tree sloth to the ever-present and ever-argumentative howler monkey. Little effort was needed, moreover, to dig out the many grubs and edible plants the soil provided. The weather was usually balmy, though in the inland zones hot, sticky summers and short, bone-chilling winters were not uncommon.

In most respects, the region furnished its earliest inhabitants with the necessities of life, leaving them free to pursue ritual, the decorative arts, and war making, which they practiced with a razor-sharp keenness. Whether they fought for glory, vengeance, or access to the best hunting grounds, these early peoples always fought hard. They built no cities or roadways. They left no pyramids or temples for their descendants to contemplate and admire. But they did forge a martial spirit and a tradition of physical courage that resurrected itself in myriad ways over the centuries.

*The Geographic Dimension*

The Paraná-Paraguay river system dominates this part of South America, running southward in a long arc across a broad grassy plain before emptying into the Río de la Plata and the sea. It draws the bulk of its flow from the eastern portion of its basin. In the northeast, its course is fed by hundreds of streams with their common origin in the Brazilian highlands of Minas Gerais. This makes for decidedly soggy terrain downriver.

The Paraná in its upper reaches is so turbulent that even steam-powered craft hugged its banks to avoid the full force of the current. At its abrupt westward bend near Posadas, the river is wide and relatively deep but changes its character again near the rapids *(salto)* of Apipé. There the Paraná briefly shoals to as little as seven feet at low water. Some miles to the west it joins with the Paraguay and then deepens and widens once again, spreading out over a mile from bank to bank. Here the Paraná is strewn with islands and sandbanks, offering a poor channel for navigation except where the more dangerous obstacles are dredged away. In general, the left bank of the river does not lend itself to the construction of ports; though long stretches are high and well-defined — such as at Corrientes — intermittent marshes prevent contact between the main river channel and the loftier ground to the east. The right bank, for its part, is regularly inundated as far south as Santa Fe. Settlements on that side of the river could be erected only at some distance from the waterway.

The Paraguay River, which flows into the Paraná from the north, is one shade darker than ginger, looking like the milk-laced yerba mate tea as it is drunk in Buenos Aires. The river flows through the sandstone plateau of northern Mato Grosso onto a plain so flat that water regularly overflows both banks. Below Asunción, immense, mazelike marshes typify the region to the east of the river, some reaching as far as sixty miles inland. Only one deep-channeled tributary, the Río Tebicuary, provides passage through these swamps.

The Paraná and Paraguay Rivers combine to set the annual rhythm of the Platine system. High waters rising on the Paraná in January and February reach Santa Fe by early April. The Paraguay gains its maximum height at Asunción in May. Its flood reaches the Paraná later that month, prolonging the annual high-water period. During the rainy season from November to January, the flood of the Paraná joins with that of the Paraguay to produce remarkably high waters to the south.

To the southeast of the Paraná lies the greenish Uruguay, which is narrower and less swift for most of its course than either the Paraguay or Paraná. The latter is a great river at all times, while the Uruguay is subject to frequent and remarkable fluctuations, sometimes sinking to a small fraction of its usual flow. The only similarity between the Uruguay and the Paraná is that the course of each is broken by a fall barrier. While on the Paraná the shoals of Apipé interfered little with the settlement of adjacent regions in Paraguay and Argentina, the succession of cascades at Mbutuí and Santa Rosa on the Uruguay created an insurmountable problem for navigation except in the rainy season. As a result, the upper reaches of the latter river remained little known or settled until relatively late in the colonial period.

Though the rivers are the most salient geographical features of the Platine region, its denizens were normally land-bound folk (the exceptions being the Payaguá Indians of the Upper Paraguay, who dwelled on floating "islands" of vegetation). In the south, early peoples built their camps near streams in the Pampa grasslands, where they could hunt rheas, armadillos, and later cattle. Only an occasional *ombú* tree interrupted this ocean of high grass, which extended a thousand miles from the foothills of the Andes to the Banda Oriental. A predilection for openness and an unwillingness to submit to any order other than that imposed by nature characterized the people who passed their lives on this vast plain.

Farther north, forests dominated the scene all the way to the swampy

Pantanal of Mato Grosso. Stands of flowering lapacho, urundey, and other hardwood trees were found in the forests interspersed with rivulets, deep lagoons, and mile after mile of creeping lianas. Holly bushes wound their way up the sides of rolling hills in the Cordillera of central Paraguay and the Sierra de Mbaracayú of the extreme northeast. Only rarely were clearings visible through the heavy foliage, but these open spaces revealed a soil striking in the redness of its clay or the whiteness of its sand. The effect was of a primeval wilderness, of a Nature that overwhelmed as much as it embraced. Amid such a baroque superabundance of plant and animal life, man seemed very small indeed.

### The Human Element

When the Spaniards arrived in the Plata in the early 1500s, they found bands of nomadic Indians, every single group of which appeared disposed to resist their incursion. This region offered little to the newcomers, who sought gold and silver as well as a settled Indian society upon which they could impose a colonial order.

Far up the Paraguay the Spaniards finally found the Guaraní, a semisedentary people, the southernmost representatives of Tupí-Guaranian-speaking Indians who populated the interior of the continent as far north as Venezuela. Each Guaraní community was composed of several mutually supporting patrilineal clans that could be quickly summoned into battle. Men and women played gender-specific roles in the organization of this warrior society. Women did most of the daily labor that kept the group alive. They wove vegetable fibers into clothing and hammocks and used digging sticks to cultivate multicolored squash, which the Guaraní ate with Indian corn and manioc root. They also brewed a powerful beer from wild honey mixed with the mashed pods of the sweet *algoroba* bush. And it was the women who tended to the needs of the very young, the very old, and often the very sick.

For men, the first priority was the shaming of enemies in battle. Yet they also provided fish and meat, which were as important for the spiritual power they conveyed as for nutritional value. Hunting was a serious and often dangerous undertaking. It required great endurance, for hunters had to spend hours in search of game, exposed to a sweltering sun, a thorny undergrowth, and swarms of biting insects. That men sometimes failed to return from such excursions increased the prestige of those who did. Men fashioned canoes from fallen logs and built thatched longhouses (malocas) that served as dwellings for up to sixty people each. The men also kept alive the history of the community as storytellers, diviners, and interpreters of dreams.

The Spaniards were primarily concerned with the military capabilities of the Guaraní. The latter was a large group, with perhaps as many as one hundred thousand individuals clustered within sixty miles of what in 1537 became Asunción, the "Mother of Cities." As the Spaniards discovered in some initial clashes, the Guaraní were formidable fighters with spear, hardwood cudgel, or bow and arrow. Taking advantage of cover, advancing stealthily on their enemies, they loosed their arrows at the last possible moment and would then rush in with their clubs to kill all but the younger women and children.

The Indians had developed a keen sense of organization for defense. Ulrich Schmidl, a Bavarian soldier of fortune who accompanied the Spaniards during their early exploration of the area, praised the Guaraní defensive preparations, especially the high wooden palisades that surrounded their communities near Asunción: "at a distance of fifteen feet from the town wall [of Lambaré, the Indians] dug pits as deep as the height of three men, one over the other, and placed into them . . . lances of hardwood, with points like that of a needle; they covered these pits with straw and small gravel, strewing a little earth and grass between, such that when we Christians pursued them, or assaulted their town, we should have fallen blindly into these pitfalls."[1] Unlike their descendants during the Paraguayan War, who rarely prepared adequate escape routes, the Guaraní cut paths through the brambles to allow withdrawal when faced with overwhelming odds. With numbers, prowess, and a knowledge of the terrain, they were the kind of allies the Spaniards appreciated.

Both groups had to contend with many enemies. Across the river in the Gran Chaco were thousands of Guaicurú marauders, whom the Guaraní excoriated as cruel and implacable opponents. No less dangerous were the Mbayá, who inhabited the forests a hundred miles to the north, and the Guayaki, even closer in the eastern hills. The Guaraní, it seemed, lived in a world of enemies and carried the scars of countless campaigns. No matter how well organized and ruthless they were, the Guaraní could never feel secure. They therefore looked to the Spaniards in expectation of a fruitful alliance, the few violent conflicts between them notwithstanding.

The Spaniards also felt pleased with the alliance. That the Guaraní seemed generous and pliant, and the women amiable, were added enticement. The Bay of Asunción, a sheltered bend in the Paraguay, was perfectly placed as a defensive position; it could serve as a base of operations for further explorations upriver and in the Chaco. Without indigenous support, the Spaniards had no hope of maintaining a presence there.

A considerable mythology has grown up around these early stages of Spanish-Guaraní cooperation. Paraguayan nationalist writers maintain that mutual respect and affection characterized the contacts between the people of the Old World and the New. The benefits of the alliance, they argue, overcame all the differences of culture between Spaniards and Indians. The latter saw the new relationship as an extension of their traditional social practices, in which members of the same kin group owed each other reciprocal labor. As each Spaniard took multiple Indian wives, the various Guaraní clans readily accepted as natural the demands for assistance.

Despite this tale of early harmony, conflict between European and Indian erupted on many occasions during the second generation. Neither side fully trusted the other. The worst violence came in the 1550s, when the Spaniards began to apportion grants of Indian labor *(encomienda)* to reward three hundred European colonists. These grants assigned the Guaraní to the colonists as permanent laborers in a system outwardly indistinguishable from slavery.

When the Indians balked, an ugly repression followed. Thousands died. This ruinous state of affairs was exacerbated by a simultaneous measles epidemic. In the end, the Spaniards quelled the revolts with the help of those Guaraní who accepted the new colonial arrangement.[2] The old alliance between Indian and European thus disappeared. In its place grew a new social order in which Spaniards led and Indians followed.

During these years the colony remained fragile. The Guaicurú had no more intention of yielding to the Spaniards than to the Guaraní. To the contrary, they conducted raid after raid against the new settlements, seized many captives, and killed those whom they could not take prisoner.

Paraguay played only a minor part in the European colonization of South America. The Spaniards began their occupation there only after the failure of their settlement at Buenos Aires. By 1580, however, they reestablished the future Argentine capital, having reached the conclusion that the interior rivers offered no access to the silver of Peru. Paraguayan settlements languished in consequence, and this indifference made possible an unusual social evolution.

*The Development of Hispano-Guaraní Society*
Spaniards arrived in the Plata with the get-rich-quick-and-return-home-wealthy attitude that marked their conquest of the West Indies and Mexico. With no intention of remaining in the region, they brought few European women with them. Liaisons with Guaraní women received the broad approval of the Indian leaders (*mburuvichá*), who hoped to forge an alliance necessary to their own future power. The Guaraní and the Spaniards in effect used each other. As a result they created a prodigious group of mestizos who took their fathers' surnames, preserved many of their mothers' customs, and built a different kind of society.

Paraguay's first provincial governor, Domingo Martínez de Irala (1509–56), illustrated the formation of this new society. From the beginning the governor legally recognized his children born of different Indian women. Each child grew up without the social stigma that the offspring of Indian-white pairings faced in other areas of the continent. His sons enjoyed many rights as Spaniards while they continued to speak and think in Guaraní. His daughters did just as well, all marrying *conquistadores*.[3]

This might suggest that Hispano-Guaraní society drew in near-equal parts from Europe and from indigenous Paraguay. Such was not the case. From the Guaraní came an appetite for certain foodstuffs and a preference for the melodic and deeply evocative Guaraní language, which even today dominates the speech of Paraguayans. The Indians also preserved a sensitivity to things supernatural, an appreciation of natural phenomena — winds, waterfalls, boulders that broke the flow of fast-moving streams — and a belief in a profusion of mischievous sprites that dwelt in the shadows behind every tree.

The Spaniards made their own contributions to this new society. They inaugurated an economy based on iron implements, chickens, draft animals, and the plow. They organized an extraprovincial trade in wheat, tobacco, and yerba mate that connected Paraguay with consumers in other areas of South America. They also created bureaucratic structures of governance that quickly transcended the traditional leadership of the *mburuvichá*. Most important, they introduced the Roman Catholic religion, which provided a new direction. The concept of a universal flood, of a Redeemer who would cleanse the people with fire, and of a land without evil *(yby marane'y)* to which all should migrate — these became part of Paraguayan thinking. Such innovations were critical. They gave Paraguayan society a European-oriented core, though it retained durable associations with the indigenous past.[4]

The near absence of new immigrants from Spain over the next two centuries allowed these early trends to consolidate, giving Paraguay the semblance of a timeless place outside history and bereft of progress. Yet the region only appeared static. In reality, it was undergoing almost constant change due to the pressure of Guaicurú raiders. The new Paraguayans — for such they ought now to be called — had to resist a continual external threat. This gave rise to a sense of identity and community.

And there were also new enemies to contend with, the so-called Mamelucos of São Paulo. These self-reliant frontiersmen earned a special place in the history of Brazil, as it was they who opened the South American hinterland, carrying the flag of Portugal thousands of miles from the coast in search of gold and Indian slaves. Rather than Portuguese, they commonly spoke a Tupí-based pidgin called *lingua geral*. The Mamelucos led lives of privation and violence, and there was little permanence in their day-to-day existence, save perhaps in matters of faith. Their religion centered on a simple if irregular adoration of saints with liberal borrowings from African and Indian precepts. Like the Hispano-Guaraní people of Paraguay, the Mamelucos were culturally ambiguous, the chief difference between the two being the much stronger sense of community displayed by the Paraguayans. Both were hard fighters, accustomed to living off the land. And at times, they were inveterate enemies.

*The Influence of the Missionaries*

The imposition of Catholic institutions might have mitigated the animosity between the Mamelucos and the Guaraní, but Christianity affected different peoples in different ways. The less-settled populations of the Pampas and the Gran Chaco actively resisted many of the efforts of the religious orders to convert them.[5] The Guaraní, however, generally welcomed the missionaries as additional allies against the Guaicurú and eventually the Mamelucos. These same priests sometimes protected the Indians against the local Spanish *encomenderos*. Protection came with many strings, however, for the clerics demanded an absolute obedience in temporal matters as well as convincing demonstrations of piety.

The Franciscans, who arrived in the 1560s, and the Jesuits, who came a half century later, were the most influential of the several orders that targeted Paraguay as a missionary field. Both were zealous in bringing the Guaraní under ecclesiastical rule and in teaching them the rudiments of the faith. This they accomplished by adapting their homilies to Indian sensibilities, offering the Indians doctrines that made Christianity seem a logical extension of pre-Columbian beliefs. For instance, they transformed a Guaraní folk hero, Paí Luma, into a cognate of Saint

Thomas. By example as much as by assertion, they converted the Guaraní to a more orderly and regimented life.

The Indians were not accustomed to working under supervision. In previous times, their labor was intermittent, undertaken only when hunger spurred them to hunt, fish, or dig tubers. Producing a surplus had no place in their thinking, and they felt ambivalent about adopting the practice as a way of life. They also resented giving up certain traditional beliefs and customs, which included polygamy, infanticide, and ritual drunkenness.

Despite some doubts on matters of detail, the Guaraní accepted that the world the priests offered had many positive points, not least a regular food supply. As for changes in the social order, the *mburuvichá* found themselves displaced by Indian councils that ruled subject to ecclesiastical consent. The Guaraní often applauded this reordering of duties, for it assured access to both Indian and European counsel. In times of strain, the Jesuit missions and the Franciscan *pueblos* offered the Guaraní a valuable sense of stability. Yet, in the end, the Indians had little choice. Whatever mitigation of their lot that might have occurred, the principle of compulsion always permeated the mission or *pueblo* environment. In this, the clerics were similar to the *encomenderos*.

In other ways, the two were decidedly different. As a matter of policy, the Jesuits sought to prevent contacts between the mission Indians and their European neighbors, whether Spanish or Portuguese. Their strategy placed the Guaraní in a position of strict subservience to the local Jesuit resident, leaving secular officials, the agents of the greater Spanish society, out of the picture. This brought about the level of obedience the Jesuits demanded, but it also guaranteed that when contacts with European outsiders did occur, they were apt to be laden with suspicion.

A series of disastrous Mameluco raids against the Jesuit missions of Guairá in the 1620s illustrates the point. Guairá was located far up the Paranapanema River, close to Portuguese possessions. The viceroy in Lima had never allocated resources to defend this area. This left the Jesuit superior, Antonio Ruiz de Montoya, to organize an evacuation south with some fifteen hundred families. A great many Indians died before the survivors managed to reconstitute themselves into thirty new communities near the great bend of the Paraná.

Subsequently, the Jesuits petitioned the Council of the Indies to permit the Guaraní to bear arms, arguing that Spain ran the risk of losing the entire region to Portugal. The council agreed to this request in 1642, allowing Ruiz de Montoya to establish a militia under the command of Jesuits who were themselves former soldiers. The Guaraní then proceeded to smash several expeditions sent against them from São Paulo. Mameluco depredations quickly declined.

From this point, whenever secular authorities sensed danger from Indian revolts, settler discontent, or invasions by the Portuguese, they fell back on the services of a Guaraní army.[6] For over a century, the principal contact the mission Indians experienced with the outside world was within a military context.

Matters developed differently in the Franciscan *pueblos*. In the densely populated areas around Asunción and the smaller south-central town of Villarrica, the Franciscans and secular priests predominated and neither group upheld the segregationist ideal of the Jesuits. Indians who lived in Franciscan *pueblos* earned income for their communities by working for Spanish-surnamed overlords together with Indians held in *encomienda*. Other *pueblo* Indians served in gangs of loggers and yerba gatherers, often at a great distance from their home communities. The Jesuits denounced such contacts between Europeans and Indians. It was the work, they argued, of self-serving friars who, like the Pharisees of old, cared more for the gold of the temple than for the temple itself.

Certainly some Spaniards moved into Franciscan *pueblos* and lived openly with Indian women. Both practices were illegal. Yet these contacts between Indians and secular society served a social function that was absent among the Jesuits. The central parts of the province, far more than in the Jesuit territories, witnessed a blending of cultures into a recognizable Hispano-Guaraní whole. From this common identity evolved a community distinct from that seen elsewhere in South America.

*Clash — and Collusion — of Empires*

Despite its isolation, colonial Paraguay was an outpost of Spain, a vanguard of Spanish imperial ambitions vis-à-vis Portugal. Likewise, though they were freebooters in search of private gain, the Mamelucos spearheaded Portuguese expansionism. The two European powers had already quarreled over the Banda Oriental far to the south at the mouth of the Plata. And they would quarrel again.

Until the beginning of the eighteenth century, the government in Lisbon had never shown much interest in Brazil. The thrust of Portuguese imperialism had been eastward, toward the commercial entrepôts of India and China. After the Dutch and British entered the East India trade in the late 1600s, however, the Portuguese had trouble competing and began to focus more on trading in the Gulf of Guinea and along the coastline of Angola. They also took another look at their Brazilian possessions.

This new interest swelled with the discovery of gold in Minas Gerais and Mato Grosso. Bringing the mining operations under effective royal administration in the early 1700s proved a serious challenge to the governor-general in Bahia. Where gold was involved, men thought of their own interests first, and the miners, like the Mamelucos before them, had a decidedly independent spirit. In the end, thanks to the clever machinations of colonial bureaucrats (and their willingness to compromise with local mining bosses), royal authority won a major voice in the administration of the Brazilian interior.

Portuguese penetration of southern Mato Grosso in the mid-eighteenth century bred sharper conflicts with Spain. The viceregal authorities in Lima and later Buenos Aires complained that these Lusophone interlopers had no right to set foot in territory reserved for Spanish subjects. The 1494 Treaty of Tordesillas had assigned Portugal only the northeastern "hump" of Brazil. The wanderings of the Mamelucos and other explorers, however, radically expanded de facto Portuguese rule along the Upper Paraná and far up the Amazon, São Francisco, and Guaporé Rivers.

The claim of effective Portuguese occupation was appropriate enough in some places, but not in all. The Spaniards had spent many decades in Paraguay without ever defining the boundaries of their control. When they began to pay attention, they were surprised at the number of restless landowners, opportunistic minor officials, violent Indians, and reticent clerics whose loyalty to Spain was questionable.

In truth, effective rule by either Portugal or Spain was always more tentative than real in the frontier areas of Paraguay and Brazil. In a sense, there were two South Americas present in this same geographic space. One was the South America of Lima, Buenos Aires, and Bahia, where a European administration functioned more or less as designed. The other South America was larger, more amorphous, and held together by connections looser than the bonds of a colonial state.

The 1700s brought the first attempts by European bureaucrats — who epitomized the South America of the cities — to foster a more rational order throughout the continent. Their work in the Platine basin, though piecemeal at first, later became direct and effective. The Spaniards and Portuguese tried several approaches, sometimes pitting their respective colonies against each other in confrontation and just as often achieving a short-term cooperation.

An example of the latter occurred in midcentury, when Spanish and Portuguese joined hands first to weaken, then to smash, the Jesuit "republic" in Paraguay. The Enlightenment officials of Portugal and Bourbon Spain considered the missionary order an impediment to building modern and more profitable regimes in South America. The interests of both empires demanded that the Society of Jesus relinquish its properties and, above all, its authority over so many Indians.

In 1750, Spanish and Portuguese officials met in Madrid and signed a comprehensive agreement based on *uti posseditis*. All Jesuit lands east of the Uruguay River were transferred to Portugal in exchange for the little port of Colonia de Sacramento at the mouth of the Plata. Seven prosperous missions and the cattle lands of several more fell like ripe oranges into the hands of the Jesuits' traditional enemies.

The transfer was difficult. Hundreds of Guaraní Indians fled across the river to the supposed safety of Jesuit territories on the western bank.

Another group stayed behind and, under a brave but foolhardy Indian official named Sepé Tiarajú, initiated an impossible fight. Sepé's struggle lasted three years (1753-56) and only came to an end when a combined Spanish-Portuguese army several thousand strong annihilated the last defenders. Their resistance turned out to be pointless, for although the ceded lands soon returned to nominal Spanish control, the Portuguese had gutted most warehouses and ranches and driven away the livestock.

The Jesuits never regained their previous influence in the Plata. They tried to portray the Guaraní War as an isolated affair, just a matter of hotheaded Indians responding to foreign pressure. This argument failed to convince Bourbon officials, who cited the war as proof of Jesuit intransigence and perfidy. Whether or not the Fathers inspired the war, its ferocity convinced Spanish bureaucrats to finally put the order in its place.

The Portuguese needed no convincing. Under the anticlerical marquis of Pombal, the Lisbon government had already adopted a regalist policy that in 1759 brought the expulsion of the Jesuits from all Portuguese territories. Spain followed suit eight years later. The Jesuit departure proved a momentous event in Paraguay. Local landowners felt vindicated. So did the Spanish government, which enriched itself through confiscation of hundreds of thousands of cattle, other livestock, church ornaments, buildings, and, of course, land.

The social ramifications of the takeover were even more profound, especially for the Guaraní. Though theoretically they continued to enjoy the protection of the Crown, in fact, the Indians suffered terribly at the hands of royal administrators sent to rule over them. These officials usually showed more interest in lining their own pockets than in promoting the welfare of their charges. The system of communal ownership that the Jesuits had introduced in order to assure an equal distribution of harvests now served royal administrators as a tool of exploitation. They opened the missions to outside merchants, who arrived at every community with ready-made clothes, trinkets, and hardware to set before the credulous Indians. The latter were obliged to buy these goods, for their administrators had guaranteed the purchase in exchange for a portion of the profit. This forced purchase of unwanted commodities ensnared the Guaraní in a cruel web of debt.

The mission Indians withstood the pressures of overwork for a time but soon began to drift out of the province, first as individuals and then in small groups. Some went north to join their Hispano-Guaraní cousins in Paraguay. Others went south to join the gauchos of the Banda Oriental and Entre Ríos. As they donned European clothes for the first time, they began perceptibly to leave much of their Indian identity behind. The parallel colonialism of the Jesuits, which was nonmestizo and communitarian in nature, disappeared. The transformation was striking, though it was no greater than that which the Plata as a whole experienced in matters social, administrative, and economic.

*The "Golden Age"*

Paraguay had changed greatly in the nearly two hundred and forty years since Spanish ships first tacked their way up the river to Asunción. A Hispano-Guaraní society now dominated the province. The Jesuit Order had come and gone. And the state — in the guise of the absolute Bourbon monarch and his agents — now expanded its role.

Previously, the economy of Spanish South America centered on the vast silver complex of Potosí, high in the mountains of Upper Peru. This enterprise involved not just the mining and processing of ore but also the transport and supply of miners. Their demand for provisions sustained a large trade between Potosí and neighboring provinces. These contacts grew over time to include not just Lima but also Chile and many parts of the Plata. Paraguay, which was much farther away than the map suggests, sent supplies of yerba mate, tobacco, and mules to the Potosí miners.

This legal commerce generated notable profits for entrepreneurs. These same individuals, however, frequently smuggled silver to entrepôts in the Platine estuary. This contraband greatly vexed Crown officials. Their own programs in the Plata required revenues from silver

*Environment and Society* 17

that were now slipping away. Faced with a growing problem, the government began to authorize private transfers of coin in exchange for goods shipped inland from Montevideo and Buenos Aires.

In light of this new trade—and in order to stave off Portuguese interference—the Crown established the Viceroyalty of La Plata in 1776. The creation of this new administrative unit signaled Spain's recognition of economic potential in a neglected area of the empire and the government's willingness to defend that area against foreign encroachment.

It also signaled the emergence of Buenos Aires as the Plata's chief emporium, the focus of modernization for the entire region (despite the deeper draft of Montevideo's port). Buenos Aires was still backward and isolated—a village surrounded on three sides by an enormous grassland. Even so, the ideals of the European Enlightenment—especially the notion of manifest and inevitable progress—were beginning to be felt there.

Given its location near the mouths of the Paraná and Uruguay Rivers, Buenos Aires seemed destined to control those inland areas that depended on the rivers for trade and communication. Yet only certain royal officials and hide merchants grasped the significance of this fact, and they were hardly typical of most *porteños* who understood the distances involved. At the time, a sailing ship coming from Europe took perhaps three weeks to cross the Atlantic to Buenos Aires. But a caravan coming from Salta took as much as four months to make the overland trip to the viceregal capital. Such vastness was not easily overcome.

The *porteños* were a rather atypical people in South America. The ties of blood and the sense of community that knitted the Paraguayans together were less in evidence in Buenos Aires. Instead, a pervasive mercantile spirit held sway. Most inhabitants were recent arrivals, a diverse group who lived by their wits and perceived little need for social discipline.

But the *porteños* could boast of something both the Paraguayans and the Portuguese lacked—a compact, relatively well-educated elite. Within a decade, this group developed an unmistakable sense of its own future role in the country—and a way to make the land reflect that vision.

The Bourbon administration gave this elite many opportunities to expand its influence in the hinterland. In 1778 the government adopted the policy of *comercio libre* as the linchpin of imperial trade. This was designed to increase revenues for Madrid by expanding the volume of transactions within the empire. *Comercio libre* aided local merchants by opening new ports, streamlining taxation, relaxing the strict licensing system of the past, and allowing unfettered commerce among the different regions of the empire.

The returns from an increased trade were potentially high, so much so that junior partners soon journeyed upriver from Buenos Aires to open branch offices in Santa Fe, Corrientes, and Asunción. Their success opened the way for a wave of Spanish-born immigrants to the northeastern reaches of the viceroyalty. These immigrants, though few in number, were the first into that region in over two centuries. They were a plucky, self-assured lot, convinced that profits could be found in Paraguay like so many nuggets in a streambed.

Though Madrid never gave the province more than passing attention, few in the Plata doubted that it contained untapped wealth. The success of Jesuit commercial enterprises had demonstrated the value of its hides, tobacco, and yerba. The newcomers from overseas provided capital, business acumen, and enthusiasm, all of which had an impact in Asunción. There the merchants received the support of every provincial governor, each of whom was anxious to outshine the others in competence and dedication to change. Together, the merchants and the royal officials transformed the Paraguayan economy.

Change came rapidly. The government declared a monopoly on the production and sale of tobacco. This swept many of the isolated Paraguayan farmers into the cash nexus for the first time. Coin flowed into the province in the late 1700s; though barter was still the most common form of exchange, even menial laborers soon demanded payment in silver.[7]

The arrival of specie made possible other business ventures. Ranches

Environment and Society 19

of considerable size sprang up in the north. Stands of wild yerba bushes (*yerbales*) were discovered and exploited. Flotillas of river craft soon ferried hundreds of yerba gatherers to the north and were supplied thanks to the merchants and their local agents.[8] Towns were founded and older ones rejuvenated to take advantage of the new traffic.[9]

The people of Paraguay had mixed reactions to these changes. The local elite became avid for imported luxuries such as silver cutlery, fine cloth, and perfumes. Most Paraguayans, however, were mistrustful of change. They were suspicious of the merchants as outsiders and resented their taking positions of importance in the Asunción cabildo. An export economy meant yielding authority to these foreign traffickers, men who spoke not a word of Guaraní and who had no sympathy for local concerns. Economic development extended the power of government into realms hitherto private, and it was not clear to Paraguayans that this was a favorable exchange.

This "Golden Age" of plenty in the Upper Plata lasted from the 1780s through around 1816. During this time, the region, like the rest of the continent, benefited from expanded markets. The port of Asunción, for example, registered an export of nearly two million *arrobas* of yerba mate in the decade from 1788 to 1798; the return on these exports alone (not counting tobacco, timber, ready-made furniture, and hides) amounted to some one hundred thousand pesos annually — a figure that would have seemed astounding only a few years earlier.[10]

So it was that Paraguay and other interior areas of South America became fully integrated into the greater colonial economy. It was a late phenomenon much influenced by events overseas. These same events had political ramifications that in years to come brought even more upheaval to the region and its people.

# The Rise of Politics

## 2

In meeting the demands of an open economy, South America's people had to adjust. Though their material well being expanded in the late 1700s, they had to work harder than before and at more specialized tasks. They also had to tolerate outsiders who dressed differently, knew how to read and write, and had curious habits and creeds. How should the native elites adjust to the new economy and, possibly, new politics?

That South Americans of all classes should ponder self-definition was predictable in such circumstances. Yet only the colonial elites could afford to act politically. The people as a whole were loyal to their families, to their villages, and to their provinces but possessed no broader patriotism. Such sentiments had to be created for them — and this the elites were prepared to do.

Hints of just how important these questions would become had been evident in Brazil as early as the late 1780s, when there was vague talk of economic modernization and a more open political order. Similar thoughts found a voice among the elites of Buenos Aires during the next decade. Manuel Belgrano, Mariano Moreno, and Manuel José de Lavardén — leading lights among the liberal physiocrats of the day — spoke for a modern system of trade in which the port city might shape its own destiny. But they had yet to utter the words "independence" or "republic."

These demands for change did not include advocating a more egalitarian social order. South America's elites understood the risks that any change in the colonial relationship might portend. They had witnessed several episodes of democratic exuberance (the Tupac Amaru Rebellion of 1780 and the Bahian Tailor's Conspiracy of 1798). They had no taste for power sharing with the lower classes. Philosophical musings on "liberty, equality, and fraternity" were one thing, concrete actions in league with blacks and Indians quite another.

As so often in the past, events in Europe hastened political change in South America. The French Revolution and the rise of Napoleon Bonaparte threw open the question of sovereignty. Who should rule in Europe: the Crowned Heads through divine right, or men of action who had the will to seize and hold power in accordance with popular wishes?

Napoleon's spectacular military campaigns in Italy and elsewhere during the late 1790s completely upset the normal patterns of politics on the Continent. Spain, which ostensibly maintained a rock-hard legitimist stance, found itself under tremendous pressure to reach a modus vivendi with France. The Spaniards felt similar pressure from Great Britain, which needed more support in the south of Europe than that afforded by the traditional alliance with Portugal. Spain's King Carlos IV wavered, then reluctantly sided with Napoleon.

The wars in Europe and the Atlantic blockade disrupted communications with the New World. In the Plata, commerce suffered a severe downturn. Shipments of mercury to the Potosí mines dropped appreciably, and silver production fell rapidly in consequence. Exports of hides and tallow decreased as well. Meager earnings were soon siphoned off to pay for scarce imports, most of which reached Buenos Aires aboard neutral vessels or through smuggling. Thus, while some local merchants in the viceregal capital made significant profits from contraband, the established monopoly merchants saw their incomes dwindle. The shortage of coin produced some confusion for internal trade; Paraguay, for instance, experienced first a slowdown and then an expansion of exports as quantities of warehoused yerba and tobacco entered the market.

Regular communications with Spain were restored by the Peace of Amiens in 1801. A strict import policy was reasserted for Spain's South American colonies, though not without opposition from Belgrano and other reformers in Buenos Aires. The *porteño* chamber of commerce *(Consulado)*, for example, echoed Lavardén's call for free trade.

The defenders of the old order enjoyed little respite. In 1803 the fragile European peace came to an abrupt end. France, Britain, and then Spain recommenced the war, and in 1805 Admiral Nelson obliterated the principal Franco-Spanish fleet at Trafalgar. The Royal Navy again cut contact between Spain and her colonies, but neutral trading vessels moved in to make up the difference.

The Platine merchants assumed that they could weather the storm as they had the earlier troubles by persuading the viceroy to relax trade regulations. The merchants supposed that they could wait out the conflict by dealing with neutral shippers. However, in late June 1806 a sixteen-hundred-man British expeditionary force landed at Buenos Aires. No one in the Plata (or in London) had thought an invasion possible, yet here were British grenadiers and marines sweeping away the Spanish regulars and sending the viceroy in precipitous flight to Córdoba.

The invaders occupied parts of the estuary for about a year. Despite the welcome that merchants, certain officials, and even the clergy initially afforded them, the British never felt at ease. Whitehall, which had not authorized the initial incursion, showed little sympathy for such an expensive, poorly planned endeavor and resented having to supply reinforcements after Montevideo was seized. In Buenos Aires itself, the British saw victory turn to defeat when local landowners cobbled together an army of eight thousand horsemen. Once organized into units, these irregulars swiftly defeated the invaders, driving many across the river to the Banda Oriental.

The Spanish victory over the British belonged not to the viceroy, nor to the regular colonial militia, but to hastily assembled local cavalry and their commander, Santiago de Liniers. A French-born officer who had served in the Spanish navy, Liniers saw his star rise steadily over the next three years, then suddenly fall. He became viceroy when his disgraced predecessor departed for Europe, and he was widely admired for his benevolence and good humor under difficult circumstances. Yet Liniers had little time to savor the honors attached to the viceregal post, for Buenos Aires had been altered by the brief British occupation. Try as they might, the Spaniards could not put the genie of political dissolution back into the bottle.

During their short stay, the British introduced unprecedented free trade, the effects of which filtered throughout the region. Their presence had made possible a more open discussion of the region's political circumstances and its future. The Spaniards had failed to defend the Plata, as the *porteños* duly and loudly noted. They also emphasized that later military success, when it came, was a product of local, rather than Spanish, efforts.

The period from the British invasions to 1816 seethed with political ferment, and Argentine historians consider it crucial to understanding what happened thereafter. Many decisions taken at the time were actually the result of outside pressure. A few men in elite circles in Buenos Aires knew of intellectual and political trends in Europe and were willing to learn more. Fewer in Paraguay and the riverine provinces (the Litoral) understood these changes and what they meant.

Events in Europe gave an immediacy to political questions. In September 1807, Napoleon invaded Portugal, prompting King João VI and his court to flee to Rio de Janeiro aboard British warships. Six months later, the emperor of the French turned on Spain, forcing the abdication of Carlos IV and the incarceration of his heir, Fernando VII. The Iberian Peninsula then erupted in rebellion. A nominally pro-Fernando junta claiming imperial authority assembled at Cádiz in the wake of the king's detention. Shortly thereafter, a British army under the Duke of Wellington landed to aid the Peninsular forces. Having been at war with Great Britain for eight of the previous twelve years, unoccupied Spain — and the empire — found itself the de facto ally of perfidious Albion.

These changes unfolded with a rapidity that many in the New World found difficult to grasp. Buenos Aires became the scene of intense political agitation. Having crushed the British in the field, the locals had no idea what to do next. Some *porteños* argued for loyalty to Cádiz to improve their position within the empire. Another group sought the establishment of a British protectorate in the Plata to forge links with a commercial empire. Another faction favored an independent monarchy under the Portuguese Princess Carlota, sister of the imprisoned Fernando. Still another faction wanted republican institutions as soon as possible. Only Liniers and — for rather different reasons — the ultraconservatives in the cabildo rejected any fundamental change in the relation with the mother country and its king.

These differences of opinion were not merely the stuff of debating societies. Shoving matches became common in the streets, and few doubted that serious violence might follow. Adding to this tension was the presence of gangs of armed men, many of whom were of gaucho and/or African extraction. No matter that the cultured figures of the city were themselves men in arms, they could not afford to ignore popular sentiment.

To prevent the outbreak of violence, the viceroy agreed to convoke a *cabildo abierto* on 22 May 1810. Although some 450 notables could participate in the meeting by right, only 200 actually did so; the rest stayed home, afraid to face mobs of wandering militiamen. Those who did attend the assembly swiftly established a self-governing regime headed by Manuel Belgrano, Mariano Moreno, and other advocates of free trade. Though formally still linked to Fernando VII, this government acted like an independent entity. Many *porteños* gave themselves over to celebration, secure that their nation — the Argentine nation — was now a reality.[1]

But was it? The *porteños* had no firm political convictions. Most had no sense of what to do next but doggedly argued the pros and cons of every point. It was easy for them to mistake the idea of nationhood for its substance and to project upon Paraguay and the Litoral the city's own exuberant but ultimately insecure vision of the future. In early-nineteenth-century Buenos Aires, "nation" meant the state or the body politic; it had not yet become synonymous with "homeland" *(patria)*, yet

*The Rise of Politics* 25

it was only on the basis of the latter concept that the *porteños* could hope to spread a revolutionary message.

### Early Divisions in the Plata

In setting their political course, the *porteños* considered themselves unassailable. Like French *philosophes*, they believed their politics arose out of pure reason rather than religion or uncontrolled passion. Since their ideas were scientifically grounded, they allowed for no compromise — just as no one would think to argue with the law of gravity. The *porteños* wore this self-assuredness like a badge of honor, though it was more like a yoke. It hindered the development of more imaginative or more sensible politics and prevented any real cooperation with the interior and Litoral.[2]

The *provincianos*, for their part, had good reason to suspect the *porteños*. In their eyes, the port city and its region already had a magnificent approach from the sea, huge herds of cattle and sheep, and the most fertile soil imaginable. That these gifts should be matched by an outsized ambition surprised no one upriver. But why should Buenos Aires be allowed to dictate policy to the *provincianos*? The recent experience of the British invasions, when Paraguayan militiamen took heavy casualties, offered little room for optimism.

Few outside the capital understood the patriotic fervor of 1810. For the average northeasterner, life had less to do with politics than with endless toil. A patch of land sufficient to graze cattle or to raise corn and manioc — this was what was important. Of politics, rural men knew little but village gossip and the simple, often erroneous statements of the local priest.[3] They had heard of the new king (though not of his imprisonment) but felt utterly removed from imperial matters. To the extent that northeasterners had any politics at all, they preferred the slow processes of natural change and opposed any artificial break with the past.

This isolation from European thinking was manifest on many levels. Few *provincianos* had ever seen a map. Most had no idea how their country might look to outsiders or of the relative position of communities within it. Buenos Aires appeared far away. Thus, it was colossal arrogance on the part of the *porteños* to claim to speak for the people of the northeast. Their money brought them influence, but it did not justify their conceit. The king at least enjoyed a traditional legitimacy for which there was religious sanction. But the inhabitants of the city of Buenos Aires only represented themselves.

In retrospect, that there should have been a clash of interests between Buenos Aires and the countryside seems obvious. The opinions described above were typical not just in the Litoral but also in all the provinces. Exceptions did exist, especially among foreign-born merchants. These men had many ties to the growing commercial traffic with Buenos Aires and looked upon the political aspirations of the *porteños* with some tolerance. As word of the May revolution spread inland, however, the merchants lost their security. Trade fluctuated wildly—and so did opportunities to enhance their influence. Everything depended on what Buenos Aires might do next, and since the new government there had just executed the once-popular Liniers, no one could be sure of anything.

Aside from the merchants, there were also landowners, militia officers, and clergymen—*provincianos* all—who wished to retain some links to the port city. In the provinces, politics was multilayered, with many shadings, subtle textures, and interests at work. Few factions reflected the traditional image of a "barbarous" countryside. Córdoba, for example, was an introspective city mired in the Catholic past, a place of spires, convents, and uneasiness about the future. The northeast, however, displayed a more hopeful attitude, as members of the tiny elite called for a political system that recognized provinces as virtual sovereign entities.

This was rather more than the federalism usually associated with the Litoral. Yet provincial sovereignty meant different things to different *provincianos*. Powerful militia officers, for example, painted their personal interests and those of their districts as being one and the same. On the whole, provincial sovereignty proved such an amorphous concept that it rarely provided the basis for anything more than passing alliances between regions. Certainly it offered little effective competition with the supposed populism of local chieftains or the unbending centralism of the *porteños*.

Buenos Aires had little patience or sympathy for the provincial position. If people inland had hesitations about the Patriot cause, then such positions, the *porteños* assumed, were built on ignorance or royalist machinations. In either case, the *porteños* felt the time had come for direct action. In June 1810 they sent emissaries upriver to announce the advent of the new order, asking each Litoral community in turn to recognize the authority of Buenos Aires as the proper substitute for the Spanish Cortes. Since the viceroyalty still existed in name, the *porteños* felt that they had every right to do so.

They had their successes. Corrientes, at the confluence of the Paraná and Paraguay Rivers, approved the *porteño* appeal right away. The merchants and ranchers who controlled its cabildo believed that immediate acquiescence would safeguard their local influence, which rested on the maintenance of the river trade.

Paraguay was another matter.

*Asunción Refuses to Budge*
In naming an agent to take power for them in the Guaraní province, the *porteños* chose Col. José de Espínola, perhaps the single most hated Paraguayan of his day. Espínola had previously gained notoriety as chief militia officer at the northern port of Concepción, where he used his connections with former governor Lázaro de Ribera to feather his own nest. He later accepted the onerous task of militia recruitment in Paraguay at the time of the British invasions.

On his native soil once again in 1810, Espínola exacerbated his poor standing among his fellow Paraguayans by reminding them that Buenos Aires had placed *him* in command over the province. Gov. Bernardo de Velasco refused to cooperate. A modest and courtly man who bred hummingbirds in his spare time, Velasco was as well liked locally as Espínola was reviled.[4] It was thus with broad support that he arrested the colonel and banished him to the far north.

Espínola refused to go quietly. He escaped and tried to raise the banner of revolt, but when no one harkened to his appeal, he fled downriver to Buenos Aires. His subsequent account of his adventures fully convinced the *porteños* of two key contentions. Espínola claimed to have been the victim of intrigue by a powerful coterie of Asunción Spaniards. Yet, simultaneously, Paraguay was ready to support the May revolution if the port city could send troops. These were both dubious claims, but many *porteños* were ready to believe them.

Meanwhile, an assembly of two hundred notables met in Asunción to swear allegiance to the regency government at Cádiz. These men, who represented the *peninsulares* on the cabildo, wanted no open confrontation. But they stressed that good relations with Buenos Aires could never take priority over provincial needs, though in every other way they intended to be flexible.

The *porteños* wanted none of it. They promptly rejected the Paraguayan stance and organized an expeditionary force commanded by Manuel Belgrano. He would make sure that the Paraguayans saw reason, through compulsion if necessary. In September 1811 Espínola died peacefully in his sleep in Buenos Aires, little realizing the trouble he had called down upon his province.

Belgrano was by training a lawyer. He had worked for a time with the local board of trade but had scant military experience. Instead, he trusted in his ability to persuade potential opponents. Belgrano's idealism, which was profound, never wavered in spite of the many reverses he experienced; it is unsurprising that later nationalist writers portrayed him in a saintly light. Yet Belgrano remains something of an enigma. His political outlook was always liberal, although his definition of that term fluctuated. Early on he expressed support for Princess Carlota and a constitutional regime. Later he endorsed a curious plan to place a descendant of the last Inca on the throne of South America. Always, however, he was enthusiastic.

Belgrano was in particularly high spirits in December 1810, when his militia force of some fifteen hundred cavalrymen crossed the Alto Paraná into Paraguay. He expected a cordial welcome from the locals and was surprised when the country people fled at his approach. Belgrano penetrated as far north as Paraguarí, where on 15 January 1811 his units encountered an ill-armed but well-mounted mass of Paraguayans numbering six thousand. In the ensuing melee, the locals broke Belgrano's forces, sending his troops in full retreat to the south toward the Paraná.[5]

Velasco, it emerged, had been warned of Espínola's machinations and of the *porteños'* steady advance. The governor and the militia commanders had time to plan a defense and opted for an old strategy. They allowed Belgrano to advance relatively close to Asunción, then they pounced on him. Governor Velasco and his Spanish-born aides, convinced that the Paraguayans had been defeated, abandoned the field and rushed to the provincial capital with news of a rout. Many of the wealthiest families in the city had already begun to load their possessions aboard riverboats when word arrived from Paraguarí that local militia had in fact triumphed.

Velasco's flight had unfortunate consequences for metropolitan Spain. It cost the governor, the only *peninsular* still seen in a favorable light, the respect he had previously enjoyed among the Paraguayans.

In March 1811, the much-chastened Belgrano withdrew from the province, having received generous terms from Paraguayan officers. His failure to sway the locals to the Patriot cause disappointed the *porteño* leadership, yet it was hardly proof of pro-Spanish feeling among Paraguayans. Faced with pressure from several directions, they had simply fallen back on their usual localism. Velasco had argued that Buenos Aires wanted the province chiefly as a manpower pool for its own ill-conceived wars of conquest, and on the surface, there seemed no denying this.

Paraguayan mistrust of *porteño* motivation did not signal any meaningful local support for a continued link to Spain. Velasco was still a Spaniard, after all, and could only be trusted so far. His loyalty to Fernando VII was real enough, though he also wanted to be a friend of Paraguay. Maintaining this posture was not always possible. He had little money to pay militiamen returning from the field and no way to pass this off as a simple budgetary matter.

His failure to pay the promised amount proved to Paraguayans that the situation had fundamentally changed. What Belgrano had suggested now did not seem so ludicrous — some kind of self-rule was not only desirable but also unavoidable. When rumors circulated that Velasco was about to accept an offer of military assistance from the Portuguese, militia officers at Asunción needed no further encouragement. In May 1811 they mutinied against the governor in a bloodless coup and seized control. They received the quiet but broad support of most Paraguayans, who feared further interference from the outside. As far as many were concerned, neither Spain nor Buenos Aires deserved Paraguayan loyalty. They were willing to negotiate many things, including friendly relations with the mother country and the port city, but ultimate power they refused to barter away. Sovereignty, they now insisted, rested with themselves.

### How Not to Build a Nation

Throughout the Plata, the groups that constituted themselves as local leaders were slow to note the permanence of their break with the mother country. For one thing, they desired British aid, which no one could guarantee if they rejected the government that was Britain's ally against Napoleon. More importantly, the various ad hoc governing bodies regarded themselves not as rebels but as the rightful heirs to Spain. Even Buenos Aires, for all of its revolutionary noisemaking, only admitted to a fully independent status six years into the struggle — and then only as part of a purposely ill-defined "United Provinces of the Plata."

A great deal had changed in the interim. Belgrano's expulsion from Paraguay was followed by a similar defeat in Upper Peru. The frustrated Patriots of Buenos Aires thereupon adopted a more conservative stance, setting aside extremist rhetoric in favor of establishment-oriented language. Their earlier use of the Jacobin term "citizen," for instance, was replaced by the more conventional "señor."

This was not the only concession to a growing conservatism. In military matters, the junta members replaced Belgrano with the more pragmatic José de San Martín (1778–1850), an American-born veteran of the

Peninsular War. San Martín, whom nationalist writers later acclaimed as Argentina's greatest hero, proved an inspirational and hard-working commander. He had spent his youth in the Misiones, where his father was *administrador* on a former Jesuit mission. Broadly recognized as a native son, San Martín got on well with the various *provincianos*, including those who only spoke Guaraní. No one mistook him for a *porteño*. Indeed, when he managed to convince rural militiamen to take one more chance on the Patriot cause, his successful recruitment seemed nothing short of miraculous.

San Martín reorganized the *porteño* forces, which on several occasions had been badly mauled by both Spanish royalist and Portuguese troops. And as he busied himself with the military, his civilian allies on the Buenos Aires junta addressed a glut of political questions. They organized a congress that included deputies from the capital and the western provinces. The Congress, which met in Tucumán in 1816, reflected the many contradictions of the age. It included young visionaries in bright uniforms and clerics in heavy cassocks, country solicitors in frock coats and richly attired, foppish landowners in varying stages of enthusiasm or disenchantment. All were emissaries of essentially sovereign states and had limited powers to negotiate on their own.

The *porteños* managed to win over this curious group by agreeing to dismantle the old administrative structures, replacing the intendancies with self-governing provincial regimes. These in turn offered San Martín several secure bases in the interior from which he launched an audacious push across the high Andes in midwinter 1817. This feat had tremendous significance, as it led directly to Patriot victories in Chile and Peru.

San Martín's successes could not have been accomplished without firm logistical and financial backing from Buenos Aires. Once his army passed over the western ranges, however, the *porteños* failed to consolidate his victories. They even found it difficult to maintain their control over nearby provinces.

In the Banda Oriental, for instance, power seesawed between Spanish royalists centered around the port of Montevideo and Patriot forces, mostly gaucho cavalrymen, who exerted a tenuous hold over the hinterland. The leader of the latter group, José Gervasio Artigas, was a former colonial militia officer with strong ties to the countryside. A man of strong if not altogether inflexible convictions, he espoused the cause of independence and took his rustic supporters with him. Artigas kept up a bloody and protracted fight against the Spaniards while his *porteño* allies harassed them by way of the river. By June 1814 the royalists gave up the fight and abandoned Montevideo.

The Spanish withdrawal from the estuary brought neither peace nor independence. For one thing, the Portuguese had already occupied large areas of the Banda Oriental along its frontier with Rio Grande do Sul. The *porteños* insisted that political power in Montevideo and the rest of the region be reserved for them as legal heirs to the viceregal government. On one occasion, the *porteños* even signed an agreement with the Spaniards that offered to return to royal control all of the Banda Oriental and a portion of Entre Ríos; though nothing came of the agreement, that it should be formulated at all suggests a lack of *porteño* confidence in Artigas.

Confronted with this dual challenge, Artigas's strength of character (and sheer stubbornness) asserted itself. He became a proponent of regional autonomy. Self-rule, he asserted, would free the new Platine states from the pernicious hold of Buenos Aires, a city he later castigated as a "new Imperial Rome, sending its pro-consuls as military governors of the provinces and [despoiling] them of all public representation."[6]

For nearly a decade, Artigas bedeviled the *porteños* and kept the Portuguese at bay. He invaded the Litoral, setting up sympathetic regimes in Entre Ríos, Corrientes, Santa Fe, the Misiones, and for a short time, Córdoba. The *Liga Federal* he established assigned political authority to local militia officers and friendly ranchers. In the Banda Oriental, he attempted to include all races, *castas*, and classes in his system. Whether free black, Indian, or poor Creole, all were Americans, he felt, and all should have some access to power. This inclusive definition of what constituted an "American" persuaded a few people in the Litoral, but it made a good many more feel uneasy. No one doubted Artigas's influence, but whether he was better seen as savior or demagogue was still debatable.

In neighboring Paraguay, his truculence brought a general disapproval, and he found little sympathy from the merchant class anywhere in the Plata. Such opposition mattered little to the Oriental chieftain. Proclaiming himself the "Protector of the Free Peoples," he worked hard to undermine the *porteños* by wrecking the commercial and institutional structures they had inherited from Spain. But in the end, Artigas left his forces overextended and incapable of fending off a major Portuguese offensive in 1816-17.

Even as he retreated toward the Misiones, Artigas left a powerful message for the people of the Litoral and the interior. His revolution was more comprehensive, more democratic, and more understandable than anything the *porteños* offered. Most importantly, it was provincial in character. It could appeal to the poorest Correntinos, Paraguayans, and Entrerrianos in a way that nothing designed in Buenos Aires ever could.

From the late 1810s, the Patriot cause as envisioned by Belgrano and Moreno was in trouble. Yet so were the conservative elements everywhere in the region. Whether royalist, republican, or seemingly apolitical, the elites feared the lawlessness unleashed by the Artiguista "hordes." Many were willing to turn in any direction in search of safety. Increasingly, the merchants, landowners, and clerics — as well as the masses — put their trust in charismatic strongmen, or *caudillos*, who exercised a personal influence over the unlettered gauchos.

The "Age of the *Caudillos*," which began in the interior and the Litoral in the second decade of the nineteenth century and spread to Buenos Aires during the 1820s, gave birth to a tentative security in the countryside. In framing their political agendas, the *caudillos* had no clear priorities. They had to switch alliances and political orientation frequently in order to survive, and death was the price if they guessed wrong. These leaders never evolved a political system of much complexity but relied on their wits and personal connections to cement different social classes into a workable whole. Since they could not transfer such arrangements to a successor, the political climate remained unstable.

Some of the *caudillos* nonetheless ruled their little *republiquetas* for extended periods of time. Gen. Estanislao López of Santa Fe was in power for twenty years (1818-38). Juan Felipe Ibarra, the governor of Santiago del Estero, held sway in his province for thirty-one (1820-51). Under such rulers, a semblance of order emerged from which both elites and masses could benefit. And this order, more than the rarified ideas of the *porteños*, gave Argentines a sense of identity and community, though not yet one of nationality.

*The Francia Dictatorship*

The national project in Paraguay was already well advanced by the 1820s, though few at the time knew that such was the case, not even its chief promoter, Dr. José Gaspar de Francia (1766-1840). The Supreme Dictator—for such was his title for the last twenty-four years of his life—had an extraordinary impact on his country. To some modern historians, he represents popular revolution at its best, having made possible an alternative economic and political development without equal in South America. Contemporary accounts, however, usually painted him in more somber colors as having fostered the worst kind of excesses while cloaking his country in an impenetrable despotism.

The contradictory opinions of Francia make sense given the shades of modern Paraguayan historiography. And many European commentators—including Thomas Carlyle—offered their own estimations of the man. That Francia could gain such a reputation, however, could not have been deduced from his early life.

His mother carried the surname Yegros, which placed her among Paraguay's most ancient and distinguished families. His father was a Brazilian of obscure origin who came to Paraguay to work as a tobacco concessionaire. He later joined the colonial militia and, like the father of San Martín, ended his public career as administrator of an Indian pueblo. Francia's detractors later spread the rumor that his father had Negro blood; certainly the future dictator felt sensitive about the charge. His relations with his father were in any case tempestuous, and the two quarreled bitterly over many things, including the mother's estate.

Francia's life was fundamentally shaped by his experiences after leaving Paraguay for the University of Córdoba in the 1780s. Córdoba was a conservative town, and the university its most conservative institution. Francia pursued a degree in theology, mastering all the medieval subjects from rhetoric to Latin to Aristotelian logic. After obtaining his doctorate, he returned to Paraguay, though not to the priestly avocation his family expected.

Instead, he practiced law. Córdoba evidently shaped him in many ways, turning him from a well-read provincial with religious leanings to an ambitious and politicized man of the world. He came to harbor visceral contempt for the people he found in authority, especially the *porteños*, many of whom had purchased high positions at the university. For all his anger and resentment, Dr. Francia possessed an appetite for hard work, which brought him material success and influence. Unlike other solicitors, he made time for the lawsuits of poor folk who spoke only Guaraní. Francia made a name for himself among these peasants and small farmers, especially outside Asunción. These *provincianos* found many reasons to trust his judgment. Though aloof and condescending with Asunceños, with the peasants he acted the part of a sagacious, paternal advocate. With his slender build, sallow complexion, and aquiline nose, he looked like an ascetic. He habitually wore a heavy black coat, tricorn hat, and outsized silver shoebuckles, all signs of an earlier age. He refused all modern trimmings—no frock coats and certainly no red *culottes* or Phrygian caps for him.

As to public demeanor, Dr. Francia understood and manipulated the prejudices of his countrymen. He never disguised his antipathy for outsiders. If most Paraguayans shared his opinions, at the same time they stood in awe of a man so versed in mathematical calculations who could speak French, possessed a thousand-volume library, and spent nights peering at the heavens through a telescope. Such a man was more than just well educated—he was a *payé apojhá*—a sorcerer.

Dr. Francia promoted this reputation. He used it to advantage in 1811 first to isolate, then to overcome, his internal opponents. As perhaps the only cosmopolitan among native-born Paraguayans, his presence on the governing junta was widely deemed indispensable. His skillful maneuvering soon displaced the few pro-*porteño* members. He then negotiated a treaty with the port city that allowed for retention of the Misiones territories, low duties on Paraguayan trade, and an unofficial recognition of Paraguayan independence—all in return for vague promises of military aid at some unstated date "if circumstances permitted."[7]

With this success in hand, Francia played the role of Cincinnatus. He resigned from the junta and withdrew to the *campo*. Far from public haunts, he renewed his earlier contacts with ranchers, Indian officials, and all who might increase his base of support. And he waited.

Francia's absence from Asunción coincided with some of the worst violence in the lower provinces. This worked in his favor. In November 1812, bewildered junta members found themselves begging him to reenter the government. Francia accepted their invitation but demanded broad concessions. The junta agreed to create a battalion of infantry responsible to him alone and to equip the unit he received with half the munitions then available in the Paraguayan capital. More importantly, he gained a virtual veto over junta decisons.[8]

Though the establishment of his supreme dictatorship was still two years away, for all intents and purposes, Francia had already assumed power. In September–October 1813, a special congress convened in Asunción to decide the future of the Paraguayan state. Dominated as it was by Francia's rural partisans, the representatives assigned the doctor of theology the right to form the new government. Like other conservatives of his day, Dr. Francia saw the new revolutionary order in South America as debased and looked to classical antecedents for republican virtue within a patriarchal structure. The Rome of Caesar and Pompey furnished his model. Francia put himself forward as consul in association with militia commander Fulgencio Yegros. Approving this, congressional deputies declared Paraguay an independent republic and sanctioned the official rupture with Buenos Aires.

Dr. Francia's influence grew even greater over the next few months, and soon he dispensed with his Pompey. Another congress removed Yegros from his consular position in 1814 and granted Francia dictatorial powers for a period of five years. Two years later, a final congress named him supreme dictator for life. Under this formulation, Paraguay evolved into a republic, though certainly not a democratic one.

Despite claims in the revisionist literature that Dr. Francia was a radical revolutionary, his political thinking had more of the reactionary in it. Like an absolutist of the Bourbon mold, he considered the most moral government that which set the most reasonable political goals. Above all, he favored the enhancement of state power over internal rivals and competing states. Having attained the highest political office, he intended to use his authority comprehensively. Not only did he proceed to formulate policy on foreign relations and the domestic economy, but he also addressed the most minute budgetary matters. In a sense, he became the father of his country, the great lord, *Caraí Guasú*, who guarded the welfare of his childlike people.

The dictator refused to change the basic socioeconomic fabric of Paraguay, save for those features relevant to the legitimization of his regime. He forced out many, though not all, foreign-born merchants. He seized the properties of local opponents, though in no greater proportion than occurred in other South American countries. He pointedly went no further. Slavery and the labor-draft for Indians continued as before, and the rural elites (save for *peninsulares*) maintained their dominance of the peasants. Indeed, since wage-earning activities (such as yerba gathering) significantly declined under dictatorial rule, the number of dependent retainers actually increased.

In all of this, Dr. Francia had the support of his countrymen. He dealt fairly with the poor while also granting privileges to landowners and the military. Francia was popular with all these groups, though unlike Artigas, he was never a populist.

In common with his *porteño* contemporaries, Francia occasionally used radical rhetoric in the early years, though in practice his actions drew more from conservatives like Francisco de Vitoria than from

Robespierre. For Francia, the failings of the European revolutionary movements outweighed their virtues. Napoleon he admired for his military acumen and for his willingness to write his own rules in politics. For the Jacobins, however, Francia had less sympathy. Of the three great principles they enunciated in Paris, only equality interested him in a detached way. Liberty was bad for discipline, and in any case inappropriate for Paraguay, where disputes were commonly settled with the knife.[9] As for fraternity, that notion sprang from the worst sort of effeminate French demagoguery. Such nonsense he considered appropriate for self-important *porteños*, but it was too sentimental, too wooly, for practical Paraguayans.[10]

The congresses that gave birth to Francia's dictatorship reflected these views. They were composed of appointees—rural smallholders who willingly left decision making to the *Caraí*. As a rule, Paraguayans accepted the power of their ruler because his strength seemed essential in a world full of enemies. Such power, such *mbareté*, was crucial to their security. Congressional deputies formally approved his actions, and thereafter he felt no need to consult them. When questions of legality arose, Francia referred to precedents in the colonial Laws of the Indies. But all real power emanated from his will alone.

The dictator's conservatism found its most palpable manifestation in his decision to establish a *cordon sanitaire* around the republic, prohibiting the entry of foreigners and the departure of those who wished to leave. This policy, in force from before 1820, kept the country isolated from the anarchy of the lower provinces, though it also kept out capital, foreign expertise, and any idea that Francia rejected. The dictator turned Paraguay in upon itself.

This policy had the effect—probably unintended—of reinforcing the Hispano-Guaraní identity of the Paraguayans. They abandoned all pretense of belonging to a greater community of Americans, Spaniards, or anyone else. This feeling, which grew more pronounced as the decades went by, became the principal element in Paraguayan nationality. Nothing comparable existed in Buenos Aires, the Litoral provinces, or Portuguese Brazil.

These countries likewise had no figure like José Gaspar de Francia. In a period dominated by young military men and liberal courtiers, Paraguay was ruled by a middle-aged pedant who combined in his person all executive, judicial, and legislative powers. Like Napoleon and Peter the Great, Francia believed himself the "Man of Providence," and he acted accordingly. He may have taken Paraguay out of the mainstream of Latin American development, but his people came to feel part of a nation in consequence.

Francia's isolationism reflected the fear that Paraguay was encircled by hostile forces. Buenos Aires had already shown its true colors by launching the Belgrano expedition. Artigas presented an even more immediate threat. His troops clashed with those of the dictator several times in the Misiones, and worse still, much to Francia's dismay, the protector actively encouraged defections from Paraguay's southern command.

This antagonism brought no open conflict of any intensity. Indeed, by 1820, with his shrinking army reduced by disease and mutiny to a mere handful of men, Artigas chose to cross into Paraguay in search of asylum. Dr. Francia took no revenge. He gave the defeated Oriental chieftain a frugal allowance and a rustic though comfortable exile in a small hamlet far to the northeast of Asunción. There, Artigas spent most of the remaining thirty years of his life.[11]

Artigas's departure did not assure peace. But the *caudillos* who succeeded him in the Litoral were more interested in fighting each other than in invading Paraguay. The dictator could never afford to take that for granted, of course, and stationed troops on both sides of the Paraná for many years. On a few occasions he made use of them. But he also had to contend with a traditional, possibly more dangerous enemy to the north.

*The Brazilian Alternative*

Events in the Platine estuary had not escaped the attention of the Portuguese, who intended to press their opportunities in the region. They worked to exacerbate the growing disorder in their neighbor's house.

Yet this strategy had a dangerous side. The quest for independence in the Plata held many perils for Portuguese Brazil; ever since the Haitian revolution, any regime that depended on slavery had reason to fear the outbreak of rebellion.

Nevertheless, Brazil derived benefits from the situation. The turn of the century had brought a dramatic expansion of British commerce with Portugal and its colonies. Trade, in turn, fostered greater political involvement for the Portuguese in European affairs, including participation in a general European war that they might better have avoided. In late 1807 a French army crossed the Spanish border into Portugal, forcing King João VI and his court to flee Lisbon in a flotilla organized by the British Royal Navy. The British happily extended this courtesy to a traditional ally, but it came with many strings attached. Within a short time, Portugal agreed to a commercial reorientation that gave Britain the status of most favored nation. British imports to Brazil soon paid lower tariffs than those of Portugal itself, and London-based firms gained extraterritorial rights that remained in force until the 1840s. The Brazilian market clearly had great potential, and the British were anxious to bolster their activities in that part of the world. In return, Brazil earned a measure of commercial (and ultimately political) stability that contrasted with the chaos then sweeping Spanish America.

João's arrival at Rio de Janeiro provided new support for the *ancien régime*. Like the Platine countries, Brazil suffered from general illiteracy and poverty, and even the elite was noticeably rustic. A few Brazilians had read Adam Smith, Jean-Baptiste Say, Montesquieu, and Raynal despite official disapproval, but it was difficult to act on such ideas where indifference and a deficient system of communication reigned. Several antigovernment groups tried to organize but failed to capture the popular imagination.

Not so the royal presence of João VI. The arrival of the monarch and his court lent new life to the colony and awakened a sense of self-worth among local residents. The king invested heavily in his new home. With Brazil as the de facto center of the Portuguese Empire, the Crown designed Brazilian copies of imperial institutions. João built roads, palaces, and public buildings; established schools and printing presses; and held dress balls. He included native-born elites in these activities. And in 1815 he gave Brazil a political status coequal with that of Portugal.

Brazilians enjoyed their new prosperity and importance. They made efforts to act more European than the Europeans themselves, trading rough colonial habits for a soft and polished urbanity. A few young Baianos, Pernambucanos, and Cariocas even talked openly of a republic. They drew inspiration from the United States and from Revolutionary France, though notably not from the Plata. The Portuguese regarded those flirtations with republicanism as subversive but were otherwise tolerant. Privately, colonial officials worried that the very progress the king had inspired was causing Portugal's grip on Brazil to weaken.

Napoleon's occupation of the Iberian Peninsula came to an end in 1814, leaving the Portuguese court free to return to Lisbon. King João, however, preferred Rio. He had become accustomed to the easygoing atmosphere of Brazil, the warm sun, the pleasant people, and the mild evenings beneath the vistas of Corcovado. A cold palace in Lisbon held no charms for him. The king understood, moreover, that Brazil had become the economic center of his empire and deserved special attention. If he left, Brazilians might refuse to submit to Portuguese dominance.

He was right. In 1817 a republican uprising in sugar-rich Pernambuco almost enveloped the entire northeast. The Portuguese military prevailed, though just barely. In 1820—five years after Waterloo—a liberal revolution broke out in Portugal, impelling the king's reluctant return to his homeland. Before departing, he advised his handsome, impetuous son Pedro to erect an independent political movement around himself, if necessary, to safeguard the Bragança dynasty in Brazil.

Local elites approved of this strategy, though for different reasons. A seamless transition from the old colonial regime, untainted by republican rule, allowed their continued domination without enflaming the passions of the lower orders. Planters and merchants favored liberal economic reforms that permitted them to pursue their own projects without Portuguese interference. They could expand and modernize their sugar holdings in order to fill the vacuum created by the debacle in Haiti as well as develop the then tiny ranching and coffee infrastructure in the south of the country. And they could also consolidate their hold over the Banda Oriental, which the Portuguese had annexed after Artigas departed. All this the elites could accomplish without abandoning their traditional control over land and labor or permitting any meaningful liberties for the poor.[12]

The drift toward this sort of independence proved unstoppable. When the liberal Cortes in Lisbon threatened to restore Brazil's colonial status, Portuguese and Brazilian forces clashed openly in the field. These encounters never amounted to much, but in their wake even many resident Portuguese pressed for independence as a way to safeguard their investments. The prince regent found it difficult to make up his mind: which was it to be, return to Portugal, as some of his European followers demanded, or stay behind and create an independent state in Brazil? Finally, in September 1822, Pedro acted and declared the independence of a new empire with himself as monarch. He suppressed pro-Portuguese elements in the far north, then celebrated that the outcome had been achieved with little force. Many of Pedro's subjects also celebrated, though only a few guessed at the extent of the political challenges ahead.

For their part, the British felt pleased. Ever interested in the free flow of trade, they applauded Pedro's declaration of independence and started their own campaign to persuade Lisbon to recognize the new Brazilian government. Three years later the effort was crowned with success.

Repudiation of colonial status did not translate into modern nationhood. Brazilians were still unsure of the country's future. As emperor, twenty-four-year-old Pedro I enjoyed the cautious support of the elites, who needed more than liked him. The alliance of convenience between the emperor, the merchants, and the great planters guaranteed freedom from Portugal at a low cost in money and lives. This contrasted markedly with the Platine experience. Yet all was not well. Pedro's tendency to emphasize dynastic matters annoyed highly placed Brazilians. So did his habit of putting metropolitan Portuguese into high positions in the new government. Rather than address these issues squarely, Pedro I chose to dissolve the constitutional assembly that he himself had only recently formed. In 1824 he issued his own constitution that defined the empire in nativist terms as "a political association of all Brazilian citizens" who formed "a free and independent nation." For some years previous, Brazilians had used the term "nation" to refer to a community of peoples rather than to a single class, but now the constitution certified that broad, if still idealized, definition.

For all its allusions to liberty, Pedro's constitution only granted political rights to certain "citizens."[13] The new franchise was broadly conceived at the parish level, yet the exercise of higher authority was limited by indirect voting and a "moderating power," which the emperor alone exercised. Under this system, real authority rested with Pedro, the appointed Council of State, and a select group of legislators. All of these figures were men of substance who believed that good government derived not from universal suffrage but from the proper management of rivalries.

In practice, local notables guided the smaller districts by arranging votes for provincial politicians in exchange for personal favors. Fraud and violence were widespread, and ministers and provincial authorities openly intervened so that official candidates carried every election through the 1850s. Ministers, deputies, and senators debated political philosophy, literature, and the country's future among themselves but enjoyed only a nominal constituency among the mass of their countrymen.

For the average person, the constitution, the emperor, and even independence itself were still distant business. Little had changed. Power remained with the same propertied class that had wielded it during colonial times. Slavery still dominated the economy. And the workday was still long, hard, and seemingly unending, save perhaps during the Lenten season, which was given over to the revelries and catharsis of the annual Carnival.

Of course, the poor everywhere tend to ignore the workings of high government. In tropical Brazil, as in Paraguay, the indifference was profound, and this was in keeping with elite interest in an ordered, deferential society. To stave off the social chaos so common in the Plata and elsewhere, the elites encouraged the common people to accept their subordination within a hierarchy in which every individual knew his place.

The monarchist option in Brazil never pretended to be revolutionary. It offered trusteeship more than representation and, for the poor, a putative protection from the infighting of an elite deeply contemptuous of the lower orders. The common people had their symbol of unity and future greatness in the person of the emperor, but little else; they themselves had no role in political decision making. Brazilian nationhood was thus like the bright gilt on a religious statuette — it was decorative and fine, but only clay lay just underneath.

Yet the state apparatus inherited from the Portuguese did permit greater administrative cohesion than was present in the Argentine provinces. According to the 1824 constitution, the emperor might dissolve the Chamber of Deputies, select members of the life senate from triple lists submitted by provincial electors, and appoint or dismiss government ministers. That he felt free to exercise such authority showed another contrast with Buenos Aires, where governors might aspire to broad powers but never attain them.

The local and regional conflicts that wracked the Plata were likewise common in Brazil, but they failed to take the form of civil war (Rio Grande do Sul providing a telling exception some time later). Though provincial strongmen exercised some influence, they generally recognized the advantages of working with the state. This contrasted with the more independent-minded *caudillos* of the Plata, who, after all, owed their prominence to the disintegration of institutions and social norms that still prevailed in Brazil.[14]

The survival of colonial models in the new Brazilian Empire was less an indication of vitality than of stasis. The lower classes still carried the weight of society, and for all the elites knew, the poor were either apathetic or full of seditious desires for emancipation or religious atavism.

A series of revolts in Minas Gerais, São Paulo, and in the north and northeast pointed out exactly how uncertain the situation was. Even the imperial capital was not altogether safe from trouble.[15] Of particular concern in this regard was the attitude of the slaves, who knew that independence held nothing for them. And many other Brazilians wondered the same thing.

# War and Nation Building

## 3

The Banda Oriental, with its excellent port at Montevideo, had been in Portuguese hands since 1817. Brazilian independence brought a withdrawal of Portuguese troops from the province, but their place was immediately taken by Brazilian forces. Pedro I insisted on preserving the southern frontiers his father had established. He also dreamed of extending Brazilian influence through the Litoral provinces and into Paraguay.

Events betrayed that vision. At the time, Buenos Aires was still dominated by reformers whose own dreams were as grandiose as those of the emperor. They saw themselves as the architects of a spirit of civilization that emerged to counter the savagery of the Pampas. This commitment to modernity, they thought, was destined to spread throughout South America. It was in this context that the *porteños* sought to take advantage in the Banda Oriental. They understood how tenuous the Brazilian position there was. But so did certain Oriental exiles then in Buenos Aires.

The news of the patriot victory over the last Spanish forces at Ayacucho reached the Plata in 1825. It had a galvanizing effect, stimulating the various exile groups and igniting rebellion against Brazilian rule in the Banda Oriental. Rebels crossed the river from Buenos Aires in April 1825 and then convinced militia units on the other side to join them. The rebels hoped not just to liberate the Oriental territories but also to instigate a wider rebellion that would destroy monarchy in South America once and for all.

What they received instead was a bloody three-year conflict, the Cisplatine War. Brazilians at once saw the hand of *porteño* provocateurs in the rebellion (and, indeed, the professed intention of the rebels to join with Buenos Aires suggested as much). As the situation deteriorated, the emperor's government declared war and proclaimed a naval blockade of Buenos Aires. Revenues of the port city fell precipitously. Though this undermined social stability, it failed to bring about the collapse of the Centralist (or Unitarian) regime. Instead, the war ground on.

For both sides the conflict was costly. The Brazilian cabinet initially welcomed the war against Buenos Aires as a way of demonstrating the superiority of the monarchical form of government. As the months went by, however, expenditures for munitions and men began to drain the imperial exchequer and yet brought no victory.

With *porteño* assistance, the Oriental rebels eventually seized control of the countryside but failed to pry the Brazilians out of Colonia and Montevideo. Then, in February 1827, imperial forces suffered a humiliating reverse at Ituzaingó in Rio Grande do Sul; only the empire's naval power prevented a total rout. For several months thereafter, weary commanders exhausted their men and materiel in a fruitless quest for a decisive engagement.

For the British, the costs of a continued war now exceeded those of open intervention. With their trade and prestige severely affected, they decided in 1828 to dispatch some vessels of the Royal Navy in a show of force. The Brazilians and *porteños* withdrew their forces from the Banda Oriental, and the province became an independent buffer state, the Oriental Republic of the Uruguay. Britain guaranteed the freedom, if not the stability, of this new state.

The Cisplatine War devastated Pedro I's authority. Despite his enthusiasm, the conflict failed to inspire a broader nationalism among his subjects. Indeed, the only imperial units to defend the "national" cause consistently and wholeheartedly were composed of recently arrived German immigrants. Heavy war expenditures brought a steep fall in the currency followed by an unchecked issuance of paper money, the inflationary effects of which made life more difficult for the average man. Instead of blaming Orientals or *porteños* for these troubles, most Brazilians blamed their Portuguese-born monarch.

Pedro I spent the last three years of his reign trying to settle his dynastic interests in Portugal, expending still more political capital in the effort. His absolutism, his lack of consideration for Brazilian interests and sensibilities, his openly flaunted mistress, and his extravagance combined to reduce the emperor's popularity among his subjects both high and low.

A mutiny in June 1828 undercut the military backing that Pedro had enjoyed. Though he retained parliamentary support for a time, his own deputies now called upon him to account for his actions and demanded compromises that he refused to consider. Rather than force civil war, he abdicated on 7 April 1831, leaving his five-year-old son Pedro as heir in a regency government that provided neither adequate budgets nor ideological solidity.

*Federalism Ascendant: Juan Manuel de Rosas*
The fiscal complications that undermined the imperial regime found parallel in Buenos Aires. The Unitarian regime had achieved some successes in the near hinterland, though the experience in the interior and Litoral provinces was clearly mixed (with Paraguay a clear loss). The war had eaten up budgets and good intentions and had contributed nothing to the development of a national spirit beyond Buenos Aires Province.

It also seriously weakened the Unitarians. Since 1810 the men of the port city had put themselves forward as the Plata's great hope. Not only did they consider the whole region rightfully theirs through inheritance from Spain but their own intelligence, experience, and the scope of their vision also convinced them that power should remain in their hands.

Such an assumption failed to convince *provincianos* who were understandably skeptical given the mounting costs of the Cisplatine War, San Martín's expedition to Chile, and the failed campaigns in Paraguay and

Upper Peru. Country people ignored the subtleties in *porteño* politics, yet the differences were critical. Bernardino Rivadavia and those closest to him were impeccably "liberal" and anglophiles. Other wealthy *porteños*, however, favored a decentralized state — one willing to guarantee their traditional privileges. These men resented Rivadavia's alliances with provincial leaders in the Litoral and interior. And as the war with Brazil dragged on, they also came to resent their funding the lion's share of the struggle.

Revolts in the interior started unraveling Rivadavia's tentative new order, but his *porteño* opponents — the Federalists — finished the job. In July 1827, as rumors spread of an internal coup, the foreign merchants in Buenos Aires abandoned the Unitarian regime. Rivadavia resigned, leaving to his successor Manuel Dorrego the tasks of arranging the peace with Brazil and restoring domestic order. Dorrego went further. He nullified the centralist constitution, reaffirmed provincial autonomy, and assumed the title of governor of Buenos Aires.

Returning Unitarian troops overthrew and executed Dorrego soon afterward. His death set off a chain reaction ending in a new rebellion by Federalist landowners. The leader of this uprising was Juan Manuel de Rosas (1793–1877), perhaps the most prosperous and innovative rancher in the region, a man equally at home fighting Indians from the saddle and managing the activities of huge (and profitable) cattle estates.

Rosas effectively crushed the Unitarians in Buenos Aires. But to retain power, he had to quell Unitarians in the interior provinces while sponsoring other provincial strongmen. It was a task that kept him busy for the next quarter century.

Rosas eclipsed the other *caudillos* of his era in part because he controlled the customs revenues for the port of Buenos Aires. Thus, he could afford to arm his troops more substantially than his opponents. But he was also a remarkably adept politician. Rosas realized that in the absence of a coherent nation-state, his best chance for survival lay in mobilizing the gauchos of Buenos Aires Province for a partisan rather than national struggle.

He was equal to the task. He knew both the city and the Pampas as well as anyone. He could throw ostriches with *boleadoras* in the morning and put together complicated statistical evaluations of hide and tallow exports in the afternoon. He took pride in speaking the language of whomever he was with. As Tulio Halperín Donghi has noted: "Rosas was the only Federalist chief to assimilate the lessons of the recent turmoil and create a style of rule adapted to the new conditions of political life. He correctly recognized that the mobilization of large portions of the population in antagonistic factions had become irreversible and that political stability depended on the total victory of one party over the others. . . . Rosas set out to build a disciplined organization capable of doing just that."[1]

Rosas brought a stability that had been absent for many years. As the "Restorer of the Laws," he fostered a political climate that was essentially colonial in its respect for class divisions. Yet fear always tinged the paternalism of this traditional order. He used sophisticated propaganda to persuade local elites of the virtues of his administration and required every individual to display the red insignia of Federalism. Churches maintained a place of honor for Rosas's portrait.

In both the city and the Bonaerense countryside, Rosas's authoritarianism assured the peace during the 1830s and 1840s. Yet for all of his cunning and political expertise, Rosas never succeeded in bringing Argentina completely under his sway. Though the provinces participated in a general federation that delegated limited powers to Buenos Aires, they had enjoyed a measure of self-government since the Congress of Tucumán. The outlying governors had no interest in trading this freedom for the more centralized structure that Rosas favored.

The shortcomings of his political program appeared obvious to all but the wealthiest Bonaerense ranchers. Though nominally a Federalist, Rosas chiefly sought to promote the cattle interests of his own province. This left him at odds with those inland areas that also had ranching economies. The favor he showed Buenos Aires made him appear more Unitarian than the Unitarians. No *porteño*-led federation could afford to integrate the *provincianos* on an equal basis with Buenos Aires — and everyone knew it.

Rosas had many domestic opponents. Classic Unitarians, for instance, remained active throughout the 1830s. Following Rivadavia, they demanded a centralized regime in Buenos Aires to serve as a beacon of modernization for the region. They promoted civil education as the instrument for the dissemination of their beliefs, yet their vision was unabashedly elitist, which explains the relatively poor reception it encountered in the *campo*.

Ironically, the Unitarians initially enjoyed their greatest military advantage in the countryside. José María Paz, their most accomplished general, read terrain as well as Rosas and fought just as hard. His capture by Federalists in 1831, however, sounded the death knell for the old Unitarians, and their leaders fled into exile in Chile and Montevideo.

Rosas found other enemies to take their place. With Federalist allies in control of Santa Fe, La Rioja, and all points between, he had felt sufficiently secure to resign and leave Buenos Aires for a two-year campaign against the Patagonian Indians. But the *caudillos* of the interior were unsatisfied with the scraps that Rosas had thrown them and demanded a new constitution that would grant them a share in the customs revenues. When Rosas returned from the south in 1835, he refused to grant the *provincianos* any such concession, which, after all, would undercut his own influence.

In Buenos Aires, Rosas demanded and received dictatorial powers (*la suma de poder público*). Any educated man who henceforth thought to dissent risked being daggered by agents of his political police, the *Mazorca*. With overwhelming authority in his hands, Rosas proceeded to renegotiate economic policy with the *caudillos*, many of whom gave in.

Provincial criticism of Rosas eventually crystallized in a new federalism based in Corrientes. That northeastern province was exceptional in several ways. Unlike Santa Fe, Entre Ríos, and Buenos Aires, which all depended exclusively on ranching, Corrientes neatly balanced its cattle industry with farming (cotton, tobacco, and food crops), extractive activities (timber and yerba mate), and a surprisingly advanced shipbuilding industry.[2]

The diversity of the Correntino economy was coupled with a small but worldly elite in the provincial capital. This group included some Unitarian refugees (and a few from Francia's Paraguay), all well read in the political theories of the day. Yet the most talented individuals in the local elite were native-born — practical men who were conversant with agriculture, trade, and the mechanical arts.

The chief, though by no means only, light in this group was Pedro Ferré (1788–1867), who for two decades symbolized the Litoral's resistance to Rosas. The son of Catalán immigrants, Ferré rejected the normal route to power via the militia and rose instead in the local shipbuilding industry, married well, and by the 1820s owned the largest shipyard in Corrientes. His position gave him access to the town's merchants, who recognized a potential spokesman. The provincial congress, which recreated the elite composition of the colonial cabildo, was likewise persuaded. It elected Ferré governor three different times (1824–28, 1830–33, and 1839–42).

Rosas detested the Correntino shipwright and dismissed him as a "Unitarian savage." In some ways, however, Ferré was more of a federalist than Rosas himself. Ferré's concept of the nation required a political and economic role for all the provinces. He insisted on the need for protectionism. His own province could never hope to attain the tremendous trading advantage that Buenos Aires enjoyed. But if the foreign portion of the *porteño* market could be redirected, then Corrientes and the other Litoral provinces might make up the loss by supplying the port city with locally produced goods. In this fashion, Argentines alone would benefit, rather than having to share with Britons, Brazilians, Orientals, and Paraguayans. Such a commercial shift could only be induced through heavy import duties imposed at the port city. This project, which had much in common with colonial mercantilism, perceived the nation as a federation of provinces in which the constituent parts assumed equal risks in order to gain equal advantages. In this, Ferré rejected the elitism of his Unitarian allies as much as he did that of Rosas.

His argument had no chance in the lower provinces, however. Merchants, speculators, and cattle breeders of Buenos Aires benefited from Rosas's free trade policy and were uninterested in alternatives. They argued that the high costs of protection made Ferré's plan unthinkable and that consumers should not have to pay in order to promote the welfare of farmers. Ferré's vision foundered on political reality.

Rosas tamed much of the interior through a blend of diplomacy and coercion. The client *caudillos* he supported recognized his sovereignty and gave him no trouble. With time, he believed he could effect the same hegemony in the Litoral provinces and the Banda Oriental. But doing so required a delicate hand.

In 1835 the Bonaerense governor introduced a significantly higher tariff at the port city, seemingly reversing his traditional policy on trade. In fact, his motivation was largely political. Federalists had lost ground among the artisan class, which was ripe for a Ferré-like protectionist solution. The new tariff widened the regime's social base at a key moment. But protectionism delivered few of the economic opportunities that its proponents promised; Buenos Aires retained most of the revenues produced and those monies that did trickle inland were appropriated by those sectors already favored by the system.

A new generation of opponents, the Men of 1837, promised a thorough reordering of society, an elimination of Spanish colonial vestiges and *caudillismo*, and the establishment of workable liberal institutions. Though they were avid readers of John Locke, Jeremy Bentham, and the Compte de Saint-Simon, they concluded that their predecessors were mistaken in trying to impose European political fashions. Argentina was an American country. It needed to develop a liberal regime with an American character.[3]

All this, of course, was anathema to Rosas. From his comfortable home at Palermo, he sneered at both Ferré and the young delinquents across the river. To the largely agrarian population of the Plata, with little communication, little participation in politics, and loyalties divided among thirteen provinces, it was difficult to see why national integration should have any appeal. The Men of 1837 promised to address broad concerns in a national fashion. They would restructure politics, bringing European immigrants, education, and culture to the countryside.

Why should such a program have any more success than that of Rivadavia? These new liberals were not romantic idealists so much as practiced revolutionaries. They had gained their maturity under Rosas, knew his strengths and weaknesses, and abjured his rigid factionalism. They claimed to be men of the future who had risen above the old partisan divisions.

And the Bonaerense governor stretched his forces rather thin in the late 1830s and 1840s. He launched campaigns in the provinces to contain his internal enemies, Ferré included. He involved himself in a none-too-quiet attempt to set up a satellite regime in Uruguay, specifically forbidden by the treaty that ended the Cisplatine War.

Rosas's intrigues in the Banda Oriental presented the Men of 1837 with an opportunity. The British had guaranteed Uruguayan independence, but only Montevideo loomed outside Rosas's orbit. In that city of refugees, the different groups of exiles met freely with each other and with European residents — including the British minister. Affecting a position of moderation and liberality, the Men of 1837 legitimized themselves in the eyes of the most important extracontinental power. They appeared *au courant* with everything European. They spoke French, English, and Italian and dressed in frock coats like the gentlemen of London. The British never officially recognized the Men of 1837 as allies but cooperated with them during the sieges and naval blockades frequent in the unsettled times. Up the river, anti-Rosas *provincianos* became aware of this patronage and began to regard the young men as a serious threat to the governor after all. Dealing with them made sense, given the appearance of meaningful foreign support. And the British and French were not the only parties to be considered. Brazil, the not-too-distant giant of South America, had finally decided to settle its own accounts with Rosas.

### *Pedro II Comes of Age*

After the abdication of Pedro I in 1831, Brazilian elites were in a position to shift the center of political gravity from the monarch to the parliament.[4] Transfer of power to provincial representatives was logical now that the absolutist Portuguese faction had faded. But in general, the regency brought little innovation.

A cause of this inertia lay in the divergence of opinion between moderates such as regent Diogo Antonio Feijó who wanted reforms through the 1824 Constitution; radicals who sought a new constitution, bypassing the life senate; and reactionaries who wanted Pedro I to return as regent until his son attained his majority. Only a tiny handful of vocal enthusiasts wanted a republic.

The 1830s saw little domestic peace. The sugar economy had declined due to foreign competition, and coffee had yet to take its place. Government expenditures caused problems for years after the Cisplatine War. Worse still were provincial revolts in the north, northeast, and far south.

Moderates, who had wished to see central power curtailed, now had to use that power to keep the empire together. Their commitment to the status quo was simple recognition of necessity. Decentralization might have had ideological advantages, but in the 1830s any real adjustment ran the risk of letting loose an avalanche of change. Members of the Brazilian elite, whether from city or province, knew enough to fear social revolution, for every barefoot street worker might be a potential Dessalines.

Out of this slow-moving process rose Dom Pedro II. An orphan by the mid-1830s, he already had many responsibilities thrust upon him, and never was parental solicitude more intense than the care taken by the Brazilian elites on his behalf. The younger Pedro had a sensitive nature and enjoyed reading, playing with his dogs, and quiet conversation with his sisters. Aside from his immediate family he had no intimates, no one with whom to share his innermost feelings. His tutors thought him exceptionally bright, though in a starchy, self-conscious way.[5] As they saw it, he presented Brazil with wonderful material from which to form a monarchy, and they impressed upon him the delicacy of his situation and that of the empire.

Another child might have rebelled against such a burden, but not Pedro II. If he were as indispensable as his tutors said, then he needed to calculate his actions with great precision. Unlike monarchs who behaved like spoiled children even in middle age, Pedro II always affected the demeanor of a grave elder. He went about every task with plodding deliberation, allowing himself no flexibility in official or private matters. He wore heavy royal vestments during long ceremonies at the hottest time of the year and never once scratched his nose.

In pinning their hopes on this lonely adolescent, the elites presumed a nation in which the monarch and entrenched privilege were the twin pillars of order. This was a reasonable conclusion given their class interests, but such a structure could never appeal to every segment of society. The Portuguese had departed, but where were the Brazilians? Thus far, regional and local concerns had always confounded a greater nationalism. Yet this boy had the potential to draw the diverse elements together. His father had surrounded himself with Portuguese courtiers. But Pedro II was a Brazilian through and through.

The emperor became the focus of loyalty and identity in widely separated areas of the realm. The people of the northeast could see themselves as subjects of Dom Pedro II, though otherwise they recognized no necessary links with the people of São Paulo, Santa Catarina, or the Amazon. In 1840 the parliament recognized his early majority, transferring to Pedro the full responsibility of his constitutional role.

The new monarch was a youthful figure unsullied by the infighting of the recent past and forward looking in his aspirations. He was incorruptible, attentive to his duties, kind, and intellectually precocious — in sum, just the person the "nation" required to foster positive change while preserving the established social hierarchy. High and low, the emperor's subjects showered him with an affection and respect that grew with time. Though widespread sympathy for Dom Pedro did not reflect an unadulterated nationalism, still it was a more developed political sentiment than anything that preceded it. Brazilians liked Dom Pedro, though they were less sanguine about the monarchy. Perhaps the more astute politicians hoped that admiration for the one would grow into support for the other.

Two important factors shaped these hopes from the final years of Pedro's minority through the mid-1840s. One was the development of party politics on a national basis. The other was the secessionist threat in Rio Grande do Sul.

The emergence of Conservative and Liberal blocs had as much to do with ties of blood and friendship as with shared ideology. In theory, the Liberals were federalists who favored local autonomy and who trusted in society's ability to correct its flaws. They demanded the abolition of the Council of State and the moderating power, opposed the appointment of life senators, and supported free trade and liberty of religion. In general, they advocated the principle that "the king reigns but does not rule."[6]

The Conservatives saw themselves as a party of order that resisted the supposedly anarchist inclination of their rivals. Conservatives, who counted among their number the great sugar planters, strongly defended central authority, the moderating power, and the Council of State. They favored life tenure in the Senate, Roman Catholicism as the official religion, and the principle that "the king reigns *and* rules."[7]

Both Liberals and Conservatives were members of Masonic lodges. Both praised the ideas of Jeremy Bentham and other European reformers (though to varying degrees). Both endorsed slavery, the established social order, and a free press. Yet contrary to what many in the government hoped, the advent of Pedro II failed to bring real cohesion, even among members of parliament. At lower levels, politics remained an uncertain blend of influence and force, with regional bosses delivering electoral votes (and national party chieftains) through their dominance of dependent clientele. Family connections, business contacts, personal loyalty, and reciprocal favors provided the key ingredients in this structure.

Most members of the Brazilian parliament shared three common characteristics. First, they were all educated in one university (Portugal's Coimbra); second, they were trained mostly in civil law; and third, they had experience as bureaucrats, magistrates, or judges. This shared background, even more than their wealth, gave the members of the elite a common outlook, making it easier for them to rise above their factional rivalries — unlike their counterparts in Buenos Aires and Montevideo. Even so, national consciousness evolved unevenly among the social groups and regions of Brazil. Nationalist feeling was present in the major port cities; it was evident a decade later when British efforts to stem the slave trade met with an indignant popular response in many areas of Brazil. Yet centrifugal forces still frustrated the growth of nationalism, and when local or provincial interests clashed with those of the nation, it was never certain which would prevail.

*The Farroupilha*

The Farrapo Revolt of 1835–45 demonstrated the perils of placing provincial interests first. In the beginning, the rebellion looked like any number of minor insurrections that had plagued the country since independence. Yet it soon took on a more ominous aspect, first, because it was broadly representative of local thinking; second, because its leadership included many former imperial officials; and third, because its republican-secessionist orientation was intrinsically appealing (and therefore dangerous) in a region bordering the Plata.

For years the ranchers in Rio Grande do Sul had chafed under interprovincial custom duties that made it difficult to compete with Buenos Aires in the jerked-beef markets of Rio and São Paulo. The Riograndense sense of Brazilianness was understated and far less defined than the sense of being part of a rich southern province of temperate grasslands and rolling hills. A deepening frustration among these gaúchos enhanced the influence of the most hard-line elements in the 1830s. In September 1835 a force of armed horsemen from the borderland with Uruguay seized the provincial capital of Pôrto Alegre. Deposing the imperial agents, the rebels (whom the press derided as ragamuffins, or "Farrapos") claimed they were saving their country from disorder, precisely like Rosas in Buenos Aires. In subsequently opting for independence, they asserted a basic incompatibility between their province and the Brazilian nation — a difference so profound that it could only be resolved through separation.

The Farrapos' lack of organization gave the central government some breathing room in 1836. A counterrevolt brought Pôrto Alegre back under loyal control, and the rebels had difficulty recovering from a series of minor battlefield reverses. Yet government armies failed to exploit these advantages with a concerted attack, and the Farrapos redoubled their efforts in the countryside.

Rio Grande's long border with Uruguay acted like a sieve through which arms, supplies, and foreign volunteers passed to the rebels. Rosas provided some of this support, and curiously, so did some of his enemies in Montevideo. The latter wished to encourage a more liberal, republican order throughout South America and saw the Farrapos as natural allies. The Bonaerense governor simply hoped to complicate the politics of Argentina's traditional enemies.

The government crushed revolts in Pará and Maranhão through intervention by troops from outside the northern region. Other rebellions in Minas Gerais and São Paulo also received a heavy dose of military repression. But the main focus of Rio's efforts was the Farrapo insurgency in the south.

In April 1838 the rebels gained an important victory over imperial forces at Rio Pardo and felt themselves more secure as a result. Yet beneath the surface, the Farrapo cause was weaker than many suspected. Military aid from Rosas and the Uruguayans was erratic. Certain liberals in Montevideo never wanted the door completely shut on the empire. Also, the imperial forces held several strategic locales, including Pôrto Alegre. In addition, though the Farrapos enjoyed popular support, they were uncertain as to what their "nation" really consisted of. Many rebels had grown up in the borderlands and felt no loyalty to either Rio or Montevideo. The Farrapo government at Piratini was thus opportunistic, willing to discuss union with Uruguay, Corrientes, Entre Ríos, or any other neighboring region. Even Francia's Paraguay was not excluded. Constructing a "nation" on such an improbably fluid basis was bound to cause problems for the Farrapo cause, and it did.

In June 1839 the rebels thrust into Santa Catarina, gathering strength, so they supposed, from local sympathizers who wanted a republic on the Farrapo model. In fact, an expanded war had serious flaws. It depended on unreliable allies, cost a great deal in terms of horses and materiel, and enjoyed indifferent support among Farrapo fighters. In the end, they could not sustain their northward advance and fell back into their home province much chastened.

The Farrapo retreat coincided with the arrival of a new imperial commander in Rio Grande do Sul, Luis Alves de Lima e Silva, the baron, later count, marquis, and duke of Caxias (1803–80). Son of an imperial regent, Caxias was destined to occupy a lofty spot in Brazil's national mythology. He often had to act as statesman as much as military man. Shrewdly competent in both roles, the nobleman learned the art of giving orders early in life. Immaculate in his dress, he was soft spoken, polite, and smoothly in control of himself. He seemed to radiate calm composure and authority.[8] He had served with the Imperial Guard and at various postings around the country. His triumphant campaign against the rebels of Maranhão was a model of counterinsurgency (itself an impressive innovation in Brazil); the victory brought Caxias the nomination as president of that province. Shortly thereafter, he became vice president of São Paulo province before returning to Rio Grande do Sul to oppose the Farrapos.

Caxias knew that much of the fight had gone out of the gaúcho rebels since they abandoned Santa Catarina. Even with the help of foreign adventurers, notably Giuseppe Garibaldi, the republican movement was now on the defensive. The Farrapo leaders sought a way out. Had Caxias insisted on a comprehensive victory, he faced the ugly prospect of an unending guerrilla war indistinguishable from brigandage. He therefore offered generous terms in February 1845. By his order, officers in the rebel army reentered the imperial military with the ranks they had held under the Farrapo regime. To satisfy Riograndense demands, the imperial government had already imposed a 25 percent import duty on Platine jerked beef. This concession rendered the Brazilian connection far more attractive to Rio Grande do Sul than association with the Plata.

Caxias had won. His diplomacy, forbearance, and military skill had restored the south to Dom Pedro with little damage to the vanquished.

Indeed, the Riograndenses appeared fully reconciled to a new life within Brazil. As the Farrapo insurgency subsided, many in the imperial government felt reassured that Brazil had finally gained control over its own destiny. Perhaps in a way it had, yet such a conclusion was more often expressed among the elites than the poor. Brazil had begun to function as a "nation" of elites, the emperor included, who shared a narrow view of the country's identity. This provided little basis for full nationalism, which would have required an appeal to all classes and regions.

Nevertheless, the state — as opposed to the "nation" — displayed more solidity than in the past. It had become a force to reckon with. In 1844 the commercial treaty with Britain expired and with it went the last extraterritorial rights enjoyed by a foreign power. Imperial politicians now felt more secure in their ability to influence foreign affairs. Having disposed of the country's internal enemies, they turned their attention to Rosas and his allies in the south. Brazilians were hardly alone in aligning against outsiders. The whole continent was reassessing the direction of politics, combining the quest for modernization with a more assertive nationalism, a willingness to look outward rather than inward, and a desire to settle accounts with foreign opponents.

*The López Family and the New Nationalism*

The most curious opening to the outside occurred in Paraguay after the death of José Gaspar de Francia in 1840. The *Caraí* had kept political power tightly in his hands and supervised government affairs, general finances, and military preparedness down to the meanest detail. His little army maintained garrisons in Asunción and several strategic locations near Paraguay's frontiers, but it had little to do. There were periodic confrontations with outside powers and with Indians, but in general a closed-door policy saved Paraguay from the trauma that the lower provinces had gone through since independence.

Yet the country paid a high price for internal stability and peace. Paraguayan society stagnated under such autarky. Many of the earlier Hispano-Guaraní cultural traits — paternalism, mistrust of outsiders, a narrow focus on community—reasserted themselves. The economy returned to self-sufficiency, barter, and reciprocity *(jopói)*. Political innovations, once so inviting, withered into nothingness after 1816.

In practice, the Paraguayan government had a simple character, for it was a republic in name only. Francia's *subdelegados* translated his wishes into policy at the local level, issuing internal passports, punishing criminals, and collecting taxes. They sometimes administered state ranches and logging operations. Country people saw their government as having a strong but efficient hand. It was legitimate because it fit into their concept of how a responsible administration should act. The regime did not clash with their traditions, it embraced them.

One of those traditions involved upholding the authority of the father figure. As dictator and therefore Paraguay's *pater-familias*, Dr. Francia had much to recommend him. As he grew older, for instance, he displayed far less vindictiveness toward his rivals. Local landowners and Spanish-born merchants who once disputed his mandate found refuge in the small hamlets of the interior; like Artigas, they discovered that Francia's benevolence increased the farther they got from Asunción. Though they had limited options, they enjoyed a quiet measure of freedom. They might study, take in pupils, practice law, engage in local commerce, or raise cattle. So long as they stayed apart from each other and took care with their public statements, Francia let them live unmolested.[9]

Though they respected the agents of the government, country people, Asunceños, and elites all preferred to keep them at arm's length. When such avoidance was impossible, most Paraguayans assumed a profoundly submissive bearing; they used every honorific while simultaneously feigning ignorance in order to escape responsibility for any problem or failure (a practice called *ñembotavy*). Paraguayans might have been successful farmers and tenacious, resourceful fighters, but they were emasculated by the Francian state. This left them their clearly defined, traditional roles but little else. Politics were beyond their preserve.

The dictator never set out to create a nation. Yet his policies succeeded in doing something rather like that. His regime served to promote a sense of identity among the Paraguayans, a broad confirmation of their status as a separate people, full of pride if not power. The flaw in the system, of course, was that it left no room for a successor. And the dictator was a very old man. In September 1840 he succumbed to dropsy, having ruled the country for twenty-six years. A short period of uncertainty followed, during which time many Paraguayans refused to believe that Francia had died. People called him *el difunto*, as if his spirit still walked the earth. Few were aware through the hot summer months that his battalion commanders had positioned themselves to dominate the country. In the end, however, their jealousies prevented them from making much headway.

In early 1841 the republic adopted a consular regime headed by two men of differing talents. The first, Mariano Roque Alonso, was a semiliterate militia officer who gained power through a barracks coup. Finding it impossible to administer a state without learned assistance, he turned to Carlos Antonio López (1787–1862), one of the last graduates of the Asunción seminary. López soon eclipsed his mentor in authority, and though a general congress in March named the two coequal rulers for a period of three years, in fact the redoubtable López ruled alone.

The new head of state had spent much of his life as a country solicitor and rancher in the small town of Rosario. Though of modest birth, López married well and, by the social standards of the Paraguayan interior, rose high in the ranks of the rural elite. He avoided politics, but because of his education, both peasants and ranchers regarded him as an enlightened man.

Their estimation was well deserved. As consul, López began to make changes in the way Paraguay was administered. He created a new state apparatus to replace the colonial structures that had been the mainstay of the Francia regime. His innovations included new ministerial positions, a reorganized treasury, and a military officer corps. He filled these posts with talented individuals, a good many of whom came from his same propertied class. He also founded a "literary academy" in 1841 that had spaces for 149 students. Above all, Carlos Antonio López was willing to experiment and to learn from past mistakes. If his basic impulses were as authoritarian as those of the late dictator, he balanced them with a more modern inclination.

Such was the case when he adjusted the legal framework of the Paraguayan Republic in 1844. In that year, he authored an up-to-date constitution, something that Francia had never done, though "up to date" for López meant minor borrowings from the French and Spanish legal tomes he had studied as a youth. He suppressed the Laws of the Indies as "being incompatible with a free and independent polity," but his constitution had nothing in it of democracy. All it offered was a fig leaf of legitimacy to cover the crude reality of his personal rule. At no point did the constitution allude to "liberty." Instead, it concentrated exclusively on the prerogatives of the executive, to whom all citizens owed "recognition and obedience." Despite a theoretical division of powers, the president was given a legal obligation to "maintain order" and to cancel, amend, or confirm legislation and judicial decisions.

López's constitution called upon him to convoke a congress every five years—but only in order to issue presidential messages, not to debate. Membership in congressional bodies was limited to *propietarios* who were required to present themselves at the appropriate time. And when they did convene, they always looked like country bumpkins out of their element in Asunción. Such men López could manipulate with ease because he knew their personal strengths and weaknesses. And he knew that they knew him and the power he could wield. Thus, when the constitution of 1844 assigned the president a ten-year term and indefinite "reelection," no complaints were voiced, no criticisms offered, just respectful applause.

Why did López feel constrained to draft such a document? His predecessor had ruled for decades by fiat, and in practice little had changed in Paraguay. Carlos Antonio López, however, saw himself as a modern man. Every contemporary regime in Europe, he observed, had crafted a legal structure appropriate to its needs and to the times. Nation building was a road to modernity and a guarantee of survival. Paraguay deserved its place among the new states of the world. At the same time,

López wanted to open the country to outside trade, and it was best that foreigners understood who set policy within its borders.

Notably absent from these considerations was any reference to Paraguay's Hispano-Guaraní character. López did not see the nation in such terms. Since colonial times, the state and the community were parallel entities that only occasionally overlapped. One was Spanish-oriented and imposed originally by the colonial empire; the other was Guaraní and directed inward as part of the country's oral culture. The modernization that López proposed had little to do with the latter.

In fact, Guaraní had no words to convey the meaning of many critically important political propositions.[10] But then the new president felt no need to consult with those Paraguayans who were unacquainted with Spanish. As an autocrat, he could afford to take such people for granted. Indeed, as part of his push for modernity, López evidently tried to prohibit the use of Guaraní surnames because he felt that they summoned up images of an Indian, hence backward, past. His son found reasons to regret this stance after war broke out in the 1860s and the use of Guaraní took on a military aspect.[11] However, the *vox populi* had no role in the organization of the new Paraguayan state.

Like Dr. Francia, Carlos Antonio López used his legal reputation as a springboard to power, but unlike the dictator, he gave in to many human weaknesses. He enjoyed eating to excess, stuffing himself with beef and manioc until he was fit only for the hammock. By the time he reached middle age, he had grown so monstrously fat that he could no longer ride a horse and had to be driven about in an open carriage escorted by a troop of guards.

López's sins were not limited to gluttony. A worse fault involved the favoritism he showed the members of his family. He obtained the bishopric of Asunción for his brother Basilio. He permitted his wife and daughters to run a money exchange out of the presidential residence, where they purchased ragged banknotes from the public at an 8 percent discount and traded them at full value from the treasury.[12] His two youngest sons, Venancio and Benigno, held high positions within the government while administering large private holdings (particularly in ranching). But it was upon his eldest son, Francisco Solano, that López showered particular affection.

The future marshal was born in the Paraguayan interior in 1826. Malicious gossip attended his birth, for rumor had it that López was not the father. Yet Carlos Antonio López did everything he could to indulge the boy, first with sweets and an occasional coin, later with the highest posts in the government. Francisco Solano responded as if all in the nation were his personal property to be played with or discarded according to whim. He had a restless nature, and it was not clear that either a father's love, or a country's isolation, could contain it.

Meanwhile, there was much work to be done. Paraguayans still remember Carlos Antonio López as the "Great Builder," and he merits that title. During his twenty-year rule, he oversaw the construction of public thoroughfares, a foundry and industrial smithy, a shipyard, a national theater, an arsenal, a legislative palace, several presidential residences and ministry buildings, and various military facilities. He inaugurated Paraguay's first railroad, which was among the first in the Plata. And he repaired and expanded older edifices, such as the cathedral, bringing them up to midcentury standards. Such projects demonstrated López's enthusiasm for the modern age of steam and iron. But they also indicated a determination that the majesty of the Paraguayan state be universally recognized. The new state edifices succeeded in this regard, for they stood out like leviathans among the brick, adobe, and thatch constructions of the capital city. Such efforts cost a great deal of money and labor, but López had access to both. He increased revenues by reintroducing taxes that Francia had let lapse. He expanded state leaseholds to peasant farmers in exchange for annual payment (or a portion of their harvest). More importantly, the state generated profits from its monopolies in yerba mate and timber and from the dozens of ranches that it operated. These enterprises brought in foreign exchange, and the government became Paraguay's dominant exporter, a force to be reckoned with in commercial, not just political, matters.[13]

As for labor, López greatly expanded the number of workers in government service. He made extensive use of convict labor, but he also enacted a broad-based conscription law—nearly universal for young men—and set the soldiers to work at state projects. The cultivation of foodstuffs for private consumption did not especially suffer; women had done much of the agricultural labor previously and now stepped in to do the rest. While many of these labor practices had colonial antecedents, Carlos Antonio López made more extensive use of them than either Francia or his Bourbon predecessors. And he gave them a clearer direction.

This widespread mobilization was bound to have significant social and political effects. In general, López managed to popularize the various state projects as being the business not just of the government but also of Paraguay as a community. His was ultimately an appeal to a national sentiment, though an ambiguous one, for López wanted obedience as much as enthusiasm. He clearly got the former—that much his bureaucrats and spies could arrange. Whether he brought about a widely felt patriotism, however, no one could tell.

The same fervor that López put into his construction plans he also put into foreign relations. The two were interconnected. In order to build a strong state, he needed to cultivate respect for his government abroad. That was not an easy task. López was naturally cautious and had little experience with diplomacy. He knew that many had never heard of Paraguay, except as some semimythical "inland Japan." He wanted good relations with all foreign powers. Yet over the years he had serious conflicts with Brazil, Buenos Aires, Britain, France, and the United States.[14] He sent his nineteen-year-old son Francisco Solano as general in chief of a military expedition to Corrientes in 1845–46. His intention was to dislodge Rosas's allies from the Argentine northeast as part of a new rapprochement with Brazil and the Unitarian factions to the south. Although the intervention failed in its objective, it demonstrated López's willingness to abandon isolationism in favor of a more activist role for Paraguay in Platine politics. Foreign respect and unconditional acceptance of Paraguay's right to exist as a nation—these were what the president sought, and he did so in an unbending, completely focused way.

*War and Nation Building* 69

## South America Faces the 1850s

Despite the elements of modernity seeping into the South American scene at the beginning of the new decade, the continent had yet to take on a modern guise. There were striking social divisions; illiterate masses, whether slave or free, felt themselves only minimally a part of a world greater than their own small communities. True, the elites were trying to construct an image of nationhood that appealed universally. They offered public processions, the waving of red, green, or sky-blue banners; loud speeches in honor of the emperor; and celebrations of the president's birthday, complete with fireworks and bullfights. The average person celebrated such events. Yet it was difficult to know whether this was an honest expression of patriotism or just an opportunity to drink *aguardiente* after a long day's work. Perhaps it was both.

In any case, the political integration the elites wished to encourage had yet to materialize. While the assertion of leadership by a wealthy upper class was á normal, rarely questioned part of South American social relations, there was still no common sense of ideals among either Brazilians, Uruguayans, or Argentines. There was no political community that held each nationality together vertically by its shared character rather than horizontally by reason of state authority. Only in Paraguay was some of this present, thanks to the distinctiveness of Hispano-Guaraní culture and the small size of the country. Francia's isolationism, followed by Carlos Antonio López's universal draft, provided catalysts to create a national spirit.

None of the nearby countries had anything similar, though. After three decades of "nationhood," Brazil had experienced few changes in its basic political and social structures. The empire looked like it had in the late colonial period, an aggregation of regional economies all oriented to the outside rather than to each other. The printing press and the various steamship lines improved communications between the various provinces, but isolation remained the dominant feature in most areas. Though Riograndenses proclaimed their renewed loyalty to the imperial system as a result of the Farrapo defeat, they still had little common ground with Sertanejos, Baianos, and other Brazilians.

Dom Pedro had done much to promote the idea of a Brazilian nation. He was widely popular, and the cultural, scientific, and political institutions he favored did enjoy some success. Yet it was difficult for him or anyone else to inspire a widely felt nationalism. Subordinated classes understood that the system upheld the interests of the elites more than their own. Their affection for the emperor was honest enough, but they remained unconvinced about the monarchy. In effect, the poor people of Brazil acquiesced in the established order, but they did not support it.

For the Brazilian elites, who saw nationhood in terms of European models, the fatalism of the masses was an inescapable annoyance. It had its good side, for apathetic subjects were unlikely to disrupt traditional privileges. But the same elites believed that Brazil was on the verge of a great material expansion in which all would share, if only all would contribute. Modernization was contingent, they thought, on the projection of Brazilian power, for only great nations like Britain and France deserved the unalloyed support of their people. "Greatness" was tied in their minds to war, just as it was for many of their European contemporaries, especially in the German states.[15] For the empire to follow suit, it had to stand firm against outside opponents, and the most obvious, most implacable foe was Rosas.

In Buenos Aires, the Restorer of the Laws had seen many enemies come and go: the early Unitarians, the British, the Patagonian Indians—he had defeated all through negotiation, stealth, and hard fighting. Yet by the beginning of the 1850s, Rosas had run out of ideas. Once praised for his innovative experiments with *saladeros*, he was now seen as part of a bygone generation, incapable of thinking beyond old despotic habits.

His exiled enemies in Chile and Montevideo were no longer quite so young themselves. But they had something that Rosas lacked, a comprehensive plan for the modernization of Argentina. The Men of 1837 all wanted to build a new society based on European immigration and on full participation in the Atlantic economy. Such a plan rejected the Argentina of the Pampas and sought a national identity that eschewed *caudillismo* in favor of an elitist democracy. Those groups in society whom the revolutionaries deemed incapable of assimilation into the new order would be pushed out onto the Patagonian frontier to eventually disappear.

Of course, this "democracy" had more in it of *porteño* hegemony than of popular sentiment, yet its proponents disguised this fact. Such deception was justified, for as they saw it, building the nation was identical to fostering human progress. Their perspective resembled that of the Brazilian elites — though significantly not that of Carlos Antonio López.

The exiled revolutionaries were under no illusions about the provinces; the *provincianos* had their own interests and would pursue them no matter what. As one exile wrote: "The *patria* for the Correntino is Corrientes, for the Cordobés Córdoba, for the Tucumano Tucumán, for the *porteño* Buenos Aires, for the Gaucho the dirt upon which he was born. The life and common interests that make up the rational sentiment of homeland is an incomprehensible abstraction for them."[16]

Yet the anti-Rosistas had every reason for optimism. Though the social conditions in the Argentine countryside had changed little since independence, the political situation now offered room for hope. Brazil, Britain, the other European states, the Uruguayan liberals, and perhaps even the distant Paraguayans might unite in a campaign to overturn the tyrant Rosas. The young Men of 1837 expected to prevail as mature Argentine statesmen in the 1850s by ousting Rosas and building a regime dedicated to civic virtue. Their belief in the possibility of near-universal progress might have seemed naive to the *caudillos*, but it was keenly felt. Like many of their European contemporaries, they defined progress in national terms so that creating a "progressive order" for them also meant creating a nation. And the means to this end, paradoxically, was violence.

War, in fact, was the major ingredient in South America's transition to a more modern political order. Not war on a restricted scale, but a grand, full-fledged showdown between old and new. In wishing to break Rosas, the Argentine revolutionaries did not merely want to replace him — they wanted to transform all aspects of Argentine politics, turning an agglomeration of weak provinces into a single nation. The Brazilian elites had a similar goal, though in their case the effort to conquer Rosas and his Oriental allies was less a matter of constructing a nation than of preserving a political order. As for Paraguay, nation building there turned on the whims of one all-powerful man, his wife, sons, and daughters. In joining the crusade against the Argentine *caudillo*, the members of the López family signaled their commitment to a "modern" vision of their country, especially of its military. At the same time, their concern was in keeping with traditional political assumptions, chief of which was that the country's neighbors wished to seize her territory and enslave her people. Building the Paraguayan nation, then, was not a matter of preserving social privileges, defining borders, or recasting political institutions. It was a matter of survival.

# II

## Uneasy Neighbors

# Paraguay Faces the Empire

## 4

The independence that came to South America in the early 1800s was not accompanied by clear territorial divisions between the new states. Border disputes plagued the continent from the Darien Gap to Patagonia and frustrated the development of good international relations. On occasion, disputes involved large or strategically important pieces of land; more often, observers attested to the obscurity of the disputes and the unimportance of the territory involved. Even more remarkable was the intensity with which contending sides pressed their respective claims, sometimes at the negotiating table, sometimes on the battlefield. The Paraguayan War, for its part, only partially originated in border disputes. Other factors far beyond the frontiers of Paraguay affected both the origin and the course of the war. Yet the country's border difficulties with Argentina and Brazil always added to the climate of mistrust in the region and made a violent clash on a large scale as likely as anything in history can be.[1]

The Paraguayan border question, like its cousin in the Banda Oriental, was tied to conflicting conceptions of nationalism. A nation defends its sovereignty up to its legal frontiers. Paraguay, which formally declared its independence only in the mid-1840s, had seen its government construct a serious and unyielding nationalism symbolized by loud claims to irascibility. The twin slogans "Independence or Death!" and "To Conquer or to Die!" were coined to meet the needs of a state that was continually at odds with its neighbors. In this way, every slip of official paper, every government publication, and every piece of currency bore the warning that the youthful Republic of Paraguay demanded the same respect accorded its larger neighbors. And the largest and most problematic of these neighbors was the Empire of Brazil.

### A Long Dispute: The Mato Grosso

Brazil and Paraguay inherited and accepted the imperial thrust of their respective mother countries. Just as Spain and Portugal made claims against each other's holdings in South America, so too did the successor states seek to gain territorial advantage.

Drawing on seven hundred years of struggle with the Moors, the Spaniards and then the Paraguayans based their claims to final sovereignty on legally and divinely sanctioned precepts. The Demarcation of 1493, which Pope Alexander VI had authorized and overseen, divided control of South America between Portugal on the Brazilian bulge and Spain throughout the rest of the continent. No further justification was necessary. The Portuguese and their Brazilian successors always displayed more flexibility in interpreting legal and diplomatic mandates than their Spanish or Spanish American neighbors. What might be written on a piece of vellum was of little consequence to them unless it worked to their advantage. What mattered most was physical presence. If their settlers could occupy an area, legal authorization would eventually follow.

Both sides prepared ornate casuistries to explain and defend their moves toward self-aggrandizement. True, the Portuguese were more actively expansionist and the Spaniards more defensive over the long run, but it made little difference in the way they behaved on the frontier. No move that vexed the other side was unworthy of consideration. Arming hostile Indian groups, razing rival settlements, falsifying charts and other documents—all were used time and again in a prolonged struggle. Sometimes competition took the form of a single interloper searching for gold or Indian slaves in an unauthorized area. At other times the full force of government policy was summoned on behalf of

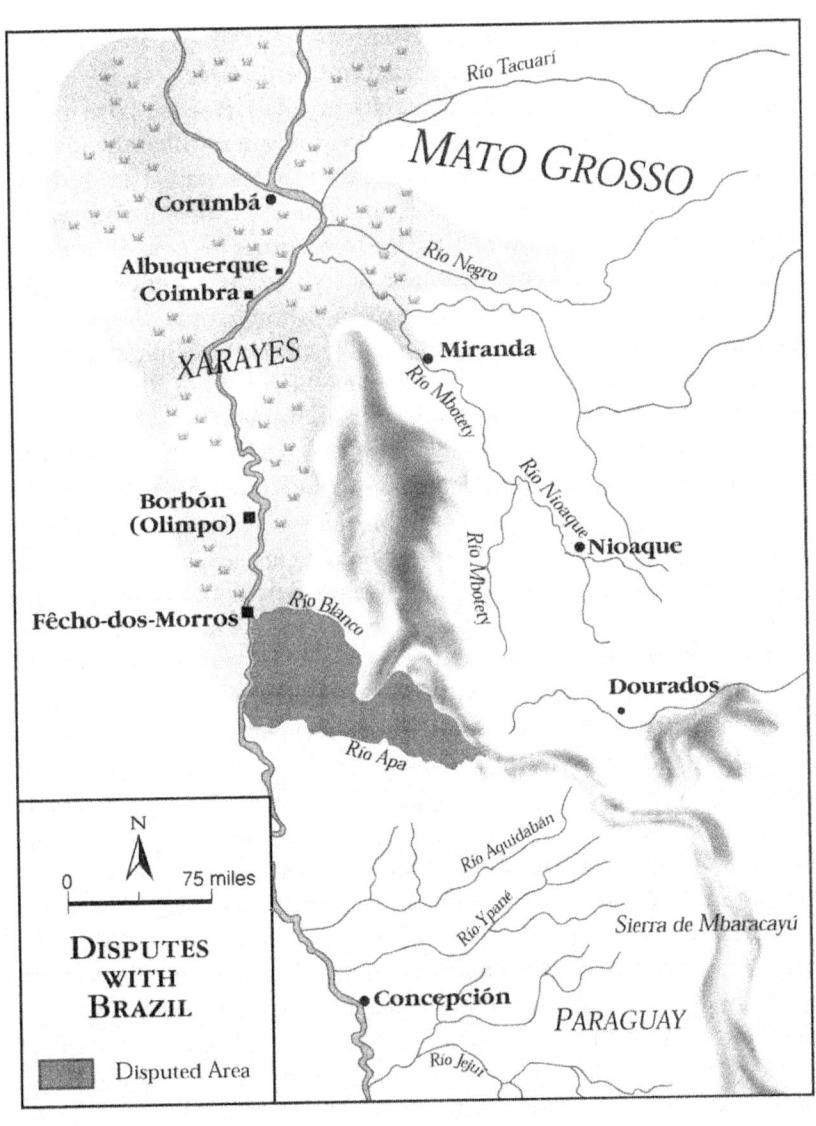

territorial expansion. Even the most desolate and rarely visited areas became the object of intense interest and competition.

Early maps of South America depict as one immense lake the region later called the Mato Grosso. This body of water, which the Indians named Xarayes, was described by explorers as spreading in all directions, unbroken except for the occasional *camalote*, or floating vegetation. On overcast days, rowers in canoes sometimes became disoriented upon the lake, for it was impossible to tell where the sky ended and the waters began. Given this obstacle, any expedition to open the center of the continent would have to be mounted from some other direction.

Lake Xarayes had a powerful hold over the minds of the explorers, even though it never existed in the way usually described. The swampy Pantanal, which covers thousands of miles of south and southwestern Mato Grosso on a seasonal basis, is generally shallow, normally less than a meter in depth. In fact, no impassable body of water prevented Europeans from penetrating the interior of South America. Yet such was the power of legend that meaningful European settlement of the southern Mato Grosso had to wait until the end of the eighteenth century.[2]

That neither Portugal nor Spain could establish clear title over this area was of little consequence to the two European governments. It turned out that the Pantanal was less a barrier than a doorway to a varied and potentially wealthy province. To the north, the swamps gave way abruptly to a vast expanse of low hills and plateaus. Fertile soil and moderate climate characterized this huge area, which possessed many creeks and rivulets, some of which flowed north to the Amazon basin and others that flowed south toward Paraguay and the sea.

As early as 1719, bands of Paulista raiders, on the lookout for Indian captives for the coastal slave markets, found signs of mineral wealth in northern Mato Grosso. Later there was a full-scale gold rush; few found anything of value. Instead, they faced tremendous physical hardship far from home. The isolation of the region, the constant fear of hostile Indians, and the need for skilled canoe pilots caused most miners to travel in expensive, well-organized convoys. Traveling in this fashion meant that it took five to seven months to reach the gold districts from São

Paulo. The Guaicurú, Mbayá, and Payaguá Indians harassed the Portuguese at every turn (the Payaguá killed six hundred men in one convoy in 1725 and four hundred more in a raid five years later). Many prospectors died of want and of tropical diseases before finding a single nugget.[3]

By 1748 the remnants of the Portuguese mining settlements in the Mato Grosso were organized into a captaincy separate from São Paulo. Settlement continued into the nineteenth century, though most of this occurred in the north, where stockraising gradually replaced mining. In the south, settlement was intermittent and uncertain, for these southern districts were home to several groups of aggressive Indians, and Spain claimed these territories as well.

The 1750 Treaty of Madrid specifically addressed the question of rival land claims in South America. It focused more on the Banda Oriental and the Jesuit missions region than on the Mato Grosso. Nevertheless, the treaty did contain a major concession to the effect that Spain now accepted the Portuguese argument that the two governments should use the principle of *uti possidetis* to determine their common frontier. Thus did the Spaniards forego their long-cherished yet hopelessly unrealistic claim on territories dominated by Portugal. Effective occupation would be henceforth an important factor in resolving outstanding border problems in the Mato Grosso and elsewhere.[4]

Within several years, most sections of the Madrid treaty had been overturned, though not the references to *uti possidetis*. No one could decide what "effective occupation" along the Alto Paraguay really meant, and various border commissioners argued the point for decades. The Portuguese accepted what was supposed to be a definitive frontier as a result of a short war (1776–77) in which Spain gained control of the entire Banda Oriental. The subsequent 1777 Treaty of San Ildefonso fixed the Mato Grosso boundary as running from the Ygurey River to its chief source in the Sierra de Mbaracayú, then by a straight line to the head of the nearest river that emptied into the Alto Paraguay, down that river to the Alto Paraguay, and up the latter waterway to the Xarayes marsh.[5]

Even this specific delineation failed to satisfy both sides. The borderline at the Sierra de Mbaracayú posed no problem, but farther west it was a different matter. For the Portuguese, "nearest river" initially meant the Ypané, and finally the Apa, while the Spaniards maintained that the Blanco was the designated waterway. No one initially had the better claim. In 1792 the Spaniards founded Fort Borbón on the Chaco side of the Alto Paraguay, just below the mouth of the Blanco. This encampment thereafter exercised some control over both banks of the river. The 1777 treaty failed to indicate, however, that Spain had any right to the left bank. The Portuguese rejected this claim, but failed to advance one of their own.

### Indian Raids and Border Disputes along the Mato Grosso Frontier

In 1801, during the sixty-day War of the Oranges, a Spanish force from Asunción penetrated the Mato Grosso and assaulted the tiny Portuguese fort at Nova Coimbra. This expedition, which had as its object the expulsion of the Portuguese from southern Mato Grosso, was well equipped in armament and personnel.

Despite these advantages, the expedition failed miserably. A heavy storm pounded the little flotilla as it neared its objective, and the water-soaked militiamen, unable to land, retreated downriver to Concepción. Memory of this fiasco, which texts in the Asunción military schools now omit, was at the time a source of much discomfort and resentment among the Paraguayans; all the more so because, in its aftermath, Indians supported by the Portuguese began a series of incursions deep into northern Paraguay.[6]

The situation along the Mato Grosso–Paraguay frontier remained tense in the two decades before 1830. Smuggling was a factor, especially after Paraguayan ranchers expanded their holdings into the isolated frontier areas just before the end of the previous century.[7] Their Brazilian neighbors had never made their own livestock ventures succeed, so the Paraguayans found it tempting to avoid their own border posts and drive their cattle, horses, and mules to Brazilian settlements, where they exchanged the animals for gold. Less commonly, Brazilian smugglers crossed into Paraguay to return the favor. Their destination was the yerba mate district east of the ranching zone. Poor Paraguayan workers sent to harvest the yerba formed a market for those who would supply them with luxury items and alcohol. Peddlers *(changadores)* coming from Asunción sometimes met this demand, but Brazilian *contrabandistas* also periodically supplied demijohns of rum and other goods.

The Francia government took exception to this illegal trade and did everything possible to stamp it out. The dictator rejected the entreaties of Brazilian diplomats who promised closer political ties but failed to guarantee an end to encroachments in the north.[8] He also rejected talk of a legal commerce, which he saw as promising nothing but a "contemptible trade in bagatelles, [amounting] to no more than some hammocks, a little bit of cotton, and some bolts of very ordinary, crude cotton cloth."[9]

He did allow supervised trade at Pilar and Itapúa in the far south of Paraguay. Brazilian merchants were active in this commerce, particularly at Itapúa, which linked Paraguay to Rio Grande do Sul by means of a circuitous route across the Misiones wastelands. To some extent, the dictator favored the Brazilians who frequented the Itapúa market; after all, some imported commodities (such as paper and gunpowder) played a necessary role in the maintenance of his government. He had his police keep a careful eye on them notwithstanding, since he always suspected that their activities served as a cover for spying.[10]

Francia's suspicions were justified. When the Brazilians were not trying to trade with Paraguay, they were trying to subvert its authority along the frontier. The Guaicurú Indians who earlier had raided Brazilian mining settlements in Mato Grosso also engaged in regular attacks against the Paraguayan north. Most of these raids involved the theft of cattle, which the Indians then sold to the Brazilians. Although Mato Grosso settlers could not always repel the marauders, when possible they encouraged their raiding to the south—far better that the Paraguayans be the victims.[11]

Some of these assaults were notably bloody. Cutting his losses, Francia ordered his militia to withdraw to Concepción during the 1820s. Most of the large ranches north of the Aquidabán River then disappeared. Even communities along the Paraguay River felt the pressure of Guaicurú raids. Referring to the now-deserted settlement of Tevegó, the dictator noted that, despite the presence of his troops, "anytime the Indians desire, they come there as to a corral of sheep, cause many deaths, plunder and take away whatever they wish."[12]

To appear not to have abandoned the north entirely, Dr. Francia left a small garrison at Fort Borbón. This camp was situated at a strong position high on the Chaco bank of the Alto Paraguay. From this point and from Concepción, Francia occasionally mounted military sweeps against Indian *tolderías* in the disputed region. Since the Guaicurú could disperse into the bush at a moment's notice, these campaigns accomplished little. But his objective was not so much to pacify the region as to keep up a Paraguayan presence, even one that was necessarily temporary.

Francia's death in 1840 brought few changes at first. The dictator had spent the last decade carefully building his dominion over the north, but this authority was always conditional, affected by Brazilian and Indian incursions, and costly to maintain. His successor, Carlos Antonio López, thought the expense worthwhile. The *yerbales* and ranch lands beyond Concepción offered Paraguay a potential source of wealth unequaled in the rest of the country, and the only way to resuscitate the economy in that region was to provide security for settlers and investors.

López met this challenge by reinforcing Borbón, which he renamed Fort Olimpo. He then founded four forts along the left bank of the Apa, each with garrisons of over a hundred men.[13] This was only the beginning of his efforts to renew control over abandoned territories. Within five years his militia had built nearly a score of such forts and subsidiary guard posts in the north, not only along the Apa but also along the Alto Paraguay, Aquidabán, and Ypané Rivers. López also offered land in this area to any peasant who would migrate there from the south.[14]

These measures worked after a fashion. The Indian threat receded and many of the old ranches began operations again. So did work in the *yerbales*, though in this case López had considerable trouble keeping enough laborers on hand, so great was their fear of Indians. He often had to resort to drafting vagrants to make up for deserters. In 1848 he went so far as to order that "from this day forward, deserters from the yerba stations will be treated to the death penalty, just as is imposed on deserters in [times of] combat."[15] By the end of the decade, the permanent non-Indian population of Paraguayans between the Ypané and Apa Rivers had grown to nearly ten thousand, a figure perhaps ten times what it had been under Francia.[16]

*An Incident at Fêcho-dos-Morros*
The middle and late 1840s saw some marked improvements in official relations between the Brazilian government and that of Paraguay. For the Brazilians, rapprochement was part of a plan to gain allies to help unseat the Rosas regime in Buenos Aires. In this, the government in Rio followed a colonial precedent: by encouraging disaffection in the Platine Litoral, the Brazilians sought to weaken *porteño* influence and give themselves a freer hand in the estuary. The collapse of the republican revolt in Rio Grande do Sul in 1845 gave a new impulse to this goal. Now was a good time to strike at Rosas.[17]

Carlos Antonio López demanded concessions for his cooperation. Brazilian recognition of Paraguayan independence, which finally came in 1844, he deemed insufficient. This had to be coupled, he argued, with an agreement on free navigation, commerce, extradition, and most important, boundaries.[18] Negotiations on these points began in Asunción in 1850.

The discussions at first proceeded amicably. Then, midway through the talks, Carlos Antonio López learned that the Brazilians had built a primitive fort, Fêcho-dos-Morros, sixty-three miles north of the confluence of the Apa and Alto Paraguay Rivers on a wooded island that rose some eighty feet above the water level of the Alto Paraguay. The island boasted more capybara and tapirs than Brazilian soldiers, but its occupation nonetheless posed a threat, for nearby at the eastern bank of the river loomed a 1,350-foot-high volcanic formation that commanded the countryside in all directions.[19] On its rounded summit, the Brazilians could establish an artillery battery that could cut off the Paraguayans from their base at Olimpo.

Was Brazil negotiating in bad faith? Certainly the decision to build a fort in the disputed territory seemed ill advised. The Paraguayan response was clear. López ordered the expulsion of the Brazilian troops from Fêcho-dos-Morros and the destruction of the fort itself. A strong detachment immediately sailed upriver, and on the morning of 14 October 1850 the Paraguayan *lanchas* opened a three-hour barrage on Fêcho. The Paraguayans were under orders to let the Brazilians escape, so although they fired a great deal of musketry and shells into the air that day, little of it was directed on the Brazilian position. In the end, the garrison of thirty-one men fled eastward to the safety of Mbayá *tolderías* and thence to Coimbra; two dead pickets and an Indian auxiliary were left behind. The Paraguayans then set the site ablaze. Brazil's reign over Fêcho-dos-Morros had lasted a scant fifteen days.[20]

Brazilian negotiators in Asunción swallowed their pride at word of this military reverse. So anxious were they to gain allies against Rosas that they signed a treaty that bound their country to the old San Ildefonso delineations. They later claimed that López had taken advantage of their momentary inability to defend the Apa line. In the end, though, the Brazilian parliament refused to ratify the treaty and in turn received only nominal help against the governor of Buenos Aires.

*New Negotiations and the Transit Question*

The attempt to establish a presence at Fêcho-dos-Morros was only a small part of the Brazilian effort to legitimize the empire's frontier claims in Mato Grosso. As López consolidated Paraguayan rule in the north, he gave stimulus to the Brazilians to reinforce and develop the settlements on their side of the line. Paraguayans later argued that such development had little to do with secure borders. Had the Apa presented a genuine barrier — had it been a Danube, a Mississippi, or a Plata — then Paraguay would have relinquished the land between it and the Blanco. The Apa, however, was little more than a stream, and López wanted the swampy land to its north as a shield. There was disingenuousness in this position: marshes abounded everywhere, and if they had never stopped Indian raids (even when the Indians were mounted on slow-moving horses), then why should they be expected to stop the Brazilian army?

At this stage, the Paraguayans were not interested in going beyond the Blanco into the Mato Grosso itself. Indeed, during the late 1840s, Carlos Antonio López had even sent an agent to Rio to suggest the neutralization of the disputed territory and thus rid both sides of any reason for confrontation.[21] Although this suggestion went unanswered and the incident at Fêcho-dos-Morros temporarily clouded good relations, López continued to press for a peaceful resolution of his dispute with the empire. Because of his prudent stance (and also because of obvious military constraints), the survival of Brazil's Mato Grosso settlements never seemed much in question. Their future as viable economic entities, however, posed a different problem, and it was on this point that the Brazilians needed a concession from Asunción.

Because of the difficulties of overland communication and supply, the imperial government had long sought to use the Paraguay River as the link between Rio de Janeiro and the Brazilian far west. The river route, however, was politically sensitive. It passed through a thousand miles of Argentine and Paraguayan territory before leading into Brazil. Imperial diplomats had never secured from López any clear agreement on transit via the Paraguay River. The Paraguayan leader feared that cooperation on this point might feed an already evident expansionism on Brazil's part. His government's newspaper, *El Semanario*, later explained his position in the following terms: "[Brazil] says 'I need to go through the territory of Paraguay in order to arrive home; this need gives me some right to impose upon Paraguay the obligation to let me pass;' . . . Paraguay responds 'I recognize that law and natural reason insist that I grant passage to Brazil, and I would gladly do so; but I have an even greater right to demand of Brazil that this [transit] not be prejudicial to me; real security [can only come] with the delineation of borders . . . make such a demarcation, give me this guarantee, and everything can be worked out.'"[22]

This diplomatic impasse sparked the establishment in 1853 of two new Brazilian military colonies in southern Mato Grosso, Brilhante and Nioaque. Under a plan sponsored by the Baron of Antonina, these colonies provided a key link in a new mixed fluvial-overland highway that connected the province to the Atlantic. The imperial government sought to counteract the bad effects of the transit problem with Paraguay by literally going around it. Yet the presence of the Nioaque and Brilhante colonies (and, ultimately, smaller colonies at Dourados and Miranda), instead of alleviating the difficulty with Paraguay, in fact aggravated it, since all these posts lay within or near the disputed zone.[23]

Carlos Antonio López matched the Brazilian forts with new forts of his own. By 1854 his troops had built eight such installations along the Apa: Arrecife, San Carlos, Observación del Apa, Observación de Quien Vive, Itaguí del Apa, Rinconada del Apa, Estrella, and Bella Vista. Another large permanent camp, also called Bella Vista, was founded at the same time some fifteen miles to the south. The reinforced Paraguayan presence in the north was not only military in character: twenty new ranches were soon in operation within twenty-five miles of the Apa.[24]

A de facto border came into existence, a border lined with bayonets. The two governments had reached no agreement on river transit. Relations between Paraguay and Brazil had become tense and so remained until 1858. On one occasion in 1855, after an acrimonious exchange of notes, the imperial government dispatched a fleet of twenty ships mounting 120 cannons to force Paraguayan acceptance of the Brazilian position on transit. Argentine authorities, who would one day regret the decision, gave the fleet commander permission to pass upriver through their territory to Paraguay. Having come this far, the Brazilians felt optimistic about settling the matter on their terms. Ironically, their efforts were wasted because no one had consulted the navigational charts of the Paraguay River to see how low it would be in February. With the Brazilian fleet unable to go beyond Corrientes, the 1855 confrontation was deemed a complete failure by many in Brazilian political and military circles. The Argentines saw no benefit in the affair for any party, themselves included.[25]

*Free Navigation on the Alto Paraguay*

On 6 April 1856, Paraguay and Brazil signed a treaty of friendship, navigation, and commerce in Rio de Janeiro. This agreement conceded free navigation to Brazil (and all other foreign powers) without any clear determination on the question of limits, discussion of which was postponed for six years.[26] Foreign Minister José Berges, who had negotiated for Paraguay at the Brazilian capital, thought that he had made as good a treaty as he was likely to get.[27] When he returned to Asunción, he learned that Carlos Antonio López thought otherwise. The president at first delayed ratification of the accord and then, after he eventually did approve it, did much to frustrate its observance; he levied irregular duties on goods in transit to Mato Grosso, and his sentinels and customs officers were encouraged to exaggerate their officiousness in dealing with foreign vessels bound for the same destination.[28]

In the end, López gave in. He had lately become involved in a thorny diplomatic confrontation with the United States over the less than diplomatic commercial activities of the local American representative. López wanted no further foreign complications.[29] In January 1858 Imperial Councilor José María da Silva Paranhos, the future viscount of Rio Branco, arrived in Asunción with what amounted to an ultimatum.

The councilor cut an impressive figure. He was well over six feet tall with piercing sky-blue eyes. His resplendent diplomat's uniform, which he used on all official occasions, shone brightly with gold brocade and included a high collar and white gloves, even in the tropical heat. Such fashion was calculated to give him a larger-than-life presence, symbolic of the enormous empire he represented. Paraguayans were sensitive to subtleties in appearance and they understood such an image. They likewise noted his balding head; his ample, carefully arranged sideburns; and his clean-shaven chin. In appearance he suggested a modern European statesman, a man who combined shrewdness and easy familiarity with power. In Paraguay, only members of the presidential family dared to put on such airs.

The empire was willing, Paranhos stated bluntly, to go to war to enforce the 1856 treaty. Francisco Solano López, whose own appearance was just as dazzling, had momentarily replaced Berges as chief negotiator for his father's government. The future marshal chose to take the councilor's threat at face value. On 12 February 1858 the two men signed a convention that ended the restrictions on Brazilian transit of the Alto Paraguay.[30]

After this settlement, the Brazilians inaugurated a state steamship line that ran up the Alto Paraguay to Cuiabá. The steamers, which included the *Marqués de Olinda*, made eight round trips annually between Rio de Janeiro and the Mato Grosso ports, carrying goods a distance of almost four thousand miles. The line continued in operation until 1864 without interference from the Paraguayans. Eventually, merchant vessels from Corrientes, Buenos Aires, Montevideo, and several Italian ports joined Brazilian and Paraguayan ships in fostering a tiny Mato Grosso trade.[31] In addition to the transit of merchant vessels, the treaty allowed three imperial warships a year to ascend the river without Paraguayan inspection or limits as to tonnage or armaments. The ships that made this voyage were not required to take on a Paraguayan pilot. Whenever possible, therefore, they sailed close by Paraguayan river defenses, the better to gain useful military intelligence. López's navy was unable to respond since Brazilian customs regulations mandated that all foreign vessels discharge their cargoes at Corumbá, more than four hundred miles south of Mato Grosso's chief strategic point, the provincial capital of Cuiabá.[32]

The 1858 agreement also included a protocol on territorial limits. Neither side took this document seriously but accepted it for convenience's sake. It identified Bahia Negra, at the juncture of the Alto Paraguay and Negro Rivers, as the border between the two countries. Bahia Negra lay seventy miles north of the Blanco in a largely uninhabited and clearly indefensible zone; its very isolation was the chief point in its favor as a line of demarcation. The protocol did not define the entire frontier, confining its writ to the west bank of the Paraguay River. Regarding the more important border dispute on the opposite bank, the protocol only called for a demilitarization of the area between the Apa and Blanco and, when necessary, for free passage during hot pursuit of Guaicurú raiders. All outstanding questions were to be addressed within the six-year delay on limits previously imposed.[33]

The six-year time frame, which was supposed to make possible a period of reflection and cooperation, failed to ease tensions between the two countries. Solano López had by then taken active charge of his country's armed forces and of government efforts to expand and modernize the Paraguayan military. He imported armaments, hired European military specialists, and built Humaitá from a minor border station near the Paraguay's confluence with the Paraná into a fortress the likes of which had never been seen in South America. And he continued to reinforce national defenses along the Mato Grosso frontier.[34]

In June 1862 the six-year delay on the settlement of that frontier expired without either side having lifted a finger to resolve their problems peaceably. Relations between Brazil and Paraguay, if formally correct, were in no way cordial; instead, they suffered from suspicion and mutual contempt. Charles Ames Washburn, the newly named U.S. Minister to Asunción, reported that Carlos Antonio López "wants the old question of boundary . . . settled, and complains that [Brazil] is crowding upon him all the time and will not come to a settlement, as by delay it is continually appropriating his territory. He has a bitter hatred of the Brazilians and a contempt of them as soldiers, and in speaking of them usually calls them *macacos* (monkeys)."[35]

Politicians in Rio de Janeiro generally reciprocated the bad feelings displayed by the Paraguayan president, but the Banda Oriental concerned them far more. The lands disputed with Paraguay would almost certainly come into the empire's hands through the course of protracted negotiations. Time was on Brazil's side, and the Paraguayans could be left to wait.

In the long litany of prewar ironies, perhaps the most telling—and the most poignant—came from Carlos Antonio López. In September 1862 the corpulent president lay on his deathbed. Fever and the constant pain of diabetes had sapped his strength, and he was anxious to pass his final hours with his family. One of his last official gestures was to nominate his eldest son, Francisco Solano López, as vice president, empowering him to exercise presidential authority until Congress met to choose a successor. Summoning a last reserve of strength, the old man struggled to voice his opinions, to give some final advice on how best to guarantee Paraguay's future safety. "There are many pending questions to ventilate; but do not try to solve them by the sword but by the pen, *chiefly with Brazil.* He pronounced the italicized words with emphasis. . . . The general remained silent; he did not answer his father, who after he had finished speaking also remained silent." Carlos Antonio López died a short while later, without speaking another word.[36]

Within days, Solano López filled the streets of Asunción with his soldiers, their rifles and bayonets at the ready. This assured his accession to the nation's highest office with a minimum of debate.[37] It also set the tone for his entire administration.

# The Misiones and Chaco Disputes

## 5

Travel accounts of the early nineteenth century generally portrayed the borderlands that separated Paraguay from Brazil's Mato Grosso province as a place of mystery, a blank on the map. The southern borderlands that separated Paraguay from Argentina, however, were so well known that they had achieved an almost legendary status. In the seventeenth and eighteenth centuries, this region, known as the Misiones, had been home to tens of thousands of Guaraní Indians grouped into communities under Jesuit control. These reductions, and the priests who operated them, fired the imagination of European intellectuals. Even the skeptical Voltaire expressed his grudging respect and gave the Jesuit missionary experiment a full chapter in his *Candide*.

Spanish settlers in the Plata regarded the Jesuits with suspicion and jealousy. The Paraguayans envied their substantial herds of cattle, the size and efficiency of their export operations, and particularly their easy access to Indian labor. Though their secular neighbors might have hated them, the Jesuits recognized the power that their missionary appeal held among the Guaraní. Even in the sparsely populated Chaco, located one hundred miles to the west, the reductions offered a practical, if not always successful, model for the assimilation of Indians into colonial society.

By the early 1800s this was all in the past. The Jesuit Order was long gone, expelled by the Crown forty years earlier. The inept administration that replaced the Jesuits in the Misiones and the military campaigns of the early national period ravaged and depopulated the region. The once meticulously cultivated fields now lay fallow. Village buildings, churches, and warehouses became so overgrown that they resembled lost Mayan ruins, fit only for ghosts and roving bands of marauders. Exacerbating this dismal state of affairs, Paraguay and Argentina actively disputed possession of both the Misiones and the Chaco.

*Colonial Antecedents*

The Spaniards divided the Jesuit territories after the expulsion of the order in 1767, but certain divisions were already implicit in the administration of the missions. Royal ordinances in 1650, 1651, and 1654 gave the governor of Paraguay the authority to appoint the priests to direct the thirty communities along the Paraná and Uruguay Rivers.[1]

Soon after Buenos Aires was separated from Paraguay in 1618, secular authorities worked out a rough demarcation that placed eighteen of the thirty mission communities under the bishop of Buenos Aires. The remaining villages, located mostly to the north of the Alto Paraná, remained under the bishop of Asunción. This demarcation — and indeed the arrogation of any authority over the region — was largely theoretical; only the Jesuit Provincial of Tucumán exercised any real authority in the Misiones, and he permitted no secular priests to enter there. Nonetheless, this division provided the basis for future territorial squabbles.

The seriousness of this matter became apparent during the eighteenth century, when civil authorities tried to pressure their ecclesiastical counterparts into making clearer delineations. Royal bureaucrats were already thinking to displace the clerics as masters of the Indian population, and their efforts to paint the priests as disloyal may be seen in this light.

In February 1724 the king issued an ordinance that directed the two bishops to settle the jurisdictional question. The bishops subsequently selected arbitrators who met at the Jesuit headquarters of Candelaria. They agreed to divide the Misiones territory along the line of its watershed, with the bishop of Asunción maintaining jurisdiction over the area that drained into the Río Paraná and the bishop of Buenos Aires over the territory that emptied into the Uruguay.[2]

Two years after this decision, the Crown ordered the transfer to Buenos Aires of the thirteen missions controlled by Paraguay. Royal officials justified this move by noting the dangers the Misiones faced from the anti-Jesuit Comuneros rebellion then affecting central Paraguay. This transfer of authority, however, failed to clarify the ambiguity in the status of the Misiones. After all, colonial officials in Paraguay never regarded the transfer as anything more than temporary; indeed, they petitioned regularly for the return of the lost missions. In 1784 the viceroy finally ordered a new partition of the Mission communities, with Paraguay receiving the thirteen villages formerly within its jurisdiction.[3]

By this time, the Jesuit Order had been expelled from the Spanish and Portuguese Empires. Their departure ushered in a period of even greater uncertainty for the Misiones. The Guaraní residents of the territory enjoyed some nominal protection from the Crown. The secular agents assigned to administer the villages, however, soon connived with outside entrepreneurs to exploit the Indians, often in shameless fashion. Some communities were forced to abandon ranching and subsistence farming and devote themselves entirely to the cultivation of yerba mate, principally for the *porteño* market. The Indian laborers involved in this received little food and worked far longer hours than they had under the Jesuits.

Confronted with disease and malnutrition, many Indians, most of them male, fled the region and thereby placed a still greater burden on those who remained. Spanish administrators tried to compensate for the loss in production by squeezing the Guaraní even more. The result was predictable: the collapse of Misiones society. In fact, the royal government had itself precipitated the disintegration of the mission communities by handing over seven of the richest missions to the Portuguese through the Treaty of Madrid in 1750.[4] Though they returned the villages seven years later (and they remained under Spanish control until 1801), prosperity and social stability never returned.

*The Misiones and Chaco Disputes* 95

At the beginning the nineteenth century, the Spaniards made a final effort to resuscitate the Misiones and bring the region back into the mainstream of Platine development. To better protect the few remaining Indians, the Crown issued a decree in May 1803 that took the ten remaining Río Uruguay missions from Buenos Aires and the thirteen Paraná missions from Paraguay and consolidated them into a separate province governed by Lt. Col. Bernardo de Velasco.[5] According to the *cédula real*, Velasco was free to act "with absolute independence of the Governors of Paraguay and Buenos Aires." The decision to create a new province might have provided a solution to the territorial dispute, but a complication arose. In September 1805 the Crown received two reports from the Council of the Indies that recommended the unification of the provinces of the Misiones and Paraguay for military reasons. The king concurred and gave orders to this effect. Now, in addition to his position as governor of Misiones, Velasco received appointment as governor of Paraguay.

Velasco's assumption of the Paraguayan governorship represented the last act in the long drama of Spain's troubles with the Misiones. In May 1810 the Cabildo of Buenos Aires proclaimed the independence of the port city and, by extension, all the provinces of the Plata, including Paraguay. Though enthusiastically welcomed by many *porteños*, this declaration failed to please everyone in the provinces and was met with open hostility in the northeast.

*Independence and Nation Building: The Misiones in Limbo*
The landed elites of Paraguay hesitated only briefly in rejecting the presumptions of the Cabildo of Buenos Aires. For them, any break with Spain had to bring a more open regime that would specifically guarantee the rights of landlocked regions. South America's political future, they felt, depended on power sharing among all its provinces rather than a monopoly of power by one province alone. From the Paraguayan viewpoint, their treatment at the hands of Buenos Aires had been uniformly bad. Not only had commercial and fiscal policies always favored the port city over the Litoral but the viceregal regime also had repeat-

edly called upon Paraguay to contribute men and materiel to dubious and unprofitable military ventures. In 1781 Buenos Aires had mobilized a thousand Paraguayan militiamen to fend off a feared British attack. Fifteen years later, royal bureaucrats in Asunción had pressured the local elites into a costly border war with Portuguese Brazil. In 1806, royal officials again called upon Paraguayan militiamen, this time to drive British invaders from the mouth of the Platine estuary. On this last occasion, the appeal for men was poorly handled in Paraguay. The interim governor illegally impressed tobacco concessionaires *(matriculados)* into the militia, and press gangs sent into the Paraguayan countryside endured open hostility. Given such a checkered history, Paraguayans naturally feared the events of 1810 and worried that answering the *porteño* call would again result in the loss of lives and property.

Underlying these suspicions, however, were complex cultural differences that separated the two peoples and set the stage for additional conflicts over the Misiones. At this time, the "nationalism" of the *porteños* was entirely legalistic: as the self-proclaimed political heir to the viceroy after 1810, the Cabildo of Buenos Aires claimed control over all the territories and peoples once governed by the Spaniards. In the view of the *porteños*, all of the Plata formed a new nation directed from Buenos Aires.

Paraguayans viewed the "nation" as a community of shared values, customs, and language. All who were raised within the Hispano-Guaraní milieu belonged to a greater Paraguayan "nation," whether they lived in Paraguay proper, in the Misiones, or even in Corrientes. Like the Kurds or the Basques, Guaraní speakers saw themselves as part of a community different from other communities within the Plata and for whom political divisions were a reality to be borne, not to be celebrated. To the denizen of a small village in central Paraguay, the inhabitants of the Misiones were close (if not necessarily trustworthy) cousins, while those in Buenos Aires were foreigners.

These concepts of nationhood, as much as legal, strategic, and commercial concerns, shaped the territorial dispute in the Misiones. Buenos Aires's first attempt to convert Paraguay to the patriot cause — the Bel-

*The Misiones and Chaco Disputes* 97

grano expedition of 1811—was launched via the Misiones. The Paraguayan victory on that occasion led to the realization that outsiders could easily repeat such an incursion if the Misiones stayed outside the orbit of Asunción. Subsequent Paraguayan governments, therefore, determined to maintain their hold on the region.

Belgrano's departure from Paraguay led to a short-lived rapprochement between the *porteños* and the Asunción government.[6] Buenos Aires needed friends in the face of Spanish resistance in Montevideo and Upper Peru, and the Paraguayans, who had ousted Velasco in June 1811, eagerly responded. The result was an agreement signed on 12 October that tacitly recognized Paraguay's independence and explicitly recognized Asunción's jurisdiction over much of the Misiones: "Until with fuller information the definitive boundary of both Provinces on this side has been established in the General Congress, the frontiers of this Province of Paraguay are to remain, in the meantime, in the form in which they are at present. Consequently, its government charges itself with the care of the department of Candelaria."[7] The agreement left undecided who should govern southern Misiones, the territory along the Río Uruguay.

Claims on paper were one thing, effective occupation of the Misiones was something else. In this respect, the Paraguayans held the upper hand. The area between the Alto Paraná and Uruguay Rivers had by 1817 become greatly depopulated owing to an outflow of Indian men in search of work in the south, continued Portuguese incursions, increased banditry, and fighting between Correntinos, Entrerrianos, Orientales, and occasionally *porteños*.[8] Given this chaotic situation, only José Gaspar de Francia's Paraguay offered hope for stability.

As heir to the Bourbons, Francia claimed sovereign rights over the Misiones, and, unlike the Correntinos and Brazilians, he worked to establish a presence there. His early occupation of Candelaria represented a crucial development, for it secured an overland trade outlet with São Borja in the Brazilian Misiones. To defend Candelaria, the dictator's men constructed a wall two meters high that ran for twelve hundred meters across a small peninsula jutting into the Alto Paraná. The Paraguayans built the wall with stones taken from the ruins of nearby missions and

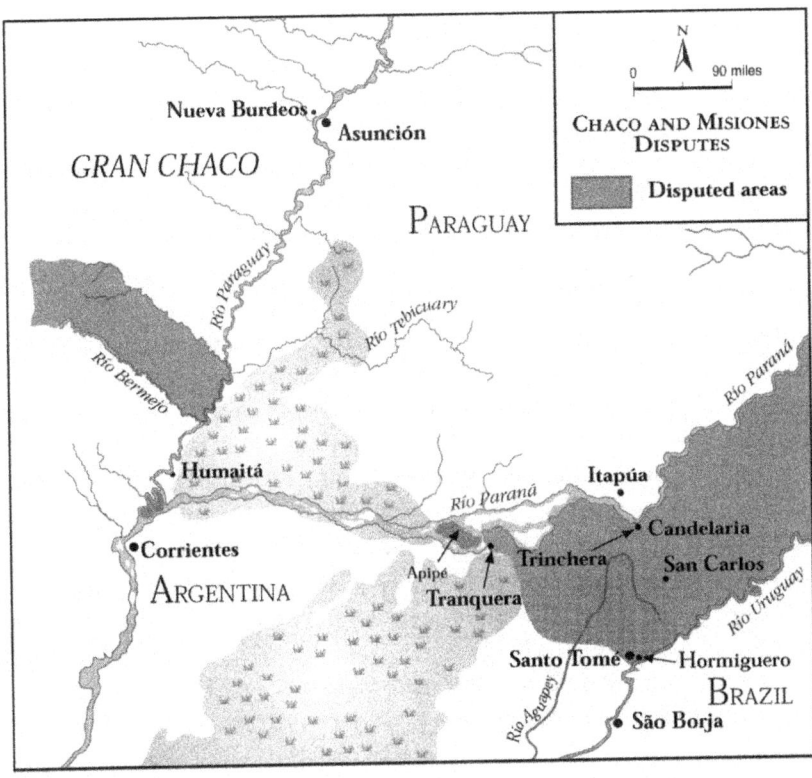

reinforced it with battlements and a series of entrenchments. A sizable garrison occupied the facility from the early 1820s onward. Francia christened this fortification San José, but it soon assumed the more common name of Trinchera de los Paraguayos (the present-day site of the city of Posadas).

In 1822 the dictator established another base camp at Tranquera de Loreto on the southern bank of the Alto Paraná fifty miles west of Trinchera. The site was well chosen. Set just above the rapids of Apipé, Tranquera stood at the narrowest point of dry land between the river and the Laguna Yberá, a vast swamp located directly to the south. The

The Misiones and Chaco Disputes   99

Jesuits had left a series of embankments in this quarter that Francia greatly widened and extended. At high water, these could be broken to unite the waters of the Yberá with those of the Alto Paraná, creating a barrier to any large military force coming from the west.[9]

Because these fortifications alone were insufficient to dominate the disputed areas in the Misiones, Francia sent his small cavalry force to patrol the zone and escort merchant caravans to and from São Borja. A small force stationed in the ruins of Candelaria supplied men for temporary guard posts at Santo Tomás, San Carlos, and periodically at Santo Tomé. While none of these measures assured Paraguayan control, they did ease trade; with his government chronically in need of paper, hardware, and munitions, this was enough for Dr. Francia.[10]

Skirmishes occurred periodically. In 1821, Paraguayan troops attacked the encampment of Aimé Bonpland, a French botanist and colleague of Alexander von Humboldt, who had come to the Misiones to study the yerba mate plant. Bonpland made the mistake of openly associating with Francisco Ramírez, the gaucho leader who then controlled Corrientes and whom Francia suspected of wanting to extend that control into the disputed Misiones. As a result, the dictator ordered his troops to destroy Bonpland's base camp at Santa Ana and arrest the hapless Frenchman, who remained a prisoner of the Paraguayans for nine years.[11]

Open hostilities erupted in the Misiones in the early 1830s at approximately the same time that rumors circulated of a scheme by the *porteño* leadership to sell Misiones territory to British land speculators. Dr. Francia left no doubt as to his sentiments concerning such a real estate transfer: "The lands between the Aguapey and Uruguay [Rivers] belong to Paraguay and not to Buenos Aires which for the past twenty years has not even thought about them. It is now clear that [Buenos Aires] has conspired to appropriate this territory and feign its sale to these Englishmen only to impede and cut the Brazilian trade with Paraguay, which has hurt them as much as they envy it."[12] Though British colonists never appeared on the scene, the incident heightened Paraguayan anxiety.

Meanwhile, the provincial government of Corrientes had concluded a treaty with the municipal council of La Cruz, a tiny port on the Alto Uruguay River, which brought the village under direct Correntino rule.[13] Although the takeover of La Cruz could have been viewed as the first step in some hostile flanking maneuver to the south, Dr. Francia displayed considerable restraint. Noting that La Cruz had nothing to do with the São Borja trade, the dictator offered to sell the port to Corrientes together with all lands south to Yapeyú.[14]

Correntino governor Pedro Ferré, however, rejected Francia's offer, dismissing it as a cover for Paraguayan expansion. Corrientes, the governor believed, had acquiesced to Paraguayan aggression all too often in the recent past, not just in the Misiones but also on the island of Apipé and in the Curupayty area just north of the Paraná River's confluence with the Paraguay.[15] Ferré ordered his militia to attack Paraguayan strongholds in the Misiones and settle the matter for good.[16]

This undeclared war of 1832–34 never escalated beyond a few minor skirmishes. Ferré hoped to exaggerate the Paraguayan threat and gain political concessions and material aid from the lower provinces.[17] As events turned out, Paraguayan resistance proved ineffectual, and after a brief campaign the Correntinos occupied Tranquera de Loreto and Candelaria in September 1832.

The Correntinos held the Misiones for less than two years. During that time, Ferré attempted to consolidate economic control over the region; he established an official yerba mate industry near the Jesuit ruins and invited all interested citizens to participate in the venture.[18] He also established a customs house to tax the Brazilian merchants who journeyed to Paraguay across the Misiones from São Borja.[19] Yet despite enthusiastic rhetoric from his neighbors to the south, Ferré received virtually no support for his occupation of Candelaria. It was only a matter of time before an avenging Paraguayan expeditionary force crossed back into the Misiones. By mid-1834 the Correntinos had given up the greater part of their recent gains, including Santo Tomé and the small port of Hormiguero (although they retained control over La Cruz). The Paraguayans reestablished a protective cordon around their trading route to São Borja, and the skirmishing came to an end. Commercial exchanges with Brazilian merchants soon resumed and thrived until the early 1850s.

### The Riograndense Option

While Dr. Francia bemoaned the intrusions of "that savage thief, the carpenter Ferré," trouble was brewing at the other end of the commercial chain in Rio Grande do Sul.[20] The Brazilian foreign ministry had made no new claims on the Misiones since the time of the Cisplatine War, opting instead to develop friendly relations with the Paraguayan dictator. There was nothing disinterested in this stance. Brazil had already gained most of what she wanted in the Misiones thanks to the Portuguese, who in 1801 had taken the former Jesuit ranches east of the Uruguay River. Gathering potential allies against Buenos Aires was far more important in the 1830s than pressing questionable claims over essentially vacant land. The imperial government therefore did nothing to discourage Paraguay's trade links with São Borja.

In formulating a policy toward Francia — and toward all the Platine regimes — diplomats in Rio de Janeiro failed to see that the interests of Riograndenses rarely coincided with those of the empire. Though the imperial government showed enthusiasm for countering the pretensions of Buenos Aires and for developing good relations with Paraguay, it repeatedly postponed legislation favorable to its own cattle ranchers in the south. This brought on the ten-year Farrapo Rebellion. Though the secessionist revolt centered in the ranching zones near the Uruguayan frontier, it also had profound effects on the Misiones.

One effect was demographic. Many who were anxious to escape the fighting in Rio Grande do Sul crossed the Uruguay River to seek refuge in Paraguayan and Correntino territory. These refugees, who included Indians and escaped slaves, became new settlers in the underpopulated area. Many merchants also joined the exodus to the right bank of the river, where they opened businesses and waited for the fighting to subside.

São Borja fell to the Farrapos in October 1835 and remained under their rule for nearly a decade. This did not remove the town from the war, however, because guerrilla forces continued to uphold the emperor's cause along the Río Uruguay. Cavalry crossed the river in pursuit of opposing troops, and these forays brought additional conflict with the Correntinos or Paraguayans.

Surprisingly, the rebellion failed to disrupt the commerce that had developed across the Misiones because all sides wished to see the trade sustained. For the Farrapos, trade with the Paraguayans and Correntinos brought much-needed revenues to their budding republic and regular imports of yerba, tobacco, and most importantly horses and mules to help the armed struggle. Mounts for the rebel cavalry were essential. As one Paulista deputy remarked: "The rebels have 12,000 horses and 12,000 horses are nearly 12,000 men. [Given the terrain and the distances involved,] whoever has the largest horse herds will win."[21] When the acquisition of horses through legal means became problematic, troops from either side raided Correntino-held areas in the Misiones and took what they needed. After one such incursion, the governor of Corrientes petitioned the imperial commander on behalf of the ranchers of Santo Tomé and La Cruz, who claimed substantial loss of livestock.[22]

The Farrapo Rebellion did little to resolve the territorial dispute over the Misiones, but it did prove that both the Paraguayans and their neighbors to the south had much to gain from peace. So too did the Brazilians — a fact that became increasingly obvious after the exhausted rebels laid down their arms in February 1845.

*The Misiones in the 1840s*

Dr. Francia had kept the Farrapos — and all other suitors — at arm's length. His death in September 1840 made possible new political realities in the Plata as a whole. A portent of the changes to come had taken place a year earlier, when the province of Corrientes rose in rebellion against the government of Juan Manuel de Rosas. If the Correntinos were to defeat the *Restaurador de las Leyes*, they needed allies, whether Farrapo, imperialist, or Paraguayan.

Rosas had long discounted the threat of an alliance between Paraguay and his enemies in the Litoral. Francia's well-known policy of noninterference in Argentine affairs had conformed to Rosas's regional interests for many years. There was no apparent reason why Paraguay would launch itself into the fray now that Francia was gone.

The situation had changed far more than Rosas realized. The new consular government of Carlos Antonio López and Mariano Roque Alonso saw itself as a force for modernization that was willing to abandon the old isolationist policy. This was merely the first step in dispelling the "inland Japan" image that Francia had so carefully nurtured and that had cost so much in terms of economic prosperity. Accordingly, the consuls plunged awkwardly forward into the thicket of diplomacy and opened negotiations with the insurgent government in Corrientes.

On 31 July 1841 the consuls affixed their signatures to a treaty of friendship, trade, and navigation with the Correntinos. That same day, both parties signed a provisional boundary agreement that set a clear demarcation in the Misiones. Paraguay received all lands north of the Aguapey River while Corrientes received control of the island of Apipé and of the Río Uruguay settlements. The river fords of Itatí, Yabebirí, and Itapúa, all on the Alto Paraná, were opened to Correntino trade, as was Pilar on the Paraguay. In recognition of the cultural and linguistic unity of the two peoples, the treaty declared that "the sons of both states will be considered natives of one and the other . . . with free use of their rights."[23]

Both governments viewed the agreements as temporary. The main objective of Pedro Ferré, who had again assumed the governor's mantle in Corrientes, was to prevent disturbances on the northern frontier so that he could concentrate his forces against Rosas. López's desire was to increase trade along the Paraná while guarding the old Misiones caravan route to São Borja.

The 1841 treaties angered Rosas but did not overly concern him, for he realized that mutual suspicion would undermine any union between Paraguay and Corrientes. López was similarly aware of the weaknesses inherent in the treaties. They might be used to stabilize conditions in the Misiones and promote the entry of foreign trading ships into the Upper Plata, but they could also involve Paraguay in a war.

A major problem of the treaties was that they depended on the continued viability of the Ferré regime. In December 1842, however, the Correntinos and their Uruguayan allies suffered a major reverse in Entre Ríos. The Rosistas then poured into Corrientes and soon seized that entire province. Ferré fled with the remnants of his army, passing through Paraguay on his way to exile in Rio Grande do Sul. This left López with a frontier even less secure than before.[24]

The 1841–42 treaties had little long-term effect on the Misiones land dispute. The language of the boundary agreement did suggest a willingness on Paraguay's part to content itself with the thirteen villages it had administered before 1803.[25] But in the chaotic environment of the 1840s, nothing was certain.

The Rosista hold on the Correntino government lasted only a few months, and soon the province again found itself at war. Between 1841 and 1845, Corrientes had five different governments, none of which could maintain the peace. At one point, Farrapo envoys signed a secret convention with the Correntinos that obligated the two parties to quash smuggling in the Misiones and to disarm and expel each other's enemies.[26]

After the Farrapo collapse in 1845, the Brazilian Foreign Ministry reverted to its earlier policy of trying to undermine Rosas in the Litoral provinces of the Plata. To that end, imperial officials assiduously courted potential allies in the region. They soon identified Joaquín Madariaga, the new governor of Corrientes, as a key figure in the anti-Rosas camp and as someone who needed their help. Madariaga's position was hardly enviable. Local Rosistas already held the southeastern corner of his province, and they aligned themselves with Entrerriano governor Justo José de Urquiza, who maintained a sizable cavalry force nearby. In response, the various anti-Rosas leaders in the Plata launched an offensive in Corrientes with the full connivance of the imperial government, sending Unitario general José María Paz to assume command of their forces in the province.

López, who by now had become Paraguayan president, also wished to join this campaign. The anti-Rosistas, as far as he knew, still honored the previous border and trade commitments made by Ferré. In any case, the alternative—a Rosista Corrientes—had to be avoided at all costs. Accordingly, López dispatched an army of several thousand men across the Alto Paraná. At the head of this force was his eighteen-year-old son, Brig. Gen. Francisco Solano López.

This was the younger López's first important foray into Platine politics. It was significant that he came on the scene as a military man, filled with expectations of battlefield glory and attired in a glittering uniform. His father remained doubtful of his son's abilities and anxious to limit the Paraguayan commitment to the Rosas opposition. He issued elaborate instructions to the untried general on when to reconnoiter, when to attack, and when to withdraw.[27] He also placed experienced officers who could offer appropriate counsel in key positions in the force.

The young commander's troops seemed hopelessly inept to General Paz, who had the opportunity to see them as they disembarked at Corrientes. "It was an unformed mass," he later recalled, "without instruction, without organization, without discipline, and ignorant of the first rudiments of war.... [Their] infantry was so rustic that it did not know how to load or fire its weapons." As for their cavalry, they had no competent officers and "were badly mounted ..., not because they had been given no horses, but because they did not care for them and destroyed them in a few days."[28]

In the end, the Rosistas decided the issue before the Paraguayan troops could enter the fray, with Urquiza's cavalry smashing that of Paz in March 1845. Solano López wisely elected to withdraw across the Alto Paraná without firing a shot. Paz followed him soon thereafter. Like Ferré before him, the general tarried only briefly in Paraguay before moving on to the safety of Brazilian territory.

With Corrientes in the hands of the Rosistas, C. A. López had reason to fear an attack from the south. His hold over the Misiones seemed precarious, and he could ill afford to remain idle. In 1849, just as Francia had done years before, López moved to assure Paraguayan sovereignty over the Misiones by dispatching a column of one thousand infantry, six hundred cavalry, and an artillery unit southward under the command of the Hungarian-born mercenary Franz Wisner von Morgenstern. This force reached the disputed area in June with instructions from López to secure the territory all the way to the Uruguay River and then, if possible, to purchase two thousand muskets from Brazilian authorities.[29] On 4 July 1849 Hormiguero fell.

Wisner immediately notified the Austrian commercial attaché at Rio de Janeiro that Hormiguero was now in Paraguayan hands and that the small port desired trade. Participating merchants from the Austrian Empire would be exempted from all duties, Wisner observed, since Emperor Franz Joseph had recently recommended the recognition of Paraguayan independence. This missive not only showed Wisner's desire for prestige among his fellow Austrians but also showed that Paraguayan interest in the Misiones now focused narrowly on the need for a commercial outlet to the Atlantic economy.[30]

López meant the expedition to keep the lines of trade between Itapúa (after 1846 called Encarnación) and São Borja open under all circumstances. The Brazilians, for their part, had no interest at that time in abandoning the appearance of strict neutrality in the various Platine disputes.[31] The trade opening desired by the Paraguayans thus received little official encouragement from the Brazilian side of the river. Wisner remained in the area only long enough to conduct a few raids against the Correntino Rosistas and their Entrerriano allies. These engagements proved inconclusive, and by the beginning of 1850 the Paraguayans returned to Tranquera, making only occasional forays against the Correntinos over the next two years. López soon came to regard the dormant trade with São Borja as not worth the risk of a military confrontation, even though he still wanted to import armaments from Brazil. In the end, Paraguay retained Trinchera and Tranquera de Loreto, but less for commercial than strategic reasons—López had no desire to see a second Belgrano expedition launched against his country by way of the Misiones.

The 1849 Paraguayan incursion was for all practical purposes the end of the São Borja trade. Ironically, it resulted in such destruction that any revitalization of the old commerce would have proven difficult. As they withdrew, the Paraguayans destroyed what they could not carry. They set fire to Hormiguero. Wisner's men seized the livestock of the Santo Tomé district, some eleven thousand animals in all, and drove them back to Paraguay.[32] These actions, as harsh as anything the area had suffered, signaled that the Paraguayans had no intention of coming back.

*The 1852 Agreements*

The fall of Rosas in 1852 brought fundamental changes in the relations between Argentina and Paraguay. Carlos Antonio López had offered support to the alliance that had overthrown the *Restaurador* and expected to reap the rewards of his cooperation. He did not have to wait long. On 17 July 1852 the new Argentine Confederation officially recognized the independence of Paraguay and its right to free navigation. Two days earlier, officials of the two governments signed a treaty that carefully defined their common border.

Article 1 of this treaty established the Alto Paraná River from Yguasú Falls (at the edge of Brazilian territory) to the island of Atajó (Cerritos) at the confluence of the Paraná and the Paraguay Rivers as the boundary between Paraguay and the confederation. With a stroke, Paraguay relinquished its claim to the entire area once encompassed by the thirteen disputed missions.[33]

Carlos Antonio López's willingness to give up an enormous stretch of land stood in sharp contrast to his earlier policy and revealed more about his relations with Brazil than with the Argentines. The question of who owned the territories between the Apa and Blanco Rivers loomed large in Asunción at this time. The Paraguayan president evidently felt that a serious conflict with Brazil was more likely than one with Argentina. Since the Itapúa–São Borja trade route would lose its raison d'être with the opening of the Paraná, he could afford to compromise on the Misiones. Thus, in exchange for a nebulous show of support from the Argentines against the pretensions of the Brazilians, he surrendered a sizable piece of the Misiones, a territory whose potential value was many times what he might have hoped to gain along his northern frontier with Mato Grosso. All looked ready for the transfer of the territory to the confederation when, at the last moment, the Argentine Congress rejected the treaty because of clauses relating to the Gran Chaco hundreds of miles to the west.

### The Chaco Question

Of all the lonely and isolated regions in Spanish South America, surely the Gran Chaco was the least known. An enormous plain covered by swamps, chaparral, and thorn forests, it extended westward from the right bank of the Paraguay River to the foothills of the Andes, a full 250,000 square miles of wilderness. Had the region been nothing more than a place of unusual fauna and desolate landscapes, the Spaniards might simply have ignored it, as they had ignored Patagonia, Arizona, and Alta California. As it was, the very mention of the word Chaco filled them with terror, for it was home to many groups of feared Indians, including the Guaicurú, Toba, and Mocobí. As one failed missionary to the region observed in the eighteenth century, "the Spaniards consider [the Gran Chaco] the theater of misery; the barbarians, in turn, their Palestine, their Elysium."[34]

Indian raids from the Chaco presented a near-constant reminder to the Spanish settlers in Paraguay of the insecurity of their position. On several occasions during the colonial period, Guaicurú marauders struck Asunción itself. To keep the Indians at bay, the Paraguayans were consistently under arms and conducted punitive raids of their own. A more effective way to prevent the incursions suggested itself to colonial authorities from the beginning, but only at the end of the 1700s did they construct permanent military posts within the Chaco.

The establishment of these forts reinforced a claim that the Paraguayans had made over the Chaco for many years. A Royal Ordinance of 1618 had assigned to the bishop of Asunción all of the Chaco territories north of the Bermejo River. Lands to the south, including the areas around the town of Santa Fe, were assigned to the ecclesiastic authorities of Buenos Aires. This left three-quarters of the Chaco theoretically under Paraguayan jurisdiction. In reality, the Gran Chaco remained the domain of the Indians, except for the occasional foray of militiamen bent on reprisal and some ineffectual missionary efforts.

In 1792 the viceroy ordered the construction of a fort on the Chaco side of the Paraguay River to check the expansion of the Portuguese from Mato Grosso and, if possible, to discourage Indian encroachments from the west. These objectives could best be realized by situating the new post as far upriver as possible. The Paraguayans accordingly established Borbón, which controlled the right bank of the river as far as Bahia Negra, within easy striking range of Portuguese settlements. From this time forward, Fort Borbón (or Olimpo) was almost continuously populated, partly by convicts and malcontents and partly by garrison troops. After independence, Borbón continued as a reminder of Asunción's authority in the Gran Chaco. Yet Dr. Francia considered this single post insufficient and subsequently established forts at Santa Elena, Monteclaro, Peña Hermosa, and much farther to the south, at Formoso and Orange. Though tiny, these installations were more than simple guard posts against the Toba and Mocobí. Even in this remote spot, the dictator intended that every neighbor respect Paraguayan sovereignty.

In August 1826 this claim over the Gran Chaco was put to the test when a river vessel with twenty-five men aboard appeared at the mouth of the Bermejo. The vessel had as its captain a Frenchman, Paul Soria. He had a commission from an association of *porteño* entrepreneurs to map the river from its headwaters in Salta province to its confluence with the Paraguay. If the river proved navigable, then it might serve to tie the provinces of the Argentine interior to those of the Litoral. Such a project conflicted with Paraguay's territorial claims. Francia's pickets on the opposite bank had standing orders to detain anyone attempting to enter the country, and they promptly arrested the entire party of Salteños and sent them north to Concepción. Francia held them as prisoners for five years before expelling them at roughly the same time he ejected Bonpland.[35]

The outposts Francia established in the Chaco stayed in place for over forty years. With the exception of Borbón, these posts were flimsy affairs, consisting of logs planted in the ground, interlaced with bamboo, filled in with clay or mud, and thatched with grass. Each had a lookout tower some sixty feet in height and open at the sides. These platforms commanded an extensive view of the river. Using signal fires or horns, troops could alert the pickets guarding the opposite bank of the river.

C. A. López at first had little inclination to change Dr. Francia's Chaco policy but was concerned with protecting Paraguay's southern frontier. As the threat from Indians receded, this increasingly meant staving off threats from Argentina. López supplemented Francia's pickets on the left bank of the Paraguay River with a tight chain of fortified posts that ran from Asunción south to below the fortress of Humaitá.

The treaty of 15 July 1852, which established the boundaries between Paraguay and the Argentine Confederation in the Misiones, also implicitly recognized Paraguayan sovereignty over all the Chaco territories north of the Río Bermejo. Article 4 read: "The Paraguay River belongs from bank to bank in absolute sovereignty to the Republic of Paraguay as far as its junction with the Paraná." Article 5 asserted: "The navigation of the Bermejo River is completely common to both states."[36]

The treaty nonetheless went on to note in Article 6 a Paraguayan demand that was sure to cause friction: "The bank from the mouth of the Bermejo to the Atajó River is neutral territory to the depth of one league; by common consent the high contracting parties cannot locate there any military camps or police posts even for the purpose of observing the savages that inhabit the shore."[37]

C. A. López had insisted on the inclusion of this clause as necessary to national defense. The proposed neutral territory commanded a clear view of the site on the left bank of the Paraguay River that the fortress of Humaitá would soon occupy. The Paraguayan government even then regarded this as a strategic zone and was anxious to strengthen its position there.

Though the Paraguayans had long regarded the Bermejo as the dividing line in the Chaco, some in Buenos Aires argued that the Pilcomayo River, lying much farther to the north, was the correct border.

While there was little historical justification for this position, López knew that the Argentines would press him on this point. The insertion of the neutralization clause made more definite the recognition of the Bermejo line, for if Argentina were later to claim the Pilcomayo, it would be impossible to evade the wording of Article 6. And, in fact, the Argentine Congress refused to ratify the treaty because of this article.

For his part, Carlos Antonio López ratified the treaty immediately and then waited impatiently for Argentine compliance. Three years later, the confederation officially rejected the treaty, and Urquiza appointed Gen. Tomás Guido to negotiate a new agreement. As a young man, Guido had been a close confidant of José de San Martín and later served as Rosas's agent at the Brazilian court in Rio de Janeiro. He was widely regarded as a tough negotiator from whom the Paraguayans could expect little flexibility.

A series of diplomatic notes from third parties had already clouded the issue. When the *porteño* newspapers recorded the text of the 1852 treaty, the Bolivian chargé d'affaires at Buenos Aires protested Article 4 as prejudicial to his nation's claims in the Gran Chaco, which, though never clearly defined, were generally seen as overlapping those of Paraguay.[38] Four days later the Brazilian minister likewise issued a protest on behalf of his government. In this case, his objections centered, first, on the treaty's reference to "Brazilian possessions," which the document had left undefined, and second, on the article that guaranteed a courier service between Encarnación and São Borja that, the minister noted, would require Brazilian approval.

The prospect of confrontation with other powers may have caused confederation officials to reconsider their commitment to the treaty with Paraguay. Many in the confederal capital of Paraná, and in Buenos Aires, were arguing that delay and renegotiation better served Argentina's interests anyway.

Meanwhile, by a decree of 14 May 1855, Carlos Antonio López further extended Paraguayan claims in the Gran Chaco by establishing an agricultural colony a short distance above Asunción.[39] Called Nueva Burdeos, the colony was the brainchild of Solano López, having recently returned from Europe with a newly professed reverence for everything French. For Paraguay to follow the lead of Napoleon III, it would have to undertake radical modernization even in agriculture. Solano López sought the immigration of some four hundred hardworking French country people who could introduce new farming techniques and habits of labor to the Paraguayan peasantry. When they arrived, however, the immigrants turned out to be townsmen from Bordeaux. Not surprisingly, they failed to adapt to the rigors of life in the Chaco, and the Asunción government did little to alleviate their distress. Food shortages at Nueva Burdeos were acute and the promised farming tools unavailable; displays of anger resulted on all sides. In the end, after precipitating a minor diplomatic crisis with Carlos Antonio López, the Frenchmen received permission to evacuate the colony, leaving behind a tiny group of Paraguayan soldiers and settlers who managed to make do where the Europeans had failed.[40]

Villa Occidental, as the Paraguayans rechristened Nueva Burdeos, became a base camp for further efforts at colonizing the Chaco, and over the next decade half a dozen satellite communities sprang up in its vicinity. These rudimentary camps also served a military function in defending Asunción from enemies, Indian or otherwise, who might approach the Paraguayan capital from the west. In this way Villa Occidental and the other posts were analogous to the Brazilian military colonies in the south of Mato Grosso.

After several years of delay, Paraguay and the Argentine Confederation signed a new treaty of trade, friendship, and navigation on 29 July 1856. Although this agreement promoted expanded commerce and affirmed the principle of free navigation in the region, it specifically postponed land settlement except for the islands of the Alto Paraná, with Paraguay receiving Yacyretá and Argentina, Apipé.[41]

The claims of the confederation had grown since 1852 to now encompass nearly the whole Gran Chaco "up to the Bolivian territory" as well as that portion of the old Misiones territory lying on and below the left bank of the Paraná.[42] For their part, the Paraguayans attached even less importance to the latter territory than they had in 1852 and were willing, as before, to relinquish it if Argentina offered concessions on postal arrangements.

The Chaco, however, was another matter. The entire thrust of López's foreign policy was to carefully open the republic to the outside world while maintaining a strong defensive posture in the south and far north. If Paraguay were to drop its claims in the Chaco, then Humaitá, Olimpo, and Villa Occidental would be rendered useless; an enemy could even threaten Asunción. Of course, as López repeatedly stated, the Gran Chaco was of little consequence: Paraguay only insisted on a thin security buffer, its "Government limiting its unconditional right to a certain marginal extent from the confluence with the Paraná up to Bahia Negra."[43] This buffer excluded the south bank of the Bermejo. The Argentines naturally expected under such circumstances to enjoy the right of navigation on the river. The Paraguayans, however, refused to accept this without a treaty on boundaries and argued that navigation on the Bermejo was still an open question. In 1853 the Correntino governor, Juan Pujol, decided to test the issue by authorizing an exploratory mission to the mouth of the Bermejo. López swiftly put a stop to this effort as "an intemperate and premature enterprise," and the schooner sent by the governor turned back to Corrientes.[44]

Two years later a more serious effort was initiated in Salta, where private investors sponsored mapping of the river's headwaters. Over the next two years, the Salteños extended these explorations of the Bermejo westward into Jujuy and Bolivia. At every stage they attracted more investors who were urged to put their capital into the construction of merchant schooners to run between Corrientes and the Bolivian frontier. As an added inducement, the company revealed that the Argentine government had granted it some valuable lands just south of the river.[45] Newspapers in communities along the Paraná echoed the optimism of these notices; editorials led potential backers to believe that only minor interference from Chaco Indians prevented the Bermejo from becoming an important and profitable commercial artery.

This was an exaggeration. The river was navigable for most of its course, but sandbars and floating vegetation posed as many problems as marauding Indians. And Carlos Antonio López had no intention of allowing free navigation on the Bermejo without exacting a high price at the negotiating table. In 1857 he declared that Paraguay's claim in the Gran Chaco extended to the *right* bank of the Bermejo, thus placing the mouth of the river entirely within his jurisdiction. Since his troops at Humaitá, Formoso, and Orange were the only military forces in the vicinity, he felt assured that his word on this matter would have force.

And it did. Yet in exchange for continued dominance of the disputed lands, the Paraguayan president squandered an opportunity for a far-better understanding with Argentina. At the end of the 1850s, the confederation needed allies in its struggle with the breakaway province of Buenos Aires. General Urquiza was willing to offer broad concessions to whomever came to his aid.[46] In April 1859 he even dispatched an envoy to Asunción to effect an agreement.

For reasons that are still obscure, López rebuffed these entreaties. His posture of aloofness, which now held little promise for his country's security, reflected his recent experience with France, Britain, and the United States. His impetuousness had almost brought war. Perhaps he felt the need for a more prudent approach to foreign affairs. Regarding the conflict between the confederation and Buenos Aires, the best he would do was to offer mediation.

*The 1860s: New Possibilities and New Disappointments*
With a new decade little had changed. Paraguayans still maintained their troops and outposts in the Misiones and at the edge of the Gran Chaco. Carlos Antonio López remained committed to his interpretation of national sovereignty, and his government continued to build up defenses in the south, especially at Humaitá. Although the Argentines had not ratified the 1852 agreements, the negotiations did coincide with a decline in the old Itapúa–São Borja trade. What remained was clearly an irregular and smalltime commerce, which gave rise to minor clashes between Paraguayans and Correntinos throughout the rest of the decade and into the 1860s.[47]

The last chance to bring about a settlement of the border disputes came in 1863, two years after the *porteño* victory at Pavón had catapulted Bartolomé Mitre to power in Buenos Aires and one year after Francisco Solano López succeeded to the Paraguayan presidency. With new men directing their respective governments, there was reason to hope that Paraguay and Argentina could make mutual concessions. Solano López suggested as much in a confidential note to Mitre on 6 June 1863 in which he offered to begin negotiations.[48] Mitre agreed, but then wavered when Solano López insisted that they hold talks in Asunción rather than the Argentine capital. This might have seemed a minor point, but minor points had impeded negotiations before. Though he expressed concern for the future, Mitre thought there was still time to arrange a friendly solution.[49]

Francisco Solano López thought otherwise. A series of incidents near the frontier had convinced him to adopt a bleaker view. For one thing, there had been new attempts by *porteño* businessmen to force open the Bermejo River.[50] There had also been cases of Paraguayan soldiers deserting posts in the Misiones and escaping across the disputed zone to Argentine territory.[51]

This inclined Solano López, like his father before him, to adopt a policy of intractability. In his mind, the issue of demarcating borders had given way to the far thornier question of which country—Argentina, Brazil, or Paraguay—should dominate the Platine basin. To Solano López, the Gran Chaco, the Misiones, and for that matter the Mato Grosso, counted for little compared with faraway Uruguay, where a civil war was threatening to bring about an intervention by the major parties. Bad feelings were already in evidence when Fray Pedro María Pellichi, prefect of the Franciscan missions in Salta, visited Asunción with a proposal to set up a new Indian community on the Bermejo. The Paraguayans refused to discuss the matter.[52]

As the disappointed friar set sail on his return trip to Argentina, he could scarcely have failed to notice military movement in the port and at the various outposts along the river. This activity was hardly routine; Solano López had, in fact, ordered a general mobilization. Throughout Paraguay, troops were assembling for intensive training. "It amazes me," his foreign minister wrote shortly afterward, "that rumors have been flying around in Buenos Aires that a Paraguayan force has invaded the Misiones. Perhaps one day the news will be true."[53] The Paraguayan diplomat could allude to such eventualities flippantly; the possibility of a war erupting over the Misiones after all these years seemed remote. Such was not the case in Uruguay, where threats had already given way to violence and where Brazil, Argentina, and Paraguay all had interests to pursue.

# 6
# The Uruguayan Imbroglio

More than Paraguay, the Banda Oriental of Uruguay suffered from its position as a buffer state between Brazil and Argentina. Both the Spaniards and the Portuguese had considered it the doorway to the riches of the Platine estuary. During the colonial period, both sides fought to control the region, which, to all outward appearances, was just empty grassland devoid of any geographical feature that might indicate its northern limit. Yet this "purple land" of wide expanses (and few inhabitants) provided the catalyst for the bloody Paraguayan War.

It was the bad fortune of the Banda Oriental that all of its neighbors coveted the territory for such a long time. Many Orientals responded to this outside interest by allowing themselves to be co-opted by one side or the other. Still more of them endeavored to profit from the uncertainty by wavering between suitors, appearing first to favor the Argentines, then the Brazilians, or vice versa. Even Uruguayans failed to grasp the ambiguities of this legacy, and it caused much confusion for outsiders.

The process of forging a nation in Uruguay involved many fits and starts. The Portuguese invasion that drove out José Gervasio Artigas in 1817 resulted in continuous military occupation through the Cisplatine War. The guns of the British navy finally forced the Brazilians and Argentines to accept the existence of an independent state in 1828. The Oriental Republic of Uruguay was a "nation," but it bore little resemblance to the peaceful, orderly federation of provinces envisioned by Artigas. For many decades, the new regime remained unstable and vulnerable to outside interference.

### The Costs of Party Factionalism

The presidency of the new republic devolved on José Fructuoso Rivera, an officer in Artigas's army. In 1835 he relinquished power to his elected successor, Manuel Oribe, one of the original "thirty-three" patriots of 1825. Rivera, however, only reluctantly parted with the presidential sash and within a few months led a revolt against Oribe. This civil war gave rise to the political parties that have dominated Uruguayan politics to the present day.

Rivera's Colorados, so named for the red pennants they carried, gained the advantage for a time. With the aid of Argentine Unitario forces, they drove Oribe's Blancos, who carried white pennants, across the Uruguay River. The Blancos sought refuge in Buenos Aires, where Rosas welcomed them for as long as he could use them. Oribe, backed by Argentine troops sent by the Bonaerense governor, mounted an offensive against the Colorados at the beginning of the new decade and by 1843 began a siege of Montevideo that would last nine years.

Argentine opponents of Rosas, like the young *porteño* publicist Bartolomé Mitre, arrived in the city to aid in its defense. Negligent of dress and reserved in manner, Mitre's most striking characteristic was his bookishness, but this attribute never prevented the young colonel from acquitting himself well in battle.[1] European adventurers also slipped into the "New Troy" to offer their services. So did certain Colorados from the countryside, who, when bested on their home ground, rallied to the support of the capital city.

Among the defenders was Venancio Flores, an *estanciero* from Trinidad and a man of considerable military experience. Born in 1808, he had already seen action in the war against Brazil and in Uruguayan civil conflicts. His political instincts reflected an older rural tradition in which politics were determined by social hierarchies and infractions by subordinates were punished by the horsewhip and the dagger. Flores cultivated a public image as a *caudillo*, a soft-spoken yet powerful figure on horseback. Like Rosas, whose understanding of nation building rested on similar assumptions, he felt a broad contempt for his gaucho followers. They were useful tools, he thought, but unworthy of his long-term trust or support. Accordingly, Flores tolerated their ferocity as a necessary evil, allowing — even encouraging — them to "play the guitar" across the necks of his rivals.[2]

Flores briefly held the post of military commander in Montevideo, even though the Colorado leadership never completely trusted him. The other Colorados learned to respect him more after 1845, however, when he was wounded in battle and took refuge across the frontier in Brazil. His imperial hosts in Rio Grande do Sul were then concluding negotiations to end the Farrapo revolt and were now free again after more than a decade to project their influence into Uruguay. Flores seemed the perfect ally to help them, even though he controlled only one faction within the Colorado Party, and not the dominant one at that. Like the rival Blancos, the Colorados drew from many elements in Uruguayan society, both rural and urban, which made it difficult to forge a political consensus within the party and frustrated relations with foreigners.

Having come close to annihilating his Colorado opponents, in 1851 Justo José de Urquiza, the powerful Entrerriano lieutenant of Rosas, shocked Oribe and others by turning against his chief and making common cause with the "*salvajes unitarios.*" Urquiza's defection dumbfounded many in the region. He had always seemed the perfect Rosista — ruthless, even brutal, in war; clearly capable; but seemingly content to stand in his master's shadow. In fact, Urquiza was extraordinarily well read with strong interests in music, dance, engineering, and public education. After becoming governor of Entre Ríos in the early 1840s, he conducted a successful land distribution program and, though many *porteños* dismissed him as a rude provincial, his idea of Argentine nationhood proved more modern, more inclusive, than anything Rosas had ever envisioned.

On 29 May 1851 agents from Brazil, Entre Ríos, Corrientes, and Montevideo met in the Uruguayan capital to sign an agreement pledging their common cause to destroy Rosas and Oribe. In short order, they assembled an army of 28,189 men, mostly cavalry, comprising 10,670 Entrerrianos, 5,260 Correntinos, 4,249 Bonaerenses, 1,907 Orientals, and 4,040 Brazilians.[3] The Brazilian troops were significant, for though they amounted to only one-seventh of the total, they promised still greater support for the future. The emperor's government had long seen the divisions in Argentina as the best guarantor of Brazilian interests in the region; now these same divisions offered a direct way to settle the score with Rosas.

On 14 October the Paraguayans received an invitation from Urquiza and the Brazilians to join this effort, but Carlos Antonio López refused anything more than a nominal military commitment.[4] The allied army now complete, Urquiza swiftly lifted the siege of Montevideo, crushed Oribe, and recrossed the Paraná. Soon thereafter he smashed Rosas's untrained levies outside Buenos Aires at Caseros, sending the governor flying to the protection of a British warship and to a life of exile.

*Brazil and the New Platine Politics*

The defeat of Rosas brought a great many benefits to the empire. Ever since independence, the Brazilians had sought an agreement assuring them access to the Platine river system. At the same time, they did everything they could to prevent the consolidation of Argentina under a strong unitary government in Buenos Aires. The Brazilians achieved these goals through Urquiza's victory.

In its alliance with the Entrerriano *caudillo*, the imperial government committed itself to provincial autonomy in Argentina—a course that the Brazilians spurned in their own country. Urquiza would have liked to impose his own regime over Buenos Aires in the same way that the former viceregal capital had once worked its will over the provinces. That goal being impractical, the Entrerriano had to satisfy himself with an Argentine Confederation formed of all the provinces save one. Two months after Caseros, Urquiza held a meeting of provincial governors at San Nicolás in Buenos Aires Province. There he called for a constitutional convention at Santa Fe. Meanwhile, he reaffirmed the old federal pact of 1831 and cut interprovincial customs duties. The convention placed the land and naval forces of the new confederation at his disposal, and Urquiza assumed office as foreign minister, in reality provisional president, of the new Argentine government.

The *Acuerdo* of San Nicolás received support in the interior and Litoral but was rejected by Buenos Aires, which went its own way after a bloodless coup d'état in September 1852. The Bonaerenses, though certain that they wanted no part of the new regime, failed to define the character of their breakaway state. An internal struggle pitted those who wished to see the province and city gain complete independence against those who aimed to transform all Argentina into a Liberal-dominated state under Bonaerense leadership.

Urquiza rejected both positions, not so much from ideology as from economics. Buenos Aires earned the lion's share of Argentina's annual tax receipts through its control of the customhouse, and the nation could not flourish without these revenues. A wealthy, independent Buenos Aires and an impoverished Argentina presented Urquiza with the bleakest of prospects, and throughout the 1850s, therefore, he sought to find ways to force the Bonaerenses to cooperate with the confederation.[5] He authorized a new federal constitution, designed by Juan Bautista Alberdi on the North American model. He also sought to federalize the city of Buenos Aires and provide for the financial reorganization of the country.

The 1853 Constitution assumed that material development would necessarily accompany the political integration of Argentina. The state had the role of "promoting industry, immigration, the construction of railroads, canals, the colonization of open lands, the establishment of new industries, the importation of foreign capital, and the opening of interior rivers."[6] Modernization was seen as the key priority, with progress and nationhood being defined as roughly synonymous terms. Yet in order to build this inclusive sense of nationality, the ambition, talent, and vision of an Alberdi were hardly sufficient — political alliances would have to be forged despite the intransigence of the *porteños*, who refused to accept federalization or the new constitution.

The Brazilians embraced the new confederal government. They pressured it into recognizing Paraguayan independence (in 1852) and continued to meddle clandestinely in partisan politics throughout the region, occasionally funneling money to select Argentines and Uruguayans. This policy was reflexive, with Brazilian diplomats seeking to perpetuate a divided Argentina over which the empire could have maximum influence, which opened the door to renewed Brazilian penetration in the Plata. Much of this was commercial and financial. The baron of Mauá, for instance, actively underwrote scores of Platine ventures throughout this period; indeed, the finances of Montevideo became dependent on the baron's bank.[7] A Brazilian diplomatic campaign was also part of the picture. The empire's representatives wanted both Argentina and Paraguay to grant free access via the rivers to Brazil's Mato Grosso province. And the Brazilians wanted to control Uruguay short of outright annexation.

The Banda Oriental took a course similar to that of Argentina. After Oribe's defeat, a faction of the Blancos had joined with the victorious Colorados to create a coalition government. This regime soon disintegrated, principally due to the intrigues of Flores, the Colorado war minister, who seized the presidency in 1855 thanks to the aid of a four-thousand-man Brazilian military force. He in turn was forced out by a new coalition of Blancos and disaffected Colorados. The Brazilian interventionists, still present on Uruguayan soil, abandoned Flores for this new Blanco-oriented coalition.[8]

Flores found asylum in Buenos Aires, where his old comrade in arms Bartolomé Mitre now held a key post in the Liberal government of the province. Mitre, the urban sophisticate, found much that was admirable and useful in Flores, the rural *caudillo*, thirteen years his senior. Both men were Masons, both were revolutionaries, and both wanted mastery over wider territories than they presently could hope to control. The exiled Colorados of Flores became the close allies of the Bonaerense Liberals and were opposed in due course by a looser alliance of Urquiza's federal movement and the Uruguayan Blancos. The Brazilians, who had temporarily withdrawn from the Banda Oriental, welcomed the opportunity to influence events, though they were no longer sure which side to favor.

### Building to a Crisis

The years 1856–59 were more than usually chaotic in the Banda Oriental and throughout the Plata. Every exile group organized regular assaults from Montevideo or Buenos Aires against their opponents on either side of the river. The Brazilians continued to interfere wherever possible. And far to the north in Paraguay, a military machine of great potential was taking shape.

A major incident occurred at Villamayor in January 1856, when *porteño* cavalry crushed a Blanco-inspired expedition against Buenos Aires. Mitre, acting as war minister, ordered the execution of the invaders, and of the 160 men who had disembarked from Uruguay, only 27 survived.[9] Two years later, a similar expedition against the Blancos was mounted from Bonaerense territory, meeting with similar results. Radicals in the Montevideo government decided that only the most severe punishment would discourage further attack; they shot, disemboweled, and lanced 152 Colorado exiles at Quinteros. The foreign community of the Plata greeted news of this slaughter with horror, as well they should have if one believes the account given by the British chargé: "On six successive days from ten to twelve of the prisoners were killed in the same way [with their throats cut], whenever the army encamped for the evening.... These executions were in some instances distinguished by excessive cruelty; for instance, the young men among the prisoners were stripped, given a certain start, and told to run for their lives, when they were pursued by men on horseback, who speared them, and after amusing themselves, cut their throats."[10]

A result of these events was to throw the Montevideo government more and more into the hands of Blanco extremists, who had already decided to drive the Colorados from the Banda Oriental. Room for political compromise in the Plata was becoming more difficult to find with every passing week. In early July, U.S. Minister Benjamin C. Yancey offered to mediate the dispute between Buenos Aires and the confederation. After a month of temporizing, however, the *porteños* issued demands that forced an end to any hope of mediation.[11] Then Gov. Valentín Alsina of Buenos Aires, who had earlier indicated a willingness to reconcile with the confederation, launched a tariff war against Urquiza's government that threatened to bring it down in short order. This set the stage for a full-scale conflict.

*Cepeda and the Paraguayan Mediation*

The Bonaerenses immediately prepared for war. The government appointed Mitre as commander of an army of nine thousand in the north of the province, and he in turn appointed Flores to command the left flank. More than half of Mitre's men were infantry, mostly inexperienced *porteño* national guardsmen. He also commanded twenty-four pieces of artillery. Ordinarily, a force of this size would have been sufficient to repulse an occasional raid, but the army sweeping down from Entre Ríos was no mere raiding party. It amounted to fourteen thousand men, including ten thousand cavalry, with thirty-five artillery pieces, under the command of Urquiza. Given the odds, Mitre could only fall back utilizing any advantages provided by the terrain, which, on the open Pampas, were few in number.

Mitre chose the arroyo of Cepeda as offering the best chance of success. This creek, located a short distance from San Nicolás, was sufficiently deep and full of obstacles to make possible a reasonable defense. Urquiza attacked Mitre's prepared positions on 23 October 1859. The balmy air soon filled with smoke, shot, and the cries of the wounded as Urquiza's men bore down. Mitre's artillery and infantry stood firm, but his cavalry, save for Flores, broke and fled under the pressure of the Entrerriano onslaught. The Uruguayan commander kept up the fight, showing much personal courage, but most of the men under him soon grew weak from fear and exhaustion. Hoping to save what he could, Mitre withdrew to San Nicolás under cover of the night with what remained of his army; from there he embarked his remaining two thousand men (and six artillery pieces) on river vessels and set sail for Buenos Aires.[12]

The confederal army held the field and seemed poised to march into Buenos Aires. Urquiza, though clearly pleased with his victory at Cepeda, realized that total victory was beyond his grasp, for he could not cover the costs of an extended occupation of the city. Having won by force of arms, he now sought a political solution. In Mitre and the other *porteño* leaders, Urquiza faced masters of the political art, men whose erudition was matched by their shrewdness. This new battle would not be so easily won.

Francisco Solano López now entered the picture. He was as unknown as his rarely visited but much-talked-about country. He was thirty-four, typically attired in a dazzling uniform, and a sojourn in the European capitals five years before had given him a passing acquaintance with the niceties of diplomacy; he was anxious to show off what he had learned. He was also eager to demonstrate that Paraguay would make itself an indispensable part of the Platine equation. Urquiza and the *porteños*, worried that nothing would come of their own negotiating efforts, accepted López's offer of mediation.[13] Talks began in November.

Solano López's decision to mediate the dispute between Buenos Aires and the confederation was a major departure from Paraguayan diplomatic practice, which had stressed noninterference. Dr. Francia, in his time, had taken this principle to an extreme; Carlos Antonio López brought a relaxation of this hard-line stance; but before 1852 the change was relative. The elder López refused to yield on border disagreements with Brazil and Argentina, and several times he sent raiding parties into disputed territories. Yet he avoided full-scale confrontations with Paraguay's neighbors. The younger López, upon his return from Europe, was unwilling to accept any check on Paraguayan foreign policy. Outsiders had respected his father's aggressive approach when it was backed by sufficient force. The young general made it his business to see that from this point forward it was always well supported. His mediation efforts after Cepeda had the same objective: to promote respect for Paraguay and its government within the ruling circles of the Platine countries and Brazil.

The young Paraguayan leader did very credible work at the negotiating table. It became clear to him from the outset that the confederation would talk peace only if Valentín Alsina, the rabidly anti-Urquiza governor of Buenos Aires, were removed from office. Not surprisingly, Alsina rejected this demand and broke off negotiations. The governor's position was hardly secure; Mitre had engineered his earlier accession in Buenos Aires as a symbolic gesture, as an expression of defiance to Urquiza and the Federalists. Alsina was not indispensable and everyone knew it.

Solano López handled the situation with considerable tact. Without giving offense to Alsina, he negotiated around the intransigent governor. He reminded the Bonaerenses that Urquiza's armies were within striking distance of their capital and that he could not prevent their advance if the truce expired. He suggested that they do the right thing. They did. The provincial legislature of Buenos Aires demanded the governor's resignation, and Alsina capitulated.

On 11 November the confederation and the city and province of Buenos Aires signed the Pact of Union that paradoxically gave the Bonaerenses everything they wanted save legal independence. Buenos Aires reentered the confederation under its own constitution and, in turn, received a specific revenue out of the national customs — no other province enjoyed such a concession. Solano López announced that the Republic of Paraguay would guarantee all the particulars of the agreement.

The Paraguayan general felt satisfied with the negotiations. His skill and tenacity had won out against ingrained animosities, and now he happily accepted the accolades of the Argentine public. *Porteño* representative Carlos Tejedor wrote to Solano López on 13 November and noted that the "diplomatic action of Paraguay in bringing together the members of the same family and allaying difficulties that until now had appeared insuperable, has contributed strongly to the solution, by peaceful means, of questions that could never have been resolved honorably for all through recourse to arms. It is a pleasure to inform Your Excellency that the Government of Buenos Aires shall conserve the pleasant impressions inspired in it by the distinguished person of the representative of Paraguay as a complement of the noble and successful mission that he has performed."[14]

These sentiments were echoed in the *porteño* newspapers and in testimonials by officials on all sides of the conflict. Urquiza went so far as to present Solano López with the sword he had worn at Cepeda.[15]

For all of the acclaim directed at the Paraguayan general, the real victor at the negotiating table was Mitre. With Alsina gone, he became the dominant figure in *porteño* politics and immediately set to work restructuring his home government into a modern powerhouse. The Pact of Union allowed him space for maneuver, and by the next time he met Urquiza on the field of battle, his troops were equal to the challenge.

*Pavón: A Prelude to War*

The leaders of the Buenos Aires government accepted reincorporation into the Argentine Confederation as a temporary expedient. They had no intention of allowing the interior and Litoral provinces to set national policy and endeavored to undermine the 1859 agreements. Urquiza did prevent Alsina from regaining power in Buenos Aires, but this meant little. Mitre dominated the *porteño* government both before and after negotiations. Urquiza decided against occupying the city of Buenos Aires, although he had several opportunities to do so; instead, he trusted that the proconfederation political factions within the city would win the day.

Mitre favored unity, but his idea of Argentine nationhood was radically unlike that of Urquiza. Like the Unitarians of old, he believed that the city of Buenos Aires should lead the rest of Argentina. Urban intellectuals could shape political culture in the country so as to make *porteño* hegemony seem altogether natural, while a modern army could neutralize Urquiza and other provincial *caudillos*.

Mitre had already begun the task of molding a new political culture. His writings, which celebrated the Patriot cause of 1810 as a harbinger of his own nationalism, enjoyed an audience in the provinces. Now came the time for building his military.

Events at the beginning of the 1860s favored Mitre. The export economy, which demand for salt beef had fueled for many years, now received an unprecedented boost thanks to an expanded market for wool, which French and Belgian carpet mills needed in quantity.[16] To profit from this demand, the Litoral provinces needed an understanding with Buenos Aires that would keep credits flowing to sheepmen and the Paraná River open to navigation. Only Mitre could assure *porteño* cooperation on this point, and Urquiza could ill afford to oppose his own *provinciano* landowners.[17]

In February 1860 Santiago Derqui was elected president of the confederation. A former justice minister from Córdoba, Derqui had fallen out with Urquiza, whom he considered as wild and untrustworthy as the gauchos of his province. Not altogether surprised by the election, Urquiza left for his Entre Ríos estates. He nonetheless retained the governorship of that province and control over the armed units stationed there.

Mitre, who became governor of Buenos Aires in May, was delighted with the change. The confederation had removed his most intractable opponent, leaving someone with whom Mitre could bargain. He now stressed the advantages of national unity, "a high and great cause" that would bring peace and prosperity to long suffering Argentina.[18]

Mitre invited both Derqui and Urquiza to come to Buenos Aires in July to celebrate the independence holidays. For two weeks he feted them, showing them schools, theaters, and Argentina's first railroad (which the *porteños* judged a marvel even though it had yet to extend beyond the city limits). Buenos Aires *was* the leader of the nation, he emphasized; its material progress left no doubt that the city had a right to that role. If the other provinces recognized this superiority, then the nation as a whole could take a similarly happy road to the future.

Derqui and Urquiza were duly impressed, if still unconvinced.[19] Mitre knew that for such propaganda to work, he had to add a plan to subvert the authority of the confederation in the provinces. In 1860 and 1861, he encouraged his followers to make their own bids for power. Mitrista revolts erupted in San Juan, Córdoba, and elsewhere. Correctly seeing the hand of *porteño* agents in these disturbances, Urquiza issued a sharp protest. Then, in a calculated affront to the newly ratified national constitution, Mitre demanded the seating of *porteño* deputies who had been elected according to provincial, rather than national, law. If the *porteño* meant to test Urquiza's reaction, on this occasion he did not have to wait long. The Entrerriano *caudillo* again took up the sword.

The ensuing battle of Pavón sealed the fate of the old order in the Plata. In military terms, it was a more difficult contest than Cepeda, for on this occasion the contending forces were more evenly balanced than two years earlier. Again, Mitre's strength was in his infantry and artillery. His mounted troops, though led by courageous officers like the Uruguayan Venancio Flores, had no real combat experience except against the Indians of the south. Mitre had learned some lessons from Cepeda, however, and now his forces boasted a few pieces of modern artillery and a much-needed medical unit. As a whole, the Bonaerense army numbered 15,500 men.

On paper, confederal forces held a slight edge with a total of 17,000 men, the better part of them experienced cavalrymen. This advantage was offset, however, by the disposition of the troops. In fact, the confederation had two armies in the field, one advancing from Entre Ríos under Urquiza's command and another coming from Córdoba under the command of Derqui; since the two were barely on speaking terms, they not surprisingly found it difficult to cooperate in battle. In addition, confederal forces were woefully lacking in arms and equipment, whereas their opponents, despite their inexperience, possessed cannons and rifles newly imported from Europe.

The battle itself was anticlimactic. Convinced that Mitre's strength necessitated a defensive posture, Urquiza encamped in the low valley of Pavón, just south of the line that separated the provinces of Buenos Aires and Santa Fe. On 17 September 1861 Mitre's infantry attacked the center of the confederal position and crushed its front lines. As expected, Urquiza's cavalry pushed their mounted opponents back precipitously on the flanks. Mitre then quickly deployed his infantry and artillery in close formation to fend off an envelopment. Colonels Wenceslao Paunero and Emilio Mitre (the governor's brother), each commanding an infantry division on the *porteño* side, distinguished themselves by their tenacious fighting at this juncture. After a short but ferocious uphill charge, the *porteños* began an envelopment of their own. Most of the confederation's artillery, some thirty-two pieces, fell into Mitre's hands. Urquiza deemed this loss crucial. He ordered his Entrerriano cavalry to withdraw to the north, leaving the remaining troops without effective command.[20]

Urquiza's retreat seemed curious at first. The engagement, after all, had cost Mitre more casualties, especially among his cavalry units. At the same time, confederal troops were still undefeated when Urquiza abandoned the field. The simplest explanation for the Entrerriano's action was that he lost faith in his ability to take Buenos Aires even if he temporarily gained an edge over Mitre. Urquiza's personal fortune was strained, his province threatened, and he was tired; on the battlefield, a stomach ailment exacerbated his malaise. He slinked back to Entre Ríos to bide his time. He remained governor of the province and head of the majority faction of the Federal Party, but he no longer seemed the man he once was.

Mitre's victory at Pavón sealed the fate of the Argentine Confederation. The *porteño* army advanced without opposition to Rosario; less than two months afterward the national government capitulated, and Derqui fled to exile in Montevideo. Most officials of the former regime resigned or offered to serve whatever government Mitre could put together.

The *porteño* governor now had more power than any Argentine politician since Rosas. In celebrating his triumph over Urquiza, Mitre rightly judged it a watershed event in Argentine history. In a letter to one of his generals, he attributed the victory to military modernization and a new shift in politics: "Pavón is not only a military victory. It is a triumph of civilization over the weapons of barbarism. History will show that Pavón was the tomb of the undisciplined cavalry.... With the bands of cavalry of both sides dissipated, the battle demonstrated that decisive victories are won only by trained infantry and artillery."[21] The civilization that Mitre referred to had taken on an iconic character in Argentina. It assigned a special place to the city of Buenos Aires in transforming and regenerating the Argentine nation, bringing it to a level comparable to that of the European countries. Such an interpretation was as shrewd as it was self-serving in that it provided justification for any course that the *porteño* leadership might pursue.

### New Trouble in Uruguay

Bartolomé Mitre's domination of Argentina remained incomplete. In Entre Ríos, still under Justo José de Urquiza, and in the provinces of the west, the power of the *porteño*-oriented government was dimly felt. In La Rioja and Catamarca, the illiterate *caudillo* Angel Vicente Peñaloza was still in open rebellion. Even provinces such as Corrientes and Santa Fe, located much closer to Buenos Aires, saw their loyalty to the new regime as conditional at best. And this disunity did not go unnoticed in Brazil and Uruguay.

The period between Cepeda and Pavón found Uruguay under an increasingly harassed Blanco administration. The Blancos identified their interests with those of Urquiza's confederation, but as the fortunes of the Entrerriano *caudillo* declined, so did their identification with his cause. A full year before Pavón, the Montevideo government began to loosen its ties to the confederation and search, gingerly at first, for rapprochement with Mitre.

Uruguayan president Bernardo Berro, a man of considerable vision, realized the development of his country would forever be constrained if its government continued to link itself overtly to either Buenos Aires or the confederation. He realized that a more palpable threat to Uruguay's sovereignty lay to the north, in Brazil.

Imperial diplomats also viewed the decline of the confederation with some trepidation. On the one hand, Mitre's ascendancy, they felt, might bring *porteño* hegemony over all the Platine states. On the other hand, many regarded the connection with Urquiza as nothing more than an expedient; perhaps the time had come for a better understanding with Buenos Aires.[22] The empire, after all, had attained many of its short-term objectives. All sides in the Plata, including Paraguay, now recognized

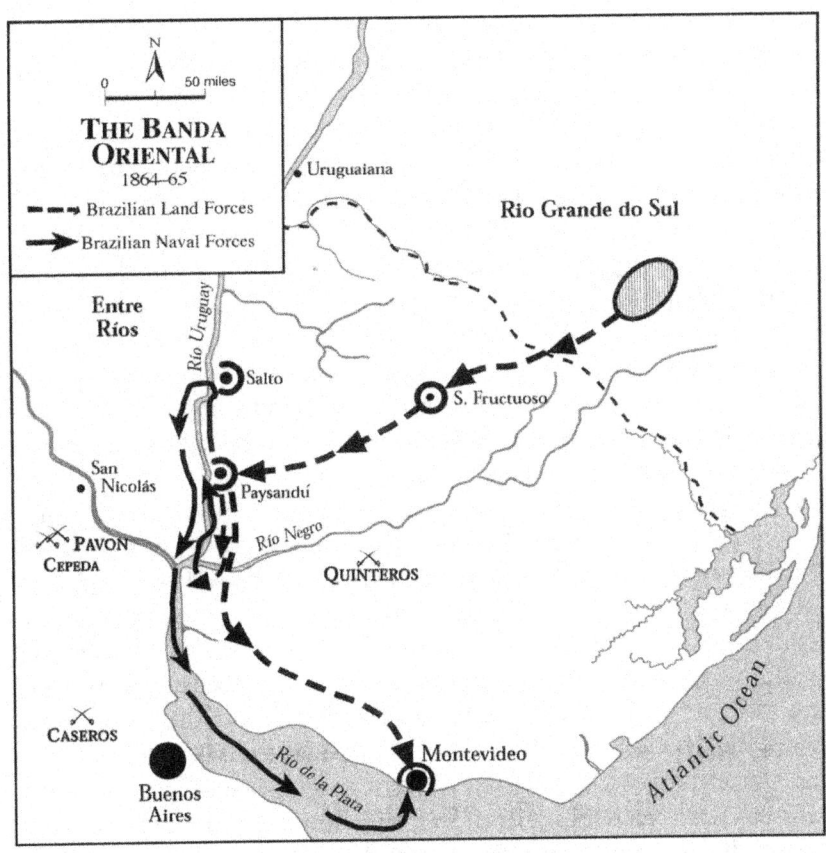

Brazil's right to traverse the Paraná, Paraguay, and Uruguay Rivers. This assured communication by water with the Mato Grosso and encouraged growth of Brazilian trade with communities in the Platine interior. Commercial exchanges had also expanded with the Banda Oriental. Since much of the trade involved cattle transfers along an unclear frontier, however, it also brought with it the possibility of conflict with Montevideo.

Berro declared neutrality at the time of Pavón. Mitre, who appreciated this stance, agreed to prevent any attacks against Uruguay by Colorado émigrés living within *porteño* territory. Yet he also had a debt to pay to Venancio Flores. The redoubtable cavalryman had bravely served Buenos Aires on many occasions and expected support in return. Mitre might have preferred to wait; he took office as president of the Argentine Republic on 12 October 1862 and had other things on his mind. Flores nonetheless pressed for an immediate hearing. And when Mitre gave him reason to expect aid in due course, Flores began clandestine preparations for an invasion of Uruguay.

The Berro government had infiltrated spies into the ranks of the exiled Colorados and soon became aware of these activities. As the months went by, anxiety grew in Montevideo to the point where Berro felt desperate. In November he sent to Buenos Aires a trusted agent, Dr. Octavio Lapido, charged with lodging a protest with Mitre.

The Argentine president promised to intern all Colorados found plotting any kind of escapade but otherwise failed to reassure Lapido and the government in Montevideo.[23] At the end of November, the Blancos intercepted an incriminating letter from Flores to a sympathetic Uruguayan who was then *jefe político* in the department of Minas.[24] Presented with this evidence of Flores's machinations, Argentine Foreign Minister Rufino de Elizalde tried to play down the affair, reminding Lapido that Flores had no legal standing in the Argentine Republic.[25] Elizalde was known not only for his composure, tact, and agreeable appearance but also for his devotion to Mitre's line; therefore his response was hardly reassuring. Mitre himself chose to stay mute. This ended the special relationship that had existed between Montevideo and Buenos Aires since 1860. President Berro braced for the attack that he knew would come.

*The Flores Invasion*

On the night of 19 April 1863, Flores landed at Rincón de las Gallinas, a small village at the mouth of the Negro River in Uruguay. He quickly gathered some five hundred gauchos and, under the banner of "Vengeance for Quinteros," set out for safer territory along the Brazilian frontier. The Blancos did not pursue Flores's little army to the north. Instead, they concentrated on meeting the greater challenge that was sure to come from Buenos Aires.

Public opinion in the latter city was solidly behind Flores. The *porteño* press, including the quasi-official *Nación Argentina*, referred glowingly to the "liberator" and his quest to free his country. Mitre's local opponents, the autonomist faction led by Adolfo Alsina, supported the majority opinion.[26] Gunrunning up the Uruguay River began almost immediately. So did public meetings designed to recruit volunteers for the Colorado intervention. Yet the national government continued to deny its involvement. Mitre himself was in Rosario when the invasion came, and although he knew of the action in advance, feigned surprise at the news.

Berro decided to try diplomacy one last time. He dispatched to Buenos Aires a figure famous in Uruguayan political circles, Dr. Andrés Lamas, a publicist, bibliophile, and diplomat, perhaps the only Uruguayan statesman to command respect from both Blancos and Colorados. A gray old gentleman of dignified appearance, Lamas had served for many years as minister in Rio de Janeiro, where he developed a personal friendship with Dom Pedro. He also knew Mitre, with whom he had worked on various exile publications in Montevideo during the 1830s, as well as Solano López, whom he met in Rio upon the young general's return from Europe in 1855.[27]

Lamas received no satisfaction in Argentina. He met with Elizalde at the beginning of May, exchanged information, and felt vexed when the foreign minister denied any complicity on the part of his government. On the thirteenth, Lamas sent a formal note to Elizalde, reminding him that real neutrality required something more than his simple assertion. The minister's written rejoinder was a model of sophistry and calculation: "General Flores has lent the most distinguished services to this country, which have placed him on a level with the most notable of its citizens. Leaving the country in the way he did has shown that he carried his delicacy to the extreme in order not to throw upon the Republic the least responsibility. . . . Flores was not under the necessity of leaving the country secretly; he, more than any, could leave not only freely but surrounded by the attentions that the Republic owes him and that the government has deemed it an honor to render him. If General Flores on leaving this country intended to go to Uruguay, it was not incumbent on the government in this case to inquire or to hinder."[28] Three days later Elizalde followed this with a note suggesting that Argentina knew how to define true neutrality and had resolved to defend that interpretation henceforth.[29]

At this juncture the European diplomatic representatives in Montevideo and Buenos Aires attempted to push for reconciliation. Both sides rejected this effort, even though the British chargé joined his European colleagues in arguing that a new civil war would greatly damage everyone's interests. Elizalde insisted that his government had observed neutrality and that the entreaties of the foreign powers were both unnecessary and unappreciated.[30] The American minister, who observed these exchanges from a close distance, later noted that such protests had had little chance of success, for when Flores departed Buenos Aires, he "had many friends to assist him, and [was] supported by nearly all the native press of the city.... [He is] the Jeff Davis of Uruguay."[31]

Having spurned the Europeans, the national government proceeded on a confrontational course with the Blancos. In early June 1863, Uruguayan police officials at the port of Fray Bentos inspected the hold of an Argentine packet steamer, the *Salto*. Finding war materiel aboard, they took the ship into custody. The authorities released the vessel soon thereafter, but the contraband arms and munitions stayed behind at a guarded warehouse in Montevideo. The captain of the *Salto*, who had initially denied the presence of contraband aboard his ship, later told the Uruguayan authorities that the materiel belonged to the Argentine government. Upon receiving this news, the Uruguayan foreign minister, Juan José de Herrera, dispatched a note to Elizalde offering to return the cases if Mitre's government would confirm the captain's claim.

Refusing to confirm the story, Elizalde denounced the seizure of the ship and called "upon the Uruguayan government for immediate and solemn reparation such as is fitting to avenge the outrage, punish the offense, and accord the indemnities owing."[32] Elizalde's strident tone masked an innovation in Platine diplomacy: he was responding not as spokesman for a liberal revolutionary movement but as minister of a sovereign state with clearly defined national interests.

Argentine nationalism, as formulated in the writings of Mitre, Alberdi, and the Men of 1837, had started to take shape in foreign-policy statements, in the newspapers, and in the rhetoric of politicians. Even now, such nationalism was not shared by Argentines in the interior or by *porteño* autonomists; neither group ever willingly made concessions to a government greater than that of their province, and neither was much liked by the Men of 1837. After gaining power in the 1850s, the latter offered Argentina a seemingly modern, representative order, but because they mistrusted popular sentiment—which had so strongly backed Rosas—they limited debate to their own elite class. The troubles in Uruguay gave them an opportunity.

Herrera swallowed his pride and gave the Argentines a courteous reply. If Uruguay had done anything requiring reparation, he wrote, then it would soon be forthcoming, but meanwhile both parties could benefit from an enquiry. He suggested that Elizalde discuss the matter with Lamas, who was still in Buenos Aires and had instructions to enter into talks with the Argentines.[33]

Elizalde would have none of it. He issued an ultimatum, which included demands for compensation, the cashiering of the Uruguayan naval commander who had first inspected the *Salto*, a twenty-one-gun salute to the Argentine flag, and the return of the war supplies. Lamas tried to sidestep the demand and formally proposed arbitration by any sovereign the Argentines might name out of a list that included Queen Victoria, Napoleon III, Victor Emmanuel II, and Dom Pedro. Elizalde rejected this suggestion, remarking how unfortunate it was that the Montevideo government had placed Argentina in the position of having to take "coercive measures to avenge the outrage."[34]

On 22 June 1863 the Argentines seized the Uruguayan steamer *General Artigas* and blockaded the mouth of the Uruguay River. The next day, the Blanco government broke relations with Buenos Aires. However, as events built to a crescendo, behind-the-scene efforts sought to prevent

*The Uruguayan Imbroglio* 137

an outbreak of hostilities. The Uruguayans released the *Salto* and returned the arms and munitions. On June 24 Elizalde wrote to Lamas to suggest that they could solve the problem with a simultaneous twenty-one-gun salute from both vessels involved. The Italian chargé at Montevideo offered his mediation at the same time, and the two parties accepted.

Having precipitated a major crisis, Elizalde now ended it, pulling back from war at the last instant while insisting that his government had never swayed from neutrality in Uruguayan affairs.[35] A more accurate statement on the nature of Argentine neutrality came from William Doria, the British chargé at Buenos Aires, who noted that "all dispassionate persons concur in the belief that clandestine assistance has been afforded to Venancio Flores by this government."[36]

The Mitre government had by now recognized Flores as a belligerent. This meant that the Colorado chieftain could legally obtain the same succor in Buenos Aires as the internationally recognized regime in Montevideo. To take active measures against gunrunning, to break up pro-Flores rallies and recruitment campaigns, and to censor rebel newspapers would have constituted a breach of neutrality as Elizalde and Mitre defined it. A more common interpretation of neutrality, as generally practiced in the nineteenth century, would have demanded taking these actions.

Why, after purposely aggravating the relationship with Uruguay, did Elizalde move so quickly toward a normal state of affairs? His change of attitude can be explained on three levels. First, the *Salto* episode had demonstrated to the Berro government that it could not interdict gunrunning operations, especially near the mouth of the Uruguay River where Flores wished to establish supply lines with Argentina. Second, the deteriorating situation had caught the attention of Urquiza, whose province was contiguous to the Oriental Republic. Mitre did not wish to see a new alliance spring up between the Blancos of Montevideo and their old ally in Entre Ríos. The *caudillo* might have suffered defeat at Pavón, but he was still a force to be reckoned with. Third, and perhaps most important, the national government suspected Brazil's intentions in Uruguay. A war with the Blancos would have stretched Argentine resources further than Mitre dared go. He was already involved in suppressing revolts in the western province of La Rioja, and his war chest was seriously depleted. If he did poorly in the west, no one could know what the Brazilians might do in the Banda Oriental. True, they had good contacts with Flores (he was at that moment organizing his cavalry along the frontier with Rio Grande do Sul). Yet they also had a long-standing relation with Lamas, who acted on behalf of the Montevideo government. One thing was certain: the empire would follow a policy congruent with its own interests, and these traditionally had been in opposition to the interests of Buenos Aires. Now was not the time to risk Brazilian intervention.

*New Diplomatic Efforts and the Paraguayan Connection*

Incidents continued to mar the prospects for peace during the winter of 1863. In August and September, the Argentine warship *Pampero* assisted pro-Flores elements landing at Fray Bentos. Again the Blancos failed to prevent the incursion. Again they protested to the Argentines. Again it did no good.

What the Blancos could not achieve with their warships on the Río de la Plata they attempted to achieve at the negotiating table. On 20 October 1863 Lamas signed a protocol with Elizalde that committed their two governments to a common interpretation of neutrality based on international law. According to Article 3 of the document, any disagreement on interpretation would be presented to a single arbitrator, the emperor of Brazil.[37] In making this agreement, the two sides thus placed final authority in the hands of Dom Pedro, hardly a disinterested party.

This very point caused great consternation to President Berro: "Is señor Lamas mad? Since when has he claimed to elevate the Emperor of Brazil into a supreme tribunal for the international affairs of the Uruguayan people?"[38] Berro was not speaking out of simple exasperation, however. His government, it emerged, had been conducting another diplomatic offensive in Asunción. Berro had reason to think that he could play a Paraguay card, for he had just received dispatches indicating Solano López's willingness to help his regime.

The Blancos had been actively trying to recruit the Paraguayans for over a year. Juan José de Herrera, the chief architect of this venture, arrived in Asunción in March 1862 on a mission to convince the aging Carlos Antonio López that their two countries had a common cause.[39] Their first meetings went well. Both men regarded the Brazilians as expansionists ready at a moment's notice to swallow disputed territories. Both feared the machinations of Mitre, whom they saw as a schemer who would set the peoples of the Plata against each other so as to inherit the shattered remains.

For all of their amiable discussions, Herrera failed to elicit any concrete promises from López, who thought his Uruguayan guest pushed a little too hard. As in 1852, the Paraguayan president preferred to hold back from any entangling alliances.[40] He was also tired. He had transferred much of his authority, especially in military matters, to his eldest son. Carlos Antonio López still issued orders, but more and more it was Solano López, the war minister, who executed them. Unlike his father, whose conservatism had long prevented an expanded role for Paraguay in regional affairs, the younger López was ambitious for himself and his country.

On 3 March 1863, Herrera, now Uruguayan foreign minister, addressed a dispatch to his colleague, Dr. Octavio Lapido, who was about to leave on a mission to Asunción. The dispatch contained detailed instructions on how to coax the Paraguayans into an alliance.

Herrera emphasized the reciprocal interest that existed between Uruguay and Paraguay, both threatened by deceitful and hungry neighbors. Their situation being common, so should be their response. This had been suggested the year before to the elder López, but now Herrera added a new element, arguing that the two countries should forge a common policy "directed to the establishment of a balance of power, protective to all in this agitated part of South America. . . . The system of balance of power has been and is one of the strongest guarantees of people's rights. . . . [It] conserves the peace because it inspires the fear of war. Uruguay and Paraguay must seek it out."[41] An alliance between the two could serve, he continued, as a magnet, drawing Argentine provinces away from Buenos Aires and Mitre. In this way Paraguay and

Uruguay might become important actors in Platine affairs, rather than passive buffer states.⁴²

Herrera understood that Paraguay's policy stressed noninterference and that any alteration was unlikely. But the situation had changed, for on the morning of 10 September 1862, Carlos Antonio López had died and was quickly succeeded by his eldest son. The latter's assertiveness and ability to grasp concepts and interests on a continental, rather than just a national, basis augured well for the Lapido mission. Solano López had experience in Europe and was aware of the political and economic benefits an effective balance of power might bring.

Herrera's appeal to the Paraguayans was born of desperation, not of a perceived opportunity. Andrés Lamas's appeals to the Argentine government regarding the activities of Flores had brought nothing but promises. The Blancos needed allies and were willing to seek them in any quarter.

Lapido arrived in Asunción in early July 1863, and over the next several weeks met frequently with Solano López and his foreign minister, José Berges. With his heavy brow, lustrous eyes, and drooped mustache, the latter appeared more like an overworked innkeeper than a seasoned diplomat, but he was in fact the most thoughtful official in the Paraguayan service. Since the early 1850s, Berges had enjoyed much success in government circles, largely owing to the skillful manner in which he presented the proposals of the younger López to skeptical foreign representatives. Unlike other Paraguayan officials, who seemed little more than lackeys, Berges spoke from clear authority, and foreigners liked dealing with him. His talks with Lapido on this occasion drew the full support of Solano López.

Perhaps the new Paraguayan president hoped to repeat the successful mediation of 1859, or perhaps he was only trying to assess a complicated situation in which he might eventually become involved. In either case, Lapido was soon able to report a qualified interest in the Uruguayan position on the part of the Asunción government. López held back from any immediate announcement of alliance, it seems, only because Berges urged caution. The foreign minister noted that the *Salto* affair had not yet run its course and that a decision of such magnitude required more reflection.[43] Solano López the general was eager to unsheathe his sword, but Solano López the president decided that it would be more prudent to wait. Lapido, who knew his man, began to draft a treaty of alliance.[44]

Toward the end of August, Berges asked to see any written proposals that Lapido might care to submit. The Uruguayan diplomat promptly sent a memorandum advocating an alliance between his country and Paraguay.[45] Solano López considered the options and told Lapido that he would await the open support of Urquiza, with whom the Paraguayans had been in correspondence. The struggle in the Banda Oriental had greatly concerned the Entrerriano *caudillo*. And Solano López was not the only one who expected him to announce his strong disagreement with pro-Flores policy. Mitre expected it as well. In order to head off any trouble from that quarter, the Argentine president had already offered to support his old foe for reelection as governor.[46] Urquiza temporized, and as a result so did Solano López.

No one had to wait for long. On 21 September 1863 Berges directed a note to Elizalde in which he asked for "friendly explanations" of Argentine actions vis-à-vis the Oriental Republic. In this missive, which he carefully backdated to 6 September, Berges maintained that his government regarded as essential the continued independence of Uruguay, "whose political existence is the [necessary] condition for the balance of power and for the peace that protects the interests of all in the Plata."[47] In a move that flabbergasted Lapido and the other Uruguayan diplomats, Berges appended to his note copies of the correspondence that the Blanco government had conducted with Paraguay. Nothing in this compilation flattered the Mitre government, and it was a breach of diplomatic etiquette for Berges to put it before the eyes of the Argentines.

The Blancos in Montevideo fumed. Such revelations could only make relations with Buenos Aires worse. Even so, the Blancos got what they wanted: a specific declaration of support from the Asunción government, a harbinger of some kind of alliance. Solano López knew exactly what he was doing when his minister released the confidential documents. He revealed the intrigues of the Uruguayans, thereby showing his independence from them while presenting himself in the most sincere and impartial light possible. Sincerity and impartiality, he hoped, might to all parties ultimately translate into indispensability, as it had in 1859. López intended to be pivotal in whatever happened next.

Foreign Minister Herrera had received detailed accounts of Lapido's diplomatic efforts in Paraguay. The 6 September note strengthened the Blancos at the moment when Herrera received news of the Lamas-Elizalde Protocol. He now felt that his government might actually contain the threat from Flores and not have to yield to Mitre or the Brazilians. He decided to take the risk and provoke both Buenos Aires and the empire. Herrera demanded that Solano López's name be added to the protocol as equal arbitrator with the emperor. The reaction in Buenos Aires was predictable. Mitre had no intention of giving in to Paraguayan pretensions, scornfully adding that "one might as well invoke the mediation of China."[48] With the protocol now as good as dead, events drifted toward a much bloodier conflict.

Smuggling to Flores continued without pause, and rumors indicated that his troops were nearing the vicinity of Paysandú. On 10 November 1863 Blanco authorities searching for Colorado infiltrators discovered a small expeditionary force among the islands of the Uruguay River. It comprised three lighters heavily loaded with arms, uniforms, and cavalry equipment and was guarded by forty-one armed men. The seizure of this materiel and the capture of the men, which occurred three days later, provoked a new confrontation. Argentine officials demanded the return of men and materiel on the dubious grounds that, as one of the islands lay adjacent to the Argentine bank of the river, the Uruguayans had violated Argentine soil in making the seizure. Montevideo responded with a sharp note, after which the British minister in Buenos Aires, Edward Thornton, offered to mediate. Both sides declined and then suspended diplomatic relations with one another in early December.[49]

Mitre ordered a redeployment of his best troops from the interior provinces, where they had just finished crushing the Peñaloza uprising, to the Litoral. He ordered the construction of modern forts on Martín García, a small island near the Uruguayan bank of the Río de la Plata, which already served as a transit station for smuggled war supplies to Flores. Yet the most important preparation that Mitre effected was diplomatic: he opened negotiations with Brazil to clarify their relations and perceived interests, and, if possible, to coordinate their actions.[50]

*The Brazilian Connection*

The imperial government had paid careful attention to Uruguayan affairs since Flores launched his invasion in April 1863. The Brazilians were perfectly aware of Argentine support for the Colorado *caudillo*, and the fact did not especially alarm them, since they too had agents within Flores's camp.

Brazil's long-term interest in weakening the hand of Argentina in the Banda Oriental involved more than strategic concerns. No one had ever adequately defined the frontier between Rio Grande do Sul and Uruguay. The inhabitants of this zone identified themselves either as Brazilians or Uruguayans; their nationalism was expedient depending on which nation was useful as a shield in a time of need.[51] Borderlanders lived their lives in much the same way whether on the Brazilian side of the frontier or the Uruguayan side. They worked in ranching, often with thousands of head of cattle to manage; spoke Spanish and Portuguese (and sometimes Guaraní) with equal fluency; enjoyed sipping *mate*, sharing tall tales, and playing the same card games as their gaucho cousins in Argentina. And they wore the same regional costume: loose baggy trousers *(bombachas)*, calf-skin boots with silver spurs, a colorful shirt with silk handkerchief about the throat, a wide but unadorned sombrero strapped under the chin, a belt studded with silver coins and a razor-sharp knife *(facón)*, and a dark blue or black poncho of delicate wool flung jauntily over the shoulder to reveal the scarlet lining.

Many borderlanders spoke of themselves as Brazilians. Yet the wealthiest owned thousands of hectares in Uruguay as well. All used the laws of the empire and of the Oriental Republic to their advantage when possible and ignored the laws when not.

By the early 1860s, as many as twenty thousand Riograndenses had settled in northern Uruguay together with their slaves. They had purchased some of the largest estates in the country, establishments that were quite impressive in terms of livestock holdings.[52] In order to make these ranches profitable, the Riograndenses needed to drive their herds to *saladeros* in Brazil. This required the cooperation of the Montevideo government, something that was not always forthcoming. Even though some of these Riograndenses as individuals had good relations with the Blanco regime, as a group they feared the measures that an unstable government might enact against them.

The Flores invasion presented the Riograndense ranchers with an opportunity. Many Colorados had served in the Farrapo armies during the 1830s and 1840s and were well known in southern Brazil. After the Quinteros massacre, hundreds of Colorados found refuge there. Now their old leader Flores expected them to join his forces in the borderlands. Cooperation with the Riograndenses was necessary in effecting this linkup; both the Colorados and Blancos knew it. This put the Riograndenses (both the borderlands ranchers and their agents in the imperial government) in the enviable position of being able to determine the specific course of the Flores rebellion, whether it was to move forward toward Montevideo or be left stillborn along the frontier.

The price they demanded for their support would be high. Riograndense leaders counted among their number some skilled politicians who were also proven fighters in the *caudillo*-like mold of Urquiza. Generals Manoel Luiz Osório (afterward baron of Herval) and Manoel Marquez de Souza (afterward baron of Pôrto Alegre) were two such men. The recognized chief of the Riograndenses was a much older man, Gen. Antonio de Souza Netto, a fearsome warrior in the Farrapo War. (Indeed, it was he who had declared Riograndense independence after the battle of Seival in 1836.)[53] He was now one of the wealthiest men in the province, having supplied the armies of Manuel Oribe with thousands of head of cattle during the nine-year siege of Montevideo. Netto thus had excellent contacts with the Blancos. Yet their decision to tax Riograndense ranchers in Uruguay had adversely affected his holdings.

*The Uruguayan Imbroglio* 145

Netto came to Rio de Janeiro in late 1863 as spokesman for the aggrieved ranchers. He stayed on in the imperial capital until April 1864, all the while offering banquets to deputies, senators, and members of the press and Foreign Ministry. His purpose was easy to discern: to convince the imperial government that direct action on behalf of the Brazilian residents in Uruguay was warranted.[54] This message, usually delivered in the most nationalistic tones possible, was soon heard in every hall of the government, including the emperor's residence in Petrópolis. Not surprisingly, the Carioca press came out in favor of Netto and the interventionists, with many newspapers reporting as fact the stories of atrocity the Riograndense patriarch supplied them.[55]

Netto's appeal failed to convince every official, though. After all, his earlier enthusiasm for the secessionist Farrapos did not recommend him as a Brazilian patriot, and there was lingering suspicion that he might return to a separatist ideal. Evidence also had come to light that Netto had sent one thousand of his gaúchos to hover near the Uruguayan border, presumably to provoke an incident, the nature of which was still unclear.[56] The problem before Dom Pedro, then, was if he refused to intervene in Uruguay, would Netto and his associates opt for a secessionist solution once more?

A newly elected Chamber of Deputies largely comprised of young Liberal Party *bacharéis* came into office on 1 January 1864. These men believed that they had received a mandate to effect sweeping domestic change, and even if the exact nature of that change was still hazy, they nonetheless felt determined to pursue it. Older Liberals, who worried what would happen if these reformists had their way, did everything they could to divert their younger colleagues with foreign affairs. The Banda Oriental crisis seemed ready-made in this respect, and indeed, the younger Liberals listened with rapt attention to Netto's arguments. Seeing that he had gained their confidence, the old general demanded sharp and immediate action, no matter what the cost. Many in the chamber, old and young alike, nodded their approval.

The majority faction among the Liberals had chosen as prime minister Zacharias de Góes e Vasconcellos, the thin-faced scion of a wealthy family from Bahia who had first entered Parliament in 1850 as a Conservative. Since then he had discovered the writings of Jeremy Bentham and John Stuart Mill and considered himself a convert to pragmatism. His commitment to the Liberal Party was lukewarm, but in the uncertain political environment of the moment, such a stance had its advantages, for he could present himself as the consensus candidate of all parties. As prime minister, Zacharias embodied not only much that was good but also much that was shortsighted in the Brazilian system of parliamentary government: "Methodical all his life, meticulous as a bureaucrat in every stroke of his pen, calling all and sundry to account by the rule of the constitutional pedagogue, he was the most implacable, and also the most authoritative censor.... In him was no trace of sentimentality; no affection, no frankness, no intimate complaisance threw their shadow over the acts, words, or thoughts of the politician. His position reminded one of a warship, with the quarter-decks battened down, the decks cleared, steam up, the crew at their posts; lonely, unapproachable, ready for action."[57] Zacharias did not long resist the call for intervention. Pressure for some military response came to a head in the parliamentary session of 5 April 1864. Radicals delivered impassioned speeches in which they laid all manner of despicable crimes at the feet of the Blanco government. Cries of horror and indignation from the audience echoed the sympathies of the various orators, and the normally complacent legislators were left jittery and clench-fisted in their chairs.

Zacharias went to the emperor and argued that the government should present Montevideo with a peremptory demand for "restitution, reparation and guarantees." Dom Pedro reluctantly agreed that Brazil should formulate a more aggressive policy toward Uruguay and left the matter to Zacharias and the foreign minister. It was a fateful decision.

In late April 1864, the imperial government dispatched José Antonio Saraiva to Montevideo with a list of specific demands. A key moderate who had opposed the hard line against the Blancos, Saraiva was, like Paranhos, a member of the Council of State and a brilliant diplomat in his own right. He had started life as an orphan, which was an advantage, for he could claim an impartiality that was rare among the servants of a patronage-ridden government. Saraiva was also talented. He had studied the workings of the imperial court as if it were the machinery of a watch and understood the complexities of diplomacy almost as well. Now his superiors charged him with delivering some hard messages to the Uruguayans. The naval squadron that accompanied him conveyed the clear impression that he negotiated with the backing of the Brazilian military.

The envoy based his complaints on the claims of Brazilians to have suffered loss of property, injury, or persecution in Uruguay since the campaigns against Oribe and Rosas. The terms Saraiva brought from Rio de Janeiro were direct. The Uruguayan government should: (1) punish all known "criminals" who occupied civil and military posts; (2) cashier and hold responsible all Uruguayan police officials who had abused Brazilian residents within the territory of the republic; (3) compensate all Brazilians who had lost property at the hands of Uruguayan authorities; (4) discharge all Brazilians who had been impressed into the Uruguayan military; and (5) issue instructions to its officials condemning all previous outrages and ordering them to comply with the new regulations and agreements. In order to soften these demands, Saraiva was to inform the Montevideo government that the empire would forcibly prevent the passage of any pro-Flores contingents out of Rio Grande do Sul; but, in a significant aside that amounted to an ultimatum, he was also to stress that the military forces then moving south to interdict the Colorados would "also serve to protect the life, honor, and property of the subjects of the Empire if, contrary to our expectations, the Government of the Republic, ignoring this final intimation, is unable or unwilling to do so itself."[58]

Saraiva knew better than to present these demands to the Blancos shorn of all diplomatic niceties. When he arrived in Montevideo at the beginning of May 1864, he purposely took his time before presenting his credentials to the Uruguayan government. President Berro's term of office had ended on 1 March, and his successor, on an interim basis, was Anastasio de la Cruz Aguirre. The new chief of state was as ardent a

Blanco as his predecessor, though he boasted little of Berro's patience and none of his polish or tact. Worse still, Aguirre's position was indistinguishable from that of the *Amapolas*, the most fanatical faction among the Blancos, who wished to resist both Brazil and Mitre to the bitter end and pinned their hopes on Solano López.[59]

The Blancos were also preparing their case. Since the end of 1863, they had redoubled their efforts to forge an alliance with Paraguay. A new Uruguayan ambassador to Asunción, the able José Vázquez Sagastume, had the task of persuading Solano López that the Brazilians and Argentines were at that moment knotting the "rope with which to strangle first Uruguay and then Paraguay."[60]

Mitre had tried to frustrate the potential alliance between Montevideo and Asunción by offering good relations with both the Brazilians and the Paraguayans. Since the Flores invasion the Argentine president had regularly sent out feelers to Solano López, hinting at some favorable resolution to the Misiones boundary dispute. He went so far as to imply that Argentina and Paraguay should cooperate against Brazil.[61] Mitre felt that this attention could block Uruguay's diplomatic offensive, but the Paraguayans remained unconvinced. Throughout early 1864 they continued to demand "clear explanations" of Argentine intentions in the Banda Oriental, but Buenos Aires always rebuffed their inquiries.[62]

Greater progress occurred in opening discussions between the Argentines and Brazilians. José Mármol, now seen as a key figure in Mitre's diplomacy, arrived as new Argentine ambassador at Rio de Janeiro in March. From the beginning his talks with officials at the Imperial Foreign Ministry went well. Within a few weeks, the emperor received him at the Summer Palace at Petrópolis. Although the Brazilians held back from any alliance, the possibility that they could work with Buenos Aires clearly interested them.[63]

The contrast with Argentine diplomatic efforts in Paraguay was striking. Mitre's failure to come to any agreement with Solano López, and the contempt with which the Argentines treated the latter's inquiries, made matters worse. The Asunción government increasingly leaned toward the Blanco outlook on Platine affairs and prepared its sizable military for any eventuality. In the same month that Mármol arrived in Brazil, Solano López established a training camp at Cerro León in the district of Pirayú, where thirty thousand men between the ages of sixteen and fifty drilled. By August he had concentrated some sixty-four thousand recruits at various points throughout Paraguay, and war-supplies flowed into the country.[64]

Aware of these developments, Saraiva issued his first note to the Blanco government on 18 May 1864. He translated the severe instructions of his government into language of great tact. He emphasized that the Oriental Republic had nothing to fear, that the Brazilian Empire sought to prevent its Riograndense subjects from participating in the Uruguayan conflict. While he clearly stated his country's demands, carefully noting that good relations were contingent upon their acceptance, he nonetheless omitted reference to the clause of his instructions that indicated war. Attached to the note was a long memorandum that enumerated and explained every outstanding claim made against Uruguay by Brazilian subjects since 1852.[65]

Herrera replied on 24 May. He attributed most of the problems the Brazilians had experienced to the vicissitudes of civil war. At the same time, Herrera posed an uncomfortable question: if the claims against the Blanco government had been building up over twelve years — at the rate of five a year — why wait until this moment of turmoil to present demands? The terms, he continued, were in any case unjust. After all, if it were true that the Riograndenses had aided Flores because of the continued persecution of the Blanco government, why did so many Correntinos and Entrerrianos also help him? The Argentine government had not tried to excuse the behavior of some of its citizens by alleging bad treatment at the hands of the Blancos. As Herrera observed, Flores and his ilk could always find followers among the "uncivilized masses of our frontiers, the Tatars or Bedouin of those regions, smugglers and malefactors . . . like the peoples that inhabit that desert, and the outskirts of countries not yet sufficiently protected by civilization."[66]

The Uruguayan foreign minister concluded by arguing that his country was interested in peace with the Brazilian Empire; when the Uruguayans had subdued General Netto and the other Riograndenses who were then helping Flores, then all outstanding problems would be settled according to the rule of law.[67] Herrera appended to his reply a statement on the forty-eight claims of the Montevideo government against Brazil on behalf of Uruguayan residents in the empire.

Over the distance of 138 years since he wrote this note, one can almost hear Saraiva's groan. The Brazilian diplomat had wanted to avoid just this sort of exchange. He had thought that the Blancos might see reason. In attempting a judicious approach, he had hoped to keep in check the hotheads in Rio de Janeiro. Herrera's reaction made this next to impossible.

*The Storm Breaks*

However pessimistic Saraiva might have felt, he replied to Herrera's dispatch with a dignified note stressing that Uruguay had recognized Brazilian neutrality on many occasions. He repeated his pleas that Blanco officials protect Brazilian residents and not mistreat them. Saraiva concluded by noting how unfortunate and untimely Herrera's note was "because the Uruguayan government sweeps away the hopes that the friends of peace build on a compromise that, saving the sacred institutions of the Republic, might assure her a future happier than the present."[68]

Thus far, Saraiva had departed from his instructions only in terms of their presentation, not in terms of their substance. Now, at the end of May, he decided to alter the whole scope of his mission. He wrote to his government requesting an extension of powers in order to explore the possibility of a full pacification of Uruguay. He no longer regarded reparations and promises of mutual respect as sufficient guarantees of future peace. War, or at least the threat of war from all the outside powers, might be the only way out. The key, Saraiva knew, was Bartolomé Mitre's Argentina and, to a lesser degree, Solano López's Paraguay. A rapprochement with at least the former power would settle the Uruguay question.

In Buenos Aires, Mitre and Foreign Minister Elizalde were having some of the same thoughts. They worried that if they failed to interpose themselves at this point, the empire would invade the Banda Oriental and leave them with no influence in Montevideo whatsoever.

On 1 June the two met with Edward Thornton, who had already advised Elizalde to reopen negotiations with the Blanco regime. Mitre now suggested that Thornton accompany Elizalde to the Uruguayan capital to confer with Saraiva on an informal basis (any official contacts being out of the question given the strained relation then existing between Brazil and Great Britain over the "Christie Affair").[69] In making this request, Mitre knew what he was doing. Inclusion of a British official lent prestige to any talks, and regardless of Thornton's contribution, discussions would then appear to have London's sanction. The president requested that the two diplomats take passage aboard a British warship, as an Argentine vessel could not then risk approaching the Uruguayan shore.

The inclusion of Thornton was well considered. Despite the fact that his government had no formal representation in Rio at the time, upper-class Brazilians respected the minister. Great Britain had guaranteed Uruguayan independence since the end of the 1820s, and in the Plata it remained the most influential extracontinental power. The British wanted to see stable trade conditions restored as soon as possible; they therefore favored a peaceful resolution to the Blanco-Colorado struggle without clear preference for one side or the other. At the same time, the minister's presence in negotiations might mitigate the impression that Argentina and Brazil were about to threaten the independence of the Banda Oriental. Thornton had considerable experience in the region. He spoke Spanish and Portuguese fluently. He had visited Paraguay in 1862 and had offered his good offices to mediate the Uruguayan conflict on several occasions during 1863 and early 1864. Now, he willingly joined Elizalde's party.[70]

After some hesitation, in which he mused that he already had his hands full with Saraiva, Herrera decided to receive the delegation from Buenos Aires. The only condition that he demanded was Andrés Lamas's inclusion in the discussions. When Thornton, Elizalde, and Lamas arrived on 6 June, they immediately set to work to convince the Montevideo public of the wisdom of making peace with Flores. As expected, the participation of the distinguished Thornton eased the anxiety that the Montevideo government felt at the thought of having Uruguay's fate determined by its two powerful neighbors. Saraiva was especially pleased and hastened to press Aguirre to accept the mediation of the three diplomats. On 10 June the president issued a decree that embodied their suggested proposals for peace. These included an amnesty for rebels, a general disarmament of those forces then in arms against the government, and provisions for open elections in which the Colorados would field candidates.[71] Far to the north, Flores accepted that outright victory was not a realistic expectation. His cavalry was sufficiently adept to allow him to raid his opponents at will, but he had no infantry and no way to consolidate any triumph against the Blancos. The mediation efforts of Elizalde, Thornton, and Saraiva seemed to offer him the best chance for future success. Flores decided to join the negotiators.

On 18 June they met to sign an agreement at Puntas del Rosario. No record exists of precisely what was said at this meeting, and this has fueled much subsequent discussion of a conspiracy. Thirty years later, Thornton remembered the Puntas del Rosario meeting as the inauguration of a triple alliance of Brazil, Argentina, and Uruguay against Paraguay.[72] Perhaps there was a touch of truth in this testimony; it seems only logical to suppose that the Paraguayan posture received attention from the gathered diplomats. Revisionist historians, however, have woven Thornton's comments into an elaborate tapestry of imperialism featuring the invisible hand of Britain behind every turn in Platine politics.[73]

Certainly, the agreement signed at Puntas del Rosario mirrored Aguirre's decree. In permitting the national debt to cover the cost of the Flores invasion, the mediators went beyond the original terms expressed in the 10 June document. The change they judged insignificant. Flores signed unconditionally, the Blanco negotiators *ad referendum*. In a separate note to President Aguirre, Flores demanded that the new agreement receive a full guarantee. To this end he suggested a change of ministry from a party to a nonparty basis within the Uruguayan government.[74] This could not be incorporated into the agreement outright since it implied equality between Flores, a rebel, and the legitimate government in Montevideo. Still, the negotiators felt that Aguirre would accept this condition as the necessary price for peace.

At first, the Uruguayan president seemed to do exactly that. He issued a proclamation to his soldiers that announced the imminent cessation of hostilities. He called personally on the three mediators to offer his thanks for a job well done. Then, when Aguirre sent officials to organize the disarmament of the Colorado forces, Flores told them that he would accept no arrangements without acceptance of the point made in his letter.

On 1 July the mediators returned to Montevideo to urge Aguirre to change the ministry as requested. They expressed amazement that he would let the opportunity for peace slip away when the outstanding issue was trivial. In truth, Aguirre did not regard it as a minor point. He was afraid that the *Amapolas* within the government would do everything they could to frustrate the agreement. After several fruitless meetings with the president, Elizalde, Saraiva, and Thornton withdrew, and the plan collapsed.

Saraiva next went to Buenos Aires to confer with Mitre. Having given up on the Blancos, the Brazilian diplomat now hoped to gain Argentine support for a joint military intervention. His work with Elizalde during the last month had run so smoothly that he felt certain he could depend on his colleague. After all, an intervention would not threaten Argentine interests because free elections and the withdrawal of foreign forces would swiftly follow. Mitre, however, held back, still fearing a wave of revolts in western Argentina. He also worried that Urquiza might oppose the intervention and thereby place the national government in the embarrassing position of supporting a foreign military adventure against Argentine-born troops. Nonetheless, he accepted Saraiva's friendly intentions, which constituted the one bright spot in the Brazilian diplomat's mission to Buenos Aires.

At the end of July, the Italian minister at Montevideo arrived in the

Argentine capital with a final appeal for renewed mediation. Saraiva, who had received word of rampant war fever in the Brazilian parliament, replied that it was too late. The Italian withdrew, and Saraiva set sail for Montevideo to confer once more with the Blancos.

On 4 August he presented Herrera with an ultimatum. He demanded that the Blancos accede within six days to the terms indicated in his note of 18 May. Failing such acceptance,

> The forces of the Brazilian army stationed on the frontier will receive orders to proceed to reprisals in the event of Brazilian subjects being subjected to violence, or menaced in life or security. It will be incumbent on the respective commanders to provide in the most convenient form the protection that they need. The Admiral Baron of Tamandaré will likewise receive instructions to protect in the same way with the forces of the squadron under his command the Brazilian consular agents and citizens injured by any authorities. . . . The reprisals and measures to guarantee my fellow-citizens above indicated are not, as Your Excellency is aware, acts of war; and I hope that the government of this Republic will avoid augmenting the gravity of these measures by precipitating regrettable events, the responsibility for which will rest exclusively on that government.[75]

As Saraiva delivered his note, detachments of the imperial army assembled along the frontier and Tamandaré's warships stood by off Montevideo.

Herrera waited until just before the expiration of the ultimatum to send his reply, which was long, polemical, and noncommittal. He asked that the diplomatic corps at Montevideo arbitrate all outstanding questions. On 10 August, Saraiva announced that his mission before the Uruguayan government was at an end; General Netto and Admiral Tamandaré had their orders to proceed. The Brazilian diplomat left immediately for Buenos Aires to formalize the entente that already existed de facto. Twelve days later, he and Elizalde issued a protocol that promised the mutual aid of Brazil and Argentina in efforts to bring about a settlement in the Banda Oriental. This move gave the empire a free hand in eliminating Aguirre's government.

The only hope left for the Blanco regime lay in the Paraguayan connection, and this hardly presented an ironclad guarantee of safety. Relations between Paraguay and the government in Montevideo had been anything but perfect during 1864; a February incident in which Uruguayan port authorities tried to forcibly inspect the Paraguayan vessel *Paraguarí* was only closed months later when Vázquez Sagastume presented his government's apologies to Solano López.[76] Also, the refusal of Brazil and Argentina to accept Paraguayan mediation in Uruguay had offended the Paraguayan leader and dampened his enthusiasm for such a role.

The Uruguayans kept trying to enlist Paraguayan aid and Berges kept responding in the affirmative, but nothing much happened. At the end of July, the Montevideo government sent one of its highest officials, Antonio de las Carreras, on a secret mission to Asunción to get definite commitment of support. Yet Carreras had no authority to make any promises, and this left Berges and Solano López uncertain as to what their next step should be.[77]

Agents of the Paraguayan government stationed in Corrientes, Paraná, Buenos Aires, and Montevideo sent in regular reports to Solano López. In consequence, he often knew more about conditions in the Banda Oriental than did Vázquez Sagastume himself. News of the rejection of Saraiva's ultimatum, however, failed to reach the Paraguayan president until 24 August, when the *Paraguarí* docked at Asunción. Aboard the ship were the new Brazilian minister-resident, Cesar Vianna de Lima, and Edward Thornton, the British minister at Buenos Aires. The latter approached Solano López to beg for calm consideration of what had occurred. He tried "with admirable dexterity" to allay the suspicion that Brazil's actions had aroused in the Paraguayan capital, all to no avail.

Responding to the entreaties of Vázquez Sagastume (and to the confidential appeals of Carreras), Solano López ordered Berges to compose a policy statement, a protest that the empire could not ignore. As part of this note, which Berges presented to Vianna de Lima on 30 August, the Paraguayans issued an unmistakable warning as to what might happen should Brazil continue on its aggressive course in the Banda Oriental: "the Government of the Republic of Paraguay would consider any occupation of Uruguayan territory by Imperial forces . . . as an attack upon the balance of power of the Platine states, which interests the Republic of Paraguay as the guarantee of its security, peace, and prosperity. That Government protests in the most solemn manner against such an act, disclaiming at once all responsibility for the ultimate consequences of the present declaration."[78]

Over the next few days, Vianna de Lima and Berges exchanged a series of notes, all highly spirited. No progress could have resulted from this correspondence because the Brazilian minister lacked the authority to make concessions of any kind. Solano López, moreover, had already determined to increase pressure on the empire. His efforts at a conciliatory stance had failed. If the Brazilians had dealt more gently with López's *amour-propre* in this matter, much of the following tragedy might never have happened.

Public opinion in Asunción, until then almost oblivious of the conflict downriver, began to turn angry. Expression of political sentiment had never been welcomed under the rule of the López family. In a society like Paraguay's, however, state orders could generate and direct popular fervor with as much ease as they could summon work parties. On this occasion, as one British observer noted:

> A body of the chief men of Asunción went to the Palace and declared their adhesion. They then went with a piquet of soldiers from the Palace to the Government Square, in procession. Here they hoisted the Paraguayan flag, under a salute of 21 guns; and afterwards all the town took to dancing, drinking, and serenading—by order, of course. Everyone, high and low, was obliged to assist at these frolics, under pain of being reported by the police as unpatriotic, which was equivalent, for the ladies, to being banished to the wilds, and for the men, to being imprisoned. Deep family affliction was no excuse for

*The Uruguayan Imbroglio*

being absent from the revels. Written manifestoes were made up, and signed by *everyone*, offering their lives and goods to sustain the cause. Even ladies and children were obliged to sign these documents; and they were got up in all the towns and villages of Paraguay, so that no one remained in the country who had not signed away life and property, without knowing why.[79]

Vianna de Lima and the Brazilian residents in Asunción knew of these demonstrations, but their countrymen in Rio doubted that Paraguayan protest went beyond mere bombast. Indeed, they greeted the protest "with shouts of laughter, and its author was recommended by the Colorados to attend to the state of his huts and settle the squabbles of his half-naked squaws at home."[80] Such gibes may have brought smiles to the faces of government officials in Brazil and Argentina, but six months later they no longer seemed so amusing.

Berges directed a final protest to Vianna de Lima on 9 September. The Paraguayans had received word that a corvette under Tamandaré's command had given chase to the *Villa del Salto*, a Blanco vessel carrying reinforcements for Mercedes (a port along the Uruguay River then threatened by Flores's cavalry), and forced it to take refuge at Paysandú, still higher up the river. Berges noted that such actions "profoundly impressed the Government of the undersigned who cannot do other than confirm by this communication his declarations of 30 August and of the 3rd instant." The Paraguayans sent no further communications but instead stepped up military preparations on a huge scale.

Given the alliance that had come to exist between Paraguay and the Uruguayan Blancos, one would have thought that both would have hastened to formalize their relation. Something quite different happened. On 30 August, the same day that he issued the protest of the Paraguayan government, Berges replied to Vázquez Sagastume's appeal with a lengthy note. After cataloguing and describing in detail all the correspondence that had passed between his office and that of the Uruguayan Foreign Ministry, Berges roundly condemned the position in which his country had been placed. Paraguay, he insisted, had been snubbed at every juncture, mislead on numerous occasions, and generally treated with contempt by the very countries it had hoped to help. Given such a background, his government had no choice but to be guided by its own counsels exclusively; though Paraguayan leaders regarded the integrity and independence of Uruguay as necessary to their own security, nonetheless they could not ally with its government.[81]

Solano López saw to it that the state gazette published this letter with the confidential communications it contained. This unprecedented step outraged many in the local diplomatic corps.[82] It is hard to understand what Solano López thought to gain from this publication. Admittedly, he never found discretion an especially heavy yoke, though he took pains to make his judgments appear calculating and shrewd. Whatever his intention on this occasion, he only managed to embarrass the Blancos.

The only voice still being raised in favor of peace was that of Andrés Lamas in Buenos Aires. Unfortunately, public opinion in the Argentine capital had moved in the same direction as that in Montevideo, Asunción, and Rio de Janeiro. Everywhere people talked of war. No political figure felt capable of protesting the drift toward violence.

The Mitre regime, however much it respected Lamas's efforts, had no intention of changing its policy toward the Banda Oriental. Elizalde declared Argentine neutrality in the event of any conflict between Uruguay and Brazil. Yet at the same time, arms and munitions continued to flow from Buenos Aires to Flores. As for the attitude of Paraguay, the Argentine government contented itself with the fact that Solano López concentrated his resentment on Brazil and left Argentina alone.

The Paraguayan president had forgotten neither the pretensions of his southern neighbor nor the border disputes in the Misiones. He had in mind Justo José de Urquiza, whose Entrerriano stalwarts still professed a pro-Blanco bias and who might be counted on should a wider war erupt in the Plata.[83] As it turned out, this assumption amounted to wishful thinking.

Brazilian troops crossed the Uruguayan frontier on 16 October 1864 and soon thereafter occupied Villa de Melo, capital of the Department

*The Uruguayan Imbroglio* 159

of Cerro Largo. If Aguirre and his associates in Montevideo thought this action would draw an immediate Paraguayan response, they were disappointed. Solano López's land forces were ready, his field commanders reported.[84] His river fleet, however, was unprepared for offensive operations, and proceeding down the Paraná to help Montevideo would certainly call for military action en route.

Solano López's vacillation might have been understandable, but Vázquez Sagastume kept plying him with exhortations to attack. He reminded him that a Brazilian steamer, the *Marqués de Olinda*, was due to enter the Paraguay River during the first weeks of November. The vessel, which made the passage between Montevideo and Corumbá monthly, was part of the empire's plan to develop the Mato Grosso.[85] Now it became the trigger for the bloodiest war ever fought in South America.

The *Marqués de Olinda* passed the fortress of Humaitá, exchanged the customary salutes, and continued northward until it docked without incident at Asunción on 11 November. It was a sizable vessel, 198 tons, with a naval lieutenant as commander and a crew of forty-three. Its passengers included Col. Federico Carneiro de Campos, the recently appointed governor of Mato Grosso, ten other Brazilian soldiers, the new Argentine consul general Adolfo Soler, and two Italian colonists. After Soler disembarked, the ship took on coal while its commander exchanged news with Vianna de Lima. By two o'clock in the afternoon, its business in the city concluded, the *Marqués de Olinda* set course again for Corumbá and eased into the muddy river with a trail of gray vapor blowing from its stack.

Upon the ship's arrival, however, a special messenger had set off by locomotive to Cerro León, where Solano López was reviewing his troops. He waited a whole day, still hesitating as to his next move. According to one account, López finally remarked, "If we don't have a war now with Brazil, we shall have one at a less convenient time for ourselves."[86] He then dispatched an aide-de-camp by express train with a message for Remigio Cabral, the commander of the war-steamer *Tacuarí*: overtake the Brazilian ship and compel its return to Asunción.

The Paraguayan steamer departed at once, and the next day its lookouts caught sight of the slower vessel steaming in the distance in the vicinity of Concepción. Cabral ordered his gunners to fire across its bow. The Brazilians immediately obeyed his shouted commands and reversed course. The *Marqués de Olinda* reached Asunción on the evening of 13 November. Even before it dropped anchor, Vianna de Lima received a note that informed him that Paraguay had severed relations with the empire.[87]

At first light next morning, Paraguayan officials boarded the ship and arrested everyone. They seized the cargo, including two thousand muskets, and removed the mail packs and two cases containing two hundred thousand milreis in paper currency. Some time later, another party led by Col. Vicente Barrios returned to the ship to confiscate its imperial ensign. The flag was sewn into a carpet and presented to Solano López to cover the floor of his office in the presidential palace.[88] This was not the last symbol of the empire's authority that Solano López would tread upon during the next five years.

# III

## The War Begins

# Military Preparedness

## 7

Nation building in South America involved much more than assigning specific identities to set people off from each other. It also involved the establishment of concrete institutions—states that sought to create independent political characters in keeping with people's needs and aspirations. Within each country, the state promoted respect for its authority through taxation, the schooling of the young, the promulgation of edicts, and other governmental functions.

Internationally, it proved harder for these new states to gain the recognition they demanded as heirs to the colonial power or as the expression of "popular" sovereignty. Border disputes invariably frustrated the common quest for status, for no one could tell where the authority of one "nation" ended and that of another began. As the disputes over Mato Grosso, the Misiones, and the Banda Oriental illustrate, such conflicts were frequent and often virulent, poisoning relations between neighbors for decades. But they fueled the development of the states' most important correlate institution—the military.

Whether viewed as a plague or as a boon to national cohesion, there is no doubt that the military played a crucial role in nineteenth-century South America. It provided an instrument through which members of the elite could legitimize their power, offered employment in certain depressed areas, brought an aspect of modernization into an otherwise backward economy, and made state policy something palpable over a wide expanse of territory.

It is useful to recall that Brazil, Argentina, Uruguay, and Paraguay shared a similar military situation. All four countries faced long periods of uncertainty during which foreigners — or local Indians — contested state authority at will and with the utmost violence. While Paraguay felt these dangers more immediately than its neighbors in the early 1800s, all experienced them in sufficient degree to prompt the creation of professional armies and navies. Beyond this general apprehension, however, the experiences of the four countries differed as sharply as their political interests.

*Brazil: The Reluctant Militarists*

One might suppose that a country as large as Brazil would build a military establishment on a commensurate scale. Yet as was true in the antebellum United States, a sizable military never received proper government endorsement. For the first forty years of its existence as an independent state, Brazil's standing army rarely rose above sixteen thousand effectives, with a reserve of *Guarda Nacional* units totaling another two hundred thousand men. The latter force, which mainly conducted police operations in the provinces, consisted of local recruits commanded by the sons of wealthy planters. The guard possessed few of the characteristics usually associated with a professional military. On occasion guard units did respectable service in that capacity, but only rarely were they deployed outside their respective provinces.[1]

The real power within the imperial military structure lay with the standing army. After 1851, the empire was divided into six military districts, each of which theoretically contained *corpos especiais* (staff personnel) and *corpos combatentes* (combat forces). The latter included cavalry, infantry, and artillery units divided into mobile forces and garrison troops.[2]

By the mid-1860s, the empire's standing army had a framework as modern as any in Europe. The artillery consisted of a battalion of engineers, a regiment of horse-drawn artillery, four battalions of foot artillery, and twelve other companies. The cavalry had five regiments, one corps of four companies, a squadron of two more, seven battalions of riflemen, and five other companies. The infantry, which made up the bulk of the troops, included nine rifle battalions of eight companies, another battalion of six, five garrison corps of four companies, another four garrison corps of two, and another two companies. Total manpower reserves for the standing army amounted to 17,600 men.[3]

On paper, Brazil's regular army looked impressive, though in practice it could rarely boast the organization or equipment that ministerial reports indicated. Its distribution was likewise curious, for the great majority of units were stationed in the far south near the Uruguayan frontier. This deployment made good sense given likely foreign contingencies as well as the remote possibility of renewed separatist conflict; but it left wide areas of Brazil essentially unprotected save for poorly trained guard units.

The Brazilian elites felt an instinctive suspicion of "creeping" militarism. They saw the disorder elsewhere on the continent and were wont to ascribe its uglier aspects to the presence of too many illiterate braggarts in uniform. Reflecting this bias, the government kept its military budgets low and its generals in the background. The emperor himself never bothered to conceal his distaste for the profession of arms (though he was scrupulously correct, even kind, with individual officers).

Nevertheless, the Brazilian military had its staunch defenders. Men like Caxias and Manoel Luis Osório were seasoned politicians as well as talented commanders. They could occasionally maneuver the government, however reluctantly, toward a more realistic military policy. This was always easier in times of political crisis, as during the campaign against Argentina's Juan Manuel de Rosas. At all other times, though, the officer corps appeared no different from other imperial bureaucracies in its penchant for bickering, its emphasis on status, and its craving for every possible coin or honor.

The officers could count some talented individuals in their midst and, as a group, displayed much the same cohesion as the *bacharéis*. The younger generation attended the Imperial Academia Militar and the Escola Militar da Praia Vermelha in Rio. The first of these two academies, founded in the reign of Dom João, taught tactics to a small cohort, usually, though not necessarily, highborn cadets. A few individuals at Praia Vermelha learned more than smart drilling on the parade ground. Some became excellent military doctors and engineers. Others read widely in foreign (especially French) tactical manuals, taking pride in their knowledge of the latest innovations in European armament.[4]

One practical result of this interest was a partial revamping of Brazil's artillery during the 1850s. Though a great many antiquated guns remained in service, the imperial government arranged for each artillery unit to receive a number of Lahitte, Paixhan, and Whitworth guns of calibers 90 to 120.[5] The better of these rifled muzzleloaders had an effective range of just under three miles and thus greatly enhanced the army's firepower. This said, target practice was much neglected in Brazil; and artillery tactics founded on the principle of concentration of fire were little practiced owing to the want of large-scale maneuvers. Still, the artillery persevered, and so did the infantry.

At the close of the Crimean War, many South American countries rushed to buy surplus materiel from Europe. The Brazilian army purchased several thousand new small arms to replace the 17-gauge flintlocks then in use.[6] The new weapons, which included Prussian-made needle rifles and Belgian carbines, were all capable of firing cartridges at a superior rate of fire. In general, such weapons could kill at half a mile and were accurate to 250 yards, five times as far as any other one-man weapon.

The needle rifle had its shortcomings. Its worst fault was the large escape of gas at the breech, which was so great that troopers found it difficult to fire the rifle from the shoulder after the first half-dozen shots. When the barrel was foul, the strain was still greater, often obliging the men to fire from the hip. It was nonetheless a remarkable weapon and eventually helped assure Prussian victory over the Danes in 1864, the Austrians in 1866, and the French in 1870–71.

Even so, the Brazilians failed to capitalize on the rifle's many advantages because they only imported a few of the newer models. Those rifles they did obtain came in many different calibers. While some of the arms were breechloaders, others were loaded at the muzzle, thus causing confusion among the regular troops, the majority of whom continued to use the older, nearly obsolete flintlocks.

The reluctance of the government to fund a larger military was understandable in a regime hard pressed for revenues. In addition, whatever the empire's interest in the Banda Oriental, little really justified an expansion of military forces. The emperor, the Council of State, and most members of Parliament believed that the nation's security was already guaranteed under the established system, which gave primary responsibility to the elite-led *Guardia Nacional*. This was a shortsighted view of military preparedness. It relegated the engineers and other regular officers to a subordinate, essentially advisory position and little more. The elites expected military men to screech like a flock of sea birds when it came to promotions and procurement, but in the final analysis, the opinions of regular officers meant little to the men in frock coats.

Coupled with the elite's mistrust of the officer corps was their near revulsion for the common soldier. The very term for an army enlisted man, *praça*, derived from the Portuguese word for the public square—with all its disreputable connotations of the street. Simply put, high society did not consider the army a fit place for the "honorable" poor (i.e., those men with access to patronage). Only degenerates and rowdies should end up in the ranks, and officers were little better than wardens.[7]

There was a good reason why undesirables predominated in the ranks. As yet, no universal draft existed, and there was no real reason for young men to join up. Starting in 1837, therefore, police officers were awarded a cash bonus for every new "recruit" they brought to the colors.[8] The police sent press gangs into the streets of every town in Brazil in search of inductees. Whether habitually drunk, delinquent, or feeble minded, the condition of such levies mattered little; the army took most of the men remanded. Even after a broader conscription began in 1865, the composition of the army changed only slightly. Wealthy and even middle-class men could hire poorer individuals to

*Military Preparedness* 169

serve as their substitutes. The practice was so common that impoverished *gente de côr* soon constituted the greater part of the soldiers in every Brazilian infantry battalion, while cowboy "vagabonds" from the south or northeast made up most of the cavalrymen. In the campaigns to come, despite continued shows of disdain from the upper classes, these men fought well.

While the standing army suffered from government indifference (or actual resistance), the imperial navy found considerable favor. In contrast to the army, the navy had an aristocratic and Anglophilic tradition that dated back before independence. Government officials responded better to admirals than to generals because the former had nothing of the parvenu about them. Besides, the lawyers, merchants, and a good many of the planters that made up the Brazilian government generally had roots in the coastal region and saw war largely in terms of protecting commercial traffic along the sea lanes. This view manifested itself in good, though not lavish, funding for the navy. By the early 1860s, Brazil's fleet had become the largest in South America. It counted forty-five vessels — thirty-three steamers (both propeller-driven and sidewheelers) and twelve sailing ships. All were reasonably well fitted with state-of-the-art guns, including 70-pounder Whitworths capable of piercing the armor of ironclads or dealing powerful blows to shore defenses.

Total manpower for the imperial navy during this period was 4,236 officers and men.[9] The crews came from a variety of backgrounds from all over coastal Brazil. The navy's greatest strength, however, was in its well-trained officer corps, which displayed the same professionalism and sophistication as the best of the army's engineers.

Of course, life in the imperial navy was in many ways unpleasant, except for senior officers, who were separated from their crews by a rigid class system. Sailors taken by pressgangs from the most squalid port districts were expected to spend long hours below deck during the hot summer months. They ate poorly, slept little, and were routinely abused by midshipmen and each other. They received minimal pay. In this, their circumstance paralleled that of the common soldiers.

Taken as a whole, the Brazilian military had serious weaknesses in the mid-nineteenth century. The standing army was small, poorly organized, and unevenly equipped. Though the officer corps boasted some talented figures, there was also much dead weight. The rank and file, for their part, were hopelessly undisciplined. The army dragooned nearly half its troops, many of them vagrants supplied by the police. Those who volunteered, or who offered themselves as substitutes, usually did so to escape hunger, homelessness, unemployment, or the law. They had neither interest in the military life nor any motivations that might be called patriotic.

Imperial officials, whose own idea of the Brazilian nation centered on political stability and the preservation of privileges, had little faith in a military structure that might potentially threaten both. Instead, they unmistakably preferred the *Guarda Nacional*, an institution that mirrored the status quo and within which existed little professionalism and no real commitment to modernization. The guard officers had their ornate swords and fancy dress uniforms, the men their bamboo lances and blunderbusses. But just as on the *fazenda* only a weak sense of loyalty connected the two groups. Real cohesion—the kind that comes from a shared identity—came only later, when the alternatives to war had been exhausted.

*Argentina and Uruguay: The Military Divided*

The germ of modernization that infected one small segment of the Brazilian military was nowhere in evidence in Argentina and Uruguay. The fall of Rosas in 1852 supposedly guaranteed unity on a foundation of political liberalism, yet real national integration under the constitution remained a distant goal. Despite the battle of Pavón, the competition between Justo José de Urquiza and Bartolomé Mitre in Argentina still colored provincial politics, especially in the Litoral. Proxies vied for government posts and positions of influence, unafraid of using force to achieve their goals. Though the unifying call of the constitution was beautiful in its conception, most Argentines remained skeptical. Even in Buenos Aires, the competition between Mitre's Liberals and Adolfo Alsina's Autonomists threatened to rend the fragile political order.

Military Preparedness   171

Such divisiveness interrupted the evolution of national military institutions in Argentina. In theory, patriotic citizen-soldiers should have stepped forward to replace the mercenaries and gaucho draftees. But nothing of the kind happened. The standing army that Mitre created in 1864 counted only 6,000 effectives, the great majority stationed in the interior provinces and along the Patagonian frontier.[10] The regulars were organized into seven infantry battalions, nine cavalry regiments, one unit of light artillery, and five companies of "newly created" artillery—the latter used as a garrison force on the island of Martín García. A high incidence of desertion took its toll on the ranks, however, and government officials conducted constant recruitment in order to keep these units near full strength.

The bulk of the men under arms in Argentina were found in the various *Guardia Nacional* units, perhaps as many as 184,478 effectives in early 1865.[11] Like its Brazilian counterpart, the Argentine guard was basically a provincial institution, though rarely a patrimonial one. Under an 1854 law, each male citizen of the confederation from age seventeen to sixty was liable for service in the guard, and versions of the same law were in vigor after Pavón. Yet the law was imperfectly and irregularly applied. A few units, especially those from Buenos Aires, did serve under national command. Aside from some Indian auxiliaries, these particular battalions proved the only reliable units in the guard, having had some rudimentary training as well as combat experience at Pavón.

The other guard units had no such preparation. Each province controlled its own militia, but with the exception of Buenos Aires—and to a much-lesser degree Santa Fe—none provided sufficient funding for its units. The result was a motley assemblage of poorly armed gauchos utterly incapable of military action on a large scale. And in the case of certain provinces, notably Entre Ríos, the local guard expressed open antagonism toward the national government.

Such divisions left little room for military development. President Mitre understood how weak his country's armed forces really were. He was also a *porteño*, however, and believed that in order to correct the country's military backwardness, he had to start with Buenos Aires. The port city at this time had just under one-tenth of the total Argentine population of 1.5 million, but it had almost all the country's merchants and most of its European immigrants. The consequent availability of both capital and skilled labor provided two ingredients for a viable military. To this was added the vision of Mitre and the native talent of his generals. One could see some solidity in the president's army, embryonic though it was. Mitre saw it too and sought to expand the efficiency and size of his military on every occasion and in every way. In 1864 the troops under his direct command numbered some eight thousand guardsmen and regulars. A year later the number had grown to fifteen thousand, largely through forced conscription in the countryside of Buenos Aires.[12]

Though they came from the poorest areas of the province, these new recruits wore blue uniforms with brass buttons and shouldered rifles of European manufacture. In their packs, along with the usual cuts of *charqui*, they carried full rations of hardtack *(galleta)*, tobacco, sugar, and even a little cane liquor. Their lives for the first time were governed by an elaborate and systematic discipline, with infantry regulations, strictly applied, that were drawn from standard Spanish precedents of 1846 (and cavalry regulations from 1834).[13]

For all their attractive appearance, these new troops were still mostly gauchos. Mitre only trusted them just so far, so he experimented with other options. He sent some of his junior officers to Europe for specialized training, recruited soldiers of fortune in Italy and France, and put pressure on provincial governors to remand an increasing number of conscripts to the national arms.[14] But he never deceived himself: creating a modern army was going to be difficult.

To put a fine point on the problem, the average Argentine soldier found it difficult to see himself as part of a "national" project. He saw no sense in soldiering on anything but a conditional and short-term basis. His nature inclined him to an impetuous courage, but patriotism was a feeling that others had to construct for him. Even without this greater sense of purpose, he remained a good soldier, brave, and inured to hardship. His normal standard of living left him content to live without many things European soldiers thought indispensable. But protracted fighting in organized units for an uncertain reward — this was frequently beyond him.

As for the Argentine navy, it existed more in name than in reality. Out of a total of nineteen vessels in 1864, only two steamers (the *Guardia Nacional* and the *Pampero*) and one schooner (the *Argos*) carried any armament, and that was substandard. Much of the remaining fleet had either been leased to private parties as merchantmen or was in dry dock. At the time of the Cisplatine War, the Argentine navy had been a formidable entity under the Irish admiral William Brown. Now it had declined so much that it was useful only for the transport of troops and horses.[15]

Neither Argentina's diminutive navy nor its untested army had developed any traditions of note, and neither institution enjoyed any respect from politicians or the public at large. Though such officers as Emilio Mitre and Juan Andrés Gelly y Obes were capable organizers, they never transferred their efficiency to the service as a whole. Unlike the Brazilian Empire, which saw a glimmer of the future in the professionalization of its military engineers, Argentina had almost no confidence. Mitre drafted plan after plan calling for reform in the armed forces — for new artillery, for commissary units and surgeons, for musical bands and staff officers. But the fractious nature of Argentine politics made progress on military matters practically impossible. As with the forging of the nation itself, great ingenuity was necessary to move ahead. Sometimes such ingenuity was at work just below the surface; more often it was not.

Across the river in the Banda Oriental, there was little talk of either nation or professional military. Every political issue — the character of the "nation" itself — was in Uruguay reduced to the partisan struggle between Blancos and Colorados. Each party maintained its own armed force. These were little changed from the gaucho bands that José Artigas led in an earlier age. The men had combat experience but no training and were poorly armed save for the usual muskets, *boleadoras*, and *facón* knives.

European immigrants with previous military experience officered a few units from Montevideo. The Spanish-born León de Palleja, for instance, headed the "Batallón Florida" under the Colorados, and he did manage to infuse his men with a measure of esprit de corps. But Palleja was an exceptional man whose discipline and attention to detail were noteworthy but also ephemeral and seemingly out of place.

The average Uruguayan soldier in 1864 related less to his country than to his immediate superior. This was not necessarily bad for discipline in any military force. In this case, however, that superior was likely the indirect agent of a foreign power. Whether he associated himself with Urquiza, Mitre, or the Brazilians, such an officer might have a legitimate claim on the loyalty of his men but could never pose as a Uruguayan nationalist. Though there were several thousand men under arms in Uruguay, a military service that was authentically Uruguayan in character had yet to evolve. What did exist was a force of men experienced in combat who were ready to fight.

*Paraguay: The Military Born*
Dr. José Gaspar de Francia had always kept his military on the tightest of leashes. It was, after all, a small institution, untrained, and woefully underarmed — exactly like the colonial militia. Paraguayan army officers could barely sign their own names. Yet in foreign circles there always existed uncertainty about just how many troops the dictator commanded, and this was a factor in staving off outside invasion. Thus, when Carlos Antonio López gained power in the early 1840s, he surveyed an army little changed since 1814.

The world was becoming a more dangerous place for Paraguay as the country slowly opened its doors. López possessed as little military experience as the garrison commanders he displaced, but unlike many Paraguayans, he believed that the old isolationism could no longer guarantee peace. As he experimented with new foreign contacts, he quietly but very intently began to improve his armed forces. In 1845 he established a national guard on the Spanish model of a semiprofessional prestige militia. Nearly all Paraguayan males between the ages of sixteen and fifty-five were supposedly registered for this force, which had police as well as military duties.[16]

Paraguay's participation in two misadventures in Corrientes during the 1840s convinced López that he had to modernize or risk seeing his country swallowed by its neighbors. The Paraguayan president was better informed than most of his countrymen, but like them he shared a near-xenophobic suspicion of foreign intentions. Although both Argentina and Brazil had recognized Paraguayan independence by the early 1850s, he still saw no reason to let down his guard in the face of "incorrigible anarchists on the one hand, and two-faced, traitorous monkeys on the other."[17] The country remained isolated and weak—far better to arm and thereby gain the respect that legal sovereignty alone could never provide.

López had chosen Franz Wisner von Morgenstern to command the Corrientes expedition of 1849. A Hungarian adventurer and sometimes tutor to the López family, Wisner had served for some time in the Austrian army. His intimate contacts with high-ranking Paraguayans opened the door for foreign military advisors in the country. And Wisner was only the first of many. In 1851, at a moment of detente between the imperial government and Paraguay, the Brazilians acceded to López's request that they provide instructors for his fledgling army. In an ironic twist, they sent Capt. Hermenegildo de Albuquerque Portocarreiro, who later commanded Fort Coimbra in the southernmost district of Mato Grosso. The captain was a talented artillery officer. He came to Asunción in the most pleasant of moods bearing an important gift: a battery of field artillery for Carlos Antonio López. Accompanying Portocarreiro was Lt. João Carlos de Vilagran Cabrita, an engineer whose daring and intricate river crossings would make possible the first major Brazilian incursion into Paraguayan territory.[18]

The Brazilian military mission was small scale. The real catalyst for Paraguayan military expansion was Solano López's European tour of 1853–54. Though only in his twenties, the younger López was already the chief military figure in his father's government—and one of the few men whom Carlos Antonio really trusted. As a student, Solano López had poured over every volume that Wisner placed before him and gained more than a casual knowledge of Jomini and other military writers of his day. His position as heir-apparent, moreover, gave him reason to suppose that he could guide the development of the armed forces much as he pleased.

Because Solano López always appraised himself in the most exaggerated and vainglorious manner, historians have tended to dismiss his claims as an organizer. His father, however, could not have found another man more dedicated to the task of military procurement. The European states had already recognized Paraguayan independence; now, thought Solano López, they had to contribute to its defense.

While accepting Solano López's basic competence, it must be recognized that he was a passionate and contradictory man, and those contradictions carried a price for his nation. His arrogance, of which much has been made, was not natural but willed; he always had to prove to himself and others that he was a man of the world, a cosmopolitan not to be bested. At heart he was a romantic who dreamed of glory for himself and his country. For many nineteenth-century South Americans, acquaintance with the majesty of the Old World brought the limitations of their own continent into clearer focus. With Solano López, it had the opposite effect. He became enthralled. And like a convert to some ecstatic religion, he convinced himself that he was a new man, partly ashamed of his past, and anxious to spread the good news. He began to copy the mannerisms of the Europeans. Even the physical aspect of his handwriting took on a florid, deliberately European style, which stood in contrast to the plain, conservative hand of his father. When the younger López put his rubric to a military requisition or decree, the force of his stroke frequently tore the paper — like a man whose hand slashes out a signature in order to hide a tremble.

On 14 September 1853 the ancient Paraguayan warship *Independencia* docked at Southampton and disgorged the young general, his brother Benigno, brother-in-law Vicente Barrios, and five or six other well-placed Paraguayans, several of them visibly seasick. The party spent three months in England, visiting factories in Liverpool and Manchester, exchanging pleasantries with British officials, and even taking in Madame Tussaud's famous wax museum.

Militarily, the most important result of López's mission in England was the beginning of a long-term relationship with the firm of John and Alfred Blyth of Limehouse, London. The Blyths acted as general agents for the Paraguayan government over the next twelve years. On López's behalf, they purchased industrial and military hardware, small arms, powder, and surplus uniforms. They undertook to arrange the education of a score of Paraguayans sent to England for advanced studies. They even sold Paraguayan cotton and yerba on the European market. The Blyth Brothers were instrumental in helping Paraguay's nascent military adopt more modern standards in armament and training. This made it possible for López to challenge his foreign rivals in a direct and convincing way.

From Britain, Solano López crossed over to the Continent, where he continued to improve his knowledge of *materia belica*. Part of his education involved learning what made great men great. In this, he particularly admired Napoleon III, whose rise to prominence he equated with his own career. That a man of a less-than-ancient bloodline should face foreign resistance and the leaden weight of aristocratic tradition and yet still bring his country to the forefront of world politics struck the young general as greatness personified. It certainly gave him pause for thought.

Solano López's grasp of the realities of the Second Empire was less than inspiring, however. He saw the glitter of Bonapartism but not the weakness of its political and military base. In the pomp of the Imperial Guard, for instance, he saw the will of a single man rather than a complex history of revolution, partisan indecision, and chance.[19] His interpretation discounted the power and influence of Napoleon's neighbors, portraying them as men of the past when their regimes, in fact, were every bit as powerful and modernizing as that of France.

On one point, however, Solano López understood European politics relatively well. A balance of power between the various states had secured the peace since 1815, and anything that threatened that balance also threatened the well being of each nation. Solano López took this principle as proven fact, assuming its applicability for the Plata (which necessarily put Brazil in the worst light). In retrospect, his approval was odd, for it contradicted the daring militarism he so admired in Napoleon III. Perhaps the young general gave in to his heart when he should have used his reason; perhaps he was simply immature. Either way, the lessons he learned in Europe had terrible consequences for Paraguay.

To the impressionable López, the avenues of Paris approached those of the Celestial Paradise in their magnificence. Roads, public buildings, bridges, even the immaculate attire of French public men were all linked in his thinking to perfection (as outlined in some barely remembered lesson on Saint Augustine). To attempt to emulate some of that grandeur in his own nation seemed natural, even obligatory: such was the proper duty of a leader.

The place to start was with the military, and while in the French capital, Solano López attached himself as closely as possible to the imperial court and army. Some officers kept the upstart at arm's length, while others were evidently amused at the young general from an obscure country. He met with ordnance specialists, picked through the newest tactical manuals, and drilled and reviewed the troops. Solano López examined the most up-to-date weaponry and basked in the attention shown him by veterans of colonial warfare in Algeria. He attended receptions and semiofficial fetes — and also joined in the licentious activities of his military hosts, visiting bordellos and gambling halls night after night.

Later, Solano López traveled to Sardinia, the Papal States, and Spain, concluding treaties of friendship and trade at nearly every stop. Finally, in mid-1854, he returned to the City of Lights to finalize plans for French immigration to the Nueva Burdeos colony in the Paraguayan Chaco. Almost as an afterthought, he entered into a fateful liaison with a beautiful paramour, Elisa Alicia Lynch. It was a relationship that lasted the rest of his life.

The gray-eyed Madame Lynch brought a degree of steadiness to the fitful López despite her somewhat checkered background. Born in 1835 into humble gentility in Ireland, she married a French army surgeon at age fifteen only to be left to fend for herself in Paris. Apparently, she succeeded through grit and a carefully cultivated charm in transforming herself into a courtesan, one of the class of kept women, often associated with the stage, that was so prominent a feature of smart Continental society in the 1850s. For Solano López, she was no mere bed partner. Her broad culture, poise, and undoubted magnetism well matched his ability to wield unchecked authority in Paraguay. Lynch made him appear more worldly, and he made her feel more secure. Many in the socially conservative Asunción later came to fear her. Lynch's blonde tresses, snobbish attitudes, and high sense of fashion made them look rather ordinary, and they hated her for it. But the general loved her as he had no other woman.

Brother Benigno voiced disapproval of the connection right from the beginning. He begged Francisco Solano to drop Lynch, but the general refused when he learned that she was pregnant. He left her instead with an ample purse, letters of introduction, and directions on how to book passage to South America. After giving birth to a son in Buenos Aires, she finally arrived in Asunción in December 1855.

Solano López had already been home eleven months by then, having departed Europe in style aboard the richly furnished *Tacuarí*. This was a 448-ton war steamer built on order through the Blyth Brothers. It had a full complement of British contract sailors and officers and eventually saw service as the flagship of the Paraguayan fleet.[20]

*Paraguay: The Military Transformed*

When the *Tacuarí* dropped anchor at Asunción in January 1855, its arrival heralded major changes for Paraguay and its military. First off the pier came the general's traveling companions, clerks, and other lackeys, all attired in frock coats of stunning weave. To the people of the capital, they seemed the epitome of modern professionals. Next came a bemedalled Solano López, who looked every inch the man who would build a military infrastructure second to none in the Plata. Finally, there was the appearance of the ship itself, so modern and imposing, the perfect symbol of a Paraguay ready to burst upon the world stage. No one missed its significance.

Though most of the *Tacuarí*'s crew soon returned to England, her captain, George Francis Morice, stayed on to help build the Paraguayan navy into a force stronger than that of Argentina. Other Britons contracted through the Blyth Brothers did much the same for the army. One of the first to arrive from London was John William K. Whytehead, who directed the labors of scores of European machinists, doctors, and technicians. A civil engineer by training, the bearded, misty eyed Whytehead proved to be a visionary not unlike Solano López. He was also as obsessive as the general, though with a more realistic sense of the country's limitations and advantages. As engineer in chief, he drove himself day and night for ten years orchestrating a program of economic and military development on a huge scale.[21] The men who worked under him came to Paraguay on two- or four-year contracts, receiving handsome pay for their efforts. They constructed public buildings, shipyards, an arsenal, an iron foundry, a railroad, and a telegraph line. In every way, they worked to modernize the government's infrastructure.[22]

Individuals who deserve specific mention in this respect included Col. George Thompson, Dr. William Stewart, and George F. Masterman, all of whom wrote memoirs of the war. A former British army officer with no previous experience in military engineering, Thompson accepted an appointment in the Paraguayan forces, first as a topographical engineer and later as a corps commander. His skill in the preparation of earthworks gave the Paraguayans a decided advantage on the defensive.

Stewart likewise had served with the British army as a member of the medical corps. He came to Asunción as a penniless survivor of an abortive colonization project and thereafter met the lonely Madame Lynch. Kept pregnant in a golden cage by Solano López, she had been mainly spurned by other British residents and basked in the attention of Stewart, a natural charmer. Thanks to her influence, he soon received the post of chief surgeon in Solano López's army. He ran military hospitals and together with Masterman oversaw the treatment of hundreds of sick and wounded. Masterman himself was a pharmacist by training and became chief apothecary in the Paraguayan forces, a position that carried a lieutenant's rank. Like Stewart, he played a major role in the wartime medical establishment and was well placed to observe the results of combat.

These British specialists and their associates earned their share of the Paraguayan payroll. The state yerba monopoly and the various government leaseholds permitted Solano López to pay cash for their services, but the government received much in return. The contracts with European engineers contained clauses that obligated them to train Paraguayan apprentices who eventually would take their place. This diffused some precious knowledge of modern industry in a country far removed from the Clyde. The apprentices commonly became noncommissioned officers in the Paraguayan army and made crucial contributions to the military buildup in the early 1860s and even more so during the long resistance thereafter.

Whytehead's projects were sound and broadly conceived. Indeed, they have inspired much favorable comment from revisionist historians anxious to discover some proof of economic development in Paraguay. But a balanced program of modernization in which all Paraguayans participated was the furthest thing from Solano López's mind. State coffers had a surplus sufficient to cover the refurbishing of the armed forces, and all the major state projects were directed toward that goal. But most Paraguayans still had no contact with the Europeans, nor did they benefit conspicuously from the changes they were helping to bring about.

One thing was certain, though: Paraguay's military capabilities were growing quickly. The greater part of the nation's artillery previously consisted of old honeycombed iron guns, "probably taken by ships for ballast and bought by Paraguay."[23] Now there were distinct signs of change. Consignments of arms of many types arrived from England and the Continent: sabers for the cavalry, iron and brass cannon, Congreve rockets, canister rounds and solid shot, and carronades. After the 1850s, foreign arms purchases continued to take up a good portion of the budget.[24] Yet more and more arms were produced locally, with the Asunción Arsenal and Ybycuí ironworks casting 12-, 24-, and 32-pounder cannon and shot of all calibers. The Paraguayans constructed wagons for the Quartermaster Corps together with fixed and mobile gun carriages. State shipyards also built the *Yporá* and *Salto Guairá* (in 1856), *El Correo* (in 1857), *Apa* (1858), and *Jejuí* (1859), all sizable, modern steamers designed for both commercial and military purposes.

Perhaps the most important innovations, however, came in the form of new training procedures for common soldiers and the establishment of large military encampments. Modern drill replaced informal slipshod discipline. Wisner earned some credit in this, though much more was due to British engineers like Thompson who doubled as military trainers.

They faced daunting challenges. Throughout the early 1850s, Carlos Antonio López built up the number of men under arms, and now with the return of his eldest son, the draft became nearly universal.[25] Men from the most isolated villages were thrown together with men from Asunción. Few except for yerba workers had any experience of working in large groups. Few had seen modern rifles; even flintlocks were foreign objects to some.

The untrained recruit's method of shooting was to cram as much shot and powder as possible into the barrel of a weapon, then looking away from the target, jerk forcibly at the trigger and hope for the best. The noisiest of reports was satisfying; few cared about the accuracy of fire. Of course, regular practice instilled more efficient habits.

Instructors of every nationality had the advantage of authority in their lessons, for they could discourage waste and inefficiency in as severe a way as necessary. Discipline in the Paraguayan army was strict, even brutal. Idle soldiers ran the risk of a flogging that would tear the flesh from their backs. Not even the youngest drummer boy claimed exemption from the rule of the lash. It went without saying that for cowardice or desertion, a man might be whipped to death.[26]

Yet for all of the harshness of military life, the average soldier rarely indulged in open grumbling or questioning of orders. He took it for granted that his lot in life demanded of him silent, unconditional acquiescence. As one eyewitness noted: "The Paraguayans were the most respectful and obedient men imaginable. From the soldier to the General, everyone squared up with his cap in hand, to his superior officer, who never returned the salute. Anyone in military costume in Paraguay was the superior officer of any civilian, and all judges, etc. had to take off their hats to any ensign.... A Paraguayan never complained of an injustice, and was perfectly contented with whatever his superior determined. If he was flogged, he consoled himself by saying, 'If my father did not flog me, who would?'"[27]

This evocation of paternalism was apt, but so was the notion that Solano López had in mind building a national army with a common national ethos. Unlike the Brazilian military, where the presence of criminals, debtors, and unemployed day laborers was the accepted norm, in Paraguay, conscription took in every able-bodied man for as long as the government required. The scorn so commonly heaped upon soldiers in Brazil thus found no parallel in Paraguay, for citizens of all stations participated in the armed forces, and the government made it obvious that soldiers deserved deferential treatment. As in the French army, officers were generally promoted from the ranks, and there were no such persons as substitutes. In fact, when wealthier men reported for service, the government obliged them to remove their shoes and go barefooted, for none but Solano López and his highest-ranking officers were permitted boots.[28] Though perhaps a mere curiosity, this doffing of shoes clearly demonstrated an inclination toward uniformity among the Paraguayans — a uniformity conducive to esprit de corps.

The military encampments the Europeans designed in Paraguay were not trivial affairs. There were already substantial garrisons at Asunción, Olimpo, Villa Franca, Concepción, and Villa Oliva, but these facilities were modest compared with those of the newer camps. The major training center at Cerro León, for instance, had barracks and parade grounds, officers' quarters, numerous corrals for cavalry horses, an armory, a hospital (with well-stocked pharmacy), supply depots and canteens, and vast herds of beef cattle for food. It was specially constructed at the terminus of the new railroad so that troops might deploy more rapidly. As a whole, the camp accommodated huge numbers of soldiers, and in late 1864 some twenty thousand were in residence.[29]

If Cerro León was impressive by regional standards, the great fortress of Humaitá became even more famous as the "Sebastopol of South America." Located fifteen miles north of the confluence of the Paraguay and Paraná Rivers, the initial settlement was founded in 1778 as a tiny government outpost set up to interdict tobacco smugglers. At the time, it consisted of two or three rough adobes on a bank overlooking a sharp bend in the Paraguay. The Gran Chaco was directly in front and Corrientes just a few hours downriver. As a strategic site, Humaitá was without equal in the region, for enemy ships could not ascend the Paraguay without passing under its guns. It was also exceptionally well protected on the south and east by marshes and lagoons. The few dry areas leading to it could be reinforced with troops in such a way as to frustrate any attack.

The camp itself came alive only after the 1855 confrontation over Fêcho-dos-Morros. The Brazilian flotilla might have caused considerable havoc at Pilar and Asunción had conditions allowed, and Carlos Antonio López was anxious that an adversary never again have such an opportunity. Under European direction, an army of workers felled the forest around the site, grubbing up the roots. They erected a line of fortifications that ran more than 6,000 feet along the left bank of the river. The line was constructed of packed abode, baked bricks, and hardwood braces. It contained scores of parapets and eight separate gun batteries. At 450 feet across at the front and 21 feet high, Battery Londres was the most remarkable of the eight. It was a long brick casement with walls nearly a yard thick, covered at the arches with packed earth. Pierced by embrasures for sixteen cannon, it then mounted two 68-pounders, two 56-pounders, three 32-pounders, and an 8.75-inch gun. The other seven batteries were mainly sited on raised platforms à la barbette, covered with straw sheds, and partly revetted with brick or earth-filled gabions. All together, Humaitá's defenses presented a formidable, though not impregnable, barrier to any enemy force approaching from the river.

*Military Preparedness*

Until the time of the American Civil War, the history of modern warfare had been one of increasing troop numbers and ever more sophisticated fortress and weapons systems. When Gustavus Adolphus introduced batteries of lightweight cannon, he revolutionized combat by making it possible to concentrate the fire of several guns on a single target and to move the guns about rapidly. Napoleon improved on this by concentrating the fire of an entire army upon a single sector of the battlefield so as to prepare the way for a decisive infantry assault. The placement of cannon at Humaitá showed that Solano López and his advisers had learned something from these European precedents, for the lighter pieces could easily be moved about to support the fire of heavier guns.

Behind the gun batteries, the Paraguayans constructed permanent entrenchments to encircle the camp in an eight-mile arc. At regular intervals they situated palisades and chevaux-de-frise, and on the southeast portion they established another set of batteries commanding the marshlands. They also set up a magazine with five hundred tons of black powder, wharves, barracks for twelve thousand troops, ample warehouses for the stocking of food and arms, a smithy, a sawmill, coal-sheds, corrals for horses and cattle, workshops, and several hospitals and clinics.[30] At the center, Solano López's men built an elegant blue and white church on the model of the Asunción cathedral. Consecrated in 1861 (and named San Carlos in honor of the elder López), it was "a splendid edifice with three towers, the middle one being 120 or 150 feet high; the interior [was] neat, and a colonnade [ran] round the exterior; there [were] four large bells hung from a wooden scaffolding, one bearing the inscription *Sancte Carole, ora pro nobis*."[31] The church's cupola was the first thing visible when ships rounded the bend from either direction; one day its outline against the rising sun would stand as a symbol of resistance, of desperation, and of a nearly unobtainable prize.

Humaitá was as much a training facility as Cerro León. Like the larger camp to the north, it saw thousands of recruits processed and made ready for combat. In general, these men had grown up in the countryside and had never lived under strict discipline. They were duly impressed by all the curious military hardware. As shipments of imported weapons arrived from Asunción, everyone had a chance to see them, though only a few could actually test their firing.

Solano López was among the few figures in South America to understand the value of the needle rifle, and even more so of the single-shot muzzleloader that came onto the market after the U.S. Civil War. The latter weapon fired the much-admired Minié projectile, which had such good range and accuracy. Solano López only managed, however, to obtain enough Wittons rifles to arm three infantry battalions and a consignment of Turner's breechloading carbines for his 250-man escort. This unit styled itself the *Acá carayá*, or monkey heads, as each member wore a leather helmet upon which was attached the tail of a howler monkey. Three or four other units, including the brass-helmeted dragoons *(Acá verá)*, eventually received percussion-cap rifles before enemy blockades cut off Paraguay's source of supply; the remaining troopers had to rely on a miscellany of flintlocks.[32] Recruits without rifles shouldered bamboo lances and marched smartly on command in their new scarlet tunics and white trousers. These young soldiers were generally small yet trimly built, sinewy figures with bright eyes like those of a Coptic mosaic. They seemed timid in the face of authority but usually enjoyed being away from home. Later observers cited their bravery, high morale, and steadfastness in combat.

The precise number of troops available to Solano López in 1864 remains a matter of conjecture. Colonel Thompson claimed at the time that the Paraguayan Army had about 80,000 men, one-third of whom were cavalry and the rest infantry and artillery.[33] Another accounting from an official source in early 1865 listed a force of 38,173.[34] This was probably closer to the mark, though it likely reflected the standing forces before full mobilization. The key factor, after all, was not how many men were under arms in Paraguay at any one time, but how much of a manpower reserve existed. Solano López almost certainly could count on upward of 150,000 men, this being nearly one-third of the country's population.[35]

Neither the Brazilians nor the Argentines could hope to mobilize so many men so quickly, though with their large populations, either could manage something similar after a rigorous recruitment. Paraguay's advantage in this sense was political, as no significant opposition to the regime existed within its borders. Moreover, when seen in narrow military terms, the country's ability to mobilize quickly and extensively imposed a burden, for the army lacked trained officers to lead so many men. Sergeants and corporals were also in short supply.

Whatever the true size of Solano López's army, its internal organization was clear enough. The infantry was divided into battalions, thirty-seven in 1864. On paper, each battalion had from 800 to 1,000 men organized into six companies. The majority of the units followed the pattern of the Second Infantry Battalion, however, which counted only 483 officers and men by midyear.[36] For its part, the cavalry was organized into twenty-nine regiments of four squadrons apiece. Each regiment had four hundred rank and file, though again, few units served at full strength, in part because they lacked sufficient horses.[37] The artillery amounted to only three regiments, and these had to handle all manner of guns, from standard steel-rifled 12-pounders to smoothbore 56-pounders for use at Humaitá.

Despite its general backwardness and lack of modern arms and materiel, the Paraguayan army was still large, and this was the key element in its reputation. Some observers—Thompson, for example—preferred to focus their criticisms on other matters, specific weaknesses in the armed forces, and the general lack of military preparedness. Most others blamed Solano López directly.

The same authoritarianism that permitted a large military in Paraguay prevented the development of a skilled officer corps. Like his father, the new president was a jealous man. He assigned promotions so sparingly that regiments were commonly commanded by a lieutenant and seldom by an officer of higher rank than captain. At the outset of the war, Paraguay's army counted but one general (López himself), five colonels, two lieutenant colonels, ten majors, fifty-one captains, and twenty-two first lieutenants. Several hundred junior grade officers and noncommissioned officers rounded out the leadership. This was hardly adequate for an army numbering in the tens of thousands. Six young men sent to France for military studies had yet to complete their first semester by the end of 1864.[38] Thus, though an imposing force by regional standards, the Paraguayan army still had glaring inadequacies — not the least of which was the fear of many officers that any show of skill on their part would bring down upon them the envy, perhaps even the wrath, of Solano López.

Conditions were no better in the navy. Though Solano López had focused on modernizing this service, it had only expanded to sixteen steamers by 1864, all of them save the *Tacuarí* converted merchant ships. These were supported by a small flotilla of sailing ships, flat-bottomed barges, and canoes. The steamers and some of the barges mounted smoothbore 4- to 32-pounder cannons, but gunners were generally neophytes.

In fact, save for the various British machinists and stokers, no one aboard these ships could be called experienced. Ships' crews tended to be small. The largest crew seems to have been that of the *Ygurey* (launched in 1862), which boasted a captain, two senior lieutenants, a sergeant, a fifer and drummer, six corporals, two pilots, and fifty-one other sailors.[39] Most steamers carried fewer than fifty crewmen, the sailing vessels around fifteen, and the barges and canoes, seven or less.

Some of these men had made the voyage to Montevideo, but most had gone no farther than Concepción or Humaitá. Therefore, no matter how many reports on naval matters Captain Morice issued and how much the Asunción shipyards worked overtime, the Paraguayans had little chance of making up for the Brazilian advantage in ships and training. They had to find their strengths elsewhere.

*Some Comparisons*

A glance at the military infrastructures of the countries under examination reveals few unimpeachable strengths. The officer corps of the Brazilian Imperial Navy and the army engineers had professional standards, if one defines those as meaning knowledge, ability, responsibility, and a sense of corporate identity. Such standards were also present to a degree in some of the *porteño* battalions of Argentina and perhaps in the escort battalion of Paraguay. Except for these tiny nuclei, however, the militaries in South America lacked the professionalism of European armed forces. South American officers might have had more ambition than talent, yet they knew which way they wanted to go and which obstacles they needed to overcome.

If one includes the *Guarda Nacional* troops, the forces available to the Brazilian Empire greatly exceeded those of Paraguay, Uruguay, and Argentina. Such numbers would normally give them an overwhelming advantage vis-à-vis any of their neighbors. But these forces could not be easily trained or concentrated. Most were poorly armed and poorly led.

The Brazilian military owed its basic disorganization to the budgetary politics of the imperial government and, more particularly, to the instinctive conservatism of Brazil's elites. The great lawyers, merchants, and landowners worried that any expansion in the standing army might disrupt their carefully constructed social order. As later events unfolded, their assumptions proved justified. This was no consolation, however, to Caxias, Osório, and others who sought to modernize the military establishment within the bounds of the imperial order. They had to content themselves with piecemeal reform.

While the imperial army had nothing of the juggernaut in it, the navy by contrast looked relatively modern in terms that any European observer would have recognized. The fleet was large, its guns formidable, and its officer class well trained. Its mission, however, centered on coastal defense. It could not easily be trained to support land forces, and its officers had little experience on interior rivers. The imperial navy was not ready, therefore, for the kind of war that Solano López thrust upon it.

If Brazil's armed forces had a certain clumsiness about them, Argentina's had yet to take a mature step. There were certainly some skilled officers in the highest ranks in Buenos Aires, but their talents were highly individual and not easily transferable to field commanders or the officer corps as a whole. Mitre tried to make some headway through the recruitment of foreign mercenaries and the purchase of modern arms, but the funds available for such initiatives were limited. Besides, the politics of the Litoral and interior provinces remained unsettled; the national government had no reason to feel confident that any program of military development would gain widespread support. Meanwhile, for the most part, the men under arms in Argentina continued to organize and comport themselves as they had under Rosas. Next door in Uruguay, the situation was broadly similar, though forward momentum there was even less conspicuous.

Paraguay was the only country in the region that could boast of its military preparedness and a full treasury. For Francisco Solano López, the center of political gravity was the army, and he treated the institution with as much favor as the isolated circumstances of Paraguay permitted. He had many successes in building the army as a result. It was large in terms of sheer numbers. Though units were untested, training had started to take on a regular form. There were still many weaknesses in armament and leadership (the lack of reliable midlevel officers was an especially thorny problem), yet the future of the Paraguayan military looked bright.

The ethos of Solano López's army was entirely different from that of the Brazilians and Argentines; it was an institution that responded to national directives rather than a coterie of provincial guards with a limited outlook. The army (and the navy) could depend on the unswerving, unquestioned patronage of the state. The two structures overlapped at so many places as to become essentially one and the same. Thus, unlike Argentina and Brazil, Paraguay could mobilize almost all of the nation's men with relative ease. The presence of Whytehead and other European engineers added another modern element to what otherwise would have been a wholly backward institution. Finally, in that nebulous area sometimes called the "will to fight," here again the Paraguayans could fall back on their strong sense of community. They had both discipline and high morale. Whether such feelings could overcome the country's geographic disadvantages, whether they alone could carry Solano López to victory, was nonetheless a decidedly open question.

# The Mato Grosso Campaign

8

The Paraguayan decision to invade Mato Grosso in December 1864 appeared to conflict with Asunción's war aims. After all, how could Uruguay, a country situated far beyond the frontier to the southeast, be defended by a concerted attack to the north? Several explanations suggest themselves. For one, Solano López was aware of the military stores that the Brazilians had built up in their Mato Grosso settlements. He also knew that the province contained thousands of head of cattle, which he likewise could use to support his army. He needed both munitions and cattle and was clearly willing to launch a quick strike in order to get them. Solano López reasoned that such a campaign would last only a few weeks, after which he could redeploy his forces to Uruguay. At the same time, he knew that if Paraguay ignored Mato Grosso, it might later prove costly. In a general war with Brazil, the empire could find a way to transfer troops from Goiás or São Paulo to reinforce the Mato Grosso garrisons. This would mean that the Paraguayans would have to fight on two fronts. If Solano López attacked Mato Grosso now, he might prevent such an enemy move until after it no longer mattered.

There was also the longstanding territorial dispute with Brazil. An audacious strike against the north might yield a secure frontier, for the Brazilians could not hope to reinforce Mato Grosso in a timely fashion except by the Paraguay River. Solano López could gain de facto sovereignty in the disputed area and thus achieve his father's old ambition of a definitive border. An attack on Mato Grosso would nonetheless take time, time that López could ill afford if he were to save the Blanco regime in Montevideo.

*The Invasion Plan*

Although one of the largest provinces in the empire, Mato Grosso still had a small population in the mid-1860s, numbering less than sixty-five thousand inhabitants, of whom twenty-four thousand were Indians and another six thousand slaves. Most lived in tiny, isolated communities, so isolated, in fact, that few Brazilians in Mato Grosso sensed the immediate danger facing them from Paraguay. And only a few in the provincial government were aware of how unprepared they were to face that danger.

On paper, the province maintained nearly four thousand men under arms as National Guardsmen, but the true figure, inclusive of Indian auxiliaries, was almost certainly less than one-third that number.[1] Many were stationed upriver at Cuiabá, far from the potential invasion sites in the south. These soldiers had little or no training in the conventional sense of the term. They had to provide their own uniforms and mounts, and although commanded by officers of the regular army, they generally acted more as independent rovers than organized troops. On raids against the Indians, they lived off the land like the *Bandeirantes* of old. Yet such independence of movement often took them far from populated areas and far from contact with other units. They could not easily respond to a large-scale assault.

The only major defensive work in the province was the small fort at Nova Coimbra. The tiny military colonies at Dourados, Nioaque, and Miranda worked well enough as observation posts but could not hope to mount any serious resistance to a determined attack; together, they had an effective force of only eighty-four men, most of whom, officers included, were regarded as the dregs of the imperial army, hardly fit even for guard duty.[2] As for naval defenses, the Brazilians did have available six small sailing vessels under the command of a captain. But only the flagship, the *Anhambaí*, carried any guns at all — two small, smoothbore cannons mounted haphazardly on the deck. The other vessels served primarily in the transport of supplies and had no military capability. All told, the Brazilians in Mato Grosso were in no position to repel any serious attack from the south. And in Cuiabá, if not on the frontier, few suspected that danger from that quarter even existed.[3]

For their part, the Paraguayans were prepared. Solano López demanded thorough and regular reports from his own frontier posts on the Apa River.[4] In 1863 he sent two secret agents into the disputed territory on reconnaissance missions. One of these men, naval lieutenant Andrés Herreros, explored the Alto Paraguay, São Laurenço, and Cuiabá Rivers as part of an open, semiofficial visit to improve trade relations. His real task was to survey Brazilian river defenses. His trip to Nova Coimbra, Albuquerque, and Dourados proved critical to what subsequently occurred, though because of low waters he failed to visit Cuiabá. The other agent, who posed as a wealthy entrepreneur looking to purchase ranch land, was in fact Lt. Col. Francisco Isidoro Resquín of the Paraguayan army. He had received orders to complete a land reconnaissance just north of the disputed area.[5]

The intelligence-gathering activities of Resquín and Herreros gave the Paraguayans some advanced understanding of the Mato Grosso terrain as well as the disposition and weaknesses of the Brazilian troops generally.[6] López now felt prepared. He had his brother, the war minister, issue a detailed plan of invasion. In typical fashion, President López's plan was many pages in length, addressed every possible contingency, and made sure that his field commanders would follow orders to the letter.[7]

López envisioned a three-pronged attack, with two columns crossing into Brazil by land and a third by the Alto Paraguay River. The riverborne force would disembark at Nova Coimbra and seize the fort there, then reembark and move north to take the villages of Albuquerque and Corumbá. The two land forces, comprising mostly cavalry, would depart simultaneously from Concepción in parallel columns. After crossing the Apa, they were to capture Dourados and the Brazilian settlements along the Mbotety (or Miranda) River. They would then make contact with the

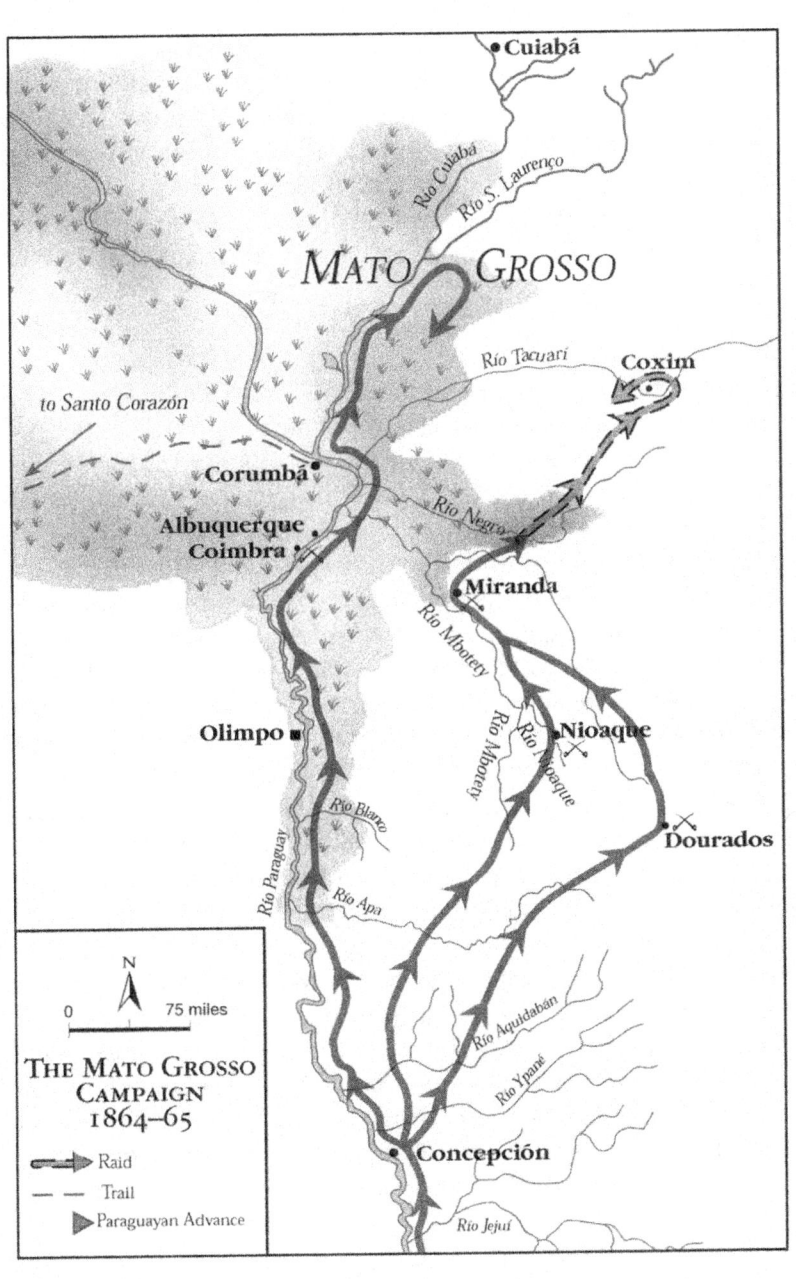

river force and together consolidate the Paraguayan gains by stationing garrisons in the captured communities. López's plan called for a strict (and unrealistic) timetable of one week to attain all of these objectives. River conditions in December made it impossible to go above Corumbá, so the Paraguayan president made no specific provision regarding any move on Cuiabá or points north. In this, López seemed to recognize that although southern Mato Grosso might be easy to take, it might not be so easy to hold.

### The Departure

López had been at his military headquarters at Cerro León for nearly a month, conferring with his officers there on the proposed offensive against Brazil. Since the seizure of the *Marqués de Olinda*, the Paraguayan capital had been swept by a war fever, which, though distinctly artificial in character, was now having the desired effect of mobilizing the populace for war. On 7 December 1864, the president returned to Asunción to amplify and focus that feeling in specific support of his Mato Grosso expedition. He quickly gathered his army. The assembled troops included his crack Sixth and Seventh Infantry Battalions (exclusively comprised of *pardo* regulars), the Twenty-seventh and Thirtieth Infantry Battalions, and two field batteries equipped with twelve rifled cannons and several 24-caliber Congreve rockets, totaling around thirty-eight hundred men.[8] Asunción had not seen this many soldiers for some time. Their scarlet tunics and brightly shining bayonets might have clashed with their rough, bare, and callused feet, but they maintained an energetic and jaunty attitude and made a favorable impression.

On 12 December López designated the commanders for the Mato Grosso expedition. Not surprisingly, he placed Resquín and Herreros in key positions, the former to lead the principal column against Miranda and the small posts on the Mbotety, the latter to command the steamer *Yporá*, which took the vanguard position in the Paraguayan flotilla. Solano López assigned all river forces to Capt. Pedro Ignacio Meza, then the senior officer in Paraguay's navy. For overall command of the expeditionary force, López chose his own brother-in-law, Vicente Barrios.

As a favored member of the president's family, Barrios enjoyed an authority far above that conferred by his military rank. He had known Solano López since they were boys and had, according to one source, "been his willing tool in outraging other people," even acting as his procurer in Asunción during the 1850s.[9] Whatever the truth of this observation, Barrios had received command and, in the Paraguayan service, this alone assured him unquestioned obedience.

His subordinate officers were also held in high regard by their men, though less for their political connections than for their military skills. The stocky Resquín, who eschewed Barrios's lustrous beard in favor of a clean-shaven chin, was typical. He was a wily fighter, having learned many lessons over the years from the Guaicurú; he was constant, loyal, and inured to personal suffering (and actually managed to survive the war).

Meza and Herreros, the two naval men, had decidedly different backgrounds and personalities. Meza was already an *anciano*, having fought in the independence struggle (though he had never commanded a warship in combat). He had the sad, wizened face of a businessman whose years of material success had been purchased with a series of peptic ulcers. Herreros, for his part, was young, dashing, and worldly—an authentic "dandy" in naval uniform and much beloved by the officers and men around him. His openhearted "slap-on-the-back" bonhomie stood in stark contrast to the saturnine manner of Meza. Had he lived longer, Herreros's effusiveness might well have brought him trouble when the Paraguayan government began to turn against its own.[10] As it was, he became Paraguay's first martyr.

Embarkation commenced on 14 December with the assembled three thousand soldiers boarding five steamers and three schooners at Asunción. Immediately before their departure, an officer standing upon a dais at the Campo del Hospital read them a triumphant proclamation:

> Soldiers! My endeavors to keep the peace have been fruitless. The Empire of Brazil, not knowing our valor and enthusiasm, provokes us to

war, which challenge we are bound by our honor and dignity to accept in protection of our dearest rights.

In recompense for your loyalty and long services, I have fixed my attention on you, choosing you from among the numerous legions that form the armies of the Republic, that you may be the first to give a proof of the force of our arms, by gathering the first laurels we shall add to those that our forefathers planted in the crown of our Fatherland in the memorable battles of Paraguarí and Tacuarí.

Your subordination and discipline, and your constancy under fatigues, assure me of your bravery, and of the lustre of the arms that I confide to your valor.

Soldiers and sailors! Carry this vote of confidence to your companions, who will join you on our northern frontiers, and march serenely to the field of honor, where, gathering glories for your country and fame for yourselves, you may show the world what the Paraguayan soldier is worth.

"Francisco Solano López"[11]

What the assembled troops thought of these rousing though somewhat mawkish words has not been recorded. That the various phrases were flowery they recognized easily enough; their own Guaraní language had an ample vocabulary of just such expansive terms, and the tradition of oral culture had a long history in their country. The proclamation, however, was in Spanish, a language whose nuances were usually lost on the average Paraguayan soldier. What mattered was its provenance: the Supreme Authority had given the order to attack the Brazilians, to drive the *macacos* out, to carry the flag northward. *Opáma!* It was enough.

For Solano López, the proclamation had a deeper, more personal meaning. He had begun it, characteristically, with a reference to himself, saying that he had tried to prevent an outbreak of hostilities, but now that the Brazilians had thrust the war upon Paraguay, he expected every man to do his duty, to "show the world" the value of the Paraguayan soldier. A hint of insecurity and self-doubt lay behind this last point, even perhaps the briefest recollection of a time a decade earlier, when, at the court of Louis Napoleon, no one had even heard of his country. Never again would he tolerate such colossal ignorance.

Perhaps these thoughts raced through López's mind as he sat upon his white charger *Mandyjú*, watching his troops embark in the blazing December sun. Bishop Palacios had already given the benediction, and the cheers had started to die down. The flotilla, still in full sight of the crowd, veered northward into the main channel of the Paraguay and set out for Mato Grosso.

*The Attack on Nova Coimbra*

The transit upriver was uneventful. Soldiers lounged together on the decks of the ships and sweated in their red tunics. With little room to move about, most men polished and repolished their bayonets, gossiped, tried to make shade for themselves, and drank prodigious amounts of cold yerba mate *(tereré)*. Naval regulations forbade them from spitting off the side into the water, nor were they officially permitted to discharge the used tea from the cow-horn receptacles *(guampas)* by tapping them against the railing. The British engineers who had modernized the Paraguayan navy had earlier insisted on these prohibitions as hygienic necessities.[12] The summer of 1864, however, was not a time for such niceties, and the officers (who themselves were drinking a great deal of *tereré*) chose to look the other way.

On 16 December the expeditionary force halted momentarily at the small port of Concepción. There, Barrios met with Resquín, who was waiting with several thousand more troops, again mostly cavalrymen. Some joined the amphibious force, which proceeded upriver after two days. In compliance with the preestablished plan, the remaining units (some three thousand to five thousand men) departed overland from Concepción at the same time. After crossing the Ypané, this force split in two, with the main group under Resquín marching on Miranda and a smaller force under Maj. Martín Urbieta moving on Dourados.[13]

As the morning star rose on 27 December, the riverborne units under Barrios reached their objective. The fort at Nova Coimbra was perched on a low, wooded bluff some fifty meters above the river's right bank. Irregular in shape, its walls and parapets were built of stone and heavy mortar, thick enough to withstand solid shot from smoothbore cannons. The walls ranged in height from two to five meters and boasted both gun and firing ports for riflemen. Yet none of these positions had overhead cover, and, in general, the fort was vulnerable to direct fire from the hills just above, where tamarind forests obscured the view.[14] Even so, an effective fusillade from this direction seemed unlikely because of the range limitations of the muskets and rifles.

The Brazilian garrison defending Nova Coimbra consisted of 115 artillerymen, not counting forty male Indians, civilians, convicts, and seventy female dependents. Besides the army garrison, two naval vessels, the British-built steamer *Anhambaí* and the smaller steamer *Jaurú*, lay at anchor nearby. The imperial commander at the fort, who also controlled these warships, was Lt. Col. Hermenegildo de Albuquerque Portocarreiro, who a decade earlier had been artillery instructor to Solano López. The colonel had little idea that the empire's relations with his former student's government had taken such a violent turn. Portocarreiro had just risen to take his breakfast when his lookouts sighted the smoke coming from the stacks of the approaching Paraguayan steamers. At 8:30 A.M. a Paraguayan sloop advanced under a white flag to a spot just below the fort. A Paraguayan officer then stepped ashore and carried a surrender demand from Barrios to Portocarreiro.

The Brazilian commander, still trying to recover from his surprise, hastily wrote a negative reply. In it he tried to buy time by telling Barrios that he had sent the Paraguayan demand on by courier to superior authorities in the provincial capital.[15] He evidently was unaware that under cover of darkness the preceding night, the Paraguayans had landed on the opposite bank of the river, established themselves on the heights, and now had several cannons trained on the fort.

Upon receipt of Portocarreiro's note, these same cannons began to spew fire upon the Brazilian position. They were soon joined by guns firing from the Paraguayan warships and from the muskets of infantry units swarming up from landing points at the river's edge. The Brazilians within the fort returned fire with gusto and kept up the cannonade until dusk, when further firing became ineffectual.

Sunset in Mato Grosso was normally accompanied by a rhythmic din of animal and insect sounds that grew louder and more hypnotic as darkness drove out the last flicker of sunlight. This night there was little such noise. The howler monkeys had fled and so had the birds. The only loud sounds to break the silence came from the occasional bark of a musket or rifle and from the shouted insults in Guaraní coming from the Paraguayan lines. Around eight in the evening, in a move that remains unexplained, Barrios reembarked his troops aboard the Paraguayan warships. There, at last, his men found a moment to wash the grime from their hands and faces. Their scarlet tunics, dirtied by mud and powder burns, no longer looked so impressive, but then, there was no one left to impress except other soldiers. Among the Paraguayans morale was high. A feeling of exhilaration had replaced the nervous excitement and tension that had accompanied the first volleys. They had survived the first day of battle and now could almost taste victory. Barrios and Meza opened bottles of wine, and there were many toasts to the glory of Solano López.

The dawn of the new day found the Paraguayans still in high spirits, ready to renew their attack on Nova Coimbra. They had seemingly placed their opponents in an untenable position and felt exceedingly optimistic. The morning of 28 December, however, brought good reason to question that hasty appraisal. Heavy solid shot had pitted the fort, but it still held and showed no outward sign of a quick capitulation. Barrios decided to mount a ground attack—if not an all-out assault, at least a reconnaissance in force.

The topography of the land surrounding the fort prevented any direct attack upon it except from one side, and there the Brazilians had planted hedges of prickly cactus. To mount a simple probe, the Paraguayans had to cut through this cactus under constant rifle fire. Even with luck they advanced only with great difficulty. The midday heat also took its toll, and many soldiers felt the onset of heatstroke.

In the end, the Paraguayan reconnaissance (if it deserves the name) was quite uneven in character. Some units withdrew precipitously to the protective line of the forest after firing only a few shots. Others blundered ahead in an obstinate if unorganized and undirected assault. In this they made some headway, though at a high price. Colonel Thompson, who had many friends among the participants in the battle, described what happened next: "Although exposed to a terrible fire of grape and musketry, [the Paraguayans ultimately] reached the walls; but they could not scale them, having taken no ladders with them. They also lost many men by the hand-grenades that the garrison threw upon them. Seven men, however, did scale the wall and got in, but they were immediately overpowered, and the remainder retreated."[16]

Having seen their men repulsed, Barrios and Meza continued to coordinate their barrage of Nova Coimbra into the late afternoon. Despite their excellent firing position, they could not tell what effect they were having. In fact, while the Paraguayans themselves had already lost 164 wounded and 42 killed, the Brazilians within the fort had yet to suffer a single casualty.[17]

Ammunition was a different matter. Portocarreiro's men had spent more than three-quarters of the available rounds for their rifles in repulsing the Paraguayans. The women in the fort had already set to work making new cartridges. Led by the garrison commander's wife, they rolled 17-mm round balls under heavy stones to make them longer in order to fit the smaller bores of the French-made rifles. Though far from perfect, the result proved serviceable, as the Paraguayans found to their regret during the assault. Now, even these makeshift bullets were running out.

Portocarreiro's position was desperate. The following morning saw the advance once again of Barrios's troops along the west bank of the river. These men quickly melted into the adjacent forest, hacking their way to good firing positions around the fort. They constructed ladders during the night and expected to use them during the course of another assault. Then one of the forward observers for the Paraguayan artillery ran to the river bank to shout a message to Barrios: the Brazilian imperial ensign, clearly visible the previous day, no longer flew from Nova Coimbra's flagstaff.

Portocarreiro and his men had withdrawn aboard the *Anhambaí* and *Jauru* during the previous evening. The Paraguayans had not detected this evacuation, which had taken place quickly and in near silence. The Brazilian commander and his men were now far away, steaming upriver toward Corumbá. As for Nova Coimbra, Barrios's men rushed its walls under a heavy cover fire from below. They then scaled the parapets and established immediate control. Inside they found eighteen Paraguayan prisoners who the Brazilians had taken the day before and who Portocarreiro had left behind in a locked room. They also found intact thirty-one cannons with substantial stocks of ammunition and powder.[18]

Military historians have criticized both Barrios and Portocarreiro for their conduct of the battle. According to one source, the latter was arrested and charged with ineptitude after he arrived at Corumbá.[19] By leaving his gunpowder dry and not spiking his cannons, he allowed valuable supplies to fall into the hands of the enemy.

As for Barrios, his critics have focused on his poor staff work (as seen, for instance, in the initial lack of ladders and in the sloppy reconnaissance efforts) and, more generally, on the timidity of the Paraguayan attack. After all, he had overwhelming strength in both men and firepower, but he used neither to great effect. Nor did he employ his naval power appropriately. In keeping Meza and his ships back a good deal of the time, he prevented their effective participation in the fight, which in turn probably cost Paraguayan lives. Worst of all, he failed to take the *Anhambaí* and *Jauru*, allowing Portocarreiro and the garrison the means to get away and warn Cuiabá. If he had placed even one of his five steamers a half-league upriver, the Brazilians could never have escaped.[20]

These criticisms aside, historians have rightly judged the attack on Nova Coimbra a major Paraguayan victory, and all over the country the soldiers and common people celebrated it as such. Whatever the original plan, the Brazilian defenders were less of a threat outside the fort than they were inside it. Better to have them flying away to the north, far away from Paraguay's borders, than having them pressing down upon the *patria* and impeding the realization of Solano López's grand design.

*Albuquerque and Corumbá*

After the hard fighting at Nova Coimbra, the Paraguayans expected further strong resistance as they pressed northward along the river. Events from this point forward, however, took an anticlimactic turn for Barrios and his troops. Not only did the Brazilians refuse to engage them in combat but the emperor's forces simply abandoned wide stretches of Mato Grosso as they fled back toward Cuiabá.

The tiny post of Albuquerque, located in a protected bend of the river some fifty miles north of Nova Coimbra, learned of the Paraguayan incursion when Portocarreiro arrived aboard the *Anhambaí* on 29 December. The "garrison" there consisted of only six men (despite the fact that the construction of fortifications at that spot was due to begin soon), so there was never any question of resistance. Instead, Portocarreiro disembarked some of his own soldiers from the overloaded steamer and ordered them to move overland to the provincial capital with the male civilians of the district. Portocarreiro himself evacuated the female residents of Albuquerque by river. As the ship departed, two smaller Brazilian vessels steaming south with reinforcements from Corumbá and that had just learned of the disaster downriver joined it. All three now turned north.

On New Year's Day, the Paraguayans reached Albuquerque. They found it abandoned but, significantly, not burnt to the ground. Perhaps the Brazilians thought that they could return soon, or perhaps they panicked and simply failed to take the time to set the place on fire. Throughout the campaign, the retreating Brazilians made this mistake repeatedly, leaving much useful materiel to fall into Paraguayan hands.

Corumbá turned out to be no more defensible than Albuquerque. Located on limestone bluffs high above the west bank of the Paraguay, the community enjoyed the best climate in the province, but no major fortification protected the town. Instead, Corumbá was known as the chief emporium of southern Mato Grosso—a valuable plum for Solano López as it constituted the terminus point for the nascent caravan trade to Santo Corazón in Bolivia.[21] Since a land dispute existed between the latter country and Brazil, possession of Corumbá might also provide

Paraguay with a key asset in forging any alliance with the government in La Paz.[22]

On 2 January an emergency committee consisting of two colonels, several junior officers, and important local notables met at Corumbá. After some heated argument, these men decided that they could not hold the town and recommended that an orderly evacuation of its two thousand inhabitants commence at once. The committee members themselves, rather than organize an orderly retreat, immediately left with their families aboard the *Anhambaí*. As the ship set course for Cuiabá, the populace of Corumbá hurried from their town into the Pantanal and the forests. They fled in abject terror, as if Barrios and his men were not creatures of flesh and blood but demons sent by Satan.

If their estimation seemed unjust initially, it later seemed altogether appropriate. On 4 January, Barrios landed four companies just south of Corumbá. They advanced and determined that the town was empty save for some foreign merchants and their families. Barrios then brought up his full force. He seized the small Brazilian vessel *Jacobina*, then in port. Afterward, while he stayed at the riverbank with Meza, he ordered patrols to enter the town.

The Paraguayan troops quickly fanned out among the few streets of the community. They made no effort to respect the neutrality of the foreigners but rounded them up with great harshness together with the few Brazilians they found. Officers dispatched patrols to nearby ranches to seize supplies, hides, and livestock and to arrest any civilians. No one was exempt. As Colonel Thompson related:

> The inhabitants had hidden themselves in the surrounding woods, and Barrios sent and brought them back. Their houses were already completely sacked, and some of the choicest articles of spoil were sent as presents to López, who did not disdain to accept them. The women were ill-treated, and Barrios himself took the lead in it. A Brazilian gentleman and his daughter were taken to him on board his steamer, and on the old man refusing to leave his daughter with Barrios, he was sent away under a threat of being shot, and his daughter was kept

on board. All whom Barrios took he put to the question, and those who did not give or did not possess the information he required were beaten by his order, and some of them lanced as spies.[23]

The sacking that Thompson alluded to went on for some time. It included not only the taking of sundry souvenirs—billiard balls, church ornaments, and the like—but also the tearing out of door hinges and the stripping of imported wallpaper from the wealthiest homes.[24] Men who would have been satisfied with chickens and dried beef carried away everything that caught their eye. In short order, the Paraguayans gutted Corumbá, leaving it fit perhaps to shelter a rough military force but otherwise shorn of everything that gave the town its life.

One can only speculate on the causes of such behavior. How was it that border disputes and balance-of-power concepts, all poorly grasped by the average Paraguayan, should translate into the brutal treatment of Brazilian civilians and the greedy seizure of their property? Was it a matter of deliberate policy? Solano López certainly regarded the Brazilians with great contempt, and the state newspapers reflected this bias, but much less so at the beginning of the war. It was only later—at the end of 1865 and in 1866—when the Paraguayans were first publicly enjoined to kill the "vile traitors and slave-mongers." The savagery seen in Mato Grosso must have resulted, then, from something else.

On one level, lack of disciplined leadership was a factor. Barrios set a poor example; he helped himself to money taken from merchants and townsmen and even sent the choicest prizes and the prettiest jewelry on to Solano López and Madame Lynch in Asunción. He also raped at least one woman in Corumbá. Their leader's actions made it clear to the Paraguayans that war justified any degree of barbarous behavior, that, indeed, their commander would forgive any undisciplined behavior and countenance any taking of revenge.

There was, however, another element at work. Paraguayan society had always centered on a patrimonial worldview that featured heavy-handed social control as part of everyday life. The police spy, the work-gang foreman, and sometimes the local priest were all part of a repressive structure that successfully channeled anger and discontent in directions that could not threaten the social order. In such an environment, bad feelings could only be expressed in nonproscribed ways — religious confession, drunkenness, familial violence. Only occasionally, as when militiamen destroyed an Indian *toldería*, were Paraguayans really allowed to unburden themselves fully, and when they did, it was with great relish. Perhaps for the Paraguayan soldiers at Corumbá, the war with Brazil was just another "big Indian fight." Fighting those they thought of as savages meant that no quarter would be offered. Yet the Paraguayan penchant for letting their worst impulses rule their actions played into the hands of Brazilian propagandists, who wanted to mask their own questionable actions in a veneer not just of respectability but also of a "civilizing mission."

*The Capture of the* Anhambaí
Barrios was well aware of the little Brazilian flotilla escaping northward toward Cuiabá, and he lost no time in sending two warships after it. The *Yporá*, with Herreros in command, took the lead. The young lieutenant had no doubt that he could find his quarry, for he knew this section of the river well from his espionage the year before. His own vessel, moreover, was a light passenger boat built in Paraguay and equipped with a powerful eighty-horsepower engine. The *Anhambaí*, although it had a head start, had only half the horsepower. It was also overloaded with civilians and soldiers from Corumbá. Herreros's companion vessel, the *Río Apa*, ran slower than the *Yporá* (though not as slow as the Brazilian ship), and was well suited to serve as an auxiliary.

On 6 January the Paraguayan vessels discovered the *Anhambaí* near the confluence of the Alto Paraguay and São Laurenço Rivers. The ship had already discharged its troops some distance below Cuiabá and was returning downriver in hopes of reaching Corumbá to complete the evacuation. Now, after sighting the Paraguayan steamers, it abruptly reversed course and entered the São Laurenço. Herreros immediately gave chase.

The most-seasoned sailor aboard the Brazilian ship was an Englishman, Josiah Baker, who had considerable experience with river vessels.[25] He knew that he could not outrun the *Yporá*, so he trained his stern-mounted 32-pounder on the approaching Paraguayan and started firing. Baker hoped to get in a lucky shot as he kept moving forward toward shallower water. One round did hit the *Yporá*'s bridge, killing an army lieutenant, but Herreros continued to close rapidly in an obvious attempt to overtake and board the vessel. Baker was a good gunner, but after he fired the thirteenth round, the crew panicked and turned the vessel sharply toward land.[26] It ran aground on a sandbar, and the men tried to flee for their lives. Colonel Thompson later recounted that the "Brazilians were terror-stricken, and many of them jumped into the water, where they were shot at; the rest were put to the sword. Captain Baker, who had been obliged to load and fire his gun himself, finding that his men would not fight, jumped into the water and escaped into the woods. Boats were sent to follow the fugitives, and all who were caught were killed."[27]

Thompson followed up this description with a specific charge of atrocity, asserting that the Paraguayan soldiers had cut off the ears from the Brazilian dead, gleefully stringing them together and hanging them on the shrouds of the *Yporá*. When the vessel returned to Asunción, the ears were removed, he claimed, by presidential order.[28] While Thompson normally took a skeptical view of atrocity tales, on this occasion he seems to have uncritically accepted a rumor then being circulated in the Argentine press. The rumor evidently originated in the doubtful testimony of a Brazilian purser who had entered Mato Grosso in early 1865 aboard the British ship *Ranger* and later wrote letters to several *porteño* newspapers. To be sure, this individual had visited the province as he claimed, but he witnessed no combat nor even set foot in occupied territory.[29] Whatever the truth of this atrocity story, it was widely believed in South America and added to the general reputation of ferocity that the Paraguayans enjoyed.

Lieutenant Herreros, for his part, acted in a disciplined manner. He quickly organized work parties that attached cables to the *Anhambaí* and eased it off the sandbar. Working in the cold water refreshed and calmed his men after the heat of combat and of the day. There was no further problem with their shooting captured Brazilians (despite Thompson's claim, the Paraguayans did take some prisoners, and these, for the moment, they treated properly). Noting the presence of still more sandbars, Herreros turned his ships around and headed out of the São Lourenço with his prize. He had shown great bravery during the battle and gained some fame among the soldiers attached to him.

Herreros, however, had nearly run out of time. On 9 January his ships reached the undefended port of Dourados near the confluence of the Alto Paraguay and Cuiabá Rivers. The Paraguayans decided to go no farther than the mouth of the Cuiabá because the waters ahead were too shallow for their steamers. The capital of Mato Grosso therefore remained safe under imperial control. Its inhabitants, however, greatly feared that the Paraguayans would shortly sweep through the entire province, probably in conjunction with a general uprising of black slaves. Though this revolt failed to materialize, the Cuyabanos never ceased to worry that the Paraguayans would forge a murderous alliance with the Indians and slaves.[30]

At Dourados, Herreros concerned himself with more practical matters. No sooner had he dropped anchor than two other vessels came into view from downriver. Captain Meza, it turned out, had dispatched the two ships from Corumbá in order to speed the transport of captured munitions and powder. Solano López urgently needed these supplies to bolster his forces in the south. Realizing that speed was of the essence, Herreros ordered his crew to join in the task of loading. The men labored through the night and into the next day.

The sun grew unbearably hot by midmorning, but Herreros refused to slow the pace of loading. When an army officer remonstrated with him, warning of the danger of accident in the intense heat, he waved off the officer's concerns and walked up to the riverside storehouses to supervise the work gangs. These storehouses, which the Brazilians used as magazines, were never built for such a purpose: rainwater seeped down the sides of the walls, the flooring was moist and uneven, and loose powder filled every crack. Herreros had just gone into one building when a thunderous blast tore it apart. Exactly what happened was never established with certainty, but given the high temperature, a static spark was the likely culprit that set off the powder (or it might have been some careless individual dragging his spur along the floor). In any event, the young lieutenant and twenty-five other Paraguayans died instantly.

On the news of their deaths, Solano López ordered an elaborate funeral service for Herreros and decreed the erection of a public monument to commemorate his deeds.[31] The mourning that ensued in the Paraguayan capital — and especially in the armed forces — was heartfelt, as Herreros enjoyed near universal esteem. His death brought home the reality that waging war inevitably carried a high price, not just for the common soldier but also for others like the handsome officer and hero beloved by all.

*The Overland Invasion*

Resquín's and Urbieta's columns made good progress after they crossed the Apa River (and this despite the fact that much of the land they traversed was flooded).[32] With 3,000–5,000 men at their command, the two Paraguayan officers enjoyed a decisive numerical advantage over their opponents. Whenever their cavalry approached, the noise of the horses' hooves was enough to cause Brazilian troops, settlers, and Indian allies to scatter into the bush. All told, the Paraguayans encountered little resistance, especially at the beginning.

The main contingent under Francisco Resquín took five days to reach the military colony at Miranda, arriving on 29 December. The Brazilian commander had received word of the Paraguayan presence the day before and had ordered his men to flee. They hastily buried some munitions and valuables before departing. An advance column of 150 Paraguayans reached Miranda within hours of their exit, finding the cooking fires still warm but no Brazilians.

It was different farther east. Maj. Martín Urbieta, who had two hundred men at his disposal, arrived at the Dourados colony the same day that Resquín's men took Miranda. Unlike his immediate superior, however, he encountered some resistance from the sixteen-man garrison — a struggle both courageous and foolhardy.

Dourados (not to be confused with the present-day city of the same name, nor with the river port located far to the northwest) was commanded by a young Brazilian lieutenant named Antonio João Ribeiro. Antonio João, as military biographers always call him, refused either to capitulate or to flee at the approach of the Paraguayans. The thirty-odd civilians of the district he ordered to withdraw immediately into the bush, accompanied by one soldier who carried a message to Brazilian cavalry units farther north.

The officer and fourteen of his men went onto the field to meet the enemy at 1:00 P.M. Answering their challengers with muskets, the small force was itself immediately fired upon. Antonio João and two other Brazilian soldiers fell dead, their bodies scored with shot in a dozen places; two others were wounded. The remaining men scattered quickly into the forest and away from Urbieta's advancing troops, who later captured most of them anyway. Dourados fell after an engagement of only two minutes' duration.[33] A new Paraguayan garrison moved in to replace the vanquished Brazilians. Urbieta then proceeded to sack and burn nearby Colonia Brilhante and the tiny Vila Vacaria cattle station during the next few days. He then moved north to rejoin the main force under Resquín.

Antonio João's sacrifice made no difference to the outcome of the Mato Grosso campaign. Yet the message he sent to his superior officers before the action contained a rousing note of defiance that became famous as the battle cry of the empire in the general conflict that followed. His words have since inspired many a Brazilian schoolboy: "I know I shall die, but my blood and the blood of my comrades will serve as a solemn protest against the invasion of my homeland."[34]

Only one major objective of the overland invasion force remained: the taking of the small post at Nioaque. On 30 December, as they attempted to ford the Feio River, Resquín's advance guard made contact with 200–300 Brazilian cavalrymen. This was the force that Antonio

João had tried to warn. Now fully ready to fight (though greatly outnumbered), they discharged their weapons at the Paraguayans, making their passage across the shallow water nearly impossible. Resquín later reported that "after a heavy volley of rifle fire and a few artillery rounds, the Brazilians retreated to the banks of the Desbarrancado River," there to make a stand.[35] They held that position, however, only long enough to destroy a small bridge and then quickly withdrew, leaving fifteen stragglers to the mercy of the Paraguayans. The Brazilians lost fifty-seven men killed and could afford no further losses. Instead, they abandoned Nioaque, which Resquín took on 2 January.

The Paraguayan commander attempted no major pursuit thereafter but allowed the enemy cavalry to fall back on Miranda (not the military colony, which had already fallen, but the small village of the same name on the Mbotety River). Unsure of what to do next, the Brazilians then headed west toward Corumbá to link up with the troops there. When they learned that their comrades had also abandoned that site, the column turned due east and quit Mato Grosso altogether. Eventually, they reached friendly territory in the province of São Paulo.

Resquín had by now reached the Mbotety. His men found the village of Miranda abandoned save for two Italian merchants and a black freedman; all the other inhabitants had fled, they claimed, when the rumor reached them that the Paraguayans were beheading every Brazilian they found. The Mbayá had also entered the picture in the eleventh hour, ransacking every abandoned building and making off with considerable loot just before the Paraguayans arrived.[36]

After securing the area, Resquín sent a flying column of three hundred cavalrymen to raid the remote military colony of Coxim, which lay above Corumbá at some distance to the northeast on the Tacuarí River. They reached this site only in late April and seized it without resistance.[37] Yet they held it only long enough to put it to the torch. The raiding party then returned to Paraguayan positions farther south.[38] They made no attempt then or later to raid Cuiabá by land. Heeding the frantic appeal of the imperial governor, troops had arrived from the northern areas of the province (and perhaps from Goiás), effectively reinforcing the town. The Brazilians nonetheless lacked sufficient strength to force the Paraguayans to relinquish their gains. Solano López's army controlled southern Mato Grosso essentially undisturbed until 1866.

*The Spoils and the Consequences*

The conquest of Mato Grosso was a mixed blessing for the Paraguayans. In terms of overall political goals, most particularly rescuing the Blanco regime in Montevideo, the victory was obviously of little use. The fighting was far removed from the Banda Oriental, and it drew no Brazilian troops from that quarter. The invasion, moreover, ate up valuable time that López could have used in dispatching troops to Uruguay. He evidently concluded, though, that securing his northern flank was of greater importance.

Some historians have argued that Solano López exaggerated the danger posed by the Brazilian forces in the north, that he "frittered his time away" in Mato Grosso when he should have launched a decisive attack across the Misiones and into Rio Grande do Sul, there to blunt the Brazilian invasion of Uruguay and save the Blanco regime. Yet this position begs the question as to what Brazilian intentions along the Mato Grosso frontier really were.

The quantity of arms and munitions the Paraguayans discovered at the various military posts—if not necessarily the quality—suggest more than a defensive posture. After all, from the Brazilian point of view, Paraguay was the natural extension of Mato Grosso, and any geographer could see that the republic stood poised like a dagger at the entrails of the empire. If the Paraguayans ever chose to move against Brazil in collusion with the other Platine states, then they could effectively blunt the westward expansionism that had started with the Portuguese and continued into the 1800s. This was, of course, a long-term policy consideration, and officials in Rio believed that, in the short run, they had time to prepare for any contingency. They stockpiled arms in Mato Grosso without a clear sense of how much this irritated the Asunción government. Had the Brazilians positioned enough men to shoulder the weapons they had stored along the frontier, then this perhaps would have justified Paraguayan fears.

As it was, Brazil did not have the men to defend the region, and Solano López knew it. Any explanation of Paraguayan actions in Mato Grosso relying primarily on a perceived need for a preemptive strike therefore misses the point. A token Paraguayan force along the Apa could have held the Brazilians back (and, given the geographical circumstances of the province, it would have been impossible for the imperial army to reinforce Mato Grosso sufficiently to make it a palpable threat to Solano López).

The desire to acquire materiel rather than strategic considerations offers a better explanation for the 1864–65 invasion of Mato Grosso. In fact, the capture of arms and munitions ultimately gave the expedition its raison d'être. Thompson insisted that Paraguay "drew from Mato Grosso almost all the stores it consumed during the war."[39] The quantities involved were impressive, for the Brazilians had been stockpiling weapons there for years.

Though no complete inventory of the materiel seized appears in the Paraguayan records, the fragmentary documentation is suggestive. At Nova Coimbra, the steamer *Salto Guairá* loaded ten bronze cannons of various calibers and several hundred cannonballs.[40] Every other Paraguayan ship carried similar numbers of armaments downriver. As for the spoils taken by the overland expedition, at the village of Miranda, Resquín's cavalry found "four cannon, 502 muskets, 67 carbines, 131 pistols, 468 swords, 1,090 lances, and 9,847 cannonballs of different calibers."[41] This in itself was sufficient to arm a full battalion, and apparently much more existed. Resquín himself was said to have observed that it looked as if "the Brazilian government had been expecting to defend the frontier simply with racks of arms."[42]

Still, it was easy to overstate the real value of these acquisitions. The fact was that not all of the captured cannons were serviceable. Many were ancient pieces, the refuse of the old colonial militia, which the governors-general had dumped into Mato Grosso to provide a false show of strength to the Indians. The harsh climate had left some cannons jammed with muck; the Brazilians made no attempt to provide regular maintenance but simply left their cannons in the rain. The foreign technicians at Asunción did, however, maintain shops capable of providing good repair for the guns, even including rifling for the iron pieces (though this was rarely done to bronze cannons). The Paraguayans were thus ready to incorporate even the most deteriorated Brazilian guns into their arsenal. They normally left behind the original, termite-ridden gun carriages and refitted the tubes with new carriages at Humaitá or elsewhere. A good many of these artillery pieces later saw service against their former owners.

Arms and munitions were not the only spoils taken by the Paraguayans. They confiscated hardware, money, foodstuffs, farm implements, carpets, bric-a-brac, and herds of cattle.[43] Colonel Thompson summed up the general picture by referring to a specific case: "The houses were all sacked by the Paraguayans, who found a great deal of booty in them. They laid waste the property of the Baron of Villa Maria, who only just got away in time himself. He managed to put a bottle of diamonds in his pocket [before he made good his escape]. He was the richest man in the province, and had a fine house and furniture, paintings, etc. He had also 80,000 head of cattle. All this was taken by the Paraguayans, together with his patent of nobility, under the Emperor's seal, which he had but lately bought. It was in a gilt frame, and afterwards adorned Mrs. Lynch's anteroom."[44]

The distance between Corumbá and Rio de Janeiro is greater than that between Paris and Belgrade, and yet the baron arrived in a record forty-seven days, bringing to the imperial capital its first word of the invasion. He was lucky. Many other Brazilian landowners and colonists in Mato Grosso, surprised by the enemy troops, passed into an uncomfortable and uncertain captivity, much like the passengers of the *Marques de Olinda*. Normally, the army sent such people down to Asunción, where state officials distributed them among the well-to-do families (though some ended up in the streets).[45] The Paraguayans set the male prisoners to work at heavy labor on various government projects, particularly at the iron foundry of Ybycuí, where overseers had them lashed for the slightest infraction. Even the foreign merchants of Corumbá, who had thought themselves safe from abuse by virtue of their nationality, saw their lives radically changed. As George Frederick Masterman noted: "All the foreigners they [the Paraguayan forces] could find were brought down as prisoners, after having been stripped of all they possessed: they were principally Germans, Italians, and Frenchmen. I saw many poor fellows working as laborers or begging in the streets, who, a few weeks before, had been wealthy merchants or landowners."[46] The poor treatment accorded prisoners in López's Paraguay was later reciprocated by the Brazilians, who treated their own Paraguayan prisoners as little better than slaves.

For better or worse, the southern reaches of Mato Grosso fell under Paraguayan control. Tiny garrisons were left in place at various spots in the occupied zone, while the bulk of Barrios's and Resquín's men withdrew toward Asunción, taking with them the remaining prisoners and all the goods and foodstuffs. They also carried away herds of cattle and enough arms and munitions to equip an army. Such supplies were much needed, for now that the war had begun in earnest, there were greater — and far bloodier — challenges ahead for the army of Solano López. Its enemies would no longer be so easily surprised.

# 9

# Neutrality Tested

The seizure of the *Marqués de Olinda* and the rapid conquest of Mato Grosso surprised and infuriated the Brazilians, few of whom had heard of Solano López before this time. Now, in turns, he was represented to them as a child, a uniformed orangutan, a rolling-eyed Asiatic ogre, and king over a mountain of skulls. That such a man should launch an attack against the empire, and even seize a piece of national territory, was unbearable. In a much-later parliamentary session, political opponents accused Prime Minister Zacharías de Góes e Vasconcellos of having failed to predict López's action; this was certainly true, he responded, but no one in either Brazil or the Río de la Plata had ever guessed that the Paraguayans would behave so rashly.[1]

What mattered now was how the empire should respond to the challenge of a new war. The Paraguayans clearly had to be taught a lesson, but that was perhaps easier said than done. On Saturday, 7 January 1865, Dom Pedro authorized the creation of a new corps, the *Voluntários da Pátria*, which consisted of those men aged eighteen to fifty who had not yet enrolled in the National Guard.[2] For legal reasons, the latter could not easily be deployed outside the Brazilian provinces. The emperor and his ministers, however, felt confident that the *voluntários* and the standing army could soon obliterate the Paraguayans and restore the honor of emperor and nation.

Volunteers fell into two groups. There were the aggressive ones, who were itching to get at the throat of the enemy, and the restless, who stepped forward to take on any job in order to escape the boredom of their home districts. From all over Brazil, men donned uniforms to show their zeal for this new conflict and their interest in the monetary awards announced in the decree of 7 January.

The first *voluntário* units to come together in São Paulo were an undisciplined and violent lot, though seemingly happy in their contemplation of new clothing. A good many were not really volunteers in any sense of the word. Like those individuals who had earlier been impressed as military "colonists" in Mato Grosso, they were simply seized on the streets by press gangs.[3]

Yet despite the poor quality of many recruits (and the questionable circumstances of their entry into the armed forces), the enthusiasm of the majority appeared genuine enough. The same was true for civilians, who offered contributions of money, slaves, and foodstuffs for the war effort.

This openhanded reaction stood in sharp contrast to the indifference displayed forty years earlier at the time of the Cisplatine War. It suggests that some sort of national feeling had sunk roots in Brazil. Even so, the show of patriotism was not entirely convincing, for a majority of contributors were members of the small (but growing) middle class. Such individuals had an interest in establishing their legitimacy as coequal citizens in an elite-oriented nation. As such, they were doing what they imagined the Germans or French would do in like circumstances. A good many seem to have had some association with the state (or else found it useful to mouth the government's anti-Paraguayan litanies). The director of a private *gymnasium* in Bahia, for instance, reserved five places in his school for twelve-year-old boys, sons of officers sent to the front. His offer could be interpreted either as nationalism or as advertising.[4]

This kind of posing, of course, was common in many countries during the nineteenth century. And it should be stressed that some contributors in Brazil had a more humble background with less to gain by their generosity. One Bahian seamstress, for example, offered to sew one hundred shirts for the use of the army and navy at no charge.[5] Perhaps she assumed that the war would last only a short time and engender few casualties. If she really believed this, then she was far from alone, for no one in Brazil guessed how long and traumatic a fight this war would become.

If the attack on Mato Grosso angered the Brazilian public and government, it also displeased the Uruguayan Blancos, who would have preferred to see the Paraguayan army on the march to Montevideo. From their point of view, Solano López had forgotten his primary objective in favor of a questionable adventure. The Blancos now had to contend with both Flores and a full-scale Brazilian invasion force without any outside help at all.

Solano López recognized the predicament faced by his allies and, in a vague sense, sincerely wished to help them. Paraguay came first, however, and any thought of timely assistance had to be subordinated to the national interest as he defined it. The occupation of Mato Grosso was a first step in pursuit of this interest; exploiting the anti-Brazilian sympathies in Argentina's Litoral provinces, and especially gaining the support of Justo José de Urquiza, was another. As Solano López viewed it, Paraguayan success in any venture in the Lower Plata depended on the Entrerriano's cooperation. Additionally, it required a neutral Argentina that would show sympathy for Paraguay at the right moment.

In contrast to the Uruguayan Blancos, who had spared no effort to convince the Asunción government to adopt their viewpoint, the Paraguayans made no systematic attempt to sway Argentine opinion. They had agents in Corrientes, Paraná, Buenos Aires, and Montevideo who periodically supplied pro-López copy to the newspapers, but their efforts rarely went beyond this. Yet Solano López thought that time was on his side. As the Brazilian intervention in Uruguay unfolded, he believed that the Argentines would disown Pres. Bartolomé Mitre's collaboration with the empire. This would soon bring an openly pro-Paraguayan position. However much Urquiza might feign reluctance, under such circumstances he would inevitably seize the opportunity to wrest power from Mitre.[6] The Brazilians, faced with a united front of Paraguayans,

Entrerrianos, and certain other Argentines and Uruguayans, would soon withdraw. In this manner Solano López would restore the proper balance of power in the Plata, establishing himself and his country in a position of unimpeachable influence.

*Playing the Entrerriano Card*

Urquiza was the key. Since August 1863, Solano López had tried to persuade the *caudillo* to abandon his mistaken policy of neutrality in the Uruguayan civil war.[7] Urquiza's own son Waldino and many other local figures had also urged him in that direction. The events of 1864 did nothing to relieve this pressure. The threat of Brazilian intervention had not just set Entrerriano sabers rattling but waving wildly through the air. *El Litoral*, the provincial scandal sheet edited by Evaristo Carriego, launched a virulent attack on Buenos Aires and nervously predicted the disintegration of the Argentine Republic should Mitre continue his dalliance with the emperor.[8] In response, the *porteño* press came close to calling Urquiza a traitor and even treated his alliance with Paraguay as an established fact: "General Urquiza is in close touch with López. It is he who is manipulating López. We are told on the authority of a witness from [Urquiza's palace at] San José that there is an alliance between these two kindred spirits and that López is providing Urquiza with money."[9]

Actually, Urquiza had yet to decide on any agreement with the Paraguayans. For one thing, he doubted whether the Blancos were worth defending. He knew Venancio Flores personally and, though they were hardly close friends, wished to avoid any direct confrontation with him and his Colorado stalwarts. In addition, Urquiza had attempted an unofficial mediation between the warring factions of the Banda Oriental in September 1864 and had been greatly irritated at the intransigence of the Blancos.[10]

The Entrerriano also questioned Solano López's trustworthiness as an ally. The Paraguayan president might possess an impressive war chest, but his army remained untested and he himself was hardly the brilliant commander he pretended to be. Urquiza had come close to facing the Paraguayans once before, in 1845, and on that occasion the nineteen-year-old Solano López had fled the field before opening a single engagement, leaving his Unitario allies — or what remained of them — to an uncertain fate in Corrientes.

More significantly, it was by no means clear that the two men shared the same political vision for the future of the Plata. While Urquiza believed in a strong Argentina composed of coequal provinces, Solano López desired weak neighbors over whom he could exercise some authority (much like Bismarck's attitude toward the Bavarians during the period of the North German Confederation). The two leaders' common interest vis-à-vis the Brazilians was a thing of expedience. Moreover, the Entrerriano felt uneasy about starting a war that he had lost once before for the sake of a short-term gain.

It was also likely that Urquiza had grown tired of fighting big battles. Since Pavón, events had cast him as a King Lear, yet he saw no reason to willingly accept that role. He might still retain his prestigious place in Platine affairs and grow wealthier by selling cattle to all buyers — but only if he eschewed the dangerous propositions of Solano López. Far better to stay neutral, provide Paraguay with indirect support, and reap the benefits from the resulting confusion.

Toward Mitre and the national government generally, Urquiza professed an unflinching loyalty. He even went so far as to provide the *porteño* leader with certain correspondence he had received from the Asunción government that depicted Paraguay in an aggressive light (while leaving his own Entre Ríos free of blame).

Mitre in turn found it convenient to express his confidence in Urquiza. On 3 November 1864 he wrote from Buenos Aires to stress that he scoffed at the malicious tales journalists were circulating about him. After reasserting his own neutrality in the Uruguayan crisis, he appealed to the Entrerriano to avoid complications by restraining the provincial hotheads who had called for action: "it is essential that all good Argentines and all men of influence . . . unite their efforts with those of the national government. . . . [W]e should be Argentines above all, pursuing a truly Argentine policy that will not be subordinated to foreign passions and interests, nor allowed to deviate due to harangues in the street that have not the slightest responsibility."[11]

Mitre's call for national unity might have been genuine, but he was less than candid with Urquiza. He made no mention of Foreign Minister Rufino de Elizalde's latest negotiations with the empire, pointedly avoiding any reference to the protocol just concluded with Rio. This agreement (as mentioned earlier) came close to bringing the two countries into formal alliance.

Urquiza's mouthpiece, *El Uruguay*, which had thus far avoided the radical tone adopted by Carriego and other opponents of Buenos Aires, denounced Mitre's links with Venancio Flores and the Brazilians. It also offered a succinct defense of Urquiza's actions: "If General Urquiza does not raise the standard of revolt, it is not because he is too old or too interested in his private fortune as his critics say. This is signal ingratitude to one to whose self-effacement the country owes its liberty and its institutions. No, if General Urquiza does not raise the standard of revolt it is because of his faith in and respect for those same institutions."[12]

Having declared his true feelings in this manner, the Entrerriano *caudillo* then wrote a solicitous letter to Mitre indicating his commitment to moderation even at this late hour: "peace [in Uruguay] should be made under the same program as at Caseros: 'neither conquerors nor vanquished.' [But] since all efforts made to end the civil war have been frustrated, ... there is truly no other way nor is there any other policy possible [for the country] whose intervention has been frustrated than to let events take their course, preserving neutrality and trying, as Your Excellency says, to avoid involving the Republic in this war, which like all civil strife is hateful and without honor."[13]

Solano López and his advisors refused to believe that this stance was anything more than a political minuet. If they failed to arrange an alliance with Urquiza, they knew that they could at least secure free passage across the Misiones to attack the Brazilians. Urquiza, they felt, wanted the same thing and was simply feigning reluctance. They therefore redoubled their diplomatic efforts in October 1864 and sent a junior official, José Caminos, on an exhaustive mission from San José to

Buenos Aires, from Montevideo to Paraná, and then to Asunción. Caminos carried a memorandum from the Paraguayan president that urged Urquiza to issue a *pronunciamento* calling for the secession of the Litoral provinces and their adherence to an anti-Brazilian alliance with Paraguay. The Paraguayans had floated this idea a year earlier, and at that time Urquiza showed some interest. Now, however, he sent only a tepid reply that promised nothing.[14] Upon Caminos's return to Paraguay, Foreign Minister José Berges deemed it unwise for him to proceed on to Cerro León to report to Solano López, who by this time had heard enough about negotiations with Urquiza.[15]

*Paysandú*

Things had not gone well for Anastasio de la Cruz Aguirre's Uruguayan forces since the intervention began. The imperial army, in the form of two extended columns of gaúcho cavalry, had crossed the border at the beginning of December. These were roughhewn men, inured to hard riding and the steamy weather that always accompanied year's end in this part of South America. The broad grasslands through which they passed were exactly like those of their own country—better fitted for range cattle, and for millions of gnats and fireflies, than for large human settlements. The Brazilians encountered few enemies or Uruguayans of any kind at first, moving slowly and deliberately southward, timing their advance to coincide with a naval expedition sent up the Uruguay River. The objective of both forces was Paysandú, a major trading center on the river and the site chosen by the Blancos to make a stand.

Paysandú was strategically important to President Aguirre and the Blanco cause. If Solano López or any other allies were to affect a rescue, they would almost certainly have to enter Uruguay from the west at that point. In addition, the stretch of land directly opposite the town on the Argentine side of the river belonged to General Urquiza, who would never tolerate Brazilian troops so close to his territory. The Blancos had to keep this door open at all costs.

The imperial government also understood the value of Paysandú and wanted it in Brazilian hands as soon as possible. Venancio Flores had already concentrated his attacks in that area since January. On 20 October he exchanged notes with the Brazilian vice admiral, the baron of Tamandaré, whose squadron subsequently steamed up the Uruguay River. Blanco control over the north withered, leaving the Montevideo regime in possession only of Paysandú and the smaller port of Salto, just to the north. On 28 November, Salto fell to Flores, leaving Paysandú isolated.[16] Immediately thereafter, the Brazilians and Colorados began a siege of the latter community.

The month-long stand at Paysandú has attained heroic proportions in Uruguay, not for its duration (Montevideo, after all, had endured a nine-year siege in the 1840s and early 1850s) but for its tragic outcome, which greatly appealed to popular notions of loyalty and self-sacrifice. At first, the defenders of Paysandú gave little thought to dying for a cause. They knew that the Blanco stronghold presented a major challenge to its enemies in spite of its isolation. Its garrison counted 1,120 men, all of them veterans in the fight against Flores. Their commanding officer, Col. Leandro Gómez, was a fifty-three-year-old Blanco partisan with a short, unkempt beard and a reputation for irascibility and hardheadedness.

On 3 December, Flores and the Brazilians found out precisely how stubborn Gómez was when they demanded his surrender and were rebuffed with great insolence. The colonel reportedly taunted Tamandaré, challenging him to bombard Paysandú as he saw fit. No matter what the Brazilians threw at the town, its garrison would never surrender. That same evening Gómez appeared before his troops on horseback with a Blanco sash across his tunic and a national flag in hand. "Will you swear," he rasped melodramatically, "to defend this *plaza* to the death?" Though his men thought him an insufferable martinet, they admired the grandiloquence and timing of Gómez's gesture and thundered their affirmation to a man.[17]

Such esprit de corps was easy to maintain at first, but as the days went by, individual doubts among the men gave way to a general feeling of regret and anxiety. The defenders did their best, however, to hide their fears from Gómez, who treated any sign of defeatism with a swift and cruel hand. The colonel was an impatient man, all the more so since he had contracted a severe chest cold and slept little as a result. His loud coughing, which could be heard from the enemy lines, had a frustrated and mournful tone, like that of a dog who could not escape his pursuers.[18]

The Brazilians carefully bided their time. They fired intermittent shells into Paysandú but left most of the aggressive penetrations to the Colorados. Admiral Tamandaré, a white-haired argumentative old man who used a block of wood for a pillow at night, saw no need to take chances. He positioned his three gunboats on the opposite bank of the Uruguay and waited. He avoided any moves that might unduly irritate Urquiza and contented himself with having prevented the one Blanco steamer, the venerable *Villa del Salto*, from leaving port.

Tamandaré also sent four hundred imperial marines to join Flores's six hundred troops for the attack. On 6 December a small column of these marines marched into the outlying district of Paysandú with banners flying and music playing. A fusillade fired by three hundred determined Blancos drove them back. Later Gómez took fifteen small cannon from the *Villa del Salto* and moved them to the forward lines to prevent a recurrence of an attack from that quarter.[19]

Such forays by the enemy failed to impress the colonel, who remained as obstinate and provocative as ever.[20] During a lull in the fighting, he invited a group of foreign naval officers to dine with him in the besieged area around the central plaza. On entering the hall, the guests discovered that a captured Brazilian flag had replaced the rug that normally adorned the room. A British officer saved the situation by lifting the flag with studied nonchalance and placing it on a chair before sitting down to eat.[21]

The Brazilian columns finally reached the outskirts of Paysandú in the last week of December. Their arrival brought the total number of men participating in the siege to nearly nine thousand. After giving Gómez a final opportunity to surrender — which he predictably declined — this combined force opened a tremendous bombardment of the Blanco positions. It lasted fifty-two hours, essentially without interruption. The Brazilians ultimately poured more than four thousand rounds into the port.[22]

Although the defenders showed much bravery, the outcome of this constant shelling was never in doubt. Despite Gómez's ferocity, the Blancos were worn thin, dispirited, and ready to call an end to their resistance. They had lost four hundred men dead and wounded and had been reduced to one musket for every two men. The supply of shot for their few remaining cannons was exhausted. And the town of Paysandú had been blasted beyond recognition, with some neighborhoods little more than rubble.

On New Year's Eve, Gómez sent a note to Flores to ask for a temporary suspension of hostilities in order to bury his dead men, whose bodies littered the ground in every direction. Flores refused. Still defiant even after all these losses, Gómez finally yielded to the pleas of his subordinates. He laid down his arms at 8:30 in the morning on 2 January 1865.[23]

The Brazilian officers to whom he capitulated counted among their number some talented and ambitious men, all of whom in short order would face Solano López. As individuals, they had reason to consider themselves honorable gentlemen. In victory, though, they behaved badly. When Gómez surrendered, he believed that the empire would provide protection for his subordinates. The Brazilians, however, turned him and four of his officers over to Gregorio "Goyo" Suárez, a colonel of Flores's army, who conducted the group to the patio of a small house near the central plaza. Suárez began shooting the prisoners, starting with Gómez himself, and bodies soon covered the patio. Additional bloodshed was avoided at the last moment when an Argentine officer, José Murature, interposed himself until higher authorities reestablished order.[24]

The fall of Paysandú brought rejoicing in the Colorado camp. There was much drinking and much talk of a sweet revenge for Quinteros; the singing, laughing, and shouts of jubilation could be heard until cockcrow. But the execution of Gómez and his officers—who had become symbols of heroic resistance in the popular mind—ultimately proved scandalous. The Brazilians offered an excuse reminiscent of Pontius Pilate when they claimed that Gómez had asked to be turned over to the Colorados, preferring to be a prisoner of his own countrymen rather than of a foreign power. He therefore had to take responsibility for his own death. Perhaps this version of events gave some comfort to officials in the Brazilian Foreign Ministry, but it failed to convince others.[25] Col. George Thompson, normally a dispassionate writer, observed acidly that the "taking of Paysandú, with the atrocities committed there, form a revolting page in the history of Brazil."[26]

Even those who had nothing to fear from the Brazilian intervention felt outraged by what had happened. Many wondered in print who would next come under the emperor's knife. Public figures expressed indignation as far away as Peru, Chile, and Bolivia, where Solano López was acclaimed as a champion against monarchist Brazil.[27] The French intervention in Mexico and Spain's unfortunate seizure of Peru's Chincha Islands had already caused many in the continent to view monarchism as a dangerous, resurgent force that had to be stopped. Certainly that feeling was evident in Argentina's Litoral provinces, where opposition newspapers that had previously castigated the Brazilians as monarchist interlopers now depicted them as outright butchers.

Such antipathies were troubling to both Mitre and Urquiza. Henceforth, it would be more difficult for the national government to maintain a façade of neutrality. Mitre still looked upon the Colorados as his protégés, but their actions and those of their Brazilian allies made it difficult for him to maintain his influence in the Litoral.

For Urquiza, the situation was even worse. Entre Ríos stood on the verge of open rebellion, and even his own son was clamoring for Brazilian blood. Urquiza's inaction up to that point had been widely seen as contributing to the Blanco's predicament. The killings at Paysandú, it was said, proved that he had lost the confidence that had sustained him on so many other battlefields.

Actually, Urquiza realized that violent action on his part would bring an open break with Buenos Aires. This he wished to avoid at all costs. As it was, he found it nearly impossible to control the wrath of his own Entrerriano supporters, and he had to use all of his threats and diplomatic skills to keep the other *provincianos* in line. He nonetheless seethed with contempt for the Brazilians, who seemed to be gloating at him from across the river.

The one obvious course open to Urquiza was to make common cause with Solano López. Throughout the siege, the Asunción government had continued to seek his support in transiting the Misiones. On one occasion, the Paraguayans even tried to interest him in an earlier Blanco plan to ally Uruguay, Paraguay, and Entre Ríos.[28]

Urquiza wanted no new alliances. He maintained his posture of fealty to the national government in part because he felt he had no other long-term option and also because his sense of personal honor prevented any room for maneuver. Once before he had tried to forge an Argentine policy that left out Buenos Aires, and that effort had resulted in civil war. He refused to repeat that mistake.

Even so, Urquiza was unwilling to surrender all strategic advantage to the empire. At the end of December, he notified Mitre that while he would tolerate neither Paraguayans nor Brazilians in Entre Ríos and Corrientes, he had no objection if either party crossed "the uninhabited territories" of the Misiones. Since Brazil was preoccupied with the Banda Oriental and had no clear interest in the Misiones, Urquiza's note implicitly benefited only Solano López.[29] Not surprisingly, Mitre rejected the idea. The established policy, he argued, extended to the Misiones as well as the rest of the Litoral, and any departure from it would constitute a "neutrality of the weak."[30] By the time he penned his response to Urquiza, however, Gómez and his men had been dead for eight days.

*The Blanco Collapse*

The fall of Paysandú presented a dilemma for Paraguay. Though it provided impetus for a Paraguayan intervention, such action would now only succor a much weakened Blanco ally; Solano López was frankly unsure whether or not he wanted to do this. However much the political schemes of Urquiza, Mitre, or the Blancos might depend upon support from his army, the Paraguayan president was adamant that he alone would time its deployment. Had Solano López advanced decisively through the Misiones and down the Uruguay in January 1865, he would have found strong support from Ricardo López Jordan and other Entrerrianos who would have willingly defied both president and governor alike. A resuscitation of the Blanco cause was not unthinkable. Instead, Solano López waited and lost a splendid opportunity.

On 16 January 1865 the Asunción government ordered a force of ten thousand men — comprising recently assembled infantry, cavalry, and artillery units — to cross the Alto Paraná and establish a base camp in the Misiones. For this purpose, they selected a spot at the edge of a swollen creek called the Pindapoi.[31] Nearly all of these recruits had seen the Alto Paraná, but very few knew anything about what lay beyond it. After crossing the river, they moved eastward along a trail leading out of the old Trinchera de los Paraguayos. Soon they passed San Ignacio Miní and what was left of the other Jesuit missions, now engulfed in weeds, bearing lifeless testimony to human ambition and to failure.

Not far from the ruins of San Carlos they finally reached the Pindapoi. In short order, the soldiers covered the grassy meadows above the creek with pitched tents, lean-tos, and semicircles of carts. Here they trained and retrained under a suffocating sun. They knew that discipline demanded of them a skill so perfectly honed that later, when in mortal danger, they would do things mechanically, as part of a unit. They therefore took seriously the close order drill that Solano López had adopted from French military manuals and practiced it over and over again. Some became ill with heatstroke as a result.[32] But everyone not in hospital worked hard, with cavalrymen learning to handle the lance and infantrymen, the musket.[33]

Most of these men came from isolated villages in southern Paraguay such as Jesús, Yuty, and San Juan Bautista. Instead of the scarlet tunic seen among the troops sent to Mato Grosso, the majority wore the long, loose shirt and the soft cotton pantaloons of the Paraguayan peasant. They had no idea why they were there and soon felt homesick and uneasy despite the resemblance of the landscape to that of their own country. They knew that the supreme government had declared war on Brazil, but surely there were no *macacos* in the Misiones. Unlike recruits in

Neutrality Tested 229

other armies, however, they grumbled little, for such behavior implied disrespect toward a higher authority that never hesitated to use the whip. Their commanding officer, gray-bearded Maj. Pedro Duarte, had been placed over them by that same authority; he would eventually tell them all they needed to know. Though in fact he possessed little information, Duarte put on a great show of building a modern army that at short notice could be dispatched anywhere, even to Montevideo. He ignored the notes that anxious Correntino officials wrote to remind him that his camp was in Argentine territory (strictly speaking, it was not, for the national government had never ratified the 1852 border agreement with Paraguay).[34]

Meanwhile, Solano López had grown impatient. With Paysandú in Brazilian hands and with the Colorados closing in on Montevideo at the beginning of 1865, he needed to push south as fast as possible to save the Blanco regime. Yet if he could not save it, then how should he proceed?

If Berges and the other men around López had not been afraid to speak plainly, they might have told him that Argentine neutrality actually worked in his favor. Mitre would almost certainly hesitate to allow Tamandaré's fleet to pass through Argentina in order to save the Brazilians in Mato Grosso. An overland expedition to relieve that province was at that point too expensive to contemplate. If Montevideo could not be relieved, the Paraguayans might at least negotiate from a strong position that left their seizure of Corumbá a fait accompli. The empire would have little choice but to accept this new reality or be lost in a maze of diplomatic head-knocking with an uncooperative Buenos Aires. The Paraguayans could effectively win their territorial dispute with Brazil without further expense.

Solano López, however, apparently never considered this. All his natural inclinations, reinforced by a history of bad relations with his neighbors, told him to strike hard and swiftly. By bringing a sizable force to the Pindapoi, he had moved a knight into the attack position on the chessboard. He meant this as a provocation, yet another unmistakable warning to those who still ignored his country's aspirations. And still the Argentine government paid no heed. Ominously, a comet with a huge, fiery tail had just become visible in the southwestern sky of Paraguay at night.[35] This traditional omen of calamitous times could also be plainly seen in Buenos Aires.

Even before the fall of Paysandú, the Brazilians had played a shrewd diplomatic game of their own, and Argentines of all political persuasions had their attention drawn to the Banda Oriental, not to the Misiones. Silva Paranhos had gone to Buenos Aires in early December to complete José Saraiva's task of obtaining an open alliance with Mitre. Knowing full well the political cost of such an agreement (and the effect it would have on Urquiza), the Argentine president refused again to deviate from his policy of neutrality. The councilor returned to Rio de Janeiro empty-handed but remained enthusiastic. As late as 26 December, he told British Minister Thornton that he was still negotiating with Mitre "for an active alliance against the Montevidean Government in which he believed he should succeed, and that when the coditions would be made public, the position of Brazil would be greatly improved." In his official report to the foreign secretary, however, Thornton dismissed Paranhos's optimism as little more than wishful thinking.[36]

The Brazilians were just as anxious to win Flores to a formal alliance that would supersede the nebulous agreements reached earlier with Tamandaré. They thought their task would be relatively easy but were surprised when the Colorado chieftain held back. Many years later, the British historian Pelham Horton Box attributed his reluctance to the emotional stress of the moment: "though far advanced along the path of treason, [Flores] was suddenly and quite unexpectedly afflicted with an attack of conscience, perhaps nothing more than apprehension. He knew the hatred that was rising against Brazil in all the countries of the Río de la Plata, and he feared to be compromised."[37]

Paranhos had no patience with such dithering. If the longhaired Flores was not strictly a puppet of the empire, he also was not the independent patriot he had imagined himself in April 1863. He owed all his major victories to Brazilian arms, and even now he could not hope to take Montevideo without imperial troops. Between 28 and 31 January, Paranhos exchanged a series of notes with Flores that effectively quashed any misgivings the latter had about his Brazilian connection. Flores acceded to the empire's demands. This included a specific commitment to oppose Solano López: "[The Uruguayan government] will afford to the Empire all the cooperation in its power, regarding as a sacred task its alliance with Brazil in the war treacherously declared by the Paraguayan government, whose interference in the internal affairs of the Uruguayan Republic is a bold and unjustifiable pretension."[38]

In addition to this important concession, Flores also had to agree to recognize the losses Brazilian subjects had incurred during the decades-long fight against Rosas. He thereby committed his country simultaneously to making good on the exaggerated claims of the Riograndense ranchers and to the pursuit of a foreign war the little republic could ill afford.

Paranhos assumed that Mitre and Elizalde would see reason once the Blancos had submitted. Yet there were many dangers inherent in victory. Above all, Flores and the Brazilians needed to prevent a repetition of the Paysandú massacre; to fail to do so would galvanize opposition in the Lower Plata. The same result might also follow if any new regime in Montevideo appeared too much the tool of the empire. The challenge for Paranhos was to steer clear of these obstacles and definitively crush the Blancos while leaving the Argentines reassured about Brazil's good intentions. Improbable as this scenario seemed, he characteristically pushed ahead, confident that he would triumph in the end.

His first step was to urge restraint among his own people. In this regard, Paranhos did his utmost to rein in the impetuous Tamandaré, whose warships had steamed back into the Río de la Plata and were then preparing to fire upon Montevideo. The councilor pressured his Colorado allies in a similar manner, letting them know by subtle and not-so-subtle means that their earlier barbarism brought no benefit to the common cause. What he needed was their cooperation while he fought the real battles behind the scenes.

At this tense juncture, the aged but still indefatigable Andrés Lamas put forward an idea that he hoped would save his native city. He argued from Buenos Aires that outside mediation was still possible. He hastened to inform President Aguirre that Mitre might be called upon to offer his services.[39] If Mitre proved reluctant, then the ministers of Great Britain, France, Italy, or some other European power might help.[40]

The talk of last-minute mediation provoked excitement in the Uruguayan capital, where many viewed it as the last chance to preserve the Blanco government. The Blancos themselves were terribly divided, with some favoring compromise and others, still smarting from Paysandú, preferring to fight to the death; a few others favored some kind of negotiation as a delaying tactic so as to give the Paraguayans enough time to arrive on the scene. President Aguirre was as indecisive as ever and failed completely to bring the various factions together. On the streets of Montevideo, the Blancos were cursing each other far more than they cursed the name of the emperor.

Other than Lamas, the only strong proponents of a new mediation effort were the European representatives in Uruguay, especially the British and Italian ministers. Over the next month, the diplomats in Montevideo pressured Aguirre to accept the inevitable and request Mitre's help. They elicited from Tamandaré a promise to cancel the bombardment of the city if the president opened negotiations. Yet nothing seemed to move him.

The European diplomats failed to realize that the composition of the Montevideo government had shifted in favor of the most fanatical Blancos. Antonio de las Carreras, who only recently had returned from his failed mission to Asunción, had succeeded the moderate Juan José de Herrera in September as part of this change. Carreras came into office convinced that only the diehard faction could save Montevideo. Aguirre hesitated to act without the full support of the cabinet. Yet despite the mounting danger of Montevideo's position, his ministers still counseled against any mediation. Perhaps this was simple stubbornness or foolish thinking, or maybe it reflected a xenophobia learned after so many bad experiences with foreigners during the Rosas era.[41]

Whatever the cause, Aguirre refused to deviate from his established

*Neutrality Tested* 233

policy, an attitude that the frustrated diplomats viewed as ostrichlike in its self-deception. On 21 January, the British chargé, W. G. Lettsom, flew into a most undiplomatic rage at the president, his patience exhausted by the Blanco leader's obstinacy. Lettsom asked Aguirre point-blank if he were planning to torch the city rather than see it fall to his enemies. The president assured him that such was not the case, but left the Englishman unsatisfied as to every other particular. One day later, Aguirre formally declined the proposal of the diplomatic corps.

Lamas, who was even more exasperated than his European counterparts, wrote a final appeal to the president on 27 January that in its bitterness captured the essence of the problem:

> Your party by spontaneously opening the doors of Government House to the Colorado Party so that all Uruguayans together might close our territory to the foreigner would have saved itself gloriously and spared our unhappy country that horrible nameless spectacle that took place at Paysandú and that Your Excellency is about to have repeated in Montevideo. Always the party above the country! As Your Excellency does, so do all the rest. I despair, sir, of the safety of our country. They are murdering her and dishonoring our name in a dispute about official posts, for in the end that is all it comes to. God knows, I do not want to do an injustice to Your Excellency, or to anyone, but in good earnest I believe that Your Excellency is sacrificing to your party the city of Montevideo. Am I mistaken? It is easy for Your Excellency to prove it.[42]

Aguirre had no other answer for Lamas and the Europeans but to again question the impartiality of Mitre and the goodwill of the empire.

His response was for once decisive, but it played directly into the hands of Paranhos, for it provided the councilor with the excuse he needed to turn aside Argentine mediation.[43] Now nothing could keep the empire from destroying the Blancos and converting Uruguay into an ally in its war against Solano López.

On 2 February, Admiral Tamandaré declared a strict blockade of the

Uruguayan capital as a prelude to a general bombardment. Paranhos, sensing that victory could be attained without further violence, convinced the admiral to grant six-days notice to enable merchant vessels to clear the port. He then arranged to extend the grace period until mid-February, when, as the councilor well knew, the Uruguayan Congress was scheduled to name a new president to replace Aguirre.

Paranhos lost no time. The British and French had already sent warships to evacuate their countrymen to Buenos Aires. The general exodus of foreigners that followed caused those who remained in Montevideo to feel terror for the first time. All agreed that a full-scale assault against the city could no longer be postponed. Paranhos knew better; it suited him to let the volatile Tamandaré rant and threaten and jab at the shoreline with his sword. He was aware that behind the scenes, the Blanco moderates were gaining the upper hand. The councilor believed that a major change in the Blanco leadership would shortly take place, either through the actions of the Uruguayan Congress or through a coup d'état. His agents in the city told him as much, and so he was prepared to wait.

On 15 February 1865 Aguirre's term of office expired, its last hours clouded by the same "vacillation and paralysis of will" that had characterized his entire administration. The Senate had been scheduled to meet the day before to confirm the election of the moderate Tomás Villalba as successor to Aguirre, but partisans of Carreras had drawn their *facones* on certain senators to prevent their attending the meeting. Without a quorum, the Senate could not conduct business and the Blanco extremists might continue their inglorious reign.

Carreras, however, failed to consider the garrison commanders who would have to face Tamandaré's guns without the benefit of popular support. Meeting hastily on the night of 14 January, these officers swore to defend any president the Senate might elect—moderate or otherwise. They sent armed soldiers to protect the individual senators, and the extremists abandoned their attempt to disrupt congressional deliberations. Villalba assumed executive power on 15 February. He at once called upon the diplomatic corps for recognition and aid. The European representatives quickly arranged for a mixed detachment of British, French, Italian, and Spanish marines to land at Montevideo, where their presence dissuaded the remaining extremists from any further thoughts of a coup.

The councilor's perseverance had won the day for the empire. He could easily have dictated the terms of the resulting peace accord, but Paranhos cleverly left the task to Villalba and Flores so as to make the agreement appear to be written by and for Uruguayans. The settlement fooled no one, least of all the Blancos, who soon fled into the interior and to Entre Ríos. Their departure meant the beginning of a virtual dictatorship for Venancio Flores, who, having already promised his full cooperation against Paraguay, could be counted among Brazil's allies in whatever happened next.

The Riograndense ranchers, in whose name the Brazilians had launched their invasion of Uruguay, felt satisfied at last. Flores gave many of their number commissions in his army and agreed to look after their business interests.[44] Gen. Antonio Netto and his supporters accepted this patronage at face value. Their many claims against Uruguay, which hitherto had filled the editorial pages of various Carioca and Paulista newspapers, seemed to disappear overnight.

Ironically, the only unsatisfied party on the Brazilian side was Tamandaré. The Blanco collapse had left the admiral with no outlet for his truculence, and he was in no mood for celebrating. He was a recognized favorite of the emperor and felt he deserved better. Paranhos offered to assuage his hurt feelings by arranging for the peace agreement to be signed on 20 February, the anniversary of Brazil's defeat at Ituzaingó in 1827.[45] Tamandaré held his temper in check, and the agreement was signed on schedule at Villa de la Unión.

Metternich once described the diplomat's task as the art of seeming a dupe without actually being one, and in this sense Councilor Paranhos had good reason to feel pleased with himself. At minimal cost he had eliminated the Uruguayan threat and had transformed the country into a friendly base for future operations against Paraguay. His actions made it possible to satisfy the Riograndense ranchers and at the same time demonstrate how shrewd diplomacy could win the day. Brazilian objectives in the Plata would henceforth be realized through his sort of negotiation, not through the force of arms. Now the councilor was free to apply the capstone to his Platine strategy by enlisting Mitre in the struggle against Solano López.

Paranhos stood at the summit of his influence. It turned out, however, that the ground beneath him was less than rock-solid. Though a Conservative, Paranhos had received his appointment as minister to Montevideo from Francisco José Furtado, a progressive Liberal who had replaced Zacharias in mid-1864. Neither Furtado nor any of his appointees enjoyed steady support among the older Liberals, who had consistently rejected their calls for reform. When news of the agreement of 20 February reached Rio de Janeiro, many of these Liberals feared that the councilor's achievements would translate into political gains for the Conservatives. At the same time, Tamandaré's partisans complained loudly in the elegant coffeehouses of the Rua Ouvidor (and in the newspaper offices) that Paranhos had sold out the empire. He had dishonored his Imperial Majesty's armed forces by talking when events called for action.

The councilor might have weathered this storm, but at this juncture, Liberal hardliners met privately with Furtado to demand the ouster of Conservatives from positions of confidence in his government. The prime minister had recently decided to name the marquis of Caxias, another longtime stalwart of the Conservative Party, to head the army against Paraguay. Caxias, who had vanquished the Farrapos twenty years earlier, was still Brazil's most famous soldier and widely seen as an indispensable figure in any military campaign. Furtado knew that he could not win on the Caxias nomination and also retain Paranhos at the Itamaraty Palace. With some hesitation, he instructed the councilor to step down. Now no longer the foreign minister, Paranhos had to watch from a distance while others reaped the benefits of the peace he had forged.

*Argentine Neutrality Challenged*

The Blanco capitulation at Montevideo was Mitre's cue for a new approach to the Brazil-Paraguay conflict. The Argentine president had long been accustomed to seeing his country at the center stage of Platine politics, but recent events in the Banda Oriental had left him nonplused. His assistance to Flores and his many overtures to the empire might reap some rewards for Buenos Aires now that the Blanco forces had disintegrated. Mitre was too shrewd a politician, however, to openly assent to Uruguay's becoming a satellite of Rio de Janeiro. Like Urquiza, he distrusted having Brazilian troops so close at hand, and however much he might respect Paranhos and other officials of the imperial government, he had no desire to see them dictating terms in a sphere that traditionally had been his.

Mitre had always left open alternative lines of policy in order to take credit for whichever one succeeded. Thus, as Paranhos's Uruguay policy began to bear fruit, Mitre tried to distance himself from the empire. His "neutrality," which had been notoriously indulgent toward Flores, now became progressively stricter.

Mitre faced a difficult domestic situation. His cabinet ministers had all been overtly pro-Colorado, and his own favorable inclinations toward Brazil were widely known. Many in Buenos Aires had celebrated the fall of Montevideo and urged the president to now move against the Paraguayans. Yet within Argentina as a whole, much sympathy still existed for the now-defunct Blanco government. Brazilian victories in the Banda Oriental had caused these feelings to refocus on Solano López, whose army still awaited its orders in the Misiones. Brazilian agents had been trying to counter this development by financing an anti-López propaganda campaign in the *porteño* press.[46] Paraguayan émigrés aided these efforts by issuing polemical tracts and holding public meetings where they called for the ouster of the López family.[47] Yet there were many Argentine public figures, not the least of whom was the brilliant jurist Juan Bautista Alberdi, who felt that Mitre's flirtation with Brazil was dangerously wrongheaded, and that the national government would be wise to lean toward Paraguay. Mitre had no intention of doing so, but he did want to exercise the utmost caution at that moment in dealing with other Argentines; Alberdi's sharp criticisms, after all, were a vivid reminder that not all Argentine citizens shared Mitre's goals.

Every observer of Platine affairs was aware that one chapter had ended and another was about to begin. The war between Paraguay and Brazil could ensue in a small way or a great way, all depending on the role of Argentina. That country's continued neutrality made a Brazilian invasion of Paraguay well-nigh impossible; but it also put a limit on any ambitions that Solano López might entertain in the region. This fact put great pressure on Mitre, who above all craved information on what his neighbors would do next.

In Asunción, Solano López also craved new information. Unlike Mitre, who always hid his worries, the Paraguayan president appeared nervous and out of sorts. The news from Mato Grosso had been good, and it had whetted his appetite for further action. The Brazilians, however, were far away, and it violated all of his aggressive instincts that he could not get at them.

Visiting the Paraguayan capital at the beginning of 1865 was Anacarsis Lanús, an Argentine arms merchant of considerable means. He had come to Asunción to obtain trade concessions for his firm from the Paraguayan government. Solano López, with whom he had many conversations, saw in Lanús a possible conduit to Mitre; he therefore talked freely with him about Paraguayan-Argentine relations and the war with Brazil. As expected, Lanús reported their discussions to Mitre, who encouraged the merchant in his role of intermediary. Mitre's message to López, addressed in an 11 January letter to Lanús, reiterated in the clearest possible terms Argentina's commitment to neutrality.[48] To show his good will, Mitre had just allowed an important shipment of arms to pass unmolested to Paraguay. This act alone might have failed to reassure the ever-suspicious Solano López, but Lanús's unflagging optimism did suggest that Mitre would keep his word.

The Paraguayan president had every intention, it now seemed, of keeping his own commitment to the Blancos, who at this point had yet to surrender Montevideo. Solano López's advice to the besieged forces was in this respect ironic but unambiguous: "Fall with the glory of Paysandú, and I shall soon reconquer your territory."[49]

On 14 January 1865 Solano López gave substance to his impatience in the form of an official note from Berges to Elizalde. It asked Argentine permission for Paraguayan forces to cross the province of Corrientes to attack Brazil in a supposedly expeditious and direct way: "The Government of this Republic hopes that the Argentine Government will consent without difficulty to this request and at once tenders the assurance that the whole transit will be effected without injury to the population and with all due consideration to the Argentine authorities."[50]

In a period characterized by many miscalculations, this letter stands out as a tragic blunder from which no good could come. No one doubted that the Argentines would protest a Paraguayan dash across the disputed Misiones, but this was all they were likely to do. Mitre could hardly be sentimental about the Misiones no matter how firmly he stood on the principle of national sovereignty. He would never abandon his policy of neutrality over such a minor infraction. As for Urquiza and the Entrerrianos, almost certainly they would welcome a Paraguayan intervention against Brazil as long as it proceeded southward down the left bank of the Uruguay and left Argentine territory alone. But a request for passage across Corrientes presented an entirely different situation. Corrientes was not disputed territory but an integral part of Argentina. Urquiza, who had tacitly supported the Paraguayans in his arguments with the national government, could never countenance their violating Argentine territory. Mitre, who had earlier resolved to keep the belligerent armies out of the Misiones, would refuse in even stronger terms any suggestion of a Paraguayan force crossing Corrientes.

Berges believed, however, that he possessed an answer to any Argentine objections. In his note to Elizalde, he cited as a precedent that both Buenos Aires and the Argentine Confederation had permitted a Brazilian naval expedition to ascend the Paraná in 1855 during the Fêcho-dos-Morros incident. As it turned out, low water had kept the Brazilian fleet from moving above Corrientes. The Paraguayans nonetheless noted the good treatment the Brazilians had received from the Argentine authorities and from merchants anxious to sell foodstuffs and other supplies. Surely, Berges argued, there could now be no complaint about any "act of just reciprocity." He delegated Luis Caminos to carry this message to Buenos Aires and to return as soon as possible with the Argentine response.

Berges was too seasoned a diplomat to feel hopeful about how Elizalde might react. Like Solano López, he had no faith in the neutrality espoused by Mitre. He regarded Duarte's force in the Misiones as the best guarantor of Argentine cooperation. War fever had swept Cerro León and Asunción, and Berges could not afford to make himself an exception. Whoever was not a friend could only be counted an enemy.

Caminos had meant to travel aboard the British ship *Ranger*, which had just arrived from Corumbá and was en route to Buenos Aires. American Minister Charles Ames Washburn had also booked passage aboard this vessel and was looking forward to some months on home leave. As it turned out, Caminos did not accompany him downriver, for the *Ranger*'s captain decided not to compromise the safety of his vessel by carrying the Paraguayan envoy.[51] It was not until early February that Caminos arrived in Buenos Aires. On the sixth of the month, he presented his note at the Foreign Ministry, retired to a nearby inn, and waited.

Caminos had come to the Argentine capital not simply as a courier but also as a special agent. He possessed authority to negotiate a loan of up to five hundred thousand pounds sterling to pay for the purchase of war supplies from Europe. His timing on this occasion, as on so many others, was decidedly poor. As Félix Egusquiza, the Paraguayan commercial agent in Buenos Aires, related in a letter to Candido Bareiro, his government's representative in London:

> The operation would have been easy to realize three or four months ago; but at this moment I consider it, if not impossible, extremely difficult, not only on account of the monetary crisis through which this market is passing, but because of the political events that are causing the fear of a general conflagration in the states of the Plata. As raising

Neutrality Tested 241

a loan here at this moment is almost impossible, it will not surprise me to see you shortly send authority to raise one in London or Frankfurt. . . . But I greatly fear the President is letting time pass and that when he wants to do so it will be too late, as is the case here, or, if not too late, it will have to be done under conditions more unfavorable than those we should obtain today. Our President has the defect of letting time pass and waiting for the last moment, and sometimes this is likely to have lamentable consequences.[52]

Again, as with the question of passage across Argentine territory, Solano López was late. On 12 February Caminos wrote to Bareiro to notify him that he had found backers for a ten-thousand-pound loan, but since this sum was obviously insufficient, he had decided to forego the offer.[53]

Elizalde, meanwhile, had responded to the Paraguayan request to cross Corrientes; although the note was dated 9 February, it seems to have been delivered into Caminos's hands several days later. As Berges anticipated, the Argentine foreign minister spurned the Paraguayan appeal. Elizalde observed that since Paraguay and Brazil had a long common border, the two countries should fight their war there and leave a neutral neighbor in peace. To accede to the Paraguayan demand, moreover, would turn Corrientes into a theater of combat, for what was granted to Paraguay would also have to be granted to the empire. As for the precedent cited by Berges, it was irrelevant: "[T]here is no reciprocity between the innocent passage by navigable waters to arrive at a pacific negotiation and the passage [by land] for an avowedly hostile object."[54]

In another note addressed on 9 February, Elizalde asked Berges to explain the concentration of Paraguayan forces in the Misiones.[55] He evidently intended to emphasize his government's rejection of the Paraguayan request for transit across Corrientes. In point of fact, neither he nor Mitre were especially worried about López's men in the Misiones. Over and over they reassured Correntino authorities that Paraguayan troop movements amounted to little more than posturing.[56] Almost to a man, officials in Buenos Aires thought that López would welcome their refusal to grant passage so that he could then advance it as an excuse for abandoning his Blanco allies.

Urquiza was the only influential figure who clearly saw the danger this correspondence foretold. The Paraguayans thought that they could still count on his support; Mitre was just as convinced that Urquiza would remain loyal to the national government as long as Buenos Aires pursued a genuinely neutral policy. The Entrerriano leader apparently inclined toward the latter course. He recognized, however, that any confrontation with Paraguay would throw the Argentine nation into an alliance with the Brazilian Empire, and this would spoil all that he had worked for. He therefore wished to do everything possible to defuse tensions between Argentina and Paraguay. "I believe," he wrote (with more hope than conviction), "that once this circumstance is averted, Paraguay will gain great advantages and place Brazil in a difficult position."[57]

Yet nothing was certain. Consequently, Urquiza sent his private secretary, the twenty-year old Julio Victorica, to persuade López that Argentine neutrality helped, rather than hindered, the Paraguayan cause. When the envoy arrived in Asunción on 16 February, however, he found the president in a somber frame of mind. Befitting his dark mood, Solano López had donned a heavy blue uniform and buttoned it to the neck in spite of the sultry, dog-day weather. "He had all the aspect of a French general," Victorica wrote, and "revealed in his behavior an irreproachable culture and correctness."[58] Yet not a hint of friendliness could be read in the president's face. Little wonder: he had just received Elizalde's two letters.

*Stepping toward the Chasm*
It sometimes seems quite impossible to stop the onset of a major war; it is like the course of the Paraná, the motion of which at times is scarcely seen, though it possesses a momentum quite irresistible. So it seemed to Solano López in early 1865. Accustomed since his childhood to abject condescension, he found it difficult to see in the Argentine rejection anything but rank hostility. He showed Victorica clippings from the *porteño* newspapers that represented his campaign against Brazil as the

antics of a buffoon in a feathered cockade. Protestations of neutrality at the official level, insults and taunts in the press: this was more than he cared to endure.

López felt particularly incensed at Elizalde's request for "explanations" of Paraguayan military movements in the Misiones. His country was at war, he told Victorica, why should he not move his troops to forward positions? More to the point, when would Urquiza drop his pretense of supporting Mitre and ally himself with the Paraguayans? Victorica later recalled that "On López telling me that General Urquiza could count on him in making himself President by overthrowing General Mitre, I made clear to him that such an offer could not be accepted by the Liberator of the Republic and the founder of her Constitution. 'Then,' said López raising his voice, 'if they provoke me I shall go ahead with everything.'"[59]

"Everything" in this context was an ominous word. As he departed downriver, Victorica reflected on this and on the many things left unsaid in his interview with the Paraguayan president. He knew that he would have nothing positive to report.

When Urquiza read the message from Solano López, his hopes vanished, for the letter accused him of having reneged on earlier promises of support on the transit question.[60] Decidedly pessimistic about the future, Urquiza offered — one last time — to mediate between Paraguay and Brazil. His offer, however, went nowhere.

For his part, Mitre clung to his earlier optimism about the Paraguayan threat. The Argentine president thought it manifestly clear that López would do nothing to threaten Paraguay's relation with Buenos Aires. Any action in Corrientes would result in an Argentine-Brazilian alliance that held nothing but disaster for the López regime. This being obvious, Mitre looked for little change in the immediate future. There was time to placate the Paraguayans as he had the Brazilians, offering them periodic concessions and praise, flattering their sense of honor, but never allowing them any permanent advantages in the diplomatic game.

By Mitre's reckoning, the time had in fact come to offer the Paraguayans a sop. He had already made many public statements defending his government's neutrality. At the beginning of March 1865, he found an opportunity to do more than talk when a flotilla of eight Brazilian warships prepared to depart Buenos Aires. Tamandaré, having concluded his Uruguayan mission, intended to steam up the Paraná to Tres Bocas, the river's confluence with the Paraguay, and there establish a blockade of López's country. An 1856 treaty between Brazil and Argentina provided that the navigation of the Platine waterways should remain free in wartime. From this it followed that ports, but not rivers, could be blockaded. Mitre, who well understood the implications of the proposed Tres Bocas operation, could either wink at this obvious contravention of the treaty or demand that the Brazilians refrain from any such action. This would force them into a dangerous frontal assault on Humaitá, for that fortress could not be bypassed if the imperial navy wished to blockade Paraguayan ports. If Mitre refused to agree to the navy's plan for a river blockade, then the Brazilians would have little room for maneuver. Tamandaré would have to attack Humaitá immediately or withdraw.

Anacarsis Lanús, who had carefully followed these events, paid a call on Mitre at this point. The merchant still wanted to do business in Asunción, but he had received word from Félix Egusquiza that the Paraguayan government was growing more hostile and now regarded an open confrontation with Buenos Aires as highly likely. The Argentine president was as calm as ever. He regarded his interview with Lanús as a fortuitous opportunity to send new reassurances to Solano López and encouraged him to depart for Asunción as soon as possible. The neutrality the Argentine government espoused had not wavered, the president insisted; if anything, it had grown more concrete.

When Lanús sailed northward aboard the *Salto* on 25 March, he carried with him a letter to Solano López written in Mitre's own hand. It revealed the Argentine president's decision to prevent the Brazilian blockade at Tres Bocas (a decision that Mitre immediately acted upon by refusing to allow Brazilian gunboats then in Buenos Aires to ascend the Paraná). The *Salto* also carried a cargo of rifles and sabers for the Paraguayan army. When he learned of the cargo, Lanús hastened at ten in the evening to inform Mitre. He warned him that such a shipment might exacerbate an already difficult situation (in truth, the merchant was irritated that the Paraguayans had purchased arms from another supplier). Mitre reacted calmly; without hesitation, he let the shipment pass, pointedly observing that "we cannot deny to Paraguay what we do not deny to Brazil."[61] He calculated that Solano López would interpret this gesture as a clear signal that Argentine neutrality was evenhanded. In a separate note to Solano López written at the beginning of April, Egusquiza confirmed that Mitre was serious about maintaining this stance and that the Argentines eschewed any thought of allying themselves with the empire.[62]

But it was already too late. On 26 February Solano López had written to Candido Bareiro that the government in Buenos Aires was definitely leaning toward the Brazilians and that an alliance between the two powers would soon be in the offing: "That event is very likely to happen, and though we can no longer count on a single dissident [in the Argentine Litoral] because General Urquiza has not fulfilled his spontaneous promises, yet if war with that country becomes inevitable, counting on the firmness and enthusiasm of my fellow countrymen, I hope to bring it to a good conclusion."[63]

*The Extraordinary Congress*

To provide the legal foundation for any action that he might take, Solano López had already decreed the convocation of an Extraordinary Congress to meet on 5 March. Paraguayans from all walks of life understood the importance of this decree, for such meetings were rare events and always preceded momentous political changes. To imagine that Solano López was influenced by public opinion or that he was swayed by a fear of parliamentary opposition is to transfer to Paraguay the principles of constitutional government as practiced in the United States or Britain. Nothing was further from the truth. The 1844 Constitution provided for a legislature that met every five years at the pleasure of the chief executive. Revisionist writers have portrayed these various congressional bodies as a form of "organic democracy." But membership was limited to established landowners who were named by local garrison commanders or *jefes políticos* and approved by the president.[64] Thus, when Solano López convoked the 1865 Congress, he fully expected its unanimous support for his position.[65]

The Congress sat for two straight weeks in the sumptuous confines of the new Legislative Palace. During that time, members passed a series of propositions that reflected the bellicosity of the moment and the ascendancy of Solano López to the status of all-powerful war leader. They conferred upon him the rank of marshal, together with a sixty-thousand-peso annual salary (his father never earned more than four thousand pesos as president) and the right to create a new officer corps with six brigadier and two major generals. In honor of his new rank, members voted him a gold commemorative sword encrusted with precious gems.[66] Solano López also received congressional approval to raise a foreign loan of twenty-five million pesos and to issue paper money in whatever amounts he saw fit.

All of these honors and privileges López accepted with feigned reluctance. He made a particular show of annoyance when members insisted that he refrain from exposing himself to enemy fire should he later become involved in battle. As Colonel Thompson remarked, "The Bishop said it was the decision and personal bravery of López which chiefly made them anxious on his account."[67]

Whatever the truth of that observation, government officials had clearly coached the congressmen. Following word for word the president's proclamations and utilizing the sharp rhetoric found in *El Semanario*, members parroted every conceivable accusation against Argentina. Buenos Aires, they asserted, had virtually declared war by refusing the passage of Paraguayan troops through Corrientes. Mitre's hostility, moreover, was demonstrated in every sarcastic story the *porteño* press printed.[68]

After hearing Berges somberly recount these and other serious charges against Argentina, the Congress named a special commission of sixteen men headed by the canon of the Asunción Cathedral to prepare a comprehensive report on Paraguayan foreign policy. Not one of these commissioners had any previous experience in foreign diplomacy, and most had never left Paraguay, but they worked hard at their task and delivered their report to Congress on 17 March. Well written and highly detailed, it constituted a virtual précis on the marshal's worldview and the threats facing the nation.

The report began by exploring the causes of the war with Brazil and by clarifying the need for the invasion of Mato Grosso. The empire was roundly denounced for its refusal to acknowledge the Paraguayan note of 30 August 1864 in which the Asunción government demanded that the Brazilians withdraw from the Banda Oriental. This demand, which the commission now specifically endorsed, revealed to the world how seriously Paraguay desired to maintain a balance of power in the Plata; by ignoring the demand to withdraw, the imperial government chose the path of war and now had to pay the price.

With reference to Argentina, the commission echoed the resentment that Solano López felt concerning the transit issue. The only possible reason for Mitre's refusal to allow Paraguayan passage across Corrientes was that he sought to injure Paraguay (and thus aid Brazil). The second note from Elizalde, in which the Argentine foreign minister asked for an explanation for the troop movements in the Misiones, only confirmed the bad intentions of the Buenos Aires government. The report cited Argentine interest in the Misiones as implicit proof that Mitre wanted to eject Paraguay from the region. In this, the Argentine president was following a long tradition of unfriendly behavior toward Paraguay that dated from independence, a tradition that, if the insulting articles in *La Nación Argentina* were any measure, had yet to run its course. The official toleration Mitre had shown a committee of anti-López revolutionaries in Buenos Aires provided additional evidence of unfriendliness. He had used these tactics against the Uruguayan Blancos and now wished Paraguay to share their fate.[69]

The commission's report then turned to the heart of the López argument by explaining the Paraguayan defense of a balance of power in the Platine basin. On this point, the report observed, Mitre had posited a radically mistaken line: "Guiding itself strictly by the principles of international law, the Argentine Government ought to help us in the war that Brazil is waging against us, thus breaking the balance [of power] of the States of the Plata; when there is a restless and malignant nation, disposed always to harm others by creating obstructions and rousing internal dissentions, all the other [nations] have the right to unite to repress and reduce [that nation] so as to make it impossible for it to work evil. It is also a principle of right that when a State finds itself unjustly pressured by a powerful neighbor that seeks to oppress it, if it can immediately, it has the duty to defend itself."[70]

Having underlined this point, the commission members opted to cloak it in a *poncho* of historical and legal precedent. Strangely citing Alphonse de Lamartine's *Histoire de la Turquie*, they described an exact parallel between events in the Platine basin in 1864–65 and the Crimean War a decade earlier. Lamartine had criticized the neutrality of Austria and Prussia in that conflict, noting that this policy in essence constituted a thinly disguised hostility toward Britain and France. The latter two countries had gone to war against Russia to defend the balance-of-power concept in Europe, just as Paraguay had now done in the Plata. The analogy between the two cases was not particularly apt. Lamartine had never recommended that the western powers attack Prussia and Austria for their alleged hostility (and thus push them into an active alliance with Russia). Yet this was precisely what commission members advised the Paraguayan government to do in regard to Argentina, whose leaders had already shown their lack of true neutrality by colluding with an empire every bit as expansionist as that of the Tsar:

> If the silence and immobility of Austria and Prussia in a question of continental interest are considered hidden aggressions, what qualifications can be given to the Argentine policy of proclaiming neutrality and openly protecting a rebellion, favoring the action of an Empire against a weak sister Republic, and encouraging discord in another nation that with generous self-abnegation rushes to the defense of the first . . . ? How can we qualify the conduct of the Argentine Government that offers a passage that is not asked and refuses one that is so-

licited as necessary or useful for the preservation of the balance of power . . . ? The Commission therefore thinks that, should war break out with the Argentine Republic because of the transit of our armies by way of our Misiones territory or by way of her own, it will not be war but simply the defense of the peace and of our own survival.[71]

With this, the commission recommended that the Congress issue a "decisive statement" expressing broad condemnation of the "antinational" policy of the Argentine government. In pursuit of even more decisive action, the commission also offered a "project of law" that the Congress approved without debate on 18 March 1865. Its adoption formally indicated that Paraguay had declared war on Argentina.

*The Paraguayans Prepare to Attack*
Though the decision for war had received unanimous approbation, many in the Paraguayan Congress secretly feared the consequences of their action. Juan Crisóstomo Centurión, who had been present in the Legislative Palace throughout this time, felt stupefied and angry: "After the vote, I was left pallid and heartsick with a great sadness, to the point that I could not resist saying, in a low voice, to my colleague and friend Natalicio Talavera, whom I found standing by my side at one of the interior doors: 'Bad tidings, my friend! Paraguay might be able to contend with one country; but with two, who are bound to make common cause, it seems to me very risky. It is a great imprudence, and . . . he that seizes much holds but little.' [Talavera] answered me with a countenance equally sad, 'What do you want, my friend? We will see what happens.'"[72]

The more common reaction in Asunción was one of unrestrained patriotic fervor. *El Semanario* announced the declaration of war on 25 March, but even before then the plazas had filled with raucous crowds cheering Marshal López and the army. A festive atmosphere, officially encouraged, soon suffused the Paraguayan capital. Celebrations occurred everywhere and there was much drinking.[73] The revelers screamed themselves hoarse, calling for the heads of Mitre, Elizalde, and the other Argentine pigs *(kurepí)*.

The objects of this scorn remained strangely unaware that their neighbor had thrown down the gauntlet. Their ignorance on this point is all the more remarkable given that Mitre's own newspaper, *La Nación Argentina*, had already reported *in extenso* on the Paraguayan congressional meetings of 5-14 March. During these meetings, several delegates had expressed the opinion that Paraguay was *already* at war with Argentina.[74] These statements should have given clear warning that something drastic was pending, but the official posture in Buenos Aires was that "the Paraguayan despot had invented a tactic as ridiculous as it was original." The marshal's threats were clearly designed as theater, part of a plan to raise loans overseas, and Argentina could safely ignore them. The cost of Paraguay's war with Brazil had exceeded the funds available in the national treasury; surely now Solano López was without the "means to launch the Quixotic expeditions with which [he] threatens [his] neighbors."[75]

Revisionist historians have claimed that Argentina's confident attitude was itself a kind of theater. Their argument closely parallels that of American historians who assert that Franklin Roosevelt knew in advance that Japan would attack Pearl Harbor in December 1941. In this case, Mitre supposedly knew that the Paraguayans would lash out at Argentina. He desired that they do so, for then he could portray his own aggressiveness — and his friendship with Brazil — as a legitimate defensive response, and this would convert what was certain to be an unpopular war into a righteous struggle.[76]

The revisionist argument gives Mitre more credit for farsightedness than he deserves. Like Paranhos and Saraiva (who found reason to regret their attitude), he had always regarded the Paraguayan threats as empty talk, and it is only with hindsight that the events of March 1865 look more serious than those that preceded it. The revisionists also err in assuming that Mitre paid close attention to his informants. The governor of Corrientes had warned him on many occasions of Paraguayan unpredictability, and these same sentiments had been echoed by his minister in Asunción and others. The Argentine president had always reassured these doomsayers, telling them that Solano López was loud but not really dangerous and that he could always be mollified with minor concessions and promises.

Mitre's dismissive attitude toward Solano López seems foolhardy in retrospect, but at the time it was hardly surprising. No diplomatic or military intelligence can be better than the judgment of its interpreters. Mitre had the *porteño*'s disdain for country bumpkins dressed in gaudy uniforms—which is exactly what he considered Solano López to be (he thought much the same about most leaders of the Platine interior and Litoral). Such men, he believed, do not make war on the Argentine Republic. Perhaps this was wishful thinking, perhaps ignorance. Conspiracy, however, it was not.

Mitre harbored great ambitions for himself and his country. Revisionists are right in supposing that he wished to forge a new hegemonic order in the Plata with Buenos Aires dominant over all the other provinces of the old viceroyalty, including Paraguay and the Banda Oriental. His plans, however, never included provoking the Paraguayans into a genuine war with Argentina.

The attack, when it did occur, came largely as a surprise to Mitre. On 29 March, Berges directed yet another note to Elizalde to tell him of Paraguay's declaration of war. He went into considerable detail to explain why the Asunción government had taken such a step and did not omit mention of the transit question, the insulting references to Paraguay in the *porteño* press, the purported aid given to anti-López revolutionaries, and the favoritism that the Argentines had shown Brazil. He also offered a novel interpretation when he argued that strict neutrality demanded either the concession of a right of "innocent transit" across Corrientes or the closing of the Paraná to Brazil.[77]

The Argentine government only acknowledged receipt of this missive on 3 May 1865.[78] The revisionists see this month-long delay as proof that Mitre manipulated the facts to serve his political interests at the expense of his country.[79] And there is probably some truth in this assertion. Mitre had carefully built a reputation for himself as a shrewd *pensador* and statesman, yet he was always capable of twisting the truth to his advantage. If he could lie about the extent of his early support for Flores, he could also lie about the threat from Asunción and when he first became aware of it. After all, Mitre had to constantly sidestep rivals in his own *Partido de la Libertad*. Adolfo Alsina, for instance, wished to see the president openly aligned with the Brazilian Empire, the better to drive Urquiza into a final, hopeless confrontation with Buenos Aires. To stave off such an eventuality, which held so many uncertainties, it was crucial for Mitre to delay the announcement of war with Paraguay in order to make the fight look less like a self-interested political maneuver and more like an expression of popular will.

Whatever the truth, the danger from Paraguay was real enough. A month earlier a young Paraguayan lieutenant named Cipriano Ayala had changed into civilian dress and hurriedly slipped out of Humaitá on the war steamer *Jejuí*. After reporting to Paraguayan agents at Corrientes and Paraná and changing ships at Rosario, he finally reached Buenos Aires on 8 April. Without delay, he presented himself at the door of Félix Egusquiza. The lieutenant then drew from his baggage several sealed dispatches that informed the commercial agent that Paraguay had declared war on Argentina.

Egusquiza wasted no time. He immediately set to work destroying his correspondence, converting his paper money to specie, and transferring title of his properties to trustworthy locals. The speed with which he accomplished these tasks did not go unnoticed by his neighbors, who spread word of his actions through every *barrio* in the city. The capital was soon abuzz with rumors of impending war. Thornton and the other foreign representatives heard these rumors and gave them ample credit. Mitre heard them as well but paid little heed at the beginning.

Lieutenant Ayala remained in Buenos Aires less than a day before boarding another steamer heading north. Once again he changed ships at Rosario, this time switching to the *Esmeralda*, a fast cargo vessel that, not coincidentally, carried a substantial shipment of arms and munitions for the marshal's army at Humaitá. Ayala, it seems, had completed most of his assignment. He had warned the various Paraguayan agents of the blow that was about to fall, and now he found himself escorting the last shipment of arms his country could expect to see for some time to come.

Back in Buenos Aires, it had finally dawned on the Argentine leadership that the rumors concerning Paraguay possessed considerable credence.[80] Some indirect evidence suggests that news of Paraguay's declaration of war had already slipped out due to an indiscrete private letter the authorities had intercepted in Córdoba. Guillermo Rawson, the Argentine finance minister, who happened to be visiting the inland city at that time, saw the letter and sent word of its contents to Mitre on 17 April.[81] The Correntino governor, Manuel Y. Lagraña, also informed Buenos Aires of the declaration of war, but again, the news came too late.[82]

Whether the Argentine president was angry with himself for having been caught unawares or found it convenient to appear more surprised by the news than he actually was scarcely mattered by the time he received these notes. There was no longer any room for speculation. Word had just arrived from Corrientes that a Paraguayan invasion force had landed.

1. José Gaspar de Francia (1766–1840). He helped foster a narrow, patrimonial form of nationalism in Paraguay. Engraving reprinted from Thomas Jefferson Page, *La Plata, the Argentine Confederation, and Paraguay* (New York, 1859), 202.

2. Carlos Antonio López (1798–1862). López "opened" Paraguay to many outside influences yet offered only a rigid authoritarianism as the best guarantee of its independence. Courtesy Javier Yubi.

3. Emperor Dom Pedro II of Brazil. He was an introverted, studious monarch whose long reign (1840–89) provided the sinews of nationhood to Brazil. Courtesy Roderick Barman.

4. Justo José de Urquiza (1801–70). The Entrerriano *caudillo*, who long resisted *porteño* pretensions in Argentina, ended by supporting the national government during the war. From a nineteenth-century lithograph.

5. Bartolomé Mitre (1821–1906). A poet, publicist, and historian as well as president, he represented the modern and the implacable in Argentine politics. From a contemporary drawing.

6. Venancio Flores (1808–68). A Uruguayan gaucho of the old school, his doubtless courage was wasted in an uncompromised pursuit of power. Courtesy Miguel Angel Cuarterolo.

7. Marshal Francisco Solano López (1826–70). The Paraguayan president (here shown with his young son) was a complex figure, by turns affectionate, brutal, and calculating. Courtesy Museo Histórico Militar, Asunción.

8. Eliza Lynch (1835–86). The Irish-born courtesan who shared Solano López's passions, insecurities, and craving for greatness. Courtesy Javier Yubi.

9. Joaquim Marques Lisboa, baron of Tamandaré (1807–97). The "Father of the Brazilian Navy" was as imposing in imperial politics as he was in naval affairs. Courtesy Biblioteca Nacional, Rio de Janeiro.

10. Charles Ames Washburn (1822–89). The U.S. minister to Asunción was an unrepentant critic of the López regime. Courtesy Billie Gammon, Washburn-Norlands Library.

11. The Paraguayan army assembled in Asunción. Engraving reprinted from Alfred M. DuGraty, *La República del Paraguay* (Besançon, 1862).

12. The fort at Nova Coimbra as it appeared in the late 1800s. From a nineteenth-century photograph.

13. The river battle of the Riachuelo, 11 June 1865. From a painting by Vitor Meireles. Museu Histórico Nacional, Rio de Janeiro.

14. Adm. Francisco Manoel Barroso (1804–82). The Brazilian naval commander was the controversial victor at the battle of the Riachuelo. Courtesy Miguel Angel Cuarterolo.

15. The Battle of Yataí, 17 August 1865.
(Uruguaiana is in the distance.)
Reprinted from *L'Illustration*.

16. The Argentine encampment near Uruguaiana. From a painting by Candido López, Museo Histórico Nacional, Buenos Aires.

17. Lt. Col. Antonio Estigarribia (d. 1870). His surrender of the Paraguayan forces at Uruguaiana ended all hope of victory in the south. Engraving reprinted from Colección Juan O'Leary, Biblioteca Nacional, Asunción.

18. Allied forces land at Corrientes following the Paraguayan evacuation. Engraving reprinted from Jorge Thompson, *La guerra del Paraguay* (Buenos Aires, 1869).

# IV

## The Paraguayan Offensive

# 10

# Corrientes under the Gun

Like its northern neighbor, the Argentine province of Corrientes was a lush, riverine province cut by broad waterways and fast-flowing creeks, many of which were so poorly drained that they merged into immense sloughs after every heavy downpour. A small population of Hispano-Guaraní *vaqueros* and peasant farmers lived in tiny, often isolated settlements wherever they could find dry land. They raised citrus fruit, maize, peanuts, manioc, tobacco, and livestock (with yerba mate taken from the Misiones)—enough to meet their own needs with a small surplus left over for export.

As in Paraguay, the social ethos was generally conservative. Most Correntinos had little use for the innovative spirit seen elsewhere in the Plata. They tended to regard as mere whimsy all the details of modern science that so enraptured the intellectuals of Buenos Aires. Instead, traditional Spanish values defined for them the exact relation between the classes, between man and woman, parent and child, priest and parishioner.

To be sure, Correntinos did understand the importance of money; they were happy to find new opportunities to enrich themselves and so permitted in their midst foreign entrepreneurs and outside *políticos* whose attitudes were distinctly "modern." Though Correntinos regarded their modernity with ambivalence, some individuals were willing to learn and, to a vague extent, redefine themselves according to the changing times. Yet only a tiny number of Correntinos were really aware that new notions of representative government, of freedom of the press and assembly, and of obligatory public education had already started to send up a few tentative shoots through the sandy soil of provincial politics.

One man who did know these things was Juan Pujol (1817–61), a tireless, sensitive, bighearted dreamer in a frock coat who governed Corrientes during the 1850s. A strong ally of Justo José de Urquiza, he began as something of an unknown but was so manifestly talented and well connected downriver that few locals found it convenient to oppose him. The political order in Corrientes traditionally resembled that of old Paraguay, with a tiny elite of landowners and merchants holding sway in patrimonial fashion over the peasant masses. That basic social arrangement was too deeply engrained for Pujol to openly challenge. In fomenting a more modern social order, therefore, he adopted a "water-upon-stone" approach, promoting steamship companies, colonization projects, and other economic and scientific ventures that he felt the elites could broadly support. He had some minor successes locally and then left Corrientes behind for new duties in the Argentine Congress.[1]

Pujol's attempts at reform were widely admired but not emulated by his successors. Instead, the province abandoned the newfound sense of optimism that he had created and in its place substituted another round of political strife. Part of this conflict reflected uncertainties at the national level—the effects of the battle of Pavón above all. But a great deal of the problem involved local jealousies that had remained hidden beneath the surface during Pujol's administration. When he left office in December 1859, he was succeeded by José María Rolón (1826–62), an unimaginative and conservative cleric who found little to admire in his own century.

Though he himself became governor as the result of a political compromise, Rolón's politics were anything but conciliatory. His opponents in the provincial legislature represented all the key political factions, but they failed to unite against him until after he adopted a policy of wholesale repression. Arrest followed arrest in every community. In late 1861, with the elites in Corrientes still divided over his policies, the black-cassocked priest faced an open rebellion in the south.[2] The rebels, many of whom were disgruntled militiamen, quickly forced his ouster and went on to provide a political opening for various "liberals," Manuel Lagraña among them. Though the victory over Rolón was complete in one sense (he died of natural causes within a year's time), it left unanswered many questions about the province's future, especially regarding its relation with the national government. Under the circumstances, few Correntinos expected peace to endure.

The feeling of apprehension that characterized this period was caused by the radical and abrupt shifts between old and new politics, shifts that Correntinos usually resented. The rural people, in particular, preferred to be left alone to their livestock and crops, their morning yerba, and their old habits. The constant interference of outsiders had aggravated local differences and was deeply resented as a result.

Paradoxically (for they themselves were foreigners), the Paraguayans in 1865 sought to take advantage of the Correntinos' resentment of outsiders. It was a feeling of indignation that was common on both sides of the Paraná River. More important, as in Paraguay, everyone in Corrientes spoke Guaraní. The use of Guaraní gave Correntinos a mindset similar to that of Paraguayans but quite different from that of other Argentines. This was why Solano López thought that the *provincia hermana* would rally to his cause; no matter what the government in Buenos Aires did, the Correntinos would choose their cousins over the "nation" that Bartolomé Mitre offered them.

### The Seizure of the Fleet

Having chosen to make war on Argentina, the marshal moved quickly to prepare his attack. He redeployed all but one thousand of his troops from the Mato Grosso, sending the greater part to Humaitá. There was a flurry of activity at the latter base at the beginning of April, but even more at the port of Asunción. There Solano López assembled a fleet of five steamers — the *Tacuarí, Ygurey, Paraguarí, Yporá,* and the recently captured *Marqués de Olinda*. Together these ships mounted twenty-three guns of various sizes — a formidable river force by any measure.

Regardless of how the Correntinos might react, López had good reason to suppose that he would need these guns to cover his incursion into the neighboring province. In fact, on the morning of 12 April, Paraguayan border guards at Paso de la Patria confirmed earlier reports that placed three Argentine warships carrying as many as four hundred men in the port of Corrientes.[3] Only part of this story turned out to be true, for one of the three ships was a British-flagged vessel, the *Flying Fish*. The contingent of sailors on the remaining two vessels numbered nowhere near four hundred, but the Correntinos evidently felt secure nonetheless. Governor Lagraña had often asked Mitre for naval assistance to fend off the Paraguayan threat. Though he scoffed at the supposed danger, Mitre ultimately gave in and dispatched two small warships, the *25 de Mayo* (six guns) and the *Gualeguay* (two guns).[4] As it turned out, this one gesture toward the defense of the port made no difference at all.

As in the Mato Grosso campaign, the Paraguayans had conceived a detailed plan of attack. It called for the seizure of the Argentine ships at Corrientes on the morning of 13 April. After depositing the captured vessels at Humaitá, the Paraguayan fleet would then steam to Fort Itapirú on the Alto Paraná and embark the advanced elements of the invasion force. The next day these troops would land at Corrientes to conquer the city in tandem with two cavalry regiments riding hard from Paso de la Patria. After all resistance ceased, the main body of Paraguay's Southern Division would arrive from Humaitá and begin preparations to advance along the Paraná toward Bella Vista and Goya.

The attack went better than expected. An hour after dawn, Correntino lookouts sighted the Paraguayan squadron coming straight for them. The appearance of so many ships together and the loud noises from their engines caused some commotion ashore. Men, women, and children came down to the river to stare. They gathered in small groups and wondered aloud what it was all about. Capt. Pedro Ignacio Meza, in command of the approaching force, soon showed them.

The Paraguayans steamed downriver parallel to the port as if it were their intention to continue toward Buenos Aires. A few miles to the south of Corrientes, they turned sharply and approached the port on the windward side (to facilitate the boarding of the two enemy ships). The sailors of the *25 de Mayo*, who were just as surprised as the local townspeople, dipped their colors in salute. Some of those on the Argentine steamer suspected the intentions of the Paraguayans, but her captain, who had only just come back on board, assured everyone that all was well, that Lagraña himself had recently said that the Paraguayans had no argument with the Argentine navy.[5] The captain failed to take any extraordinary steps, and his men, to their regret, stood back from their main guns. This allowed the *Ygurey* and *Yporá* to slip in unopposed from port and starboard.

The fusillade started at once. Paraguayan riflemen fired one quick volley that peppered the *25 de Mayo*'s deck with Minié balls. In response, the shocked Argentine sailors drew cutlasses and tried to fire back with their own rifles, but boarding parties quickly overwhelmed them. The captain, first mate, and forty-seven crewmembers fell prisoner, while others who tried to escape by jumping overboard were shot to pieces as they swam. Twenty-eight men died.[6]

The *Gualeguay* proved a more difficult catch, if only because it was tied close to the shore, which meant that the Paraguayans could only board from the side facing the river. The *Marqués de Olinda* offered light covering fire for this effort while troops from the *Paraguarí* closed in to effect the boarding. The captain and crew of the *Gualeguay* gave no thought to fighting and rushed ashore at once.[7]

As a last gesture of bravado, a drunken Paraguayan corporal gleefully fired one salvo from his cannon into the town proper.[8] While the smoke cleared, the Paraguayans took both Argentine vessels in tow and turned north into the main current of the Paraná. The entire action had lasted just under an hour and cost the marshal's navy one officer and ten men wounded; none were killed. By 9:00 A.M. the seven ships had disappeared upriver.

The attack on the port left the inhabitants of Corrientes in a state of complete bewilderment. The *Gualeguay* and *25 de Mayo*, whose brief presence had provided them with a sense of security, were now gone, taken before their eyes. Instead of offering resistance, most Correntino guards along the riverbank had stood motionless, as if mesmerized by the swift maneuvering of the steamers. The harbormaster managed to fire two or three rounds from a small cannon he kept at the customshouse, but this effort was "more symbolic than effective."[9]

The capture of the two Argentine ships left Corrientes with nothing to prevent a full-scale invasion. The sense of surprise in the town gave way to panic by midday, with many residents hastily packing their valuables onto carts and wagons and departing for the interior of the province. No one stopped to bury the bodies that washed up along the riverfront (and which soon filled the bellies of crocodiles). One eyewitness, a Correntino cavalry officer recently returned from an expedition into the Argentine Chaco, succinctly summed up the reactions of his fellow provincials on this first day: "*¡Oikoú los paraguay, añama ñandé rerajhá!* [The Paraguayans have come and the devil is upon us!]."[10]

While Governor Lagraña had warned the national government of Paraguayan intentions, he had done precious little to prepare the town's defense. Faced with imminent invasion, he decided to abandon Corrientes. This was a sound move. Any Paraguayan invasion force was sure to proceed southward along the Paraná, and Lagraña thought it possible to organize some defense along its anticipated route farther south. Though nervous, the governor also had the foresight to send word to intercept the *Esmeralda*, then en route to Humaitá with a large shipment of arms. Had the marshal delayed his surprise attack by a single day, this shipment, which young Lieutenant Ayala had so carefully shepherded, would have reached the Paraguayans. As it was, thanks to Lagraña's quick thinking, the *Esmeralda* turned back near Bella Vista and Ayala was arrested.[11]

Among the governor's last acts before joining the line of fleeing townspeople was instructing the municipal council not to resist the Paraguayans but to cooperate with them in order to ensure public safety and protect property.[12] At the same time, however, Lagraña issued a call for all men between the ages of sixteen and sixty to take up arms against

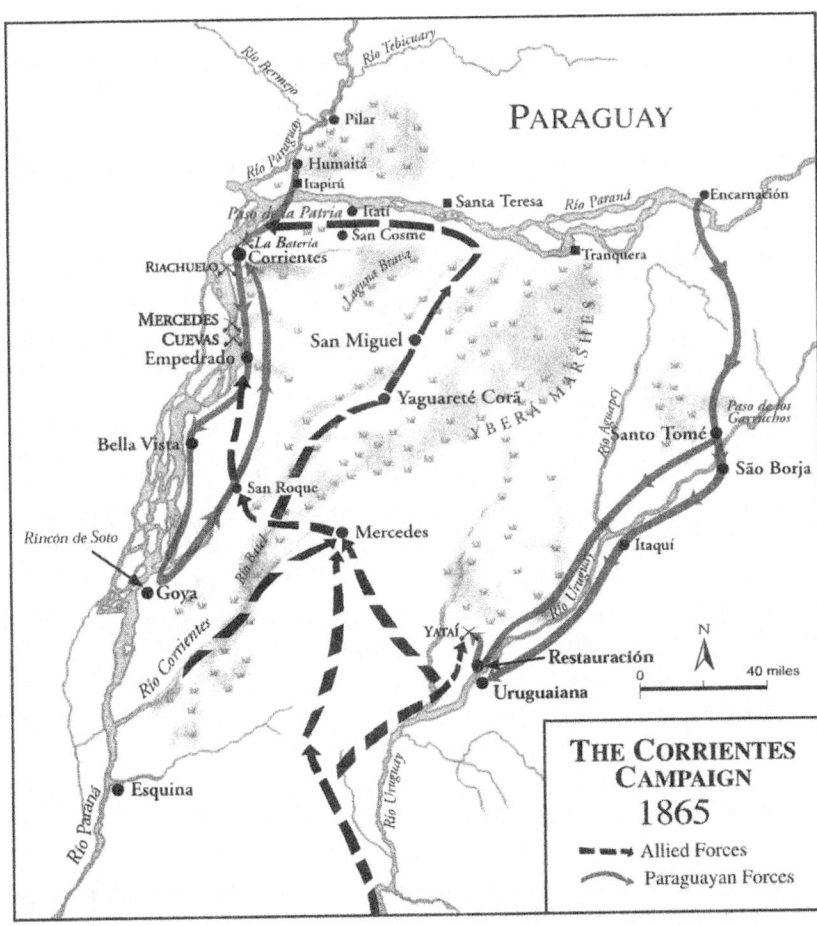

the invaders.[13] He himself demanded the right to command all available units while he tried to set up a functioning government at the town of Empedrado.

When troops actually began assembling farther south, however, it soon became obvious that real authority there rested with the old Urquicista general Nicanor Cáceres (1812–70), who took his given name from a lieutenant of Alexander the Great. This veteran officer was as

*Corrientes under the Gun* 263

brave and as bearded as his namesake, and as ruthless in war. He had fought campaigns in Corrientes as early as the 1840s and had developed a reputation for ferocity combined with an acute knowledge of the terrain. As one Correntino historian put it, Cáceres was as unbeatable on his home ground as "the armadillo of our countryside, which in his own burrow is invincible."[14] Now, as the Paraguayans advanced, many in the province looked to him to save the day.

Meanwhile, Captain Meza towed the two Argentine ships to Humaitá, where cheering troops greeted the arrival of the victorious Paraguayan squadron. "Death to the *porteños!*" the soldiers cried, echoing the same words used only hours before at Corrientes.[15] Without delay, Meza steamed to Paso de la Patria, where Gen. Wenceslao Robles and three thousand men awaited him. As planned, at five the next morning, the Paraguayan ships again approached Corrientes and in the morning twilight landed the invasion force. There was no resistance. Robles's men spread through the streets, seizing government buildings, the port district, and the marketplace. A large number of women and children, frightened by the dramatic advent of Robles's men, sought refuge in the confines of the church, but the Paraguayan commander let them know that they had nothing to fear and could return unmolested to their homes.[16]

The cavalry units from Paso de la Patria arrived several hours later only to find that their waterborne compatriots had already secured their common objective.[17] The two units then moved to establish a defensive perimeter along the southern approaches to the town, but no counterattack occurred, nor even any sniping. As the sun set over the Gran Chaco on that first day, the Paraguayan troops across the river in Corrientes settled back in their positions to brew their yerba and to eat their portion of beef and biscuit. All were relieved that it had been so easy. That night they slept comfortably.

*The Occupation Begins*

The Paraguayans understood that the military conquest of Corrientes would not in itself bring victory over Buenos Aires and the Brazilian Empire. For that, Solano López needed friendly supporters in the Litoral provinces. From the beginning of his invasion, therefore, he sought to build a political alliance with those Correntinos who would see the justice of the Paraguayan cause. Identifying such a faction seemed an easy enough matter; after all, the Correntinos and the Paraguayans were neighbors and thought they understood each other well. Any detail or specific matter that remained fuzzy could be clarified with information supplied by spies. Yet the marshal failed to grasp how very complex Corrientes was.

The internal politics of the province reflected the several different approaches to nationhood in Argentina in the 1860s. Though Correntino elites shared a conservative social agenda (especially regarding religion and the subordination of the lower classes), they disagreed about which group among them should administer the province. Roughly speaking, three strong factions competed for power.

The most important group, led nominally by Lagraña, affiliated explicitly with President Mitre's Liberals. These men considered themselves modernists on all the key national issues: construction of railroads and telegraph lines, nationalization of customs receipts, and promotion of immigration as a solution for the country's backwardness. Though clearly ascendant in provincial politics by the mid-1860s, the Liberals were themselves divided, mostly due to family interests and personal jealousies. Sometimes they refused even to speak to each other.

A second faction, less divided but also less powerful, consisted of allies and former allies of Urquiza. These men, who thought of themselves as authentic federals, took the pre-Pavón Argentine Confederation as their model for the nation. More than other Correntinos, they resented the heavy hand of Buenos Aires, which they saw as inevitably oppressive of local enterprises. In the 1850s these "Autonomists" dominated the province under Juan Pujol. Many national politicians had considered the latter a probable successor to Santiago Derqui as president of the confederation and had brought him south to prepare his candidacy. Pujol served as senator and then as interior minister, but he died young, in 1861, and his hopes for broad-scale reform came to naught. In Corrientes his partisans only managed to retain the support of ranchers in the south and southeast, an area that in its topography, culture, and political forms more closely resembled Entre Ríos than it did the rest of the province.

The weakest of the three factions in 1865 was made up of members of the old Federal Party. Many of these men had once supported Juan Manuel de Rosas and now espoused a frankly reactionary line. They favored an extreme interpretation of provincial autonomy tantamount to independence for individual provinces except in matters of defense. This outlook enjoyed scant support among the younger generation of Correntino politicians, who regarded its adherents as irredeemably old fashioned.

Characteristically, the Paraguayans pinned their hopes for success in Corrientes on this latter group. This was, in part, simple expediency. As the weakest of the "out groups," the Federals had little to lose from forming an alliance with the Asunción government; they had no obvious patron, nor any prospects of finding one, within Argentina. Moreover, their distinctive interpretation of autonomy reinforced Paraguay's ascendancy in the Plata since it rejected on ideological grounds any stance that gave Buenos Aires a commanding role over the other provinces. The Federals also deeply mistrusted the Brazilians, whom they saw as backward monarchists, born opponents of the "American cause."[18]

Even before the invasion, José Berges had already sponsored several Correntino Federals then present in Asunción with whom he wanted to work. One of these, Victor Silvero, was the young, handlebar mustached editor of a rabidly anti-Mitre newspaper that had constantly vexed Governor Lagraña and his political allies. The Paraguayan agent at Corrientes identified the editor as the best friend his government had in the province: "Silvero is no merchant of phrases, and if he has spoken out against Brazil . . . , it is because he really holds these convictions, and these harmonize with his private interests and with those of the province in general. Silvero is a man who has dignity, and as such, in his political beliefs he is firm and constant. . . . That I have not had to make use of any monies to assure *El Independiente*'s stance against Brazil and in favor of our cause is due in large part to the efforts of Silvero."[19]

Berges also picked Sinforoso Cáceres, a major cattle dealer, who like many Correntinos dating back to colonial times, had enjoyed excellent business relations with the Paraguayans. In this case, Cáceres had supplied cattle to the troops stationed at Humaitá ever since the beginning of the war with Brazil; as Charles Washburn laconically observed, he "had a partnership with Mrs. Lynch, and through her influence with López was able to secure very profitable contracts."[20] But Cáceres, though he "might irritate certain *doctores* in the city [of Corrientes, was likely to be] well-received in the countryside, where he had many relations."[21]

Immediately after the fall of Corrientes, José Berges sought out Silvero and Cáceres and arranged for their conveyance to the conquered town. While Solano López and his officers normally looked to straightforward military solutions to complex problems, the Paraguayan foreign minister had in mind a more subtle policy of coaxing Corrientes into a pro-Paraguay stance. He knew that many in the province hated the *porteños* exactly as the Paraguayans did; hatred of the Brazilians ran still deeper.[22] Through friendly treatment and generosity on the part of the invading forces, the Correntinos might come to see Paraguay as a natural ally. Berges believed, moreover, that the old Federals would be instrumental in granting their fellow Correntinos at least the illusion of alliance in the struggle against Buenos Aires and the empire.

Berges may have hoped for more. López Jordan and the other Entrerriano dissidents were not far distant to the south. As yet, there was no clear inkling of how the Autonomists in southern Corrientes might react. Perhaps with their help, the Paraguayans might yet reach Montevideo.

This was, of course, pure speculation. For the moment, however, Berges held the upper hand in setting state policy in the occupied provincial capital, and he wanted to make a show of goodwill. If he failed, not only were the Correntinos certain to align themselves with the national government, but he also would lose out to his uniformed rivals. Those officers, he fully expected, would be blind to any political opening that might later develop. Fighting alone made sense to them. Whether this was also true of the marshal remained to be seen.

Berges, Silvero, Cáceres, and a team of Paraguayan assistants arrived in Corrientes on 16 April. The next day, drumbeats and the shouts of heralds summoned the townspeople to the public square in front of Government House; from there Robles's officers led the various notables down the street to the Chamber of Commerce building, where three hundred of their number received instructions to hold an impromptu election to replace Lagraña. Silvero and Cáceres had already announced their candidacy for office in this new government, and there existed little doubt as to Paraguayan preferences. At the last moment, an aged Federal named Teodoro Gauna stepped forward to join the other two in forming a triumvirate—la Junta Gubernativa—to administer Corrientes for the foreseeable future.[23]

Most Argentine sources paint the *junta* as a clique of unscrupulous opportunists and collaborators who had no real standing among Correntinos.[24] In truth, though the inhabitants of the province failed to receive the *junta* with enthusiasm, they were not altogether displeased with those whom the Paraguayans had chosen. Some thought that these servants of the occupation might open a new and better avenue for trade. Others thought they would act as useful middlemen between the townspeople and the Paraguayans.[25]

Many Correntinos sympathized with the marshal's troops, with whom they could easily converse in Guaraní.[26] Correntinos also regarded the Paraguayans as disciplined and orderly, for they seemed to respect the rights and property of locals. This offered a sharp contrast with the behavior of other armies that had seized the town in earlier decades.

The Correntino reaction shows that the concept of Argentine nationalism as Mitre understood it had yet to sink deep roots in the northeast. Even before coming to power, the Argentine president recognized the weakness of the Liberal agenda in the interior and Litoral provinces. Like Urquiza, Juan Bautista Alberdi, and others, he sought to remedy this in part by stressing the contributions that the provinces had made in forging a modern Argentina (and the benefits they could enjoy if they all worked together).

In his various historical writings, Mitre reminded the people of the northeast that José de San Martín had been born in Corrientes and that the great liberator, more than any other man, had given his country a vision of the future that went beyond the province or *republiqueta*. This image of San Martín beckoning to his native province convinced some people in April 1865, but not many. Most Correntinos, especially in the lower classes, remained skeptical now that war had come. They had little use for a *porteño*-dominated nation-state, so they waited to see if the marshal offered them anything better. A few of the province's wealthiest men took exactly the same attitude, such that the Paraguayans had no lack of potential clients.[27]

Berges was acutely aware, however, of how conditional any Correntino support might be. He knew that many friendly people in the province still viewed the Paraguayans as having been "baptized late and very badly." Berges therefore did not base his strategy exclusively on the *Junta Gubernativa*. Shortly after arriving in the occupied city, he sought out and interviewed Santiago Derqui. The former president of the confederation had retired to a small ranch outside of Corrientes after the defeat of his old ally Urquiza at Pavón. Though he lived quietly and avoided politics, Derqui was just the sort of senior statesman who might bridge the gap — if that were still possible — between Solano López and the Entrerriano *caudillo*. Evidently, however, the ex-president had no intention of doing anything of the kind; in his report of their meeting, Berges made the unlikely claim that the two had avoided all talk of politics.[28] Even so, the Paraguayan foreign minister never quite gave up on Derqui and treated him with great consideration throughout the time of the occupation.

For Berges to make any real headway in Corrientes, he needed the cooperation of General Robles and his men more than anything else. On the surface, Robles followed point-by-point the political line set down by Berges. In his 19 April proclamation to the Correntino people, for example, he announced:

You have practical proof that we have only come to [help] you reconquer that freedom wrenched from you by *porteño* demagoguery. . . . The [*junta*] you have elected will have the firm support of the soldiers I have the honor of commanding. The enemies of our common happiness wish to divide us from the cause of democracy and make us instruments of Brazilian conquest. [But] now, loyal to the tradition of our fathers, we will have the glory of fighting together against the Empire, traditional enemy of the principles of Americanism. . . . On our side you will sustain your independence, and together we will show throughout the Argentine Republic that we recognize no enemy save General Mitre and his clique.[29]

Despite these words, however, Robles had his own ideas of how to govern a defeated province. A middle-aged soldier with deep-set eyes and jet-black hair, he had enjoyed a notable career during the time of the elder López. Now he was the most senior officer in the Paraguayan army, and like so many who had benefited from the military buildup of the 1850s, he was keenly sensitive to anything or anybody who might come between him and his superiors. His opportunities for further fame and honors could only come with victory over the Argentines. And that was a matter not of fair words or political compromise but of fighting. Robles assumed that the marshal shared this inclination and would cheerfully approve any measure the general thought necessary.

From the beginning, for instance, the Paraguayans required that Correntinos accept Paraguayan paper currency, which was valued at an implausible thirty-four pesos to the gold ounce.[30] Some merchants rejected these bills as legal tender until the day General Robles ordered the arrest of an entire community of Chaco Indians when they refused to take the paper money as payment for horse fodder and firewood. He had them all shot in full view of the merchants.[31] Though this act ended the grumbling from the shopkeepers, it did little to inspire confidence in Berges's stated desire for continued open trade, by then a hopeless goal anyway.[32]

Robles's men believed from what had happened in Mato Grosso that they could abuse the Correntinos, take their possessions, and be forgiven by the marshal of any excesses notwithstanding. Robles had already examined the Correntino archives, sending some crucial documents north to Asunción, including a detailed map of the province that indicated the location of the most prominent ranches.[33] Armed with this intelligence, the Paraguayans now moved on those estates closest to Corrientes and carried off their livestock. Raids near Itatí, Caacatí, San Luis, and San Cosme netted hundreds of head of cattle and horses, which were quickly transferred to the main Paraguayan forces just north of Empedrado.[34]

In the town of Corrientes itself, Berges was at pains to depict the unpleasantness associated with these seizures as a passing phase. If the Paraguayan soldiers engaged in unauthorized looting, he claimed, this resulted from a misinterpretation of orders rather than from any general disdain for the locals — and he would not tolerate such abuses in the provincial capital. He paid indemnities to the few merchants in town who reported bad experiences with the soldiers.[35] T. H. Mangels, a British wholesaler, received a full ten thousand pesos from the Paraguayans after a group of Robles's men ransacked his warehouse.[36] Berges apologized and, as a palliative, arranged to give passports to anyone who wished to leave. This was hardly a satisfactory solution, though, since it excluded the detained families of Argentine army officers.[37] The truth was that few people wished to abandon Corrientes just yet. Berges continued to exercise great influence in the administration of the town (though not the province), and his word went a long way toward reassuring the populace.

*Argentine Reactions*

Manuel Lagraña was understandably less convinced about Paraguayan intentions. When he informed the national government of the invasion on the morning on 13 April, he wrote: "this declares the war of vandalism. It is useless to reflect [any further]. Our fatherland must through necessity and honor accept the war to which we are provoked."[38] Most Correntinos, the Liberals excepted, were not yet inclined to follow his lead. They reacted instead with quiet fearfulness, then momentary panic, and finally ambivalence, when the Paraguayans swept into their province.

In Buenos Aires the news of the invasion brought a very different reaction of unreasoning white-faced rage. *Porteño* newspapers such as *El Nacional, La Tribuna, El Bonaerense,* and Mitre's own *Nación Argentina* reflected the general opinion when they styled Solano López an "imbecile," a "sinister tyrant," a "broken down emperor of a barefoot nation," and a "tropical Caligula."[39] Crowds gathered everywhere, shouting for revenge. Musical bands quickly joined in, playing such martial tunes as "El Tala," "A la lid," and "La Carcajada," while men of every age bellowed out their intention of joining up.[40] The American consul in Buenos Aires, who had witnessed a similar enthusiasm among his fellow Yankees when the Confederates attacked Fort Sumter, likened the show of fervor to a religious experience and noted in the *porteños* "unmistakable demonstrations of joy as if a Divine Messenger, with love and healing in his wings, had descended from the heavens. Bonfires, rockets, crackers, and all the improvised paraphernalia of great and glorious occasions were conspicuous in every street of the city."[41]

The Paraguayan attack caught President Mitre unaware. Outwardly, he was as incensed as his fellow *porteños*. Yet he was also a calculating politician who prized clear-headedness, especially in himself. His instincts told him that Solano López would not have behaved with such impetuousness; there had to be some other explanation, and just possibly that explanation—whatever it was—could be turned to Argentina's advantage.

For the moment, Mitre kept these ideas to himself and assumed the public pose that the throng demanded. He gave a rousing patriotic speech at his residence. It was full of angry recriminations and promises of swift action against Paraguay: "to the barracks in twenty-four hours, to the field in fifteen days, and to Asunción in three months."[42] On 16 April he issued a proclamation that called upon all citizens to support the national cause. "As for myself," he concluded, "I will not rest until the peace that was treacherously broken is restored, and the honor of the Argentine nation is vindicated."[43]

That same day, Mitre ordered the formation of new infantry units for the National Guard, four battalions of 500 men each from the city of Buenos Aires, and another four from the province. A day later he called upon the interior and Litoral provinces to contribute another eleven battalions—for a proposed total of 9,500 infantrymen—to form the backbone of the national army.[44] These troops would join the nearly 10,000 cavalrymen then being assembled in Entre Ríos and southern Corrientes. On 24 April the first battalion of *porteño* infantry, commanded by Gen. Wenceslao Paunero, left for the northeast.

Mitre had always trusted his own judgment far above that of his informants. He still thought it just possible that the marshal would repent of his actions and, after making some effusive apologies, make everything right. One year earlier, Mitre had insisted to Lagraña that the Paraguayan leader would act rationally even when pushed into a corner: "Señor López will reflect long and hard before adopting measures that might produce a war in which he has much to lose and nothing to gain."[45] The effusion of blood in April 1865 proved Mitre wrong. Yet despite all the evidence coming from the northeast, the Argentine president still hoped for some backdoor arrangement with López that would save face for all concerned.

Lagraña, for one, knew that that time had passed. So too did the town fathers of Rosario, who organized a mass demonstration, arrested the Paraguayan consul (José Rufo Caminos), and tore from the Consulate building the shield bearing his national arms. This they dragged through the streets together with a portrait of the marshal. Upon reaching the Paraná, they shot both icons full of holes before casting them into the river. They then composed and published a "solemn act" that gave a full account of the proceedings.[46]

The Brazilians, though they had yet to issue an official statement, grasped the importance of what had occurred right away. They had already opened some contacts with the Argentine military. In a letter to Lagraña dated 17 April, War Minister Juan A. Gelly y Obes notified the desperate governor that a full division of three thousand Argentines and Brazilians was on its way to Corrientes.[47] This claim of reinforcement was almost certainly an exaggeration, for it was hardly likely that the minister had Brazilian troops at his disposal. Yet, to the extent that words could reassure Lagraña, mention of imperial forces helped — but not much.

As the Correntino governor brooded about the future, Robles started to move. He left the Third and Twenty-fourth Infantry Battalions, together with several small artillery pieces, to protect the port of Corrientes and established a new base nine miles to the south. The site was well chosen, with the majority of his twenty-five thousand men encamped on a high cliff overlooking the spot where a large stream — the Riachuelo — emptied into the Paraná. From this easily defensible point, the Paraguayans could conduct raids into the interior and as far south as Bella Vista.

Lagraña had already left Empedrado for the relative safety of San Roque, a tiny community in the dead center of the province. All he and his government could do was wait. Correntino irregulars and some of the units attached to Nicanor Cáceres harassed the Paraguayans as best they could, but real resistance could only begin when Urquiza and the Brazilians committed their forces.

The Entrerriano chief had long since accepted as inevitable a coming confrontation with Paraguay. Now that it was here, he gave every sign of loyalty to Buenos Aires: "The moment has arrived when words must give way to deeds. Now it falls to our lot to fight once more under the flag that united all Argentines at Caseros. . . . I look forward to the moment of clasping your Excellency's hand and placing myself personally under your orders."[48] According to Julio Victorica, Mitre received this note with the succinct exclamation, "We reap the fruit of a great policy."[49]

And so they had. The Paraguayans still held out hope that Urquiza would switch to their camp. Indeed, Berges was still sending correspondence (which Urquiza refused even to open), begging him to join their fight against Brazil. Urquiza, however, had retreated too far to turn around now. He had suffered a diplomatic defeat at Mitre's hand over the transit question in the Misiones. And he had sold horses to the imperial army.[50] Writing from exile in France, Alberdi contemptuously observed that Urquiza had sunk back to the level of a local *caudillo*, beholden to Mitre as he had once been to Rosas.[51] Just as predictably, Foreign Minister Elizalde expressed great satisfaction at this same development: "When the present Argentine government was formed we had ranged against us much of the Interior of the country, Paraguay, Uruguay, Brazil, and almost all of the foreign diplomats. Our entente with General Urquiza weakened our enemies and we were able to proceed slowly but surely with independent policies and, with the elements we had on our side either to defeat or to conciliate our enemies. We made friends with the foreign representatives, we made a friend of Brazil and by letting things take their course in Uruguay we saw a hostile government disappear to be replaced by a friendly one."[52]

For the moment, therefore, the *porteños* could count on the backing of many key political figures in the Litoral who would follow Urquiza's lead with little argument.[53] Those who hitherto opposed Mitre now saw him as the only alternative to a Paraguayan victory. Even the English-language *Standard*, which had favored Solano López's war on Brazil, came out strongly in favor of the national government: "The foreign element is of great influence and will now pronounce unanimously for President Mitre and the Argentine cause. If Buenos Aires had first declared war the case would be exactly opposite. But López has broken with all the usages of civilized nations by seizing the fleet and invading Argentine territory before any declaration of war. President Mitre is a pet of good fortune, for nothing could render him more popular than the present conjuncture, and his sword will carry in its victorious career, besides the weight of past glories, the irresistible impulse of public opinion in a righteous cause."[54] The Argentine president believed he could convert all this positive feeling into something durable that would outlast the struggle with Paraguay. And unlike the marshal, whose procrastination and missteps had already cost him dearly, Mitre understood when to strike.

Popular feeling in favor of the war was likely to wane when the public learned how poor the Argentine military response had been thus far. Lagraña had struggled with some sort of mutiny, the details of which even now are unclear.[55] In the south, Gen. Nicanor Cáceres had yet to gain firm control over his men, a great many of whom were reluctant to heed the call to arms; and as for Urquiza's ten thousand men, there was good reason to doubt that they would ever fight. Mitre realized all of this. Master publicist that he was, he knew he could stave off doubt for only a short period — but that would be enough time to conclude a formal alliance with the Brazilian Empire.

*The Triple Alliance*

The Paraguayan invasion of Corrientes served as a catalyst in South American politics. Before April 1865, Paraguay's war with Brazil encompassed little more than an isolated front in Mato Grosso. Few thought that the empire could respond effectively even if Adm. Baron de Tamandaré managed to force the Paraná and Paraguay Rivers — a highly unlikely scenario given Mitre's hardening stance on neutrality.

The fall of Corrientes, however, changed the political configuration in the Plata in a basic way. In Uruguay, the Colorados had effectively subdued the Blancos. The famed cavalry of the Litoral provinces, following Urquiza's lead, had now placed themselves under the orders of the government in Buenos Aires.[56] This left the Paraguayans boxed in on three sides with few friends in the immediate vicinity and no real hope of succor from Correntino or Entrerriano rebels. Solano López was on his own.

The Brazilian minister in Buenos Aires, Francisco Octaviano de Almeida Rosa, moved speedily to sign a politico-military alliance with Argentina. He met with a group of key notables (of whom Urquiza was one) and began complex negotiations without specific instructions from Rio de Janeiro. By 24 April, Octaviano reached an understanding with Mitre on the terms of the proposed alliance; the two men at once informed Uruguayan president Venancio Flores, who likewise affirmed his support for the agreement.[57] The Triple Alliance Treaty was signed on 1 May 1865 and ratified unanimously by the Argentine Congress twenty-three days later. Brazil and Argentina exchanged ratifications on 12 June, and Uruguay was added the next day.

The Triple Alliance agreement guided the Allied nations in their struggle against Paraguay for the next five years. Its terms, as revealed in public fora, were high minded and moderate, though absolutely focused on the objective of final victory. The Allied signatories maintained that the López government callously threatened the peace and security of their respective countries. Consequently, according to Article 6 of the treaty, they vowed not to lay down their arms until the marshal quit the scene. Since the war was to be directed specifically against López and not against his people, the Allies vowed to accept the aid of all friendly Paraguayans (Article 7); indeed, a Paraguayan Legion of anti-López "patriots" was already being organized in Buenos Aires for that purpose.[58] Article 8 pledged the Allies "to respect the independence, sovereignty, and territorial integrity of the Republic of Paraguay." In the end, the Paraguayan people would "choose the Government and the institutions that suit them without any one of the Allies annexing them or imposing its protectorate on them as a result of the war."[59]

The liberal tone of these words reflected the careful scripting of Mitre and his foreign minister. They depicted the war as the product of historical necessity, as the inevitable clash between a barbarous, despotic regime that "for twenty years has been sharpening the sword" and a republic that "throughout Spanish America was distinguished as civilized, progressive, and as always opening its arms to outsiders."[60]

The implicit reference to a civilization-versus-barbarism dichotomy, which drew its inspiration from Domingo Sarmiento's famous essay *Facundo*, was as obvious then as it is today. Less obvious, perhaps, was the fact that it was demonstrably false. "Civilization" was present in both systems and in both countries—as Mitre well knew from his contacts with Solano López during the mediation of 1859. As for "barbarism," if that term meant the violent irregularity of rural politics, again, that was more typical of Mitre's own western provinces than it ever was of Paraguay. To suggest that the Allied side was entirely virtuous and the Paraguayans entirely "savage" amounted to a claim of disinterestedness on the part of the former—and nothing was further from the truth in 1865.

Specifically, the Allies argued that their war was directed solely against Solano López, yet both Mitre and the Brazilians had other, more substantial, aspirations than they initially revealed; they left secret the sixteenth, seventeenth, and eighteenth articles of the treaty of alliance. These articles, it later emerged, granted the senior Allies the full extent of their territorial demands on Paraguay while leaving the country nominally independent.[61] Mitre clearly wanted even more territorial concessions in the Chaco. The Brazilians, however, refused to allow him more land than was initially stipulated during the early negotiations. In a dispatch written while these talks were still in progress, Edward Thornton noted the expansionist proclivities of Elizalde and his president:

> I had supposed that on the arrival here of Señor Octaviano, the Brazilian Minister, who had come here sooner than he had intended at the invitation of the Argentine Government, negotiations would at once [have] been entered into for a formal alliance with Brazil as regards the war against Paraguay; but at first there was an evident coolness between Señor Octaviano and the Argentine Government. I can only attribute it to the stipulation demanded by the former that both parties should declare that they would respect the independence of the Republic of Paraguay. Both Mitre and Señor Elizalde have at different times declared to me that for the present they wished Paraguay to be independent, that it would not suit them to annex Paraguay, even if the Paraguayans should wish it, but that they were unwilling to make any engagement to that effect with Brazil; for they did not conceal from me that whatever their present views on the point, circumstances might change them hereafter, and Señor Elizalde, who is about forty years old, said to me one day though in mere conversation that he "hoped he should live to see Bolivia, Paraguay, Uruguay, and the Argentine Republic united in one Confederation, and forming a powerful Republic in South America."[62]

Thornton, who like all British diplomats in the Plata had long favored a buffer-state for promoting peace in the region, had no sympathy for the Argentine view on this question. The British government, as a sign of its displeasure, opted to publish his report at the end of June 1865.

Despite the distances involved, it was still odd that the report's contents elicited so little comment in South America, for they clearly showed that the marshal was right in suspecting Mitre's intentions.[63] They also showed that, far from instigating the war, the British regarded a violent conflict in the worst possible light and wanted nothing to do with it. The alliance, the British believed, was a sloppy and entangling piece of diplomacy, for in wedding Brazilian interests to those of Argentina, the treaty sought to join oil to water. No one, after all, could predict the war's outcome, Mitre's claims of a three-month campaign notwithstanding. The only thing the British government regarded as certain was that the Platine trade they had done so much to promote was sure to suffer.[64]

The Brazilians had no interest in seeing Paraguay swallowed by their Argentine ally and pointedly refused to approve any such plan. Speaking before the Imperial Parliament some ten years later, José Antonio Saraiva explained his government's opposition to Argentine expansionism in concise terms: "I recognize that the Argentines wish to form a great State on the margins of the Plata. That desire is natural. Facing Brazil, whose territory extends 1,200 leagues along the Atlantic, . . . it is natural that the Argentines want to constitute a strong nationality. Suppressing the little republics that more than once have affected the peace of those regions. But the Argentine Government knows that those small republics wish to be independent and that the interest of Brazil consists in sustaining that independence. Later, when Brazil becomes a giant, it can afford to be indifferent to Platine unity."[65] Even though the Brazilians rejected Argentine plans for territorial aggrandizement, it would not have been politic to admit that such discussions had taken place. Octaviano understood the explosive character of the treaty's territorial provisions as they stood and insisted that all such references remain secret until after the Allies had crushed López.

H. G. Lettsom, the British minister at Montevideo, did not feel bound by any such considerations. Given a copy of the treaty in confidence by the young Uruguayan foreign minister, he transmitted it in toto to London, where in early 1866 the government published it as part of a parliamentary blue book. This time the British government's revelations caused a furor in South America, where many who previously had espoused neutrality now leaned sharply against the Allies. Little wonder; the terms of the treaty that touched on territorial matters were specific, unambiguous, and extensive.

Article 11 declared the Paraná and Paraguay Rivers permanently open to commercial and naval traffic. In fact, for the most part, the rivers had already been open since the mid-1850s, though to be sure, there were times when Carlos Antonio López harassed Brazilian vessels passing through his territory. Article 14 held that Paraguay, if defeated, should bear the entire cost of the war. Article 16 provided for the settlement of land disputes "in order to avoid the arguments and wars to which boundary questions give rise." The boundaries of Paraguay and Argentina were set at the Paraná and Paraguay Rivers up to Brazilian territory; in other words, in the event of Allied victory, the Argentines would receive the whole of the Misiones territory south of the Alto Paraná and the whole of the Gran Chaco as far north as Bahia Negra. Villa Occidental and all the lands opposite Asunción would come under Argentine control. Thornton, who regarded as farfetched the claims made in Article 16, wrote to the Lord Russell that "Señor Elizalde has stated to me that although the Argentine Government appears to claim the right bank of the river Paraguay as far up as the Brazilian frontier, they are willing to acknowledge that Bolivia has a right to an intervening space from the Brazilian frontier to the river Pilcomayo, and they would even consent upon certain conditions to cede to Bolivia as far down as the river Vermejo; but both the Brazilian and Argentine Governments think it very desirable that Paraguay should at no point have dominion over both banks of the river of that name."[66]

The empire set its boundary with Paraguay at the confluence of the Paraguay and Apa Rivers in the west and at that of the Alto Paraná and Ygurey Rivers in the east. The two points would be linked by a line running along the crest of the Sierra de Mbaracayú. In sum, the two allies recognized each other's most extensive claims against Paraguay.

By an additional protocol, Argentina and Brazil agreed to dismantle Humaitá and eliminate forever all of Paraguay's war-making capabilities. Article 18 concluded the treaty, declaring that its various details should remain secret until its principal objective — the elimination of the López regime — was attained. However, word of the treaty's contents leaked after several months. The result, as Octaviano and his colleagues had foreseen, was that Paraguayan resistance stiffened in every way, for now the Paraguayan people saw that more than simple politics guided the ambitions of their enemies: Paraguay's survival as a nation, as a community, was at stake. Given this fact, it mattered little that the marshal was irresponsible. The Paraguayan people would follow him, if necessary, down the long, painful trail to Armageddon.

*Delaying Actions*

A treaty is one thing; planning and conducting a military campaign quite another. The Allied armies now had a major theater of operations in which to fight the Paraguayans. But could they coordinate their actions to good effect? Roseate promises of easy victory were certainly reassuring, yet no one considered the financial and political costs of waging war. Thus far, no one had thought in practical terms at all.

As the need for an overall strategy came into sharper focus, General Paunero arrived in the Litoral. His mission necessarily took the form of a holding action until the general mobilization throughout Argentina was complete. All the Argentine forces — including Urquiza's Entrerrianos — received orders to execute maximum delay against Robles's army while avoiding decisive combat.

The Allies enjoyed some advantages even at this early stage. For one thing, the marshal had failed to concentrate all his forces in the west and had instead left ten thousand men at the Pindapoi to prepare an incursion along the Uruguay River. Had the Paraguayans combined their forces and moved boldly on Bella Vista and Goya, nothing could have stopped them. They would have taken Paraná and gone on to threaten Santa Fe, Rosario, and the east of Entre Ríos.

The Paraguayans exhibited another weakness at the divisional level — the indecision of General Robles. He had no experience with the type of conventional warfare he was now pursuing. As a result, he favored slower, more conservative tactics. He obviously expected the Argentines to mount a counterattack, though, as he should have recognized, they were in no position to mount offensive operations. True, Robles's cautious approach aided his reconnaissance efforts on his peripheries and thereby gained for the Paraguayans a degree of safety that they otherwise would not have enjoyed. But it also lost valuable time.

After 1 May, the Allies adopted a long-term strategy that called for a direct confrontation with the Paraguayans along the Paraná River followed promptly thereafter by the recapture of Corrientes, the passage across the Paraná to Paso de la Patria, and then up the Paraguay to Asunción. All this would be the task of the main Allied armies then being assembled, organized, and trained at the small Entrerriano town of Concordia, opposite Salto on the Uruguay River.

For the time being, the province of Corrientes had to defend itself with five thousand irregulars. One-fifth of this number — almost all cavalrymen — were positioned near the Misiones frontier, where they carefully watched Duarte's activities on the Pindapoi; if the Paraguayans made any precipitous moves, the irregulars had orders to slow them by whatever means necessary. The Correntino commander in the east, Col. Simeón Paiva, realized that his men would show only a limited enthusiasm for obeying these instructions. He therefore had to be satisfied with keeping desertions to a minimum.

Similar problems plagued the Correntinos in the west. Though on paper Nicanor Cáceres had at least four thousand irregulars under his command, in reality the number varied from day to day. These troops operated without artillery and without logistical or medical support. They often refused to obey their officers. Experience had taught Cáceres not to expect too much of his men. He himself was a cunning old guerrilla who knew well enough how to dodge, retreat, and circumvent, but he also knew these men, and he wisely avoided pushing them too hard. Instead, he gave up land in order to gain time, making only minor forays against the Paraguayan left. Maintaining contact in this way helped restrict Paraguayan reconnaissance to a thin semicircle around the front and flank of Robles's vanguard column, which had limited itself to long-range patrolling. Though his troops outnumbered their Argentine opponents eight to one, Robles continued to ease forward only gingerly.

Cáceres, whom the *porteños* still dismissed as a gaucho rustic, now began to reap benefits from these delaying tactics. His war of movement played to the strengths of Mitre and his generals, who wished to avoid any decisive battles at this stage. And the frequency of sniping and small-scale ambushes began taking a toll on Paraguayan morale.

On 28 April, Cáceres's irregulars and Robles's main force clashed for the first time along the edge of the San Lorenzo River, a narrow and unremarkable waterway located halfway between Empedrado and Bella Vista. The Paraguayan general had dispatched the six-hundred-man Twenty-first Cavalry Regiment to reconnoiter along the riverbanks and seize whatever livestock could be found. One squadron of about fifty troopers was moving through tall grass when it suddenly found itself surrounded by two or three hundred Correntino cavalrymen. The Correntinos shouted in Guaraní for the Paraguayans to surrender. One officer, Col. Fermín Alsina, hastily sent over a note to the same effect, threatening the Paraguayans with extermination (the *degüello*) should they refuse. Yet this was exactly what the squadron did. José de Jesús Páez, the lieutenant commanding the Paraguayan horsemen, refused to parley and instead attacked at once. His men dashed through the front line of the Correntino cavalry and, with their lances stabbing to the left and right, made good their escape into the bush. The Paraguayans lost four men killed and perhaps a dozen wounded. They left behind the herds of cattle that they had taken earlier in the day.

This action at San Lorenzo, which lasted less than an hour, was typical of the clashes that occurred on a daily basis for the rest of the Corrientes campaign.[67] General Robles remained with his infantry in a defensive position at Riachuelo, all the time receiving reinforcements from the north. Berges and the *Junta Gubernativa* promised to send some reliable Correntino troops to join the Paraguayans as part of this buildup.[68] By the second week of May, the Southern Division reached a peak strength of twenty-five thousand men — far greater than anything the Argentines could muster. The size of these units mattered little, however, for Robles's inaction had already cost him too much time. More than three weeks had passed since the beginning of the campaign, and he had yet to advance even as far as Empedrado.[69] Nicanor Cáceres could afford to feel sanguine. His small band of irregulars had effectively delayed the Paraguayan army.[70]

When Robles finally decided to move on 11 May, he struck out in a curious direction. The Paraguayans abruptly pushed inland, away from the Paraná and toward the marshlands at the center of the province. Within twenty-four hours, the army turned again, first to the south and then to the southwest, before finally entering Empedrado on the fourteenth. This odd maneuver might have fooled a few Argentine pickets, but its execution took three days, whereas Empedrado would certainly have fallen in just as many hours.

On 15 May the long-anticipated advance began in earnest as the Paraguayans, now formed into a single column, pushed south in the direction of Bella Vista. The vanguard, commanded by Col. José María Aguiar, had already been bloodied in the many minor encounters with Cáceres. Now, however, it boasted an important advantage hitherto unavailable. Robles brought most of his artillery well forward in the column where it could directly support the advance guard. As soon as Aguiar met resistance, his men wheeled their cannons into position and fired on the Correntinos at close range. Cáceres, who could not take many casualties, invariably withdrew. By this deft use of artillery, the Paraguayans kept their own losses low. More importantly, they saved wear on their horses, without which no forward momentum was possible.[71]

The Paraguayans took Bella Vista on 20 May. They found the village largely deserted, its inhabitants gone. Even so, there was something restful about the place they left behind. Many of the sweet orange and tangerine trees that made the community famous in the northeast were bearing fruit just then. The few blooms that remained on the trees were enough to fill the air with a light perfume that seemed wildly out of place in a country at war. As at Corumbá, the Paraguayans went from door to door filling their rucksacks with whatever spoils they could find.

They then slept soundly by their campfires. Having come nearly eighty miles through backswamps and sloughs littered with brush and downed timber, the soldiers were tired and footsore.

Robles allowed his men two days rest, then started them south once again. The harassment they encountered this time was far less than earlier; Cáceres wrote Paunero that desertions plagued him terribly and that what remained of his exhausted forces could not continue their delaying operations much longer.[72] Still in good spirits after a long march, the Paraguayans took up new positions along the Santa Lucía River, some forty miles south of Bella Vista, on 26 May. They were poised to walk into Goya, this time convinced that Argentine resistance had evaporated. Events back at Corrientes were to prove them wrong.

The Argentine predicament in the region had been exacerbated by bad intelligence all along. General Paunero, an old, white-bearded officer who shared the same unusual given name with his Paraguayan opponent, had far more experience of the world and of the military art than his counterpart.[73] Yet this did not stop him from misconstruing the situation in the northeast.

Paunero had counted from the beginning on the active support of the Brazilian fleet. After the attack of 13 April, Admiral Tamandaré had sent ten vessels to Bella Vista to begin preparations for a blockade upriver. Paunero's First Division arrived in town on 2 May only to discover by messenger that, though Entrerriano recruitment had gone well, Urquiza would not be able to deploy his troops for some time to come. This was unfortunate, for word had just arrived from Cáceres that the Paraguayans had withdrawn from Empedrado and had even abandoned their base camp on the Riachuelo. To Paunero, these tidings could only mean that Paraguayan indecision, even cowardice, had finally rebounded to Argentina's favor. He promptly asked the imperial navy to provide passage for his two-thousand-man force so that he could cut off Robles's retreat and destroy the Paraguayan interlopers before they could reach Paso de la Patria.

In fact, the enemy had no intention of withdrawing. Acting under the marshal's specific orders, Robles had transferred to the port of Corrientes all the men he deemed unfit for a forced march to the south. This was the "withdrawal" that Cáceres had reported. Thus, when Paunero set out from Bella Vista, he imagined himself to be in pursuit of a retreating army, only to discover on arrival at Empedrado that the Paraguayans even then were bearing down on him.

There was nothing left to be done. Paunero reembarked his men aboard the Brazilian steamers and returned to Bella Vista without having once made contact with Robles's forces. The swiftness of the Paraguayan onslaught made it impossible for him to attempt any resistance at Bella Vista, and so, rather embarrassed, he again withdrew, this time to an old *saladero* just north of Goya called the Rincón de Soto.

*The Raid on Corrientes*

On 19 May the much-flustered Paunero received a reinforcement of two infantry battalions and a squadron of artillery. This gave his First Division a total of some thirty-five hundred men and twelve guns, not counting Cáceres's five thousand mounted irregulars.[74] Though still distinctly inferior to Robles's army, this force at least was capable of effective action. The Brazilians still had ten vessels in the area, and perhaps Paunero could take advantage of their firepower—though this was by no means certain, as the Paraguayans could simply move out of range. The Argentine commander initially planned to land at Bella Vista but abandoned the idea when Robles preempted him. This left two possible options. In keeping with his mission of delaying the Paraguayan advance, Paunero might set up a defensive position across from the Paraguayans on the Santa Lucía River. Though Robles's men could storm or outflank his division, their losses would be heavy. But Paunero was also likely to lose many men.

Another option involved using the Brazilian fleet to transport his men upriver and land them behind the Paraguayans to wreck havoc in their rear. Robles had established a line of communications that stretched one hundred miles back to Corrientes and was nearly undefended along its entire length. The Paraguayan had relied on Meza's ships to ferry men and supplies to the front lines; this made sense initially, when the enemy fleet had yet to react, but now no one could tell when the imperial navy might choose to take offensive action.

This uncertainty worked to Paunero's favor. So did the fact that Marshal López had left only a token force to garrison the port of Corrientes — an unforgivable error given the thirty thousand men held in reserve at Humaitá. Had López used these troops to reinforce Corrientes and defend Robles's lines of communication, Paunero would have had to yield even more ground. Instead, the Argentine commander became the happy recipient of some important news. At midnight on 23 May, Brazilian vessels captured a small Paraguayan canoe that was attempting to work its way down the Paraná to Robles; its crew, when forced to talk, informed Allied officers of the true situation at Corrientes: the port had only a skeletal defense force and one warship at anchor.[75] Paunero at once decided to mount a major raid to coincide with 25 May, Argentina's independence day.

His plan called for the First Division to leave the Rincón de Soto aboard nine Brazilian and two Argentine vessels, then land and capture the provincial capital under the covering fire of the navy. Nicanor Cáceres, who was already hard pressed, received an order to contribute fifteen hundred cavalrymen who would by-pass the Paraguayans on the east, ride hard on Corrientes, and support the landing force on the river.[76]

This part of the plan, which the Correntino general strenuously opposed, was ill considered. It required that his men move a distance of 110 miles through partly contested territory, join a battle in progress, and then withdraw just as quickly by the same route. Exhausted men fight poorly. Moreover, as Cáceres gruffly pointed out to his *porteño* superior, their participation was unnecessary to a successful raid. It added nothing while drawing away from the delaying operations in the south. Paunero, however, overruled Cáceres and made preparations for the attack.

The Allied landing force consisted of approximately four thousand officers and men. This included Paunero's First Division, which then had twelve hundred infantrymen and one hundred artillerymen; Brazil's

Ninth Infantry Brigade, under the command of Col. João Guilherme Bruce, which in addition to thirteen hundred infantry had another fifty artillerymen; and twenty-three hundred naval crewmen, including gunners commanded by Adm. Francisco Manoel Barroso, a white-whiskered old salt only recently arrived from Montevideo. The Paraguayan defenders, who would also have to contend with Cáceres's fifteen hundred cavalry, had two infantry battalions and three old bronze field guns of small caliber in battery for a total of sixteen hundred men.

The raiding force arrived off Riachuelo in midafternoon on 24 May. The Paraguayans had already left their nearby base camp, and Paunero felt reassured that he could surprise his enemies without fear of detection. In fact, the Paraguayans learned of his presence almost immediately.[77] At 7:30 A.M. the next day, the Allied ships again got under way, and after rounding a bend just below Corrientes, they became visible to sailors aboard the Paraguayan ship *Pirabebé*. As the British-flagged *Ranger*, this vessel had previously plowed the river as far north as Corumbá and was well known in the region. Solano López had authorized her purchase only a short time earlier and was happy to add her to his fleet. At 120 tons, though, she was one of his smaller steamers and not likely to put up a good fight. As the Paraguayan prisoners had maintained, no other ship was then in port. The *Pirabebé* fired two shots, both of which missed, and then retired posthaste toward Humaitá to warn the troops there. She steamed past Corrientes without stopping though her crew did signal the Paraguayan garrison of the impending attack.

At 10:00 A.M. the Allied fleet moved into view off Corrientes. The streets of the town, though sandy and rutted, were laid out on a perfect grid; this allowed the fleet to fire along straight lines into Corrientes and make difficult any movements by the defending Paraguayans. General Paunero and Admiral Barroso, however, had decided to keep such firing to a minimum and concentrate it only on the points where they intended to land troops.

The place chosen for a landing was several miles north of the port at a spot called La Batería de San Pedro. After their invasion six weeks earlier, the Paraguayans had erected a small fort at this site, which guarded the approach to Paso de la Patria. One of the two available Paraguayan battalions had moved up earlier to guard this site upon receiving news of Paunero's approach. They were ready when, at four o'clock in the afternoon, two companies of Argentine infantry landed directly in front of them.[78]

One of these companies was organized as a unit called the Legion Militar, comprising mostly Italian and French mercenaries recruited in Europe at the time of the troubles in the Banda Oriental. Some of these men had fought in the Crimea, and all had been told that the struggle against Solano López was the same as their own against the hated Austrians. To a man, they were anxious for the fray to begin. Their commander, Maj. Gianbattista Charlone, had formerly served in the Italian forces and, like many adventurers in the Garibaldi mold, had cultivated a dashing appearance and an air of self-assurance. He too was ready to fight. Before his legion could advance, however, he had to cancel the supporting fire of his Brazilian allies, who had accidentally rained shells among his men.[79]

Still more died when they tried to assault the small fort. Paraguayan resistance proved sharper and more sustained than anyone on the Allied side would have guessed. Charlone received a serious wound when a Paraguayan trooper struck him across the head with a saber as he tried to rush the enemy position. His men pulled him to safety, but several were lanced in the process. More common were the casualties suffered on both sides from musket and rifle fire.[80]

Though the Paraguayans looked grimy and ill attired compared to the Legión Militar, there was nothing sloppy about their fighting. They maintained unit cohesion amid the smoke and confusion and even when pressured at close quarters. Already the Allies were beginning to note and admire the fighting qualities of López's men.[81]

The most impressive show of Paraguayan doggedness came an hour and a half into the fight. The marshal's commander at Corrientes, Maj. José de la Cruz Martínez, was a young, dyspeptic-looking officer with a thin, almost comical moustache and no experience of war. He sent his reserve battalion forward to reinforce La Batería without understanding the artillery arrayed against him. Given the constant bombardment, the battalion made it only as far as the Poncho Verde Creek, still a quarter mile to the south. The creek, which was filled with slow-moving, greenish water, could only effectively be crossed at one stone bridge. Since they could go no farther, the Paraguayans decided to hold the bridge in order to disrupt any Allied moves on Corrientes. The defenders at La Batería, seeing what had happened, abandoned the fort and fell back to the bridge to join their comrades.

Martínez, who observed these developments from the tower of the legislative palace in Corrientes, had no time to plan an elaborate defense, but what his men lacked in preparation, they made up for in stamina. They brought forward two of their three bronze guns just before the Argentines attacked en masse. The Paraguayans fired their cannon and muskets and brandished their cutlasses at the enemy. Acrid black-powder smoke engulfed their position; neither side could see what they were firing at. Many defenders fell back bloodied, reeling into the Poncho Verde, where they were drowned.

The Argentines fought well for a time, concentrating their rifle fire with good effect on the thinning ranks before them. But when the Paraguayans still refused to break, the attacking force fell back to regroup and strike again. At just that moment, Colonel Bruce and his Brazilian Ninth Infantry arrived. The colonel brought with him a two-gun battery that at once proceeded to fire grapeshot directly into the Paraguayan position. This proved too much even for Martínez. He signaled his men to abandon the bridge, leaving behind the corpses that littered it at both ends. That night no one could cross the bridge without stepping on the bodies of the fallen.[82]

The Paraguayans retreated through the town to a point about one mile east. There, in a forested area, they halted, regrouped, and awaited aid from Humaitá. Berges, the *Junta Gubernativa*, and scores of pro-López Correntinos had already preceded them to Las Lomas, where they found refuge at Teodoro Gauna's summerhouse. The Paraguayans had lost some four hundred men and the Allies just over three hundred.[83]

As it turned out, the Allies lacked sufficient naval support to stay in

Corrientes. They definitely had no wish to pursue Martínez away from the river and the protection of naval guns. Instead, they marched into town and seized a huge quantity of Paraguayan arms and munitions.[84] Then, during the night, they celebrated with drinks and fireworks. The Correntinos showed little interest in these festivities nor any sign at all of friendship for their *porteño* liberators.[85] Some of the townspeople kept their distance because they worried about Paraguayan retributions, but a majority thought the raid an unqualified victory for no one save the Liberals. In fact, the Brazilian and Argentine troops wrecked at least a score of houses and made off with whatever spoils were lying within — hardly the kind of behavior calculated to build support for the Allied cause among the Correntinos.[86] As for Cáceres, whose participation Paunero had deemed so crucial, he failed to arrive until the next day.

To achieve maximum disruption of Paraguayan movements, Paunero wished to station the Brazilian fleet forward, directly in the channel that separated Corrientes from Paraguay. This would prevent any quick reinforcement for Martínez from the opposite bank of the Paraná. Admiral Barroso demurred, however, saying that his fleet had no pilots familiar with that stretch of the river. He feared that his ships might run aground or come under the Paraguayan guns at Paso de la Patria.[87]

Though no great comment was made at the time, Barroso's refusal to heed the Argentine request was only the first instance of what was to become a chronic problem: without an overall commander, the naval and land forces operated independently, and their leaders could not or would not subordinate their individual interests to a common goal. Jealousy played a role in all this as did mistrust, both of which augured badly for the future.[88]

Reluctantly, Paunero reembarked his troops aboard the Brazilian transports. The Correntinos, who had neither welcomed nor shunned the Argentine raiders, came out of their houses to stare at the troops. Paunero told them that he would provide transport for anyone who wished to leave, but few locals took him up on his offer. By the morning of the twenty-seventh, the Allied forces were steaming southward, once again looking for Robles.

The *porteño* press celebrated the raid of 25 May as a great triumph for Argentina, and indeed, Paunero had much to feel good about. As a spoiling action, his raid was completely successful. It confused the overconfident Paraguayans and frustrated their plans for a continued advance to the south. Now they had to worry about similar Allied attacks in their rear, and this worry, in turn, justified a reappraisal of their entire strategic position. The government in Buenos Aires had ordered Paunero to delay Robles in every way possible; his raid on Corrientes accomplished this better than the harassment of the main Paraguayan columns had hitherto done.

Despite Paunero's success on 25 May, he could not afford to bluster. He had sustained heavy losses without really diminishing the numbers of Paraguayans facing him. And, without sufficient naval support, he could never hope to hold Corrientes. Thus, though he might claim a significant victory for Allied arms, he still had much to worry about. Word soon spread throughout the army, moreover, that the Paraguayans fought like jaguars and would not yield to superior arms.

### The Marshal Overreacts

When Solano López learned of Paunero's attack on Corrientes, he flew into a rage. The main part of his fleet was at anchor at Asunción, unable to respond to this obvious threat to Paraguay proper. The marshal had men ready at Humaitá but no way to get them in sufficient numbers across the river to Martínez. Flustered, he summoned his scribe and dictated an elaborate dispatch to Robles, who at that moment was still positioned along the Santa Lucía. López ordered his general to decamp and return in haste to Corrientes together with the entire Southern Division: "There is no need to effect a forced march, but you must not lose time. It is understood that you cannot leave a single man behind, but instead [rush] to reinforce our troops.... If General Urquiza should appear to pursue you, attempt to avoid contact and fight only if you have no choice, always keeping in mind that the further you pull him [into Corrientes], the further will he be from his base of supply, whereas you will be approaching and finally uniting with us."[89]

The marshal had incomplete information when he composed this dispatch, and he sent it off without waiting for an update. In point of fact, Martínez had reoccupied Corrientes; Paunero's army had withdrawn to Esquina, a town far to the south of Goya; Cáceres had melted back into the hinterland away from the Paraguayans; and neither Urquiza nor Mitre could promise reinforcements any time soon. There was no threat.

Such was his character, however, that López could not bring himself to reverse his order. Robles had been set to march on Goya. He was finally beginning to feel his oats as a fighting general, and his men were rested. Yet now came this baffling instruction to turn around, abandon the field, and retrace his path northward to Corrientes.

Robles simply could not believe it, for once the offensive had begun, it was his duty to sustain it. The general assumed, therefore, that the marshal had issued his order without full knowledge of what had happened back at the provincial capital.[90] The general equivocated for a time, then sent his own messenger to ask for a clarification. When the query reached Asunción, Solano López lost his temper. How dare this general question his orders? Worse still, he began to think that Robles was not merely foolish but actively undermining Paraguayan war aims. His suspicions were confirmed to him when he learned that Robles had occupied Goya on 2 June. On that same day, the marshal announced his decision to leave for the front to take personal command of his forces in the field.[91]

The Paraguayan general had not meant to appear insubordinate, but Goya had always loomed large in his strategic plans. It possessed the best port in the immediate vicinity. The Allies had left it undefended, and yet the Paraguayans could easily bring the town under their own defensive umbrella from their camps on the Santa Lucía. Most important of all, Goya was located along the shortest and best-trod route to the Uruguay River, which meant, in effect, that only a few days' march now separated Robles from his Oriental friends. It is easy to see why he was reluctant to part with such a valuable prize.

Solano López had no patience with "unruly" field commanders. By his actions, Robles had planted the seed in his president's mind that something had gone badly awry with the Southern Division. On 4 June the general received confirmation of the earlier order. In language that was terse and biting, Solano López reminded him of his place, stating that his failure to obey promptly had frustrated the military timetable elsewhere.[92]

Why should the marshal insist now on the course of action outlined on 26 May? Robles, after all, was right — the situation had changed. In looking for an answer, we need to recall that the López regime was atavistically focused on the power and prestige of the chief executive. Any suggestion of fallibility brought the entire system into question. Solano López reacted instinctively to protect himself, his family, and the established order. He might change his mind, but no one would change it for him.

It is also unclear how much reliable intelligence he had received. Martínez had reported; his men had started to clear the corpses from the battleground and from the mucky waters of the Poncho Verde. Eighty-three soldiers wounded in the battle were being cared for in a converted convent at one side of town. Aside from this, the only news worthy of attention was the arrival, some miles to the south, of the British ship *Dotterell* and the Italian ship *Veloce*, both of which intended to sail on to Asunción to evacuate their respective compatriots. The Brazilians, who insisted on the inviolability of their blockade, tried to hold up their passage, though only for a short time.[93] There was no further evidence of enemy activity.[94]

The marshal had also heard from Berges, however, and in his note the foreign minister stressed that Barroso's warships were still lurking near the Riachuelo. Perhaps Solano López suspected that another Allied assault was in the offing. In any case, he had given Robles an order twice and now expected to see it obeyed.

Robles felt chastened, even a little afraid. He forgot all about the military implications of abandoning Goya and, after setting a few buildings ablaze, turned his army around.[95] On 13 June the Southern Division reached Empedrado. The weird movement of the Paraguayan column perplexed Paunero, who at first assumed that Robles meant to attack San Roque on his way to the Uruguay. When the Paraguayan commander made no move in that direction, the main Argentine forces held back, leaving Cáceres's irregulars to ambush a few enemy stragglers. In any case Paunero was considering urgent calls to bring his troops to join the Allied buildup at Concordia and wished no confrontation at the time. Little else happened as the Allies pondered their next move. Meanwhile, Robles received an order to encamp his forces along the Paraná at the Rincón del Peguajó. His mission now was to prevent the passage of the Brazilian fleet — a ludicrous assignment for an army.

The Allies had reason to feel perplexed, for in truth, the Paraguayan movements made no sense. In the two months since the war began in Corrientes, Robles had marched roughly two hundred miles into Argentine territory but had yet to fight a major battle. What he had accomplished had little strategic value if he failed to push forward. Instead, he withdrew because of a brief but violent raid behind his back. And now, oddest of all, he was holding a riverbank in order to keep seven Brazilian warships at bay. None of this was useful, none of it necessary.

The Paraguayans fared no better in their political offensive. Berges and Silvero were hard-working individuals who struggled incessantly to convince the Correntinos to adhere to the marshal's cause. With the followers of the Federal Party — and their extended families — they enjoyed some success. The *junta* also managed to recruit several hundred men to serve with the Paraguayan army.[96] These forces were just as irregular as those who served with Cáceres and fought in the same ruthless way. They served as scouts and foragers for Robles and were particularly effective in stemming Mitrista resistance in the departments of Itatí, San Cosme, and Yaguareté Corá.[97] Even so, their numbers were tiny and their support precarious.

Ordinary Correntinos — the people that Berges and the *junta* desperately wished to sway — remained indifferent to the Paraguayan appeals. Their attitude of uncertainty was understandable, but the Paraguayan tired of waiting for their conversion. The marshal had little use for political gestures when military solutions were freely at hand. Now that the battle of La Batería was over, he grew tired of the seemingly endless banter in Corrientes and demanded that his officers get on with the war. Under such pressure, Berges's hopes for rapprochement between the two Guaraní-speaking peoples were sorely tested. He tried to address the concerns of the Correntinos by establishing a ten-member committee to investigate allegations of Allied theft and mayhem growing out of the 25 May raid. Merchants, especially foreigners, filed scores of complaints with this committee, which continued to operate until the end of August.[98]

In the intervening months, the *Junta Gubernativa* repeatedly attempted to serve as a conduit between the Paraguayans and the Correntinos in the south of the province. Berges encouraged Silvero and his associates to think of themselves as allies, not puppets. One result early on was that they openly sought to contact Nicanor Cáceres and encourage his defection from the national government.[99] They also made several clandestine attempts to open negotiations with his old patron Urquiza, and on at least one occasion, now understood only in outline, they tried to tempt some key *porteño* officers to turn against Mitre and his Brazilian friends.[100] None of these efforts had any success. And as the cold South American winter months passed, the *Junta* members began to lose the little amount of legitimacy they had built up in the province. They also learned how expendable they really were. More and more, the trio found themselves turning to Berges as someone who might protect them, as much from Solano López as from the Allied armies. For his part, the foreign minister felt no compunction at passing off every failed policy in Corrientes as specifically their work.

*The March to the Uruguay*

Ever since the attack on Corrientes, the Paraguayan force stationed on the Pindapoi had been waiting to join the fight. Maj. Pedro Duarte, aware of the distances involved, supposed that at some point his army of ten thousand would be ordered south to link up with that of Robles. The Argentines were perfectly aware of his presence, but the dispatch of

Col. Siméon Paiva's irregulars into the Misiones was all they could manage by way of defense. No one imagined that such poor troops would stop Duarte once he started to move. The Brazilians were still too far away to provide support, yet to the surprise of the Allies, the Paraguayan major failed to advance.

The map of northeastern Argentina suggests two possible strategies for Duarte's army. In one scenario, it could drive through the lightly held Misiones directly into Rio Grande do Sul, probably at São Borja, and continue south as an independent force until it crossed the Uruguayan frontier. At that point, friendly Blancos would rise and link their operations to those of the marshal. Given the disposition of the imperial forces, most of which still clustered around Montevideo, this approach had much to recommend it.

A safer, though more time-consuming, strategy would involve Duarte's force as one arm of a giant pincer movement across the provinces of Corrientes and Entre Ríos. His force would act as counterweight to that of Robles, driving down the Uruguay just as the general's troops drove down the Paraná. Somewhere below the Laguna Yberá, the two forces would come together and destroy any remaining Argentine units between them. They then would move on as a single formation into friendly territory in Uruguay. Both strategies required a clear timetable that synchronized Duarte's movements with those of Robles. To achieve such coordination, Duarte should have started his march before 13 April. But he remained immobile, nervously awaiting orders.

Other than advancing in the general direction of the Banda Oriental, Solano López had no operational plan to achieve his military goals. He expected to be carried from victory to victory by the bravery of his troops and the sheer incompetence of his enemies. The Mato Grosso campaign had demonstrated the vulnerability of Brazilian arms. But there the Paraguayans enjoyed the advantage of surprise. Rio Grande, the marshal hoped, would prove that even with sufficient time for preparation, his enemies would still crumble at the approach of his army.

This was a dangerous assumption. The marshal's lack of concrete plans was astonishing for a man who had read Jomini and who had done so much to prepare his armed forces in training and weaponry. In this case, not only did he fail to synchronize Duarte's movements with those of Robles but he even went so far as to relieve Duarte at the last moment, replacing him with an inexperienced lieutenant colonel.

The new commander was Antonio de la Cruz Estigarribia, a tall, youngish officer whose black beard had yet to be marred by a single gray hair. Although not particularly wealthy, he came from a well-connected family (one of his relatives had been Dr. Francia's personal physician) and enjoyed the many privileges of elite life in the 1850s. But he had little aptitude for the military. Instead, he owed his advancement in the army to connections and to his unfailing submissiveness to the president. As one of his own subordinates later observed, Estigarribia might have been "a sergeant with the epaulettes of a lieutenant colonel," but he was always willing to keep himself in Solano López's shadow.[101] During the latter's mediation between Buenos Aires and the Argentine Confederation in 1859, Estigarribia acted as his military assistant. At the beginning of the war with Brazil, he was still serving as presidential aide-de-camp. Then in quick succession, he was transferred to the far south to take command at Encarnación before finally arriving at the Pindapoi on 27 April to take over from Duarte, who stayed on as second in command.[102]

The troops in the Misiones saw in the appointment of Estigarribia the triumph of political connections over efficiency, and they felt uncomfortable. Duarte, whom the men regarded as a soldier's soldier, had been with them since the beginning and had overseen their training and organization. They still itched to get into action. With a "political" commander like Estigarribia to lead them, however, they were far more uneasy about the task before them.

Estigarribia was no more comfortable than his men. He understood better than they how meager his real experience of command was and chose to make up for it by ridiculing Duarte behind his back. He made life so difficult for his subordinate that even written communication between the two became strained—a fact that later played to the Allies' advantage.[103]

Though by the end of April most of the men along the Pindapoi were reasonably well trained, they still had few arms relative to their compatriots on the Paraná. Estigarribia could boast only five cannon, calibers 3 and 5, and one mortar, caliber 10. For a force about to mount an invasion, this was woefully inadequate artillery. Estigarribia's superiors in Asunción evidently felt, however, that the sheer weight of his ten-thousand-man force was more than enough to cover any contingency, and indeed, the Allies had no comparable armed force anywhere nearby. The most Colonels Paiva and Isidoro Reguera could do was to follow Estigarribia's movements and perhaps steal some of the cattle grazing along the Pindapoi.

On 5 May the first Paraguayan units, organized into a "brigade" under Major Duarte, began a reconnaissance in force, marching south through rolling hills. Heavily wooded in places, this was some of the fairest land in the northeast. Light breezes kept its climate pleasant except in the hottest months, and even then it was more comfortable than the adjacent river valleys. Its beauty and pleasant airs aside, this part of the Misiones impressed the Paraguayans by its emptiness. As the threat of war mounted in 1864, the small farmers and ranchers of the region relocated farther south. Even those tiny groups of refugees that had taken up residence in the ruins of the old Jesuit missions were nowhere in sight.

Duarte's men periodically spotted some of Paiva's troops but made no contact. On 7 May the Paraguayans reached the former mission town of Santa María, now an abandoned ruin save for one or two families who proved outwardly friendly. They informed the major that he would encounter no Correntino or Brazilian troop concentrations before reaching Santo Tomé on the Uruguay River. Armed with this information, Duarte sent to Estigarribia for reinforcements. The colonel, who had stayed behind with the main Paraguayan force, immediately sent two squadrons of lancers to help Duarte dislodge any enemies he might find. Using lancers as shock troops was certainly unconventional, but the major was glad to get the help, which brought the size of his command to 664 men.

The marshal's instructions directed Estigarribia to move with all dispatch to the Paso de los Garruchos, an isolated bend on the Uruguay some distance from Santo Tomé. Solano López wanted the colonel to avoid all inhabited areas during the first stage of the campaign. Duarte's reconnaissance, however, took him forty miles south of the point indicated; it was well that he went so far, else he would not have learned how weak Allied defenses really were. A false rumor had it that a full division of infantry and cavalry was waiting in ambush.

On 9 May, having advanced twenty-eight miles through wooded country from Santa María, Duarte's brigade caught sight of the Uruguay River, glistening and curving gently like a crescent moon in the direction of Buenos Aires. The next day Duarte ordered twenty-three of his best horsemen to move forward into Santo Tomé. This was only a probe, designed to ferret out enemy stragglers and determine the disposition of any larger forces; Duarte still thought it likely that they would encounter sizable Allied units. In order to prevent their being heard, the horsemen received orders to use only their lances and avoid all gunfire. Yet as they came to the edge of town, the Paraguayans turned a corner and ran headlong into an Argentine mounted patrol, probably from Paiva's command. The Paraguayans instantly charged, killing one officer and driving the other horsemen from the field.[104] Duarte's men then entered Santo Tomé, which they found deserted save for several old women and three or four Italian merchants. One of the Paraguayan soldiers returned to the major with this news, and Duarte quickly brought up the remainder of his troops.

Santo Tomé hardly amounted to much—a score or two of little houses built of wood and adobe and thatched with palm leaves, and a half-dozen more substantial dwellings built partly of stone. Each house had its own small grove of orange trees intermixed with guavas, sweet limes, and the omnipresent mango, under which no grass could grow. The sleepy port district of Hormiguero was located a mile farther to the southeast. Though still small and underutilized, it was well situated to control the upper reaches of the Uruguay. Only São Borja, above the opposite bank a few miles downriver, had any claim to greater prominence. That town was still in the hands of the emperor's forces, and Duarte had no idea how many enemy troops were there.

As it was, the major had his hands full assessing the situation at Santo Tomé. While he was composing an extensive report for Estigarribia, however, he was happily surprised by the arrival of several well-dressed Uruguayans, army officers of the former Blanco regime. These men had earlier left Montevideo and journeyed to Paraguay through the Misiones in order to offer the marshal their support in driving the Brazilians from their homeland.[105] Their arrival at Santo Tomé gave added significance to Duarte's expedition, heartening his men, who reasoned that there must be many more potential allies in the Uruguayan hinterland and in Entre Ríos. Flores and the Brazilians had spent five months suppressing the Blancos, however, and a general uprising against the new order was now most unlikely. The men who came to Santo Tomé posed as heralds of a new round of fighting in the Banda Oriental, but in fact they were simply exiles. Duarte, who could not judge one way or the other, incorporated them into his brigade. They were to serve him faithfully over the next months.

Heavy rains delayed both Paraguayan and Allied movements for some days (though, as usual, rumor had thousands of Brazilian cavalrymen coming from the east). When the rains abruptly cleared on 17 May, Duarte temporarily retreated north toward Santa María, halting at a small encampment called Caazapava, where he ordered his men to dig a series of trenches. Reinforcements still had not arrived from Estigarribia. Spies had revealed to him, though, that the various Correntino cavalry units had finally reconstituted themselves into a fighting force of at least one thousand, and these horsemen were rapidly approaching the Paraguayans from the southwest. Given the presumed threat from imperial forces on the other side of the river, Duarte opted to pull back and tempt his enemies into a frontal assault, giving him the tactical advantage of a prepared defensive position.[106]

This was a wise move. Paiva, in fact, had already arranged for 500 Brazilian troopers to cross the Uruguay at São Borja to join his advance on Santo Tomé. When he learned of Duarte's retreat, however, he erroneously concluded that the Paraguayans were pulling back to the Pindapoi. Pushing ahead to cut them off, he missed his rendezvous with the Brazilians.[107] Lack of coordination between the two allies made it impossible to strike decisively at Caazapava. As the various units tried to regroup before attacking, they discovered that Duarte had finally received reinforcements — 452 cavalrymen and 385 infantrymen — and could not now be vanquished without serious loss to the Allies.[108]

Having missed the moment, Paiva and the Brazilians withdrew to Santo Tomé to plan their next move. Meanwhile, on 21 May Solano López sent word to Colonel Estigarribia to get on with his attack. Strangely, the marshal expressed little anger at the vacillating officer, simply reiterating his previous orders. Estigarribia was to move his command south of the Uruguay, crossing the bulk of his forces at the Paso de los Garruchos, and take São Borja. A secondary force along the right bank of the river was to protect his line of communication. Duarte would command this latter force.

As always, the major started out first, securing the river crossing without incident on 27 May, then moving on to retake Santo Tomé three days later. The Correntinos had learned of the Paraguayan advance from the few remaining refugees escaping south. Colonel Paiva, who had nothing to match the enemy's fifteen hundred men, wisely opted to avoid contact, save for a single incident in which some of his men exchanged fire with the Paraguayan vanguard and managed to shoot Duarte's kepi from his head.[109] Paiva's decision to pull back rather than take a stand at the river's edge was perfectly sound, especially as his Brazilian allies had yet to make an appearance.

The absence of the imperial forces worried rather than reassured the Paraguayan commander back at the Pindapoi. Despite the urgency of his orders, Estigarribia still hesitated to commit his full contingent, delaying his departure until the afternoon of 31 May 1865. His "Uruguay Division" now counted some eight thousand men in eight infantry battalions of seven hundred men each, three cavalry regiments of six hundred men each, one artillery squadron of five guns, and several engineering units to handle canoes and forty supply wagons.[110] At that time, the Brazilians had no soldiers west of the Uruguay River and relied on the sporadic reports of Correntino refugees fleeing Santo Tomé for intelligence. These frightened people always exaggerated the size of the Paraguayan force, some putting it as high as twenty-five thousand men.

Ignorance of the true strength of the enemy vexed the Brazilian military (as indeed it did the Paraguayans), but instead of acting with prudence, imperial forces scoffed at the antics of their opponents. These Riograndeses had not fought at La Batería and still regarded the marshal and his army with contempt. One rumormonger in Pôrto Alegre even claimed that the true commander of the Paraguayan forces was the Neapolitan general Bosck (a possible reference to Ferdinando Bosco, who had served Francis II in his recent campaign against Garibaldi).[111] Above all, no one felt that the Paraguayans themselves presented any real challenge.

Gen. David Canabarro, the thickly built Brazilian commander of the northern stretches of the Uruguay, held the same disdainful views as his men. Again and again he laughed at the Paraguayan army, which he thought full of "children and ancient men with hardly any teeth."[112] As an old cavalry officer from the Farrapo Revolt, he had the usual gaúcho disdain for peasant soldiers who walked rather than rode on horseback and who could never be trusted to obey an order.[113] The fall of Corrientes had taught him nothing, nor had the approach of Estigarribia. When the time came, he felt confident that the Paraguayans would turn and run.

Canabarro's experience and skill in the saddle, though certainly respectable, could only take him so far. He might loudly disparage the enemy while speaking words of kindness and encouragement to his men. He realized, all the same, that his own units were both inexperienced and under strength. In 1864, when the empire launched its invasion of the Banda Oriental, it sent to Paysandú the only organized military force in Rio Grande do Sul—a division of cavalry and infantry under Gen. João Propício Menna Barreto. The departure of this expeditionary force left an uncomfortable void in provincial defenses. Locals had to make up the difference with existing reserves. This meant that a brigade of less than five thousand untrained Guarda Nacional had to defend the entire length of the river as far south as Uruguaiana. As individuals, these guardsmen were exactly like Canabarro in his youth — resourceful, cagey, and accustomed to hard living on a sparse diet but almost incapable of acting together as a disciplined unit. Recognizing this weakness in his forces, Canabarro sought to bring as many men as possible under his command. He scoured the countryside looking for recruits and impressed young teenagers and even slaves. He also tried to obtain reinforcements from other commands, meeting with little success.

Commanders in other areas of Rio Grande do Sul failed to offer aid because they faced the same problems as the general. All the recently recruited guardsmen were familiar with flintlock muskets, but they had never before seen the imported percussion-cap rifles then being issued. It took some effort to master the loading and firing of such weapons, but the Brazilians had no time.

Another problem concerned recruitment of the *Voluntários da Pátria*. When the idea of forming these volunteer units initially came up in January 1865, the imperial government set terms of enlistment at three months.[114] By May, many volunteers (who were mostly foreign born) had taken their pay and departed. Few showed any interest in reenlisting, especially since authorities could promise them neither prompt pay nor a ready supply of equipment.

Only the First Infantry Battalion of Volunteers, then disembarking at the port of Rio Grande, responded to an appeal from Canabarro. Rio Grande was over two hundred miles distant, however, and at this late hour, only a forced march could get the unit to São Borja before the Paraguayans.

Estigarribia arrived near Santo Tomé on 7 June, having again — for no discernible reason — chosen to bypass the Paso de los Garruchos. Two days later, while his engineers prepared canoes to cross the Uruguay River, the exhausted soldiers of Brazil's First Infantry Battalion of Volunteers set up camp eight miles east of São Borja.

At midmorning on 10 June, Brazilian pickets spotted a large column of Paraguayans approaching the Uruguay River from the west. At a prearranged signal, Estigarribia's men launched canoes into the water.

They then scrambled aboard in groups of twenty-five and made for the opposite bank as fast as they could paddle. At this one site—the Paso de Hormiguero—the Uruguay was nearly six hundred yards wide, and the Paraguayans had to work against a strong current.[115]

A river crossing in full daylight is usually ill advised. Estigarribia outmaneuvered his opponents by having sent across a battalion of infiltrators the previous night. These men kept in the tall grass and waited quietly for the same cannon shot that sent their comrades to the water's edge. As the canoes neared the east bank, the hidden soldiers were to spring out and flank the Brazilian defenders before they could respond.[116]

The Brazilians had already moved one hundred men into position at the Paso de Hormiguero. When the main crossing began that morning, they fired a volley into the canoes as soon as they came within rifle range. The Brazilian fire proved effective. The Paraguayans slowed, then returned to the west bank and started out once more, this time directed to a point farther south. By now, their comrades had placed dozens of rafts and various floats onto the water and were furiously paddling eastward. They obviously had in mind landing at multiple sites.

The Brazilian field commander, Maj. José Rodrigues Ramos, decided on a desperate maneuver. He split his small force into four platoons and sent them to intercept the various landings individually. This made a coordinated defense more difficult. The east bank of the Uruguay was wooded right down to the water and had a narrow clearing only at the port, called San Borjita. Ramos's platoons failed to get through the heavy vegetation in time to prevent or even slow the landings. To make matters worse, as the Brazilians attempted to maneuver, Estigarribia's hidden battalion—perhaps five hundred men—came at them unexpectedly from the north.[117] As his men began to waver, Ramos yielded to the inevitable and called for a retreat into the town of São Borja, more than a mile distant. His southernmost platoon was cut off and in danger of annihilation when, at the last moment, a body of Brazilian cavalry arrived from Itaqui and managed to rescue them. Both units then dashed back to join Ramos on the outskirts of the town.[118]

The Brazilian retreat allowed Estigarribia to land his full contingent on the east bank.[119] The first units across were the Seventeenth Infantry Battalion and the Twenty-seventh Cavalry Regiment, which together totaled fourteen hundred men. In short order, two more battalions of infantry and one of cavalry crossed over to join the fray.

The first Paraguayans ashore drove steadily toward São Borja. The same cavalry unit that had saved Ramos's platoon an hour earlier furiously attacked the Paraguayan right flank; Estigarribia's men recoiled slightly, and in the confusion Ramos struck at their left flank, causing several more casualties. São Borja, it seemed, would not fall easily.

Capt. José de Rosario López (no relative of the marshal) was the Paraguayan field commander that day. Still unsure of how many Brazilians stood in his path, he decided to bring up his artillery and pound the town. This caused a delay of some minutes as his forward units shifted to clear a field of fire. Ironically, the Brazilian defenders facing him at that moment numbered less than a hundred and probably could have been dislodged without serious effort.

The delay proved costly to López, for it permitted Brazil's First Infantry Battalion of Volunteers to move into position alongside Ramos. The Paraguayans fired twice into the town, but then were stunned to see the volunteers rushing directly at them. López's riflemen soon beat the Brazilian infantry back with minor losses. By this time, though, it was clear that neither the Brazilians nor the Paraguayans would win a victory that day.

Fearing that his vanguard would become separated from the bridgehead, Estigarribia ordered Captain López to withdraw to the river at sunset.[120] This ended the day's fighting, which had lasted five hours. Twenty-two Brazilians had died and another sixty-four were wounded. Paraguayan losses, though officially reported at three killed and twenty-four wounded, certainly amounted to far more.[121]

Night brought no celebrations, either in São Borja or in the Paraguayan camp. Estigarribia wanted to expand the bridgehead before the Brazilians could mount a counterattack. He still believed that enemy reinforcements would soon arrive from the interior of Rio Grande do Sul. In consequence, his engineers labored through the night and the next day to ferry troops, horses, cattle, and all kinds of equipment and baggage to the eastern bank of the river. By dusk on 11 June, Estigarribia had across five infantry battalions, four cavalry regiments, all the artillery, and most of the cattle. This left Duarte in Santo Tomé with the remaining twenty-five hundred men and the canoes. From now on, the major's mission was to stay in contact with Estigarribia's main force and parallel its movement as the two columns marched south along their respective sides of the Uruguay River.[122]

The Brazilians, it turned out, had no reinforcements. They spent a nervous night evacuating civilians and the wounded from São Borja. Some of the forward units lit bonfires and roasted meat so as to give the Paraguayans the impression that their numbers were still considerable.[123]

The various Brazilian commanders met the next morning and concluded that, despite all the courage their men had shown, São Borja could not be held. Rather than waste lives, they ordered their men to abandon their makeshift trenches and follow the civilians eastward. The Paraguayans occupied São Borja on the morning of 12 June and immediately set to work sacking the place.[124] The private homes, which were low and carefully whitewashed, all had decorative sashes to the windows as in England. Without exception, each was brutally torn apart, their clean and sober aspect done away with in an hour's time. Every man, from Estigarribia down, felt justified, even exhilarated, by this looting. This was the celebration the Paraguayans had missed the day before. Little did they know that on the Paraná, just below Corrientes, their country had just suffered a terrible defeat.

# The Battle of the Riachuelo

## 11

The 25 May raid on Corrientes demonstrated an important weakness in the marshal's strategy: without complete control of the Paraná River, his fleet could not keep Gen. Wenceslao Robles adequately provisioned and the latter's drive on Entre Ríos would fail for want of supplies. As it stood, Adm. Francisco Barroso's warships were on the Paraná River just opposite the mouth of the Riachuelo, itself split by an island into northern and southern channels. From that station, the Brazilian naval forces could make constant trouble for the Paraguayans and had proven as much by transporting Paunero's troops into Corrientes at the time of the raid. They might do so again at any time. Solano López decided to deal with this threat before any additional warships arrived from Buenos Aires or Rio de Janeiro.

On 9 June 1865 the marshal stepped off the gangplank of his flagship onto the pier at Humaitá. After a short welcoming ceremony, he called a meeting of his senior officers to discuss an attack on the enemy fleet. Representing the navy at this session were Capt. Pedro Ignacio Meza, commander of the fleet; Capt. Remigio Cabral, second in command; and Lt. Pedro V. Gill, commander of the *Yberá*. For once the marshal asked his subordinates' advice: when and how should the assault take place?

To a man, the naval officers argued for an early morning attack, at least two hours before daylight, to take full advantage of the element of surprise.[1] In this they echoed the words of John Watts, chief engineer of the *Tacuarí*, who several years earlier had served in a similar capacity in the imperial navy. On the voyage downriver, Solano López had sought his counsel regarding a plan of attack against the enemy squadron; the marshal was pleased to hear him call the Brazilians inept and Admiral Barroso an obvious poltroon. A direct attack before daylight, the British engineer indicated, stood every chance of sweeping them all away.² With a half-dozen accurate shots from the *Tacuarí* or her sister ships, the whole balance of naval power in the Plata could shift in the Paraguayans' favor.

Watts and the naval officers were clearly right about the attack plan, but tactical detail would interfere with its realization. Among the army officers present at the meeting was Franz von Wisner, the sly Hungarian who had commanded Paraguayan forces in 1849. Colonel Wisner had never really proven himself as a leader of men in combat, yet he remained one of the best military engineers in the Paraguayan service. On this occasion, he rose to point out to the assembled officers that even with surprise in their favor, the navy still had to face heavy enemy firepower. Barroso's fleet at that moment consisted of eleven warships with sixty-eight guns as opposed to Meza's nine ships with forty-four. Wisner proposed that they make up the difference by having Meza's men tow six *chatas* into battle behind them. These were small, double-prowed punts strengthened with layers of planking, undecked, drawing a few inches water, and standing hardly half a foot above the surface. This left just enough room for three or four sailors to operate a single mortar or 8-inch gun. The *chatas* had no motive power of their own, so the Paraguayans would have to tow them into firing position. For this reason, Meza opposed their deployment, arguing strongly that they would restrict his speed and maneuverability.³

In the end, Solano López approved Wisner's plan. He went a step further, ordering Col. José María Bruguez to set up three batteries of artillery (twenty-two guns of mixed calibers and a few Congreve rockets) along the left bank of the Paraná just north of the Riachuelo. These guns, which the colonel had to move quickly from Humaitá, would provide supporting fire for the Paraguayan fleet.⁴ In addition, the marshal

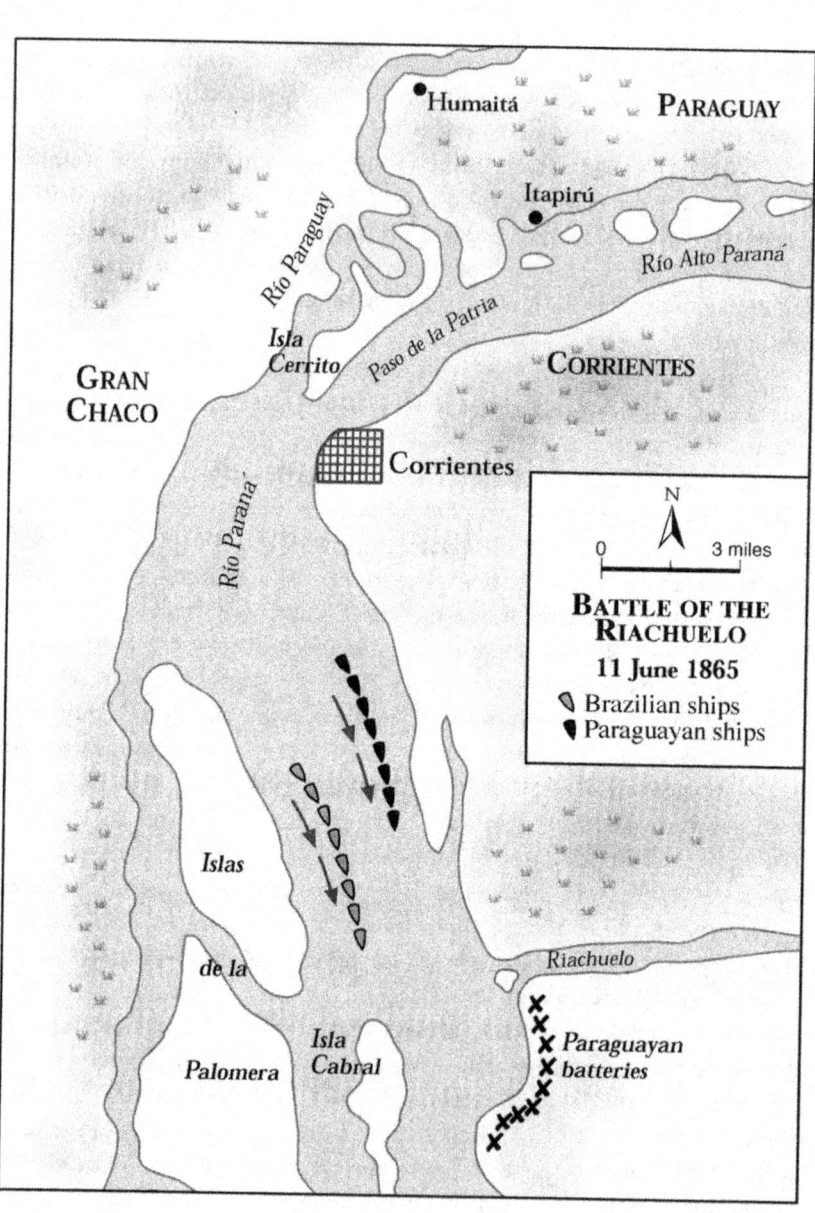

ordered Meza to supplement his forces with men from the Sixth Marine Battalion, called *Nambí-í* ("Little Ears"), who were to assist in the capture of enemy vessels. This unit, comprised entirely of Paraguayan blacks from the small town of Laurelty, had already proven itself during the fighting in Mato Grosso.[5]

Together with the sailors of the attack force, these men spent 10 June loading ammunition onto the steamers and listening to rousing speeches. The marshal, full of enthusiasm for the coming fight, leavened his words with choice Guaraní insults, urging his soldiers and sailors to surge forth and drive the monkeys into the river. The men responded with honest delight. They forgot for a time all their previous apprehension and felt confident, ready for battle. López told them to bring prisoners back from their victory. "What do we want prisoners for? We will kill them all," came the thunderous response. "No," chuckled the marshal, "bring some prisoners."[6]

The plan was for Captain Meza to depart on the night of 10 June with nine ships towing three *chatas*. He had to pick up three additional *chatas* at Paso de la Patria and then move on to attack the Brazilian fleet at the Riachuelo just before daybreak. The sun would come up behind the Paraguayans as they steamed past the Brazilians and fired as many broadsides into them as possible. Meza would then execute a quick turn, and each Paraguayan steamer would come alongside an enemy vessel and fire once more before beginning boarding operations. By this time, the demoralized Brazilians would be stumbling over each other to get into the water to swim to the Chaco shoreline. As on 13 April, the Paraguayans would crown their victory by towing the captured steamers to Humaitá.

The marshal's plan had many arguable points. Unlike his own fleet, that of the empire was designed as part of a blue-water navy. The Paraguayans, who had not read of Admiral Farragut's recent accomplishments on the Mississippi River, hoped that the Brazilians would find it difficult to maneuver once the fighting began. The Brazilian seamen, moreover, were still inexperienced in river operations, and whatever action they had seen at Paysandú would not prepare them for the sort of battle that Solano López had in mind.

Admiral Barroso, however, was better organized than the Paraguayans believed. The empire had declared a blockade against Paraguay as early as 26 January 1865, and Brazilian warships had been in Correntino waters since late April. By now, Barroso understood the condition of that section of the Paraná better than the Paraguayans, who for all their knowledge of the river were still apt to run their ships onto the shifting sandbars that the Brazilian's pilots had already sighted.[7] Also, with Tamandaré in Buenos Aires, Barroso could organize his strategy without interference from his usually cantankerous superior.

The Brazilians had several other advantages. The imperial fleet consisted entirely of well-armed, screw-propelled steamers, all of which had been built as warships. Those vessels on station with Barroso included the *Amazonas, Jequitinhonha, Belmonte, Parnahyba, Ypiranga, Mearim, Yguatemí, Araguari, Beberibé, Ivaí,* and *Itajaí*. The latter two vessels had gone downriver to Bella Vista at the end of May but were close enough that Barroso could call them back in an emergency. The remaining nine ships lay anchored on the Chaco side of the river within five miles of Corrientes. At that time, Barroso had no Argentine ships in his command.

The Brazilians had excellent visibility from their place on the river, while two nearby islands afforded them a measure of protection from any force bearing down from the north. Barroso had all his men maintain a semialert status, with imperial marines constantly watching for suspicious moves from the opposite bank. He thought a naval assault likely at any moment and posted a picket ship just upriver. Underlining his concern, the admiral issued a clear directive on 30 May: "Maintain maximum vigilance. Have armed and alert men at combat posts at all hours of the day and night. No audio signals after the hours of darkness and reduce use of lights that can be seen from a distance to a minimum. Attach boarding nets, fires banked, artillery laid out at minimum elevation and ready, with ammunition at gun positions."[8] Barroso had no intention of being caught unaware.

By contrast, of the eight Paraguayan vessels that were to take part in the attack, only the *Tacuarí* had specifically been constructed as a warship. The rest were converted merchantmen and had boilers located above the water line, vulnerable to enemy fire. The 300-ton *Salto Oriental*, which the Paraguayans had recently purchased from Anacarsis Lanús, and the 120-ton *Pirabebé* were propeller driven. All the rest were sidewheelers and thus unsuited to the boarding operations that played such a key role in the marshal's plan.

In many ways, Meza commanded less a flotilla than an assortment of ill-matched vessels, each one answerable to a captain of limited experience. Even so, every Paraguayan vessel counted among its crew a British naval engineer, all of whom had seen duty at sea. Not one, however, had ever been in action in a river battle. The *chatas* might help, as would the Paraguayan shore batteries, but Meza would still need surprise to inflict decisive damage on the enemy.

*Blood on the Water*

The Paraguayan flotilla got underway just after midnight on the night of 10–11 June 1865. The timing was terrible because Meza's ships would be unable to engage the Brazilian fleet before daylight. As planned, Meza took the three *chatas* in tow at Paso de la Patria, but as he departed downriver, Lieutenant Gill discovered that the metal peg that connected the *Yberá*'s shaft to its propeller had broken. Without it, the shaft could not properly drop into the keel, and maneuvering became impossible. Repairs would take time, so Meza decided to continue on without the three-hundred-ton vessel. Col. George Thompson observed that Gill "was so vexed at not being able to go, that he absolutely cried."[9]

The morning of 11 June was cool and crisp along the Paraná River. The sun shone brightly, burning away the early fog so that the view on the water was clear far into the distance. All was quiet in occupied Corrientes. A few Paraguayan troops patrolled the water's edge and there were some minor movements in the port. Still, all seemed calm enough as Sunday Mass began. Then, as church bells pealed out the hour of nine, the soldiers along the river's edge raised an excited cry: they had sighted Meza's fleet. Within moments so had Barroso's picket ship, the *Mearim*. The seamen aboard quickly gave the signal "enemy in sight" followed by a second signal reporting that a formation of eight Paraguayan ships was steaming downriver toward them.

Barroso had more than enough time to react. Messboys were still clearing away dishes and mugs from breakfast when the *Mearim* gave the alarm.[10] As she returned to her assigned place in the Brazilian formation, the admiral's flagship signaled "clear for action," then "full steam in boilers," and finally "raise anchors." Crews on every ship of the fleet responded in a well-drilled manner, securing hatches, stacking additional ammunition next to their Whitworth guns, and taking up battle positions. Though their coal supplies were limited, only the day before, the men had brought a quantity of chopped hardwood from the Chaco for use as fuel.

As the excitement mounted, the marines prepared their rifles. Barroso strapped on his sword and looked through his spyglass at the *Lópezguayo* fleet coming toward him. All sources agree that he appeared stolid; yet while some claim that this was because he was undaunted, others thought he was petrified by the approach of the enemy. In the action that followed over the next several hours, Barroso's behavior was only one of many things open to interpretation.[11]

The impressive British-built *Tacuarí* led the Paraguayan squadron, followed by the *Paraguarí, Ygurey, Yporá, Marqués de Olinda, Pirabebé, Salto Oriental*, and *Jejuí*. No sooner had the men aboard these ships sited Corrientes than they realized that all hope of surprise was gone. The Paraguayans could only manage a speed of ten knots, and even with a two-knot current in their favor, this hardly seemed enough to protect them from well-aimed Brazilian guns. Captain Meza kept to the left bank, where Bruguez could provide some protection and where the river's deepest channel guaranteed better maneuverability. Deviating so far to the left compromised the original plan of attack, for instead of the full broadsides the marshal had envisioned, Meza could only hope for some lucky shots.

The Paraguayan ships opened fire at 9:25 A.M., with the *Tacuarí*'s eight cannon blasting away. The Brazilians responded with double loads of grape and solid shot as the other ships went past. In fifteen minutes Meza's squadron was out of range to the south. The gray smoke from the gunfire and the many billowing stacks hung over the water like an immense shroud so that that no one could verify the extent of damage to either side. The pilot of the *Parnahyba* indicated many years later that the smoke was so thick that Admiral Barroso could not make out the enemy position and was surprised to see the Paraguayan steamers some distance downriver.[12]

The *Mearim* reported that its gunners had sunk a *chata*, though no one could confirm the deed.[13] The *Jejuí*, the last ship in the Paraguayan formation, had its boiler pierced by shot, but after halting for a short time just opposite the Riachuelo shore positions, its British engineer improvised a metal patch, and the steamer soon returned to its place in line. Other Paraguayan ships also took hits, though none were seriously damaged. The Brazilians must have had their Whitworths elevated too high, for Paraguayan soldiers later collected pieces of iron shell a full five miles east of the river.[14]

Barroso's ships suffered only moderate damage. Shot and fragments embedded themselves in the superstructure of several of his steamers, but no vessel was knocked out of action. A few imperial marines and sailors received wounds in this first exchange of fire. One Paraguayan soldier aboard the *Yporá* was decapitated by a cannon ball.[15] No one else was killed.

The battle thus far bore little resemblance to the plan outlined at Humaitá two days earlier. Meza's flotilla had departed too late to achieve a predawn surprise. When the two forces finally did engage, Meza hugged the left bank of the Paraná, too distant from the Brazilians for his fire to be effective. He then compounded his mistake. Instead of executing a quick turn and immediately reengaging, as the marshal had ordered, the old man hove to in front of the Paraguayan encampment at Riachuelo and waited; his ships did not anchor but used their engines to keep station. At 10:00 A.M. Meza released his *chatas*, which in effect became part of the army's shore defenses. Uncertain of his next move and unwilling to make a decision without first consulting his commanders, the captain called a council of war aboard his flagship *Tacuarí*.

Events had already made the marshal's plan impractical, and Meza needed to think of a way to salvage the day. Solano López's anger with Wenceslao Robles for disobeying orders had been palpable, and the captain had no desire to place himself in a similar situation. Still, he was a man of little flexibility and even less imagination. Fat and sickly, and at an age when most Paraguayans quietly sip yerba with family members under the shade of a mango tree, Meza was now being called upon to make vital command decisions. He was unequal to such stress.

The lull in the fighting presented options to both sides. Barroso could have turned north and proceeded to attack Asunción, although holding the city was beyond his means. Colonel Thompson reported that the marshal's British engineers had only set sixteen of ninety guns into properly constructed parapets at Humaitá in April; little work had been done on the fortifications since that time. In addition, Barroso knew that many of Humaitá's guns had been ferried south to Corrientes after the 25 May raid. Therefore, it was unlikely that Humaitá could prevent the Brazilians steaming to the Paraguayan capital.

Barroso, however, thought this option too speculative. He had made no plans to exploit an opportunity such as now presented itself and had no orders to go beyond his blockading mission. He was low on ammunition and supplies. If he did move north, Meza eventually would follow and the battle between them might recommence in waters less friendly to Brazil than those of Corrientes. Everything seemed to suggest that Barroso should attack the Paraguayan flotilla sooner rather than later.

Meza had been hoping for precisely this decision. If the Paraguayans held their position, then perhaps it would entice the enemy into a frontal assault. In such a case, the strength of the Paraguayan shore batteries could deliver the victory that had been planned for the navy alone. Meza needed to be careful, however. Some of Robles's scouts had reported several Brazilian ships in the vicinity of Bella Vista, and if the Paraguayan fleet tarried too long at Riachuelo, these steamers might close from the south just as Barroso came at them from the north.

One of his British experts had suggested to him that he sink several launches in the main channel so as to bottle up the entire enemy fleet, but Meza refused to listen.[16] To make matters worse, his officers informed him that someone had forgotten to load the grappling hooks he had intended to use to help board, capture, and tow the enemy steamers. Flustered and not knowing what to do, Meza turned to his most trusted officers. All of them, Paraguayan and foreigner alike, recommended that he resume the fight without delay. Meza gave the order to prepare for battle. As his captains rushed to return to their vessels, however, lookouts signaled the approach of the Brazilian ships.

Barroso made his decision. He heralded his attack by raising two signal flags, the first of which echoed Lord Nelson's signal at Trafalgar: "Brazil expects that every man will do his duty." This Barroso followed with "Attack and destroy the enemy at the closest possible range."[17] Having thus invoked the memory of one of the great naval commanders, he plunged forward into the fray. Yet whereas Nelson always scrupulously informed his subordinates of his plans, Barroso left his officers bewildered, with no idea of how their admiral intended to organize the attack.

The first ship in the Brazilian line, the *Belmonte*, steamed toward the mouth of the Riachuelo, followed by the *Jequitinhonha*. The third steamer, Barroso's flagship *Amazonas*, pulled sharply out of line to the port side. This turn, which the admiral later defended as necessary to establish better control over the movements of his fleet, caused nothing but confusion. The next six vessels followed in his wake, leaving the *Belmonte* and the *Jequitinhonha* to rush at the Paraguayans alone and unsupported.

Barroso realized his mistake instantly but failed to communicate the fact to his subordinates. When he saw the resulting disarray, he headed downriver once again, repeated the signal to attack, and led his seven ships toward the northern opening of the Riachuelo. By then, however, it was too late for the two ships that had gone forward.

The *Jequitinhonha*'s commander, Capt. Joaquim José Pinto, had spotted the *Amazonas* moving away and in response ordered his own vessel to turn back and follow. He had six 32- and one 68-pounder guns, sufficient firepower to do ample damage to the enemy vessels. But Pinto had no idea of Admiral Barroso's intentions, and rather than strike at the Paraguayans, he thought it best to regain his position in line. To that end, he guided the *Jequitinhonha* on a wide turn to the east but soon perceived the flagship moving rapidly away from him. Pinto then decided to rake the Paraguayan shore batteries. This required another turn to the east. In the midst of this maneuver, the *Jequitinhonha* ran aground on a sandbar. At 647 tons, she was the second-largest vessel in the imperial fleet and carried over two hundred marines. That she was now caught, seemingly helpless, proved a major bit of luck for the Paraguayans. Bruguez, who had witnessed everything from his position on the bluff, found the ship's range within a few minutes and began to pour shot into it.

Among the first casualties was the ship's Santafecino pilot. His death left the steamer unable to maneuver away from the sandbar, and thus unable to deploy all her guns. At that moment the bewhiskered Capt. José Segundino de Gomensoro, who acted as commander of the marines aboard, took over the *Jequitinhonha*'s defense and rallied his men. He continued to fire the guns that would still bear on the enemy, converting the ship, as it were, into a stationary battery.

The *Belmonte*, meanwhile, was having troubles of her own. Having entered the northern channel of the Riachuelo without noticing that the other ships had altered course, her commander, Lt. Joaquim Francisco de Abreu, chose to complete a firing pass before returning to the fleet. At 11:20 A.M. the *Belmonte* engaged the entire Paraguayan force in a solitary duel. For the next twenty minutes, the ship came under merciless fire from Bruguez's artillery before finally retiring at the southern end of the Riachuelo into the main channel of the Paraná.[18] Abreu's bold action carried a high cost: nine of his crew lay dead and another twenty-three were wounded. Thirty-seven great holes riddled the ship's wooden hull, nearly half of them at the water line. Aware that the vessel might sink, Abreu ordered his men to beach the *Belmonte* on one of the small islands and attempt repairs, out of range of enemy fire.

As the *Belmonte* withdrew, the *Amazonas* was closing with the Paraguayan fleet. Barroso reached the Riachuelo's northern channel at 11:25 A.M.. He slowed to eight knots to allow the other ships to come together in tight formation before giving the order to open fire.

The full firepower of both fleets now engaged at close range. The air filled with heavy shot, and the noise, which sounded from a distance like an unending chorus of kettledrums, blotted out the cries of the wounded on every ship. Clouds of smoke permeated the scene, and not a man had clear eyes.

The *Araguarí*, center ship in the Brazilian formation, approached the mouth of the Riachuelo around 11:45. As she came closer, Captain Meza signaled his ships to close and board without delay.[19] The *Marqués de Olinda*, *Tacuarí*, and *Paraguarí* pushed forward but were beaten back by grape and canister. The firing continued until the last Brazilian ship, the *Parnahyba*, passed into the southern channel at around 12:15 P.M.. Even then, Paraguayan sharpshooters continued to direct fire from hidden spots on the islands and along the riverbank. The imperial marines suffered more casualties from Minié balls than from the earlier cannonade.

Despite the heavy firing, neither the Brazilians nor the Paraguayans lost any ships in the fifty-minute action. The *Belmonte* was no longer operational, but the *Jequitinhonha* still defied the superior firepower of the Paraguayans and continued to resist. The *Mearim* had sunk another *chata*, the only Paraguayan loss. Both sides did suffer extensive damage, with the *Tacuarí*, for instance, taking a 68-pounder shot in the insulation of her boiler just inches from the boiler itself.[20]

Barroso could see the wounded and dead on the decks of his ships, yet he judged the attack reasonably successful. He wanted to swing upriver for a second, more devastating pass, but his pilot advised against it; the water, though generally high in June, was too shallow at that point to permit a wide turn. Reluctantly, the admiral steamed south to find deeper water. As before, no one thought to signal instructions to the remaining Brazilian vessels, but each one, save for the *Parnahyba*, turned downriver after the *Amazonas*.

The Paraguayans on shore may have thought they had won a great victory. Meza, the sweat dripping from his face, felt dazed and uncertain, for the Brazilian fleet was still operational and still posed a threat. In addition, the Paraguayans had yet to capture a single enemy ship. Perhaps, Meza thought, they might make good by taking the *Jequitinhonha*, but even that seemed doubtful. Hesitatingly, he gave the order to board her. Three of his steamers at once responded and edged toward the beached vessel. Captain Pinto, still blasting away, repulsed Paraguayan attacks again and again. Though his casualties were already heavy, it began to look like he would run out of shot before he ran out of gunners.

By this time the *Parnahyba* was also engaged. Her commander, Lt. Aurélio Garcindo Fernandes de Sá, had seen his friend's vessel go aground and resolved to rescue her after completing his initial pass. He failed to notice that the rest of the fleet had headed south until after he began to turn in the direction of the *Jequitinhonha*. Perhaps he ignored the advice of his own pilot, for as he turned, his rudder ran against the riverbank and bent sideways, nearly wrecking the ship's steering capability. Garcindo ordered his men to raise sails to try to continue upstream in spite of the damage, but this effort proved useless.

As the *Parnahyba* veered into the firing zone, Meza's gunners had little difficulty in finding their target. They shot off what was left of her rudder, causing the ship to drift helplessly toward them. The Brazilians took more and more losses. In fighting between wooden vessels, splinter wounds always constituted a high proportion of the casualties, and this action proved no exception. Worse still — as Allied surgeons were later to find — those hurtling pieces of wood could never be extracted easily because their shape gave them barbed ends. The results for the sailors who survived usually involved terrible scarring.

Having failed to capture the *Jequitinhonha*, Meza turned his attention to Garcindo's disabled ship. The *Tacuarí*, *Paraguarí*, and *Salto Oriental* steamed out at 1:00 P.M. to begin boarding operations. Scores of *Nambíí* were anxious to tear into the Brazilian seamen and take their prize home to Humaitá. Garcindo had one final option, born of desperation and courage: as the *Paraguarí* moved across his bow, he gritted his teeth, fired his boilers a final time, and without a working rudder still managed to ram the enemy vessel amidships. The crewmen of both steamers lunged and fell as Garcindo found his mark: he split the hull of the *Paraguarí* to the waterline. As water began to pour in, the Brazilians had the momentary satisfaction of seeing the marshal's soldiers falling into the cold water.[21]

After considerable effort, the *Paraguarí* managed to break loose and steam for a nearby island to beach herself in order to avoid sinking. The *Tacuarí* and *Salto Oriental*, joined by the *Marqués de Olinda*, pressed the attack. This time Garcindo had no more tricks. What happened next has been obscured partly by poor memory, partly by deliberate deception, and partly by the fog of war. The Paraguayans initially seem to have had difficulty with the boarding, for the high side-wheel housings on their own ships made it next to impossible to jump directly onto the *Parnahyba*. Meza's failure to bring grappling hooks now exacted its cost, for while both sides continued to fire with cannon and musket, the ships kept drifting apart. Exasperated and crazed with anger, some of the Paraguayans then vaulted overboard between the vessels and, with their cutlasses still clutched in their hands, scrambled aboard the Brazilian steamer. The imperial marines shot the first few, but others soon took their place. Several of the Brazilian marines showed uncommon valor as the number of Paraguayan boarders grew.[22]

As the more audacious among them fell, the Brazilians broke. Some jumped into the water and the rest fled below deck, sealing the hatches behind them. This left the *Parnahyba*'s crew virtual prisoners, for the Paraguayan marines, now several hundred in number, swiftly secured the wheelhouse and cut down all who continued to resist. A Paraguayan sergeant, laughing in exaltation, amused himself by marching up and down the deck, beating the reveille on a drum he found there. A few Brazilians rushed out at this sound with fixed bayonets, then just as quickly either rushed back or jumped overboard. At this, the Paraguayans burst out in laughter, thus saluting "the terrified *kambá* as they tumbled over each other in their eagerness to get below."[23]

The Paraguayans controlled the ship from the stern to the mainmast; they tore down the imperial ensign and began to celebrate their victory by trampling upon it and shouting to all who could hear. Garcindo, who was still forward, supposedly ordered the firing of the ship's magazine, but water had splashed onto the powder and the fuses failed to set it off. His men were in the midst of lighting still more fuses when a familiar report erupted behind them.[24] The *Amazonas* had returned.

Barroso had been gone for more than an hour. When he finally found water deep enough to turn he moved swiftly, feeding his coal reserves to the furnace and leaving the rest of the fleet behind as he steamed upriver. At 1,050 tons, with four 32- and two 70-pounder guns, his ship was the largest and most formidable craft on the river, and the admiral had every intention of using his superiority. With the *Parnahyba* in distress, he headed straight at her four attackers. As he came up to the besieged ship, his gunners fired grape across her deck, tearing off limbs and heads and spraying everything topside with Paraguayan blood.[25] Some men jumped into the river. Others stayed long enough to see Garcindo's crew bursting out from the holds and fighting to regain control of the main deck. This time it was the Paraguayans who broke, though not before showing the Brazilians how bravely wounded men can fight.[26]

Nor were the Paraguayans alone in their courage. Antonio Luiz de Hoonholtz, commander of the *Araguari* and later baron of Teffé, wrote to his brother ten days later to note how inspiring Admiral Barroso's own comportment had been: "When I saw the *Amazonas* pass majestically between our line and that of the enemy, it made my soul rise, and when I found the erect figure of Barroso atop the bridge, standing impassive during that hailstorm of projectiles, megaphone in hand and stroking his long white beard that blew in the wind . . . , for the first time I felt enthusiasm for this brusque and uncommunicative chief, who had never before inspired me with sympathy or confidence. Now, in this place of death, I doffed my cap and cried out, 'Long live Admiral Barroso!' As he went by, though he heard me not, he . . . bellowed in a strong and clear voice, 'Follow in my wake! Victory is ours!'"[27] Perhaps this evocation of bravery was overstated, but it was doubtlessly heartfelt. Colonel Thompson, whose knowledge of the engagement was secondhand, had little good to say of either Barroso or his men, suggesting with contempt that in any country save Brazil, the admiral would have been court-martialed for cowardice.[28]

Whatever Barroso's qualities as leader, he certainly had a fine pilot in the person of Bernardino Guastavino, an Italian-born Correntino, and between them they certainly did good work.[29] The *Amazonas* continued to press its attack, turning its guns on the smaller *Jejuí*. Heavy shot passed through the latter's hull, sending a shower of splinters below deck and causing water to gush in. The ship broke apart shortly thereafter, and what remained of her crew swam ashore to the protection of Bruguez's artillerymen.

Barroso then chose his targets one by one. He first rammed the *Marqués de Olinda*, then shot her boilers through, which blew scalding water in every direction and killed all her stokers. With the *Marqués* out of action, Barroso swung to the side and did the same to the *Salto Oriental*, all the time heedless of Paraguayan fire. Soon the *Salto* fell backward with a considerable list until she caught upon a bank and began to split open, her deck heaped with dead and dying men.

Meza had by now lost his nerve and was almost raving one moment, almost crying the next. His officers could do nothing with him. He managed to order the *Tacuarí* to maneuver out of range, and as he fled, his remaining ships, the *Ygurey*, *Pirabebé*, and *Ypora*, closed behind him. Barroso, whose victory was now in sight, focused at length on the *chatas*. With his marines firing their rifles at will, he slaughtered the crews of each in turn and finished by sinking one and taking the other four in tow. By this time, he was nearly out of fuel.

Meza made one last futile attempt to wrest some advantage from what had become a disaster. He ordered one last assault on the *Jequitinhonha*. Gomensoro had little ammunition left but used what he had to good effect against the remnants of the Paraguayan flotilla. A stray pistol shot from one of the enemy's tops hit Meza between the shoulder blades and penetrated his left lung. Mortally wounded, he fell forward onto the deck of the *Tacuarí*. As his weathered face changed color and he slipped into unconsciousness, command passed to Capt. Remigio Cabral, who broke off the attack.[30]

The *Mearim* and *Beberibé* had already started to close with the Paraguayans, and the *Araguari*, *Yguatemi*, and *Ypiranga* were not far behind. Meza's senseless attack on the *Jequitinhonha* only succeeded in making the Paraguayan retreat more difficult. The *Beberibé* and *Araguari* pursued Cabral until he was well past Corrientes, while the remaining Brazilian ships stayed behind to protect Pinto's crew from the enemy shore batteries. The two pursuing vessels maintained contact until around 5:00 P.M., and as the sun set, they returned downriver to the fleet. Cabral continued on to Humaitá.

*After the Battle*

The Paraguayans had been confident of victory, and the first news of the battle helped confirm their feeling of optimism. Their confidence disintegrated, however, when they caught sight of Meza's steamers limping toward them in the morning fog on 12 June. Cut cordage and disordered rigging hung from the splintered yards of every vessel, and the many wounded were clearly visible. An eager crowd of soldiers hurried across the slippery pier to bring the wounded and dead on shore. Much whispering went on, "for it was as much as a man's life was worth to spread bad news."[31]

Captain Meza died eight days later, thus escaping the wrath of Solano López, who was livid that his orders had been disobeyed once again.[32] The Paraguayan president had no forgiveness for the dead, no spot of understanding for an old man of whom too much had been asked. And Meza should have expected no sympathy. His defeat had cost his country dearly, and now, with the Brazilians in control of the river, Paraguayan strategy required a complete revision. The marshal never forgave this setback, and at his express order, only sergeants, corporals, and ten common soldiers from each ship accompanied Meza's body to the cemetery, where they interred him in a shallow grave without honors.[33]

In truth, Solano López had to share responsibility for the defeat at the Riachuelo. He had rushed the deployment of his fleet when there was no reason to do so. He had burdened his ships with the towing of the ineffective *chatas*. He sent an inferior force against a superior one and tried to preplan all steps of the operation, which left Meza with no flexibility to adjust as the battle developed.

The Paraguayans saw nearly one thousand of their men wounded and around two hundred killed in the battle, including two ship captains. One was Lt. Ezequiel Robles, brother of General Robles and commander of the *Marqués de Olinda*, who woke to find himself in a hospital, a prisoner of the Allies. The lieutenant, still defiant, though now missing an arm, tore the bandages from his amputated limb and thrashed at his captors, choosing to bleed to death, so he said, rather than remain their captive.[34] This gesture offered just the sort of death the marshal expected of his officers. But such loyalty, no matter how handsome or decorous, would not recover his fleet.

The battle of the Riachuelo cost the Paraguayans four steamers: *Jejuí, Salto Oriental, Marqués de Olinda,* and *Paraguarí,* almost twelve hundred tons in all. Every ship that took part in the engagement against the Brazilians sustained heavy damage and had to return to Asunción for repair. Salvage crews later returned to the scene of the battle and recovered the ruined hulk of the *Paraguarí,* but after they towed it to the Paraguayan capital, engineers there found the damage too extensive to mend.

This left the Paraguayan navy with thirteen vessels, all of them tiny save for the *Ygurey, Tacuarí, Yberá,* and the two Argentine steamers captured on 13 April. The four ships that survived the fight at the Riachuelo remained out of service for some time. For the rest of the war, even simple harassment of Allied shipping on the Paraná was difficult. The marshal could not acquire new vessels from overseas as long as the Brazilian blockade held. It was unlikely that his shipwrights could supply him with anything better than *chatas,* and insufficient guns were available even for these. Thus, in this one river battle, Solano López lost the better part of his offensive capability, for without naval support, his land forces could never advance boldly to the south. As George F. Masterman put it: "The tide had turned, such easy prizes as the *Marqués de Olinda* and the riverine towns were to be gained no more, and from that day forward, although there were occasional slight successes, . . . it was evident that the sun of López was setting, amid storm and tempest, forever. It was not so much the loss of the four ships, but the loss of an opportunity which could never occur again, of capturing fine vessels and heavy guns, which made the defeat of Riachuelo so serious."[35]

For the Brazilians, the fighting was not quite over, since they still had to support Pinto, who had remained under the fire of Bruguez's guns even after dusk. Admiral Barroso suffered 104 men killed, 148 wounded, and another 40 missing.[36] Yet he justifiably claimed to have won a great victory. Six of his ships remained operational, while the severely damaged *Parnahyba* was now safely under tow. The admiral ultimately abandoned the *Belmonte* and the *Jequitinhonha*, though his engineers spent the whole night and most of the next day trying to pull the latter off the sandbar. Pinto and his crew escaped, though they left behind much material the Paraguayans found useful, including two 68-pounder guns, four 32-pounder guns, two brass 5-inch howitzers, and a quantity of swords, watches, and instruments. The Paraguayans also sawed out the ship's main yard, which they then took as a souvenir to Humaitá; it later became the center column of a dance rotunda.

The battle of the Riachuelo showed the two contending navies at their best and worst. Despite some obvious lapses, both sides displayed considerable courage and determination as well as surprisingly superior levels of seamanship and marine engineering. These technical and tactical qualities were more than offset, however, by an almost complete absence of skill at maneuvering. Neither side operated well on the water and it showed. Thus, given that the Paraguayans and Brazilians were equally matched in the intangibles, the latter won the day because they had superior materiel and better luck.

The Brazilians never followed up their victory on the river with an amphibious assault. For one thing, Barroso's stocks of fuel, powder, and shot were now seriously depleted. Little remained to support a direct attack on Bruguez. It must also be remembered that Barroso was a naval officer and little inclined toward operations on shore. From his perspective, the crucial task now was to get south of the enemy batteries and begin the repair and resupply of his fleet. On 14 June he steamed downriver, only to be informed that Bruguez's artillery had also moved, though no one knew where.

Three days later the *Araguari* reported seeing new batteries being built on a bank at Mercedes, just north of Empedrado. Bruguez had received reinforcements of three infantry battalions and enough guns to bring his total number to thirty-six. He had chosen this new site well, for here the navigable channel was narrow and Barroso could only get through by running a gauntlet of fire from the Paraguayan position. This he did on 18 June, speeding by as Bruguez's gunners did their best to stop them. The Brazilians got through with only minor damage to their steamers. Two men died, however, including the commander of the *Beberibé*, who was shot through the head.[37] There were also considerable wounded among the imperial marines, who had crowded on deck to return small-arms fire and were picked off as a result.[38]

Barroso anchored his ships just south of Bella Vista that same day. He was soon joined by the *Ivaí* and by the Argentine steamer *Guardia Nacional*, and with their help the admiral managed to reestablish the river blockade. Colonel Bruguez, however, was not to be outdone so easily. He again moved his artillery and infantry units south through wooded country to Cuevas, just below Barroso's position. Again he placed his cannons on a high bank overlooking a narrow spot on the river. There he waited for the Allies to push past, hoping that this time his artillery would be effective. Barroso, however, had no intention of embarking for that kind of fight again, at least not right away. For the moment his fleet was safe, and as the Paraguayans could wait, so could he.

# The March into Rio Grande

## 12

The Paraguayan defeat at the Riachuelo brought predictable responses. Solano López was enraged, his people saddened. The satisfaction in the Allied capitals, however, was intense. Even so, it took some time for most observers to grasp the implications of so broad a victory.

In Rio de Janeiro, the emperor and his ministers were jubilant when they heard of Adm. Francisco Barroso's achievement. Dom Pedro, though inwardly elated, was temperate and dignified in his bearing, offering simple thanks to the officers and men of the imperial navy. The members of his government showed no similar restraint. The *Jornal do Commercio* churned out a series of official paeans, including a glory-drenched piece of verse written by the abolitionist leader Joaquim Nabuco.[1] The minister of the navy eventually commissioned the painting of a gigantic tableau of the battle that stressed all its heroic aspects (and none of its folly).[2] Crowds gathered in the streets of every major city in the empire. They celebrated long into the night with laughter, dancing, flowery speeches, and generous libations of *cachaça*. Everyone confidently predicted an early victory over the strutting dictator of Paraguay.

In Buenos Aires, the popular reaction was one of muted relief—now López could be defeated without a serious commitment of men and materiel. The official press, which echoed this sentiment, rejoiced in Paraguay's "humiliation" and offered words of praise for Brazilian valor.[3] As for the leaders of the Argentine government, behind their smiles, many were worried. President Mitre and Foreign Minister Elizalde tempered the happy news with the knowledge that this was a Brazilian, rather than an Allied, triumph. In any new arrangement of power to come out of the battle, the empire would have the upper hand. So while they offered fulsome congratulations to Barroso and his men, Mitre and his associates quietly maneuvered to retain as much influence as possible within the alliance.

What few in Buenos Aires realized at the time was that the outcome of the battle delivered a major political victory to the Argentine national government. Previously, the anti-*porteño*, anti-alliance feeling in the Litoral provinces was deep enough to inspire hope for any number of uprisings. Regional dissidents had in mind launching these rebellions whenever the Paraguayan forces reached Entre Ríos. Yet now the Brazilians dominated the Paraná River almost as far as Tres Bocas, and Gen. Wenceslao Robles was standing still.

Marshal López's decision to concentrate on military action while leaving aside his political appeal to the people of the Litoral was shortsighted. His friends, if such they were, had to depend on themselves. In these circumstances, even the members of the *Junta Gubernativa* in Corrientes regretted their previous enthusiasm. They quietly went about their business, but the fire that characterized their thoughts and actions earlier had gone out. Having expended few lives and little capital in the campaign so far, the national government nevertheless reaped the reward of seeing this regional opposition weakened, ready to be disposed of altogether.

A weakened opposition is apt to be desperate, however, and willing to cause all kinds of mischief as it recedes from center stage. In the Litoral, the political figure who suffered the most from this was Justo José de Urquiza. For two months he tried, with limited success, to mobilize units to support the national cause. As early as 19 April, he issued a call to arms in his native province, and there was no reason to question the sincerity of his efforts then or later.[4] Moreover, as Mitre's designated lieutenant in the region, he had behind him all the prestige and authority of the national government. This extended to command over the forces of Generals Paunero and Nicanor Cáceres and Colonel Paiva. Yet with all his power and influence, Urquiza still failed to recruit men who could think like Argentines first and *provincianos* second. Ricardo López Jordan spoke for many Entrerrianos at this time when he spurned his governor's appeal: "You call on us to fight against Paraguay. Never, my General, for that nation is our friend. Call on us [instead] to fight the Brazilians and *porteños* and we will be ready — for they are our enemies. We still hear the cannons of Paysandú ringing in our ears and I know where the true feeling of our people lies."[5]

More common than outright rejection of the old *caudillo* was a passive compliance by many men of military age who joined Urquiza, collected their pay, and deserted at the first opportunity. On paper, Entre Ríos fielded a formidable army of eight thousand to fight against Paraguay (three thousand more than Mitre had requested). In fact, few could be trusted to carry out their orders.

Urquiza's position was decidedly weak, and he tried various means to keep his head above water. He politely ignored pressure to send his unreliable troops northward to aid Paunero and instead used soothing words to calm both the *porteños* and his own irate followers. He also attempted to suborn the Paraguayan military leaders. Mitre approved this, though he considered unlikely any major defection from the marshal's camp.[6] Urquiza eventually penned a series of notes to Robles in which he pointed out that, with twenty-two thousand men in his command, the Paraguayan general and not Solano López was the real power in his country; if only he would turn his back on the marshal, then the war would end. Robles, who had yet to begin his retreat, spurned these overtures with contempt. This ended Urquiza's clandestine contacts with the Paraguayans but not his troubles.

For one thing, the Entrerriano governor disagreed on basic military strategy with Mitre and the various Argentine field commanders, notably Paunero. The latter favored extensive harassment of the enemy no matter where they were bound. Urquiza was more cautious and had far more respect for the fighting quality of the Paraguayan soldiers, perhaps because he saw in them the same rustic bravery of his own gauchos.

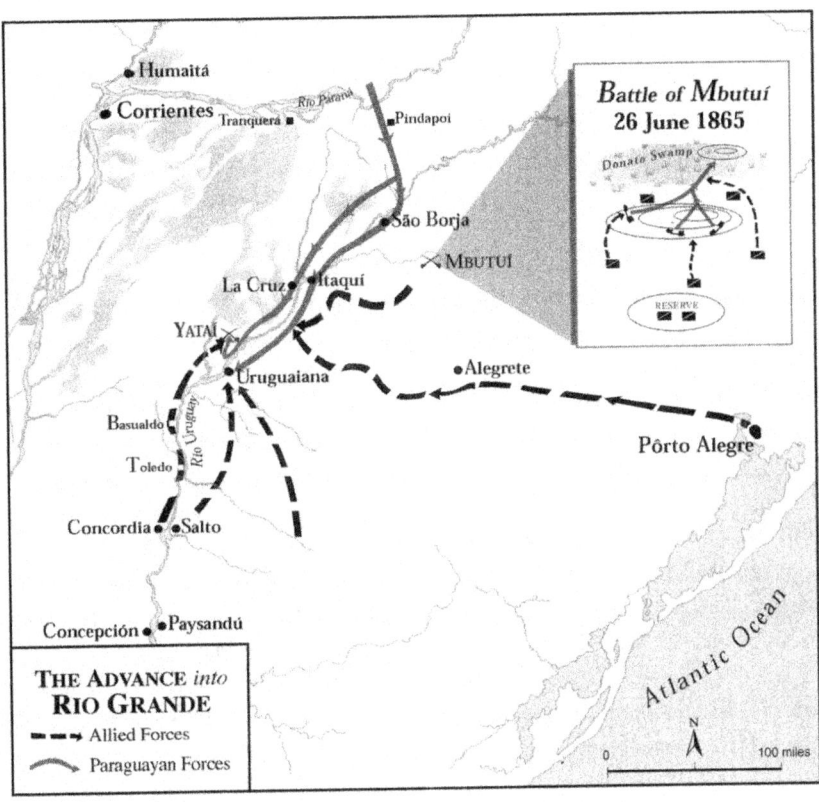

He felt that Estigarribia's column alone could subdue the greater part of his province and wanted to withdraw in order to concentrate Allied forces along the Uruguay.

The first manifestation of a problem with Paunero came in early June. Urquiza had encamped the bulk of his army at Basualdo, near the border of Entre Ríos and Corrientes. At that time, Robles was still closing on Goya and Maj. Pedro Duarte had advanced almost to Santo Tomé. Urquiza expected the two enemy forces to join at any moment and so ordered Paunero to proceed to Basualdo without delay. As the latter was

*The March into Rio Grande* 331

about to comply, however, he learned of Robles's abrupt withdrawal and wisely elected instead to follow the Paraguayans northward.[7]

Urquiza regarded this as insubordination. He believed that Robles wished to entice the Allied advance guard across the Río Corrientes in order to entrap and destroy it before moving south once again. He sent Paunero a sharp reprimand on the very day of the Paraguayan debacle at the Riachuelo.[8]

Urquiza remained convinced of the accuracy of his appraisal even after news reached him of the Brazilian victory. He could appear to do no other, for any compromise with the *porteños* on matters of strategy or tactics would further erode his base of support. Mitre, who was assembling troops sixty miles south at Concordia, had to choose between Urquiza and Paunero. Reluctantly, for he knew the political costs involved, he chose to support the latter. As Paunero started his pursuit of Robles, Urquiza received orders from Mitre to likewise advance to the Río Corrientes. The president believed that this advance would encourage Cáceres and other Correntinos who might then begin wide-scale resistance to the Paraguayans. Red-faced, Urquiza insisted that the maneuver would ruin the effectiveness of his cavalry.[9] Though he did not mention it at the time, he doubtless thought that Paraguayan movements down the Uruguay would vindicate his more conservative strategy as the correct one.

### Mbutuí

The hydrographic features of the Uruguay River do not lend themselves to fighting a decisive naval battle like that of the Riachuelo. Although the river was navigable for most of its length, above Salto and Concordia several series of rocky shoals prevented the passage of all but canoes during most of the year. Even at high water, passage for vessels of over six-feet draft was nearly impossible. In 1865 this made it impractical for the Allies to mount a naval expedition against the oncoming forces of Duarte and Estigarribia.

The most extensive and visually impressive series of shoals and cascades was located at Mbutuí, roughly halfway between São Borja and Itaquí. As the waters of the Uruguay pass through this *salto*, they hurled themselves in myriad patterns through fissures in the rocks. The clouds of spray, iridescent with rainbows, formed a permanent layer of vapor over the lush vegetation, and the roar could be heard from many miles away. At one end of the shoal, half hidden in mist, lay the confluence of the Uruguay with the Mbutuí River, an obscure waterway originating in the hill country a hundred miles east. Few Paraguayans had ever heard of it. It was near this river — some miles inland — where they next faced the Allies.

The occupation of São Borja coincided with Captain Meza's defeat at the Riachuelo. As at Corumbá, the Paraguayans sacked the town, but unlike events at the Mato Grossense community, this was less undisciplined looting than a systematic collection of the "spoils" that Solano López had promised. Soldiers went house-to-house seizing everything of value and reserving the best loot for the marshal and Madame Lynch. The Paraguayan officers took their turn with deference to rank, followed by the soldiers themselves who seized whatever remained. Estigarribia sent a sizable share across the river to be divided among Duarte's troops.[10]

Pedro Gay, the canon of the local church, echoed the dismay of the town's *vezinhos* when he reported in detail the awful ravaging of his vicarage.[11] The only dwellings that escaped a ransacking by the invading force belonged to resident foreigners, though they too had many complaints. One French merchant went out to remonstrate with Estigarribia, noting that his place of business enjoyed the protection of his country's flag. The colonel, who was too busy to bother with the hapless shopkeeper, replied, "Yes, yes, the [*tricouleur*] has not ceased to be beautiful, it is the most beautiful flag after that of the Republic of Paraguay; but if this Frenchman wants respect for his house he should stay within it, for all who flee are enemies of the Supreme Government."[12]

The vandalizing of São Borja yielded relatively little of military value. The three days spent in plundering the town might better have been spent pursuing the imperial forces or establishing a secure perimeter. As happened, the Brazilians had no units close enough to mount a counterattack against the Paraguayan salient, so the colonel had all the time he needed to pursue other priorities.

The defeat at the Riachuelo had no immediate effect on Estigarribia's command. The troops at São Borja were less concerned with the strategic implications of a battle on the Paraná than with the general lack of provisions. Their quartermasters had failed to squeeze much out of the adjacent countryside. The colonel therefore decided to go farther out, sending foraging and reconnaissance parties — some of which consisted of several hundred horsemen — in several directions. One such party, led by Capt. José del Rosario López, went north to São Mateus and there seized two thousand head of cattle and horses before returning to São Borja on 14 June.[13] The next day Estigarribia ordered Captain López to intercept a convoy of arms known to be moving east toward Alegrete.

López's column of four hundred men included several Correntino and Uruguayan volunteers who earlier had joined Estigarribia. One of these, Justiniano Salvañach, had served the former Blanco government as an army major and now acted as adjutant to López. Expecting to guide the marshal's forces through Rio Grande do Sul and Uruguay, he was perfectly happy to pursue convoys so long as it took him south toward his homeland.

In this case, the convoy managed to escape, but in the process of searching for it, López and Salvañach penetrated nearly sixty miles into the heart of Brazil's Rio Grande do Sul. They engaged in one brief skirmish with the Brazilian Twenty-eighth Cavalry Regiment but otherwise saw no action. The local population melted away whenever the Paraguayan troops came near.

The López column returned to São Borja on 22 June only to discover that Estigarribia had evacuated the town three days earlier and was now on the march to Itaquí. Lacking specific orders or information, Captain López rode south to rejoin his commander's column. In the process, he and his men crossed over the Mbutuí River at a point some miles inland from the shoals.

The river at this spot was a wide creek running along the south edge of a large marsh, the Donato Swamp, into which it partly drained. Because of heavy rains, the creek was in full flood during late June, and López detoured some distance to the east to find a spot for fording. With Estigarribia many miles away near Itaquí, he was more isolated than ever before.

On 25 June, López's column fought a new action with the Twenty-eighth Cavalry. The latter unit had been attempting for some days to link up with the First Brigade, the main Brazilian force in the region. Col. Antonio de Fernandes Lima and his thirty-five-hundred-man brigade were in fact moving up from the southeast. Having earlier failed to prevent Estigarribia's occupation of São Borja and now learning that the Paraguayans had driven the Twenty-eighth Cavalry from the field, he resolved to exact a terrible vengeance the next day.

Brazilian and Paraguayan accounts differ on every critical detail of the ensuing battle of Mbutuí, including the actual site. While standard Brazilian sources place the fighting thirty miles south of the Mbutuí River, the Paraguayans maintain that it occurred near the river itself.[14]

Whatever the geographical truth, when Captain López saw that a large enemy force was deploying against him, he ordered his troops to dismount and establish a defensive position atop a lightly wooded hillock. The Donato Swamp was to his back, which made it difficult for Fernandes to get behind him. The Brazilian commander was forced to make a frontal assault.

López's decision to stop and fight revealed a pattern of behavior that proved all too common among Paraguayan officers throughout the war. Though he was on a reconnaissance and resupply mission and should have been concerned at all costs with getting back to Estigarribia with information on enemy movements, he instead elected to dismount and dig in. Worse still, he positioned himself with a major obstacle to his rear. Though it safeguarded his rear from a Brazilian attack, the swamp also made impractical any retreat. Captain López, like many Paraguayan commanders, displayed no subtlety in combat; he gave no thought to losing a little in order to gain a little. For him, war was always a matter of victory or death.

Fernandes wished to launch his attack at daybreak but had difficulty in confirming the Paraguayan dispositions. A thick, cold fog that looked like a broth of gray slush had set in, and it was impossible for the Brazilian colonel to see more than a few yards ahead. He finally began his attack around 8:00 A.M., just as the scene began to clear. Incongruously, however, he advanced in piecemeal fashion, a serious mistake. In failing to coordinate his five regiments so that they assaulted the Paraguayans simultaneously, he gave López the opportunity to repulse each unit in turn. As the Brazilians learned to their dismay, this played to the Paraguayans' greatest strength, for they invariably fought well on the defensive.

Again and again the Brazilian horsemen surged forward, first against the enemy's right flank, then the left. Fernandes's men carried modern carbines known for their range and accuracy. These rifles soon had a terrible effect upon the Paraguayans, who for the most part were armed with lances and flintlocks. Had the Brazilian commander committed the two regiments he held in reserve, he might have swept López's position at the outset of the engagement. As it was, the Paraguayans withstood eleven assaults. Each time, the Brazilians wore them down a bit more, until finally the First Brigade broke the Paraguayan right wing, which was commanded by Salvañach. With Minié balls whizzing all around him, the Uruguayan major fled into the swamp; he reappeared alone and disoriented in Misiones a full month later.[15] At the same time, the Brazilians cut down most of López's mounted cavalry, leaving the remaining Paraguayan horsemen to pull back into the swamp to regroup.

Despite their losses, the Paraguayan center and left wing held firm for more than an hour. Sensing victory, Colonel Fernandes pressed his attack. He felt certain the enemy would break under added pressure, and indeed, the Paraguayan left started to waver. These were mostly infantrymen — lean, tough troops accustomed to long marching but not to wave after wave of galloping, cursing gaúchos. In the end, the Paraguayan infantry melted into the Donato, leaving behind many corpses. Strikingly, López's center still showed no sign of weakening.

After another hour, Fernandes broke off the attack. He probably wished to mount a final charge with the aid of his reserve units but chose to rest his troops before doing so. López, his men no less spent, nevertheless ordered all the survivors to withdraw north to join their fellows who were already seeking a refuge among the high reeds.

As the Paraguayans looked for firm ground amidst the water and muck, another brigade of the imperial army, the Fourth, arrived to reinforce Fernandes with two more regiments of cavalry and one of infantry. After a short interval, the Brazilian commander confidently ordered the combined force to strike the remaining Paraguayans.

López had nearly abandoned hope. His exhausted men, having climbed atop a dry outcropping, were barely able to lift and load their muskets. The bodies of the wounded and slain were all about, half sunken in the mire. The captain expected to see his command obliterated. He was relieved, therefore, to observe the unsteady, slip-shod progress of the enemy cavalry through the mud, reeds, and *camalotes*. At the last minute, Fernandes decided that he should not risk his mounted units in such terrain and called off the attack. For a time, he considered sending in his infantry but gave up the idea as impractical. Besides, there was still Estigarribia's force somewhere to consider.

The battle was over. López's command suffered 116 killed and 120 wounded out of a force of 400.[16] His willingness to endure such losses confirmed the worst fears of the Allied commanders — the Paraguayans would be intractable in combat, difficult to defeat.[17] Mitre's press tried to put a good face on this fact, but it was not easy.

As word of the Paraguayan resistance spread to Concordia and points south, Captain López and his remaining 160 men made their way through the marshes to the Uruguay River. They salvaged few of their muskets and even fewer horses. Most men left behind pieces of their uniforms and kit, and some arrived at the river nearly naked. Everyone who waded through the waters emerged with their legs covered with leeches, the creatures looking like tiny wineskins filled with red *carlón* wine. The soldiers eventually found Estigarribia, who was still trudging south unaware that anything had happened.

Despite the bravery of their opponents and the admiration it inspired among the Allied soldiers, it was the Brazilians who gained victory at

Mbutuí. They retained control of the field, while the Paraguayan detachment, badly mauled, fled the scene. Fernandes claimed to have lost forty killed and seventy-eight wounded, though his overall casualties were probably two or three times that number.[18]

In terms of the campaign as a whole, the battle was relatively unimportant. The main Paraguayan force was still advancing, and Fernandes's action at Mbutuí did nothing to slow its progress. Indeed, while the First and Fourth Brigades should have been striking at Estigarribia's rear, the Paraguayan colonel entered Itaquí unopposed.

*What Next?*

The move of the main Paraguayan force south from São Borja proceeded without incident, but it was hardly a comfortable experience. The men were hungry and cold, soaked by freezing rain every day. No one could find dry firewood. Pacing in his tent, Colonel Estigarribia had other worries. The advance guard of his army had reached the mouth of the Mbutuí on 22 June and drove off the small force of Brazilian defenders they found there. Now nothing stood in Estigarribia's way — yet he felt perplexed. His orders allowed him to advance as far as the *salto*, but the marshal made no mention of his advancing farther.

Now was not the time for Estigarribia to test his president's patience. Solano López had reacted with profound irritation at Paunero's raid of 25 May on Corrientes and blamed his officers for their failure to prevent it. He grew suspicious when General Robles resisted his orders to retreat from Goya. And Captain Meza's defeat at the Riachuelo sent him into an uncontrollable rage.[19]

Solano López now decided to sack Robles and recall Francisco Resquín from Mato Grosso. The latter officer, now a general, would assume command of the Southern Division. Historians traditionally have interpreted this change of command as a sign of the marshal's anger at Robles's supposed insubordination combined with a fear that the general might defect.

The truth was more complicated. Robles never acted in open opposition to Lopez's orders — though he certainly thought the retreat from

Goya ill advised. He had received missives from Urquiza and other Allied officers, some of whom were Paraguayans. These men all urged upon him a treasonous course of action, but he rejected all of them, even threatening to shoot anyone foolish enough to bring him further notes from Fernando Iturburu, the émigré commander of the Paraguayan Legion.[20] Robles's real problems began on 14 June when he learned of his brother's death at the battle of the Riachuelo. The news upset him terribly. He visibly sunk into depression, drank heavily, and ignored communications from Corrientes. The weather aggravated him. The chill had grown profoundly, such that when a man rested upon a flat stone, it felt as if he had sat in a puddle of cold water. This increased everyone's feelings of helplessness, including those of the general.

At about this time Lt. Col. Paulino Alén arrived at Robles's camp from Humaitá. The newcomer, who had arrived to take over the position of chief of staff for the Southern Division, also received instructions from Solano López to report on the situation. Alén was frankly shocked by the general's bad mood and indiscreet mutterings. The colonel thought to cheer him with the formal presentation of the National Order of Merit, which the marshal had authorized and consisted of a decorative sash with golden star. Instead of lifting his spirits, however, the decoration had the opposite effect. Robles turned on his new subordinate with an almost biblical fury, demanding that the honor be given to his dead brother, who had really earned it. Alén begged him to set aside his modesty and accept the decoration — it came from the supreme government and ought not be ignored. To this the general growled: "If they don't like it, they can go ahead and shoot me. . . . What value is there in such rubbish? Do you think perchance that such a trifle will please me? What I want is clothes for my poor soldiers who are shivering from the cold! What does the life of one man matter? And at the end of it all we have no weapons."[21] A wise commander in chief might have been willing to let such an outburst pass without comment, for it clearly arose from an understandable grief and frustration. For the marshal, however, it simply added fuel to an already blazing fire. Knowing that Robles headed a demoralized and possibly rebellious army, he sought to reestablish discipline indirectly. Transferring Alén to Robles's camp was only the first step. On 30 June, Resquín arrived at Southern Division headquarters, not as the new commanding general but rather as Robles's second in command. In this post Resquín began to restore morale while paving the way for the early exit of Robles, who was now drinking a full bottle of cognac a day.

Resquín himself was a big, brown-faced man, whose square shape and deliberate stride gave him the appearance of solidity, courage, and correct military bearing. Yet his fear of Solano López affected his performance in the field. He had been successful in Mato Grosso, but in the end, his pliability was what mattered to the marshal.

During this same period, Humaitá sent the Southern Division a reinforcement of one cavalry regiment and two infantry battalions. One of these units—the Fortieth Infantry Battalion—later gained fame under a brilliant if ruthless officer, Col. José Eduvigis Díaz. Like Alén, Díaz was a trusted agent of the marshal. Both officers received a proper, if not a hearty, welcome from Robles, who was glad of their company and the chance to march south again.

Several weeks passed before Resquín judged the army fit to move. In that time he spent every waking moment retraining it, pushing the soldiers to the breaking point with drill and more drill. When he was finished, it was his army in all but name. Robles hardly knew what had happened, only that López had instructed him to hold his position.

In fact, the marshal had ordered the Southern Division to remain at Empedrado to guard against a new assault from the Brazilian fleet, a preposterous assignment. Barroso was completely inactive at that time and, in any case, how could cavalry and infantry units counteract the movements of a naval force? Of course, by ordering Robles to stand still, the marshal made it simpler to later portray him as an erratic sot who avoided taking the offensive. That such a charge was unjust might have been obvious to anyone outside Paraguay (though, to be fair, something similar had also been said of Union general U. S. Grant at Vicksburg only two years earlier). In the end, however, it hardly mattered.

On 21 July 1865, Gen. Vicente Barrios, now the Paraguayan war minister, arrived at Corrientes with sealed letters from Solano López. These contained orders to arrest Robles, turn his command over to Resquín, and proceed south against the Allies with all dispatch. Arrested two days later in camp, Robles made no protest. He handed his sword to Barrios and went with him quietly. In an elaborate trial at Humaitá five months later, Robles found himself accused of incompetence and collusion with the enemy.[22] His execution by firing squad in January 1866 came as a surprise to no one.

### The Mutiny at Basualdo

Colonel Estigarribia knew nothing of Robles's plight or of the marshal's decision to rearrange the Southern Division's command structure. He did know that his own force of seventy-five hundred men was isolated. While he was afraid to go forward without orders, he was more afraid to stand still. In itself, Itaquí held little for the Paraguayans, but not far distant lay the Uruguayan border, beyond which the Blancos even now might be awaiting their liberators.[23]

Major Duarte's column kept roughly parallel with that of Estigarribia and occupied the Correntino hamlet of La Cruz on 5 July. On the whole, Duarte had thus far enjoyed more success than his compatriots to the east of the Uruguay River. His intelligence was better; he knew, for instance, that the Correntino irregulars attached to Colonels Paiva and Reguera had moved seven miles south of La Cruz and were still retreating. They were badly demoralized. The two colonels had sustained the failing courage of their men by an unending series of threats and cajolings, but even these efforts had reached their limit.

The Allied position on the Correntino-Entrerriano frontier disintegrated on 3 July when Urquiza's eight-thousand-man army mutinied at Basualdo. The *caudillo* was absent from camp at the time, on his way to Concordia to confer with President Mitre and Allied commanders. The mutiny seems to have started with groups of from one to two hundred cavalrymen shouting *vivas* to Urquiza and *mueras* to Brazil and the national government. Mass desertions followed at once. A clique of disaffected officers went from unit to unit spreading the same message:

"Comrades! The Captain General has gone home and we should do the same. Don't be foolish, don't be taken in!"[24] Soon, virtually the entire Entrerriano army abandoned the camp. The deserters, taking their arms and horses, headed home, leaving behind a few sick men and a small Correntino contingent that could not hope to fend off the Paraguayans by itself.[25]

Urquiza was livid when news of the mutiny reached him. In a letter to Mitre he tried, however, to put as good a face as possible on the situation: "False rumors about the reason for my journey, the [reckless] products of the press recalling our past differences . . . , and the effects of drink exacerbated this [state of affairs, which perhaps] would not have happened had I been present or at least would have been controlled sooner. You can imagine the disgust I feel for what has occurred in the army on the night of my journey, precisely when I was reflecting that the example of our loyalty would inspire others."[26]

The mutiny, however, caused great consternation in Buenos Aires. Allied strategy depended on the concentration of cavalry forces in Entre Ríos. Now, supposedly "crack" units from Nogoyá and Victoria had deserted en masse. Mitre knew better than to appear alarmed, but he realized the danger the situation presented to the alliance with the empire.

Even more serious was the effect on Mitre's alliance with Urquiza. As Edward Thornton observed, the mutiny showed clearly how far the old *caudillo*'s prestige had fallen in the province and concomitantly how much that of López Jordán and other opponents of the war had grown.[27] For Mitre to help Urquiza, he needed to avoid any measure that might undercut the latter's authority in Entre Ríos. He could not, for instance, bring in *porteño* troops to replace the Entrerrianos without making a bad situation worse, for any resulting unpleasantness might in turn necessitate the deployment of Brazilian forces in the province—an eventuality certain to ignite civil war.

The one remaining advantage for the national government was that no Paraguayan force could readily take advantage of the mutiny. The Southern Division was far away and immobilized by command troubles. Estigarribia had just arrived at Itaquí—on the wrong side of the river—

and chose to concern himself with looting rather than strategy. He directed his mule trains and the greater part of his army away from the river in order to avoid marching through the back swamp. That movement took him farther away from Duarte, who could not move south without Estigarribia's specific permission.

The major was sorely tempted to move anyway, for on 6 July, 378 Entrerriano deserters arrived from Basualdo to place themselves under his command. Duarte held off accepting these new recruits, for he knew that only the marshal could make decisions that involved the shifting politics of the region. Yet Solano López, far away at Humaitá, could not effectively guide events on the Uruguay. Though evidently informed of the Basualdo mutiny, he had limited communication with Estigarribia and Duarte and no way to improve the efficiency of his mounted messengers. It was another opportunity lost.

Ever since Pavón, Urquiza had noticed his power slipping away. Now he found himself clutching at phantoms even in his home province. He might still increase his wealth by the sale of horses to Mitre's cavalry, but this could have no positive effect on his standing with the Entrerrianos, many of whom now wondered whether he was selling mounts to the Brazilians as well. With his influence gone and the situation in disarray, the *caudillo* did the only realistic thing. Without consulting the national government, he issued a decree granting a general furlough to all the troops who had deserted. He knew that this contradicted Mitre's wishes but saw little choice: *obedezco pero no cumplo*. On 7 July, Urquiza lamented to the president, "You must know that I only made such a grave decision . . . because there was no other way to counteract the bad morale and disorder among those elements that should return to the nation's defense and Your Excellency can rest assured that they will do so even if I have to sacrifice myself if necessary."[28]

The Basualdo mutiny had not been spontaneous, although it easily could have been. López Jordán, who lived nearby, had involved himself in the mutiny at some level and now simply tapped into a widespread antiwar — or more properly, anti-Brazilian — feeling in the Litoral and turned it to his political advantage.

The disappearance of Urquiza's fighting forces posed serious strategic problems for the Allies. The *caudillo* set out at once for San José, Victoria, and Nogoyá to try to lift morale in those quarters. Yet he hardly expected his efforts to meet with success. In order to stave off the threat from Duarte, therefore, the Allied high command decided to detach Venancio Flores from the main camp at Concordia and send him north.

### The Paraguayans March South

On 14 July, Estigarribia advanced again, now with full authorization from the marshal, who ordered a movement twenty miles downriver to the Uruguay's confluence with the Ybycuí River, there to await further instructions. Duarte departed La Cruz at exactly the same time, still keeping parallel with the main Paraguayan column across the river. Even so, the two units stayed in sight of each other only rarely, a fact that made joint operations impossible.

The Brazilians also maintained contact with Estigarribia's force after it left Itaquí. They had a good notion of where the colonel was bound and conducted an active defense. On paper, they had between seven and nine thousand troops at their disposal for the task.[29] The First Division, still commanded by Gen. David Canabarro, took up positions along the southern bank of the Ybycuí to prevent the enemy from crossing this relatively wide river. Meanwhile, the First Brigade, which had already bested the Paraguayans at Mbutuí, received orders to stay north of the river and attack Estigarribia's left flank whenever the column attempted to cross. In effect, the Brazilians were preparing a trap.

As it happened, Canabarro's men failed to arrive at the Ybycuí until the twenty-first, three days after the Paraguayans. Estigarribia, who by now had made a habit of ignoring the marshal's orders, failed to stop at the river and instead moved to establish a bridgehead on its southern bank. Unwittingly (for he had no knowledge of the First Division's movements), the colonel selected a spot some three miles east of the Brazilian defenders. His men constructed a pontoon bridge to facilitate the passage of the artillery, and by the morning of 20 July, he led his entire contingent across.

As General Canabarro approached the Ybycuí, he was surprised to learn that the Paraguayans had marched a full fifteen miles farther south and were well on their way to Uruguaiana. Taken aback by Estigarribia's swiftness, Canabarro met with Gen. João Frederico Caldwell, overall commander in Rio Grande do Sul. The two generals decided to establish a new defensive line still farther south at Touro Passo Creek just above Uruguaiana. The Brazilian failure to stop the Paraguayans at the Ybycuí left no credible defense possible, and any effort at the Touro Passo could only amount to a short-lived holding action. Caldwell and Canabarro knew this, as did the inhabitants of the small Riograndense communities in Estigarribia's path. Every newspaper in the empire trumpeted their fears, and commentators asked openly whether imperial forces could contain the Paraguayan threat in Rio Grande do Sul or anywhere else.[30]

Estigarribia reached the Touro Passo on 28 July after several inconclusive clashes with Brazilian forces. With Canabarro and Caldwell in disarray just to the south, the colonel halted to wait for further orders from Humaitá. And, indeed, within a day Duarte and a small escort crossed the Uruguay with a messenger from the marshal. Solano López expressed both anger and satisfaction at Estigarribia's progress: "Since you have not obeyed my orders and have [instead] passed beyond the Ybycuí, I now order you to continue your march to Uruguaiana, where [Brazilian] supplies await you, and then you will move on to Alegrete, taking care, as before, not to camp within the towns, so as to avoid being besieged by the enemy."[31]

It was obvious that Solano López had in mind a major foraging operation—Alegrete being a key livestock region—before launching an invasion of the Banda Oriental. This approach, which resembled his undertaking in Mato Grosso, revealed the limits of the marshal's strategic thinking. Instead of drafting overtures to the Uruguayan Blancos and Entrerriano rebels, he busied himself with securing the army's sources of supply, which was surely a concern but not the highest priority for the leader of a nation at war.

Estigarribia's own imagination carried him no further than new spoils. He paid little attention, for example, to Duarte's request for new

*The March into Rio Grande* 345

instructions to cover the changed circumstances. Instead, the colonel sent his subordinate back across the Uruguay without clear instructions. Estigarribia believed that he could reach the major at a moment's notice and had little concern that the enemy might interfere. As things turned out, he never saw Major Duarte again.

The Brazilians had known for some time that the river itself was a weak link between the two Paraguayan columns. Now, with Estigarribia encamped north of the Touro Passo, they boldly moved forward to sever the link. It was all the work of an ingenious young artillery lieutenant, Floriano Peixoto, who commandeered several small river craft, turned them into a makeshift flotilla, and used them to completely disrupt communications between Estigarribia and Duarte. Of the three vessels involved, only the *Uruguai*, a little steamer of thirty-five tons, had any claim to being a warship, the other two vessels being little more than launches.[32]

In Floriano's capable hands, however, they became a formidable naval force. The lieutenant embarked aboard them a special unit, which, like Paraguay's *Nambi-í*, was composed entirely of black troops. Dressed in spectacular uniforms that featured green vests, red trousers, blue jackets, and bright, scarlet fezzes, these *Zuavos Baianos* proved to be excellent fighters.[33] With their help as gunners, Floriano trained his three small cannons on the Paraguayan canoes in the river and coolly shot them to pieces. His own talents as a gunner had already been noticed by his superior officers, but no one, least of all the Paraguayans, suspected that he might maneuver his vessels with such dexterity.

Duarte and Estigarribia tried to strike back on two occasions. At Touro Passo, the latter erected an artillery battery overlooking the river and tried to entice Floriano into range of the superior Paraguayan firepower. When the lieutenant's boats rushed toward the shoreline and fired into the Paraguayan position, it was Estigarribia who pulled back. As for Duarte, he organized an assault force of canoes to attack Floriano under cover of darkness, but the attempt failed and the canoes scattered. The Brazilian officer's skill and audacity prevented the Paraguayan commanders from coordinating their efforts and sowed the seeds of their ultimate defeat.

### Estigarribia Takes Uruguaiana

Armed with new orders from Solano López, Estigarribia crossed the Touro Passo on 2 August 1865, encountering no resistance; General Caldwell had already decided six days earlier that his troops were too few and too ill prepared to make a stand at the creek. Uruguaiana was the last Brazilian community of any significance before the Uruguayan border. From there the Paraguayans could launch an invasion of the richest cattle lands in the empire while raising the flag of revolt in the Banda Oriental. The Brazilian commanders understood the strategic importance of Uruguaiana as well as the great risk they took in giving it up without a fight. After all, they had prepared the town for defense, stockpiling food and munitions, all of which they now abandoned. The town itself offered rich spoils for the Paraguayan soldiers, who, cold and dog-tired, looked forward to the takings as a respite from the march.

The Brazilian decision not to defend Uruguaiana was sound enough despite the risks it involved. If Caldwell and Canabarro had defended the town with the inferior force at their disposal, it likely would have been overwhelmed. Alegrete might then have fallen, leaving the door open to the rest of Rio Grande do Sul and the Banda Oriental. Far better, they thought, to give up Uruguaiana and play for time. Their position could only improve as Allied reinforcements reached the theater. Colonel Thompson, who was contemptuous of the Brazilian commander's inability to defend the Riograndense towns, nonetheless gave his grudging approval of Caldwell's decision to pull back from Uruguaiana: "[The Brazilians allowed Estigarribia] to sack their towns, ill-treat their women, and destroy everything before him, without doing more than sending a few skirmishers to watch him. If they left the honor, lives, and property of their countrymen and country-women entirely out of the question, and looked at it in [sic] a purely military point of view, they did right, as they would have had much more trouble in fighting him than they had afterwards in besieging and starving him out, though they had superior forces."[34]

For his part, Colonel Estigarribia knew that he could expect no reinforcements from Paraguay and hoped that Blanco armies would soon join his victorious soldiers. The odds against this happening were long, and it seemed best to the colonel not to dwell on the likelier alternative. As for his men, for once there was sufficient firewood and provisions to meet their needs. They even traded their tattered uniforms for new shirts and pantaloons taken from Brazilian stores and enjoyed fresh yerba for the first time in weeks.[35] Let the marshal handle questions of strategy; for their part, they obeyed orders.

By instructing Estigarribia to march on Alegrete, Solano López thought to encourage the Uruguay Division's forward momentum. The colonel had already taken too much time at São Borja and Itaquí. Now he tarried again at Uruguaiana. On 16 August the imperial high command replaced the overcautious Caldwell with another general, Manoel Marquez de Sousa, the count of Pôrto Alegre. Like Canabarro, the new commander was a man in his sixties with long experience in the military; unlike his fellow Riograndense, however, he had sided with the emperor during the Farrapo Revolt and thereby earned promotion after promotion. He had commanded the Brazilian forces against Juan Manuel de Rosas at Caseros in 1852. Then, at the end of the decade, he had retired with all the prestige and accolades his government could accord him.

Pôrto Alegre was as meticulous in his military planning as he was in dress. Having been called out of retirement, he did not panic now but carefully weighed his advantages and disadvantages. He saw at once the weakness of Estigarribia's position. If the Paraguayan colonel delayed his march for any length of time, as he had already done at São Borja, then Uruguaiana would become a trap, snapping shut upon him. Pôrto Alegre hoped, therefore, that the enemy force would stay at the town, consume all the available rations, and grow complacent. In the meantime, the Allies prepared a siege.

# V

# The Tide Turns

# Missteps in the South

## 13

Major Duarte's column continued its southward march through knee-high grass toward the lower provinces, encountering no significant opposition. Colonels Paiva and Reguera had pulled back toward Concordia and allowed the Paraguayans to advance unhindered. Perhaps the Correntinos thought to weaken Duarte's lines of communication by pulling him farther away from his base camps above the Alto Paraná. Perhaps they believed themselves so weak that withdrawal was their best option. Duarte, of course, had to face more risks, since every day he put more distance between his forward position and Paraguay. Yet he kept moving. Unlike Lt. Col. Antonio Estigarribia, he had no intention of second-guessing the marshal and pushed through the wild open country from La Cruz. He always kept the river in sight and always buttressed his main column with wide-ranging patrols on the right flank. Finally, at the beginning of August, his troops entered Restauración (Paso de los Libres), the last town before the Entrerriano frontier, just opposite Uruguaiana.

No one could have predicted the calamities that would soon follow. The Paraguayans refrained from looting at Restauración and did little to irritate the few locals remaining in the vicinity. For Duarte, this was more a matter of common sense than of humanitarianism; far more than his immediate commander across the river, he recognized that the goodwill of the Correntinos and Entrerrianos was necessary for any victory.[1] With this in mind, he kept a tight rein on his men, paid (or tried to pay) for any goods taken, and always spoke reassuring words to the civilians he encountered while on campaign.² Whereas the Brazilians were confirmed enemies and could be thrashed accordingly, he might yet convince these Argentines to join the Paraguayan cause.

Duarte wanted to keep every option open. Despite the relative proximity of Estigarribia, the two columns found it difficult to maintain contact. Lt. Floriano Peixoto's activities on the Uruguay River interfered with all their efforts, clearly demonstrating a major weakness in Paraguayan thinking. Why should any Argentine — or, for that matter, Uruguayan — rally to Solano López's call if his troops could not stop such an insignificant river force? And without Argentine or Uruguayan aid, the Paraguayans had little chance of victory.

Estigarribia appeared oblivious to the dangers of standing still, but Duarte had few illusions about his position. Rather than remain in occupation of Restauración, he moved three miles north to a hill he considered more defensible. He ordered extensive patrolling on all sides. Even so, he felt edgy, overextended. Though he scrupulously obeyed the marshal's orders, he found no comfort in the fact; his president could never reach him in an emergency. As for Estigarribia, even under the best of circumstances, his aid could only be tentative, given the river that lay between them. The colonel might feel safe in Uruguaiana — or at least so tired and distracted that he ignored the danger — but Duarte felt nervous and knew why. To his south, not many miles distant, Venancio Flores's cavalry was riding toward him.

*Preparing for the Big Fight*

The Allies had exchanged land for time ever since the fall of Corrientes in April. Wenceslao Paunero's raid of 25 May had been a brilliant stroke, completely disrupting Paraguayan timetables and overall strategy. The battle of the Riachuelo likewise damaged the marshal's hopes for an early victory. On both occasions, however, the Allies failed to capitalize on their advantages for simple want of manpower.

Bartolomé Mitre was doubtlessly more comfortable as a man of letters than as a battlefield commander, yet he was an exceptional military organizer. The mutiny at Basualdo slowed, but did not stop, his plans for offensive action. The Triple Alliance Treaty had assigned him the role of commander in chief, and the Argentine Congress granted him leave to assume command in the field. Now Mitre used all his powers to build a fighting force second to none in the Plata.

Mitre worked unceasingly to harness the country to the task of mobilization.[3] It was not easy. The national government had only just established the Argentine army in January 1864. It had yet to crystallize into anything substantial despite the call to recruit every male between the ages of seventeen and forty-five. Real military power remained in the hands of the National Guard, itself a weak provincial institution. Buenos Aires alone had a guard with any pretensions of modernity, and in the present circumstances Mitre was, in effect, demanding that the provinces align their military forces behind those of his own province. This was not an approach destined to be well received in the Argentine interior.

More often than not, provincial governments held back the troop contingents demanded of them, invariably citing financial difficulties. In truth, even at the beginning, the war against Paraguay engendered popular misgivings, especially in the west of the country, where local officials risked an uprising if they acceded to the national government's demand for soldiers. A spirit of enthusiasm and a sense of offended national honor often inspire young men, but such was not the case throughout Argentina. Many in the interior simply did not consider themselves part of a "nation," or at least not part of the same Argentina that Buenos Aires dominated.[4]

There were exceptions to this trend. The widow of Gregorio Araóz de Lamadrid (once the most influential Unitarian general in Tucumán and Salta) wrote Mitre to offer her paltry military pension as contribution to the national cause.[5] But she was hardly representative. Far more people were suspicious of *porteño* objectives and wondered how far the national government might push them. In addition, the majority of those conscripted came from the peripheral sectors of provincial society—unemployed gauchos who, like the title character in José Hernández's *Martín*

*Fierro*, chafed under the demands of military discipline and deserted before reaching the theater of operations. A starry-eyed feeling of patriotism was not part of their world.⁶

Mitre busied himself with building a consensus in favor of the war. From the Argentine Congress he obtained a clear long-term commitment to the campaign, pressing the legislators hard, appealing in every way to their emotions, from vanity to love of country.⁷ On a more confidential level, the president wheedled influential congressional leaders, offering them detailed promises of patronage and vivid warnings of what would happen if they failed to cooperate. It was an impressive orchestration. In short order he gained solid — if not unanimous — political and financial backing from Congress.

Mitre understood how delicate the situation was. His cajoling of congressional and provincial leaders was nonetheless sinuous and effective, and for a man who all along had doubted the warlike intentions of Francisco Solano López, his political instincts now served him well. He knew whom to push hard, whom to bribe, and whom to leave alone. He delegated the onerous task of organizing conscription to individuals of proven loyalty, while carefully distancing himself from the hateful image of the press gang. With great skill, Mitre argued the "national" option, expressing in every communication that Paraguay had launched the war against all Argentines, not just his own *porteños*, and that all needed to contribute to final victory. The progovernment press repeated these appeals and stressed that civilization's "crusade" against barbarism was worth every effort.⁸

Mitre's successes outweighed his failures in this early stage of mobilization, but not by much. In his own province, he mustered thousands of men quickly and deployed them with relatively little fuss to Concordia. He personally attended to the minutest details of their provisioning and transport from Buenos Aires and Rosario.⁹ He provided mounts purchased from Bonaerense *estancieros* and foodstuffs and clothing from Anacarsis Lanús, Marshal López's former armorer.¹⁰ He supplied weapons and shot in various calibers, six packets for each soldier.¹¹ He provided new uniforms, blankets, and surplus woolens left over from the Crimean War and the U.S. Civil War.

Mitre also increased his recruitment of foreigners into the Argentine army. Some of these were resident in the Plata, others came directly from Europe.[12] A few of these individuals, such as the Italian Gianbattista Charlone, the Englishman Ignacio Fotheringham, and the Pole Roberto Chodasiewicz, played major roles later in the war.[13]

Since government resources could produce only a portion of the capital he required, Mitre experimented with various schemes to raise war revenue internally. He soon discovered that support for the war was paper thin, even among *porteño* oligarchs. The national government attempted to secure monies from private citizens through bond sales, yet when Vice President Marcos Paz opened a subscription list in Buenos Aires, no one showed any interest.[14] When private citizens made proposals, the special guarantees and rate of interest they demanded made the offers unacceptable.[15] In the end, only major foreign residents showed any willingness to contribute; Thomas Armstrong, director of the Argentine Central Railway, gave fifty thousand pesos to Paz's fund (though easing the way for possible future contracts with the government probably had as much to do with his generosity as any show of patriotism).[16]

Behind the scenes, both Mitre and Foreign Minister Elizalde began to negotiate for foreign loans. The imperial government, itself deeply indebted to the British Rothschilds, made available a loan of one million pesos to the Argentine national government on 31 May 1865 (the Brazilians issued a second loan for the same amount eight months later).[17] The Bank of London was another early lender, and for its trouble earned a high 18-percent interest on the monies it passed to the Mitre regime. These various loans (which later formed a key element in the analyses of revisionist historians) were most welcome by the Argentine War Ministry in 1865, for they made possible much-needed financial backing at a critical time.[18] Even so, the loans were difficult to raise. The baron of Mauá was in England throughout this time but, given his disillusionment with the various political turns in the Banda Oriental, was of little help in arranging loans for the Allies. Prudent European financiers, moreover, displayed little interest in bankrolling South American wars when they could make certain profits in overseas railroad construction and in the India trade.

Having paved the way for a strong response to the Paraguayan invasion, Mitre left for the front in mid-June, arriving at Concordia on the eighteenth. He immediately set to work turning the ramshackle camp at the edge of town into a model military installation. His men erected tents in regular rows, dug latrines, and prepared hundreds of small campfires.[19] They leveled out a parade ground, unloaded a train of two score wagons, and set up a serviceable canteen. The surgeons and medical personnel soon had a hospital and dispensary in full operation. Just as busy were the local sutlers, who hawked their various wares among the soldiers with as much energy as their counterparts in the marketplaces in Buenos Aires and Montevideo. Thanks to Mitre's detailed attention, Concordia began to look the part of a nineteenth-century military encampment—far less grand than Sebastopol, but certainly impressive.[20]

The Argentine contingents at Concordia were unusual to say the least. The best and the meanest of the country were crowded together. Here were thieves and ne'er-do-wells forced into service alongside volunteers from the most prosperous families of Buenos Aires, young men who had enjoyed all that money could buy. There were, of course, individuals of privileged background who did not wish to join the campaign despite all the clamor; they had easy recourse to substitutes, often immigrants, who advertised their availability for service in the newspapers of both Buenos Aires and the provinces.[21]

Mitre's task at Concordia was the same as Duarte's at the Pindapoi—to take an inexperienced, amorphous body of men and transform it into a strong, dependable, and motivated army. The Argentine president, however, was under severe time constraints. The longer he delayed sending his troops into action, the farther the enemy was likely to advance. Yet Mitre refused to be rushed into battle. His own *porteño* battalions had received adequate, if not extensive, training and were ready for combat after a fashion. The same could not be said for the provincial troops—men who were apt to fight like their gaucho grandfathers, with much heart and little cohesion. Compared with all previous wars in South America, this conflict required that enormous numbers of men be brought under arms, and Mitre was anxious to see those in his command function well together.

The infantry's training at Concordia involved hour after hour of close-order drill. No one, then or now, had yet devised a better system to inculcate the habit of instant obedience, so necessary to unit cohesion during the noise and smoke of battle. The infantry also practiced complex maneuvers such as forming a line of battle and changing the direction of that line by ninety degrees. Following the geometrically precise configurations suggested by Jomini and others, the infantrymen formed and reformed themselves into large defensive squares that no enemy could supposedly penetrate.

The cavalry, for their part, attacked stationery targets with saber and lance and practiced quick movements at full regimental strength. Through practice, it was hoped, the Allied units could all maneuver effectively against the Paraguayans on the battlefield.

Training of this kind, however, took time, and Mitre had little to spare. In addition, the Argentine president had to cope with the problem of command and control of coalition forces. The Uruguayans under Flores presented no problem, for like their leader, many had previously fought with Mitre and understood his temper and inclinations. The Brazilians, however, were quite another matter.

Though the imperial government had every wish to live up to the letter of the alliance, the Brazilian admirals and generals had serious doubts about the wisdom of combined command, or at least of combined command under the Argentine president. Senior officers resigned themselves to obeying Mitre but in their own minds insisted that such obedience also advance the interests of the empire. Whenever cooperation with the Argentines conflicted with their duty to Dom Pedro, they would do as they chose without any open display of insubordination.

This attitude, implicitly adopted by all Brazilian commanders, handicapped operations many times during the next three years. The Argentines and Brazilians were traditional enemies, and any alliance between them, irrespective of any common military goal, was sure to be fraught with mistrust and veiled antagonism.

At Concordia, the mistrust was already evident. Mitre was calling for the concentration of all Allied forces to challenge Marshal López with the strongest hand possible. Yet all the while, Estigarribia was rampaging through southern Brazil. The men of the imperial forces had to march away from the scene of Paraguayan depredations, while their countrymen were making an immediate sacrifice in blood and property — and all this for the sake of an alliance that most thought unnatural in the first place.

The reunion of the Allied armies came only on 23 June. On that date, Gen. Manoel Luiz Osório authorized the passage across the Uruguay River of the first contingent of Brazilians, some eight thousand men in fourteen battalions. These soldiers were among Brazil's best troops. Many had seen combat in Uruguay the year before, and as the majority were Riograndenses, they called upon a tradition of soldiering going back generations. They favored the gaúcho style of fighting. Like their Spanish-speaking cousins on the Pampas, they preferred the lance, the boleadoras, and the wild, uncoordinated cavalry charge. Mitre intended to forego this way of fighting in favor of something more modern, more capable of crushing the Paraguayans speedily and at low cost. Sensible though this might have been, the president knew that forcing his Brazilian troops to conform would bring as much trouble as it would alleviate.

General Osório arrived at Concordia on 6 July, one day after Admiral Tamandaré and nearly a week after a thunderstorm had blown down every structure in camp. Like the admiral, Osório possessed a distinguished military record. Born in Rio Grande do Sul in 1808, he had fought in the Cisplatine War as a young officer and had risen in rank during the Farrapo Revolt. In 1852 he commanded a gaúcho lancer unit that, under heavy fire, captured a five-gun battery at Caseros. Though portly and silver haired by the time the conflict with Paraguay began, Osório still maintained his reputation for efficiency and courage. Richard Burton, himself a fanatic of sorts, remarked toward the end of the war that the general was "brave to temerity; horse after horse has been shot under him, and the soldiers declare that he bears a charmed life, and shakes after battles the bullets out of his poncho."[22]

Whatever the legends surrounding Osório, he was highly regarded by government leaders in Rio de Janeiro, who trusted him with posts of importance. He served, for instance, as the empire's representative at the council of war convened at the time the Triple Alliance was signed. More than other Brazilian generals, he grasped that military operations would necessarily carry the imperial forces far from Rio Grande do Sul. His troops had to forget their local loyalties and concentrate instead on defeating the Paraguayans along the Paraná before advancing to the agreed-upon prize, Humaitá. He therefore broadly supported Mitre's concept of a new, heightened discipline among the Brazilian troops. As more *voluntários* arrived, he put them through a rigorous program of drill such as few had ever seen.

The contacts between Osório's men and the Argentine and Uruguayan troops in camp were abrasive at times, but in the main they treated each other with a wary respect. When Justo José de Urquiza visited Concordia in the last week of July, he expressed an admiration for the apparent cohesion of the Allied units. The total force now numbered 20,000 men, of whom 12,180 infantry, 3,000 cavalry, and 756 artillerymen (with thirty-two pieces of rifled cannon) formed the Brazilian army of 15,936, exclusive of the 1,000 Riograndenses detailed to act under command of Venancio Flores.[23] Over 80 percent of Mitre's command, therefore, was Brazilian—a fact that everyone noted.

Without question, this army looked imposing. There were thousands of troops, and each day more supplies arrived by land and river. Urquiza failed, however, to note how many men were sick in hospital. Osório had brought 600 seriously ill men with him to Concordia. Several had the pox.[24] And the number of sick was growing. As the correspondent for the London *Times* reported in early August: "The Brazilian troops

*Missteps in the South* 359

were attaining considerable perfection in their exercises and maneuvering, but sickness was prevalent, and the cold weather was severely felt by them. Nearly 2,000 were sick, including those in camp and those [evacuated to] Montevideo. All were weary of the stationary camp life, and anxious to put in practice the lesson they had been receiving in warlike exercises."[25]

The desire to get on with the fight, though keenly felt, had to be tempered with the realization that these were mostly green troops, smart on the parade ground but still untested in battle. Their careful deployment was Mitre's key concern, and he was not about to be pushed into a premature confrontation with the forces of Estigarribia, Duarte, or Resquín. He wanted to plan his war meticulously.

*Cuevas*

The Allied buildup at Concordia should have coincided with an intermittent naval bombardment of Paraguayan positions on the Paraná. Admiral Barroso had been bloodied at the Riachuelo and Mercedes, however, and although events there dealt his enemies a greater blow in terms of ships and lives, he refused to tempt fortune. Colonel Bruguez's artillery represented a potent threat just to the south at the bluffs of Cuevas, and no one needed to remind the admiral of his own extended position relative to any Allied land force. His ammunition was low, and after Mercedes, his men were worn out. All these factors combined to keep his vessels out of action for nearly two months, while his men rested and he took stock of his situation.[26]

Observing all this from a distance was Barroso's superior, the baron of Tamandaré, still in Buenos Aires. The baron had taken no great pleasure from Barroso's sudden jump to fame. True, the imperial navy had won a stunning victory at the Riachuelo, but Tamandaré, the most senior officer in the service, had played no role in it. He cheerfully accepted the praises of Argentine government officials and the good wishes of people in the street, but inwardly he resolved to make it clear that the fleet belonged to him. After all, he reasoned, no navy has two commanders, and in the war now unfolding, many factors had to be considered, not the least of which was the relationship with Brazil's Argentine allies. Only he could deal forthrightly with such subtle and calculating politicians. Of one thing he felt sure: unlike the vacillating diplomats attached to the Imperial Foreign Ministry, he was the emperor's servant, the man through whom the imperial will would express itself. If others in the Brazilian government failed to share this estimation, that was their concern.

Tamandaré had a habit of always placing a strategic gloss on his actions. In this case, he believed that the Brazilian fleet, then nominally pursuing its blockading mission above Cuevas, should sail south to link up with Allied land forces near Goya. This would take them past Bruguez's shore batteries. The narrowness of the channel made a night transit impossible, so they would have to face the Paraguayan guns in broad daylight.

On 9 August 1865 Admiral Barroso issued orders to make ready to depart for the Rincón de Soto in accordance with Tamandaré's instructions. The ships weighed anchor promptly at nine o'clock the next morning. Later that day they paused along the Chaco side of the river to pick up several families of Correntino woodcutters, who informed them that something was afoot in Bella Vista and Cuevas. Many Paraguayan soldiers had moved into both locations, though exactly how many was unclear. Bruguez's batteries, it turned out, now counted thirty-two cannon (smoothbore pieces of six, nine, eighteen, and thirty-two caliber, and rifled pieces of twelve and twenty-four caliber) and eight Congreve rocket stands facing the Paraná. Two new battalions of infantry bolstered the Paraguayan artillerymen, ready to add the fire of sixteen hundred rifles.[27]

At 10:00 A.M. on 12 August, Barroso took his fleet of eighteen vessels past the Paraguayan batteries. Because of differing boiler capacities, the Brazilian vessels could not steam at a uniform speed; the admiral therefore ordered his smaller ships to stay close to the larger ones, which would provide cover fire. Despite the warnings of the woodcutters, Barroso still believed that Bruguez could only mount a few small pieces. Even before the Allied ships came into range, however, the sky started to fill with smoke, shot, and sound.[28]

Bruguez had chosen his position well. The bluffs above the river at

*Missteps in the South* 361

Cuevas were high and the river relatively narrow. Even so, visibility became a problem for the batteries almost immediately. Each Allied vessel took thirty to forty-five minutes to traverse the Paraguayan front, and gun crews on land and water were busy the whole time. Barroso had learned his lesson from the engagement at Mercedes and this time kept his hatches closed, with nonessential personnel well below deck. This precaution saved many lives.

First in the Brazilian formation came the *Ivaí*, which recoiled from her own firing and from the Paraguayan shells that tore into her side. She took forty hits. The admiral's flagship, the *Amazonas*, took a like number, and the *Ypiranga* and *Itajaí* took thirty apiece. The Argentine steamer *Guardia Nacional* escaped with twenty-six hits and had two of its own guns dismounted in the exchange.[29] An officer aboard the latter vessel left a striking, even frightening, account of the action:

> We were going at one-fourth speed downstream when our bow-chaser threw a grenade into the enemy's battery of four pieces *á fleur d'eau*. The firing then became general, and the enemy poured on us a perfect storm of grape, shell, congreves, shot and musketry, which lasted 45 minutes. One shot struck our wheel, knocking over the four helmsmen, when Admiral Murature himself took charge of the wheel, but the pilot's voice ahead could not be heard in the awful roar of 50 guns of the enemy and ours in reply. We followed in the wake of the *Amazonas*. Another shot struck Adjutant Ferré, carrying off his left leg, and he died from the wound the next morning. . . . Enrique Py was killed in like manner by a shot through the forward bulwarks, his father looking on and unable to save him: he died at 7 P.M. begging to be remembered to his poor mother. One shell and a dozen cannon-shot struck our prow and gunwales; fourteen more in the keel, mostly between wind and water, one of these killing a poor fellow who was below sick, and going clean through us; two more injured our paddles, and another entering the fire room killed a fireman. Our fore funnel was injured, also the forward boat, armory, main-mast, admiral's gig, and sides.[30]

The last Allied ship, the *Ypiranga*, steamed out of range at 7:00 P.M., just as the twilight gave way to an indigo sky. Barroso then turned his attention to his losses: seventeen killed and thirty-five wounded for the Brazilians, four dead and five wounded for the Argentines. Significantly, the Allies lost no ships nor had any of their vessels put out of service.[31] The admiral concluded with relief that shipwrights in Buenos Aires could soon refit his entire fleet.[32]

On the Paraguayan side, losses were minimal: ten dead and twenty-five wounded. The batteries and their accompanying infantry units behaved exactly as Colonel Bruguez had hoped, and he himself led the way, manning a rocket stand throughout the fight.[33] Though he sunk no enemy vessels, his gunners had done fine work, and he looked forward to their doing still more when a reinvigorated Paraguayan army began its march south once again.

After the Allied fleet dropped anchor off the Rincón de Soto, Admiral Tamandaré dispatched a report on the combat at Cuevas to the imperial government. In it, almost unnoticed at the time, he elaborated a new policy that profoundly affected the subsequent conduct of the war: "The downriver movement of the fleet was necessary so as not to be in a position of having the rear guard cut by [Bruguez's] battery and thus out of communication. It is necessary that the fleet always move parallel to the movements of the enemy rear, as long as this [army] is not contained by our own."[34] Put another way, Tamandaré would no longer allow the imperial navy to operate farther upriver than the front lines of the Allied army.

From the baron's perspective, a cautious approach had the benefit of placing clear boundaries on all naval operations and kept his risks to a minimum. Like other Brazilian naval officers, he detested the restrictions of river operations, especially the need to depend on foreign pilots. More to the point, Tamandaré trusted few of the men with whom he had to work. His arguments about strategy and tactics ultimately came less from intellectual differences with allies or subordinates than from his unspoken desire to shift the burden of casualties to the land forces. He was jealous of his prerogatives, moreover, and wanted no innovation that might diminish his authority. He wanted, and demanded, to make war his own way.

Tamandaré's new policy was excessively cautious. His navy had won a major victory at the Riachuelo and then had blasted its way through several well-positioned shore batteries without the loss of a single ship. Brazil could have controlled the river. Barroso had proven, moreover, that by keeping as many soldiers and sailors below deck, many lives could be saved without sacrificing overall effectiveness. Tamandaré never recognized this. He purposely kept his ships back when they might have offered effective support by steaming upriver to harass the Paraguayans from the rear. The baron probably saved some ships as a result, but he also consigned thousands of Allied troops to death on the battlefield later in the war — men who might not have died had their efforts been covered by naval gunfire. Indeed, the decision to hold the fleet to a line parallel with the Allied armies almost certainly added to the duration of the war — to the detriment of both sides.

*Yataí*

Setting precise military priorities was not only a naval problem. In the east, as Estigarribia advanced into Rio Grande do Sul, the Brazilians pressured Mitre to release troops from Concordia to help drive the enemy back into the Misiones. The president reluctantly detached Flores and ordered him north in response. Mitre promised that these same units would soon pivot and strike Estigarribia as well. This seemed credible. The Flores unit, designated the Army of the Van, had strength enough to pursue both goals, especially if reinforced en route. Flores commanded some four thousand men and twenty-four guns.[35]

By every measure, the Army of the Van had a rough go of it. The Allied force crossed a dozen streams and rivers, an exhausting task that called for the unloading of wagons and the repacking of their contents aboard rafts, which horses and oxen then dragged to the opposite bank, where soldiers would load the wagons once again.[36] The freezing rain refused to let up, and the men were soaked through from beginning to end. They could not light fires. Most nights, they sat huddled together on the wet fields and ate cold rations of stringy beef without bread or hardtack. Consequently, there was much sickness, a few deaths, and a number of desertions.[37] Yet thanks to Flores's constant prodding and unflagging optimism, the column moved forward.

Reinforcements from several commands joined the army before it had gone far. The mounted irregulars of Colonels Paiva and Reguera (now commanded by a Correntino general, Juan Madariaga) were among the first to arrive. This was the only force that had maintained some contact with Major Duarte's troops since their departure from Santo Tomé.[38] The Correntinos had observed the three thousand Paraguayans making camp above Restauración and judged that they would not immediately resume their march. Thus reassured, the Correntinos hastily moved to link up with Flores.

At roughly the same moment, the Allied high command attached General Paunero's force from the Paraná to join the Army of the Van as it moved north. Paunero had been largely inactive since the 25 May raid, although more than once he had tried to reach Urquiza and had been disheartened by the mutiny in the latter's camp. Now Paunero's troops—including the dashing Charlone—double-timed through the swampland of central Corrientes until the first units linked up with Flores on 13 August.[39] The Army of the Van now counted four Uruguayan infantry battalions (one of them comprised entirely of black troops from Montevideo) and three cavalry regiments, the Twelfth Brazilian Infantry Brigade, and Paunero's First Corps of three Argentine divisions for a total force of over eight thousand men. Madariaga supplied just over two thousand more cavalrymen.[40]

Though the Allies outnumbered Duarte's forces by over three to one, Flores could not feel certain of victory. In combat, he displayed a boxer's pugnaciousness, but still he had only scant knowledge of his foe. He had yet to face the Paraguayans in battle and knew little of their prowess save for what the Brazilians had told him, and their accounts were hardly reassuring. Colonel Estigarribia, moreover, remained close at hand and might somehow rush across the Uruguay to rescue his fellow Paraguayans no matter what Floriano's little flotilla could do. On only

Missteps in the South   365

one point did Flores have any room for comfort: he held twenty-four artillery pieces to none for Duarte. Yet as events were to demonstrate, the Uruguayan general failed to use his superior firepower and depended instead on infantry to carry the day.

Reports from Correntino and Entrerriano sympathizers gave Duarte some knowledge of Flores's objective only a few days after he left Concordia.[41] Realizing the danger, Duarte passed the information on to Estigarribia together with an urgent appeal for help. Estigarribia, however, did not believe that the reports reflected anything more than jitters. He ordered Duarte to continue his aggressive patrolling and told him that reinforcements would come by canoe if the need arose.[42] Estigarribia evidently tried to send two small cannon, but these disappeared without a trace.[43]

Persuaded that no reinforcements were coming, Major Duarte had already ordered his units to a low hill three miles north of Restauración. The knoll was partly covered by an orange grove, which afforded a minor degree of protection. The major himself took possession of a small cottage belonging to a French immigrant. This building served as his command post over the next few days. Yataí Creek, a tributary of the Uruguay River, lay immediately to the Paraguayan rear. The creek was then so flooded that at its confluence with the Uruguay, it seemed more ocean than rivulet and was utterly impassable. By opting to defend this particular position, Duarte left his men with no obvious line of retreat. Victory for the Paraguayans could thus only come by luring the Allies in and destroying them wave upon wave.

This deployment initiated a battle of annihilation. Duarte positioned his three infantry battalions onto the reverse slope of the hill, leaving behind one company from each posted on the crest. He took personal command of his two cavalry regiments, which he concentrated on the left flank, leaving the right flank open.

Common military practice would have had the defending force place its main body on the forward slope of the hill mass in order to maintain long-range observation and fields of fire. But Duarte had no artillery and little use for an unobstructed field of fire. He assumed that the Allies would rain shot at will on his units and pulled them back beyond the line of sight for better security.

Duarte's had a flawed notion of safety. The hill, after all, was only slightly elevated, and, having left his right flank exposed, he could do little to prevent Flores from moving cannon close to that position and enfilading the Paraguayan line. As he had no other way to compensate for his own lack of firepower, Duarte sought to shield his men by moving them behind the rise. This might have bought some time, but it could not affect the outcome of any engagement where the numbers so heavily favored the enemy. In retrospect, it would have been better for him to have recrossed the Yataí and then defended behind that obstacle, but like Captain López at the Mbutuí, he chose a more dangerous tactic.

The situation had become desperate. Duarte sent out daily patrols, hoping that he might at least be able to react quickly should they bring word of an enemy approach. And indeed, sharp clashes with forward elements of the Army of the Van took place on 9 and 16 August. Duarte then received a small delegation sent by Estigarribia to survey the scene and report back; the major pointed out the difficulties of his situation once again, but his words made as little impression on these men as on their colonel. They departed by canoe in the late afternoon of the sixteenth, taking with them Duarte's last communication to his commanding officer.[44]

The Paraguayans dug in. The near-frozen ground made the work difficult, especially given the dearth of shovels, though this was only one of many worries. A sense of foreboding had swept through their ranks as Flores took Restauración and made ready for an assault. Even from a distance, the Allies appeared rested and ready for combat — not so the outnumbered Paraguayans. As night fell few slept, instead they kept alert in the cold air, mindful of the words of the eldest among them: *Ñande kupy ojoivy vovémante japytu'u* (when death comes, there will be time enough for rest).

One man was already dead: a surly German (or Frenchman — the sources differ on this point) sent by Flores as an emissary. With a smirk he demanded that the Paraguayans yield, and even offered the major

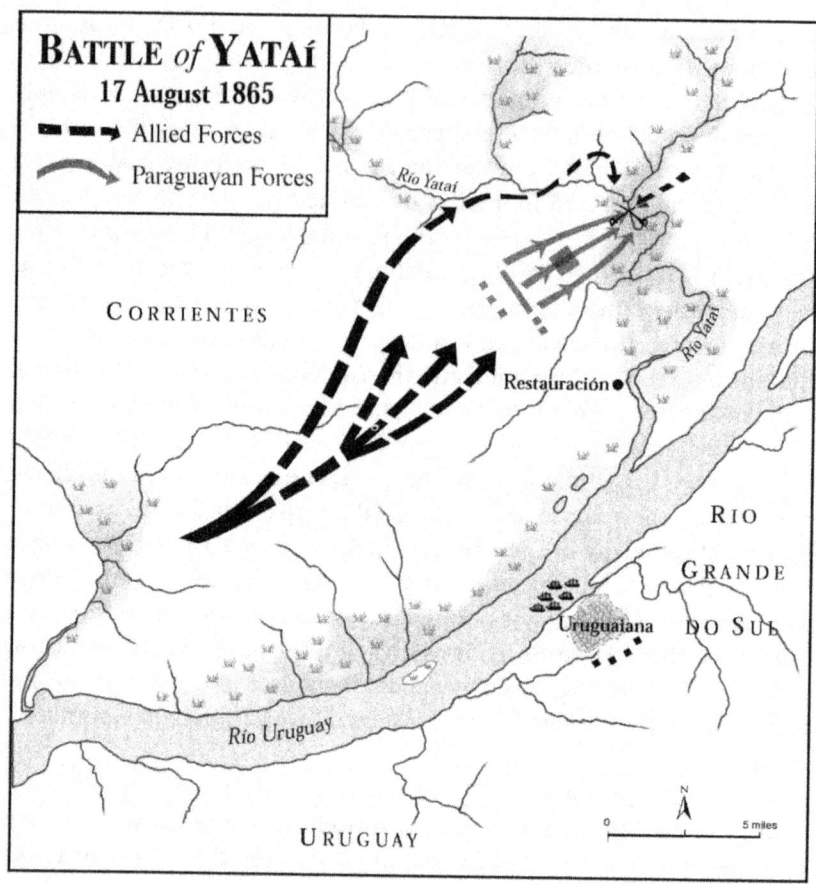

twenty thousand pesos to arrange the surrender. Duarte scornfully rejected the bribe and directed instead that the intruder be summarily shot. As he was led to an adobe wall, the German heard the angry reproach of Duarte, who shouted for all to hear that no Paraguayan ever submitted without orders.[45]

The short, bloody, and decisive battle of the Yataí took place on the morning of 17 August 1865. Four battalions of red-pantalooned Uruguayan infantry, commanded by Spanish-born Col. León de Palleja, led the way at 10:30 A.M., sweeping into the Paraguayan forward positions with fixed bayonets. The day was cold and foggy. As visibility was poor, the Uruguayans had difficulty approaching the enemy. Mitre later contended that Palleja attacked prematurely, for he started without artillery support and saw his men quickly repulsed by a storm of musketry.[46]

General Flores cursed as he saw the movement unfold. He then called a hurried meeting of senior officers to confirm his battle plan. He ordered General Paunero to deploy his Argentine corps behind and to the left of Palleja. The Brazilian Twelfth Brigade moved into position on the extreme right. Oddly — since it weakened the potential concentration of Allied firepower — Flores decided to disperse his artillery pieces among the two Argentine divisions and cavalry reserve. The Paraguayans had no artillery and thus no obvious defense against a focused barrage; had the Allies concentrated their heavy guns, they could have more effectively supported the Uruguayan assault.

As it was, the Uruguayans advanced at noon with only sporadic artillery support. The Paraguayans fought resolutely at the forward outposts, killing many of the oncoming infantry and dying in great numbers for their efforts. Before an hour had passed, the surviving Paraguayans withdrew to their main defensive line where Duarte was waiting.

The Allied advance, at first seemingly unstoppable, now stalled directly opposite the main Paraguayan force. Clearly, though, the Allies might push forward again at any time. Duarte seized the moment. He still had cavalry at his disposal, and these he ordered to charge the enemy's right flank. They lunged ahead with lances and sabers flailing from side to side and within moments met the Allied cavalry. The Uruguayan horsemen were taken by surprise. They had expected the Paraguayans to keep low and fire from protected positions while avoiding a challenge in the open. Yet here they were unexpectedly surging forward. The Uruguayans hesitated, then began to break.[47]

Flores responded to this crisis like a seasoned veteran. He instantly ordered the Argentine First Cavalry Regiment from Paunero's reserve to reinforce the Uruguayan cavalry. The tide turned at once. The combined Allied cavalry savaged Duarte's horsemen with a fury born of years of fighting on the Pampas. They killed the Paraguayans by the score. A few managed to slip away and gallop toward their own lines, only to be shot from their saddles by Uruguayan infantry.[48]

As the Paraguayan cavalry disintegrated, the Argentine First Corps bore down on Duarte's exposed flank. This attack, directed by Paunero, was focused and overwhelming, with Allied troops slicing their way through the enemy position at several places. Soon Duarte's line ceased to exist. About one hundred Paraguayans dashed to the edge of the Yataí and attempted to swim to a place of safety on the other side but were picked off before they could get far. Another two or three platoons tried to retreat across the flats toward a local cemetery, continuing a harassing fire against the Allies as they moved. In short order, they too were killed.

Though surrounded and faced with a hellish fire, the remainder of Duarte's men refused to throw down their arms. As Colonel Thompson observed, "no human power could make the Paraguayans surrender [at the Yataí], . . . even single individuals would rather fight on, with certain death before them."[49] Charles Ames Washburn, though no friend of the marshal's army, agreed with Thompson's estimation: "In this battle, as in so many others, it would not infrequently occur that one Paraguayan would be surrounded by a dozen of the enemy, all calling on him to surrender, to which he would make no response but fight on until he was killed; or, if by chance he was disarmed during the unequal contest and forcibly made a prisoner, he would take the first opportunity when his hands were free to seize a musket or bludgeon of any kind, and kill as many as possible, until he himself was knocked senseless."[50] Paraguayan stubbornness and self-sacrifice mystified the Allied officers, who would have preferred to take more prisoners. The common soldiers, though, had no time for such fine points. To them, the slaughter of the

Paraguayans was a logical and necessary response to their fanaticism.⁵¹ The Allied troops did not recoil, therefore, from carrying out a massacre that lasted two hours.

Historians might be tempted to interpret the bloodletting that followed the battle of the Yataí as some variation of homicidal mania. But the Uruguayan soldiers were not frenzied lunatics running amok, slashing and cutting indiscriminately with their sabers. As at Quinteros, their killing was deliberate and mechanical, like the habitual slaughter of cattle on the open Pampas. The fear on the faces of the Paraguayan prisoners brought no sympathy, their nervous cries no pity. Over and over again the Uruguayans plunged their *facones* into the throats of their enemies, tearing through flesh, sinew, and bone to sever heads off clean. In every direction the fields were wet with blood.⁵²

Even so, Duarte and some twelve hundred of his men were taken prisoner. Most were eventually marched Buenos Aires, where the populace gawked openmouthed as the Paraguayans passed by. The *porteños* had never learned to think of these dejected figures as human beings and treated them accordingly.

When first captured, the wounded Duarte was taken before General Flores, who insulted him with vulgar words and shouted that he would receive "four bullets" for having shot his envoy. The Paraguayan major brought himself to attention and in a low voice replied, "I will take [the bullets] as if they came from your own hand." This remark unloosed another tirade of invective from Flores, who continued with his threats until General Paunero gently interceded on behalf of the defeated commander.⁵³

Duarte was taken away first to Concordia, where Mitre refused to see him, and then on to Buenos Aires. In every town and village, he received quiet respect from both military men and civilian officials.⁵⁴ After a few months in the Argentine capital, Duarte transferred south to the small town of Dolores, where he spent the war years as manager of a large cattle station. He saved enough from his earnings to go into partnership with a local *estanciero*. Returning to Paraguay a rich man in the

*Missteps in the South* 371

early 1870s, Duarte later served as war minister and commander of the Paraguayan army. Unlike so many others of his generation, he died in his bed.[55]

Few of his twelve hundred compatriots experienced any clemency. In a controversial move, the Allies enrolled several hundred of those vanquished at the Yataí directly into units of the Allied armies.[56] The majority of the Paraguayan prisoners, however, were ultimately distributed more or less evenly among the Brazilians, Argentines, and Uruguayans and spent the rest of their days as virtual slaves on distant *estancias*. Few ever returned to their homeland.[57]

The battle of the Yataí was over. When Allied burial details and local people counted the dead, they discovered seventeen hundred Paraguayan bodies, many of them headless. Another three hundred of the enemy had been wounded. One Argentine soldier, who later painted a panoramic depiction of the scene, noted that the hospital for the Paraguayans in Restauración "was set up in a mudbrick building of two large rooms, both bereft of whitewash, and without any furniture or sign that they had ever been inhabited. A door had been taken from its hinges to serve as a table [and all around were wounded Paraguayans] . . . thrown onto the floor without any covering save for their own clothes, which luckily they still had, though in tatters. That assemblage of old men and boys had already had their wounds bandaged, [but even so] they maintained a profound silence."[58]

For their part, the Allies officially admitted 83 killed and 257 wounded, though the number was probably much greater.[59] In addition to prisoners, the Allies took four flags, a quantity of arms and munitions, eight wagons, and some lean horses — poor spoils for so many lives lost.

The real significance of the victory was strategic. With Major Duarte's force destroyed, Estigarribia was completely isolated, cut off from any hope of help from Paraguay. Yataí proved to an unbelieving public in Argentina that the Allied armies could work together to crush the Paraguayans and that more victories were in the offing. The alliance with the Brazilian Empire thus grew more palatable throughout the Litoral provinces and elsewhere. Mitre and the national government had every reason to feel satisfied.

Duarte's professionalism and his bravery in the face of insurmountable odds drew admiration from many quarters, even in the enemy camp. In the end, though, Allied organization and the power of numbers proved more than a match for Paraguayan courage. Solano López, still working with only minimal information in Humaitá, should have learned a lesson from this battle and suspended "offensive" operations.

# The Siege of Uruguaiana

## 14

Antonio Estigarribia was alone. He had ignored Major Duarte's pleas for help, yet the destruction of the latter's forces at the Yataí still hit him like a thunderbolt and made him see clearly how untenable his own position was.[1] He had some seven thousand men in his command at Uruguaiana, and given the disposition of the enemy, it seemed certain that these troops would now face a desperate siege. Logic demanded that the Paraguayans do everything possible to avoid this fate by slipping away before the Allies could surround them. With this in mind, on 19 August, the colonel loaded his wagons and dashed northward toward home.

Estigarribia wanted to initiate a general retreat, but he failed even to get past the first Allied lines. Within hours of starting, his forces met the Brazilian Seventeenth Cavalry Regiment, a Riograndense unit determined to stop the Paraguayans from fleeing. The gaúchos refused to give ground, firing energetically at the enemy who limped rather than charged forward. When Estigarribia fell back to regroup, other units of Gen. David Canabarro's First Division appeared from the east and took up positions for an attack. This prevented any Paraguayan escape. To fight at this juncture would have risked a major engagement, precisely the sort of fighting for which Estigarribia had no stomach. Instead, he ordered his men back to Uruguaiana, where at least they could brood over their troubles from behind a series of trenches. The Paraguayans worked for several days to build rafts for a possible escape across the Uruguay River before abandoning the idea as impractical.

The Allies now had the Uruguay Division where they wanted it — isolated, hungry, and beyond hope of rescue. The one chance the Paraguayans had was to attack without delay, break through the enemy lines, and escape north to Encarnación or somehow regroup with Francisco Resquín's force. After 19 August, however, Estigarribia made no moves in that direction.

The colonel's bullheadedness and penchant for inaction, seen previously at the Pindapoi and more recently when Duarte begged for help, now brought new suffering to his men. When the Paraguayans first entered Uruguaiana on 5 August, theirs was a robust force, tired perhaps but still formidable. Some soldiers, perhaps encouraged by the Salvañach brothers, imagined that their presence would spur a Blanco rebellion across the border in Uruguay. Estigarribia had brought his men this far — it had to be for some reason. Surely the Blancos would rise in force to meet them and together the two armies would sweep the Brazilians from the Banda Oriental, as Marshal López had foreseen. In was a vain hope. Venancio Flores's loyalists and the Brazilian occupying army had already effectively crushed the Blanco guerrillas, particularly in those areas abutting the Riograndense frontier. Even those Uruguayans who might have favored a new rebellion could gauge the sheer number of Allied troops coming together against Estigarribia. They wanted no part of a military fiasco when their own political fortunes were so weakened. Their rebellion could wait for another day.

At Concordia, Bartolomé Mitre was already weighing the political benefits and the possible hazards of any future triumph at Uruguaiana. An outstanding victory over the Paraguayans — especially if it were bloodless — would lend him prestige as commander in chief. This in turn would give Argentina — his Argentina rather than that of the *caudillos* — the authority to destroy Solano López without yielding anything of consequence to the empire.

Brazilian officials had their own idea of how to wring profit from a victory over Estigarribia. In this instance, their ambitions had to coincide with those of the emperor, who was very much an interested party. Dom Pedro had already shown that he was a proud man who viewed the invasion of his country as a personal affront. When the Paraguayans sacked São Borja, he announced his intention of going south to join the fight. This suggestion appalled his ministers. The radical Liberals, who had dominated Parliament since August 1864, had been displaced by a more moderate faction led by the Marquis of Olinda in May 1865, but the new cabinet stood little chance of survival without the active support of the emperor. This required him to stay in Rio de Janeiro and exercise his moderating power.[2]

Pedro, however, was adamant: if his ministers vetoed his departure for the front, then he would abdicate, enlist as a *voluntário*, and go to war as an ordinary citizen.[3] At this his ministers relented, and in exchange the emperor agreed to adjourn the legislative session for eight months. This left his ministers free to concentrate on the war without worrying about parliamentary opposition.

Dom Pedro arrived in Rio Grande do Sul in late July. After a lavish reception by various provincial leaders at Pôrto Alegre, the imperial party moved inland, reaching the small hamlet of Caçapava on 11 August. There, Dom Pedro rested in rustic surroundings, anxious to join the fight but prevented from going forward by nervous advisers.[4] Annoyed by the cold and the isolation of the village, he grumbled a great deal and was only partly mollified by the arrival of his son-in-law, the count d'Eu, who came with news of Europe and family. Above all, Pedro wanted to move on to Uruguaiana and the fighting.

For the emperor, the war with Paraguay had all the hallmarks of a crusade. Though he might feel well disposed toward individual soldiers — including the few Paraguayan prisoners who passed his way — he had no doubts that the conflict had become a personal duel with López. Honor was at stake. For a monarch, especially one from a country whose political institutions were recognizably fragile, this fact superceded all others. Dom Pedro could ill-afford halfway measures in the struggle against Paraguay because they might make him look weak.

Yet at the same time, he was temperamentally unsuited to the role of warrior. As he demonstrated in subsequent decades, the emperor regarded the military with thinly disguised contempt. He complained that the army ate ravenously from the exchequer with little to show for it save gaudy uniforms and inflated bellies. He thought many of his officers thickheaded poseurs. And, at bottom, he believed that civilized men could always find ways to promote their countries' welfare without an appeal to the martial spirit. It might have been crucial for the emperor to appear inflexible at Uruguaiana, but in his heart of hearts, he was willing to place the decision making in the hands of others.

Such ruminations, of course, meant nothing to Allied troops in the field. Their task was to smash Estigarribia and then move on to Corrientes, Humaitá, and Asunción. The battle of the Yataí had left them with a feeling of invincibility, and their growing numbers assured them every practical advantage. The Army of the Van, which was poised to cross the Uruguay, alone counted eight thousand infantry, four thousand cavalry, and forty cannon, and Allied troops continued to pour in.

Flores craved the glory of another victory close on the heels of his triumph at the Yataí. On 19 August he sent Estigarribia a captured Paraguayan officer who carried a demand for surrender. The Allies, Flores insisted, directed their war against the "tyrant" López, not the long-suffering Paraguayan people. He promised the men surrounded at Uruguaiana fair treatment as prisoners and stressed that in the new order of things, their commander might assume his proper role as "one of the first men of the Paraguayan Republic."[5]

The colonel, however, refused to yield. He received a similar demand from Canabarro on the same day, and fatigued though he was from the abortive breakout, he took time to compose ornate rejections to both enemy commanders. Estigarribia intended to go on fighting until the marshal ordered otherwise.[6]

By now, the Paraguayans had exhausted Uruguaiana's stocks of canned food, yerba, flour, black beans, dried beef, manioc, and demijohns of liquor. The town's few remaining cattle had disappeared, followed by its chickens, dogs, and finally its rats.[7] Only a supply of lump sugar remained, and this became the sole ration for many of the besieged troops.

As Paraguayan morale deteriorated, the Allies tightened the ring around the town. Heavy rains brought high water to the Uruguay River, and Admiral Tamandaré managed to get two warships over the rapids at Salto. These vessels joined the *Uruguai*, still commanded by Lieutenant Floriano, in transporting Flores's infantry and artillery from the Argentine side of the river, while the mounted units stayed on in Corrientes to support Juan Madariaga against any trouble that Resquín might make in the northwest. By 4 September, the entire Army of the Van, save for the cavalry, was on Brazilian soil.[8]

Flores moved swiftly to join General Porto Alegre, who had assumed command of all imperial forces facing the Paraguayans. When the two commanders met, Pôrto Alegre politely but adamantly insisted that the Uruguayan concede control over all Allied troops. Under the terms of the alliance treaty, just as Mitre was overall commander in Argentina, so a Brazilian officer had to have overall command within the borders of the empire.

Flores wanted none of it. He insisted that as the newly "elected" president of Uruguay, he could accept no subordinate role under a foreign general. Moreover, since neither Mitre nor Pedro II was then present, he had the right and duty to command, not Pôrto Alegre. Then Tamandaré arrived off Uruguaiana with several more warships. Never one to avoid an argument, the admiral thought to add his own loud opinion on the command question, but this accomplished nothing other than add to the general sense of irritation in the Allied camp.[9]

More than the question of command separated Flores from the Brazilians. The Uruguayan *caudillo* favored an immediate assault on the Paraguayan position. Pôrto Alegre, more realistically, wanted to extend the siege and force the Paraguayans into submission through starvation. Between these positions there was little room for compromise, so Flores and the Brazilians opted to wait for Mitre and the emperor. They could make the final decision together.

Although the Allies grew stronger every day, glaring problems still complicated life for their soldiers in the field. They experienced shortages of food, clothing, firewood, and forage for the thousands of horses the Brazilians brought in. The rains continued to hamper supply and kept the men wet, uncomfortable, and in a foul temper. The army had made inadequate preparations for the treatment of the sick, with the result that simple coughs and fevers developed into incapacitating illnesses. At any one time, hundreds of Allied troopers were unfit for duty.[10]

On 30 August the sun came out over Uruguaiana, the first break in the bad weather for some time. The two contending armies, which previously had only glimpsed each other through thick fog, now saw each other plainly. The Allies noticed that the Paraguayans had gutted many houses and used the furniture and fence posts for firewood. They had also expanded the line of entrenchments begun by the Brazilians more than a month before. The Paraguayans looked ragged, but they still appeared capable of resistance. Indeed, some minor artillery duels had occurred as well as regular sniping, but it counted for little. The Paraguayans could now observe how many troops were ranged against them—at least seventeen thousand men and forty-two artillery pieces (not to mention the guns aboard Tamandaré's warships).

Estigarribia, who saw the same things as his men, refused to let mere numbers decide the contest. On 4–5 September he received another series of notes from the enemy commanders, and again he spurned their surrender demands, pointedly ridiculing the contention that they only wished to liberate the downtrodden people of Paraguay: "As your Excellencies show such zeal in giving the Paraguayan nation its liberty, . . . why have you not begun by freeing the unhappy Negroes of Brazil, who form the greater part of its population, and who groan under the hardest and most terrible slavery, to enrich and keep in idleness a few hundreds of the grandees of the Empire? Since when has a nation, which by its own spontaneous and free will elects the Government which presides over its destinies, been called a nation of slaves? Doubtless since Brazil has undertaken the affairs of the River Plate, with the decided desire of subjugating and enslaving the sister Republics of Paraguay, and perhaps even Paraguay itself."[11] Estigarribia ended this missive by comparing his own situation to that of Leonidas at Thermopylae. Whereas the Spartans effectively delayed the Persians through their sacrifice and saved Greece as a result, the Paraguayans could gain nothing by a similar gesture at Uruguaiana. The Allies enjoyed complete superiority in artillery, with which they could pound Estigarribia without serious loss on their own side. The colonel knew this, but nonetheless dared the enemy to fire away. "So much the better," he wrote, "the smoke of [your] cannon shall be our shade."[12]

Defiant words do not win battles, nor does an expressed willingness to immolate oneself. In truth, Estigarribia cringed at the notion of fighting while his troops were demoralized and incapacitated from hunger. Moreover, he had no orders from Solano López. Like every officer in the Paraguayan service, he hesitated to openly contradict the marshal on any military matter, and though he might have taken it upon himself earlier to cross the river at São Borja rather than at Garruchos, the situation at Uruguaiana seemed quite another matter. So he waited nervously in his command post, unsure of what to do next.

Mitre arrived at Uruguaiana on 10 September. Three more Brazilian warships came up the river at the same time and were on hand the next day when the emperor rode in from São Gabriel. The Allied troops had no way to offer him a regal welcome, for his arrival coincided with a heavy downpour. As the honor guards lined up to salute their sovereign, they could barely keep their faces forward and eyes opened for all the rain that blew onto them. Pedro II, clad in a poncho of blue cloth trimmed with gold around the hole and wearing long camp boots, waved to the men with as much graciousness as he could muster.[13] Shaking the water from his white hair, he then hurried into the quarters previously prepared for him and his staff. He wanted Mitre and Flores to meet with him straight away, but they begged his indulgence until the rain let up. Pedro and the other Allied leaders still had to settle the question of command.

The emperor had no military experience but did possess considerable presence of mind. Under the terms of the May agreement, he could claim command of all Allied forces in Brazil, and personally might have felt inclined to do exactly that, at least for a time. But a widely accepted interpretation of the 1824 Constitution disallowed any military role for him that might endanger his life. After all, he was a monarch, not a professional soldier. The war minister, count d'Eu, Auguste of Saxe-Coburg and Gotha (his other son-in-law), and all his chief advisers, in fact, begged him to recognize this obvious fact and do nothing that might put the dynasty at risk.

The cold, wet weather and the constant badgering from his underlings wore down Pedro II's resistance even before he arrived in camp, and now he signaled his willingness to compromise.[14] Instead of relinquishing command to a Brazilian subordinate, he turned to his nominal equal, President Mitre of Argentina, who continued as general in chief of the Allied armies, including those that stayed behind at Concordia under Gen. Gelly y Obes. Paunero, Pôrto Alegre, and Flores retained command of their respective units. Though the emperor was disappointed, he consoled himself by attending various command meetings, where he freely offered his opinions. Henceforth, however, his influence on military matters was indirect at best.[15]

When the first meeting of the Allied leaders took place in the afternoon of 11 September, the monarch took stock of his comrades in arms. "I have seen Mitre, Flores, and Paunero," he noted in a letter to his wife. "The first is the most cultured, the second an old and very ugly mulatto [caboclo], the third a friendly soldier with white hair and beard."[16] André Rebouças, a young military engineer from Bahia who observed this first encounter, wrote that Dom Pedro clearly dominated the meeting: "The Emperor, with his great height, spoke to his subjects, to Mitre, to Flores, to Paunero, . . . in fact to all who surrounded him, seeming to say: acknowledge that I am in truth the first citizen of South America."[17]

Rebouças's effusiveness was natural enough. After all, of the seventeen thousand Allied troops then surrounding Uruguaiana, more than twelve thousand were Brazilian, and they provided a most extravagant backdrop for the emperor's visit. In a sense, he was acting not as a politician but rather as the guest of honor at a meticulously choreographed spectacle, full of color, pomp, and martial music. Mitre, in his crumpled uniform and broad-brimmed hat, looked in contrast like a low-ranking officer.

Yet, though Dom Pedro would have been loath to admit it, in truth, Mitre held more than a marginal share of power at Uruguaiana. His only rival among the Argentines — Urquiza — was far away in Entre Ríos, sulking. Flores hardly counted; in fact, at Uruguaiana he spent more time playing with his dog Coquimbo than he did in consultation with his Allies. As for the Brazilians, though powerful in terms of sheer numbers, they were divided on the command question. Who should give the orders in this theater — Pôrto Alegre, Tamandaré, Caxias, the war minister, or the emperor himself? Rather than settle this divisive question and move on to the attack, Dom Pedro opted to give Mitre continued operational command over the Allied armies and thus endorsed the Argentine president's direction of the war. As a result, Mitre felt confident that he could carry through his long-term design, which included taking the campaign to Paraguay proper and making sure that any military action served his interests and those of Buenos Aires.[18]

Only one chapter remained to be written at Uruguaiana. The Allies attempted several more times to convince the Paraguayans to surrender, even sending Fernando Iturburu and other officers of the Paraguayan Legion to confer with Estigarribia in Guaraní.[19] When these efforts failed, Mitre, Flores, and the other commanders drafted a plan for the final assault. It called for a heavy bombardment of up to two days duration, assisted by naval guns, to be followed by a mass infantry attack.[20]

The assault was never carried out. On 18 September, Estigarribia observed the Allied units moving into attack positions just after dawn. It was a gray, cheerless morning with a film of fog spread low along the horizon. No amount of mist, however, could disguise what was about to happen. Marching bands struck up brassy patriotic airs and battle flags by the dozen were unfurled and tilted menacingly toward the Paraguayan lines. As a tactic designed to undermine what was left of the colonel's composure, it worked well enough. He imagined his entire command slaughtered, the town afire, and the enemy laughing over his corpse.

These thoughts finally broke Estigarribia. His malnourished and ragged soldiers might even then have attempted a defense, but their commander had already accepted defeat in his heart. He had received no instructions from Humaitá. Now, under a flag of truce, the Allies sent him one last ultimatum, a demand for surrender signed by Pôrto Alegre (though prepared by all the commanders).

Despite his previous bluster, Estigarribia had little left with which to bargain and no time at all. Resquín was not coming, nor were any friendly Uruguayans or Entrerrianos likely to appear over the horizon. Instead, an overwhelming Allied force was bearing down on his beleaguered army, and the enemy's artillery was in clear view, ready to fire.

Estigarribia, hollow eyed and exhausted, sat at a table and penned a response to the ultimatum. He proposed specific terms: (1) that all enlisted men in the Uruguay Division, sergeants included, would surrender and be accepted as prisoners according to the laws of war; (2) that officers and notable civilians could depart with their arms and equipment and go wherever they pleased; if they chose not to return to Paraguay, then the Allies would provide sustenance for them for the duration of the conflict; and (3) that those Uruguayan officers serving with the Paraguayan forces would become prisoners of the empire and not of Flores, who might otherwise have had "Goyo" Suárez execute them as he had done with Leandro Gómez at Paysandú.[21]

The colonel had no reason to hope that the Allies would grant these concessions and expected the same treatment meted out to Duarte's men. The Allies, however, agreed to the first and third terms, rejecting only the demand that Paraguayan officers be set at liberty.[22] Dom Pedro had a hand in this generous response; he fancied himself a man without vindictiveness toward the Paraguayan people and wanted to show this in as magnanimous a way as possible. Also, as emperor of Brazil, he wanted no part in devastating the town of Uruguaiana, which the Allied generals were poised to do.

Estigarribia surrendered without further delay, ordering his men to assemble and lay down their muskets. He did not consult his subordinate officers but simply informed them that relief was impossible and that he was following the only course left to him. He then turned from them and presented his sword to the Brazilian war minister, who with elaborate ostentation passed it to Dom Pedro.

Allied soldiers filled the streets of Uruguaiana to watch the Paraguayans line up by units and stack their arms in the central plaza. The vanquished troops, many of them almost naked, passed silently by, glaring with ferocious eyes at the Brazilians and Argentines, from whom they expected a quick death. The Allies captured three hundred horses, twenty wagons, six cannons, a quantity of powder, and over three hundred thousand cartridges. They also took seven battle flags, which would have been eight had Maj. José López (of Mbutuí fame) not burned his unit's colors rather than see them fall into enemy hands.[23] The Uruguayan colonel Palleja, who had commanded the first wave of Allied attackers at the Yataí, witnessed the scene and reported a total of 5,545 Paraguayan prisoners taken. Another 1,500 had died of starvation or illness or had deserted.[24]

Most observers had never seen such a miserable collection of human beings. The emperor, writing to the countess of Barral, declared the "enemy unworthy of being beaten — such a rabble!"[25] Another witness noted with wry contempt that even the most emaciated Paraguayans carried a well-chosen assortment of plunder stripped from the town. The Allied troops soon relieved them of their loot, which included an incongruous accumulation of sugar bowls, butter knives, candlesticks, and a "thousand other bagatelles that they believed to be made of gold or silver."[26]

Many among the prisoners were drafted straightaway into the Paraguayan Legion or the regular Allied armies. The rest were sent to Buenos Aires or Rio "to be stared at," just like those captured at the Yataí. "There was hardly an officer in any of the three armies who did not end up with a *Paraguayito* [for his manservant]."[27] At the same time, photographers in the Allied camp did a brisk business creating portraits of officers with drawn swords or lances dangled over supposedly dejected Paraguayan captives.[28]

Colonel Estigarribia, Father Duarte, as well as the Salvañach brothers and the other pro-López Uruguayans became celebrities in the Allied camp, where they were the objects of great curiosity. Over the next several days, these prisoners enjoyed the benefits of fraternization, especially with junior officers and war correspondents, who with rapt attention listened to their opinions of Solano López and of the now-concluded siege. They ate and drank well and basked in the praises of their counterparts, who spoke with all sincerity of them as a "gallant enemy." In the end, all the high-ranking prisoners were given their choice of a final destination. No one among them wished to return to Paraguay; they understood the fate the marshal had in store for defeated officers.

Father Duarte seems to have dropped out of sight for a time, though only after a bitter encounter with Pedro Gay, vicar of São Borja, who actually tried to throttle the Paraguayan priest for his ransacking of Gay's parish in June. Startled witnesses had to forcibly separate the two clerics to stop their fisticuffs.[29] Afterward, some vague indications placed Duarte in Buenos Aires for the remainder of the war, and he returned to Paraguay in 1870 to take up duties as curate at the Church of San Roque in Asunción.[30] The Salvañach brothers, however, retired without fanfare, first to Brazil and then to the Uruguayan countryside, only to reappear to some notoriety when the Blancos launched their bloody "Revolution of the Lances" in the early 1870s.[31]

Estigarribia chose to go to Rio de Janeiro. There, far more than at Uruguaiana, he found audiences appreciative of his tales of combat. For several weeks police had to push back crowds who came to gape at him through the window of the modest house the imperial government provided him.[32] But soon the crowds dissipated. This left Estigarribia in the guise of a tragic figure, alive perhaps, but without family or fatherland. He resurfaced in March 1869, when he unsuccessfully petitioned the emperor to allow him to serve as guide to the imperial forces then invading the Cordilleras of central Paraguay.[33] The colonel never regained the esteem of his countrymen, who thereafter associated his name with treason. He died of fever in December 1870, only days after returning to Brazilian-occupied Asunción.[34]

The significance of the colonel's surrender at Uruguaiana was not lost on the Allied leadership. At relatively little cost in terms of lives and materiel, they had eliminated a sizable enemy force and wrecked any possibility of a renewed Paraguayan offensive. Solano López now had to forget his plan to rescue Uruguay from Mitre, Flores, and the Brazilians. As linking up with the Blancos had always been his chief goal in the south, this meant that Paraguay from this point onward could only adopt a defensive strategy. The Allies hoped that the marshal would realize that victory—however he might define it—was no longer possible—he would have to rethink his war aims or face annihilation. Since only lunatics purposely set out to destroy themselves, Mitre and his generals had every reason to hope for an early peace.

The mood was celebratory at Uruguaiana. The emperor toured the liberated community, visited with its returning inhabitants, and distributed alms among the poor. Both he and Mitre joked with their respective soldiers, who responded with similar good humor. All looked forward to eliminating Resquín and seizing Humaitá.

Among the more conspicuous witnesses to this happy scene was Edward Thornton, who reached the Brazilian encampment on 22 September. The British minister had come up from Buenos Aires with instructions from his government to meet with Pedro II and present him with a letter from Queen Victoria, the reassuring contents of which helped smooth over the bad feelings associated with the Christie Affair. The emperor was gracious and appreciative. With relations between Great Britain and Brazil now reestablished, his officials could bask in the appearance of support from Europe's foremost power.

The "support" was more apparent than real. Thornton, who as always was interested chiefly in promoting trade, showed little concern for Brazil's war aims and even less that his presence at Uruguaiana might be misconstrued by both the Brazilians and their enemies. In South America, however, such details never went unnoticed. If anything, Thornton's visit made the emperor's sense of accomplishment all the sweeter.[35]

Word soon spread of the events at Uruguaiana. Letters of congratulation poured in from all parts of Argentina and Brazil.[36] There was an ironic danger to the Allied cause in all this expression of good feeling. If the press — or the Allied leaders themselves — touted the victory too much, it gave more of a reason for draftees in the Argentine interior (or in the Brazilian northeast) to resist conscription. Why should anyone fight at such a great distance from home if the issue were no longer in doubt?

News of Estigarribia's capitulation had its deepest impact in Paraguay. Solano López had been out of contact with his Uruguay Division since before Yataí, though he sent regular communications down to the Uruguay River.[37] None of these messages got through.[38] The marshal must have understood the hopelessness of Estigarribia's situation once the Allied armies began their siege. But his belief in Paraguayan tenacity, as exemplified by Duarte's sacrifice at the Yataí, blinded him to what was really happening at Uruguaiana and to the limits of what his men could endure.

To Solano López, so accustomed to political and personal intrigue, only conspiracy could explain Estigarribia's reprehensible deed. With little evidence in support, he noted as fact the rumor that the colonel had sold his garrison for three thousand pesos.[39] No other interpretation was henceforth permitted. And for those that still might waiver, the marshal left no doubt that consequences would be dire: "Gathering all his principal officers, [López] broke forth in curses and maledictions of Estigarribia as a traitor, a purchased knave, whose name and memory were deserving of universal execration. He then turned upon those present, and in terms of the most bitter invective told them that they were all traitors to a great extent; . . . and that they might count that at the least defection, the least sign of disobedience, . . . they should feel his heavy hand upon them."[40]

The marshal's fury against Estigarribia took the form of public ritual in Paraguay. The official press raged against the colonel, for whom "the Almighty in His terrible judgment [will guarantee] a most-deserved punishment." Popular manifestations of anger occurred not only in Asunción but also in the most isolated *pueblos* in the republic. The Paraguayan troops occupying the southern stretches of the Mato Grosso echoed the condemnation.[41] Even Estigarribia's dutiful wife called him a coward and petitioned the government for leave to change her name.[42]

All this orchestrated condemnation had a cathartic effect. That it was invariably coupled with expansive praises for the marshal's military genius helped López regain his composure (though, to be sure, for several days he remained so incensed that even his young son, on whom he doted, was afraid to go near him). Now, with the taste of bitterness in his mouth, López did the only thing he could do: he ordered a retreat from Corrientes.

Even before the ink on the order was dry, the marshal penned an elaborate missive to Mitre, one of several that he wrote during the course of the war. These letters make intriguing reading, for they serve as benchmarks for Paraguayan thinking at key moments. On this occasion, López was concerned with the fate of those of his men who had fallen into Allied hands at Yataí and Uruguaiana. He accused the Allies of gross mistreatment of prisoners, of "barbarous and atrocious acts" against their persons, and of illegally pressing them into the enemy armies, thus "rendering them traitors in order to deprive them of their rights as citizens, and to take away the most remote hope of their ever returning to their country and families, whether through an exchange of prisoners or by any other transaction."[43] After defending his own record of correct treatment of prisoners and noncombatants, he summarized his complaints by claiming that the Allies had unleashed a war of "extermination and horrors," which could only be answered in like fashion: "I invite your Excellency, in the name of humanity, and of the honor of the Allies, to lay those barbarities aside, and to place the Paraguayan prisoners of war in the proper enjoyment of their rights as prisoners, . . . [else] I shall no longer consider myself bound by any consideration, and will with repugnance, make the Argentine, Brazilian, and Oriental citizens [within the Paraguayan Republic] liable to the most vigorous reprisals."[44]

Mitre's response came a few days later. The Argentine president categorically refuted the marshal's charges. He denied mistreating Paraguayan prisoners and maintained that those who had joined the Allied arms had done so of their own free will (this last being manifestly untrue). Then, in carefully chosen words, he turned Solano López's accusations around, arguing that Paraguayan rather than Allied soldiers had committed barbarous deeds in Corrientes and Rio Grande, acts for which the Asunción government would someday be held responsible. Noting the marshal's warning of reprisals, Mitre concluded with a warning of his own: "Should Your Excellency employ means contrary to those recognized in warfare, [you] will have deliberately placed yourself beyond the pale of the Law of Nations, and will authorize the Allies to proceed as Your Excellency insinuates."[45]

This interchange was significant in that it defined for both sides what the future conduct of the war would likely encompass. Though Mitre and Solano López (not to mention the Brazilians) continued to allude to the cultivation of "humanity" and "civilization" as a guiding principle, in fact, both men now wedded themselves to the fighting of a merciless war.

The Paraguayan thrust to the Uruguay River was only an early chapter in a terrible struggle, and it was ill considered. If the marshal ever had a campaign plan—which is doubtful—then it depended to an irrational extent upon supposed allies in Uruguay and Entre Ríos. To be fair, such failings are common in the history of war; campaign after campaign, invasion after invasion have collapsed because those apparently suffering under the yoke of tyranny refuse to rise and make common cause with their liberators.

Given the long odds, Solano López owed it to his field commanders to provide understandable instructions. Military operations should be directed toward the attainment of a clearly defined, decisive, and obtainable objective—precisely what was missing in López's campaign along the Uruguay. Even if Estigarribia and Duarte had been better commanders, without a clearly defined objective, they could never have achieved lasting results. As it was, their operational and tactical mistakes were many, from Estigarribia's unwillingness to support Duarte at a critical juncture to the deployment, not once but twice, of major forces in defensive positions with impassable obstacles to the rear. The decision to defend Uruguaiana when withdrawal was still possible was perhaps the worst mistake of all, and it was made because the colonel lacked the resolution to proceed without orders.[46]

The Brazilians, for their part, did little right at first. Their knowledge of the terrain should have given them many opportunities to execute hit-and-run assaults against Estigarribia as Paiva and Reguera had done against Duarte. Lieutenant Floriano's action in cutting Paraguayan communication across the Uruguay was brilliant, but it could have come much earlier. And General Canabarro had several opportunities to attack the Paraguayans in relative force after São Borja but failed to do so.[47]

After Estigarribia reached Uruguaiana, however, it was quite a different story. With a limited force, the Brazilians managed to contain all the Paraguayan units, and on the one occasion when the colonel tried to escape, he was driven back with minimal effort. Thereafter, the organizational skill of Mitre combined with ever-increasing numbers of Allied troops and good overall generalship to assure a successful siege. Disease, hunger, and poor morale within the Paraguayan lines did the rest.

The Paraguayan campaign along the Uruguay River was ill conceived and ill executed. The marshal dispatched Estigarribia into Rio Grande do Sul without giving him an obvious way out. Perhaps Solano López supposed that the devotion of his soldiers would afford an adequate substitute for a well-wrought plan of campaign. Though he heaped abuse on Estigarribia for having refused to fight, the marshal ultimately had himself to blame. He created and maintained a military system absolutely dependent on the dictates of higher authority. Then, without providing either a clear mission or meaningful support, he sent a sizable portion of his army to an unknown fate.

# Retreat to Paso de la Patria

## 15

The surrender of the Uruguay Division might have ended Paraguay's chances for success in the lower provinces, but it by no means crippled Solano López's army. Francisco Resquín's Southern Division still counted nearly seventeen thousand men on the Paraná and was in no sense beaten.[1] Real victory for the Allies could only come with the destruction of this force and the invasion of Paraguay proper. The thousands of troops at Humaitá just might waver in the face of an Allied onslaught if their fellows in Corrientes were defeated or laid down their arms as Estigarribia had done at Uruguaiana.

After the arrest of General Robles in July, the Southern Division pushed south again toward Bella Vista. Along the way, the Paraguayans hunted down and killed a band of Toba Indians who had sold meat to the Brazilians but otherwise saw no combat.[2] Soldiers nervous after their long spate of inactivity were ready to vent their frustrations in any direction. The tranquil vision of Bella Vista's orange groves no longer calmed them. On the contrary, this time the Paraguayans were edgy, ready to fight, yet instead of battle they got another tedious march. Their main column advanced down the Paraná according to the marshal's precise, mechanical, overly detailed instructions, which stressed flank security above all else. Such control proved unnecessary, however. The tedium of the long passage went unbroken save for the sighting of an occasional Correntino horseman who shadowed their movements from a discreet distance.

Then, on 25 July the Paraguayan vanguard got its wish. Largely by accident, it came upon a farmhouse held by twenty-five hundred of Nicanor Cáceres's irregulars and stormed their position right away. Solano López had hoped to force a decisive engagement in this part of Corrientes, but the "Red Armadillo" refused to give him the battle he wanted. Instead, after taking a few casualties, Cáceres retreated east toward the headwaters of the Corrientes and Batel Rivers.[3]

The marshland into which his troops fled was the most inaccessible in the province. Everywhere were lakes and ponds thickly overgrown with the *Victoria regis*, an aquatic plant the color of malachite with leaves so extensive they concealed the clear water beneath. The few dry outcroppings afforded the Correntinos just enough room for a cramped refuge. Mounted troops with no experience in the region hesitated to travel in such watery territory that, according to the old Guaraní folklore, abounded with elves and hobgoblins. Cáceres, though, felt perfectly at home there. He set up camp, licked his wounds, and awaited new opportunities for raiding.[4]

*An Uneasy Presence*

Resquín's troops entered the village of Bella Vista on 2 August. The townspeople who had previously fled and returned were none too happy to see them. Except in the town of Corrientes, the authority of Foreign Minister José Berges and the *Junta Gubernativa* was completely overshadowed by the Paraguayan military, which tended to treat locals more like the enemy than potential friends. The Paraguayans had already arrested the wives and children of prominent figures at Corrientes and sent them to Humaitá as hostages.[5] It seemed unlikely that they would abstain from such practices farther south.[6] Though they kept their voices low, most Bella Visteños prayed that the national government would counterattack and drive the invaders away. While they still saw President Mitre as an untrustworthy and potentially domineering overlord, at least he was not then pressing on their throats.

As Col. José Bruguez marched southward to challenge the imperial fleet at Cuevas, the better part of the Southern Division settled into garrison duty at Bella Vista. It proved an uncomfortable experience for the locals. The soldiers seemed to consider it their right to demand food and drink from town residents, some of whom protested their loyalty to the *Junta Gubernativa*, all to no avail.[7] The troops were particularly hard on the fifty-two foreign residents of Bella Vista, mostly Frenchmen and Italians, who saw their foodstuffs and wares "requisitioned" to the last nail.[8] One merchant, a North American, ultimately had his pleas heard thanks to U.S. Minister Charles Washburn's intercession, but not before the Paraguayans had wrecked his place of business.[9]

Resquín also had the authority to impress the men of the town as recruits. Several weeks earlier, the *Junta Gubernativa* had decreed that all men from seventeen to fifty years of age were eligible for conscription. The trepidation this decree caused in Bella Vista drove many into the marshes with Cáceres, leaving a sullen population of women and children behind.[10] No one could now remember a time when Correntinos thought of the Paraguayans as their brothers.

The Southern Division stayed in the vicinity of Bella Vista for just over two months. It fought no major battles and accomplished little of benefit to the war effort other than standing by to reinforce Bruguez if necessary. When the Brazilian steamers ran past Cuevas on 12 August, Solano López directed Resquín south again to the Santa Lucía River, just above Goya.

*On the March South*
Once again, the Paraguayans advanced cautiously—unnecessarily so, for no Allied force of any size blocked their way. Gov. Manuel Lagraña had set up a provincial government at Goya, but since it had few troops attached to it, he was ready to leave at a moment's notice. Yet the Paraguayans did nothing more than probe the northern edge of town.

When Solano López learned of the defeat at Yataí, he ordered Resquín to withdraw from the left bank of the Santa Lucía "to avoid surprise by the enemy."[11] These orders reflected the effect on the marshal's thinking not only of Major Duarte's defeat but also of General Paunero's 25 May raid on Corrientes. They also reveal the Paraguayan leader's longing to take operational control of the army, pushing aside field commanders who were either too cautious or, as with Resquín, a bit too successful. In fact, Resquín was prudent and subservient to a fault, having learned from experience that a measure of self-abasement was necessary in dealing with Solano López. On this occasion, the marshal had called for circumspection — and so it would be.

In fact, the danger of a major Allied attack in the west was less than all this caution suggested; after all, the principal enemy concentrations were over a hundred miles away on the Uruguay. Even so, the Paraguayans could hardly risk marching too far south without resupply. Resquín was particularly worried about the lack of good mounts. Those horses brought from Humaitá were scrawny and weak, and Resquín's cavalrymen had ridden them too hard. Santa Lucía afforded limited pasturage for the large number of animals that accompanied the invasion force. On 3 August, Resquín notified Solano López that many horses had perished as a result, leaving some four thousand of his men without mounts. This fact forestalled any thought of resuming the march.[12]

The marshal, however, was not ready to give up. He announced that he soon expected to come personally to Corrientes with an additional twenty-two thousand men and all the horses he could find in Paraguay. Meanwhile, he authorized Resquín to take every horse the Correntino ranchers had, no matter how old or defective. This gave official sanction to looting on a wider scale than ever before, and the Paraguayans swept the countryside taking everything that moved on four feet, from blooded horses to half-lame oxen. Correntino collaborators regularly acted as *baqueanos* on these raids, greedily participating in some of the worst abuses. In this way, poor, marginalized individuals took their measure of revenge for the years of contempt that they had been subjected to by prosperous ranchers.

In fact, the burning of ranch houses and the seizure of livestock either through need or as a means of intimidation aroused lasting resentment among the Correntinos in the south-central region of the province, where hitherto indifference or passivity toward the invaders had been the rule. Hungry and unpaid, Resquín's troops tended to appropriate whatever caught their eye. They even despoiled Bella Vista's principal church, stealing the silver crown and vestments from the statue of the Virgin.[13]

Though Resquín needed additional horses, he had less need for the additional troops that López had promised; so far, he had no mission for those men already in his command, and reinforcements added new burdens. Finding food for the newcomers posed a serious problem. When they did discover cattle in a few spots, the Paraguayans showed great imagination in preparing meals from beef, including grilled ribs and stews (*jukysy so'o*) as well as the more elaborate ground-meat soup (*so'o josopy*). Even so, they sorely missed the vegetables, manioc root, and Indian corn that were daily fare at home. The sweet oranges, once available in abundance, had long since been eaten. As a result, some soldiers began to show signs of scurvy, with bleeding gums, aching joints, and listlessness. Many more had diarrhea and a few had measles, a disease that threatened the division as a whole. Medical support, which was always inadequate, had little hope of coping with the problem; untrained practitioners simply advised afflicted soldiers to keep clean and quiet and to stay as warm as possible. This last suggestion was sensible but impractical. The men had to use cow dung for fuel, and Resquín moved his entire force several times in search of firewood.

Reinforcements from Humaitá poured in during his advance — at least two cavalry regiments and an infantry battalion. Following the marshal's instructions, the Paraguayans had pressured the *Junta Gubernativa* to support this buildup.[14] Victor Silvero and the other members had difficulty meeting these demands, for no matter how much they professed their loyalty to the cause, they could not fill their fellow *provincianos* with any enthusiasm, especially after Riachuelo. The *Junta* ultimately raised a force of eight hundred men, but only by dragooning the majority into service. This contribution was all it could offer. Even symbolic contributions were important, however, and this effort did add to the number of troops available to Resquín. Despite his own uncertainty, the Correntino commander, Maj. Juan Francisco Lovera, promised that his men would more than carry their weight.[15]

### Friction among the Argentines

The Allied forces just to the south had nothing comparable in strength to the Paraguayans at first. While Cáceres, Simeón Paiva, Isidoro Reguera, and Juan Madariaga managed the active harassment of the enemy, it was Governor Lagraña who prepared the overall defense of the province. He had survived the Paraguayan invasion and had relocated several times in southern Corrientes. At Goya, Lagraña attended to the details of recruitment and logistics, attempting to emulate Mitre's earlier success at Concordia. He had few reliable men, however, and too little experience.

The national government clearly preferred to work around Lagraña by sending most supplies and money to the Argentine forces at Restauración.[16] Mitre rightly believed that hopes of victory in Corrientes rested on concentrating forces for a strong offensive. Any materiel diverted to the west would weaken the main force's ability to attack Resquín in good time. Nor was there any reason to suppose that Lagraña could hold Goya if the Paraguayans pressed forward. Supplies sent to the governor might well end up in enemy hands.

Moreover, Lagraña, though a Liberal and a Mitrista, could not be expected to uphold the interests of Mitre's Argentina in so trustworthy a manner as a *porteño* like General Paunero.[17] Throughout July, the governor persisted in begging the national government for assistance: "In three and a half months of daily action against the enemy, withstanding all the rigors of the [winter] season, the Correntino soldier has given every proof of his patriotism; but it has been with great delay that he has received clothing [and other supplies] from the Government. The uniforms sent up to now have only amounted to 4,000, leaving 1,500 men without."[18] Lagraña finally received his uniforms in mid-August, though not before Paunero gained assurances that a "competent person" would handle their distribution to the Correntino troops.[19] The general's subsequent insistence on an inventory of supplies at Goya was tantamount to accusing Lagraña of corruption, and indeed, someone evidently siphoned off supplies. The governor, who could afford to react with consternation but not with rage, wrote Vice President Marcos Paz that he would gladly open his books for inspection any time the government named.[20]

This fight within a fight looked inconsequential at the time, but it clearly illustrated how much discord existed between people supposedly united in a common cause. It was not just a question of personalities or of civilian versus military authority. In the minds of many in Corrientes, the proposed destruction of the Paraguayan army, while cause for righteous celebration, also inspired doubts about the future. Would the province recover any autonomy at all, or would it henceforth become a satellite of Buenos Aires? Would it have to endure a long Allied occupation? Who could ensure that Brazilian (and Argentine) troops would act less maliciously toward Correntino property than the Paraguayans? And who would pay for war-related expenses?

Lagraña and the various Correntino military commanders, though increasingly aware of these concerns, still had a war to wage. And to combat the marshal's army, they were willing to use the methods of the enemy. The irregular forces under Cáceres and others had survived since April largely by foraging. Mitre had sanctioned these activities as military necessities, and at the end of July, he suggested confiscating all livestock before the Paraguayans could get them.[21] Lagraña agreed, and three weeks later ordered the requisition of all horses in the province. The order clearly endorsed Correntinos seizing the property of other Correntinos, a hard policy that receipts from the national government could do little to redress.[22] Lagraña knew perfectly well that his order would cause depredations to increase generally, for the soldiers nominally under his authority, if unleashed, would take much more than horses.

This inaugurated — or, more accurately, extended — a tragic period in the Corrientes campaign during which contending armies mounted raids not so much against each other as against isolated ranches and farms in the interior, where horses, cattle, and foodstuffs were believed present. Some landowners saw their homes torn apart first by the Paraguayans, then by the Correntinos, and finally by deserters from both sides. After such raids, little remained besides broken bits of household utensils and charred ruins.[23]

### The Retreat Begins

Solano López intended to assume personal command of the Southern Division but chose to postpone his arrival until Colonel Estigarribia broke free of the encirclement at Uruguaiana. In another highly elaborated campaign plan, the Paraguayan commanders would set out to flank the Allies at the Rincón de Soto. Afterward, they would join the two columns of the army and move south once again, presumably to Montevideo.[24] Resquín, however, had no independent knowledge of what was happening on the opposite side of the province. Indeed, he had no clear idea of how many troops were with Lagraña at Goya. Resquín was an able enough officer, but his commander left him little room for taking independent action; he could do little but wait for the marshal's orders.

It took more than two weeks for news of Estigarribia's surrender to reach Resquín. The Paraguayan commander had noticed increased enemy patrols along his left flank but otherwise had no clear indication that the situation had changed. The only action of any significance during this interval occurred near Yaguareté Corã in mid-September. The 800 men of Major Lovera's expeditionary force had just completed an exhausting reconnaissance west of the Laguna Yberá. Settling into their tents and hammocks on the night of 20 September, they posted several unreliable sentinels. Just as the sun peeked over the horizon the next morning, Allied cavalrymen discovered the entire unit asleep and rushed the slumbering forms without warning. Ninety Correntinos died and another 371 surrendered. The survivors, including Lovera, escaped into the swamp and carefully made their way home, glad that their war had come to an end.[25] The national government lost not a single man in the engagement. This was the only occasion during the entire war where sizable units of Argentines faced other Argentines in open combat.[26]

Writing to Berges, the marshal expressed both consternation and understanding at the destruction of Lovera's command: "I am very sorry that the training camp of the Correntinos has evaporated; though I never believed in their ability to resist, even so they would have served greatly to give spirit to the country. . . . The *Junta* should now think of raising another [such force]."[27] He subsequently ordered new mobilizations in those areas closest to the port of Corrientes, but it was already too late.

On 6 October, having learned of Estigarribia's defeat only hours earlier, Marshal López ordered the withdrawal of Paraguayan troops from Corrientes. There was no longer any doubt about the course of the war; to salvage anything from their ill-fated offensive, the Paraguayans had to regroup, preferably behind the strong defenses at Humaitá.[28]

War Minister Vicente Barrios arrived at Resquín's headquarters two days after the marshal issued the evacuation order. He came by steamship, but his instructions directed the Southern Division to march overland. The one exception was Bruguez's Second Artillery Regiment, which embarked immediately aboard the *Pirabebé* in order to prepare batteries at Mercedes and the Riachuelo to cover the retreat.

Resquín needed no encouragement to depart. He could read a map and knew that without Estigarribia's army to the east, his own force was dangerously overextended. The Allied armies under Mitre would soon be in a position to threaten him unless he moved quickly.

The Southern Division began its march northward on 6 October 1865. The former vanguard of the force, mostly cavalry, now acted as a rearguard, but it had little to do. Cáceres, who had learned of the events at Uruguaiana at about the same time as Resquín, could have thrown his full force against the Southern Division, slowing its retreat. His men were still badly undersupplied, however, and he chose simply to maintain contact with the Paraguayans. He made no effort to delay them long enough for Mitre's army to close in; the main Allied units, of course, were still far away near the Uruguay River at this time.

The best chance to bottle up the Paraguayan force within Corrientes lay with the imperial fleet. If Admiral Tamandaré's ships could slip past the enemy batteries, they could move above the port of Corrientes and prevent Resquín's retreat across the Paraná. Such a maneuver might hold him in place long enough for the Allied armies to attack in force from the south and east. However, the admiral had already adopted the strategy of keeping his riverine forces abreast of the main land units. He was therefore unwilling to steam north of the Rincón de Soto, which was close to Lagraña's base at Goya.

In retreat, the Southern Division only averaged ten miles a day. The sandy soil of Corrientes was ill suited to heavy wagons and ox-carts, which, even with their seven-foot-high wheels, still got stuck. At the best of times, passage was difficult, but now the rains had swollen the creeks and rivers, hampering every operation. And as if this were not enough, the marshal ordered his army to sweep through the few remaining ranches that his troops had not yet plundered and drive the livestock north. The Paraguayans slaughtered those animals they could not take, leaving nothing behind for the Allies. This tactic was in one sense imprudent, for it needlessly prolonged the risk of attack. It did succeed for a time, however, in disrupting Allied supply, for as one observer noted, it left the "whole province a similar foodless waste as the Palatinate and the Shenandoah valley were in former times."[29]

The Argentines and Brazilians should have been able to acquire livestock from Urquiza's ranches in Entre Ríos. True to form, however, the *caudillo*'s underlings did everything in their power to hold up their sale. As a result, Mitre's men had to slaughter numbers of the army draft animals — a practice that slowed the Allied advance all the more.[30]

Of course, the true victims in all of this were the Correntino ranchers, great and small, who lost everything through the Paraguayan's scorched-earth operation. As a British naval officer on the South American station put it, "the Paraguayan campaign in Corrientes reads like an incursion of devils, for there was no opposition, no fighting, to excite their fury; all was done in cold blood." In the end, the way northward into Paraguay was left "white with the bleached bones [of the dead cattle]."[31]

### At the Port of Corrientes

Curiously, the provincial capital itself was little affected by these depredations. From the beginning, Paraguayans had treated the town with a far lighter hand than the countryside. They placed no encumbrances, for example, on Correntino merchants, who for the most part operated their businesses as before, if on a reduced scale. A small number managed to find means of obtaining letters of credit from Buenos Aires, a fact that Berges clearly winked at.[32]

Berges consistently tried to inculcate a spirit of normalcy in the community. He also made a great show of helping those Correntinos whose homes the Allies had damaged on 25 May. In this he enjoyed the support of local collaborators, not just the members of the *Junta Gubernativa* but many ordinary Correntinos as well.[33] For some, suspicion of Buenos Aires outweighed bad feeling toward Asunción, and the old Federals did everything they could to play upon that feeling. *El Independiente*, though hardly an unbiased source, still reflected many people's thinking when it published article after article praising the Paraguayans as defenders of provincial autonomy and the balance of power. The newspaper serialized a biography of José Gervasio Artigas, whom many considered the father of federalism in the region.[34] No one could have missed the implication that, though the Plata now had a new "father" (Solano López), the argument against the pretensions of Buenos Aires remained the same as ever.

The most striking aspect of life under Paraguayan rule was the relative ease with which the townspeople of Corrientes expressed their opinions. Berges forbade as seditious any display of pro-Allied sentiment but otherwise let people speak fairly openly. He trusted in the fractious nature of local politics to keep the most dangerous elements in check, knowing full well that most Correntinos favored a passive, more moderate course. A surprising number lent their voices to a wide-ranging discussion on the future politics of the province.

This situation offered a sharp contrast to Paraguay itself, where the López family had long since wiped out dissent. The Correntinos even felt sufficiently comfortable in 1865 to question the justice of Paraguayan dictates. A few bemoaned the detention of wives and children of pro-Allied figures. More tellingly, when the Paraguayan military authorities arrested businessman Wenceslao Díaz Colodrero on suspicion of espionage, a body of twenty-six notables, including Santiago Derqui and the Italian consul, stepped forward to demand his release. Díaz Colodrero, they insisted, was a longtime Federal and a friend of the Paraguayans who had "done nothing, even indirectly, to harm the noble cause of defending the Republic."[35] The marshal agreed and set the man at liberty shortly thereafter.[36]

The brief experiment with "open" politics under the occupation ended once fortune turned against the Paraguayan military. The *Junta Gubernativa* stumbled for weeks, increasingly unsure of its political role and all the while ceding more administrative authority to Berges. The Correntino Federals who composed the *Junta* believed that they enjoyed the marshal's confidence. In fact, Solano López used the Federals as cat's-paws and then discarded them as their usefulness waned. Berges had long advised him to acknowledge something more than a passing independence for the *Junta*, to grant that body a few trifling subsidies and some control over the Correntino levies. But the marshal refused to sugar the pill of conquest and now paid the price. As for his Correntino collaborators, by early October, Silvero, Gauna, and Sinforoso Cáceres were thinking less of new campaigns than of flight.

*In the Misiones*

At Uruguaiana, the bulk of Mitre's army remained unaware that Resquín had already started to withdraw. The only Allied force of any size on the Argentine side of the Uruguay River was the Correntino cavalry, which previously had kept pace with Estigarribia while avoiding any engagement. Mitre had instructed them to guard the northwestern approaches to the town during the siege. This left them well placed to attack any Paraguayan units coming from the Misiones to reinforce the defunct Uruguay Division. Now the Correntinos went on the offensive.

On 26 September the Correntino troops advanced to the Aguapey River, having retaken Santo Tomé unopposed a few days earlier. If they were going to encounter resistance anywhere, it would be between this point and the Trinchera de los Paraguayos, still sixty miles distant.

The next morning, advance units from both sides collided just south of San Carlos. The Paraguayans, thirty-five in number, never anticipated seeing so many Correntinos in an area supposedly cleared by Estigarribia and Duarte. Rather than attack, they repaired to their old camp near the abandoned mission a short distance away. With no time to prepare a defense, they nervously discharged a volley of musketry before the enemy came into range. Colonel Reguera assumed that the Paraguayans had exhausted themselves with this one fusillade and from across a broad field called upon them to surrender. Much to his surprise, they ignored his demand and, dropping their muskets, mounted their sorry horses and rode with total abandon straight at him. The Paraguayans cut down three Correntinos with their sabers and wounded another ten. Reguera's troops, in turn, shot and killed twenty of the enemy in a matter of minutes, leaving the rest on the field with their bodies bloodied and limbs askew. None escaped. Several mixed units of Paraguayan cavalry and infantry appeared from the north when they heard the gunfire but melted back into the bush once they grasped what had happened.

Reguera's men were weary, and their colonel decided against pursuit. He halted at the ruined mission and sent out pickets. In his official account of the engagement, he reflected on the suicidal courage of the Paraguayans. "The enemy," he wrote, "never give in to anyone and prefer death to surrender. They are worse than the Indians of the Pampa."[37] By now, this was hardly a novel observation, but Reguera understood its implications better than most Allied officers. A dying enemy soldier told him that the marshal had just deployed four thousand fresh troops to Encarnación.[38] To advance, he would likely have to engage this army, a prospect that a commander in his position should have found daunting.

The trails from the Aguapey through the Misiones provided the traditional invasion route into Paraguay. The ill-fated Manuel Belgrano came this way in 1810. So did José Gervasio Artigas a decade later, though as a refugee, not a prospective conqueror. The Paraguayans had these earlier precedents in mind as they organized their defenses. Although Solano López believed that the main Allied push would occur in the west, still he could not afford to leave the Misiones completely unprotected. He had already removed the families of Correntino ranchers in the Misiones who had sold him horses. Now he ordered his troops out of Trinchera and across the Paraná to Encarnación, leaving a tiny residual force behind. Simultaneously, he established a new camp called Santa Teresa, located on the river's right bank equidistant between Paso de la Patria and Encarnación. This new camp, the marshal hoped, would block any large force attempting to advance into central Paraguay. He also left a small garrison at the strategically important Tranquera de Loreto. There, the Paraguayan guards could observe enemy movements and sound the alarm if necessary. For the next three years, this small encampment served as the only Paraguayan installation in what later became the Argentine province of Misiones. As for the Allies, they moved into the areas vacated by Solano López and collected some one thousand horned cattle and horses that he had neglected to drive north in time.[39] They raided the Paraguayans sporadically thereafter but mounted no serious attacks in this theater, leaving the main action for their armies in the west.

*Evacuation of Corrientes*

The Allied columns along the Uruguay postponed their northward advance into Corrientes until the end of September. In part, the delay was caused by continued problems in supply and training. Few of the newly arrived *voluntários* could properly load and fire their weapons. Mules and oxen were also in short supply, and as hauling each gun required a team of six animals (with another six for the caisson), the artillerymen simply had to wait.

But politics also played a crucial role in the army's delay. The elimination of Estigarribia's division had caused many people in the Litoral to reevaluate their stand on the war. López could no longer win — that much was clear. But as the military struggle ebbed, the political struggle intensified. If Mitre had already won, the Correntinos and Entrerrianos asked, then why should they expend more lives and property for the national cause? Far better to go home and let the *porteños* mop up what remained of the Paraguayan army in Corrientes.

Allied victories gave Mitre an important political edge in the provinces, but such leverage was as impermanent as the wind. The Brazilians, for the moment, had sincerely committed themselves to the alliance with Buenos Aires.[40] Yet the closer Mitre stood with the imperial government, the more worried he became about his own countrymen. Within his own government there were many protests about the supposed bad behavior of Brazilian troops while on Argentine soil.[41] And these complaints seemed trivial compared with those of a more narrowly political character. *El Republicano*, a pro-Urquiza weekly of Concordia, summed up the opinion of many in the Litoral when it noted: "We can have much love and veneration for our fatherland, but a people cannot forget their dislikes. The republican spirit among men might keep quiet a day, a week, a month, but in the end the powder magazine will [explode]. . . . By any chance has the current war been unpopular only in Entre Ríos? Have not disaffections occurred throughout the Argentine Republic? Call upon the province of Entre Ríos for a people's war, call upon her to restrain the power of the monarchy, and we can then ask whether there is one remaining Entrerriano, just one, who has not stepped forward at the call of the fatherland."[42]

In such circumstances, keeping his troops loyal posed as great a challenge for Mitre as annihilating Resquín's army. Thus, the Argentine president kept in close communication with his field commanders and with governors of distant provinces who had promised further reinforcements. He visited units to boost morale (and to remind the soldiers that much remained to be done). And he continued to have sulfurous words in the *porteño* press for Paraguay and her leader.

Despite his labors, Mitre had less than complete success in keeping his army together. Governor Urquiza, still smarting from the Basualdo mutiny, managed to muster another six thousand of his *provincianos* and assembled them at Toledo as prelude to a planned rendezvous with the main Allied force. The *caudillo* pinned all his hopes for a continued role in the war on this new army. Yet, in the late evening of 4 November, his men made the same fateful decision as their compatriots at Basualdo. Beginning with eight hundred regulars from Nogoyá, Diamante, and Victoria, the troops simply saddled their horses and rode off into the night. This time, not even Urquiza's presence could stem the tide of desertion, and within five days the Entrerriano camp looked like a ghost town.[43]

Mitre received the news of the Toledo mutiny with little outward alarm. Had the Entrerrianos deserted earlier, it might have had disastrous consequences, but now it hardly mattered. To Urquiza, he wrote that the victories at Uruguaiana and Yataí had sealed Solano López's fate, and new contingents were no longer needed to prosecute the war: "As for the rest, and if it provides any consolation to you in the midst of so many setbacks, I take great pleasure in recognizing the patriotic efforts you have made [in favor of] the National Government. . . . [I]f your efforts have not met with the results they merited this was exclusively due to forces beyond you control."[44]

In truth, the mutiny vexed Mitre more than he cared to admit; thus, he thought, did the tree of indiscipline bear its fruit. And there were other alienated soldiers in his army, men who could easily be drawn down the same path as the Entrerrianos. Quietly, but with great firmness, Mitre insisted that Urquiza and other loyalists hunt down the deserters and bring the guilty parties before firing squads.[45] After this was done, the president then offered an incentive to those men who had not joined the mutiny. From now on he planned to dedicate himself wholeheartedly to their welfare, looking after their food, shelter, and smaller comforts with as much energy as he could manage. He promised, in essence, to trust them more if, in turn, they displayed the soldierly behavior he expected. Mitre began to build an understanding with his men, even an enthusiasm and élan, by making life as bearable for them as possible and letting the soldiers do the rest.

That was an unenviable task, and he never did convince everyone. Moreover, Mitre had to face wretchedly bad weather in November and December. Though the chill of winter had long since given way to the heat of spring, still it rained and rained. The wet times brought hordes of stinging gnats and mosquitoes and the now-omnipresent chiggers, which laid their eggs beneath the toenails of many a city-born soldier. Everyone suffered. And there was never enough food.[46]

The main Allied force now counted thirty-seven thousand men organized into eleven infantry divisions, two cavalry divisions, and various units of artillery and engineers plus musicians, medical personnel, chaplains, staff officers, and volunteers of every stripe.[47] This was as large a military gathering as had ever assembled in this part of the world. Its very size, however, reduced its mobility. It was notoriously difficult to move large numbers of men over soggy ground. The Argentine president, who had a healthy respect for nature's power, did not even try but instead elected to delay his departure again and again. The Allies had entered the isolated village of Mercedes in mid-October, then advanced no farther for three weeks. From such a distance, they could not directly affect events farther north.

The specter of a reinvigorated Allied army put real pressure on the Paraguayan commander, who urged his soldiers to hasten their retreat no matter what the cost. Resquín's men trudged on and on through the mud, driving confiscated livestock before them, foraging for food wherever they could find it. All the time, they imagined well-armed Allied cavalry nipping at their heels. Those who had fallen ill with stomach ailments, influenza, and measles grew sicker, and a great number died. As in all wars, stragglers met the worst fate; those who strayed too far from the column or fell behind it were killed without mercy by Cáceres's men, who, like their commander, had grown casually ruthless during the course of the campaign. Despite these travails, the Paraguayans kept to their relentless pace. Most passed through Empedrado by the last week of October after having dragged their guns from the batteries at the Riachuelo. They then crowded into Corrientes to await transportation to Humaitá.[48]

The port might have sunk into the same chaos as had befallen Bella Vista, but the Paraguayans and the local inhabitants reached an understanding that kept trouble to a minimum. On 20 October, a committee of foreign residents addressed a letter to Berges and the *Junta Gubernativa* regarding the delicate problem of keeping order during the evacuation.[49] Luckily, two Italian warships were in port at the time, and Berges agreed to leave behind two companies of infantry to act as police on condition that the Italians promise to ferry the infantrymen upriver to Paso de la Patria.[50] The marshal later painted this as a selfless offer, the proof that Paraguay respected the rights of local noncombatants; and, indeed, more Correntinos feared the "theft, murder, and violations" expected of the Allied soldiers than had ever feared the Paraguayans. No one wished to see a repetition of the excesses of 25 May.

As it happened, the Italians refused to transport López's men, for that would have involved them in a breach of neutrality. They did, however, deploy a company of their own marines that kept the peace in town for several days. Meanwhile, the Paraguayans brought ships and carts from the north and evacuated nearly one hundred of their Correntino allies. These included some soldiers and merchants, the editor of *El Independiente*, and the members of the *Junta Gubernativa*. The old man Teodoro Gauna, who accepted his exile with heartfelt regret, wept bitterly as his homeland receded into the distance.[51] He never saw Corrientes again.

Some four hundred Correntinos who had initially sided with the *Junta* recanted their support at the approach of the first Allied troops. Like Lovera, they received clemency with few questions asked.[52] Governor Lagraña, who arrived at the provincial capital in early November, expected to find the place sacked. In fact, all he found to grumble about was that the cashbox at the Government House had been looted, the furniture taken, and the doors of the building torn off their hinges. Those Correntinos who had stayed during the seven-month occupation had relatively few complaints (especially when compared to their loud demands for reimbursement of expenses incurred after the Allies took possession of the community).[53]

Solano López selected Paso de la Patria as the chief embarkation point for his forces in Corrientes. Located just opposite the Paraguayan fort of Itapirú, it was the logical spot from which to get the army to Humaitá with the least trouble. The river, however, was a mile and a half wide at this point with strong currents. Ferrying therefore required more than a few vessels. The marshal's navy assembled every available craft for the task by 27 October; two steamers, several barges, a plethora of *chatas* and canoes — anything that could float — moved into position at Paso de la Patria and started to embark troops. Bruguez's Second Artillery Regiment departed first, together with the sick and wounded. Then came all the cavalry regiments. Resquín had emplaced Bruguez's artillery pieces along the northern bank of the Paraná to shield the landing site from Brazilian interference, which was expected at any time.

The crucial moment came at 11:00 A.M.— one hour into the operation — when most of Bruguez's guns were aboard barges midway across the water. The sun had risen high in the sky, and the Paraguayans were plainly visible from some distance. Suddenly, six Brazilian warships steamed into view at Tres Bocas; they had left their anchorage south of Corrientes when word reached them of the Paraguayan crossing. At the same time, Resquín's rear guard signaled that enemy cavalry had commenced an assault, presumably in force. It seemed that the Allies had well timed their interdiction after all, and there was little that Resquín could do to stop them. As Thompson related, the people "who saw this gave up the army as lost, thinking that the Brazilians would never allow it to cross the river, and that it would soon be overtaken and destroyed by the Allied armies."[54]

The Paraguayan general suspended the evacuation and made ready for the worst. He dispatched all his available artillery west toward Corrientes to repulse what promised to be a major attack. Simultaneously, the two Paraguayan steamers *Yporá* and *Pirabebé* surged forward as their crewmen primed their cannon.

Then came the surprise. The Brazilian vessels, which greatly outgunned their opponents, turned sharply and pulled back downriver without firing a shot. Why they acted so was initially unclear. Then further reports from the Paraguayan rearguard confirmed that the cavalry assault had been a mere feint, that no mass of Allied troops was advancing. The imperial naval officers, whether through timidity or because of previous orders, proved singularly apprehensive at any hint of danger. Without adequate land reconnaissance, they could never be sure that the Paraguayans had not erected hidden batteries. Moreover, despite their many months in the region, they had yet to gain an adequate knowledge of navigation above Tres Bocas. With this as an excuse, they abandoned the idea of any direct challenge to the Southern Division's crossing. U.S. Minister Washburn spoke for many observers when he contemptuously recalled this example of Brazilian inaction: "[They] had it in their power to cut off [Resquín's] retreat; . . . throughout the war [they] seemed to think that all the science and strategy in war was expressed in the proverb of a golden bridge for a flying enemy, did not think it expedient to destroy the only means of escape for the Paraguayans. . . . They chose rather to bear the ills of a longer war."[55]

After the Brazilians withdrew, Resquín resumed operations, working day and night until 4 November, when the final infantry units passed over. The soldiers took with them nearly one hundred thousand head of confiscated cattle.[56] At one point, the Brazilian ships eased close enough to fire a few rounds, but these all fell short of the escaping troops. General Cáceres marched into Corrientes at the same time and proclaimed it liberated territory. The townspeople, who wondered what new ordeals his arrival portended, mainly celebrated their deliverance from behind closed doors. Cáceres tried to assault the last enemy units at Paso de la Patria, but the defenses erected by Col. José Díaz held without losses to either side. In truth, Cáceres no longer had his heart in the fight. Like other Correntinos, he had already shifted his thoughts to the equally daunting battleground of provincial politics.

Thus did the last Paraguayan troops leave Corrientes. High water, pelting rains, and simple confusion had plagued the retreat from beginning to end, but now it was over, and the Allies had done little to prevent its completion. The main Allied columns even now were 185 miles to the south. And as for Brazilian warships, their efforts were more or less negligible. The navy made no attempt to stop the *Yporá* and *Pirabebé*, which, having fulfilled their mission, sailed past Tres Bocas and up the Paraguay River to Humaitá. The Paraguayan sailors then joined in a grand ball held at the fortress to celebrate the outcome of the evacuation. The men of the Southern Division, all happy participants at the fiesta, were safe and would fight again another day.

*Aftermath*

The Corrientes campaign had come to an inglorious end, and with it ended Paraguay's ill-considered crusade to liberate the Banda Oriental and restore a "balance of power" to the Plata. From this time forward, Solano López had to formulate a defensive strategy to fend off Allied armies that were sure to invade his homeland. Yet by assuming the defensive, the marshal elicited the popular fervor of his countrymen in a new way. The feeling of patriotism, which had expressed itself only fleetingly in Corrientes, found far greater impetus once the Allies set foot in Paraguay. Love of country was no longer an empty phrase to the men of the marshal's army. No longer did obedience and attention to duty alone motivate them. Now, all their most cherished feelings, their love of family and community, their traditional values, all came under the shadow of the Allied sword. In response, Paraguayans found a strength in themselves for which the Allies had no obvious counterpart. It sustained López and his people for another four years of blood and tragedy.

Argentine commentators have always claimed that the Paraguayan occupation left an indelible mark upon Corrientes. In fact, the familiar patterns of Correntino politics reasserted themselves almost immediately after Resquín departed. Lagraña gloried in a momentary nimbus of victory, but the national government could not save him from the disunity of his own Liberal faction. Nor could it prevent his being replaced in the December elections by Evaristo López, an obscure rancher from Goya and — of all things — an anti-Paraguayan Federal.

López was only the screen behind which stood a coterie of large landowners from the south of the province. Within this group, Nicanor Cáceres held the real power, and thanks to Urquiza's patronage, he expected to retain it. Whether the Entrerriano *caudillo* was really in a position to help those outside his own province was unclear. All sides expected Mitre to attempt to manipulate local politics, but they also knew that it was not a great priority for him. Cáceres had time to reinforce his already strong following among those Correntinos who resisted subordination to Buenos Aires. He took for himself the posts of provincial police chief and commander of the militia, then withdrew to his estancia in Curuzú Cuatiá, from where he guided Correntino politics until 1868.[57]

Whether Federal or Liberal, every Correntino politician understood the need for supporting the national cause. This required that provincial militia units continue to serve in the field throughout the Paraguayan campaign. It also meant supporting thousands of Allied troops moving up from Mercedes, selling them food, providing them with billets, and in every way making them feel comfortable while discouraging them from mixing too deeply in Correntino affairs.

While the politics of war played out, Mitre's great Allied army finally made some progress. It crossed the swollen Corrientes River between 5 and 12 November, a feat for which Allied military engineers felt justifiably proud.[58] Two more flooded rivers, the Batel and the Santa Lucía, blocked the way northward, but Argentine and Brazilian engineers under Col. João Carlos de Vilagran Cabrita fashioned rafts and bridges from felled trees and got the whole army across.[59]

Mitre had already learned of Resquín's escape and no longer had a reason to hurry. Yet it was still in his interest to move forward steadily to Corrientes, for the more he delayed, the more chances there were for desertion. Mitre was also worried that the Paraguayans might mount extensive raids along the Alto Paraná. Given the right conditions, they could threaten the provincial capital once again and, if they caught Cáceres napping, might wreck his command far more effectively than they ever had in the field. With this concern in mind, the Argentine president pressed forward when the sun finally came out.

Yet all was not well in the Allied ranks. Mitre had saddled Venancio Flores with rear-guard duties ever since Uruguaiana, and it was not much to the Uruguayan's liking. He clamored for a new mission, one that would put his Army of the Van at the center of action. Mitre and the Brazilians had no intention of granting their hotheaded friend the honor of serving as the real, not merely nominal, vanguard of the Allied forces but were perfectly happy to assign him a key auxiliary role. They allowed him to detach his units from Mercedes and advance to the northeast parallel to the main force. This took him through the thickets and tangled vines of central Corrientes, past Yaguareté Corã and San Miguel.[60]

At the latter village, Flores joined Uruguayan cavalry units coming from Restauración and the Misiones and then drove due north. He reached the Alto Paraná in the third week of December, emerging just opposite the much-disputed island of Apipé. By that time, his men were fatigued and not a little disoriented as they stumbled into the village of Itatí on the twentieth. They had spent a month trudging through the marshlands during the hottest time of the year and now hardly knew where they were.[61]

Meanwhile, the main body of the Allied army continued northward. Even though the Paraguayans were long gone, the journey was still slow going. Cannons had to be pulled across spongy marshes and long expanses of matted evergreens. Carts and wagons bogged down, horses went lame, and men grumbled in the unfamiliar country. One source noted that the column under the command of General Gelly y Obes had to replace all its horses on four different occasions during the march.[62]

And that was not all. Resquín took so many head of cattle that temporary food shortages developed among the Allied troops. Though food supplies eventually reached them by way of the river, the Allies had yet to create an effective system of distribution; as a result, some units ate better than at home, while others hardly ate at all.

Despite the Allies' logistical problems, the march involved a curious measure of pageantry. Salutes fired, flags unfurled and fluttered, and there were regular displays of close-order drill. The different musical bands took every opportunity to compete with each other, loudness being given an equal footing with harmony. The Allies held dances at every village where officers could find female partners (Lagraña's daughters participated at one such affair).[63] And in a show of color rarely seen in such parts, the different army commanders donned magnificent formal uniforms of every hue, from gray to butternut to navy blue to spotless white; these they sometimes wore on the most incongruous occasions, even in the heat of battle.[64]

In general, the Argentine soldiers felt an uneasy tolerance for their Brazilian allies. Official policy had it otherwise, but in truth the Argentines were troubled with so many mixed-blooded speakers of Portuguese marching through Corrientes. Perhaps the more intelligent observers from Buenos Aires were influenced in this by the weight of historical prejudice. But the men on the march were more likely influenced by a nagging fear: if the Brazilians were to make quick work of the marshal's army, then who could get them out of Argentina? For their part, the Brazilians reciprocated much of the mistrust but tried to get along with their hosts anyway. And indeed, they were perfectly willing to keep the Argentines guessing about their final intentions.

The order of march had a length of nearly six days. This left troops spread along a thin line opposite the Paraná River, all moving slowly but steadily in the direction of Corrientes. The main units reached this destination by mid-December. First the Brazilians and then the Argentines set up camps according to a pre-established plan. Imperial forces under General Osório bivouacked a comfortable twenty-three miles northeast of the port at Laguna Brava. The Argentine units, commanded by Generals Paunero and Emilio Mitre, established themselves just to the west of the Brazilians at Ensenadas. And as for Flores, after resting at Itatí, his Uruguayans moved inland a short distance and organized a camp at San Cosme.

Corrientes now became the nerve center for the campaign against Paraguay. A large hospital with cream-colored walls was constructed as was a major supply depot. Allied politicians and military figures took rooms at the town's several hotels, while soldiers converted government buildings into operational barracks. Local innkeepers and foreign-born sutlers learned to benefit from the cash flow of war, and prices for everything from beef cutlets to ornamental spurs shot up accordingly. Restaurateurs reflected the changing times by renaming dishes with their new customers in mind; Kidneys "à la Mitre" and Green Beans "Brasileiras" became standard fare at certain establishments.[65] In spite of the profits that accompanied the Allied presence, the Correntinos never became unalloyed supporters of the war. They always maintained a certain distance between themselves and outsiders. Allied officers duly noted their reticence, concluding that the port teemed with the marshal's spies.[66] But it was only the Correntinos being themselves.

General Cáceres patrolled the transit points at Paso de la Patria for a number of weeks, but as he had little to report to his superiors, he ended by furloughing the majority of his troops. The Paraguayans escaped cleanly. Happily, they conducted no raids on Corrientes as of New Year's Day 1866, though many suspected that this could change at any time. Mitre and his staff now turned confidently to the next stage of the war. Humaitá awaited, and they began to contemplate its destruction.

# Conclusion
## *The End of the Beginning*

Francisco Solano López's decision to invade Brazil and Argentina was based on hurt pride, the desire to rectify borders, and the fear that Buenos Aires and Rio de Janeiro were moving dangerously close to realizing their national goals in the Plata. If Bartolomé Mitre and the Brazilians had their way, he maintained, they would soon eliminate all regional rivals, his own country included. They would then divide Paraguay and the Banda Oriental between them. That the two giants would inevitably clash with each other was a logical inference, and López doubted this result not for a moment. By the time Brazil and Argentina came to blows, however, it would probably be too late. His nation—the Republic of Paraguay—would already have ceased to exist.

Historians have reproached Solano López for his many miscalculations, but his intuition on this occasion was correct. The Brazilians did harbor hegemonic ambitions in the Plata. Mitre's cohort did wish to consolidate *porteño* rule in Argentina irrespective of the price. Given these inclinations, the marshal thought it wiser to attack without delay, using the army to smash his enemies before they smashed him. Afterward, he could reestablish a balance of power in the Plata while guaranteeing the security of his nation. Seen in this light, the Paraguayan offensive of 1864–65 was less the product of one man's wild ambition than of a traditional, broadly felt fear of encirclement.

In choosing the path to war, Solano López eschewed another stance that was likewise grounded in the Paraguayan historical experience: the willingness to implicitly support Brazil against Argentina or vice versa. Dr. José Gaspar de Francia had adopted this strategy when he left the door partly open to Brazilian trade in the 1820s and 1830s. Carlos Antonio López did much the same two decades later, siding first with Justo José de Urquiza and the empire in displacing Juan Manuel de Rosas, then countering Brazilian pretensions at Fêcho-dos-Morros.

Appearing to side with one power and then with another had served Paraguayan interests well over the years. But Solano López had different ideas for his country. In this, he was encouraged by Vásquez Sagastume and other Blanco agents, who needed all possible assistance to repel the invaders of Uruguay. They argued that Paraguay had a pivotal role in restoring the proper order of things in the Plata. In a sense, they were right, for Paraguay's model of nationhood included strict and powerful links between the leader and the masses — links that had a traditional basis and that other people in the Plata might well understand and emulate. If they did, then all of Mitre's plans for a greater Argentina might fail, and all of Brazil's pretensions in the region might be frustrated.

In any case, López himself was soon repeating the same words as his Uruguayan supplicants. He urged his people to prepare for the worst. And it came. Mitre's thinly disguised support of Venancio Flores followed by Brazil's invasion of Uruguay in September 1864 pushed the Paraguayan leader over the edge.

Rescuing his allies in the Lower Plata involved much more than words. Militarily, Paraguay was the best organized, though clearly not the strongest, of all the contending countries. The marshal, who fancied himself a first-rate general, had spent the better part of a decade adding to his military infrastructure, purchasing warships, and training his troops. He assumed that Paraguayan armies could vanquish the Allies, all the while giving heart to thousands of Correntinos, Entrerrianos, and Uruguayans who would rally to the common cause.

Solano López was certainly right in thinking that the Litoral provinces harbored many potential allies. The Paraguayan seizure of Mato Grosso brought nothing but praise in that quarter, and such regional figures as Victor Silvero and Ricardo López Jordan confidently expected to see their own people join the Paraguayan army as it marched south to Paysandú and Montevideo. Even Urquiza inclined in favor of Solano López — or so it seemed at the time.

Having taken the lands north of the Apa River, the marshal hesitated over his next move. Thus far, his government was still at peace with Buenos Aires. This fact suggested two possible approaches: either do nothing and allow Argentine neutrality to shield Paraguay from any Brazilian invasion by way of the river, or attack immediately — probably through the Misiones — into Rio Grande and finally on to Uruguay. The first option had much to recommend it, for the empire had no hope of mounting an overland invasion of Paraguay in the immediate future; López might even retain his prize in Mato Grosso. But if he failed to move, then he ran the risk of leaving his Uruguayan allies — and perhaps Urquiza — in the lurch. If Paraguay wished to play its proper role in the Plata, then sooner or later he had to take the offensive.

The marshal's plan was ambitious but not insane. Its slender logic rested for the most part on the resilience of the Blanco Party in Uruguay and on the putative support of Argentine "allies" in the intervening territory. Yet, to paraphrase Proudhon, the fecundity of the unexpected far exceeds the statesman's prudence; when Solano López did eventually drive south, he missed his opportunity by three months. Paysandú had fallen. Flores had assumed the presidency at Montevideo. And, for better or worse, Urquiza had cast his lot with the national government.

Compounding the political difficulties this new situation presented for Paraguay was the marshal's major strategic blunder: rather than attack Brazil by way of the Misiones, he ordered Gen. Wenceslao Robles to seize the port of Corrientes. Its invasion swiftly drove Argentina into an alliance with the empire and left the people of the Litoral with no real alternative to Mitre's leadership.

Solano López followed this decision with one misstep after another. To begin with, he never clarified his overall objective to his subordinate commanders but instead left them to ponder his next move. He then divided his army into two columns that were incapable of mutual support. He entrusted command of these two columns to weak (and in the case of Antonio de la Cruz Estigarribia, incompetent) officers who failed utterly to inspire their men or rise above the challenges of their mission. The marshal further hampered their movements by issuing detailed instructions from which they dared not deviate. They could neither advance nor maneuver without specific orders from Humaitá, which was several days away by steamer or coach.

Poor strategy translated into poor performance in the field. Unnecessary delays, misplacement of advance columns and reconnaissance units, and impossible defensive postures all followed one upon the other with devastating effects for Paraguay. In addition, Gen. Wenceslao Paunero's raid of 25 May on Corrientes upset Solano López's timetable for advancing to the south. His subsequent decision to withdraw in order to guard against further raids confused his field commanders even more.

The marshal conceived one opportunity for strategic innovation — at the Riachuelo. But his ineffectual naval commander squandered his chance for a surprise victory by attacking several hours late and by failing to eliminate a Brazilian picket ship before it gave the alarm. The Paraguayans then steamed well past the imperial fleet instead of coming alongside for the assault. Though the Brazilians reacted with confusion at first, in the end, the ill-considered Paraguayan maneuver gave Adm. Francisco Barroso the time he needed to move decisively. His destruction of Capt. Pedro Ignacio Meza's flotilla ended Paraguay's hopes of major offensive action on the river and basically limited the marshal to land operations thereafter.

For all of the skill that Barroso displayed at the battle of the Riachuelo, the Allies also made many mistakes. Neither Argentina nor Brazil had ever fought a sustained military operation over such a wide area. Neither country managed to mobilize its troops effectively. The Argentines were completely unprepared for the attack of 13 April and lost nearly all their small fleet in consequence. They then watched helplessly as a key town of their northeastern provinces came under foreign rule. The only bright spot in the national government's defense came from Paunero's 25 May raid and from Gen. Nicanor Cáceres, Col. Simeón Paiva, and Col. Isidoro Reguera, who effected maximum delay against the Paraguayan columns advancing south. Their exertions gave Mitre the time he needed to raise, organize, and train his land forces for a counterattack.

In the beginning, the Brazilians matched the Argentines in their poor defense. Though the Riograndenses had the advantage of being on their home ground, their operations against the Paraguayans were consistently sluggish with no obvious direction or unity of command. As a result, from São Borja through Uruguaiana, the Paraguayans encountered little resistance. Only at Mbutuí did the gaúchos mount a successful assault, and on that occasion, they greatly outnumbered the enemy. Apologists might suggest that the Brazilians planned to lure the Paraguayans into an isolated position far from any hope of support. In fact, the Brazilians failed to attack because of the numbers against them and because they could not coordinate their units in time. Instead of closing with the Uruguay Division, they argued among themselves. Lt. Floriano Peixoto's courageous actions on the river confounded Paraguayan communications across the Uruguay, but it could not make up for the poor generalship the Brazilians displayed in Rio Grande.

Estigarribia's own lack of initiative at Uruguaiana was palpable. It rested on three factors: the fatigue of his men, the lack of supplies, and the absence of orders from Humaitá. Every day the colonel hesitated, the Allies grew stronger. Soon it became impossible to contemplate a dash into the supposedly friendly Banda Oriental. Escape northward was also ruled out. Estigarribia's spirits sunk even lower when word came that Venancio Flores had crushed Maj. Pedro Duarte's command at the Yataí. When the Paraguayans surrendered after a siege of several weeks, it came as no surprise to anyone save Solano López.

By October 1865 Mitre had constructed a large, if untried, army at Concordia. Though it represented many different and oftentimes conflicting interests, this force was more formidable than all of the Paraguayan units left in Corrientes. Yet for a variety of reasons, Mitre delayed its deployment against Gen. Francisco Resquín. The Argentine president left the real fighting to Cáceres and his guerrillas and instead gave full attention to the broader organization of the Allied army. The Correntino irregulars had carried much of the burden of defense thus far. They were intrepid enough to harass the Southern Division and keep Resquín guessing, but General Cáceres never deceived himself into thinking that his men alone could defeat such a force.

Only the imperial navy had the power and the opportunity to gain a decisive advantage by closing the Paraguayan escape route from Corrientes. Yet Admiral Tamandaré adopted a policy that kept his warships even with the line of Allied advance on the land. To be sure, Brazilian vessels did steam forward at the last juncture but then refused to challenge Resquín's crossing of the Paraná. They thereby assured more trouble for Allied forces in the future. The failure to engage the Paraguayans at Paso de la Patria ranked as the single worst mistake the Allies made during the early phases of the war.

Success in Corrientes did not bring a comprehensive victory over the Paraguayans. Their army was, after all, anything but defeated. Humaitá loomed as the greatest defensive complex in the region, and if it were not impregnable, it surely looked the part. Not a single observer believed that Humaitá would fall without a dramatic Allied assault, something far more massive, far more intense, than anything thus far contemplated.

Gaining this new objective involved political as well as military costs, and no one expected the alliance between the national government and the empire to function smoothly. The Argentine soldiers distrusted their Brazilian comrades and each other; at any time, Mitre's army was likely to splinter into its constituent parts, as the mutinies at Basualdo and Toledo demonstrated. The Brazilians, for their part, were just as suspicious of the men from Buenos Aires. Manoel Luiz Osório and the other generals chafed under Mitre's direction. Many of their soldiers felt homesick, and it was a long way back to São Paulo, Rio, or Recife. The one thing certain about the alliance was that every party intended to pursue its own interests.

As for the marshal, he could take comfort in the loyalty of his men. The Allies were badly mistaken if they thought that these thrice-whipped soldiers were resigned to their defeat. On the contrary, what the Paraguayans lacked in dash and fire they more than made up for in constancy and in their willingness to bear up under the most trying conditions. Theirs was a psychology of extremes: *¡Vencer o morir! ¡Independencia o muerte!* Like the Japanese or the Norsemen, the Paraguayans detested the battle half-won as much as the outright defeat — and there remained much for them to do. In this the marshal understood his countrymen far better than did Mitre or Emperor Pedro II. Except for the Uruguay Division, the Paraguayan army was intact, and its men were ready for whatever eventuality. Throughout the country, the people were united behind their president; his war aims — now that the army was back on Paraguayan soil — seemed concrete, personal, and intimate to them. Solano López controlled the southern Mato Grosso with its difficult but potentially important overland route to Bolivia. And he controlled his people. This was all that he needed for the time being, for Paraguay, as he well knew, would endure, come what may.

# Notes

*Abbreviations*

AGN-BA   Archivo General de la Nación, Buenos Aires

AGPC   Archivo General de la Provincia de Corrientes, Argentina
  -CO   Correspondencia oficial
  -EA   Expedientes administrativas

AHI   Arquivo Histórico do Itamaraty, Rio de Janeiro

ANA   Archivo Nacional de Asunción
  -CRB   Colección Rio Branco
  -SH   Sección Historia
  -SJC   Sección Judicial Criminal
  -SNE   Sección Nueva Encuadernación

APEMT   Arquivo Público do Estado do Mato Grosso Sul, Campo Grande, Brazil

BNA   Biblioteca Nacional, Asunción
  -CJO   Colección Juan O'Leary

BNRJ   Biblioteca Nacional, Rio de Janeiro

HAHR   *Hispanic American Historical Review*

IHGB   Instituto Histórico e Geográfico Brasileiro, Rio de Janeiro

JSG   Juan Silvano Godoi Collection, University of California, Riverside

MG      Manuel Gondra Collection, University of Texas, Austin

MHM     Museo Histórico Militar, Asunción
        -CGA    Colección Gill Aguinaga
        -CZ     Colección Zeballos

MHNM    Museo Histórico Nacional, Montevideo

MM-AI   Museo Mitre, Archivo Inédito, Buenos Aires

NARA    National Archives and Records Administration, Washington, D.C.

PRO     Public Records Office, London
        -FO     Foreign Office

SDGM    Serviço Documental Geral da Marinha, Rio de Janeiro

WNL     Washburn-Norlands Library, Livermore Falls, Maine

1. *Environment and Society*

1. Cited in Harris Gaylord Warren, *Paraguay: An Informal History* (Norman, 1949), p. 22.

2. Florencia Roulet, *La resistancia de los guaraní del Paraguay a la Conquista española (1537–1556)* (Posadas, 1993).

3. It was not until 1604 that the mestizo descendants of the early *conquistadores* gained legal access to government posts within Paraguay, though in practice they had exercised such authority for at least twenty years before this time. See Tomás de Garay to Viceroy, Asunción, 12 Oct. 1598, cited in Efraím Cardozo, *El Paraguay colonial: Las raíces de la nacionalidad* (Buenos Aires and Asunción, 1959), pp. 155–56. Regarding Martínez de Irala's career in Paraguay, see Rodrigo de Lafuente Machaín, *El gobernador Domingo Martínez de Irala* (Buenos Aires, 1939). As for the experiences of his children and descendants, see Alfredo J. Otarola, *Antecedentes históricos y genealógicos: El conquistador don Domingo Martínez de Irala* (Buenos Aires, 1967), pp. 120–31.

4. Ruben Bareiro Saguier has suggested the intriguing comparison between the Hispano-Guaraní people of Paraguay and the Métis of Canada. See his

"Le Paraguay, nation des Métis," *Revue de Psychologie des Peuples* (Caen) 4 (1963): 442–63.

5. James Schofield Saeger, *The Chaco Mission Frontier: The Guaycuruan Experience* (Tucson, 2000).

6. In 1679, for instance, a Portuguese expedition established a fort at Colonia de Sacramento on the left bank of the Río de la Plata. Taken completely by surprise by this incursion, the Spanish governor at Buenos Aires demanded Jesuit help, and the Fathers responded by sending a militia force of three thousand men. This Jesuit army smashed the Portuguese by storming the fort, killing two hundred defenders, and taking the survivors hostage. The Indians received not one *real* for their services to Spain and had to immediately march back to their missions, lest the Spanish denizens of the Lower Plata take fright at their presence. See Warren, *Paraguay*, pp. 97–98.

7. See, for example, Manuel García de Arce to Cristobal de Aguirre, Villarrica, 18 Dec. 1793, in the Archivo del Banco de la Provincia de Buenos Aires, 031-2-1, no. 24. It should be noted that tax payments were commonly made in coin by this time. See "Actas del Cabildo de Asunción," 22 Apr. 1793, ANA-Actas del Cabildo.

8. Thomas Whigham, *La yerba mate del Paraguay, 1780–1870* (Asunción, 1991).

9. See "Report of Gov. Fernando de Pinedo," Asunción, 14 July 1773, ANA-SH vol. 139, no. 1.

10. Thomas L. Whigham, *The Politics of River Trade: Tradition and Development in the Upper Plata, 1780–1870* (Albuquerque, 1991), pp. 112–13, 118.

2. *The Rise of Politics*

1. A broad definition of "nation" is employed throughout this study because the historical actors involved had mixed views on what they considered a "nation" to be. Though the origins and character of the nation-state have received attention from scholars for more than a century, ample disagreement still exists on basic terms. No one doubts that Icelanders constitute a "nation," but do Basques? And what of Alsatians, Kurds, Bosnians, and Navajos? Imprecision dominates the arguments of even the most sophisticated students of this question, and one is left convinced that the debate centers more on labels than realities.

The most widely read theoretical works on the topic include Ernest Renan, *Qu'est-ce que c'est une nation?* (Paris, 1882); Max Weber, "The Nation," from *Max Weber: Essays in Sociology* (London, 1948), pp. 171–79; Joseph Stalin, *Marxism and the National and Colonial Question* (London, 1936); Eugen Lemberg, *Geschichte des Nationalismus in Europa* (Stuttgart, 1950); Federico Chabod, *L'idea di Nazione* (Bari, 1962); John Alexander Armstrong, *Nations before Nationalism* (Chapel Hill, 1982); Benedict R. O'G. Anderson, *Imagined Communities: Reflections on the Origin and Spread of Nationalism* (London and New York, 1991); and Eric Hobsbawm, *Nations and Nationalism since 1780: Programme, Myth, Reality* (Cambridge, 1992). Works that deal with the subject in a Latin American context include Gerhard Masur, *Nationalism in Latin America* (New York, 1966); D. A. Brading, *Los orígenes del nacionalismo mexicano* (Mexico, 1980); François-Xavier Guerra and Mónica Quijada, eds., *Imaginar la nación* (Muenster and Hamburg, 1994); Diana Quattrocchi de Woisson, *Un nacionalisme de deracines: L'Argentine—pays malade de sa memoire* (Paris, 1992); Florencia Mallon, *Peasant and Nation: The Making of Post-Colonial Mexico and Peru* (Berkeley and Los Angeles, 1995); and Mark Thurner, *From Two Republics to One Divided: Contradictions of Postcolonial Nationmaking in Andean Peru* (Durham, 1997).

2. In describing this tendency as a long-term historical phenomenon among *porteños*, Nicolas Shumway draws attention to their peculiar use of the word *intransigente* as a positive value. Even in today's Argentina, the term connotes principle, morality, and an uncompromising defense of truth in the face of ongoing criticism. Many in Buenos Aires during the 1820s epitomized this spirit of self-righteousness, and it hurt them politically in the rest of the region. See Shumway, *The Invention of Argentina* (Berkeley, 1991), p. 40.

3. In 1808, for example, the parish priest at the little Paraguayan town of Guarambaré earned himself some trouble when he spread the ludicrous story that a son of Tupac Amaru had been crowned king of the Americas and was on his way to Paraguay. That some actually believed this tale was proof of the profound ignorance of outside affairs. See "Summary Trial of Father Juan Antonio Jara," Asunción, 26 February 1809, ANA-SJC vol. 404.

4. A sympathetic, if somewhat tragic, portrait of Velasco can be found in J. P. and W. P. Robertson, *Letters on Paraguay*, 3:342–49.

5. See anonymous, "Documentos relativos a las batallas de Paraguarí y Tacuarí [1811] en poder de la viuda de Antonio Tomás Yegros," ANA-SH 334, no. 16.

6. Cited in Isidoro de María, *Rasgos biográficos de hombres notables de la república oriental del Uruguay* (Montevideo, 1939), 1:64. See also John Street, *Artigas and the Emancipation of Uruguay* (Cambridge, 1959), passim.

7. "Treaty of 12 Oct. 1811," ANA-SH 214, no. 1.

8. "Agreement of Fulgencio Yegros, Pedro Juan Caballero, and José Gaspar de Francia," Asunción, 16 Nov. 1812, ANA-SH 216.

9. Benjamín Vargas Peña has noted that in the strictest sense the Guaraní language lacks a word for "liberty" and the term most commonly used in its place, *amojha eñó*, carries the idea of self-isolation as a positive value. Even today, the public veneration for "independence" suggests nothing about freedom, except in the sense of being left alone. See Vargas Peña, *Los orígenes de la diplomacia en el Paraguay* (Asunción, 1996), p. 52.

10. Francia touched on this question of political culture in a letter to his port commander at Pilar: "These convulsions [at Buenos Aires] are the consequence of exalting the passions of a people who even now vacillate as to their fortune and destiny. They have yet to come together, [and their deliberations] have no popular form. For this reason, I established here the great Congresses ... to permit the people to unite and [work] under one agreed-upon system. This has not happened in Buenos Aires, and it is for this reason that each faction that prevails has different ideas [from its predecessor, which caused a great] commotion. Today's faction will probably not be the last, for everything has gone this way since the beginning." See Francia to José Joaquín López, Asunción, 24 May 1815, ANA-SNE 3410.

11. Francia's not entirely disinterested gesture had an ironic quality: by unexpectedly offering aid to the champion of regional autonomy, the dictator seemed to give succor to the Oriental cause, an expression of support that would be offered again in different circumstances by another Paraguayan head of state. Regarding Artigas's relations with the Paraguayans and his thirty-year exile in the town of Curuguaty, see miscellaneous documentation in JSG, doc. 6, no. 1; and E. de Salterain y Herrera, *Artigas en el Paraguay (1820–1850)* (Montevideo, 1950).

12. In this context, it is useful to remember that European liberalism had originally been a bourgeois ideology chiefly concerned with eliminating the absolute authority of kings and the privileges of the aristocracy. In Brazil, however, liberalism was associated with the elites, who found in the new ideas a powerful weapon against the economic abuses of the mother country but who had little or no use for its radical social agenda. See Emilia Viotti da Costa, *The Brazilian Empire: Myths and Histories* (Chicago and London, 1985), pp. 6–9.

13. That the term "citizen" should receive precedence over "subject" connotes an atypical borrowing from the French Revolution. See Roderick J. Barman, *Brazil: The Forging of a Nation, 1798–1852* (Stanford, 1988), pp. 123–26.

14. Political trends in the Riograndense grasslands of the extreme south often mimicked Oriental patterns — and *caudillismo* was thus evident in Rio Grande if not elsewhere in Brazil. See John Charles Chasteen, *Heroes on Horseback* (Albuquerque, 1995), pp. 21–35, 43–59.

15. Imperial forces smashed another short-lived republican revolt in Pernambuco in 1824 at roughly the same time that local units suppressed millenarian movements just to the north. Neither republicanism nor the adoration of Saint Sebastian were finished, however, and minor outbreaks continued to occur over the next decades. See Barbosa Lima Sobrinho, "A Confederação do Equador do centenário ao sesquicentenário," *Revista do Instituto Histórico e Geográfico Brasileiro* 306 (Jan.–Mar. 1975): 33–112; and Hendrik Kraay, "As Terrifying as Unexpected: The Bahian Sabinada, 1837–38," HAHR 72:4 (Nov. 1992): 502–27.

## 3. War and Nation Building

1. Tulio Halperín Donghi, *The Contemporary History of Latin America* (Durham, 1993), p. 110.

2. Whigham, *Politics of River Trade*, pp. 107–96, passim.

3. The generation of 1837 included such important figures as Domingo Faustino Sarmiento, Bartolomé Mitre, and Juan Bautista Alberdi. Despite their differences in temperament and outlook, all were committed to seeing Argentina transformed from a geographic concept into a modern American nation. This "American" orientation explains why they were so attracted to the romantic European nationalists like Mazzini, Kossuth, and Guizot (who stressed the unique

character of their own national experiences) and to the example of the United States, which had seemingly carved out its own destiny irrespective of European antecedents. See Domingo Faustino Sarmiento, *Viajes por Europa, Africa, y Estados Unidos*, 3 vols. (Buenos Aires, 1922), vol. 3, passim. More generally, see David Viñas, *De Sarmiento a Dios: viajeros argentinos a USA* (Buenos Aires, 1998).

4. See José Murilo de Carvalho, "Political Elites and State-Building: The Case of Nineteenth-Century Brazil," in Daniel H. Levine, ed., *Constructing Culture and Power in Latin America* (Ann Arbor, 1993), pp. 403–28; Eul-Soo Pang and Ron L. Seckinger, "The Mandarins of Imperial Brazil, "*Comparative Studies in Society and History* 14:2 (1972): 215–44; Eul-Soo Pang, *In Pursuit of Honor and Power: Noblemen of the Southern Cross in Nineteenth-Century Brazil* (University AL, 1988); and Roderick and Jean Barman, "The Role of the Law School Graduate in the Political Elite of Imperial Brazil," *Journal of Interamerican Studies and World Affairs* 18 (Nov. 1976): 432–49.

5. Pedro's scholarly inclinations stayed with him his entire life. He became a great patron of the arts and sciences and an active correspondent with Victor Hugo and Alexander Graham Bell, among others. Pedro gave a great deal of his own time to the study of languages, including Tupí, Arabic, English, French, and Sanskrit, and he published passable translations of Renan, Longfellow, and the Hebrew-Provençal poets. And he never missed a meeting of the Brazilian Institute of History and Geography, a scholarly society that he founded that is still in existence today. See Roderick J. Barman, *Citizen Emperor: Pedro II and the Making of Brazil, 1825–91* (Stanford, 1999).

6. Viotti da Costa, *The Brazilian Empire*, p. 69.

7. Jeffrey D. Needell, "Party Formation and the Emergence of the Brazilian Monarchy: 1831–1857," presented at the Latin American Studies Association, Chicago, 25 Sept. 1998 (revised draft, Jan. 1999).

8. Today, Caxias is the patron of Brazil's armed forces, a figure of towering proportions. His name has become synonymous with the upright officer and citizen who never breaks the law—hence the popular term *caxias*, which refers to individuals who follow regulations without mistrust, doubt, and evasion.

9. The dictator jailed many opponents in the early 1820s but few afterward. Some languished in jail with heavy irons, but a few managed to arrange some variation of house arrest. Mariano Antonio Molas, for example, enjoyed suffi-

cient freedom in captivity to be able to write Paraguay's first modern history, *Descripción histórica de la antigua provincia*, which was eventually published by his sons in Buenos Aires in 1868, nearly thirty years after Francia's death. Other individuals had a much rougher time of it, however. See Ramón Gil Navarro, *Veinte años en un calabozo; o sea la desgraciada historia de veinte y tantos argentinos muertos o envejecidos en los calabozos del Paraguay* (Rosario, 1863).

10. This is not true of contemporary Paraguay, where the members of the Academia Nacional del Guaraní have proposed all sorts of words to cover such "foreign" notions as autobiography *(oguekovemombe'u)*, democracy *(porokua pavé reko)*, and telephone *(ñe'émbyryha)*. Very few of these terms have made their way into the popular consciousness, however, and most Paraguayans continue to call them by their Spanish equivalents. The same process has led over time to the development of a part-Spanish, part-Guarani patois called *jopará*, which is so common in today's Paraguay as to be essentially a third language. The best Spanish-Guaraní dictionary remains that of Antonio Guasch and Diego Ortíz, *Diccionario castellano-guaraní, guaraní-castellano*, 6th ed. (Asunción, 1986). For general thoughts on the many ambiguities of the language, see F. Ricardo Mello Vargas, *Enigmas de un idioma llamado Guaraní* (Buenos Aires, 1989).

11. The father's plan to eliminate Indian surnames clearly failed if we are to accept the evidence of the 1871 census in the largely Indian *pueblo* of Yaguarón. See "Censo general de la república del Paraguay según el decreto circular del Gobierno Provisorio de 29 de septiembre de 1870," Archivo del Ministerio de Defensa Nacional, Asunción.

12. Regarding the business ventures of the López women, see, for example, "Contract of Juana Carillo de López and Pedro B. Moreno," Asunción, 13 Jan. 1864, ANA-SNE 3266.

13. John Hoyt Williams, *The Rise and Fall of the Paraguayan Republic, 1800–1870* (Austin, 1979), p. 132.

14. Peter A. Schmitt, *Paraguay und Europa: die diplomatischen Beziehungen unter Carlos Antonio López und Francisco Solano López, 1841–1870* (Berlin, 1963).

15. Fichte and Hegel, for instance, both thought war the necessary dialect in the evolution of nation-states. As one deputy at the 1848 Frankfurt Assembly put it, "Mere existence does not entitle a people to political independence; only the

force to assert itself as a state among others." Cited in Michael Howard, *The Lessons of History* (New Haven, 1991), p. 39.

16. Esteban Echeverría, *Dogma socialista* (Montevideo, 1846; reprint, Buenos Aires, 1947), p. 119.

### 4. Paraguay Faces the Empire

1. Diego Abente correctly notes that the Paraguayan War was "not directly related to specific boundary disagreements," yet such a contention downplays the importance of a critical dynamic. That Paraguay should seek stable international relations was inherent in its geographical position. Finding only modest success in this quest, its government was bound to feel suspicious of any foreign initiatives (even when such initiatives concerned small matters); such suspicion, in turn, was all too easy to translate into violence. See Abente, "The War of the Triple Alliance: Three Explanatory Models," *Latin American Research Review* 22:2 (1987): 47–69.

2. Maria de Fátima Costa, *História de um país inexistente: O pantanal entre os séculos XVI e XVIII* (São Paulo, 1999).

3. A. J. R. Russell-Wood, "The Gold Cycle, c.1690–1750," in Leslie Bethell, ed., *Colonial Brazil* (Cambridge, 1987), p. 200.

4. G. Kratz, *El tratado hispano-portugués de límites de 1750 y sus consecuencias* (Rome, 1954); Jaime Cortesão, ed., *Do tratado de Madri a Conquista dos Sete Povos (1750–1802)* (Rio de Janeiro, 1969); Jerry W. Cooney, "The Last Bandeira: The Struggle for Paraguay's Eastern Marches, 1752–1777," paper read before the Conference on Latin American History, Seattle, 10 Jan. 1998; Cooney, "Dubious Loyalty: The Paraguayan Struggle for the Paraná Frontier, 1767–1777," *The Americas* 55:4 (Apr.1999): 561–78.

5. Gordon Ireland, *Boundaries, Possessions, and Conflicts in Latin America* (New York, 1971), pp. 117–19. The geography of the disputed zone in the south of Mato Grosso was poorly understood even at the end of the eighteenth century; most of the earliest maps to get the basic features right came out of the 1780s and are still to be found in Portugal. "Carta limotrofe do Paiz de Mato Grosso e Cuyaba ... levantado pellos Officiaes da Demarcação," 1780–82, Gabinete de Estudos Históricos de Fortificação e Obras Militares, Lisbon, 4591/1A-10A-53; anonymous, "El

derecho del Paraguay a las tierras en disputa con el Brasil," [1863?], MG 1984; Duarte da Ponte Ribeiro, "Questões de Limites do Brazil com a República do Paraguay," Rio de Janeiro, 6 June 1862, AHI lata 279, maço 5, p. 10.

6. John Hoyt Williams, "The Undrawn Line: Three Centuries of Strife on the Paraguayan-Mato Grosso Frontier," *Luso-Brazilian Review* 17:1 (1980): 17–40.

7. Some idea of the scope of this new cattle frontier and its effects on the contraband trade with Brazil can be garnered from Renée Ferrer de Arréllaga, *Un siglo de expansión colonizadora: Los orígenes de Concepción* (Asunción, 1985).

8. The chief Brazilian diplomat, Antonio Manoel Correia da Camara, at one point promised the Paraguayans that the emperor would indemnify them for the abuses of certain Brazilians who had encouraged Indian raids out of Mato Grosso. Correia da Camara to José Norberto Ortellado, Itapúa, 16 June 1825, ANA-CRB I-29, 26, 10, no. 7.

9. Francia to Ramírez, Asunción, 24 Mar. 1824, cited in Ron Seckinger, *The Brazilian Monarchy and the South American Republics, 1822–1831* (Baton Rouge, 1984), p. 99.

10. Thomas Whigham, "The Back-Door Approach: The Alto Uruguay and Paraguayan Trade, 1810–1852," *Revista de Historia de América* 109 (Jan.–June 1990): 45–67.

11. Chiara Vangelista, "Los Guaikurú, españoles y portugueses en una región de frontera: Mato Grosso, 1770–1830," *Boletín del Instituto de Historia Argentina y Americana Dr. Emilio Ravignani*, 8 (1993): 55–76; Nidia R. Areces, "Los Mbayá en la frontera norte paraguaya: guerra e intercambio en Concepción, 1773–1840," *Años 90* 9 (1998): 56–82.

12. Decree of Dr. Francia, Asunción, 2 Oct. 1823, ANA-SH 237, no.2.

13. Decree of López, Asunción, 22 May 1843, ANA-SH 256, no. 12.

14. Ferrer de Arréllaga, *Un siglo de expansión colonizadora*, p. 159.

15. Decree of López, Asunción, 16 Sept. 1848, ANA-SH 282, no. 18.

16. John Hoyt Williams, "Paraguayan Isolation under Dr. Francia: A Reevaluation," *HAHR* 52:4 (Oct. 1972): 112.

17. "Memorandum sobre o estado das nossas relações com o Paraguay," Duarte de Ponte Ribeiro, [Rio de Janeiro?], 31 May 1845, AHI lata 281, maço 1, p. 3. In 1846 the Brazilians conducted a hydrographic survey of sorts in the disputed area of Mato Grosso. The engineer who organized this effort, Maj. Henrique de

Beaurepaire Rohan, was permitted to travel through Paraguay thanks to the detente between the two countries. "Viagem de Cuyabá ao Rio de Janeiro pelo Paraguay, Corrientes, Rio Grande do Sul e Santa Catharina," *Revista Trimensal de História e Geographia*, segunda serie, tomo segundo, vol. 9 (1847).

18. "Act of Recognition of Paraguayan Independence by Brazil," [1844], AHI lata 240, maço 2. In the immediate aftermath of Brazilian recognition, some minor commerce ensued between Mato Grosso and Paraguay (mostly chocolate, coffee, saltpeter, and sarsiparilia), but this was ephemeral. "Entradas of Olimpo and Gabilán-cue," 1845, ANA-SH 267, no. 2.

19. U.S. naval captain Thomas Jefferson Page, who visited this sugarloaf mountain three years later, found it worthy of close inspection. At its base, it was surrounded by "closely matted and almost impenetrable masses of vegetation," but this grew thinner toward the top. At its summit, "a stunted and scattering growth offered no obstacle to a clear and uninterrupted view of the country." Page, *La Plata, the Argentine Confederation, and Paraguay* (New York, 1859), pp. 163–64.

20. Gen. Silveira de Mello, "O Incidente de Fêcho-dos-Morros em 1850: Um Capítulo da História do Forte de Coimbra," *A Defesa Nacional* (set. 1954): 77–85. See also Efraím Cardozo, *El imperio del Brasil y el Río de la Plata* (Buenos Aires, 1961), p. 45.

21. Cecilio Báez, *Resumen de la historia del Paraguay desde la época de la conquista hasta el año 1880* (Asunción, 1910), pp. 96–97; R. Antonio Ramos, *Juan Andrés Gelly* (Buenos Aires and Asunción, 1972), pp. 341–51.

22. *El Semanario* (Asunción), 17 Feb. 1855.

23. David Wood, "An Artificial Frontier: Brazilian Military Colonies in Southern Mato Grosso, 1850–1867," *Proceedings of the Pacific Coast Council on Latin American Studies* 3 (1974): 95–108.

24. Williams, "Undrawn Line," p. 31.

25. Francisco Pico to Juan María Gutiérrez, Montevideo, 10 Jan. 1855; and Tomás Guido to Gutiérrez, Asunción, 10 Feb. 1855, in Biblioteca del Congreso, *Archivo del doctor Juan María Gutiérrez: Epistolario*, 7 vols. (Buenos Aires, 1982–89), 3:146–50, 171–72.

26. "Treaty of Friendship, Navigation, and Commerce," Rio de Janeiro, 6 Apr. 1856, in *Archivo diplomático y consular del Paraguay* (Asunción, 1908), pp. 87–96.

27. Luis G. Benítez, *Cancilleres y otros defensores de la república* (Asunción, 1994), pp. 59–79.

28. Williams, *Rise and Fall of the Paraguayan Republic*, p.159. See also Tomás Guido to Juan María Gutiérrez, Asunción, 27 June 1856, in Biblioteca del Congreso, *Archivo del doctor Juan María Gutiérrez*, 4:203–5; and Foreign Minister Nicolás Vásquez to Amaro José de Santos Barboza, Asunción, 17 Nov. 1856, ANA-CRB I-29, 29, 20, no.18.

29. The dispute with the United States, which eventually involved the dispatch of an expeditionary force to the Paraguayan frontier, has been the object of considerable historical debate. Pablo Max Ynsfrán, *La expedición norteamericana contra el Paraguay, 1858–1859,* 2 vols. (Buenos Aires and Mexico City, 1954, 1958); Thomas O. Flickema, "The Settlement of the Paraguayan-American Controversy of 1859: A Reappraisal," *The Americas* 25 (July 1968); Robert D. Wood, S.M., *The Voyage of the Water Witch* (Culver City CA, 1985), pp. 83–87; Clare V. McKanna, "United States Relations with Paraguay, 1845–1860" (master's thesis, San Diego State College, 1968).

30. "Fluvial Convention between Brazil and Paraguay," Asunción, 12 Feb. 1858, ANA-SH 322, no. 16.

31. The opening of the Mato Grosso trade caught the attention of merchants in Paraguay and also Argentina. "Efectos de la libre navegación," *El Comercio* (Corrientes), 27 Nov. 1856.

32. Commercial Report of British Consul Henderson for the year 1857, Asunción, 25 Jan. 1858, PRO-FO 59/19.

33. "Special Protocol . . . to the Convention of 12 Feb. 1858," cited in Juan I. Livieres Argaña, *Con la rúbrica del mariscal*, 6 vols. (Asunción, 1970), 5:67–69.

34. Solano López to Colonel Resquín, commander of Concepción, Asunción, 4 Sept. 1862, ANA-SNE 2834.

35. Washburn to William Seward, Asunción, 24 Apr. 1862, NARA M128, no.1.

36. Fidel Maíz to M. L. Olleros, Arroyos y Esteros, 12 Sept. 1905, cited in M. L. Olleros, *Alberdi a la luz de sus escritos en cuanto se refiere al Paraguay* (Asunción, 1905), p. 341.

37. The emergency congress called on 16 October to decide the matter of succession met with a substantial unit of soldiers assembled as a guard of honor.

Few doubted the meaning of such a force, and after some ephemeral debate, Solano López was elected president with the same rights and privileges his father had enjoyed. The two men who questioned his right to the office on constitutional grounds found themselves consigned for a time to a local dungeon. See anonymous memoir, [1871?], MG 2034; and Fidel Maíz, *Etapas de mi vida* (Asunción, 1986), pp. 223–25.

5. *The Misiones and Chaco Disputes*

1. Pelham Horton Box, *The Origins of the Paraguayan War* (Urbana, 1930), p. 56.
2. Alfred Marbais DuGraty, *La República del Paraguay* (Besançon,1862), pp. 109–11.
3. Alejandro Audibert, *Los límites de la antigua provincia del Paraguay* (Buenos Aires, 1892), pp. 320–22.
4. Jaime Cortesão, *Tratado de Madri: Antecedentes, Colonia do Sacramento* (Rio de Janeiro, 1954), passim.
5. Box, *Origins of the Paraguayan War*, p. 58.
6. Belgrano's defeat was used by the Mitre government some fifty years later to drum up *porteño* resentment against Paraguay. Juan Bautista Alberdi, *Mitre al desnudo* (Buenos Aires, 1961), pp. 12–13, 65, passim.
7. Box, *Origins of the Paraguayan War*, p. 59.
8. The remaining Indian inhabitants of the Misiones attempted without much success to find some faction that could effectively protect them. *Colección de datos y documentos referentes a Misiones como parte integrante del territorio de la provincia de Corrientes*, 3 vols. (Corrientes, 1877), 1:188–202, 233–65; John Hoyt Williams, "The Deadly Selva: Paraguay's Northern Indian Frontier," *The Americas* 33:1 (July 1976): 13–24; Alfredo J. Erich Poenitz, "Las misiones orientales después de la administración de Chagas: el colapso de su sociedad, 1821–1828," *Encuentro de Geohistoria Regional* (Resistencia, 1996), pp. 411–25.
9. Norberto Ortellado to Francia, Itapúa, 16 Nov. 1822, ANA-SH 235, no. 12; Victor Martin de Moussy, *Description Geographique et Statistique de la Confédération Argentine*, 3 vols. (Paris, 1860–64), 3:693. Tranquera remained under Paraguayan military occupation until the 1860s. José Zacarías Mendez to Commandant of Concepción, Tranquera, 10 Aug. 1864, ANA-SNE 3069.

10. Whigham, "Back-Door Approach," pp. 45–67.

11. Philippe Foucault, *El pescador de orquídeas: Aimé Bonpland, 1773/1858* (Buenos Aires, 1994).

12. Francia to Commandant of Itapúa, Asunción, 22 Dec. 1831, ANA-SH 241; Francia to Commandant of Concepción, Asunción, 18 Aug. 1832, ANA-SNE 3412.

13. "Treaty of La Cruz," 28 May 1830, Archivo Histórico y Administrativo de Entre Ríos, Sección Gobierno, ser. 3, carpeta 1, 9, nos. 70–71.

14. Francia to Delegado of Pilar, Asunción, 11 Aug. 1832, ANA-SH 241.

15. The heavily wooded island of Apipé, which was strategically located just to the west of Tranquera de Loreto in the Alto Paraná, had been disputed since colonial times, when both Asunción and Corrientes claimed the right to issue licenses for logging there. The *Actas Capitulares* of Corrientes allude to many expeditions there in search of timber. AGPC-Actas Capitulares 23 (1760–69), 25 (1776–82), and 27 (1790–99); Alberto Rivera, "Contribuciones a la historia de la isla Apipé," *Revista de la Junta de Historia de Corrientes* 7 (1976): 79–104. With reference to the Curupayty dispute, see "Auto of Joaquín de Alós," Asunción, 20 Apr. 1789, ANA-CRB I-29, 35, 53; [José Falcón (?)], "Memoria documentada de los territorios que pertenecen a la República del Paraguay," Asunción, 29 Feb. 1872, MG 64; and Belisario Saraiva, *Memoria sobre los límites entre la república Argentina y el Paraguay* (Buenos Aires, 1867).

16. Marco Tulio Centeno, "San Juan de Hormiguero: Crónica de su orígen y desarrollo; Antecedentes de la refundación de Santo Tomé (Corrientes)," *Primer Encuentro de Geohistoria Regional: Exposiciones* (1980): 98–103; John Hoyt Williams, "La guerra no-declarada entre el Paraguay y Corrientes," *Estudios Paraguayos* 1:1 (Nov. 1973): 35–43.

17. In a letter to the governor of Santa Fe, Ferré stressed the pernicious effect of Paraguay's connection with São Borja "through which passes all news of our political affairs and through which Francia obtains all manner of arms and munitions.... [T]his can only mean that the Dictator thinks big, that he wishes to take advantage of our domestic quarrels." Ferré to Domingo Cullen, Corrientes, 1 Sept. 1832, in Pedro Ferré, *Memorias del Brigadier General* . . . , 2 vols. (Buenos Aires, 1921), 1:422–23.

18. Decree of Pedro Ferré, Corrientes, 9 Oct. 1832, in *Registro Oficial de la Provincia de Corrientes*, 8 vols. (Corrientes, 1929–31), 3:103–4.

19. Whigham, "Back-Door Approach," p. 58.
20. Francia to Delegado of Itapúa, Asunción, 7 Aug. 1834, ANA-SH 242.
21. *Jornal do Commercio* (Rio de Janeiro), 27 July 1841.
22. Joaquín de Madariaga to the Baron of Caxias, Corrientes, 1 Oct. 1844, AGPC-EA 1844, legajo 71. Similar raids were conducted against refugees living under Paraguayan protection. See Miguel Ferreira de Sampayo to José Gabriel Valle, Itapúa, 6 May 1842, ANA-SH 247.
23. Treaty of Boundaries, Asunción, 31 July 1841, ANA-SH 245.
24. Manuel Florencio Mantilla, *Crónica histórica de la provincia de Corrientes*, 2 vols. (Buenos Aires, 1928–29), 2:83–84.
25. The terms of the 1841 boundary treaty may account for the fact that European observers included maps that indicated this partition as though it were definitive. DuGraty, *La Republique du Paraguay*, enclosure; Benjamin Poucel, *Le Paraguay Moderne et l'interet général du commerce fondé sur les lois de la géographie et sur les enseignements de l'histoire de la statistique et d'une saine économie politique* (Marseilles, 1867).
26. This document is known only in its Rigrandense version, for no copy has yet come to light in Corrientes. See "Secret Convention of Friendship," Corrientes, 29 Jan. 1842, Arquivo Histórico do Rio Grande do Sul, Arquivo Alfredo Ferreira Rodrigues, Caixa 213, no. 17.
27. Instructions of Carlos Antonio López, 9 Dec. 1845, ANA-SH 272, no. 22 (and in JSG box 5, carpeta 7).
28. Cited in Mantilla, *Crónica histórica*, 2:140–44.
29. López to Wisner, Asunción, 23 Jan. 1849, ANA-SH 286.
30. Wisner to Hipólito Sonnleitheur, Hormiguero, 8 July 1849, ANA-SNE 1449. Military aspects of the 1849 invasion are summarized in *El Paraguayo Independiente* (Asunción), 13 Oct. 1849.
31. [Francisco Solano López?] to Col. Basilio Antonio Ojeda, Paso de la Patria, 15 Sept. 1849, ANA-SNE 2003.
32. The figure of eleven thousand animals is derived from a cattle census taken earlier in the year. See Report of Pedro Virasoro, Santo Tomé, 9 June 1849, AGPC-EA 1849, legajo 102. On the general destruction of the Uruguay River settlements by the Paraguayans, see Centeno, "San Juan de Hormiguero," pp. 159–62.

33. At the same time, the new Argentine government gave up its claims on the eastern missions as part of the price to help overthrow Rosas; small loss as these territories had already been incorporated into Brazil's Rio Grande do Sul Province. Hector B. Petrocelli, *Las misiones orientales: Parte del precio que pagó Urquiza para derrocar a Rosas* (Buenos Aires, 1995), pp. 117–25. See also Liliana Brezzo, *La Argentina y el Paraguay, 1852–1860* (Buenos Aires, 1997), pp. 68–69.

34. Martin Dobrizhoffer, *Historia de los Abipones*, 3 vols. (Resistencia, 1967–70), 1:221.

35. The correspondence concerning Soria's Bermejo expedition and the fate of the men that accompanied it can be found in ANA-CRB I-29, 34, 20, nos. 1–17; and I-29, 23, 27, nos. 1–19. Several of those taken captive by Francia left accounts of their time in Paraguay, most notably the Italian Nicòla Descalzi, whose manuscript diary can be found in AGN-BA VII-17-6-1, doc. 80. In J. Anthony King, *Twenty-Four Years in the Argentine Republic* (New York, 1846), pp. 243–47, one finds a parallel account by the Englishman Lucas Crecer.

36. "Treaty of Boundaries," Asunción, 15 July 1852, ANA-CRB I-30, 6, 34.

37. Box, *Origins of the Paraguayan War*, p. 63.

38. Charles Hotham to Earl of Malmesbury, Buenos Aires, 26 Aug. 1852, PRO-FO 59, 2, no. 23. Bolivian claims were only decided after a disastrous war with Paraguay in the 1930s.

39. Decree of López, Asunción, 14 May 1855, ANA-SH 317, no. 17.

40. Correspondence and other documentation concerning the operation and ultimate failure of the Nueva Burdeos colony can be found in ANA-SJC 1466, 1764, 1856; ANA-SH 299, no. 1, 324, no. 19; ANA-SNE 749, 2746; AGPC-CO 1856, legajo 151; and in "Simple historia de la ex-colonia francesa en el Paraguay," Museo Mitre, doc. 33-3-11. See also Henri Pitaud, *Les Français au Paraguay* (Bordeaux, Paris, 1955), pp. 57–66.

41. Ireland, *Boundaries, Possessions, and Conflicts*, p. 29.

42. Box, *Origins of the Paraguayan War*, pp. 65–66; Consul Henderson to Lord Clarendon, Asunción, 21 July, 8 Aug. 1856, PRO-FO 59, 14, nos. 17, 20.

43. See *El Semanario*, 28 Mar. 1857.

44. Vicente G. Quesada, *La provincia de Corrientes* (Buenos Aires, 1857), p. 94. For an official Brazilian view of the Paraguayan-Correntino rivalry in the Gran Chaco, see Duarte da Ponte Ribeiro, "Observações sobre a rivalidade dos Corren-

tinos com os Paraguayos . . . (Rio de Janeiro, 28 Jan. 1855)," AHI lata 271, maço 3, no. 2.

45. Box, *Origins of the Paraguayan War*, pp.66–67.

46. Consul Charles Henderson to Lord Malmesbury, Asunción, 12 Feb. 1859, PRO-FO 59, 20, no. 3.

47. Isidoro Resquín to Carlos Antonio López, Encarnación, 3 Mar. 1855; Ambrosio Dandrea, Italian merchant, to López, Encarnación, 1856; and Pedro Duarte to War Minister, Encarnación, 30 Sept. 1863, ANA-SH 380 (II). See also Berges to Candido Bareiro, Asunción, 21 Sept. 1864, ANA-CRB I-22, 11, 1, no. 430.

48. Solano López to Mitre, Asunción, 6 June 1863, in Bartolomé Mitre, *Archivo del general Mitre*, 28 vols. (Buenos Aires, 1911), 2:12–13.

49. Mitre to Solano López, Buenos Aires, 16 June 1863, in Mitre, *Archivo*, 2:14–16.

50. See Venancio López to Alejandro Hermosa, Asunción, 29 Dec. 1862, ANA-CRB I-30, 23, 175.

51. See, for example, Miguel González to Francisco Solano López, Tranquera de Loreto, 13 Mar. 1863, ANA-CRB I-30, 16, 7, no. 1.

52. Solano López to Félix Egusquiza, Asunción, 6 May 1864, cited in Arturo Rebaudi, *La declaración de guerra de la república del Paraguay a la república Argentina* (Buenos Aires, 1924), p. 221. Pellichi's own account of his work among the Chaco Indians has been reprinted in Pellichi et al., *Misioneros del Chaco occidental: Escritos de franciscanos del Chaco salteño, 1861–1914* (San Salvador de Jujuy, 1995), pp. 13–63.

53. José Berges to Egusquiza, Asunción, 21 May 1864, cited in Box, *Origins of the Paraguayan War*, p. 208.

### 6. *The Uruguayan Imbroglio*

1. Given Mitre's reputation as a scholarly figure, it might seem odd that his first published book was a technical manual on modern artillery, but the guide was up-to-date, thorough, and attractively written. It was as enthusiastically received as his later literary and historical works. See Mitre, *Instucción práctica de artillería* (Montevideo, 1844).

2. Uruguayan poet and publicist Juan Carlos Gómez remarked that those who study Flores "will find behind his every act of war some clear political move, the

price of an ambition that marches tenaciously toward its goal." *El Siglo* (Montevideo), 28 Dec. 1872. Biographies of Flores include Alfredo Lepro, *Años de forja: Venancio Flores* (Montevideo, 1962), and Washington Lockhart, *Venancio Flores, un caudillo trágico* (Montevideo, 1976).

3. Ricardo Levene, *A History of Argentina* (Chapel Hill, 1937), p. 437.

4. *El Paraguayo Independiente* (Asunción), 29 Nov. 1851.

5. The best study of this period remains James R. Scobie, *La lucha por la consolidación de la nacionalidad argentina, 1852–62* (Buenos Aires, 1979).

6. Article 67, inciso 16, of the Constitution of the Argentine Confederation (1 May 1853).

7. Richard Graham, "Mauá and Anglo-Brazilian Diplomacy, 1862–1863," *HAHR* 42:2 (May 1962): 199–211.

8. Box, *Origins of the Paraguayan War*, pp. 77–78.

9. Box, *Origins of the Paraguayan War*, p. 78.

10. Edward Thornton to Lord Clarendon, Montevideo, 16 Feb. 1858, cited in Box, *Origins of the Paraguayan War*, p. 79.

11. Yancey to President Buchanan, Buenos Aires, 22 Aug. 1859, NARA M69, no. 14. Yancey's account of these times can be found in his papers, which are in the Duke University Special Collections Library (MSS 63–152), and the Southern Historical Collection, Library of the University of North Carolina at Chapel Hill (MSS 59–195).

12. William H. Jeffrey, *Mitre and Argentina* (New York, 1952), pp. 127–40.

13. Solano López to Foreign Minister Baldomero García, Asunción, 6 Oct. 1859, cited in Livieres Argaña, *Con la rúbrica del Mariscal*, 6:15.

14. Cited in Arturo Bray, *Solano López* (Buenos Aires, 1945), p. 132.

15. Bray, *Solano López*, p. 136.

16. Haydee Gorostegui de Torres, *Argentina: La organización nacional* (Buenos Aires, 1972), pp. 40–60.

17. David Rock, *Argentina, 1516–1982* (Berkeley, 1987), p.123.

18. Urbano de la Vega, *El general Mitre (historia): Contribución al estudio de la organización nacional y la historia militar del país* (Buenos Aires, 1960), p. 89.

19. Urquiza to Mitre, Buenos Aires, 20 July 1860, in Mitre, *Archivo*, 7:117–18.

20. Mitre's account of the battle can be found in Mitre to Juan A. Gelly y Obes,

Carioga, 22 Sept. 1861, in Mitre, *Archivo*, 9:9–13, passim. Urquiza's report on the engagement to his War Minister (Diamante, 20 Sept. 1861) can be found in William Dusenberry, "Urquiza's Account of the Battle of Pavón," *Journal of Inter-American Studies and World Affairs* 4:2 (1962): 249–55.

21. Cited in Rodolfo Rivarola, *Ensayos históricos* (Buenos Aires, 1941), p. 391.

22. Cardozo, *El imperio del Brasil*, pp. 66–68.

23. Elizalde to Lapido, Buenos Aires, 12 Nov. 1862, cited in Cardozo, *El imperio del Brasil*, p. 85.

24. Lapido to Elizalde, 24 Nov. 1862, cited in Cardozo, *El imperio del Brasil*, p. 86.

25. Elizalde to Lapido, 25 Nov. 1862, cited in Cardozo, *El imperio del Brasil*, p. 86.

26. *La Tribuna* (Buenos Aires), 25 Apr. 1863, revealed the interventionist sentiment so common in the Argentine capital, noting that "Oriental and Argentine parties are identical in their goals and principles, such that the Colorado Party is the Liberal Party of Argentina, just as the Blanco Party is that [which here favors] tyranny."

27. Lamas was favorably impressed—if somewhat disturbed—with the Paraguayan's interpretation of Platine politics and carefully noted the younger López's allusions to Argentine expansionism: "Don't laugh, señor Lamas, the idea of reconstructing [the old viceroyalty] is in the soul of the Argentines; and, as a result, it isn't just Paraguay that needs to stand guard; your country, the Oriental Republic, needs to get along with my own in order to prepare for any eventualities." See Pedro S. Lamas, *Contribución histórica: Etapas de una gran política* (Sceaux, 1908), pp. 251–56.

28. Elizalde to Lamas, Buenos Aires, 13 May 1863, cited in Box, *Origins of the Paraguayan War*, p. 89.

29. Elizalde to Lamas, Buenos Aires, 16 May 1863, cited in Box, *Origins of the Paraguayan War*, pp. 89–90.

30. British Chargé William Doria to Lord Russell, Buenos Aires, 14 May 1863, PRO-FO 6/245.

31. Robert C. Kirk to William H. Seward, Buenos Aires, 10 Dec. 1864, NARA M14, no. 89.

32. Elizalde to Herrera, Buenos Aires, 8 June 1863, in *Documentos diplomáticos elativos a la detención del paquete argentino "Salto" en las aguas de la república ori-*

ental del Uruguay por el vapor de guerra nacional "Villa del Salto." (Montevideo, 1863), no. 3.

33. Herrera to Elizalde, Montevideo, 9 June 1863, in Box, *Origins of the Paraguayan War*, p. 93.

34. Cited in Box, *Origins of the Paraguayan War*, p. 94.

35. "Protocol of 29 June 1863," in *Documentos diplomáticos relativos a la detención del paquete argentino "Salto,"* no. 37.

36. Doria to Lord Russell, Buenos Aires, 28 July 1863 (dispatch no. 72), PRO-FO 6/245.

37. Protocol of 20 Oct. 1863, in Andrés Lamas, *Tentativas para la pacificación de la república Oriental del Uruguay, 1863–1865* (Buenos Aires, 1865), pp. 13–15.

38. Juansilvano Godoy, *Monografías históricas* (Buenos Aires, 1895), 1:157.

39. Decree of C. A. López, Asunción, 12 Mar. 1862, ANA-CRB I-30, 1, 71.

40. Aureliano G. Berro, *De 1860 a 1864: La diplomacia, La guerra, Las finanzas* (Montevideo, 1922), pp. 122–45.

41. "Despatch of Juan José de Herrera," Montevideo, 3 Mar. 1863, in Luis Alberto de Herrera, *La diplomacia oriental en el Paraguay* (Montevideo, 1990), pp. 338–39.

42. Herrera, *La diplomacia oriental* pp. 353–55.

43. Lapido to Herrera, Asunción, 20 July 1863, in Herrera, *La diplomacia oriental* pp. 389–91.

44. Efraím Cardozo, *Vísperas de la guerra del Paraguay* (Buenos Aires, 1954), pp. 105–15.

45. Lapido to Herrera, Asunción, 20 Aug. 1863, in Cardozo, *Vísperas de la guerra*, pp. 404–6. See also, "Proyecto de Tratado de amistad, comercio y navegación entre el Paraguay y el Uruguay, presentado por el enviado del gobierno uruguayo," Asunción, Aug. 1863, ANA-CRB I-30, 26, 59, no. 2.

46. Lapido to Herrera, Asunción, 27 Aug. 1863, in Herrera, *La diplomacia oriental*, pp. 406–8.

47. Berges to Elizalde, Asunción, 6 Sept. 1863, ANA-CRB I-30, 23, 33. See also *Correspondencias oficiales relativas a los sucesos de la república Oriental del Uruguay cambiadas entre los Exmos: Sres. Ministros de Relaciones Exteriores de la república del Paraguay y de la confederación Argentina* (Asunción, 1864), pp. 3–4. The U.S. minister to

Asunción, for instance, noted in early October that López expressed strong resentment of the conduct of the Argentine government "in permitting [Flores] to organize, arm, and depart for the avowed and known purpose of invading a friendly state. . . . There are so many French and English in the Banda Oriental, or Uruguay, that in case of any serious or long continued war President López fears foreign intervention and that the imperial philanthropist, Louis Napoleon, may attempt a similar part in the La Plata countries to what he has played in Mexico." Charles Ames Washburn to William Seward, Asunción, 6 Oct. 1863, NARA M128, no. 1.

    48. Warren, *Paraguay*, p. 211.

    49. Box, *Origins of the Paraguayan War*, p. 101.

    50. In fact, since mid-November 1863, Paraguayan agents had been repeating the rumor that Mitre was secretly forging an alliance with the Brazilians (a story that clearly had some validity). See Juan José Soto to Félix Egusquiza, Montevideo, 19 Nov. 1863, MG 2010ap; and Soto to Egusquiza, Montevideo, 3 Dec. 1863, MG 2010au.

    51. Spencer L. Leitman, "Cattle and *Caudillos* in Brazil's Southern Borderland, 1828 to 1850," *Ethnohistory* 20:2 (spring 1973): 189–98.

    52. Charles Ames Washburn, *History of Paraguay with Notes of Personal Observations and Reminiscences of Diplomacy under Difficulties* (New York and Boston, 1871), 1:504.

    53. "Testimony of Teófilo Ottoni, session of Imperial Parliament," Rio de Janeiro, 27 June 1865, in Camara dos Diputados, *Perfis Parlementares 12: Teófilo Ottoni* (Brasília, 1979), pp. 825–51, passim.

    54. Helio Lobo, *Antes da Guerra (A Missão Saraiva ou os Preliminares do Conflicto com o Paraguay)* (Rio de Janeiro, 1914), p. 32.

    55. See Carlos Miguel Delgado de Carvalho, *História Diplomática do Brasil* (São Paulo, 1959), pp. 81–82.

    56. Box, *Origins of the Paraguayan War*, p. 113.

    57. Box, *Origins of the Paraguayan War*, pp. 120–22.

    58. Lobo, *Antes da Guerra*, pp. 72–74.

    59. Anastacio de la Cruz Aguirre to Solano López, Montevideo, 14 Mar. 1864, ANA-CRB I-30, 5, 16, no. 1.

60. Cardozo, *El imperio del Brasil*, p. 171.

61. Mitre to Solano López, Buenos Aires, 16 May 1863, in Rebaudi, *La declaración de guerra*, pp. 132–33.

62. Berges to Elizalde, Asunción, 6 Jan. 1864, ANA-CRB I-30, 23, 40; Elizalde to Berges, Buenos Aires, 16 Jan. 1864, in Rebaudi, *La declaración de guerra*, p. 151; Berges to Elizalde, Asunción, 6 Feb. 1864, ANA-CRB I-30, 23, 42.

63. Thornton to Lord Russell, Buenos Aires, 24 Mar. 1864, PRO-FO 6/250, no. 24.

64. Berges to Lorenzo Torres, Asunción, 6 Mar. 1864, ANA-CRB I-22, 12, 1, no. 71.

65. *Correspondencia e documentos relativos at missão especial do Conselheiro José Antonio Saraiva a Rio da Prata em 1864* (Bahia, 1872).

66. *Documentos diplomáticos: Misión Saraiva* (Montevideo, 1864), pp. 14–27.

67. *Documentos diplomáticos: Misión Saraiva*, p. 28.

68. Box, *Origins of the Paraguayan War*, pp. 130–31.

69. Britain had suffered a rather poor relationship with Brazil ever since London pressured the latter country into curbing its slave trade. When the Brazilian government failed to apologize for past grievances (or to return cargo stolen from a British vessel), Her Majesty's Minister to Rio William Dougall Christie retaliated in 1862 by ordering a British warship to seize Brazilian merchant vessels in the vicinity of the imperial capital. The emperor promptly broke off relations with Britain. See Richard Graham, "Causes for the Abolition of Negro Slavery in Brazil: An Interpretive Essay," *HAHR* 46:2 (1966): 123–37.

70. Berges to Herrera, Asunción, 6 Feb. 1864, ANA-CRB I-30, 23, 48; Thornton to Lord Russell, Buenos Aires, 25 Apr. 1864 (dispatch no. 35), PRO-FO 6/250. At the end of the 1860s, Thornton went to the United States, where he earned the respect of his American counterparts. His adroit diplomacy helped resolve the dispute over the depredations wrought by the British-built Confederate raider *Alabama*.

71. Decree of Aguirre, Montevideo, 10 June 1864, cited in Lobo, *Antes da Guerra*, pp. 164–65.

72. Joaquim Nabuco, *La guerra del Paraguay* (Paris, 1901), pp. 46–47.

73. José María Rosa, *La Guerra del Paraguay y las Montoneras Agentinas* (Buenos Aires, 1974), pp. 147–51; León Pomer, *La guerra del Paraguay: ¡Gran negocio!* (Bue-

nos Aires, 1968), pp. 116–21; Atilio García Mellid, *Proceso a los falsificadores de la historia del Paraguay* (Buenos Aires, 1964), 1:492–94.

74. Lobo, *Antes da Guerra*, p. 175.

75. *Jornal do Commercio* (Rio de Janeiro), 20 Aug. 1864.

76. Berges to Juan José Brizuela, Asunción, 21 Apr. 1864, ANA-CRB I-22, 12, 1, no. 86.

77. Carreras's mission to Paraguay is described in an unpublished commentary written twenty-five years later by Joaquín Requena, a former confidential agent of President Aguirre. Requena commentary (Montevideo, Apr. 1889), in MHM-CZ carpeta 141, no. 16.

78. Berges to Vianna de Lima, Asunción, 30 Aug. 1864, ANA-CRB I-30, 24, 26. See also Gregorio Benites, *Anales diplomático y militar de la guerra del Paraguay*, 2 vols. (Asunción, 1906), 1:94–96.

79. George Thompson, *The War in Paraguay with a Historical Sketch of the Country and Its People and Notes upon the Military Engineering of the War* (London, 1869), pp. 20–21.

80. George Frederick Masterman, *Seven Eventful Years in Paraguay* (London, 1869), pp. 89–90.

81. Berges to Vázquez Sagastume, Asunción, 30 Aug. 1864, ANA-CRB I-22, 11, 1, no. 410.

82. The U.S. minister suggested to his colleagues that they compose a joint protest. Washburn to Seward, Asunción, Sept. 1864, NARA M128, no. 1. Antonio de las Carreras felt even more scandalized. Carreras, "Notes upon the Situation of the Oriental Republic from August 1864 to February 1865," WNL.

83. Urquiza's followers—among them journalist Evaristo Carriego, Spanish-born cleric Domingo Ereño, rancher Ricardo López Jordan, and writer José Hernández (author of the great Argentine epic *Martín Fierro*)—were more dependably pro-Blanco than Urquiza himself. The Entrerriano *caudillo* had just accepted a loan from the baron of Mauá that provided him with funds for his private business ventures. The baron, who had excellent relations with Mitre and especially Lamas, was interested in peace and willing to advance money to any party, including Urquiza, who could be persuaded to adopt a similar stance. *La Nación Argentina* (Buenos Aires), 27 Oct. 1863.

84. Wenceslao Robles to Solano López, Campamento Cerro León, 19 Oct. 1864, ANA-SNE 748.

85. A schedule for 1860 that lists the *Marqués de Olinda*'s stops can be found in *La Unión Argentina* (Corrientes), 5 Jan. 1860.

86. Thompson, *War in Paraguay*, p. 25.

87. Berges to Vianna de Lima, Asunción, 12 Nov. 1864, ANA-CRB I-22, 11, 1, no. 452.

88. Gustavo Barroso, *A Guerra de Lópes* (São Paulo, 1929), pp. 39–47.

### 7. Military Preparedness

1. Fernando Uricoechea, *The Patrimonial Foundations of the Brazilian Bureaucratic State* (Berkeley, 1980), passim. See also the extensive descriptions of the standing army in Paulo de Queiroz Duarte, *Os voluntários da patria na guerra do Paraguai* (São Paulo, 1982), 1:129–74.

2. Charles J. Kolinski, *Independence or Death! The Story of the Paraguayan War* (Gainesville FL, 1965), p. 51.

3. Augusto Tasso Fragoso, *História da Guerra entre a Tríplice Aliança e o Paraguay* (São Paulo, 1957), 2:44–45. José de Lima Figueiredo, in *Brasil Militar* (Rio de Janeiro, 1944), p. 59, simplifies this recounting by assigning the standing army a total of twenty-two battalions of eight hundred men each. It is noteworthy that the number of men under arms in the regular units had actually shrunk by one-tenth since 1861. See Francisco de Paula Azevedo Pondé, *Organização e Administração do Ministério da Guerra do Império* (Brasília, 1986), pp. 278–79.

4. The Real Academia Militar was founded in Rio de Janeiro in 1810 and underwent periodic changes, especially during the 1850s in response to a new law that required formal education for promotion. Though the law had little real effect except in engineering and artillery, it brought on a flurry of institutional adjustments. A "Curso de Infantaria e Cavalaria" was created in Pôrto Alegre in 1853. Two years later, civil and military engineering were separated from the then Imperial Academia Militar, with officer training ultimately going to Praia Vermelha (established 1857). In 1859 the capital also saw the founding of an Escola de Tiro in Campo Grande, a technical school for sergeants, cadets, and junior officers. See Jehovah Motta, *Formação do oficial do exercito: Curriculos e regimes na Academia Militar, 1810–1944* (Rio de Janeiro, 1976), passim.

5. Nineteenth-century caliber designations cause no end of bewilderment for the modern student of military history. Normally, caliber was based on bore diameters (land-to-land measurement), which had little to do with the length or weight of the projectile employed—unlike many of today's shells. In the case of Minié balls for small arms, the European product was often made of paper-patched soft lead, so that the unpatched bullet might be smaller than bore diameter. The diameter of the patched bullet was usually .005 inches less than the groove diameter to allow for black powder fouling. Thus, the granulation of powder would determine the bullet chosen. South Americans commonly used European rather than U.S. designations, but this was not always the case, thus adding to the general confusion. As for smoothbore flintlocks, still in general use during the 1860s, the term "gauge" was most often seen, this referring to the number of lead balls of a specific diameter in a pound. The higher the number of the gauge, the more balls required to weigh a pound, and thus the diameter of each was smaller. On this and other questions of caliber and range, see W. W. Greener, *The Gun and Its Development* (Fairfax VA, 1995).

6. See "Instrucções para a Acquisição de armamento na Europa," in Polidoro da Fonseca Quintanilha Jordão to Francisco Antonio Raposo, Rio de Janeiro, 6 Feb. 1863, in Mario Barretto, *El centauro de Ybycui* (Rio de Janeiro, 1930), pp. 175–77.

7. See Peter M. Beattie, "The House, the Street, and the Barracks: Reform and Honorable Masculine Social Space in Brazil, 1864–1945," HAHR 76:3 (1996): 439–73.

8. Kolinski, *Independence or Death*, p. 50; Hendrik Kraay, "Reconsidering Recruitment in Imperial Brazil," *The Americas* 55:1 (1998): 1–33.

9. Juerg Meister, "Die Flussoperationen der Triple-Allianz gegen Paraguay, 1864–1870," *Marine Rundschau* 10 (Oct. 1972): 600–601.

10. Juan Beverina, *La guerra del Paraguay (1865–1870): Resumen histórico* (Buenos Aires, 1973), pp. 99–101.

11. Beverina, *La guerra del Paraguay*, p. 101.

12. As in post-1865 Brazil, it was possible for men of means to hire substitutes (here called *personeros*) to fulfill their military obligations in exchange for pay. These substitutes were frequently poor immigrants with families to feed. See

*Memoria presentada por el ministro de Estado en el Departamento de Guerra y Marina al Congreso Nacional en 1866* (Buenos Aires, 1866), app. B, p. 6.

13. Augusto G. Rodríguez, *Reseña histórica del ejército argentino, 1862–1930* (Buenos Aires, 1964), p. 34. Francisco Seeber, who served as a lieutenant in the National Guard, tells how he stayed up all night pouring over the tactical manuals and how, the next morning, he met with his men on the training grounds outside Buenos Aires. There he ordered them to complete a series of drills only to be told that they had learned the same drills earlier. "No matter," he told his sergeant, "I want these things repeated until ... the movements can be executed with precision." Thus he hid his embarrassment that such rustic troops knew more than he. Seeber, *Cartas sobre la guera del Paraguay* (Buenos Aires, 1907), p. 28.

14. Forced conscription *(la leva)* was established in the provinces as early as the 1820s. See Ricardo Rodríguez Molas, *Historia social del gaucho* (Buenos Aires, 1968), pp. 278–81; and Richard W. Slatta, *Gauchos and the Vanishing Frontier* (Lincoln, 1983), pp. 126–36.

15. D. Fermín Eleta, "Guerra de la Triple Alianza con el Paraguay en 1865," in Armada Argentina, *Historia marítima argentina* (Buenos Aires, 1989), p. 393.

16. López Decree of 26 Aug. 1845, ANA-SH 272, no. 13.

17. C. A. López comment cited in Alfredo Mota Menezes, *Guerra do Paraguai: Como construímos o conflito* (São Paulo, 1998), p. 74.

18. Antonio da Rocha Almeida, *Vultos da pátria* (Rio de Janeiro, 1961), p. 183.

19. The rumor never quite went away that, like Louis Napoleon, Solano López was eager to make himself emperor, supposedly even designing a crown for the occasion. Yet no one has ever proven that he was serious about the matter. See Charles Ames Washburn to Elihu B. Washburne, Buenos Aires, 1 Jan. 1864, WNL.

20. Juan B. Otaño, "Nuestra vieja marina de guerra," *Revista Militar* 8:73 (1931): 4342–47.

21. Josefina Plá, "Whytehead: ser o no ser," *Estudios Paraguayos* 6:2 (1978): 9–19.

22. Plá, *The British in Paraguay, 1850–1870* (Richmond UK, 1976), pp. 21–27; John Hoyt Williams, "Foreign Técnicos and the Modernization of Paraguay, 1840–1870," *Journal of Inter-American Studies and World Affairs* 19:2 (1977): 233–57.

23. Thompson, *War in Paraguay*, p. 54.

24. In 1864 Solano López also tried to buy "all sorts of arms" from the United

States, though it is unclear if any shipments could have reached him before Appomattox; the American contact for these abortive purchases was George Woodman, brother of the business partner of Minister Washburn's own elder brother, Cadwallader. See Charles Ames Washburn to Elihu B. Washburne, Asunción, 3 June 1864, WNL.

25. An 1862 recruitment measure called for the enlistment of men from all the *villas* and *partidos* of the country. See Decree of Solano López, Asunción, 13 Nov. 1862, ANA-SNE 2326.

26. Cecilio Báez, "El uso del azote en el Paraguay durante la dictadura," *Revista del Instituto Paraguayo*, 9:58 (1907): 473–85.

27. Thompson, *War in Paraguay*, p. 57.

28. The barefooted status of Paraguay's soldiery were commented upon by all outside observers. Alison Owings, *Frauen: German Women Recall the Third Reich* (New Brunswick NJ, 1993), pp. 208–9, cites the reaction of German women at the approach of U.S. occupation troops in 1945, noting that even in large columns, their marching was quiet because their boots lacked the hobnails of their Wehrmacht counterparts. The barefoot troopers of Solano López, by contrast, were as quiet as ghosts even when passing in review.

29. Berges to Juan José Brizuela, Asunción, 22 Dec. 1864, ANA-CRB I-22, 12, 2, no. 1.

30. The 500 tons of gunpowder seems an unlikely figure, but an 1864 reckoning of munitions held at the much-smaller camps at Asunción, Concepción, Salvador, Villa Franca, Villa Oliva, and Bellavista del Apa noted total powder reserves of 12,166 *arrobas* (152 tons). See "General Holdings of Arms and Munitions," Asunción, 16 Feb. 1864, ANA-CRB I-30, 27, 49, no. 6.

31. Richard Burton, *Letters from the Battlefields of Paraguay* (London, 1870), p. 317.

32. Thompson, *War in Paraguay*, pp. 53–54.

33. Thompson, *War in Paraguay*, p. 52.

34. "Fuerza efectiva del ejército paraguayo," [Asunción, Jan. 1865?], ANA-SH 344, no. 22.

35. Burton, *Letters from the Battlefields*, p. 9.

36. "Fuerza efectiva de la segunda batallón de infantería," Asunción, 31 August 1864, ANA-SNE 955.

37. It should be noted in this context that each man required a minimum of two animals, for as Colonel Thompson noted, there "were at this time, in the whole of Paraguay, perhaps 100,000 horses, only half of which could gallop two or three miles. The Paraguayan horses were never good, and a terrible disease of the spine had latterly carried off the greater part of them, attacking generally the best animals." *War in Paraguay*, p. 53.

38. Williams, *Rise and Fall of the Paraguayan Republic*, p. 203.

39. Williams, *Rise and Fall of the Paraguayan Republic*, p. 205.

### 8. *The Mato Grosso Campaign*

1. In 1863, provincial authorities claimed a public force of 4,600 men in active service in Mato Grosso. This figure was clearly exaggerated, and in any case, by mid-1864, many regular troops had been withdrawn to support the Brazilian intervention in Uruguay. See Herculano Ferreira Penna, *Relatório Apresentado a Assembleia Legislativa Provincial de Matto Grosso* (Cuiabá, 1864), pp. 11–14. Another source, written much later, noted a total defensive force of only 871 men (though perhaps this refers to regulars). See Genserico de Vasconcellos, *A Guerra do Paraguay no Theatro de Matto-Grosso* (Rio de Janeiro, [1921?]), p. 19.

2. In October 1861 the district commander of Nioaque expressed an opinion echoed by many then and later: "What can we do with such useless soldiers? They spend more time complaining than they do in service." Cited in Wood, "An Artificial Frontier," p. 104. In all fairness, a posting to one of the military colonies involved arduous labor, and the imperial government did next to nothing to alleviate the sufferings of the colonist-soldiers. See Robert Wilton Wilcox, "Cattle Ranching on the Brazilian Frontier: Tradition and Innovation in Mato Grosso, 1870–1940" (Ph.D. diss., New York University, 1992), pp. 93–94.

3. A long letter written from Cuiabá on 30 Sept. 1864 made no mention at all of any Paraguayan threat, though its anonymous author made lengthy reference to Kayapó and Coroado (Bororó) Indian depredations, "horrible acts" that called for quick military action. *Jornal do Commercio* (Rio de Janeiro), supplement, 9 Nov. 1864. *Imprensa de Cuyabá* (Cuiabá), 27 Oct. 1864, did report in detail on Paraguayan meddling in the Uruguay crisis, but it offered no hint of a threat to Mato Grosso.

4. For examples of such reports, see Solano López to Resquín, Asunción, 4

Sept. 1862, ANA-SNE 2834; Elías Giménez to Senior Colonel of the Plaza of Asunción [Venancio López?], Estrella del Apa, 31 May 1864, ANA-SH 360, no. 3, and José Zacarías Mendoza to Commander of Concepción, Puesto of Eyúa [on the Aquidabán river], 15 Aug. 1864, ANA-SNE 3069.

5. Jorge Maia de Oliveira Guimarães, *A Invasão de Mato Grosso* (Rio de Janeiro, 1964), p. 54.

6. The real extent of Paraguayan knowledge of Brazilian preparedness was revealed later in a letter from Venancio López, the war minister, to his brother-in-law, Col. Vicente Barrios, Asunción, 20 Dec. 1864, ANA-CRB I-30, 21, 96–101, no. 6.

7. See "Instructions to Col. Francisco Resquín, commander of the column [marching on] Miranda and the Mbotety River," Asunción, 13 Dec. 1864, ANA-CRB I-29, 25, 25; "Instructions to Capt. [brevet Maj.] Martín Urbieta, commander of the expedition against Dourados and [the posts on] the Brilhante River," Asunción, 13 Dec. 1864, ANA-CRB I-29, 25, 26; and "Instructions to Col. Vicente Barrios, commander of the division in operations on the Alto Paraguay River," Asunción, 13 Dec. 1864, ANA-CRB I-29, 25, 27.

8. There is some disagreement as to the number of Paraguayan troops in the riverborne force; Col. George Thompson, who was an eyewitness, noted three thousand men and two field-batteries. *War in Paraguay*, p. 32. Jorge Maia de Oliveira Guimarães, a Brazilian national guardsman during the war, emphatically maintained that the force numbered over five thousand. *Invasão de Mato Grosso*, p. 67.

9. Washburn, *History of Paraguay*, 2:393.

10. His friend Juan Crisóstomo Centurión recalled a private conversation with Herreros in 1863 during which the naval lieutenant called Madame Lynch "that grand whore" and warned that Paraguay had become suffocatingly militarized under Solano López. Had he made these remarks later in the war, it could easily have resulted in his execution despite his good family connections. Juan Crisóstomo Centurión, *Memorias o reminiscencias históricas sobre la guerra del Paraguay*, 4 vols. (Asunción, 1987), 4:153–55.

11. Proclamation of Solano López, Asunción, 15 Dec. 1864, ANA-SH 339, no. 32.

12. Regarding the consumption of *tereré* on board ship, see George Francis Morice to Francisco Solano López, aboard the steamer *Río Blanco*, 21 July 1856, ANA I-29, 30, 37, no. 8.

13. One author reports as fact the rumor that an additional two cavalry regiments of five hundred men each went overland across the Apa at this point to aid Barrios's river force. If true, almost certainly these units failed to make the rendezvous at Coimbra because of the intervening floods and either returned to Concepción or joined Resquín's mounted forces farther east. See Maia de Oliveira Guimarães, *Invasão de Mato Grosso*, p.59.

14. Loren Scott Patterson, "The War of the Triple Alliance: Paraguayan Offensive Phase—A Military History" (Ph.D. diss., Georgetown University, 1975), pp. 61–67.

15. *El Semanario*, 7 Jan. 1865. Although the Paraguayan state newspaper corrected Portocarreiro's error, in fact, he addressed his return note not to Vicente Barrios but to Vicente "Dappy." Whether this mistake was the result of Barrios's poor penmanship or of Portocarreiro's nervousness is unclear, but the Brazilian stubbornly continued in his reports to refer to "Dappy" for some time to come.

16. Thompson, *War in Paraguay*, pp. 34–35. See also the *Imprensa de Cuyabá*, 12 Jan. 1865.

17. Louis Schneider, *A Guerra da Triplice Aliança contra o governo da República do Paraguai*, 2 vols. (São Paulo, 1945), 1:175–84. In an unusually generous move, Solano López later assigned monthly pensions to the families of two sublieutenants who died valiantly in the assault on the fort. See "Decreto of Solano López," Asunción, 6 Jan. 1865, ANA-CRB I-30, 3, 17.

18. A precise accounting of the armaments taken at Coimbra can be found in Centurión, *Memorias*, 1:52–54. Considerable private property was also abandoned at Coimbra by the Brazilians, including "the most costly set of surgical instruments" the British pharmacist George Frederick Masterman had ever seen. *Seven Eventful Years in Paraguay*, pp.92–93.

19. Thompson, *War in Paraguay*, p. 35. Portocarreiro was ultimately absolved, it seems, by a military tribunal in Rio de Janeiro. (Rather than admit to a gross lack of preparation for which they themselves might ultimately have to take responsibility, the generals preferred to forget the whole matter.) Another veteran of the war, who later became a major figure in the Brazilian abolitionist movement, claimed that Portocarreiro, in fact, had never been arrested, despite Thompson's recollections to the contrary. See Antonio de Sena Madureira, *Guerra do Paraguai: Reposta ao Sr. Jorge Thompson, autor da "Guerra del Paraguay" e aos anotadores argentino D. Lewis e A. Estrada* (Brasília, 1982), p. 11.

20. Masterman claimed that Barrios and his men were so drunk when the battle began that they issued no intelligible orders, virtually ensuring an unorganized assault. The Briton was absent from the Mato Grosso campaign and other sources fail to corroborate his story, but it might have happened. *Seven Eventful Years in Paraguay*, p.93.

21. Within weeks of the fall of Corumbá, officials in the Matogrossense capital convinced themselves that the Bolivians had already joined with Solano López (and would soon send him material aid over this route from Mojos). See Alexandre Manoel Albino de Carvalho to President of the Province of Goiás, Cuiabá, 16 Feb. 1865, APEMT livro 209, no. 11.

22. There seems to be no direct evidence to suggest that Solano López wanted to forge an anti-Brazilian alliance with Bolivia. Even so, such an agreement made sense geopolitically, and as the Paraguayans were usually forced by their geographical circumstance to think in such terms, it is likely that the president gave some passing attention to a Bolivian connection at this time. See C. E. Akers, *A History of South America, 1854–1904* (London, 1912), p. 136.

23. Thompson, *War in Paraguay*, p. 36. Another British contemporary claimed that Barrios was as interested in money as he was in sex and military information: "Some of the rich *estancieros*, who did not yield as much money as Barrios expected, were tied naked on the brass guns and left in the sun for hours; others were shot or flogged for the same reason." Masterman, *Seven Eventful Years in Paraguay*, pp. 93–94.

24. For an eyewitness account of these events, see Laroza, "comerciante estrangero establecido en Corumbá, escribe sus acontecimientos ocurridole durante la guerra," [1866?], ANA-SH 341, no. 13. For similar testimonies and reports, see *Imprensa de Cuyabá* (Cuiabá), 5 Mar., 6 Apr. 1865.

25. Thompson, *War in Paraguay*, p. 36, mistakenly claimed that Baker acted as commander of the *Anhambaí*. José Israel Alves Guimarães was the captain, but since he was killed early in the engagement, it is probable that Baker assumed his role. It was Baker, in any case, who mounted the *Anhambaí*'s only meaningful resistance.

26. According to Brazilian sources, the stern gun became dismounted during the course of the engagement and was thus inoperable; this gave the crew no choice but to abandon the fight. See Tasso Fragoso, *História da Guerra entre a Tríplice Aliança*, 1:269.

27. Thompson, *War in Paraguay*, p. 36; Pedro V. Gill, who commanded one of the Paraguayan steamers that had fought at Coimbra, confirmed Thompson's account some twenty-three years later, noting that when Herreros captured the *Anhambay*, his men threw the remaining crewmembers off the side to drown. They then chased down and knifed those who had managed somehow to get ashore. See "Testimony of Pedro V. Gill," Asunción, 24 Apr. 1888, MHM-CZ carpeta 137, no. 10.

28. Thompson, *War in Paraguay*, p. 36.

29. Thomas Joseph Hutchinson, the British consul at Callao in the late 1860s, explained the origin of the atrocity stories:

> In the month of January, 1865, a small steamer, called the *Ranger*, was sent up by the Brazilian authorities in Buenos Ayres, to communicate with, as well as bring supplies and correspondence to, their forts at Cuyaba, Coramba [sic], and other ports of Brazil, in the upper waters of the river Paraguay. This steamer was commanded by a North American gentleman of my acquaintance, Captain Harrison. On board of it, besides the master and crew, were, only as passengers, Captain Parish, R.N., brother of my colleague at Buenos Ayres, . . . and a Brazilian purser, charged with some commission from his government. As soon as they had entered the limits of Paraguayan territory at Tres Bocas, . . . the purser got into a shivery-shakery condition,—now and then looking with timid glances over the ship's side toward the Paraguayan shore, and locking himself up in his cabin whenever the anchor was let down at a Paraguayan port. The steamer stopped five days at Coramba,—the highest port reached,—during which the purser never went on shore. . . . Yet, although he did not budge out of the steamer while she was up in the river Paraguay, he had no sooner returned to Buenos Ayres than he wrote a letter to the newspapers [here Hutchinson refers to *La Tribuna* (Buenos Aires), 22 Jan. 1865], stating that he had seen in the streets of Coramba (wherein, I need scarcely repeat, he had not put his foot) Paraguayan soldiers walking about the town, wearing necklaces made of the ears of Brazilians. . . . This atrocious calumny was at once contradicted by Captain Parish and Captain Harrison, as regarded the fact of the purser not having gone on shore, and therefore not having the opportunity of seeing such a thing if it existed. Whereas Messrs. Parish and Harrison, although both in the town every day, saw nothing of the kind.

*A Short Account of Some Incidents of the Paraguayan War, a Paper Read before the Liverpool Literary and Philosophical Society,* 1871, pp. 21-22.

30. Chief of Police José de Matos to Pres. Alexandre Manoel Albino de Carvalho, Cuiabá, 11 Mar. 1865, APEMT Caixa 1865 G.

31. Decree of López, Asunción, 20 Jan. 1865, in *El Semanario* (Asunción), 21 Jan. 1865.

32. Colonel Thompson noted that "the country was very much flooded by the river at the time of the invasion, and the Paraguayans had to ride and march through water, sometimes for days together. On this account they pushed no further north than to about the same latitude with Barrios." *War in Paraguay,* p. 38.

33. Martín Urbieta to War Minister, Colonia of Dourados, 30 Dec. 1864, cited in *El Semanario,* 7 Jan. 1865.

34. While giving Antonio João's bravery its due, it must also be admitted that his image has subsequently grown far out of proportion to his role at the time of the war. One Brazilian military historian described him as "the maximum expression of nationality, . . . the living example of the greatness of Brazil [as expressed] in its generosity, its ideals of justice, of beauty, and of heroism." Vasconcellos, *A Guerra do Paraguay no Theatro de Matto-Grosso,* p. 33. The hagiographical aspects of this portrayal have sometimes outweighed common sense. See, for example, Raul Silveira de Mello, *A Epopéia de Antonio João* (Rio de Janeiro, 1969), which at 554 pages may be the longest account ever written of a two-minute battle.

35. See Francisco Isidoro Resquín, *Datos históricos de la guerra del Paraguay con la Triple Alianza* (Asunción, 1971), pp. 14-15 (MS copy, 1875, ANA-SH 356, no. 21).

36. The Indians sacked more than half of the town's eighty-four houses. See Francisco Resquín to War Minister, Village of Miranda, 14 Jan. 1865, cited in *Boletín [del Ejército],* no. 5 (28 Jan. 1865), in MHM-CGA carpeta 21, no. 12.

37. *Imprensa de Cuyabá,* 18 May 1865.

38. A month later the provincial governor of Goiás dispatched a force of cavalry to free Coxim from the forces of "that new Attila." Little did the governor realize that the Paraguayans had already left. See "Carta particular," Goyaz, 26 May 1865, published in the *Jornal do Commercio,* 1 July 1865.

39. Thompson, *War in Paraguay,* p. 39.

40. "Razón numérica de los cañones de bronce y municiones traídos del fuerte de Coimbra por el vapor *Salto Guayrá,* Cuartel del Primer Batallon," 5 Jan.

1865, ANA-SH 343 no. 18. For similar documentation, see "List of arms taken at Fort Coimbra to be taken aboard the steamers *Salto Guayrá* and *Independencia*," Coimbra, 31 Dec. 1864, 1 Jan. 1865, ANA-CRB I-30, 21, 81–85.

41. Cited in Thompson, *War in Paraguay*, p. 39. Sena Madureira again accuses Thompson of exaggerating the numbers, claiming that even in an equestrian-oriented province like Rio Grande do Sul, no one would find 1,090 lances in storage in 1865. *Guerra do Paraguai*, p. 12. The fact remains, however, that Thompson drew his statistics from an official source, the Paraguayan *Boletín [del Ejército]*, no. 5 (28 Jan. 1865), which presumably reported the same information that was received at Asunción.

42. Alfredo d'Escragnolle Taunay, *Memórias do Visconde de Taunay* (São Paulo, 1960), p. 188. There is no doubting the importance that the Paraguayans placed in the capture of these arms. See José Berges to Juan José Brizuela, Asunción, 14 Jan. 1865, ANA-CRB I-22, 12, 2, no. 26.

43. For example, see "List of [confiscated] goods to be transported to Paraguay, Guardpost of Nioaque," 27 Jan. 1865, ANA-SNE 775. With respect to the cattle taken, a surprising number evidently stayed in ranches under Paraguayan control in the south of the province and were not, in fact, driven farther south into Paraguay. See Wilcox, "Cattle Ranching on the Brazilian Frontier," pp. 105–9.

44. Thompson, *War in Paraguay*, p. 38.

45. Thompson, *War in Paraguay*, p. 38. See also "Lista de los individuos ex-brasileros que han pasado a la Villa de Concepción," Guardpost of the Ex-Colony of Miranda, 15 Mar. 1865, ANA-SH 345, no. 4 [lists 137 individuals including *criados*]; and "Lista nominal de los individuos brasileros traídos de la ex-colonia de Dorados," Casalcué, 24 Mar. 1865, ANA-SNE 3063.

46. Masterman, *Seven Eventful Years in Paraguay*, p. 94. Not all prisoners expressed terror at the arrival of the Paraguayans. Escaped slaves welcomed them, some even offering their services as guides. See Martín Urbieta to Francisco Solano López, Santa Gertrudis, 5 Jan. 1865, ANA-CRB I-30, 11, 74. The majority of the Brazilian prisoners in Mato Grosso, however, cringed at the thought of Paraguayan captivity and did everything they could to escape. One group of four managed to flee toward Cuiabá in February 1865 only to be retaken and sent to the public works. "Court-martial of Benedicto Martines et al.," Corumbá, 20 Feb. 1865, ANA-SJC 1860, no. 7.

9. *Neutrality Tested*

1. Lobo, *Antes da Guerra*, p. 34 (refers to session of 4 August 1866). Zacharías's remarks on this point were disingenuous. He knew perfectly well that a great many observers had foreseen Paraguay's aggressive intentions. See, for example, Charles Ames Washburn to Elihu B. Washburne, Asunción, 6 Feb. 1864, WNL. Now that the dogs of war had indeed been unleashed, the sharp-tongued U.S. minister to Asunción continued to make accurate—if unpropitious—predictions. To his fiancée he wrote: "We are not disposed down this way to let you have all the war and fighting in North America. On the contrary, Paraguay is going to war with Brazil and I suppose the river will be blockaded in the course of two or three weeks by a Brazilian fleet and your Charlie may be unable to send any more letters." Washburn to Sallie Cleaveland, Asunción, 13 Nov. 1864, WNL.

2. Imperial Decree, Palace of Rio de Janeiro, 7 Jan. 1865, in *Jornal do Commercio* (Rio de Janeiro), 9 Jan. 1865.

3. J. J. Chiavenato, *Os Voluntários da Patria e outros mitos* (São Paulo, 1983), pp. 25–36.

4. See Dr. Abilio Cesar Borges to President of Bahia, Bahia, 18 Feb. 1865, Arquivo Público do Estado da Bahia, Seção do Arquivo Colonial e Provincial, maço 3669 (as collected by Hendrik Kraay).

5. See Antonio Firmino de Saa Guimarães to Provincial President, Bahia, 13 Feb. 1865, Arquivo Público do Estado da Bahia, Seção do Arquivo Colonial e Provincial, maço 3675. There were many other examples of a similar nature from every corner of the empire.

6. See José Berges to Juan José Brizuela, Asunción, 22 Dec. 1864, ANA-CRB I-22, 12, 2, no. 1.

7. Octavio Lapido to Herrera, Asunción, 27 Aug. 1863, in Herrera, *La diplomacia oriental*, 2:406–8.

8. See F. J. McLynn, "General Urquiza and the Politics of Argentina" (Ph.D. diss., University of London, 1976), p. 163.

9. McLynn, "General Urquiza and the Politics of Argentina," p. 163. See also *El Nacional* (Buenos Aires), 23 Oct. 1864.

10. Urquiza to Atanasio Aguirre, Concepción del Uruguay, 17 Sept. 1864, in Mitre, *Archivo*, 2:80–81.

11. Mitre to Urquiza, Buenos Aires, 3 Nov. 1864, in Mitre, *Archivo*, 2:83.

12. Reprinted in *La Nación Argentina*, 8 Nov. 1864.

13. Urquiza to Mitre, Concepción del Uruguay, 9 Nov. 1864, in Mitre, *Archivo*, 2:84–85; see also Mitre-Urquiza Letters, MHM-CZ carpeta 150, no. 1.

14. Berges to López, Asunción, 10 Nov. 1864, ANA-CRB I-30, 13, 46. Several members of the Caminos family, all highly regarded members of the Paraguayan elite, acted as agents for the López government in its dealings with Urquiza. See Ramón Cárcano, *La guerra del Paraguay: Acción y reacción de la triple alianza*, 2 vols. (Buenos Aires, 1941), 1:123–24.

15. Cardozo, *El Imperio del Brasil*, p. 474.

16. W. G. Lettsom to Earl Russell, Montevideo, 14 Dec. 1864, in "Correspondence Respecting Hostilities in the River Plate, 1864–1868," *British and Foreign State Papers* (London, 1882), 66:1215. See also Robustiano Lavraña to Aniceto Lescano, Punta del Chañas, 11 Dec. 1864, ANA-CRB I-30, 23, 187. Pro-Mitre politicians throughout the Litoral celebrated the fall of Salto, though they were careful to disguise their jubilation. In Corrientes, for instance, the provincial governor held a fiesta to officially honor the close of the legislative session, but most observers read the event as an open celebration of Flores's victory. See Miguel G. Rojas to [Berges?], Corrientes, 16 Dec. 1864, ANA-CRB I-30, 5, 19, no. 2.

17. Rafael A. Pons and Demetrio Erausquin, *La defensa de Paysandú* (Montevideo, 1887), p. 341; *Nueva Numancia: Datos y documentos históricos sobre la defensa y toma de Paysandú* (Concordia, 1865), pp. xxv–xxxiii.

18. Juan L. Cuestas, *Páginas sueltas* (Montevideo, 1897), 3:367–69.

19. Pons and Erausquin, *La defensa de Paysandú*, pp. 342–46.

20. Gómez had already resigned himself and his men to eventual immolation "in favor of the holy cause." See Gómez to Domingo Ereño, Paysandú, 9 Dec. 1864, MHNM tomo 3254.

21. *Jornal do Commercio*, 4 Jan. 1865. On another occasion, Gómez beheaded fifteen Brazilian prisoners and hung their still-dripping heads above his trenches in full view of their compatriots. See José Maria de Silva Paranhos, *A Convenção de 20 de Fevereiro demostrada a Luz dos Debates do Senado e dos Successos de Uruguayana* (Rio de Janeiro, 1865), p. 45.

22. Field Marshal João Propicio Menna Barreto to War Minister Henrique de Beaurepaire Rohan, Arroyo Negro, 7 Jan. 1865, in *Jornal do Commercio*, 7 Feb.

1865. According to a later discourse by Paranhos, some of the shells fired into Paysandú had been obtained the week before in Buenos Aires. *Jornal do Commercio,* 9 June 1865. Mitre denied that such a sale or transfer could have taken place given his country's official policy of neutrality. See Elías S. Giménez Vega, *Actores y testigos de la Triple Alianza* (Buenos Aires, 1961), pp. 29–30.

23. Orlando Ribero, *Recuerdos de Paysandú* (Montevideo, 1901), pp. 92–96; Augusto I. Schulkin, *Historia de Paysandú: Diccionario biográfico* (Buenos Aires, 1958), 2:77–90; and especially, Ernesto de las Carreras to Antonio Díaz, Buenos Aires, 16 Sept. 1878, in Antonio Díaz, *Historia política y militar de las repúblicas del Plata* (Montevideo, 1878), 11:129–33.

24. Ribero, *Recuerdos de Paysandú,* pp. 85–87. Some Brazilian sources adamantly insist that Gen. Mena Barreto tried to protect Gómez. See, for instance, Lemos Britto, *Solano Lopez e a Guerra do Paraguay* (Rio de Janeiro, 1927), pp. 59–63. In either case, Suárez's actions were not really unexpected, as several members of his immediate family had fallen victim to Gómez's wrath against the Colorados. See Silva Paranhos comments in Schneider, *Guerra da Triplice Aliança,* 1:95.

25. Gómez's execution remains controversial in Uruguay. The tale of his wishing to be turned over to the Colorados is probably a fabrication. The one source for the story is Ribero, *Recuerdos de Paysandú,* and he recorded the testimony of his brother Atanasio, a civilian participant who was taken prisoner along with Gómez and his general staff officers. Atanasio was the only man that "Goyo" Suárez spared, and coincidentally, the house where Gómez and the others were shot belonged to the Ribero family. Because of this, virtually all Blanco historians — and at least one important Colorado historian — have dismissed his account out of hand. See Eduardo Acevedo, *Anales históricos del Uruguay* (Montevideo, 1933), 3:283–85.

26. Thompson, *War in Paraguay,* p. 31. Spanish naval officers at Paysandú shared this sense of outrage and responded to the execution of Gómez and others by giving asylum to those Blancos who managed to reach the safety of their frigate, the *Wad-Ras.* Antonio de las Carreras to Martín de Hernández, Montevideo, 18 Jan. 1865, in *Nueva Numancia,* pp. 55–58. The Spaniards repeated this gesture after Montevideo's fall, transporting some three hundred Blanco refugees (including ex-President Aguirre) to Entre Ríos. See Miguel Angel de Marco,

"La estación naval española y los sucesos de Paysandú (1864–1865)," *Res Gesta* 6 (1979): 17–25.

27. The Chilean foreign minister expressed deep concern about events, though as late as February 1865 he was still urging a peaceful solution "in consonance with [traditional] American friendship." Alvaro Covarrubias to Berges, Santiago de Chile, 23 Feb. 1865, ANA-CRB I-29, 29, 11, no. 16. By May, Chilean sympathies, official and otherwise, had moved distinctly in favor of Paraguay, whose government was lauded for its strong stand against an encroaching Brazilian Empire. See *El Mercurio* (Valparaiso), 12 May 1865. A pro-Paraguayan sentiment was discernible in Peru and Bolivia throughout this same period.

28. See Berges to Alfred M. DuGraty, Asunción, 23 Dec. 1864, ANA-CRB I-22, 11, no. 476.

29. Urquiza to Mitre, San José, 29 Dec. 1864, in Mitre, *Archivo*, 2: 7–90. The Entrerriano governor was still making this argument more than a month later. See Urquiza to Mitre, San José, 8 Feb. 1865, MM-AI no. 208.

30. Mitre to Urquiza, Buenos Aires, 9 Jan. 1865, MM-AI no. 204.

31. Centurión, *Memorias*, 1:298. The Brazilians, who were vaguely aware that a Paraguayan force had entered the Misiones, believed the contingent was far larger than it actually was, some said as many as one hundred thousand men. See *Jornal do Commercio*, 21 Jan. 1865.

32. See Pedro Duarte to War Minister, Pindapoi, 25 Feb. 1865, ANA-SNE 3272. Officers often stayed up until midnight to memorize these drills and the various *ordenanzas* of the army. See "Informes del general Don Bernardino Caballero, ex-presidente de la República," in "Testimonios de la guerra del Paraguay contra la Triple Alianza (II)," *Historia Paraguaya* 38 (1998): 412.

33. Duarte to War Minister, Pindapoi, 21 Jan. 1865, ANA-SNE 3268.

34. See Pascual Isasa to Pedro Duarte, Santo Tomé, 31 Mar. 1865, ANA-CRB I-30, 26, 38, no. 2. See also Francisco Lezcano to Juan Antonio Lezcano, Santo Tomé, 16 Jan. 1865, ANA-CRB I-30, 24, 1, no. 1.

35. *El Semanario*, 28 Jan. 1865, observed that Dom Pedro should not expect the same good fortune from this apparition as Carlos V enjoyed in 1519–21, when a similar sign heralded Cortés's conquest of Mexico.

36. Edward Thornton to Lord Russell, Buenos Aires, 26 Dec. 1864, in "Correspondence Respecting Hostilities in the River Plate," 66:1224–27.

37. Box, *Origins of the Paraguayan War*, p. 226.

38. Flores to Silva Paranhos, Colorado, 28 Jan. 1865, cited in Box, *Origins of the Paraguayan War*, p. 226.

39. Lamas, *Tentativas para la pacificación de la República Oriental del Uruguay*, p. 54.

40. Given the complexity of regional disputes, it is understandable that historians have forgotten the petty jealousies of the European diplomats on station in the Plata and the squabbles of their respective governments. Any suggestion that they should cooperate among themselves in the interest of peace was bound to cause friction. As late as November, for instance, British Minister Thornton complained that his Italian counterpart, Signor Barbolini, was "moving heaven and earth to bring about an Italian protectorate [in the Banda Oriental]." See Thornton to Washburn, Buenos Aires, 16 Nov. 1864, WNL.

41. The hardline faction was willing to go to great lengths to obstruct any negotiations. On 21 January, Aguirre met with the British and French admirals, with Carreras acting as interpreter. The naval officers tried to impress upon the president the hopelessness of his situation, but they noticed that the foreign minister purposely mistranslated their words so as to rob them of their urgency. See Thornton to Russell, Buenos Aires, 25 Jan. 1865, in "Correspondence Respecting Hostilities in the River Plate," 66:1235-36.

42. Lamas to Aguirre, Buenos Aires, 25 Jan. 1865, cited in Box, *Origins of the Paraguayan War*, p. 231.

43. Carlos Oneto y Viana, *La diplomacia del Brasil en el Río de la Plata* (Montevideo, 1903), pp. 239-40.

44. Around two thousand Brazilians, officers and men, eventually served in Flores's army. See Tasso Fragoso, *História da Guerra entre a Tríplice Aliança*, 1:109.

45. According to Box, Paranhos "was above such cheap sentimentality.... But a chronological revenge was a small price to pay for the sullen silence of Tamandaré." *Origins of the Paraguayan War*, pp. 237-38.

46. Some of the anti-Paraguayan propaganda in the *porteño* press (especially in Hector Varela's *La Tribuna*) antedated the attack on Mato Grosso. See Berges to Félix Egusquiza, Asunción, 6 Nov. 1864, ANA-CRB I-22, 12, 1, no. 190.

47. A sizable proportion of the Paraguayan community in Buenos Aires was represented by these émigré groups, which had impotently castigated the Asun-

ción government from afar for over a decade. See Luciano Recalde, *Carta primera al presidente López del Paraguay* (Buenos Aires, 1857); "!Hasta el Paraguay!" in *El eco español* (Buenos Aires), 1 Nov. 1862; and, especially, Manuel Pedro de Peña, *Cartas del ciudadano . . . a su querido sobrino Francisco Solano López* (Buenos Aires, 1865). Curiously, Brazilian agents made few contacts with these groups, which they thought riddled with López spies. See "La prensa de Buenos Aires y los paraguayos rebeldes," *El Semanario*, 1 Apr. 1865.

48. Mitre to Lanús, Buenos Aires, 11 Jan. 1865, in Mitre, *Archivo*, 2:61–62.

49. José Berges made a similar observation later that year, noting that "we never really counted much on the Oriental [i.e., Blanco] contingent, and it is only with the efforts of our own soldiers that we can carry forward the holy cause of conserving our sister republic's autonomy and thus sustain the principle of a balance of power . . . , which is the basis of tranquility and prosperity for all." See Berges to Miguel Rojas, Asunción, 15 Mar. 1865, ANA-CRB I-22, 12, 2, no. 59.

50. Berges to Elizalde, Asunción, 14 Jan. 1865, ANA-CRB I-22, 11, no. 491. See also MHM-CGA carpeta 72, no. 1.

51. López to Candido Bareiro, Asunción, 1 Feb. 1865, cited in Rebaudi, *La declaración de guerra*, p. 322.

52. Félix Egusquiza to Bareiro, Buenos Aires, 11 Feb. 1865, in Rebaudi, *La declaración de guerra*, p. 36.

53. Cited in Box, *Origins of the Paraguayan War*, p. 255.

54. See Elizalde to Berges, Buenos Aires, 9 Feb. 1865, MHM-CGA carpeta 72, no. 9.

55. Elizalde to Berges, Buenos Aires, 9 Feb. 1865, in *Memoria presentada por el Ministro de Estado en el Departamento de Relaciones Exteriores al Congreso Nacional de 1865* (Buenos Aires, 1865), pp.173–75.

56. See, for example, Mitre to Manuel Y. Lagraña, Buenos Aires, 9 Jan. 1865, in Rebaudi, *La declaración de guerra*, p. 258; and Mitre to Lagraña, Buenos Aires, 31 Jan. 1865, cited in *El Independiente* (Corrientes), 29 Apr. 1865.

57. Cited in Julio Victorica, *Urquiza y Mitre: Contribución al estudio histórico de la organización nacional* (Buenos Aires, 1906), p. 481.

58. Victorica, *Urquiza y Mitre*, p. 481.

59. Victorica, *Urquiza y Mitre*, p. 483.

60. Solano López to Urquiza, Asunción, 26 Feb. 1865, cited in McLynn,"General Urquiza and the Politics of Argentina," p. 187.

61. Cited in Rebaudi, *La declaración de guerra*, pp. 21-22.

62. Cited in Rebaudi, *La declaración de guerra*, pp. 22-23.

63. López to Bareiro, Asunción, 26 Feb. 1865, cited in Benites, *Anales* 1:138.

64. "Law that Establishes the Political Administration of the Republic of Paraguay," 13 Mar. 1844, ANA-SH 266, no. 5. For a particularly sarcastic judgment on the legislative branch in Paraguay (in which the anonymous author compares Solano López to the Haitian emperor Soulouque), see "Lo que es un congreso en el Paraguay," *La Tribuna* (Montevideo), 25 Mar. 1865.

65. Indeed, when the representatives from the interior arrived in Asunción, they hurried to the various government ministries to "get their cue as to what they were to say in Congress. These cues were given upon every subject." See Thompson, *War in Paraguay*, p.42. See also an anonymous memoir of these events, miscatalogued at the University of Texas Library as "Correspondencia del Dictador al Delegado de Ytapúa," MG 2034.

66. *El Semanario* 11, 18, 25 Mar. 1865.

67. Thompson, *War in Paraguay*, p. 43.

68. Coming from a country where state control of the one newspaper was taken for granted, it is altogether possible that members actually believed that the entire Argentine press was shackled to the Mitre government. In fact, some of the editorials most insulting to Paraguay and the López regime were written by Mitre's political rivals. See, for example, *La Tribuna* (Buenos Aires), 22 Jan. 1865.

69. *El Semanario*, 25 Mar. 1865.

70. *El Semanario*, 25 Mar. 1865.

71. *El Semanario*, 25 Mar. 1865. No one on the committee ever questioned whether Lamartine, a popular historian, poet, and novelist, had any bona fides as an expert in international law. Then again, the Paraguayans were clearly less interested in international law than in ideological questions broadly considered. The unfavorable allusions to Russia, for instance (and the inevitable comparisons with Brazil), highlighted the political rhetoric of many Latin American "liberals" at this time, most notably in Chile. See, for instance, Benjamín Vicuña Mackenna to Mitre, Santiago, 1 Jan. 1865, in Mitre, *Archivo*, 21:36-41.

72. Centurión, *Memorias*, 1:235.

73. Colonel Thompson recorded: "López had dances going on every night in 'improvised saloons' in the public squares. These were divided into three com-

partments, for three classes of people—the swells, the 'golden combs,' and the common people. The 'golden combs' [kyguá verá] was a name given to a class invented at the beginning of the dancing mania, and consisted of all the third class girls who had any pretension to good looks, and were tolerably loose in their morals. They all wore immense combs in their back-hair. They were brought forward by the Government to spite the ladies, most of who refused to dance at these places, though under danger of their lives. They were, however, obliged to go and look on for a short time." *War in Paraguay*, pp. 43–44. See also "Testimony of Sr. Serafino," [Steamer *Salto*, Mar. 1865], in *La Nación Argentina*, 17 Oct. 1865.

74. *La Nación Argentina*, 20–21 Mar. 1865.

75. *La Nación Argentina*, 20–21 Mar. 1865.

76. José María Rosa, "¿Como se complicó la Argentina en la triple alianza?" *Cuadernos de Marcha* 35 (Mar. 1970): 5–29. In seeking to absolve the marshal of responsibility for the impetuousness of his declaring war on Argentina, certain Paraguayan writers have long argued the same thing. See Juan E. O'Leary, *El centauro de Ybycui* (Paris, 1929), pp. 87–91.

77. Berges to Elizalde, Asunción, 29 Mar. 1865, ANA-CRB I-22, 11, 1, no. 510.

78. Juan Crisóstomo Centurión claims that the 29 March note was written by none other than López himself. He also claims to have been "informed by people who had good reason to [know]," that Mitre received word of this note in good time but delayed making it public in order to arose patriotic feelings against the Paraguayans (whom he could then paint as vandals who had attacked without a previous declaration of war). Centurión, *Memorias*, 1:241–42. One could just as easily argue that the long delay was engineered by Solano López in order to gain more time to negotiate for foreign loans, to assure the arrival of military supplies, and above all, to maintain the element of surprise before the attack.

79. José María Rosa notes that one "would have to accept that the Argentine Government was the worst informed in the world" in order to take Mitre's word on this matter. "¿Como se complicó la Argentina?" p. 29. Yet the fact remains that as late as 10 April, Mitre was arguing that his government needed to maintain "good neighborliness" with both Brazil and Paraguay. Mitre to Hilario Ascasubi, Buenos Aires, 10 Apr. 1865, Museo Histórico Nacional, Buenos Aires, doc. 2648.

80. On 12 April, Thornton wrote to Lord Russell to say that he had spoken "of the rumor to General Mitre and Señor Elizalde who at first disbelieved it, but

they now give it credit, and the latter told me yesterday that a friend of his had seen a copy of the note from the Paraguayan Government containing the declaration of war. His Excellency expects to receive this note by the Argentine steamer *Salto* which is expected in a day or two from Assumption." See PRO-FO 6.255, dispatch no. 23.

81. Guillermo Rawson to Mitre, Córdoba, 17 Apr. 1865, in Mitre, *Archivo*, 1:299.

82. Lagraña sent the national government a copy of the Correntino newspaper *El Independiente*, which published the declaration of war in its edition of 21 April; by this time, Corrientes was already under Paraguayan occupation. See Trinidad Delia Chianelli, *El gobierno del puerto* (Buenos Aires, 1975).

### 10. Corrientes under the Gun

1. Juan Pujol, *Corrientes en la organización nacional*, 10 vols. (Buenos Aires, 1911), passim.

2. Raimundo Fernández Reguera, *Apuntes históricos referentes a la gloriosa revolución de noviembre, que dió por resultado la libertad de la heróica provincia de Corrientes en 1861* (Corrientes, 1862), pp. 1-40. See also Mantilla, *Crónica histórica*, 2:261-67.

3. Commander Miguel Lezcano to Brigadier General [Wenceslao Robles?], Paso de la Patria, 12 Apr. 1865, ANA-SNE 786.

4. Mitre had agreed in principle to this request at the end of January, but the *Gualeguay* failed to arrive until the end of February and the *25 de Mayo* until mid-March. See Mitre to Lagraña, Buenos Aires, 31 Jan. 1865, MHM-CZ carpeta 150, no. 2.

5. Vicente D. Constantino, *Vida ye servicios militares del guerrero del Paraguay, capitán de fragata Don. . . .* (Buenos Aires, 1906), p. 10.

6. Enrique Roibón, "13 de abril de 1865: Narración dedicada al historiador de Corrientes, doctor don Manuel F. Mantilla," *La Reacción* (Corrientes), 11-13 Apr. 1899; anonymous review, *La Verdad* (Saladas), 22 July 1905. Two of the sailors taken from the *25 de Mayo* were North Americans; only one survived Paraguayan captivity to be rescued a year and a half later by U.S. Minister Charles Washburn. See Washburn to Solano López, Paso Pucú, 26 Dec. 1866; and Washburn to Berges, Asunción, 17 Oct. 1867, both in WNL.

7. See Lino A. Neves, captain of steamer *Gualeguay*, to Gelly y Obes, Buenos

Aires, 21 Apr. 1865, cited in Luis D. Cabral, *Anales de la Marina de guerra de la república argentina*, 2 vols. (Buenos Aires, 1904), 1:598–600.

8. The corporal, who had acted on impulse, was put in chains on the spot. Authorities at Humaitá later had him flogged for his rash and impertinent act. See Manuel Trujillo, *Gestas guerreras* (Asunción, 1923), p. 11.

9. Andrés René Rousseaux, "La defensa de Corrientes," *Todo es Historia*, no. 226 (Feb. 1986): 48. See also Pedro Y. Meza to War Minister, Itapirú, 13 Apr. 1865, in *El Semanario*, 15 Apr. 1865.

10. Cited in Pedro Bonastre, *El coronel don Desiderio Sosa* (Corrientes, 1899), p. 46.

11. The Argentine authorities later exonerated Ayala of criminal charges. He spent the war years working as a brick mason in Buenos Aires. See Rebaudi, *La declaración de guerra*, pp. 20–21.

12. Report of Municipal Council, Corrientes, 15 Apr. 1865, ANA-CRB I-30, 23, 218, nos. 1–2.

13. Decree of Lagraña, Empedrado, 14 Apr. 1865, in *La Nación Argentina*, 24–25 Apr. 1865.

14. Hernán Félix Gómez, *Vida de un valiente* (Corrientes, 1944), pp. 31–32. Like Gen. Francis Marion, the "Swamp Fox" of revolutionary South Carolina, the "Red Armadillo" *(tatú pyta)* of Corrientes enjoyed a phenomenal reputation for backcountry fighting. Cáceres owned a forty-thousand-hectare ranch outside of Curuzú Cuatiá, where, unlike many provincial landowners, he actually resided. This rural orientation and his quickness with the *facón* were enough to earn Cáceres the hostility of Correntino liberals, who saw themselves as "civilizers" and the gaucho followers of Cáceres as things to be expunged. See Severo Ortíz, *Apuntes biográficos del general de la nación Nicanor Cáceres* (Buenos Aires, 1867), pp. 28–29, 163–64; and "Perfiles de los militares más notables del Ejército argentino," *La Nación Argentina*, 11 Dec. 1866.

15. On 16 April a Paraguayan crew took the *25 de Mayo* and the *Gualeguay* to Asunción for repairs and incorporation into the navy. Days elapsed before the vessels reached their destination because the latter had to be towed (at a scant three miles an hour). See telegram, [Alejandro Hermosa] to War Minister, Humaitá, 16 Apr. 1865, ANA-SNE 2327; and Ciriaco Molina to Venancio López, Villa Franca, 18 Apr. 1865, ANA-CRB I-30, 19, 68, no. 1.

16. Eugenio Bogado to Solano López, Corrientes, 17 Apr. 1865, ANA-SH 431, no. 2.

17. Ironically, many of the horses used by these units had been sold to the Paraguayans the previous year by Correntino suppliers. See Miguel A. Rojas to Treasury Minister, 15 Nov. 1864, ANA-SNE 818.

18. These Federals openly conflated the political posture of the empire with that of Buenos Aires. After the war started, they even lumped their opponents together as "unitarian *brasileros.*" See *El Independiente* (Corrientes), 30 July 1865.

19. Miguel Rojas to Berges, Corrientes, 24 Jan. 1865, ANA-CRB I-30, 3, 31, no. 1. For more details of Silvero's career and personality, see *El Progreso* (Corrientes), 25 Dec. 1864, 23 Mar. 1865.

20. Washburn, *History of Paraguay,* 2:20.

21. Telegram, Berges to Solano López, Corrientes, 18 Apr. 1865, "Correspondencia telegráfica entre el Mariscal López y José Berges," unpublished *copiador*, BNA-CJO.

22. Correntinos had roundly applauded the seizure of the *Marqués de Olinda* a few months earlier, and virtually no one in the provincial capital supported Brazil in its war with Paraguay. See Miguel Rojas to Berges, Corrientes, 1 Dec. 1864, ANA-CRB I-30, 5, 18, no. 2.

23. *Aviso municipal* of Juan A. de los Santos, Corrientes, 19 Apr. 1865, AGPC Fondo Mantilla, legajo 20. Four other candidates (Colodrero, Contreras, Díaz de Vivar, and Virasoro) put their names forward as possible *junta* members, but between them they polled only twenty-four votes out of three hundred. See Berges to Solano López, Corrientes, 20 Apr. 1865, "Correspondencia telegráfica entre el Mariscal López y José Berges."

24. The Argentine general José Ignacio Garmendia, who authored one of the most detailed accounts of the Corrientes campaign, failed to correctly note the names of the *junta* members, whom he nonetheless vilified as turncoats. *Campaña de Corrientes y de Rio Grande*, vol. 2 of *La guerra del Paraguay* (Buenos Aires, 1904), p. 103. Manuel Florencio Mantilla, the classic historian of Corrientes, mentions them only once, calling the adherents of their party "blind [men] who bowed before the foreign enemy." *Crónica histórica,* 2:275.

25. *Junta* members received as many official petitions as Berges or the Paraguayan military commander. See, for example, Victor Silvero and Sinforoso

Cáceres to Berges, Corrientes, 5 June 1865 (regarding passage to Chaco settlements), ANA-CRB I-30, 9, 61; and Cáceres to Berges, [Corrientes, 1865?] (regarding petition of the Spaniard Manuel Vicente Fernández, who wished to depart for Buenos Aires), ANA-CRB I-30, 9, 76.

26. Schneider, *Guerra da Tríplice Aliança*, 1:219

27. Among those members of the local elite who cautiously welcomed the new regime were Cayetano Virasoro, close relative of a former governor; Antonio Díaz de Vivar, a major landowner, local chief of the Federal Party, and longtime friend of Urquiza; and Roberto Guy Billinghurst, a merchant of long standing in Corrientes who had enjoyed many trade contacts over the years with the Paraguayan government. See Wenceslao Nestor Domínguez, *La toma de Corrientes: El 25 de mayo de 1865* (Buenos Aires, 1965), p. 17.

28. Berges to Solano López, Corrientes, 18 Apr. 1865, "Correspondencia telegráfica entre el Mariscal López y José Berges."

29. Proclamation of Robles, Corrientes, 19 Apr. 1865, in *El Uruguay* (Concepción del Uruguay), 4 May 1865.

30. See Decree of the *Junta Gubernativa*, Corrientes, 9 May 1865, in *Ocupación de Corrientes por fuerzas paraguayas, 1865* (Corrientes, 1929), pp. 7–8. See also "Apuntes de Don Pedro Igarzábal" (for 7 May 1865), cited in Domínguez, *La toma de Corrientes*, p. 62.

31. Mantilla, *Crónica histórica*, 2:278; Solano López to Berges, Asunción, 27 Apr. 1865, ANA-CRB I-30, 12, 9, no. 11. For more on the difficulties occasioned by the forced acceptance of Paraguayan currency, see Judge José Ballejos to the *Junta Gubernativa*, Empedrado, 8 July 1865, AGPC-CO 1865, legajo 209.

32. The *Junta Gubernativa* sought without success to stimulate the provincial economy of Corrientes by suspending the *contribución directa*, placing a moratorium on fees charged for stamped paper, and restoring the functions of the customshouse to Correntino (rather than national) control. Documents cited in *Ocupación de Corrientes por fuerzas paraguayas*, pp. 8–9, 21–23. In order to spread word of its decrees and laws, the *junta* habitually made use of a small river vessel previously used to transport oranges downriver. See Berges to Solano López, Corrientes, 23 Apr. 1865, "Correspondencia telegráfica entre el Mariscal López y José Berges."

33. The Argentines initially reported that the Paraguayans had seized the entire archives for transport to the marshal's camp, but the national government ultimately disavowed this charge once Corrientes was retaken. See *La Nación Argentina*, 8 Nov. 1865.

34. Nicolás Gallardo to [Victor Silvero?], San Cosme, 24 Apr. 1865, ANA-CRB I-30, 23, 155, no. 2; José María Aguiar to Solano López, Campo en la Capilla [near Empedrado], 26 Apr. 1865, ANA-CRB I-30, 11, 40; and Antonino Benítez to *Junta Gubernativa*, Corrientes, 24 Apr. 1865, AGPC-CO legajo 208. A brother of Sinforoso Cáceres acted as agent for the Paraguayans on several of these occasions; he was supposed to work out arrangements for the reimbursement of ranchers whose livestock was confiscated but most often had to stand by while the Paraguayans took what they wanted without pay; this practice was later sanctioned by the *junta* as a military necessity. See *Junta* decree, 14 July 1865, in *El Independiente* (Corrientes), 16 July 1865.

35. Berges to Robles, Corrientes, 25 Apr. 1865, ANA-CRB I-30, 23, 156. Not everyone was mollified by these gestures, though they hid their resentment. A British observer noted that Paraguayan discipline was "remarkably good; drunkenness, theft, and disorder being on all hands admitted to be unknown. It is true that when they want anything from a shop they come and take it, but invariably in an orderly manner, and even sometimes propose going through the form of paying for it, but I do not hear of the arrangement being satisfactory to both parties in the transaction." F. J. Pakenham to Edward Thornton, Corrientes, 17 May 1865, in Kenneth Bourne and D. Cameron Watt, eds., *British Documents on Foreign Affairs*, pt. 1, ser. D, *Latin America, 1845–1914*, vol. 1, *River Plate, 1849–1912* (n.p., 1991), p. 184. A local source was less elliptical, noting with contempt that such "thieves" and "beggars" were hardly the sort of people best suited to "carry the banner of civilization to the peoples of the Río de la Plata." See "Ejércitos paraguayos o sean cuarenta-y-cinco mil lismoneros," in *La Esperanza* (Corrientes), 3 Dec. 1865.

36. Burton, *Letters from the Battlefields of Paraguay*, p. 285.

37. Thompson, *War in Paraguay*, p. 161.

38. Lagraña to Mitre, Lomas, 13 Apr. 1865, in *La Nación Argentina* (Buenos Aires), 17–18 Apr. 1865. See also Lagraña to Juan Andrés Gelly y Obes, Corrientes, 13 Apr. 1865, in *La Tribuna* (Montevideo), 17–18 Apr. 1865.

39. See, for example, *La Nación Argentina*, 2 May 1865.

40. Miguel Angel de Marco, *Bartolomé Mitre: Biografía* (Buenos Aires, 1998), p. 324.

41. Consul Hinton Rowan Helper to Seward, Buenos Aires, 17 Apr. 1865, NARA M70, no. 11. The greatest — and most arrogant — show of anger against Solano López came from members of the city's rising middle class, individuals who enjoyed seeing their names in print in a country where scarcely 10 percent of the population could read.

42. Cited in *El Nacional* (Buenos Aires), 17 Apr. 1865.

43. Proclamation of Mitre, Buenos Aires, 16 Apr. 1865, in *La Nación Argentina*, 17-18 Apr. 1865.

44. Decree of Mitre, Buenos Aires, 17 Apr. 1865, in *La Nación Argentina*, 17-18 Apr. 1865.

45. Mitre to Lagraña, Buenos Aires, 21 Apr. 1865, ANA-CRB I-30, 21, 151-62.

46. *La Nación Argentina* (Buenos Aires), 24-25 Apr. 1865.

47. Juan A. Gelly y Obes to Lagraña, Buenos Aires, 17 Apr. 1865, in Juan Beverina, *La guerra del Paraguay: las operaciones de la Guerra en territorio argentino y brasileño*, 7 vols. (Buenos Aires, 1921-33), 2:437-38.

48. Urquiza to Mitre, Concepción del Uruguay, 19 Apr. 1865, in Mitre, *Archivo*, 2:114.

49. Victorica, *Urquiza y Mitre*, pp. 487-88; "The War in South America," *The Times* (London), 21 June 1865.

50. Just before the fall of the Paysandú, Urquiza's business partner Mariano Cabral sold some thirty thousand horses to the Brazilian cavalry, and sales had continued briskly ever since. See Fermín Chaves, *Vida y muerte de López Jordan* (Buenos Aires, 1957), p. 130.

51. Alberdi, *El Brasil ante la democracia de América* (Buenos Aires, 1946), p. 140 (letter written from Paris in July 1865).

52. Elizalde to Domingo Faustino Sarmiento, Buenos Aires, 11 Oct. 1865, cited in Luis Alberto de Herrera, *La culpa mitrista*, 2 vols. (Buenos Aires, 1965), 1:157.

53. Urquiza pressured his supporters to accept the alliance with the national government, and only a few openly demurred. The journalist Evaristo Carriego, for instance, whose pro-Blanco diatribes had represented an extreme interpre-

tation of Urquicismo, now found himself unwanted in Entre Ríos. Police closed his newspaper, *El Litoral*, and he himself took flight downriver aboard a British ship. See Domingo Comas a Urquiza, Paraná, 20 June 1865, AGN-BA Archivo Urquiza.

54. *The Standard* (Buenos Aires), 18 Apr. 1865.

55. Gelly y Obes to Lagraña, Buenos Aires, 17 Apr. 1865, cited in Beverina, *La guerra del Paraguay*, 2:437–38.

56. In reference to Urquiza's call to arms, see Manuel Basavilbaso to the secretary of the *Jefatura Política* of Gualeguay (Entre Ríos), Concepción del Uruguay, 19 Apr. 1865, Archivo Histórico y Administrativo de Entre Ríos, Paraná, División Gobierno, Sección C, Comandancia de Gualeguay, carpeta 42, legajo 6.

57. Thornton to Lord Russell, Buenos Aires, 24 Apr. 1865, in "Correspondence Respecting Hostilities in the River Plate," pt. 3, no. 19.

58. Juan Bautista Gill Aguinaga, *La asociación paraguaya en la guerra de la triple alianza*, pp. 44–48; Escragnolle Doria, "A Legião Paraguaia," *Nação Armada* 69 (Aug. 1945): 40–45.

59. Triple Alliance Treaty, Buenos Aires, 1 May 1865, AHI 389.4.1.

60. *La Nación Argentina*, 19 Apr. 1865.

61. The irony of the secret clauses of the Triple Alliance Treaty is that, extreme though they were, they specifically abjured what the Paraguayans most feared—the extinction of their nation through partition between Brazil and Argentina. Such a drastic measure would have eliminated a useful buffer state, thus leaving the empire directly facing an Argentina that was unlikely to play the role of permanent ally.

62. Thornton to Russell, Buenos Aires, 24 Apr. 1865, in Box, *Origins of the Paraguayan War*, pp. 270–71.

63. The same expansionist tendencies were exhibited during the secret ratification debates in the Argentine Congress, in which certain members maintained that Article 8 of the treaty contradicted their own constitutional provision providing that "new provinces may be admitted to the nation." See Box, *Origins of the Paraguayan War*, p. 271.

64. Privately, Thornton and other British officials favored the Allies for the simple reason that British interests were greater in Argentina and Brazil than in

Paraguay. This opinion was not always shared by the Foreign Office, which felt more vexed than anything else. The British public, for its part, was either indifferent or confused, with a sizable number of readers who daily scanned *The Times* accepting the Allied argument that their side represented civilization and progress and just as many who defended Paraguay as a "gallant little nation." See Leslie Bethell, *The Paraguayan War* (London, 1996), pp. 25–27.

65. Cited in Nabuco, *La guerra del Paraguay*, p. 346.

66. Cited in Box, *Origins of the Paraguayan War*, p. 271.

67. Fermín Alsina to Lagraña, San Lorenzo, 28 Apr. 1865, cited in José Fermín González, *Corrientes ante la invasión paraguaya* (Corrientes, 1916), p. 130; Robles to Berges, Riachuelo, 30 Apr. 1865, ANA-CRB I-30, 10, 13, no. 10.

68. Efraím Cardozo, *Hace cien años: crónicas de la guerra de 1864–1870 publicados en "La Tribuna,"* 13 vols. (Asunción, 1971–82), 1:206. The *Junta Gubernativa* later issued a call to arms for all Correntino men between the age of seventeen and fifty (decree of 12 July 1865), tried explicitly to reorganize the province's National Guard units in order to support the Paraguayans (decree of 19 July 1865), and imposed penalties for those men who ignored the appeals (decree of 2 October 1865). Most Correntinos ignored the appeals notwithstanding. Decrees cited in *Ocupación de Corrientes por fuerzas paraguayas*, pp. 21, 30–31. See also *El Independiente* (Corrientes), 16 July 1865.

69. His men, who felt increasingly restless, had instead spent their time being entertained by the military band and by a group of camp followers (whom Robles euphemistically called "guests"); evidently, some soldiers had produced a supply of homebrew, which threatened discipline in a keen way and added to Robles's worries. See Robles to Berges, Corrientes, 2 May 1865, ANA-CRB I-30, 10, 13, no.12.

70. See Wenceslao Paunero to Gelly y Obes, Bella Vista, 12 May 1865, Biblioteca Nacional, Buenos Aires, Sección manuscritos, doc. 15.525.

71. Colonel Thompson observed that the absence of good cavalry mounts was a serious problem for the Paraguayans throughout the war; many of the Paraguayan horses suffered from a spinal disease, which made them unfit for service after only a short time, and remounts taken from the Correntinos were not always available. *War in Paraguay*, pp. 52–53.

72. Patterson, "War of the Triple Alliance," p. 134.

73. José I. Garmendia, *La cartera de un soldado (Bocetos sobre la marcha)* (Buenos Aires, 1891), pp. 251–95.

74. Tasso Fragoso, *História da Guerra entre a Tríplice Aliança*, 2:70.

75. Cardozo, *Hace cien años*, 2:38.

76. Beverina, *La guerra del Paraguay*, 1:104.

77. One eyewitness noted that "the news [of the Allied presence] went about as if by some mysterious telephone; no one knew how it [originated] and even less how it spread, but in every home it was known and commented upon." See E. R. Cristiano [Enrique Roibón], "25 de mayo de 1865," *La Libertad* (Corrientes), 24 May 1903; and, more generally, "Asalto y toma de la ciudad de Corrientes," *La Nación* (Buenos Aires), 25 May 1915.

78. Manuel Aranda, commentary, Puesto de las Olivas, 31 June 1865, MHM-CZ carpeta 149, no. 3.

79. Thompson, *War in Paraguay*, p. 67.

80. See Paunero to Gelly y Obes, Corrientes, 26 May 1865, in *La Nación Argentina*, 31 May 1865 (reprinted in *El Siglo* [Montevideo], 2 June 1865). The Paraguayans, not very convincingly, claimed a loss of 120 dead and 83 wounded for themselves, while Allied losses, they claimed, were "much more considerable, both in terms of deaths and wounded." See José de Jesús Martínez to War Minister, Lomas, 26 May 1865, in *El Semanario*, 27 May 1865.

81. Of this action Charlone later wrote: "I can give assurances that I have never witnessed a harder fight, and that the Paraguayans are good soldiers and only abandon their posts [when forced out] by shell or bayonet.... [T]o defeat the Paraguayans, we will have to kill them all, for when the field is equal, troops like this are invincible." See Gregorio Benites, *Primeras batallas contra la Triple Alianza* (Asunción, 1919), pp. 43–45.

82. Domínguez, *La toma de Corrientes*, p. 25; Daniel Cerri, *Campaña del Paraguay* (Buenos Aires, 1892), pp. 19–22.

83. Centurión, *Memorias*, 1:262. In a report to Paraguay's representative in Paris, the minister of the treasury inverted the losses, claiming a total of between 400 and 500 casualties for the Allies and 203 for the Paraguayans. See Mariano González to Candido Bareiro, Asunción, 9 June 1865, BNA-CJO.

84. The items taken included nearly three hundred rifles and a like number of steel-tipped lances. See Parte oficial de Paunero, Corrientes, 26 May 1865, in *La*

*Reforma Pacífica* (Montevideo), 2 June 1865; and Paunero to Gelly y Obes, on board steamship *Pavón* at the Rincón de Zebellos, 29 May 1865, in *La Nación Argentina*, 8 June 1865.

85. Juan Bautista Charlone to Gelly y Obes, Corrientes, 26 May 1865, Biblioteca Nacional, Buenos Aires, Sección Manuscritos, doc. 15.039.

86. See "Records of the Fiscal Commission," [May–Aug. 1865], ANA-CRB I-30, 26, 60, nos. 1–104; and Victor Silvero testimony, cited in Rebaudi, *La declaración de guerra*, pp. 10–11.

87. Francisco Manoel Barroso to Paunero, aboard steamship *Biberibe* at Corrientes, 25 May 1865 (11 in the evening), MHM-CZ carpeta 150, no. 45, pp. 198–99.

88. Mitre thought the 25 May raid a serious error because it had been launched without any serious attention being given to combined operations with the Brazilians or to the role of Cáceres's men. See Estanislao Zeballos, "Batalla de Corrientes," MHM-CZ carpeta 141, no. 26.

89. López to Robles, Asunción, 26 May 1865, cited in Cardozo, *Hace cien años*, 2:42–44.

90. Robles himself became aware of these events a day and a half after Paunero's withdrawal. See General Order of Robles, Santa Lucía, 29 May 1865, in "Copiador de Notas de Robles (Apr.–May 1865)," ANA-SNE 2373.

91. Proclamation of López, Asunción, 2 June 1865, ANA-SH 343, no. 9.

92. This was doubtless a reference to operations that had just started in the Misiones. See Solano López to Robles, Asunción, 2 June 1865, in Cardozo, *Hace cien años*, 2:53–55.

93. W. F. Johnson, commander of HMS *Dottorell*, to José Berges, off Corrientes, 1 June 1865, ANA-CRB I-30, 22, 64, no. 7; Cardozo, *Hace cien años*, 2:45–48. A short time before the Paraguayan ship *Pirabebé* had fired on the *Dottorell* but missed her mark; the commander of the former vessel apologized after the British hoisted the Union Jack, sending a note saying that poor visibility had caused him to mistake her for a Brazilian warship. See Toribio Pereira to W. F. Johnson, off Corrientes, 13 May 1865, ANA-CRB I-30, 22, 64, no. 5; and *The Times* (London), 3 July 1865. The British ship continued on to Asunción to evacuate those British subjects who wished to leave.

94. "Memoir of José N. Alsina," [1889?], MHM-CZ carpeta 141, no. 34.

95. Lagraña to Gelly y Obes, Esquina, 7 June 1865, MHM-CZ carpeta 150, no. 45, p. 202.

96. The Correntino "division" had ten officers and 130 men on 29 May 1865. Robles to [War Minister?], Santa Lucía, 29 May 1865, ANA-SH 448, no. 1. The number eventually grew to around 900 according to one deserter who crossed to the Allied lines in September. See Testimony of Juan de la Cruz Arom, García Cué, 15 Sept. 1865, MM-AI doc. 7.614.

97. That these troops fought under the Paraguayan flag demonstrated the hypocrisy in the marshal's denunciation of Mitre's sponsorship of the Paraguayan Legion. See Cardozo, *Hace cien años*, 1:206; and Memoir of Commander Manuel Vallejos, [28 May 1889], MHM-CZ carpeta 141, no. 12.

98. For examples of major claims against the Brazilians, see Testimony of Juan Canepa, 5 Aug. 1865, ANA-CRB I-30, 26, 60, no. 46; and Testimony of Luis Patri, 8 Aug. 1865, ANA-CRB I-30, 26, 60, no. 100.

99. See, for example, Sinforoso Cáceres to Nicanor Cáceres, 27 Apr. 1865, in *La Nación Argentina*, 10 May 1865.

100. León Pomer, *Cinco años de guerra civil en la Argentina* (Buenos Aires, 1986), pp. 27-28.

101. Recuerdos del Sargento Mayor Justiniano Salvañach, [Asunción, 1888], MHM-CZ carpeta 141, no. 3, p. 9.

102. Centurión, *Memorias*, 1:298.

103. Pedro Rueda, *Biografía militar del General Don Pedro Duarte, ministro de guerra y marina de la república del Paraguay* (Asunción, 1890), pp. 8-10.

104. Cardozo, *Hace cien años*, 2:20-21.

105. Cardozo, *Hace cien años*, 2:24. Desertors from Paiva's force were also coming to Duarte to ask his protection throughout this time. See Vicente Barrios to Solano López, Asunción, 10 June 1865, ANA-SNE 2824.

106. Fr. Blas Ignacio Duarte to Bishop Manuel Antonio Palacios, Pindapoi, 19 May 1865, Natalicio González Collection, Spencer Library, University of Kansas, Lawrence, MS E222: b, pp. 49-50.

107. Tasso Fragoso, *História da Guerra entre a Triplice Aliança*, 2:116.

108. Estigarribia to Solano López, Pindapoi, 21 May 1865, ANA-CRB I-30, 11, 63, no. 3; Patterson, "War of the Triple Alliance," p. 266.

109. "Recuerdos de Pedro Duarte," [1888], MHM-CZ carpeta 121, no. 2.

110. The sources disagree as to the number of troops in the Uruguay Division. Schneider, *Guerra da Triplice Aliança*, 2:288, gives the total Paraguayan strength as twelve thousand men and six antiquated guns. Given the specific number of

units in Estigarribia and Duarte's formations (on this point there is no disagreement), ten thousand men seems a more reasonable estimate.

111. See *Diário do Rio de Janeiro*, 29 July 1865.

112. Col. Antonio Fernandes Lima to David Canabarro, Paso de Mbutui, 24 Apr. 1865, in Walter Spalding, *A Invasão Paraguaia no Brasil (Documentação Inédita)* (São Paulo, 1940), pp. 146–47.

113. Ivo Caggiani, *David Canabarro de Tenente a General* (Pôrto Alegre, 1992), pp. 163–85.

114. Regarding this early period of enlistment of *voluntários* in São Paulo, see *Correio Paulistano* (São Paulo), 12, 14–15, 17–18, 22 Jan. 1865; and Célio Debes, "São Paulo e a Delagração da guerra do Paraguai," *Revista do Instituto Histórico e Geográfico do São Paulo* 62 (1966): 133–42.

115. Estigarribia to War Minister, San Borjita, 10 June 1865, ANA-SNE 3269.

116. Sérgio Roberto Dentino Morgado, "O Combate de São Borja," *Revista do Exército Brasileiro* 129:1 (Jan.–Mar. 1992): 40.

117. Tasso Fragoso, *História da Guerra entre a Triplice Aliança*, 2:122.

118. David Canabarro to War Minister, [Itaqui?], 10 June 1865, in *Diário do Rio de Janeiro*, 11 July 1865.

119. "David Canabarro," *Jornal do Commercio*, 5 Jan. 1866.

120. A few Paraguayans were still trading shots with the enemy as late as 10:30 at night. See Paunero to Gelly y Obes, Cuartel General en marcha, 15 June 1865, AGN-BA Documentos de la Biblioteca Nacional, legajo 758, doc. 15.535.

121. Osório Tuyuty Oliveira Freitas, *A Invasão de São Borja* (Pôrto Alegre, 1935), p. 78. See also List of Killed and Wounded, San Borjita, 10 June 1865, ANA-SNE 3269.

122. Solano López himself later noted that Duarte's mission was "none other than to move down the right bank of the Uruguay in order to protect Estigarribia's movements [on that flank]. If necessary, Duarte's column could pass over to the left to join the principal forces should they [come under attack] by superior forces." See Solano López to Resquín, Humaitá, 26 Aug. 1865, ANA-SH 343, no. 15.

123. "Recuerdos del Sargento Mayor Justiniano Salvañach," p. 4.

124. Antonio Estigarribia to War Minister, São Borja, 12 June 1865, ANA-SNE 3269. See also Estigarribia to Solano López, São Borja, 14 June 1865, in "Diario Militar de Antonio Estigarribia," *O Diario do Rio Janeiro*, 6 Dec. 1865.

11. *The Battle of the Riachuelo*

1. Memoirs of Capt. Pedro V. Gill, [Asunción, 1888], MHM-CZ carpeta 137, no. 10; Ricardo Scavone Yegros, "Testimonios sobre la guerra del Paraguay contra la Tripla Alianza," *Historia Paraguaya* 37 (1997): 260–62.

2. Washburn, *History of Paraguay*, 2:65–66.

3. Juan B. Gill Aguinaga, *La batalla del Riachuelo* (Asunción, 1968), p. 2; Enique Roibón, *Guerra del Paraguay: Llegada a la escuadra aliada al puerto de Corrientes, Reflexiones respecto al Combate del Riachuelo* (Corrientes, 1910), pp. 9–17.

4. "Combat naval du Riachuelo," *Revue Maritime et Coloniale* 15 (1865): 215.

5. Benigno Riquelme García, "El capitán Pedro Ignacio Meza: Comodoro infortunado de la Marina de otrora," *Historia Paraguaya* 12 (1967–68): 41.

6. Thompson, *War in Paraguay*, p. 72.

7. Barroso's flagship, the *Amazonas*, had run aground only a few weeks earlier, and the admiral was none too keen on this happening again. Patterson, "War of the Triple Alliance," p. 197.

8. Inácio Joaquim da Fonseca, *A Batalha de Riachuelo* (Rio de Janeiro, 1883), p. 10; Miguel Calmon, *Memorias da Campanha do Paraguay* (Pará, 1888), 44–45.

9. Thompson, *War in Paraguay*, p. 73.

10. Report of Antonio Valentino, pilot of the *Parnahyba*, [San Fernando, Paraguay, 21 Apr. 1888], MHM-CZ carpeta 137, no. 3.

11. Brazilian sources commonly portray him as heroic beyond belief. See, for example, Viscount of Ouro Preto, *A Marinha d'Outrora* (Rio de Janeiro, 1981), pp. 95–106; Raul Tavares, *Commemoração da Batalha Naval do Riachuelo* (Rio de Janeiro, 1912); and Francisco Duque Guimarães, "A Batalha Naval do Riachuelo (1865–1965)," *Revista Marítima Brasileira* 50 (Apr.–June 1966): 95–115. U.S. Minister Washburn summed up the opinion of many foreign observers when he wrote that Barroso was "too frightened to give an order. He sat in his cabin, literally paralyzed with fear and unable to speak. When appealed to by a subordinate to give orders to the fleet, he sat transfixed and speechless." *History of Paraguay*, 2:72.

12. See Valentino Report, [1888], MHM carpeta 137, no. 3.

13. Carlos Penna Botto, *Campanhas Navais Sul-Americanas* (Rio de Janeiro, 1940), p. 88.

14. Thompson, *War in Paraguay*, p. 79. The Whitworths were capable of firing a projectile the distance Thompson mentions, but only under good conditions;

given the indifferent training of the Brazilian crews and the confusion of the moment, it seems unlikely that the guns could have achieved near-optimum range. General Robles noted on the nineteenth that his men had been engaged for more than a day recovering such projectiles, some of them as large as "sixteen inches long and five-and-one-half inches wide." See Robles to Solano López, Rincón de Peguajó, 19 June 1865, ANA-SH 447, no. 7.

15. Trujillo, *Gestas guerreras*, p. 13.

16. Testimony of George Gibson [machinist aboard the *Marqués de Olinda*], Humaitá, Aug. 1865, ANA-SH 448, no. 1.

17. Carlos Balthazar de Silveira, *Campanha do Paraguay: A Marinha Brazileira* (Rio de Janeiro, 1900), p. 15.

18. One of the gunners firing onto the Brazilian fleet as it passed near the shore was José Dolores Amarilla of Bruguez's command, who left a valuable though unpublished record of the engagement. See "Fojas de servicios del oficial veterano . . . ," BNA-CJO.

19. Gill Aguinaga, *La batalla del Riachuelo*, p. 7.

20. Thompson, *War in Paraguay*, p. 76.

21. In his report, which contains a vivid account of the ramming, the Italian pilot of the *Parnahyba* claimed credit for this improvised attack, and in truth, every Brazilian success that day was due in part to river pilots, none of whom were Brazilians. See Valentino Report, [1888], MHM-CZ carpeta 137, no. 3. See also Report of Santiago Guidice, aboard the steamer *Cosmos*, 4–5 Apr. 1888, MHM-CZ carpeta 137, no. 2.

22. Two of the their number, João Guilherme Greenhalg and Marcílio Dias, became the posthumous objects of considerable veneration. It was fitting—and certainly useful—that the seaman Dias was a young man of color, and thus well suited to represent the slavish loyalty associated with traditional Brazil, whereas Greenhalg, the son of an immigrant, was cast as a hero of the new Brazil, virile, courageous, forward looking. Between them, they made service to emperor and country seem appropriate to old and new, poor and affluent, black and white. See Levy Scavarda, *Greenhalg no Centenário da Batalha Naval do Riachuelo* (Rio de Janeiro, 1965); Arquivo Nacional, *Dados biographicos inéditos de Marcilio Dias, um dos herois da batalha naval do Riachuelo (11 de junho de 1865)* (Rio de Janeiro, 1929); and Didio Costa, *Marcílio Dias: Marinheiro imperial* (Rio de Janeiro, 1959).

23. Masterman, *Seven Eventful Years in Paraguay*, p. 103.

24. Fonseca, *A Batalha de Riachuelo*, p. 51. Garcindo's account of the battle can be found in his "Parte oficial," written aboard the *Parnahyba*, just below the Riachuelo, 13 June 1865, SDGM Documentos Pessoais do CMG Aurélio Garcindo Fernandes de Sá, no. 0062.

25. Valentino Report, [1888].

26. *The Standard* (Buenos Aires), 24 June 1865. Tales of Paraguayan fanaticism during the battle, whether exaggerated or not, became common fare in the Allied camps. Thompson tells of one Paraguayan marine who, having leapt across the gap between his own small vessel and a Brazilian steamer, "split an officer's head through to the neck with his cutlass when, finding himself alone, he jumped through the opposite porthole and escaped." *War in Paraguay*, pp. 79–80. Most Brazilian writers claim, plausibly enough, that the incident never took place. See Sena Madureira, *Guerra do Paraguai*, p. 16.

27. Antonio Luiz von Hoonholtz to Frederico José von Hoonholtz, gunboat *Araguarí* (off Chimbolar), 22 June 1865, in Antonio Luiz von Hoonholtz, *Memorias do Almirante Barão de Teffé* (Rio de Janeiro, 1910), pp. 37–38. Barroso's official report on the engagement downplays the admiral's own role and, indeed, generally criticizes Brazilian tactics, implying that victory came about mostly through luck. See "Parte detallado del Almirante Barroso," aboard the gunboat *Amazonas* (off the Riachuelo), 12 June 1865, in *La Reforma Pacificador* (Montevideo), 23–24 June 1865.

28. Thompson, *War in Paraguay*, p. 79. In a country that was anxious for heroes, the emperor let it be known that he agreed with Hoonholtz's account. He made Barroso the baron of Amazonas some time later. Several crewmembers of the *Parnahyba*, however, were later court-martialed for cowardice during the battle and doubtlessly felt themselves ill used compared to the supposedly tremulous admiral. See *Defeza do Immediato da Canhoneiro Parnahyba . . . Felippe Fermino Rodrigues Chaves* (Rio de Janeiro, 1867). Lieutenant Garcindo, himself accused of cowardice by those men who had jumped overboard to escape the Paraguayan boarding parties, made no secret of his contempt for their actions and their claims against him: "A coward doesn't trade in death, only in shame," he wrote his wife. See Garcindo de Sá to his wife, aboard gunboat Nitheroy, 11 Oct. 1865, SDGM Documentos Pessois do CMG Aurélio Garcindo de Sá, 077.

29. Report of the widow of Bernardino Guastavino, pilot of the *Amazonas*, [Montevideo, 1889], MHM-CZ carpeta 137, no. 1. Guastavino received six different medals of valor from the Brazilian government. When he died some years later at the age of fifty-four, Tamandaré attempted to organize a national subscription in order to offer a pension to his indigent family; when contributions failed to materialize fast enough, Dom Pedro sent one hundred milheis of his own money. Even so, Guastavino's widow never forgave Admiral Barroso, whom she said claimed credit for all of her husband's deeds in service of the emperor. See Gill Aguinaga, *La batalla del Riachuelo*, pp. 8–9. Curiously, one of the Paraguayan ships, the *Salto Oriental*, also counted Correntino pilots in her crew. See E. R. Cristiano [Enrique Roibón], "El combate del Riachuelo," *La Libertad* (Corrientes), 1–2 July 1908.

30. Report of Capt. Remígio Cabral, second in command of the Paraguayan Squadron at the Riachuelo, [Asunción, 1888], MHM-CZ carpeta 137, no. 11.

31. Masterman, *Seven Eventful Years in Paraguay*, p. 107.

32. "If only the steamers had not retired," wrote the marshal to Berges, "then the thing would have had another name. . . . [Even so,] the day's events have not been less glorious as a result." See Solano López to Berges, Humaitá, 12 June 1865, in Fonseca, *A Batalha de Riachuelo*, p. 70.

33. According to Masterman, as Meza lay dying, the marshal sent to tell him, "for his comfort," that if he survived he would be shot for cowardice. *Seven Eventful Years in Paraguay*, p. 105. In relating this same story, Trujillo quoted Solano López as saying that "if [Meza] had not died of one bullet, he would have died of four." *Gestas guerreras*, p.16.

34. Theotonio Meirelles, *A Marinha de Guerra Brasileira em Paysandú e durante a Campanha do Paraguay: Resumos Históricos* (Rio de Janeiro, 1876), pp. 71–72. George Gibson testified that Robles had been tipsy during the battle but had fought courageously notwithstanding, had taken shots to the left breast and right arm, and was more dead than alive when the Brazilians carried him from the ship's "saloon." Gibson himself managed to hide along the Chaco shoreline during several days of utter misery, after which he and a few comrades fashioned a raft from palm fronds and paddled their way to freedom in Corrientes. Though they were well received by Wenceslao Robles and other Paraguayan officials, when they returned to Humaitá, the marshal's men put each man into irons as the

price of desertion. It was only after much protest from other British engineers working with the government that Solano López relented and released Gibson from a most-undeserved captivity. "Testimony of George Gibson."

35. Masterman, *Seven Eventful Years in Paraguay*, p. 107.

36. "Report of Casualties during the Battle against the Paraguayan Squadron, 11 June 1865," in *Jornal do Commercio*, 7–8 July 1865. See also Battle Report of João Guilherme Bruce, aboard steamer *Amazonas* off Chimbolar, 26 June 1865, IHGB lata 33 ("Documentos: Batalha do Riachuelo").

37. "Combate de Merces," *Diário do Rio de Janeiro*, 6 July 1865. See also Aurélio Garcindo Fernandes de Sa to [Naval Minister], gunboat *Parnahyba* off Chimbolar, 19 June 1865, SDGM Documentos Pessoais do CMG Aurélio Garcindo Fernandes de Sa, no. 0074.

38. Regarding the combat at Mercedes, see Cecilio Echeverría to Emilio Mitre, Rosario, 26 June 1865, MHM-CZ carpeta 149, no. 110; and Alberto Ariel Domínguez, "Empedrado y la división sur del ejército paraguayo," paper read before the Congreso Nacional de Historia Argentina, Buenos Aires, 23 November 1995.

## 12. The March into Rio Grande

1. Joaquim Nabuco, "Aos Bravos de Riachuelo," *Jornal do Commercio*, 30 Sept. 1865. See also "O Que Fazia o Rio a 11 de Junho de 1865," *Revista do Instituto Histórico e Geográfico de São Paulo* 16 (1911): 431–32.

2. In 1876 the imperial government sent the studies for this commemorative painting to Philadelphia as part of Brazil's contribution to the world exposition. See Rangel de S. Paio, *Combate Naval de Riachuelo: Historia e Arte, Quadro de Victor de Meirelles, Notas para os Visitantes da Exposição* (Rio de Janeiro, 1883); *Salão-Riachuelo: Exposição do Quadro Combate Naval do Riachuelo em Benefício do Hospital da Santa Casa de Misericordia da Corte* (Rio de Janeiro, 1883); and F. J. de Santa-Anna Nery, *Salon de 1883: Combat Naval de Riachuelo, Tableau Militaire de Victor Meirelles* (Paris, 1883).

3. *La Nación Argentina*, 21 June 1865.

4. Proclamation of Urquiza, 19 Apr. 1865, in *El Nacional* (Buenos Aires), 21 Apr. 1865.

5. Cárcano, *La guerra del Paraguay*, 1:213–14.

6. Mitre to Urquiza, Concordia, 7 July 1865, in Mitre, *Archivo*, 2:223–25.

7. Paunero to Urquiza, Esquina, 12 June 1865, in Mitre, *Archivo*, 2:183–85.

8. Urquiza to Paunero, Basualdo, 11 June 1865, in Mitre, *Archivo*, 2:179–80.
9. Urquiza to Mitre, Basualdo, 21 June 1865, in Mitre, *Archivo*, 2:192–94.
10. Patterson, "War of the Triple Alliance," pp. 283–84.
11. Gay wrote:

> The desk, the dressers, and the cabinets were broken into with an ax, without bothering to use the keys found in every lock. In an instant all the furniture was tossed about. Books and papers were thrown onto the tables and floor, church ornaments, clothes, and household utensils dispersed in every direction. Meanwhile, having found a keg of sugar, a sack of manioc flour, and another of rice in a nook, the [Paraguayan friar Santiago Esteban Duarte] called in some soldiers who were at the door and told them to take what they could find; then and there they tore into the sacks of sugar and flour and began to eat by the mouthful. All this time the friar and the Colonel [Estigarribia] went carefully through the entire house expecting to find the church silver hidden within.... [I]n the desk they found several [*porteño* and Carioca] newspapers that boasted satirical drawings of the great López. These vile servants of the Paraguayan despot foamed at the mouth when looking at the caricatures of their idol [but they sent all the newspapers on to the marshal anyway]."

See Gay Papers [1865] IHGB lata 404, doc. 27. See also João Pedro Gay, *Invasão Paraguaia na Fronteira Brasileira do Uruguay* (Caxias do Sul, 1980), pp.73–74.

12. Gay, *Invasão Paraguaia*, pp. 74–75. See also "Delgação Consular Italiana em Pôrto Alegre pide Indemnização aos subitos Italianos por prejuizos sofridos na invasão paraguaia em São Borja," in Gay Papers [1865], IHGB lata 404, doc. 28; and "Oficio a José Joaquim Fernandes Torres, encaminhando o pedido de indemnização de Luis Pitaluga, súbito italiano, pelos danos sofridos com a invasão paraguaia," Pôrto Alegre, 20 Feb. 1867, Francisco Inacio Marcondes Homem de Melo Papers, BNRJ.

13. Tasso Fragoso, *História da Guerra entre a Triplice Aliança*, 2: 27. One Paraguayan source, evidently quoting from official accounts, claimed that the number of animals taken approached eight thousand. See Vicente Barrios to Solano López, Asunción, 8 July 1865, Natalicio González Collection, Spencer Library, University of Kansas, Lawrence, MS E222:6, pp.7–10.

14. Oliveira Freitas, *A Invasão de São Borja*, pp. 107–11; Cardozo, *Hace cien años*, 2:92–94; Juan E. O'Leary, "Recuerdos de gloria: 26 de junio de 1865, Mbutuy," in *La Patria* (Asunción), 26 June 1902.

15. The Paraguayans initially reported that he had been killed. See "Diario militar de Antonio Estigarribia," [25 June 1865], in *Diário do Rio de Janeiro*, 10 Dec. 1865; when they learned the truth, Paraguayan authorities agreed that Salvañach's abandonment of the field was justified under the circumstances, and they sent him to rejoin Estigarribia at Itaqui. See Barrios to Solano López, 8 July 1865, pp.15–16.

16. See the "Recuerdos del Sargento Mayor Oriental Justiniano Salavañach"; and *El Semanario*, 15 July 1865. A Brazilian account gives Paraguayan losses at 130 dead, 200 wounded, plus two battle flags, all the horses, and "a great quantity" of arms and munitions captured. See Theotonio Meirelles, *O Exercito Brasileiro na Campanha do Paraguay* (Rio de Janeiro, 1877), pp. 62–63.

17. "They fight like lions," remarked one Brazilian officer in a letter to Canabarro. "It is the most disciplined and orderly force I have seen. They never surrender, and you see how we took only one prisoner. A hundred or more died. Nothing can be done against the Paraguayan Army." See Lt. Col. Zezefredo Alves Coelho de Mesquita to David Canabarro, June 1865, cited in Cardozo, *Hace cien años*, 2:94.

18. Patterson, "War of the Triple Alliance," p. 298. Meirelles's claim of twenty-nine Brazilian dead and eighty wounded almost certainly understates the true figure (see *O Exercito Brazileiro na Campanha do Paraguay*, p. 63), but Estigarribia's assertion that López put five hundred Brazilians "out of action" wildly overstates the number of casualties. See "Diario militar de Antonio Estigarribia," [23 June 1865], in *O Diario do Rio de Janeiro*, 10 Dec. 1865.

19. Nothing is so difficult as to prescribe beforehand to a general the line of conduct he shall pursue during the course of a campaign, yet this is what Solano López constantly did—with predictably bad results. The marshal, who prided himself on his knowledge of military history, always ignored Napoleon's second maxim, which held that plans of campaign may be modified *ad infinitum* according to circumstances—the genius of the general, the character of the troops, and the topography of the theater of action.

20. Cardozo, *Hace cien años*, 2:78.

21. Centurión, *Memorias*, 1:286–88.

22. Decree of Solano López [condemning Robles to death together with two assistants], Paso de la Patria, 6 Jan. 1866, ANA-CRB I-30, 28, 2, no. 11; "Causa seguida al Brigadier Ciudadano Wenceslao Robles," ANA-SH 447, no. 7; "Relación de las causas seguidas al Brigadier Wenceslao Robles," ANA-SH 448, no. 1; "Destitución de Robles," *La Nación Argentina*, 9–10 Aug. 1865. With more hope than common sense, the Brazilians spread the unfounded rumor that Robles had been involved in an attempted coup d'état "together with sixty officers." See *O Diario do Rio de Janeiro*, 10 Feb. 1866.

23. Itaqui suffered less destruction than São Borja, but foreign residents there still found much to complain about to Estigarribia and later to Brazilian authorities. See *La Tribuna* (Montevideo), 22 July 1865; *O Diário do Rio De Janeiro*, 30 July 1865; and *La Nación Argentina*, 5 Aug. 1865.

24. Chaves, *Vida y muerte de López Jordán*, p. 137; Joaquín María Ramiro to Juan A. Gelly y Obes, Paraná, 8 July 1865, Biblioteca Nacional, Buenos Aires, doc. 14.938.

25. See Manuel Navarro to José María Domínguez, Nogoyá, 10 July 1865, AGN-BA; Archivo Urquiza; *El Independiente* (Corrientes), 30 July 1865; and especially Beatríz Bosch, "Los desbandes de Basualdo y Toledo," *Revista de la Universidad de Buenos Aires*, 4:1 (1959): 213–45.

26. Urquiza to Mitre, Puntas de Basualdo, 5 July 1865, in Mitre, *Archivo*, 2:220–21.

27. Thornton to Lord Russell, Buenos Aires, 13 July 1865, PRO-FO 6, no. 256.

28. Urquiza to Mitre, Trocitos, 7 July 1865, in Mitre, *Archivo*, 2:225.

29. Tasso Fragoso, *História da Guerra entre a Triplice Aliança*, 2: 44, cites the figure of sixty-five hundred men, while Cardozo, *Hace cien años*, 2:123, claims nine thousand.

30. *Jornal do Commercio*, 4 Aug. 1865.

31. Cardozo, *Hace cien años*, 2:138.

32. The imperial government commissioned the *Uruguai* in Rio Grande during the early 1850s (and then had the ship reassembled above the Salto Grande rapids) as part of a failed campaign to stimulate the Alto Uruguay trade. See "Tabela das Passagens no Vapor Nacional *Uruguai*, 1862–1864, Alfandega de Uruguaiana," Seção Alfandegas, Arquivo Histórico de Rio Grande do Sul, Pôrto Alegre;

and Espiridião Eloy de Barros Pimentel, *Relatório Apresentado pelo Presidente da Provincia de São Pedro do Rio Grande do Sul* (Pôrto Alegre, 1863), p. 58.

33. Spalding, *A Invasão Paraguaio no Brasil*, p. xxviii.

34. Thompson, *War in Paraguay*, p. 86.

35. Antonio Estigarribia to Solano López, Uruguaiana, 7 Aug. 1865, in "Diario militar de Antonio Estigarribia," *Diario do Rio de Janeiro*, 15 Dec. 1865.

13. *Missteps in the South*

1. As Elizalde remarked: "The plan of the enemy is not a military plan, but a political one. He comes seeking insurrection in Entre Ríos and the Oriental Republic." See Elizalde to Mitre, Buenos Aires, 18 Aug. 1865, in Bartolomé Mitre, *Correspondencia Mitre-Elizalde, 1860–1868*, 2 vols. (Buenos Aires, 1980–90), 1:169–70.

2. One eyewitness, a French immigrant, noted that the Paraguayans asked only for food and otherwise avoided disturbing the peace of the community. See "Declaration of Jean-Baptiste Verdier, *colono* in Paso de los Libres, 24 Apr. 1888," MHM-CZ carpeta 141, no. 15, p. 3.

3. All male citizens from seventeen to fifty years of age (with the exceptions of judges, school principals, postmasters, doctors attached to hospitals, and single sons of widowed mothers) were now required to serve in the National Guard. See "Conscription Law," Buenos Aires, 8 May 1865, in Congreso de la Nación Argentina, *Diario de sesiones de la Camara de Senadores, 1865* (Buenos Aires, 1892), p.37.

4. On the difficulties of organizing the guard in Tucumán, see Gov. José Posse to Marcos Paz, Tucumán, 19 June 1865, in Universidad Nacional de la Plata, Instituto de Historia Argentina, Ricardo Levene, *Archivo del Coronel dr. Marcos Paz*, 7 vols. (La Plata, 1959–66), 4:16–18. The governor of La Rioja for his part reported that towns in his province would become depopulated at the mere mention of conscription, and indeed, after Mitre insisted that the province participate in the draft anyway, troops there murdered their officers and deserted. See Julio Campos to Gelly y Obes, Rioja, 23 June 1865, Biblioteca Nacional, Buenos Aires, doc. 15.358. See also María Haydeé Martin, "La juventud de Buenos Aires en la guerra con el Paraguay," *Trabajos y Comunicaciones* 19 (1969): 145–49.

5. Miguel Angel de Marco, *La guerra del Paraguay* (Buenos Aires, 1995), p. 47.

6. The American consul in Buenos Aires noted that "few volunteers come forward to offer their services to the Government; and in order to form an army of sufficient numbers, the authorities are now pressing into the ranks all the poor and unprotected men of the country. Consular protections are in greatest possible demand." See Helper to Seward, Buenos Aires, 12 Aug. 1865, NARA M70, no. 12.

7. "Speech of the President of the Argentine Republic," Buenos Aires, 1 May 1865, in *British and Foreign State Papers* (1865–66), 56:1170.

8. See *La Nación Argentina*, 9 May 1865.

9. Mitre insisted, for example, that the men encamped at the relatively treeless Concordia receive enough charcoal to keep themselves warm in the winter chill. See Mitre to Gelly y Obes, Concordia, 10 Aug. 1865, in Levene, *Archivo del Coronel dr. Marcos Paz*, 4:90–91.

10. Pomer, *La guerra del Paraguay*, pp. 297–309.

11. Mitre to Gelly y Obes, Concordia, 10 Aug. 1865, in Levene, *Archivo del Coronel dr. Marcos Paz*, 4:90–91.

12. This process of encouraging foreign participation in the Argentine military began in the 1850s, when the confederal government recruited Crimean War veterans from Britain and Sardinia. Though ostensibly brought in as *colonos*, these men were cast as potential "monitors" for the army. See Juan Bautista Alberdi to Juan María Gutiérrez, Paris, 2–7 Sept. 1856, in Biblioteca del Congreso, *Archivo del doctor Juan María Gutiérrez*, 4:235–44. Starting in 1862, the Mitre government went one step further by contracting mercenaries in France and Italy. In charge of these efforts was a personal friend of the president, Col. Hilario Ascasubi (better known in elite circles as a poet than as soldier), who operated mainly from Paris. See Mitre to Ascasubi, Buenos Aires, 6 June 1864 [sic—1865], in Levene, *Archivo del Coronel dr. Marcos Paz*, 4:125; Ascasubi to Marcos Paz, Paris, 6 Sept. 1865, in Levene, *Archivo del Coronel dr. Marcos Paz*, 4:140–44; León Pomer, *Cinco años de guerra civil en la Argentina*, pp.139–41; and Bénédict Gallet de Kulture, *Quelques Mots de Biographie et une Page d'Histoire: Le Colonel Hilario Ascasubi* (Paris, 1865).

13. Ignacio H. Fotheringham, *Vida de un soldado o reminiscencias de las fronteras* (Buenos Aires, 1998), passim.; Harris Gaylord Warren, "Roberto Adolfo Chodasiewicz: A Polish Soldier of Fortune in the Paraguayan War," *The Americas* 41:3 (Jan. 1985): 1–19.

14. As Paz ruefully observed some months later, "Disillusion is frequent when it is a matter of an individual's purse." See Paz to Mitre, Buenos Aires, 27 Dec. 1865, in Mitre, *Archivo*, 5:21.

15. *La Nación Argentina*, 22 Apr. 1865. See also F. J. McLynn, "Consequences for Argentina of the War of Triple Alliance, 1865–1870," *The Americas*, 41:1 (July 1984): 89–90.

16. *La Nación Argentina*, 29 Apr. 1865. *The Times* of London, in its issue of 19 June 1865, noted that wealthy foreigners were not the only ones who saw their prospects improve as a result of the Paraguayan War: "immigrant prosperity [has] not been affected; the war benefits [poor foreign immigrants] . . . because they are exempt from military duty and face an increased demand for labor." For a list of domestic lenders, see *Memoria presentada por el Ministerio de Estado en el Departamento de Hacienda al Congreso Nacional* (Buenos Aires, 1866), p. xic.

17. McLynn, "Consequences for Argentina," pp. 90–91. See also Thornton to Lord Russell, Buenos Aires, 8 June 1865, PRO-FO 6, no. 256. The Rothschild loans to Brazil were the subject of considerable debate. See *Correspondencia entre o Ministerio da Fazenda e a Legação em Londres concernente ao empréstito contraído em 1865* (Rio de Janeiro, 1866).

18. Pomer, *La guerra del Paraguay*, pp. 266–67. For another, less sensationalistic view of the importance of these loans, see Bethell, *The Paraguayan War*, p.25.

19. Mitre himself took up residence in Concordia proper, where he entertained local residents as well as visiting dignitaries. See Antonio P. Castro, "El general Mitre estableció su cuartel general en Concordia," *La Nación* (Buenos Aires), 1 Nov. 1936.

20. Aníbal S. Vásquez, *La reunión del ejército aliado en Concordia* (Paraná, 1937), pp. 13–15.

21. For examples of advertisements for *personeros*, see *El Cosmopolita* (Rosario), 6 Mayo 1865; and *La Esperanza* (Corrientes), 13 Jan. 1866.

22. Burton, *Letters from the Battlefields*, p. 385.

23. *Brazil and River Plate Mail* (London), 7 Sept. 1865.

24. Vázquez, *La reunión del ejército aliado*, p. 17.

25. *The Times* (London), 21 Aug. 1865.

26. Calmon, *Memorias da Campanha*, 1:54–61.

27. See José María Bruguez to Berges, Cuevas, 12 Aug. 1865, ANA-CRB I-30, 10, 5, no. 1.

28. For details on the subsequent battle, see "Parte oficial do Chefe da Esquadra Brasileira [Francisco Manoel Barroso] sobre a passagem de Cuevas," [Rincón de Soto, 13 Aug. 1865], in *Diário do Rio de Janeiro*, 4 Sept. 1865.

29. Garmendia, *Campaña de Corrientes y de Rio Grande*, p. 217.

30. Cited in Robert C. Kirk to William Seward, Buenos Aires, 26 August 1865, NARA FM69, no. 16. For more on the steamer *Guardia Nacional* during this engagement, see Cabral, *Anales de la Marina de guerra*, 1:3–6, 12, 16, 21.

31. Barroso to Tamandaré, aboard the steamer *Amazonas* (off the Rincón de Soto), 13 Aug. 1865, in Laurio H. Destéfani and V. Mario Quartaruolo, *Comodoro Clodomiro Urtubey* (Buenos Aires, 1967), pp. 142–44. See also *Jornal do Commercio*, 4 Sept. 1865; and "Fojas de servicio del coronel don Martín Guerrico," [Buenos Aires, 26 Feb. 1880?], MHM-CZ carpeta 137, no. 9, p. 2.

32. Inácio Joaquim da Fonseca, *O Combate de Coevas em 12 de Agosto de 1865; conferencia* (Rio de Janeiro, 1882), passim. An interesting illustration of the passage can be seen in "O bravo 1. tenente D. Carlos Balthazar de Silveira, comandante do rodízio de proa do vapor *Magé*, na passagem de Cuevas," in *Bazar Volante* (Rio de Janeiro), 8 Apr. 1866.

33. *El Semanario*, 19 August 1865; Carmelo Bruguez to Berges, Asunción, 1 Sept. 1865, ANA-CRB I-30, 10, 23.

34. Tasso Fragoso, *História da Guerra entre a Triplice Aliança*, 2:93; Patterson, "War of the Triple Alliance," p. 237.

35. Again, considerable discrepancies exist concerning the early composition of the Army of the Van, but Beverina's estimate of four thousand seems the most plausible figure. *La guerra del Paraguay*, p. 121. Tasso Fragoso, *História da Guerra entre a Triplice Aliança*, 2:197, provides the figure for the number of guns.

36. "Candido López Notes, [1887?]," in Franco María Ricci, *Candido López: Imagenes de la guerra del Paraguay* (Milan, 1984), p. 114.

37. León de Palleja, *Diário de la campaña de las fuerzas aliadas contra el Paraguay*, 2 vols. (Montevideo, 1960), 1:61–63. Unpublished notes on earlier Palleja editions can be found as part of the papers of the Archivo del Centro de Guerreros del Paraguay (1914–15), MHNM tomo 87.

38. As Duarte revealed in one of his last letters to Asunción, he was well aware of both the size and potential of this force (and of that of both Paunero and Flores as well). See Duarte to War Minister, Restauración, 9 Aug. 1865, ANA-SNE 3269.

39. Flores to Mitre, San Joaquín, 15 Aug. 1865, MHM-CZ carpeta 149, no. 10.

40. "Detalles sobre la batalla del 17," in Antonio H. Conte, *Gobierno provisorio del brigadier general Venancio Flores y la guerra del Paraguay: Recopilación* (Montevideo, 1887), pp. 195–97.

41. Estigarribia to War Minister, Uruguaiana, 7 Aug. 1865, ANA-SNE 3269.

42. Thompson, *War in Paraguay*, p. 88, has Estigarribia questioning his subordinate's courage on this occasion, telling Duarte "that if he was afraid, someone else should be sent to command in his stead." Beverina, *La guerra del Paraguay*, p. 123, doubts that the interchange ever occurred, arguing instead that the colonel's haughty words were invented by the marshal's propagandists after the battle as a way to explain the defeat of Duarte, who fought like a lion, and to discredit Estigarribia, who surrendered rather than fight.

43. A year later the French consul, Auguste Parmentier, went on a hunting trip along the flooded Yataí and discovered the two missing cannons stuck fast in deep mud. Local officials arranged to pull out the two pieces, which they subsequently sent south to Buenos Aires. See "Declaration of Jean-Baptiste Verdier," p. 6. For his part, the marshal expressed shock and anger that Estigarribia had done so little to help his comrade. See Solano López to Francisco Isidoro Resquín, Humaitá, 26 Aug. 1865, ANA-SH 343.

44. Rueda, *Biografía militar del general Don Pedro Duarte*, pp. 14–15.

45. Ironically—since at the time he had no idea the battle had already been lost—the marshal sent word to Duarte that he endorsed his decision to execute the man. See Francisco Bareiro to Duarte, Asunción, 22 Aug. 1865, ANA-SNE 1702. See also Interview with General Pedro Duarte, Asunción, 14 Apr. 1888, MHM-CZ carpeta 129.

46. See Mitre to Elizalde, Concordia, 2 Sept. 1865, in *Correspondencia Mitre-Elizalde*, 1:180.

47. See "Declaration of José Luis Madariaga," [Paso de los Libres?], 24 Apr. 1887, MHM-CZ carpeta 141, no. 14, p. 5, passim.

48. See "Rectificación: Lo que dijo el General Duarte," Casa de la Independencia, Asunción, Colección Carlos Pusineri Scala. See also "Descripción del combate por un testigo ocular [Leopoldo Pellegrini]," in Beverina, *La guerra del Paraguay*, 3:545–46.

49. Thompson, *War in Paraguay*, p. 88. In an 18 August account, Venancio Flo-

res used almost exactly the same words to describe the ferocity of his Paraguayan opponents. See Flores to Mitre, Paso de los Libres, 18 Aug. 1865, in "Battle of the Yatay," clipping, NARA FM69, no. 16; additional reports on the action are found in the MHNM tomo 105. While the gaucho Flores grudgingly respected his enemies, to the sophisticate Mitre their behavior reflected the total "abdication of reason" instilled in Paraguayans since Jesuit times and refined to a terrible degree by Dr. José Gaspar de Francia and the two López. See La Nación Argentina, 24 Aug. 1865.

50. Washburn, History of Paraguay, 2:81-82.

51. Paunero to Marcos Paz, Yataí, 18 Aug. 1865, in Levene, Archivo del Coronel dr. Marcos Paz, 4:104-5.

52. One Correntino veteran who visited the site of the battle some decades later remarked that people crossing the field could still kick up human crania and tibia. See Benjamín Serrano, Guía jeneral de la provincia de Corrientes correspondiente al año 1910 (Corrientes, 1910), pp. 593-95.

53. Interview with Pedro Duarte, Asunción, 14 Apr. 1888; and Juan E. O'Leary, "Recuerdos de gloria: 17 de agosto de 1865, Yataí," in La Patria, 18 Aug. 1902.

54. Diário do Rio de Janeiro, 14 Sept. 1865; and especially Duarte to the Editor, Buenos Aires, 29 Aug. 1865, La Tribuna (Montevideo), 30 Aug. 1865 (in which the major himself acknowledges the good treatment he received). In the same issue, the editor comments that the man's actions were little better than those of an assassin and he clearly deserved no special consideration.

55. Rueda, Biografía militar del general Don Pedro Duarte, pp. 17-19.

56. The Allies routinely denied the fact that Paraguayan prisoners brought into their armies were forced into service. Though the majority of such men were either too frightened or too prudent to desert to the López forces immediately, a good number did so some months later—to the great consternation of their Allied sponsors. The combat record of those who stayed with the Allies was conspicuously undistinguished, especially compared with those Paraguayans who fought with López. Mitre thought the idea of incorporating Paraguayans directly into the Allied ranks was ill conceived and disassociated himself from its execution. Mitre to Paz, Capihiquisé, 4 Oct. 1865, in Mitre, Archivo, 5:330-31.

57. Prisoners from Yataí and Uruguaiana, many with open wounds, were still passing through Buenos Aires as late as October. See El Pueblo (Buenos Aires),

2 Oct. 1865. See also Palleja, *Diário de la campaña*, 2:87–88. A few Paraguayans did manage to escape northward into the forests and thence to Humaitá, where, according to one less-than-reliable Uruguayan source, they received four bullets each for not having died in battle. See Manuel Martínez to José Luis Gómez, Montevideo, 26 Mar. 1916, Archivo del Centro de Guerreros del Paraguay, MHNM tomo 88.

58. "Candido López Notes [1887?]," in Ricci, *Candido López*, p. 116. In fairness to the Allies, they had prepared modern and well-staffed hospitals but were simply overwhelmed with the number of sick and wounded soldiers with whom they had to contend. Regarding the hospital in Concordia, for instance, see *La Nación Argentina*, 4 Aug. 1865.

59. Tasso Fragoso offers the official tally of casualties in *História da guerra entre a Triplice Aliança*, 2:216. Enrique D. Mosquera, *De Yatay a Uruguayana* (Buenos Aires, 1945), p. 25, counters with a more believable Allied loss of 390 dead and 246 wounded, while Thompson, *War in Paraguay*, p. 88, claims flatly—and unconvincingly—that the Allies had 2,500 casualties. In a letter written just after the battle, Flores begged for a steamship to evacuate the many casualties. Flores to Mitre, [Paso de los Libres?], 20 Aug. 1865, MHM-CZ carpeta 150, no. 12.

14. *The Siege of Uruguaiana*

1. In their subsequent denunciations of Estigarribia, both Berges and the marshal cited his abandonment of Duarte "when only one small and insignificant steamship impeded his passage" as proof of a criminal ineptitude. See Solano López to Resquín, Humaitá, 10 Sept. 1865, ANA-SH 343, no. 15; and Berges to Cándido Bareiro, Asunción, 13 Nov. 1865, ANA-CRB I-22, 12, 2, no. 71.

2. Joaquim Nabuco, *Um Estadista do Imperio: Nabuco de Araujo, Sua Vida, Suas opinhões, Sua época*, 2 vols. (Rio de Janeiro and Paris, 1897), 2:293–97.

3. *Jornal do Commercio*, 9 Apr. 1871.

4. Pedro II to Dona Teresa Cristina, Caçapava, 24 Aug. 1865 [as extracted by Roderick J. Barman], Arquivo Grão Pará, Petropolis.

5. Cardozo, *Hace cien años*, 2:176.

6. See Estigarribia to Flores, Uruguaiana, 20 Aug. 1865; and Estigarribia to Canabarro, Uruguaiana, 20 Aug. 1865, in Centurión, *Memorias*, 1:312–13. See also Estigarribia letters, MHM-CGA carpeta 117, no. 2; and MHM-CZ carpeta 150, no. 17.

7. Patterson notes that one steer had provided a day's rations for forty men,

twenty noncommissioned officers, or ten officers. "War of the Triple Alliance," p. 343. When the cattle ran out, the Paraguayans ate anything they could find, including insects; they even drank kerosene. See Seeber, *Cartas sobre la guerra del Paraguay*, p. 55.

8. The transport of men and supplies across the river, and the subsequent siege operation against Uruguaiana, is described by an eyewitness serving with the Uruguayan forces in "Servicios militares del teniente coronel Abdón Giménez y Suárez," Archivo de los Guerreros del Paraguay (1914–15), MHNM tomo 94.

9. Regarding the command issue, see Augusto Fausto de Souza, "A Redempção da Uruguaiana: Historia e considerações acerca do successo de 18 de Setembro de 1865 na provincia do Rio-Grande do Sul," *Revista do Instituto Histórico e Geográphico Brasileiro* 50 (1887): 8–10, passim.

10. In his personal account, the Uruguayan colonel Palleja wrote of daily deaths and sickness from exposure and tainted food. *Diário de la campaña*, 1:98–103.

11. Colonel Thompson was inclined to think this letter the work not of Estigarribia but of his chaplain, Santiago Esteban Duarte. See Estigarribia to Commander in Chief of the Division in Operation on the River Uruguay, to the Representatives of the Vanguard of the Allied Armies, Uruguaiana, 5 Sept. 1865, in Thompson, *War in Paraguay*, p. 91.

12. Thompson, *War in Paraguay*, p. 92. Some doubt exists as to whether one of the Salvañach brothers, Father Duarte, or Estigarribia himself actually composed this note, though it carried the latter's signature alone. See *Diário do Rio de Janeiro*, 17 Sept. 1865.

13. *Anglo-Brazilian Times*, 9 Oct. 1865.

14. Forty years later a minor controversy arose when an Argentine newspaper quoted an aged veteran as saying that the meetings between Mitre and the emperor were full of rancor, with Dom Pedro shouting at the Argentine president, "I give orders, you obey!" See *La Nación* (Buenos Aires), 2–3 Dec. 1903. Brazilian commentators testily denied that such an interchange ever took place. R. J. Barman, in a private communication to the author (8 June 1998), suggested that the veteran had overheard a dispute not between the emperor and Mitre, but between the marquis of Caxias and Brazilian War Minister Angelo Moniz da Silva

Ferraz, whose antipathy for each other was well known. Silva Ferraz physically resembled the emperor, and perhaps this explains the confusion of the veteran, whose story was repeated on many occasions by those who sought to cast the Brazilians in the worst light. See, for instance, Juan E. O'Leary, *Historia de la guerra de la Triple Alianza* (Asunción, 1992), p. 114. The truth of the matter was that, in public, relations between the Argentine and Brazilian heads of state were always proper and friendly. See *Jornal do Commercio*, 22 Dec. 1903. Judging from the reception the emperor gave Mitre on the occasion of the latter's visit to Rio in 1872, the two men certainly appreciated each other's company, spending hour after hour discussing the merits of Dante Alighieri. See Ricardo Saénz Hayes, "Los compañeros de Uruguayana: Mitre y Dom Pedro II," *La Prensa* (Buenos Aires), 4 Jan. 1942; and Pedro Calmon, "Mitre y el Brasil," in *Mitre: Homenaje de la Academia Nacional de Historia en el Cincuentenario de su muerte (1906–1956)* (Buenos Aires, 1957), pp. 65–66.

15. Nabuco, *Um Estadista do Imperio*, 2:268–74.

16. Pedro II to Dona Teresa Cristina, Uruguaiana, 12 Sept. 1865 [as extracted by Roderick J. Barman], Arquivo Grão Pará, Petropolis.

17. André Rebouças, *Diário e Notas Autobiográficas* (Rio de Janeiro, 1938), pp. 92–93 (11 Sept. 1865). Rebouças, perhaps the most influential mulatto in Brazil, later became the chief firebrand in his country's abolitionist movement. See Inácio José Verissimo, ed., *André Rebouças através de sua autobiografia* (Rio de Janeiro, 1939).

18. Ricardo Piccirilli, "El general Mitre y la toma de Uruguayana," *La Nación* (Buenos Aires), 24 Jan. 1943. Several Brazilian parliamentarians chose to regard their government's willingness to allow Mitre to continue in command as a sell out. See *Protesto do Senador Visconde de Jequitinhonha contra a Intervenção dos Alliados no Sitio e Rendição da Cidade de Uruguayana* (Rio de Janeiro, 1865); and *Breve Analyse dos Protesto e Contraprotestos relativamente a Intervenção dos Alliados no sitio e rendição da villa da Uruguayana* (Rio de Janeiro, 1865).

19. See José Segundo Decoud, war diary [1865], MHM-CGA carpeta 117, no. 3.

20. See "Capitulação da Uruguayana," AHI lata 281, maço 1, p.16; "Plan de ataque de Uruguayana," *Jornal do Commercio*, 14 Oct. 1865; and Mitre, *Archivo*, 4:51–58.

21. Cited in Garmendia, *Campaña de Corrientes y de Rio Grande*, p. 386.

22. "Despatch of War Minister Silva Ferraz," Uruguaiana, 18 Sept. 1865, in *The Times* (London), 6 Nov. 1865.

23. Cardozo, *Hace cien años*, 2:226–27. Major López, incidentally, was one of the few Paraguayan officers who managed to escape from Allied captivity after the siege and returned to again serve under the marshal at Encarnación. Regarding the harrowing adventures of López and the other escapees, see Francisco Cárdenas to War Minister, Encarnación, 22 Nov. 1865, ANA-SNE 657.

24. Palleja, *Diario de la campaña*, 1:146–47. See also Paranhos, *A convenção de 20 de Fevereiro*, pp. 248–50; and Flores to Francisco A. Vidal, Uruguaiana, 19 Sept. 1865, Archivo del Centro de Guerreros del Paraguay, MHNM tomo 77.

25. Pedro II to the Countess of Barral, Uruguaiana, 19 Sept. 1865, in Alcindo Sodré, *Abrindo um Cofre* (Rio de Janeiro, 1956), p. 95.

26. See "Cándido López Notes [1887?]," in Ricci, *Cándido López*, p. 120.

27. Palleja, *Diario de la campaña*, 1:154; Helper to Seward, Buenos Aires, 26 Sept. 1865, NARA M70, no. 12.

28. Many such photographs found their way into Seção Iconográfica, BNRJ. A few were reprinted, albeit poorly, in Mario Barreto, *A Campanha Lopezguaya* (Rio de Janeiro, 1928).

29. Conde d'Eu, *Viagem Militar ao Rio Grande do Sul* (São Paulo, 1936), p. 154.

30. In 1874 Duarte returned to the role of military chaplain and fell prisoner once again when revolutionary troops occupied the Paraguayan capital. See Silvio Gaona, *El clero en la guerra del 70* (Asunción, 1961), p. 103.

31. Abdón Arozteguy, *La revolución oriental de 1870* (Buenos Aires, 1889), 1:x–xi, 47, 63–64, passim.

32. *The Times* of London probably understated the fact when it reported on 6 Nov. 1865 that Estigarribia had "been the object of an intense curiosity on the part of the Fluminenses, to whom his magniloquent despatches had made him doubly interesting."

33. See "Petition of Antonio de la Cruz Estigarribia," [Santa Catarina?], 8 Mar. 1869, IHGB lata 483, document 5.

34. "Death Notice of Estigarribia," Dec. 1870, ANA-CRB I-30, 30, 24, no. 1. A full generation would pass before a distant relative, José Félix Estigarribia, brought honor to the family name through his successful leadership of the Paraguayan army during the Chaco War (1932–35).

35. Regarding the British Minister's visit to Uruguaiana, see Thornton to Earl Russell, River Uruguay, 26 Sept. 1865, in Kenneth Bourne and D. Cameron Watts, eds., *British Documents on Foreign Affairs: Reports and Papers from the Foreign Office Confidential Print*, pt. 1, vol. 3, *Brazil, 1845–1894* (New York, 1991), pp. 82–83; *La Nación Argentina*, 28 Sept. 1865; and *Diario do Rio de Janeiro*, 6 Oct. 1865.

36. See Manuel Lagraña to Marcos Paz, Curuzú Cuatiá, 21 Sept. 1865, in Levene, *Archivo del Coronel dr. Marcos Paz*, 4:178–79; and Pedro J. Portal to Paz, Jujuy, 23 Sept. [sic.—Oct.], in Levene, *Archivo del Coronel dr. Marcos Paz*, 4:182. Heroic verse written to celebrate the end of the siege appeared in many Brazilian newspapers. See, for instance, "Himno da Uruguayana," *Jornal do Commercio*, 4 Oct. 1865.

37. See Francisco Bareiro to Estigarribia, Asunción, 12 Aug. 1865, ANA-SNE 1702; and Bareiro to Estigarribia, Asunción, 22 Aug. 1865, ANA-SNE 755. As to personal correspondence, Estigarribia's wife, Ramona Ramírez, wrote him a loving letter from Asunción on 5 August (in which she acknowledges his letter of 20 May); see ANA-SNE 1702.

38. In late October the commandant of Encarnación reported the return of three Paraguayan soldiers who had been sent south on 20 September with dispatches for Estigarribia. The soldiers got as far as Yapeyú, where they learned of the surrender, and retraced their steps as quickly as possible. See Bareiro to Barrios, Asunción, 30 Oct. 1865, ANA-SNE 768. In the end, at least a score of Paraguayans managed to escape their Allied captors at Uruguaiana and made their way to Humaitá with detailed information about the siege. One captain from San Miguel who had served with Estigarribia told López that, with few exceptions, all the Correntinos in the Allied camp were unwilling participants. Like the Entrerrianos, they still favored the marshal's cause. See "Deposition of Cándido Franco," Paso de la Patria, 18 Jan. 1866, ANA-SJC 1797, no. 1.

39. Thompson, *War in Paraguay*, p. 95.

40. Washburn, *History of Paraguay*, 2:87.

41. Martín Urbieta to War Minister, Nioac [on the Mbotety], 27 Oct. 1865, ANA-SNE 664.

42. Washburn, *History of Paraguay*, 2:88.

43. Solano López to Mitre, Humaitá, 20 Nov. 1865, in *El Semanario*, 25 Nov 1865. The Paraguayan troops who escaped insisted that those conscripted into

the Allied armies did so only under duress and would never have voluntarily joined their country's enemies, even given "the high salaries offered them." See Deposition of Pablo Guzmán, Paso de la Patria, 11 Mar. 1866, ANA-SJC 1797, no. 1. The "desertion" of Paraguayan inductees into the Allied forces remained a notable problem for Paunero, Palleja, Flores, and other commanders. See *The Standard* (Buenos Aires), 6 Jan. 1866.

44. *The Standard*, 6 Jan. 1866.

45. Mitre to Solano López, Bella Vista, 25 Nov. 1865, ANA-SH 261, no. 1. Nearly a month later the Brazilian war minister issued a statement that upheld Mitre's previous comments and denied that any prisoner had been enslaved. See "Note of Antonio Moniz da Silva Ferraz," Rio de Janeiro, 22 Dec. 1865, in *Diário do Rio de Janeiro*, 25 Dec. 1865.

46. One staff officer noted that "Paraguayan generals had no independent authority, and could do nothing without receiving orders from López, who directed the war from Humaitá; these orders, sent either by steamship or mounted messenger [inevitably] took many days in arriving." See "Datos tomados en Buenos Aires el 6 de enero de 1888 . . . del coronel paraguayo [Juan Crisóstomo] Centurión," MHM-CZ carpeta 118, nos. 1–2.

47. The imperial war minister held the old gaucho responsible for the initial Paraguayan penetration into Rio Grande do Sul, but the proposed investigation of his actions was cancelled due to the insistence of the marquis de Caxias; Canabarro was still greatly shaken by the accusations and died a saddened man in Apr. 1867. See "Ordem do Dia, no. 21," [3 Oct. 1865], in *Ordens do Dia do Segundo Corpo* (Rio de Janeiro, 1877), pp. 83–97; *Jornal do Commercio*, 13 Dec. 1865; and Nabuco, *Um Estadista do Imperio*, 2:216–25.

15. *Retreat to Paso de la Patria*

1. "Fuerza efectiva," Campamento Empedrado, 15 July 1865, ANA-SH 344, no. 2. This document lists 16,692 soldiers in seven infantry battalions, seven cavalry regiments, and an artillery unit.

2. *La Nación Argentina*, 19 July 1865.

3. Severo Ortíz, *Apuntes biográficos*, pp. 175–77.

4. Nicanor Cáceres to Manuel Hornos, Campamento Muchas Islas, 25 July 1865, 4:30 P.M., in *La Nación Argentina*, 2 Aug. 1865. Cáceres, in fact, had only just

received a note from Manuel Lagraña in which the governor reminded him to hold back from fighting in order to coordinate his activities with the rest of the Allied armies. See Lagraña to Cáceres, Monte Punta, 17 July 1865, in Levene, *Archivo del Coronel dr. Marcos Paz*, 4:40–41.

5. Many of these individuals spent the next four years in detention, though not always degradation. In a letter of March 1867, U.S. Minister Washburn noted that he had recently passed to the Allied camp, where he received some thirty pounds sterling from Modesto J. Méndez of Corrientes; this money was to be sent on to Méndez's fellow *provincianas* in Paraguay, this being the latest of several shipments of cash. Washburn to Victoria Bar de Ceballos, Asunción, [10?] Mar. 1867, WNL. Washburn later acknowledged receipt of a package of clothing and two ounces of gold sent him by Roberto Guy Billinghurst under flag of truce and meant for the benefit of Correntino women being held at San Juan Bautista. The Paraguayan counterparts of these women found no comparable source of succor. See Washburn to Roberto Billinghurst, Asunción, 28 Sept. 1867, WNL. For one particularly poignant case, that of Carmen M. de Pavón, see anonymous, "Romance of the War," *The Standard*, 25 Sept. 1869.

6. Francisco Ferreira to Desiderio Onieva, Bella Vista, 24 July 1865, in *La Nación Argentina*, 4 Aug. 1865; D. Fernández to Cecilio Echavarría, Goya, 29 July 1865, Biblioteca Nacional, Buenos Aires, doc. 15.050; Francisco Sánchez to Commandant of Encarnación, Asunción, 2 Aug. 1866, ANA-SNE 1730. It is noteworthy that the *Junta Gubernativa*, not the Paraguayan command, initiated the arrest of certain individuals "for political crimes" and mandated their transfer to Humaitá. See *Junta Gubernativa* to Berges, Corrientes, 19 Aug. 1865, ANA-CRB I-30, 23, 158.

7. Augusto Luis Scotto, "La invasión paraguaya en Bella Vista," *El Liberal* (Corrientes), 20–26 Jan. 1925. In the early 1980s, Correntino historian Federico Palma, then in his seventies, recalled his grandmother saying that the Paraguayan soldiers she saw in 1865 "were always hungry, and always anxious to eat *our* food." Interview with the author, Corrientes, Apr. 1982.

8. See Interrogation of Italians Pietro Morello, Stefano Livieres, and Gaetano Trabucco, Bella Vista, 13 Sept. 1865, ANA-SNE 1696; B. Ferreyra to *Junta Gubernativa*, Corrientes, 11 Oct. 1865, ANA-CRB I-30, 26, 49; and *La Tribuna* (Buenos Aires), 27 Oct. 1865.

9. Louis Jaeger Papers (1865–66), ANA-CRB I-30, 4, 53, nos. 1–13; Washburn to Berges, Asunción, 6 Mar. 1867, WNL. For a similar case involving a British trader in Bella Vista, see John Gannon to Edward Thornton, Buenos Aires, 31 Aug. 1865, ANA-CRB I-30, 24, 9.

10. Decree of the *Junta Gubernativa*, Corrientes, 12 July 1865, in *La Nación Argentina*, 2 Aug. 1865.

11. Cardozo, *Hace cien años*, 2:203.

12. Cardozo, *Hace cien años*, 2:148. The Allies had known of Paraguayan weaknesses in horses for some time but were unable to exploit the situation. See Nicanor Cáceres to Paunero, Ambrosio, 14 July 1865, in Levene, *Archivo del Coronel dr. Marcos Paz*, 4:32–33.

13. Lagraña to Juan J. Méndez, Goya, 6 Aug. 1865; and Lagraña to Marcos Paz, Goya, 6 Aug. 1865, both in *La Nación Argentina*, 15 Aug. 1865. The Paraguayans later maintained that Correntino irregulars were responsible for the sacrilege. See *El Semanario* (Asunción), 28 Oct. 1865.

14. Solano López to Berges, Humaitá, 12 July 1865, ANA-CRB I-30, 12, 12, no. 14.

15. Berges to *Junta Gubernativa*, Corrientes, 8 July 1865, ANA-CRB I-30, 6, 54; *Junta Gubernativa* to Berges, Corrientes, 10 July 1865, ANA-CRB I-30, 23, 163, no. 2. Regarding Lovera, see Solano López to *Junta Gubernativa*, Humaitá, 9 Aug. 1865, ANA-CRB I-30, 21, 141; and Lovera to *Junta Gubernativa*, Racitos, 6 Aug. 1865, ANA-CRB I-30, 21, 143.

16. General Paunero resented the fact that a civilian like Lagraña should have access to military supplies and advised that logistical support be taken out of his hands. See Paunero to Paz, Batel, 20 July 1865, in Levene, *Archivo del Coronel dr. Marcos Paz*, 4:51.

17. In one letter to Marcos Paz, Paunero denounced Lagraña for being interested solely in local elections, due to be held later that year, and of therefore ignoring the national cause during war. See Paunero to Paz, Monte Punta, Río Corrientes, 18 July 1865, in Levene, *Archivo del Coronel dr. Marcos Paz*, 4:42–44.

18. Lagraña to Paz, Goya, 28 July 1865, Levene, *Archivo del Coronel dr. Marcos Paz*, 4:66–67.

19. Paunero to Paz, Paso de Ayala, 12 Aug. 1865, Levene, *Archivo del Coronel dr. Marcos Paz*, 4:94–95.

20. Paunero to Paz, Yataí, 18 Aug. 1865, in Levene, *Archivo del Coronel dr. Marcos Paz*, 4:94–95.

21. Mitre to Lagraña, Concordia, 25 July 1865, in *Documentos que justifica la lejitimidad de la deuda contra el gobierno de la nación por suministros hechos al ejército de vanguardia nacional en Corrientes en armas contra el del Paraguay* (Buenos Aires, 1870), p. 7.

22. Lagraña to Paunero, Goya, 17 Aug. 1865, in *Documentos que justifica la lejitimidad de la deuda contra el Gobierno de la nación*, p. 8.

23. Dispatch of Luis Antonio González, commandant of San Cosme, Costa de Corrientes, 16 Aug. 1865, ANA-CRB I-30, 23, 165. See also Ortíz, *Apuntes biográficos*, p. 177, passim.

24. "Proyecto de combate a librarse la provincia de Corrientes," Headquarters [Corrientes?], 29 Sept. 1865, Natalicio González Collection, Spencer Library, University of Kansas, Lawrence, MS E222.6, pp. 38-40.

25. See *Junta Gubernativa* to Solano López, Corrientes, 26 Sept. 1865, in *Diario do Rio de Janeiro*, 22 Nov. 1865; and Solano López to Resquín, Humaitá, 25 Sept. 1865, ANA-SH 343, no. 15; Lovera continued to follow the orders of the *junta* over the next month, then abruptly defected to the Allies. He led a small, anti-Paraguayan rebellion in the department of San Luis before Resquín's abandonment of the province. See Berges to Resquín, Corrientes, 15 Oct. 1865, ANA-SNE 1696; and *La Tribuna* (Buenos Aires), 8 Nov. 1865.

26. Garmendia, *Campaña de Corrientes y de Rio Grande*, pp. 416-19. See also Resquín to Berges, Quevedo, 17 Sept. 1865, ANA-CRB I-30, 9, 103; and Eugenio E. Moreno to Resquín, Saladas, 22 Sept. 1865, ANA-CRB I-30, 22, 144. There had already been several skirmishes in which small numbers of Correntinos had fought each other, and on one such occasion, Nicanor Cáceres reported capturing twenty-four Paraguayans and one Correntino "volunteer"; the latter man he executed by shooting him in the back, *sic semper traditoribus*. See Cáceres to Lagraña, Paso de Flores, 17 June 1865, AGPC-CO 1865, legajo 209.

27. Solano López to Berges, Humaitá, 25 Sept. 1865, ANA-SNE 668. For his part, Lagraña expressed satisfaction that turncoats were receiving their just desserts and that their defeat "would serve as a lesson to those who might wish to join the units of the barbarian invaders." See Lagraña to Paz, Curuzú Cuatiá, 25 Sept. 1865, in Levene, *Archivo del Coronel dr. Marcos Paz*, 4:187-88.

28. "Order of the Day," Humaitá, 6 Oct. 1865, in *La Nación Argentina*, 1 Nov. 1865; and Carlos Sarmiento, *Estudio crítico sobre la guerra del Paraguay* (Buenos Aires, 1890), pp. 18-23. Resquín's memoirs are nearly silent on his retreat from

Corrientes, an operation in which he held command from beginning to end. Almost certainly he regretted the whole ill-conceived episode. *Datos históricos,* pp. 27-28.

29. *Anglo-Brazilian Times,* 7 Nov. 1865.

30. The war correspondent of *The Standard* noted in the issue of 3 Jan. 1866 that the situation for provisions was remarkably bad: "It must be borne in mind that we have already an unprecedented number of soldiers and sailors to feed, . . . to say nothing of the constant additions that are being made to their numbers, whose sole and only food is beef. The inhabitants of the devastated districts have also to draw their subsistence from the four departments that were not invaded. As for grain or any of the plants that contribute to the nourishment of man, in peaceable times a scanty supply was all that was ever thought of; this year nothing, absolutely nothing, has been planted."

31. A. J. Kennedy, *La Plata, Brazil, and Paraguay during the Present War* (London, 1869), pp. 36-37.

32. See Rafael Gallino to Sinforoso Cáceres, Corrientes, 26 Aug. 1865, ANA-CRB I-30, 23, 244, nos. 1, 2.

33. See *Junta Gubernativa* to Berges, Corrientes, 1 Oct. 1865, ANA-CRB I-30, 23, 161.

34. *El Independiente,* 3 Aug. 1865. The life of Artigas was perhaps not the best analogy since soldiers loyal to the Oriental chieftain had behaved with supreme contempt for local elites during their occupation of 1814-20. Berges rewarded *El Independiente*'s loyalty by frequent (and unpublicized) contributions of money. See telegram, Berges to Solano López, Corrientes, 29 Apr. 1865, in Rebaudi, *La declaración de guerra,* p. 14.

35. Petition of Citizens of Corrientes, Corrientes, 7 Aug. 1865, ANA-CRB I-30, 21, 144; Derqui to Solano López, n.p., 7 Aug. 1865, ANA-CRB I-30, 21, 68; Esteban Palacios, Tomás Bedoya, and Venancio Ferreyra to Berges, Corrientes, 12 Aug. 1865, ANA-CRB I-30, 22, 26.

36. Solano López to Berges, Humaitá, 14 Aug. 1865, ANA-CRB I-30, 12, 13, no. 2. Díaz Colodrero later served as government minister in the Federal regime of Evaristo López.

37. Cited in Cardozo, *Hace cien años,* 2:241. See also Enrique Castro to Mitre, Trinchera, 3 Oct. 1865, MHM-CZ carpeta 150, no. 25.

38. Cardozo, *Hace cien años,* 2:241.

39. Enrique Castro to Bautista Castro, Apipé, 14 Nov. 1865, in José Luciano Martínez, *Vida militar de los generales Enrique y Gregorio Castro* (Montevideo, 1901), p. 205. *The Times* of London, in its issue of 4 Dec. 1865, places the figure of animals captured at an unlikely thirty thousand.

40. Instructions of War Minister Angelo Moniz da Silva Ferraz to the Baron of Pôrto Alegre, Uruguaiana, 30 Sept. 1865, IHGB Coleção Marqués de Paranaguá, lata 312, pasta 4.

41. See, for example, Elizalde to Mitre, Buenos Aires, 13 Dec. 1865, in *Correspondencia Mitre-Elizalde*, 1:295.

42. Cited in *La Tribuna* (Buenos Aires), 30 Nov. 1865.

43. McLynn, "General Urquiza and the Politics of Argentina," pp. 212–15. A few of the deserters were hunted down and forcibly reintegrated into the army, but they numbered only one hundred men out of six thousand. See Pedro Caminos to Government Minister, Victoria, 13 Nov. 1865, AGN-BA Archivo Urquiza; and Bosch, "Los desbandes de Basualdo y Toledo," pp. 229–75.

44. Mitre to Urquiza, Costa del Arroyo Batel, 15 Nov. 1865, in Mitre, *Archivo*, 5:373–74.

45. Regarding the capture and court-martial of one such deserter, see Antonio Hernández to José Joaquín Sagastume, Diamante, 13 Nov. 1865, AGN-BA Archivo Urquiza, 7-14-4-12.

46. One soldier travelling with the Uruguayan contingent noted the inadequacy of provisions, remarking on 7 December that "General Flores bought up today all the fruit of an orange grove, but when it arrived, hardly one orange fell to each man." See *The Standard*, 6 Jan. 1866.

47. Mitre established a *Comisión sanitaria* that, in the wake of Yataí, found itself with much more work than it could manage. At Mercedes, doctors attempted to set up an infirmary capable of treating five hundred patients but ended up turning to hospitals in Goya, which could be supplied by the river. See Miguel Angel de Marco, "La sanidad militar argentina en la guerra con el Paraguay (1865–1870)," *Revista Histórica* (Buenos Aires) 4:9 (1981): 65–67.

48. See Rafael Machaín to Ildefonso Machaín, Corrales, 25 Oct. 1865, ANA-CRB I-30, 20, 13, no. 6.

49. See Aristófanes Caimi et al. to Berges, Corrientes, 20 Oct. 1865, ANA-CRB I-30, 23, 62.

50. See Berges to Caimi, Corrientes, 21 Oct. 1865, ANA-CRB I-30, 26, 71.

51. Cited in *El Paraná* (Paraná), 15 Nov. 1865; and *La Nación Argentina*, 8 Nov. 1865.

52. Cáceres to Mitre, Capilla del Señor, 24 Oct. 1865, in Levene, *Archivo del Coronel dr. Marcos Paz*, 4:248. The new Correntino administration found it convenient to forget the pro-Paraguayan sympathies of several hundred townspeople, and even those initially accused were ultimately "rehabilitated." See José Miguel Guastavino, *Incidente del doctor don Ramón Contreras en 1865, sospechado de traición a la patria* (Buenos Aires, 1882). The only exceptions to this were Victor Silvero, who survived the war but not the animosity of his neighbors, and Sinforoso Cáceres, who saw his considerable properties (including a large *saladero*—"Las Palmitas") seized by government order. Dardo Ramírez Braschi, personal communication with the author, Corrientes, 18 May 1999.

53. *Documentos que justifica la lejitimidad de la deuda contra el Gobierno de la nación*, passim.

54. Thompson, *War in Paraguay*, p. 96; *Jornal do Commercio* (Rio de Janeiro), 5 Dec. 1865.

55. Washburn, *History of Paraguay*, 2:91.

56. Colonel Thompson later noted that these cattle "almost all died, either of fatigue, want of food, or from eating a poisonous herb . . . which abounds in the south of Paraguay, and which only animals reared in the district have the instinct to avoid. The number of dead animals on the ground about Itapirú and a few leagues beyond it was terrible during some months." See *War in Paraguay*, p. 97; and Thomas Whigham, "Cattle Raising in the Argentine Northeast, c. 1750–1870," *Journal of Latin American Studies* 20:3 (1988): 313–35.

57. F. J. McLynn, "The Corrientes Crisis of 1868," *North Dakota Quarterly* 47:3 (1979): 45–58; Dardo Ramírez Braschi, *Evaristo López: Un gobernador federal* (Corrientes, 1997). Cáceres, it is true, left on several occasions for the Paraguayan front in 1866–67 but never strayed for long from his interests in Corrientes. As for the political movement that he symbolized, though it grew less evident as the years went by, it never completely disappeared from Correntino consciousness. At the beginning of the 1880s, for instance, a British visitor to La Cruz noted: "We were crossed on the square by a number of mounted Gauchos—of a truculent type almost extinct in more civilized Buenos Aires—armed with lances, and booted and spurred, and all adorned with sashes and ribbons round their hats of the

bright crimson which, in the days of Rosas, was the badge of Federalism." See Horace Rumbold, *The Great Silver River: Notes of a Residence in Buenos Aires in 1880 and 1881* (London, 1890), p. 220.

58. See "Cándido López notes on the November passage" in Ricci, *Cándido López*, p. 122. See also Palleja, *Diário de la campaña*, 1:261-69, which gives a detailed description of the transit of all these rivers.

59. See Mitre to Paz, Costa de Batel, 16 Nov. 1865, in Levene, *Archivo del Coronel dr. Marcos Paz*, 7:82-84.

60. Flores to Mitre, Caaguazú, 13 Nov. 1865, MHM-CZ carpeta 150, no. 30.

61. Enrique Castro to Bautista Castro, Apipé, 14 Nov. 1865, in Martínez, *Vida militar de los generales Enrique y Gregorio Castro*, p. 205.

62. Beverina, *La guerra del Paraguay*, 5:26.

63. Palleja, *Diario de la campaña*, 1:202-3. The Allied soldiers rarely saw women in the first months of the Corrientes campaign. As Dominguito Sarmiento, son of the future president, remarked, women were "unknown luxuries.... [W]henever a ship passes by with some [on board], the soldiers gather along the shoreline to stare at such a curiosity." See Domingo Fidel Sarmiento to Domingo Faustino Sarmiento, Concordia, 29 July 1865, in Domingo Fidel Sarmiento, *Correspondencia de Dominguito Sarmiento en la guerra del Paraguay* (Buenos Aires, 1975), p. 25.

64. Such displays were a visible expression of status—the higher the status, the more elaborate the uniform—and there were many generals who needed to be outshone. Paunero, for instance, made sure to wear an immaculate white uniform with sky-blue tunic and broad-rimmed felt hat. See "Cándido López notes," [Nov. 1865], in Ricci, *Cándido López*, p. 124. Most modern generals claim to dress for *where* they are, regardless of status, while most of their predecessors of the 1800s clearly dressed for *what* they were, regardless of place. Regarding dress uniforms of the Paraguayan conflict, see de Marco, *La guerra del Paraguay*, pp. 135-39; Horacio J. Guido, "Triple Alianza: la otra guerra. Uniformes, alimentos, y sanidad," *Todo es Historia* 288 (1991): 86-88; Roberto C. Da Motta Teixeira, "Brazilian and Paraguayan Uniforms of the 1865-70 War," *Tradition* 69 (1978): 12-14; and Julio María Luqui-Lagleyze, *Los cuerpos militares en la historia argentina: Organización y uniformes* (Buenos Aires, 1995), pp. 195-216.

65. Kolinski, *Indendence or Death*, p. 110. In an unusual—though not altogether

unexpected — coincidence, in 1982, Correntino coffeehouses rechristened their sandwiches after the "Exocet" missile, which the Argentine Air Force had used to sink the HMS *Sheffield* during the Falklands conflict.

66. See Wilhelm Hoffman to [wife?], aboard steamer *Araguarí* [at port of Corrientes], 28 Dec. 1865, in Carlos Ficker, "Deutsche Kolonisten im Paraguay-Krieg," *Studen-Jahrbuch* (São Paulo) 14 (1966): 29–31.

# Index

Abreu, Joaquim Francisco de, 318
Acá carayá, 187
Acá verá, 187
Aguapey River, 100, 104, 403
Aguiar, José María, 284
Aguirre, Anastasio de la Cruz, 148–49, 153, 154, 156, 160, 223, 233–35
Alberdi, Juan Bautista, 121, 238, 239, 268
Albuquerque, 194, 204
Alegrete, 334, 345, 348
Alén, Paulino, 339, 340
Alexander VI, 78
algoroba, 6
Alonso, Mariano Roque, 65, 104
Alsina, Adolfo, 135, 171, 253
Alsina, Fermín, 283
Alsina, Valentín, 125, 127, 128
Amapolas, 149, 154
*Amazonas*, 312, 317, 318, 319, 321–22, 362
Amazon River, 14, 58

*Anhambaí*, 193, 200, 203–5, 207–10
Antonina, Baron of, 88
Apa River, 82, 84, 85, 90, 194, 199, 280, 418
Apipé Island, 4, 98, 101, 113, 413, 436 n.15
Apipé Falls, 98
Aquidabán River, 83, 84
*Araguarí*, 312, 319, 322–23, 326
Aráoz de Lamadrid, Gregorio, 353
Argentina, xv, 111–12, 117, 247, 249, 360, 419; disunity in, 341; politics of, 50–56, 71–73, 119, 143–44, 154, 220, 375; reactions to war, 251, 275–76, 353; relations with Uruguay, 171–74
Argentine-Brazilian rivalries, 49–50, 57, 232, 341, 414, 434
arms purchases, 168–69, 178, 182, 187, 239, 313, 354
Armstrong, Thomas, 355
Arrecife, 88

Artigas, José Gervasio, 34–35, 39, 41, 64, 118, 401, 404, 427 n.11, 500 n.34
Asunción, 4, 7, 13, 19, 38, 82, 86, 104, 112, 115, 139, 140, 149, 157–58, 161, 180, 181, 184, 187, 189, 196, 197, 215, 240, 247, 250, 253, 259, 282, 316, 325, 385; commerce of, 20
Atajó Island, 108
Atajó River, 111
atrocities, 205–7, 370–71, 453 n.23, 454–55 n.29, 458 n.21
Austerlitz, xii
Austria, 107, 249
Autonomist Party, 171, 265, 267
Ayacucho, 48
Ayala, Cipriano, 253, 262

bacharéis, 146, 167
Bahia, 15, 147, 218, 381
Bahia Negra, 90, 110, 114, 280
Baker, Josiah, 208
balance of power, 141–42, 157, 178–79, 248–49, 411
Bank of London, 355
Barral, countess of (Luisa Margarida de Barros), 384
Barreiro, Candido, 241, 242, 246
Barreto, João Propício Menna, 303
Barrios, Vicente, 161, 177, 196, 197, 199, 202, 205, 340, 341, 399
Barroso, Francisco Manoel, 288, 291, 294, 308; at the Riachuelo, 312–28, 340, 360–64, 419, 479 n.28
Basualdo, 331, 341–44, 353, 405, 421

Batallón Florida, 175
Batel River, 392, 412
Batería de San Pedro, 288, 289, 296, 303
*Beberibe*, 312, 323, 327
Belgrano, Manuel, 21, 25, 30–31, 32, 107, 404
Bella Vista, 88, 260, 262, 274, 281, 283–86, 316, 327, 361, 391–93
*Belmonte*, 312, 317, 318, 319, 326
Bentham, Jeremy, 55, 59, 147
Berges, José, 88, 117, 141, 142, 156, 157, 158, 223, 240, 241, 242, 252, 266, 267, 268, 269, 283, 290, 294–96, 392, 399, 408
Bermejo River, 109, 111, 114–15, 280
Berro, Bernardo, 132, 133, 134, 139, 148
Bismarck, Otto von, 221
blacks, 34, 36, 311, 379
Blanco Party, 119, 120, 123, 124, 134, 137, 141, 142, 145, 147, 150–53, 158, 174, 213, 219, 224, 232, 233, 235, 236, 239, 243, 248, 276, 297, 334, 345, 375, 418
Blanco River, 82, 87, 90
Blyth Brothers, 178, 180–81
Bolivia, 112, 113, 204, 227, 280, 422, 453 n.22
Bonaparte, Napoleon, 22, 24, 32, 40, 41, 43, 186, 483 n.19
bonds, 355
Bonpland, Aimé, 100, 110
Borbón (Olimpo), 82, 84, 110, 111

Bordeaux, 113
border conflicts, xvii, 77–117, 159, 165, 431 n.1
Bosco, Ferdinando, 303
Bourbons, 16–20, 39
Box, Pelham Horton, 231
Brazil, xv–xvi, 40, 41–47, 69, 70, 117, 119, 144–51, 158, 166–71, 219, 224–27, 240, 247, 251, 276, 294, 298, 341, 360, 379, 386, 416, 419
Brilhante, 88, 211
Brown, William, 174
Bruce, João Guilherme, 288, 290
Bruguez, José María, 309, 314, 318, 323, 326, 327, 360, 361, 363, 393, 399, 409
Buenos Aires, xv, 9, 15, 18, 19, 21–22, 27, 28, 32, 34, 40, 48, 50–56, 60, 69, 72, 85, 86, 90, 96–98, 100, 109, 116, 117, 121, 122, 125, 127, 128, 132, 134, 137, 139, 140, 149, 151, 154, 159, 190, 219, 221, 223, 241, 243, 244, 245, 247, 254, 257, 264, 266, 272, 292, 298, 308, 312, 328, 353–54, 356, 360, 397, 401, 412, 414, 416
Burton, Richard, 359

Caacatí, 271
Caazapava, 301
cabildo, 20, 29, 30, 54, 96, 97
cabildo abierto, 25
Cabral, Remígio, 160, 308, 323, 324
Caçapava, 376

Cáceres, Nicanor, 263, 274, 276, 282–88, 291, 293, 295–96, 330, 332, 392, 393, 396, 399, 407, 410–12, 415, 420, 421, 466 n.14
Cáceres, Sinforoso, 267, 268, 402
cachaça, 328
Cádiz, 24, 30
Caldwell, João Frederico, 345, 347, 348
caliber, 447 n.5
camalotes, 80
Caminos, José Rufo, 222–23, 273
Caminos, Luis, 241, 242
Campos, Federico Carneiro de, 160
Canabarro, David, 303–4, 344–45, 347–48, 374, 377, 390
Candelaria, 94, 98, 101
Carlos IV, 22, 24
Carlota Joaquina, Princess, 25, 30
Carlyle, Thomas, 36
Carreras, Antonio de las, 156, 233, 235
Carriego, Evaristo, 220, 222, 470–71 n.53
Caseros, 121, 222, 274, 348, 358
castas, 34
Catamarca, 132
caudillismo, 35, 41, 46, 51, 53, 55, 72, 73, 130, 132, 138, 142, 144, 145, 269, 341, 343, 375, 378, 400, 406
Caxias, duke of (Luis Alves de Lima e Silva), 62–63, 167, 190, 237, 429 n.8
Centurión, Juan Crisóstomo, 250, 451 n.10

Cepeda, 125–26, 128, 130, 132
Cerritos. *See* Atajó Island
Cerro León, 150, 160, 184, 186, 241
changadores, 83
Charlone, Gianbattista, 289, 359, 365
chatas, 309, 311, 313, 315, 324, 325
chiggers, 407
Chile, 33, 50, 53, 71, 227
Chincha Islands, 227
Chodaesiewicz, Roberto, 355
Christie Affair, 152, 386, 444 n.69
Cisplatine War, 49–50, 57, 174, 218, 358
"civilization versus barbarism," 28, 48, 131, 277, 354, 389, 469 n.35
Clausewitz, Carl von, xii
Coimbra, University of, 59
Colonia de Sacramento, 15, 49, 425 n.6
Colorado Party, 119–20, 123, 124, 134, 135, 138, 144, 152, 153, 158, 174, 224, 234, 276
comercio libre, 19
Comuneros Revolt, 95
Concepción, 29, 82, 84, 110, 161, 184, 189, 194, 199
Concordia, 282, 332, 337, 341, 344, 351, 354, 356–60, 364, 371, 375, 381, 396, 420
Congreve rockets, 182, 196, 361
conscription, 169, 170–71, 172, 183–84, 387, 485 n.4
Conservative Party (Brazil), 59, 147, 237

consulado, 23
contributions, 218–19, 353–55
Córdoba, 23, 28, 34, 37, 72, 129, 130, 254
Corrientes (province), 34, 53–55, 69, 72, 88, 97, 101, 104, 105, 115, 176, 185, 219, 220, 240, 242, 244, 247, 248, 251, 254, 257–307, 308, 331, 332, 388, 389, 391–92, 394, 396–415, 421
Corrientes River, 332, 412
Corrientes (town), 4, 19, 29, 90, 271, 401–2, 418
Corumbá, 90, 160, 194, 196, 203, 204–7, 212, 216, 230, 284
Council of State, 59, 147, 169
Council of the Indies, 13
Coxim, 212, 455 n.38
Crimean War, 168, 204, 289
Cuevas, 327, 360–64, 393
Cuiabá (town), 90, 193, 194, 203, 204, 208, 209, 212
Cuiabá River, 194, 196
Curuzú Cuatiá, 412, 466 n.14

Danube River, 86
Davis, Jefferson, 136
Demarcation of 1493, 136
Derqui, Santiago, 129–31, 269, 402
Desbarrancado River, 212
Dessalines, Jean-Jacques, 57
Diamante, 406
Díaz, José Eduvigis, 340, 410
Díaz Colodrero, Wenceslao, 402

discipline, military, 171, 183, 186, 198, 354, 469 n.35
Dolores, 371
Donato Swamp, 334–37
Doria, William, 138
Dorrego, Manuel, 51
*Dotterell*, 294
Dourados, 88, 193, 194, 199, 210
Duarte, Pedro, 230, 241, 282, 296–302, 307, 331–32, 341, 343–46, 351, 356, 365–68, 370, 372–75, 387, 389, 394, 403, 420
Duarte, Father (Santiago Esteban), 384–85, 482 n.11

Egusquiza, Félix, 241, 245, 246, 253
*El Bonaerense*, 272
*El Correo*, 183
El Independiente, 267, 401, 408
elites: Argentine, xv, 18–19, 21; Brazilian, xv–xvi, 43–47, 56–57, 71, 73, 167, 190; Correntino, 258, 265; Paraguayan, 20, 64; Riograndense, 145
Elizalde, Rufino de, 134–39, 143, 151–55, 222, 232, 240–42, 251, 252, 275, 278, 280, 329, 355
*El Litoral*, 220
*El Nacional*, 272
*El Republicano*, 405
*El Semanario*, 87, 247, 250
*El Uruguay*, 222
Empedrado, 271, 274, 283, 284, 294, 326, 340, 407

Encarnación (Itapúa), 107, 112, 375, 403, 404
encomienda, 8, 11, 13
Ensenadas, 414
Entre Ríos, 17, 34, 53, 61, 98, 105, 107, 120–21, 125, 138, 150, 172, 220–23, 236, 240, 266, 267, 273, 282, 297, 329, 330, 331, 341, 345, 389, 400, 405
*Esmeralda*, 253, 262
Espínola, Jose de, 29–30
Estigarribia, Antonio de la Cruz, 298–307, 331–32, 337–78, 342–45, 347, 351, 352, 364–65, 367, 372, 374–75, 377, 379, 382, 383, 387, 389, 390, 398, 402, 403, 419
Estrella, 88
Eu, count d', 376, 381
Extraordinary Congress, 246–50

*Facundo*, 277
Farragut, David, 311
Farroupilha, 60–63, 70, 102–3, 105, 145–46, 237, 303, 348, 358
fazendas, 171
Fêcho-dos-Morros, 85–87, 185, 240, 417, 433 n.19
Federalists, 28, 51–56, 127, 131, 265–66, 267, 295, 401–2, 411, 412, 502–3 n.57
Feijó, Diogo Antonio, 57
Feio River, 211
Fernandes Lima, Antonio de, 335–36, 337, 338

*Index* 509

Fernando VII, 24, 25, 31
Ferré, Pedro, 54–55, 101, 102, 104, 105
Flores, Venancio, 119–20, 123, 134–39, 143, 144, 145, 148, 150–51, 153, 219, 220, 222, 223, 224, 226, 232, 236, 238, 301, 359, 364, 365, 366, 369, 370, 371, 375, 377, 381, 382, 386, 412, 414, 420, 439–40 n.2
*Flying Fish*, 260
Formoso, Fort, 110, 115
Fotheringham, Ignacio, 355
France, 22, 56, 69, 71, 113, 115, 173, 178, 227, 233, 235–36, 249, 333
Francia, José Gaspar de, 36–49, 54, 63, 68, 83, 84, 98, 101, 102, 104, 126, 175, 298, 417
Franciscans, 11–13
Franz Joseph (emperor), 107
Fray Bentos, 136, 139
free navigation, 85, 89–92, 115, 122, 132–33
Furtado, Francisco José, 237

galleta, 173
Garibaldi, Giuseppe, 62, 289, 303
gauchos, 17, 34, 72, 144, 172, 330, 357, 358
Gauna, Teodoro, 268, 299, 402, 408
Gay, Pedro (father), 333–34, 385, 482 n.11
Gelly y Obes, Juan Andrés, 174, 273, 381, 413
*General Artigas*, 137
gente de cor, 170

Gill, Pedro V., 308, 313
Góes e Vasconcellos, Zacharias, 146–47, 217
Goiás, 192, 213
"Golden Combs," 463–64 n.73
gold rush, 80–81
Gomensoro, José Segundino de, 318, 323
Gómez, Leandro, 224–28, 383, 458 n.21
Goya, 260, 281, 285, 293, 331, 338, 339, 360, 393, 397, 398, 400, 411
Gran Chaco, 8, 82, 84, 93, 109–15, 179, 185, 262, 264, 270, 280, 311, 361
Grant, Ulysses S., 340
Great Britain, 22, 42, 56, 63, 71, 97, 100, 115, 121, 124, 152, 178, 182, 233, 235–36, 249, 316, 386, 471–72 n.64
Guaicurú Indians, 8–11, 81, 83, 84, 90–91, 109
Guairá, 12–13
*Gualeguay*, 260, 261, 262
guampas, 199
Guaporé River, 14
Guaraní Indians, 6–17, 93, 95
Guaraní language, 10, 33, 37, 67, 97, 144, 198, 259, 268, 283, 311, 382, 430 n.10
Guaraní War, 16
Guarda Nacional (Brazil), 166, 169, 190, 193, 217
*Guardia Nacional*, 174, 327, 362

Guardia Nacional (Argentina), 172, 273, 353
Guastavino, Bernardino, 322, 480 n.29
Guayakí Indians, 8
Guido, Tomás, 112
Gustavus Adolphus, 186

Haiti, 42, 44
Halperín Donghi, Tulio, 52
Hernández, José, 353–54, 445 n.83
Herrera, Juan José de, 136, 137, 140, 141, 143, 150, 152, 155
Herreros, Andrés, 194, 196, 197, 207–10, 451 n.10
Hispano-Guaraní society, 9–11, 17, 40, 63–64, 67, 70
Hoonholtz, Antonio Luiz de (baron of Teffé), 322
Hormiguero, 101, 107, 300
horses, 103, 166, 271
Humaitá, 111, 115, 185–87, 245, 253, 259, 262, 281, 288, 292, 308, 309, 316, 320, 373, 386, 392, 395, 399, 407, 409, 411, 415, 419, 421
Humboldt, Alexander von, 100

Ibarra, Juan Felipe, 36
*Independencia*, 177
Indians, 6–13, 16–17, 51, 63, 78, 98, 109, 114, 166, 193, 207
Irala, Domingo Martínez de, 9–10, 424 n.3
isolationism, 27, 40–41
Itaguí del Apa, 88
*Itajai*, 312, 362

Italy, 22, 138, 154, 160, 173, 212, 233, 402, 461 n.40
Itamaraty Palace, 237
Itapirú, Fort, 260, 409
Itapúa (Encarnación), 83, 104
Itaquí, 305, 334, 342, 348
Itatí, 104, 295, 414
Iturburu, Fernando, 339, 382
Ituzaingó, 49, 236
*Ivai*, 312, 362

*Jacobina*, 205
*Jaurú*, 200, 203
*Jejuí*, 183, 253, 314, 315, 322, 325
*Jequitinhonha*, 312, 317, 318, 319, 320, 326
Jesuits, 11–13, 15, 93–95
Jesús, 229
João VI, 24, 42–43, 168
Jomini, Antoine Henri, 177, 297, 353
jopoí, 64
*Jornal do Commercio*, 328
Junta Gubernativa, 268, 283, 290, 295, 329, 392, 393, 395, 399, 401, 402, 408, 468 n.32

kambá, 321
Kennesaw Mountain, xii
kurepí, 251

La Cruz, 101, 103, 341, 344, 351
Lagraña, Manuel Y., 254, 259, 262, 265, 271, 273, 274, 275, 393, 396–98, 400, 408, 411, 413
Laguna Brava, 414

Lahitte guns, 168
Lamartine, Alphonse de, 249–50, 463 n.71
Lamas, Andrés, 135, 137, 138–39, 141, 152, 159, 232, 233, 234, 239, 441 n.27
Lambaré, 7
Lanús, Anacarsis, 239, 245, 313, 354
lapacho, 6
Lapido, Octavio, 134, 140, 141, 142, 143
La Rioja, 53, 132, 139
Latin, xvi
*La Tribuna*, 272
Laurelty, 311
Lavarden, Manuel José de, 21, 23
Legión Militar, 289
Legión Paraguaya, 277, 339
Leonidas, 379
Lettsom, W. G., 234, 279
Liberal Party (Argentina), 122, 124, 171, 253, 265, 268, 271, 396, 411, 412
Liberal Party (Brazil), 59, 146, 376, 428 n.12
Liga Federal, 34
Lima, 15
Lingua geral, 11
Liniers, Santiago de, 23, 25
Lisbon, 43, 44
Litoral, 24, 27, 28, 34, 35, 40, 50, 51, 96, 104, 110, 144, 191, 219, 227, 228, 246, 252, 268, 276, 281, 329, 343, 372, 405, 418

loans, 241–42, 355
Locke, John, 55
looting, 205–7, 215, 284–85, 307, 333–34, 347, 384, 394–95, 453 n.23, 482 n.11, 497 n.7
López, Basilio, 67
López, Benigno, 67, 177, 180
López, Carlos Antonio, 65–70, 84–87, 89, 91, 92, 104, 106, 108, 112, 115, 121, 126, 140, 141, 175, 176, 183, 185, 280, 417
López, Estanislao, 36
López, Evaristo, 411
López, Francisco Solano, 116, 135, 156–57, 176–81, 184, 228–29, 237, 239, 242, 244–50, 259, 265, 269, 281, 300, 328, 339, 341, 354, 358, 385, 387–91, 401–2, 411, 416, 422; Allied characterizations of, 272; chosen as president, 434–35 n.37; as commander, 106, 292–97, 309–11, 315, 324–25, 348, 373, 394, 418–19; desires to be emperor, 448 n.19; early career of, 68–69, 89–92, 112, 159–60, 441 n.27; and Mato Grosso campaign, 192, 194, 196, 198, 203–6, 214, 216; as mediator in Argentina, 126–28; and support for Blancos, 139–42, 149–51, 219, 220, 221, 273; and the Triple Alliance Treaty, 275–78
Lopezguayo, 314
López Jordán, Ricardo, 228, 267, 330, 342, 343, 445 n.83

López, José del Rosario, 306, 334–37, 367, 384
López, Venancio, 67
Lovera, Francisco, 396, 398–99, 408
Lynch, Elisa Alicia, 174–80, 181, 206, 215, 267

Madariaga, Joaquín, 105
Madariaga, Juan, 365, 378, 396
Mamelucos, 10–11, 14
Mangels, T. H., 271
Maranhão, 61
Marion, Francis, 466 n.14
Mármol, José, 149
*Marqués de Olinda*, 90, 160, 161, 196, 215, 260, 261, 314, 319, 321, 323, 325
Martínez, José de la Cruz, 289–93
Masons, 123
*Martín Fierro*, 353–54
Martín García, 144, 172
Masterman, George F., 181–82, 216, 325
Mato Grosso, 4, 14, 78–92, 109, 116, 160, 165, 192–216, 217, 219, 229, 230, 248, 259, 260, 270–71, 297, 340, 387, 417, 418, 422
matriculados, 97
Mauá, baron of (Irineu Evangelista de Sousa), 123, 355, 445 n.83
Mazorca, 53
Mbaracayú Hills, 6, 81, 288
mbareté, 40
Mbayá Indians, 8, 81, 86, 212

Mbotety River, 194, 196, 212
mburuvichá, 9–10, 12
Mbutuí, battle of, 332–38, 384, 420
Mbutuí Falls, 332–33, 338
Mbutuí River, 334
*Mearim*, 312–15, 319
medical, 181, 184, 356, 372, 414, 500 n.47
Men of 1837, 55–56, 71–73, 137, 428–29 n.3
Mercedes, 158, 326–27, 360, 399, 407, 412–13
mercenaries, 173, 289, 486 n.12
Metternich, Clemens Wenzel Lothar von, 236
Métis, 424–25 n.4
Mexico, 227
Meza, Pedro Ignacio, 196, 197, 202, 205, 209, 260, 264, 308, 311, 313–16, 319, 320, 323, 324, 333, 338, 419
militarism, 167, 179, 191
military, 29, 33, 34, 65, 67, 69, 70, 91, 106, 121, 128, 165–91
Minas Gerais, 4, 14, 47, 61
Minie balls, 187, 319, 336
Miranda, 88, 193, 196, 199, 210, 212, 214
Misiones, 34, 38, 41, 83, 93–108, 116, 159, 165, 228, 238, 240, 242, 248, 298, 299, 336, 404, 418
Mississippi River, 86
Mitre, Bartolomé, 134, 219, 221, 227–28, 232–34, 268, 341, 343, 369, 371–72, 396, 402, 405–7, 417–18,

Mitre, Bartolomé (*continued*)
420–22; and Argentine neutrality, 238–39, 243–44, 246, 251–52; at Cepeda, 125; early career of, 119, 123, 138, 140, 142–44; as military organizer, 171–72, 329–32, 352–54, 356–57, 359, 360, 364, 375, 415, 439 n.1; at Pavón, 129–32; reactions to war, 272–73, 275, 277–79, 283; support for Flores, 149, 151, 154, 159; at Uruguaiana, 378, 381–82, 386, 388, 390, 412, 492–93 n.14

Mitre, Emilio, 130, 174, 414
Mocobí Indians, 109, 110
moderating power, 45
monarchism, xvi, 27–28, 43–47, 57–59, 266
Monteclaro, 110
Montesquieu, baron of (Charles Louis de Secondat), 42
Montevideo, 18, 23, 33, 34, 48, 53, 71, 90, 119, 121, 124, 134, 138, 143, 147, 154, 159, 219, 230, 232, 234, 235, 267, 279, 356, 360, 398, 418
Moreno, Manuel, 21, 25
Morice, George Francis, 181, 189
Murature, José, 226, 362
music, 272, 381, 382

Nabuco, Joaquim, 328
*Nación Argentina*, 135, 248, 251
Nambí-í, 311, 320, 346

Napoleon III, 113, 137, 178
nationalism: Argentine, xv, 97, 137, 173–74, 221–22, 259, 265, 353–54; Brazilian, xv–x, 45–47, 49, 58, 60–63, 70–71, 218; Paraguayan, xiv–xvi, 25, 36, 62–63, 69, 77–78, 97, 184, 411, 417; Uruguayan, 118–19
nationhood, xiv–xvi, 25, 36, 62–63, 66, 70, 72–73, 97–98, 165–66, 425–26 n.1, 430–31 n.15
navy, 170, 174, 181, 189, 207–10, 308–27, 360–64
needle rifles, 168, 187
Negro River, 134
Nelson, Horatio, 23, 317
ñembotavy, 64
Netto, Antonio de Souza, 145–46, 155, 236
neutrality, 217–254
Nioaque, 88, 193, 211
Nogoyá, 342, 344, 406
Nova Coimbra, 82, 86, 176, 193, 194, 199–203, 214
Nueva Burdeos, 112, 179

Observación del Apa, 88
Observación de Quien Vive, 88
Olimpo (Borbón), 82, 84, 184
Olinda, Marquis of (Pedro de Araujo Lima), 376
ombú, 5
Orange, Fort, 110, 115
Oribe, Manuel, 119, 121, 145, 148

Osório, Gen. Manoel Luiz (baron of Herval), 145, 169, 190, 358–59, 414, 421

Pact of Union, 127
Páez, José de Jesús, 283
Pai Luma, 11
Paiva, Simeón, 282, 297, 299, 301, 302, 330, 341, 351, 365, 390, 396, 420
Paixhan guns, 168
Palacios, Bishop (Manuel Antonio), 199
Palleja, León de, 175, 369, 384
*Pampero*, 174
Pantanal, 6, 80
*Paraguarí*, 156, 260, 261, 314, 319–21, 325
Paraguay, xiv–xv, 8–13, 24, 27, 29–32, 35, 36–41, 63–70, 77–117, 127, 128, 139, 156, 179–91, 219, 228, 243, 379, 391, 416, 417
Paraguay River, 4–5, 81, 82, 84, 85, 88, 192, 209, 280, 411
Paranapanema River, 12
Paraná River, 4–5, 13, 14, 30, 31, 41, 91, 94, 104, 121, 129, 160, 243, 245, 252, 259, 260, 261, 273, 274, 280, 282, 291, 295, 307, 308, 312, 318, 329, 351, 391, 400, 404, 412, 414
Paraná (town), 112, 219, 223
Paranhos, José María da Silva, 89, 231–32, 234–38, 251
Paris, 179–80

*Parnahyba*, 312, 315, 319, 320–22
Paso de Hormiguero, 305
Paso de la Patria, 264, 282, 285, 289, 291, 404, 408, 409, 415, 421
Paso de los Garruchos, 300, 302, 304, 380
Patagonia, 71, 72, 77, 172
Paunero, Wenceslao, 130, 273, 281, 285–87, 292–93, 330, 352, 365, 369–71, 381, 394, 396, 414, 419, 420
Pavón, 116, 128–32, 138, 171, 172, 221, 258, 269, 343
Payaguá Indians, 5, 81
payé apojhá, 37
Paysandú, 143, 128–32, 138, 171, 172, 221, 258, 269, 303, 311, 330, 383, 418
Paz, José María, 53, 105–6
Paz, Marcos, 355, 397
Peace of Amiens, 23
Pearl Harbor, 251
Pedro I, 43–45, 49, 50, 56
Pedro II, 50, 71, 139, 146, 147, 167, 169, 357, 422, 429 n.5; and Brazilian nationalism, 135, 137; reactions to the war, 217, 328; in Rio Grande do Sul, 376–78, 380–83, 492–93 n.14; youth and early career, 56–60
Peixoto, Floriano, 346, 352, 365, 390, 420
Pellichi, Pedro María (father), 116
Peña Hermosa, 110
Peñaloza, Angel Vicente, 132, 143
peninsulares, 30, 31, 39

Index 515

Peru, 9, 33
Peter the Great, 41
Petropolis, 149
Pilar, 83, 104, 185
Pilcomayo River, 11–12, 280
Pindapoi Creek, 229, 230, 282, 296, 298, 299, 302, 356, 375
Pinto, Joaquím José, 317, 320, 323, 326
*Pirabebé*, 288, 314, 323, 399, 409, 410
Piratini, 61
Pirayú, 150
Plata River, 86, 144, 231, 232
Pombal, marquis of (Sebastião José de Carvalho e Mello), 16
Poncho Verde Creek, 290, 294
porteños, 18, 23, 25, 27, 33, 34, 36, 39, 40, 50, 52, 72, 96, 97, 98, 110, 121, 123, 126, 129, 130, 137, 172, 189, 264, 269, 272, 330, 342, 353, 354, 356, 396, 405, 416
Pôrto Alegre, 60, 61, 376
Portocarreiro, Hermenegildo de Albuquerque, 176, 200, 203, 204
Portugal, 14–17, 32, 41–44, 59, 78, 80, 95
Posadas, 99
Potosí, 17, 22
praça, 169
Praia Vermelha, 167, 446 n.4
press: Argentine, 135, 219, 221, 238, 243–44, 247, 248, 272, 292, 328, 337, 387, 463 n.68; Brazilian, 146, 328, 387; European, 359; Paraguayan, 159, 206, 247

protectionism, 54, 55
provincianos, xv, 27, 28, 33, 37, 50, 53, 56, 330, 353, 395, 406
provisions, 395, 500 n.30
Prussia, 168, 249
Pujol, Juan, 114, 258, 265
Puntas del Rosario, 153

Quinteros, 124, 134, 220, 371

railroads, 68, 129, 181, 185, 355
Ramírez, Francisco, 100
Ramos, José Rodrigues, 305
ranching, 16, 51, 52, 53, 60–62, 84, 145, 371, 394–95
*Ranger*, 208, 241, 288
Rawson, Guillermo, 254
Raynal, Guillaume Thomas Francois, 42
Rebouças, André, 381
recruitment, 169, 217–18
Reguera, Isidoro, 299, 341, 351, 365, 390, 396, 403, 420
republicanism, 405
Resquín, Francisco Isidoro, 383, 386; in Corrientes, 338–41, 391–92, 395, 400, 407, 409, 411, 420–21; in Mato Grosso, 194, 210, 212, 214
Restauración (Paso de los Libres), 351, 365–67, 396
revisionism, 182, 246, 251, 252
Revolution of the Lances, 385
Riachuelo, battle of, 308–27, 332–33, 339, 352, 360, 364, 395, 419

Riachuelo Creek, 274, 285, 288, 399, 407
Ribeiro, Antonio João, 211–12, 455 n.34
Ribera, Lázaro de, 29
Rinconada del Apa, 88
Rincón de Peguajó, 295
Rincón de Soto, 286, 287, 361, 363, 398, 400
*Río Apa*, 183
Rio de Janeiro, xv, 24, 42, 60, 87, 89, 91, 102, 107, 112, 135, 146, 149, 151, 215, 237, 276, 359, 384, 385, 416, 421
Rio Grande do Sul, xv, 34, 46, 49, 60–63, 70, 85, 102–3, 120, 139, 144, 213, 223, 236, 297, 303, 304, 306, 334, 345, 347, 358–59, 364, 389, 390, 418, 420
Rio Pardo, 61
Rivadavia, Bernardino, 51, 56
Rivera, José Fructuoso, 119
Robespierre, Maximilien François Marie, 40
Robles, Ezequiel, 324, 339
Robles, Wenceslao, 324, 332, 418; in Corrientes, 264, 268–71, 274, 281–84, 286–87, 292–94, 308, 329, 330; downfall of, 315–16, 338–39, 391; execution of, 341
Rolón, José María, 258–59
Roosevelt, Franklin Delano, 251
Rosa, Francisco Octaviano de Almeida, 276, 277, 281
Rosario, 65, 131, 253, 273, 281, 354

Rosas, Juan Manuel de, 61, 86, 112, 137, 148, 167, 171, 191, 348, 417; and Corrientes, 103, 104–6, 266; downfall of, 119, 120–21, 171; early career of, 50–53; politics of, 54–56, 71–73
Rothschild family, 355
Rua Ouvidor, 237
Ruiz de Montoya, Antonio, 12–13
Russia, 249, 453 n.71

Sa, Aurelio Garcindo Fernandes de, 320–22
Saint-Simon, count of (Claude Henri de Rouvroy), 55
Saint Thomas, 11
saladeros, 71
Salta, 110, 116, 353
Salto, 282
*Salto*, 136–38, 245
*Salto Guairá*, 183, 214
*Salto Oriental*, 312, 314, 320, 323, 325
Salvañach, Justiniano, 334, 336, 375, 384–85
San Carlos, 88, 100, 229, 403
San Cosme, 271, 295, 414
San José, 99, 220, 222, 344
San Juan, 129
San Juan Bautista, 229
San Lorenzo River, 283
San Luis, 221
San Martin, José de, 32–33, 36, 50, 112, 269
San Miguel, 413
San Nicolás, 125

San Roque, 295
Santa Ana, 100
Santa Catarina, 58, 61, 62
Santa Elena, 110
Santa Fe, 19, 34, 53, 109, 121, 130, 172
Santa Lucía, 393, 394
Santa Lucía River, 286, 292, 412
Santa María, 299–301
Santa Rosa Falls, 5
Santa Teresa, 404
Santiago del Estero, 36
Santo Corazón, 204
Santo Tomás, 100
Santo Tomé, 100, 101, 103, 108, 300–304, 307, 331, 403
São Borja, 98, 100, 102, 104, 107, 112, 115, 297, 300–307, 333–34, 380, 385, 390, 420
São Francisco River, 14
São Gabriel, 380
São Laurenço River, 194, 207
São Mateus, 334
São Paulo, xv, 10, 13, 47, 58, 60, 81, 192, 212, 218, 421
Saraiva, José Antonio, 147–48, 150, 154, 155, 231, 251, 279
Sarmiento, Domingo Faustino, 277
Saxe-Coburg and Gotha, Auguste, 381
Say, Jean-Baptiste, 42
Schmidl, Ulrich, 7
Sebastopol, 185
Sepé Tiarajú, 16
Seival, 145
Sherman, William Tecumseh, xiii

Silvero, Victor, 266–67, 268, 295, 395, 402
slavery, 39, 42, 45, 47, 59, 102, 456 n.46
Smith, Adam, 42
smuggling, 17–18
Soler, Adolfo, 160
Soria, Paul, 110
Sousa, Manoel Marquez de, count of Pôrto Alegre, 348, 378, 381–83
Spaniards, 6–11, 13, 14, 23, 30, 31, 34, 48, 78, 80, 78, 80, 94, 95, 227
Stewart, William, 181
Suarez, Gregorio "Goyo," 226, 383, 459 n.25
substitutes, 447–48 n.12
Sumter, Fort, 272
Syracuse, xiii

*Tacuarí*, 160, 180, 189, 260, 309, 312, 314, 315, 319, 320, 323, 325
Tacuarí River, 212
Tailor's Conspiracy, 22
Talavera, Natalício, 250
Tamandaré, baron of (João Marques Lisboa), 155, 224; in the Banda Oriental, 231, 233–37; at Concordia, 358; naval strategy of, 245, 360, 363–64, 400, 421; at Uruguaiana, 378, 379, 382
Tejedor, Carlos, 127
tereré, 199
Tevegó, 84
Thermopylae, 379

Thompson, George, 181, 183, 187, 188, 202, 205–6, 214, 215, 227, 247, 313, 316, 322, 347, 370, 409
Thornton, Edward, 143, 152–54, 156, 231, 253, 278–80, 386, 444 n.70
Thucydides, xiii
Toba Indians, 109, 110, 391
Toledo, 406, 421
Touro Passo Creek, 345, 346
trade, 10, 25, 28, 42, 54, 63, 68, 82–83, 96, 101–2, 108, 115, 128–29, 133
Trafalgar, 23, 317
Tranquera de Loreto, 99, 107, 404
Treaty of Madrid, 15, 81, 95
Treaty of San Ildefonso, 81, 86
Treaty of San Nicolás, 122
Treaty of Tordesillas, 14
Tres Bocas, 245, 329, 409–11
Trinchera de los Paraguayos, 99, 107, 229, 403
Triple Alliance Treaty, 276–81, 353, 359
Tucumán, 33, 72, 94, 353
Tupac Amarú, 22, 426 n.3
Turner's carbines, 187
Turkey, 249

Unitarians, 49–54, 105, 119, 128, 353
United States, 53, 69, 89, 115, 246, 393, 434 n.29
Upper Peru, 32
Urbieta, Martín, 199, 210–11
Urquiza, Justo José de, 154, 281, 365, 382, 400, 411, 417–18; and Basualdo mutiny, 341–43; breaks with Rosas, 115, 120–23; at Concordia, 359; in Corrientes, 105–6; politics of, 138, 159, 219–23, 227, 268–69, 329–30, 445 n.83; and relations with Buenos Aires, 125–32, 171; and relations with Paraguay, 240, 243, 244, 246, 274–76, 292, 296; and Toledo mutiny, 405–6
*Uruguai*, 346, 378
Uruguaiana, 345, 347–48, 351–52, 374–91, 398–99, 402, 406, 412, 420
Uruguay (Banda Oriental), xvi–xvii, 14, 23, 33, 34, 44, 48–49, 55, 61, 70, 72, 89, 117, 118–161, 165, 174–75, 191, 213, 221, 223–37, 248, 275–76, 281, 293, 297, 345, 352, 356, 416, 420
Uruguay River, 15, 94, 96, 98, 102, 135, 137, 281, 300, 337, 377, 389, 390, 400, 402
urundey, 6
*uti posseditis*, 15, 81

Vázquez Sagastume, José, 149, 156, 158, 160, 417
*Veinticinco de Mayo*, 260–62
Velasco, Bernardo de, 29, 30, 96
*Veloce*, 294
Vianna de Lima, Cesar, 156–57
Viceroyalty of La Plata, 18, 96
Vicksburg, 340
Victor Emmanuel II, 137
Victoria (town), 342, 344, 406

Victoria, Queen, 137, 386
victoria regis, 392
Victorica, Julio, 243, 274
Vilagran Cabrita, João Carlos de, 176, 412
Villa de la Unión, 236
Villa de Melo, 159
*Villa de Salto*, 158, 225
Villa Franca, 184
Villalba, Tomás, 235–36
Villa Maria, baron of, 215
Villamayor, 124
Villa Occidental, 113, 280
Villa Oliva, 184
Villarrica, 13
Vitoria, Francisco de, 39
vizcacha, 3
Voltaire (François-Marie Arouet), 93
Voluntários da Patria, 217–18, 304, 404

War of the Oranges, 82
Washburn, Charles Ames, 91, 241, 267, 370, 393, 410
Watts, John, 308–9
Wellington, duke of (Arthur Wellesley), 24
Whitworth guns, 168, 170, 315, 477–78 n.14
Whytehead, John William K., 181
Wisner von Morgenstern, Franz, 107–8, 176–77, 183, 309–10
Witton's rifles, 187

Xarayes, Lake, 80–81

Yabebirí, 104
Yacyretá Island, 113
Yaguareté Corã, 295, 398, 413
Yancey, Benjamin C., 124
Yapeyú, 101
Yataí, battle of, 364–73, 377, 387–88, 393, 406, 420
Yataí Creek, 366–67
*Yberá*, 308, 325
Yberá Marshlands, 99, 100
yby marane'y, 10
Ybycui Iron-Works, 183, 216
Ybycui River, 344–45
Yegros, Fulgencio, 38
yerbales, 20, 84
yerba mate, 20, 39, 68, 95, 101, 144, 257, 316, 377
Yguasú Falls, 108
*Yguatemí*, 312, 323
Ygurey, 189, 260, 261, 314, 323, 325
Ygurey River, 81
Ypané River, 82, 84, 85
*Ypiranga*, 312, 323, 362–63
Ypora, 183, 196, 207–8, 260–61, 314–15, 323, 409–10
Yuty, 229

Zuavos Baianos, 346

In *Studies in War, Society, and the Military*

*Military Migration and State Formation*
The British Military Community in Seventeenth-Century Sweden
Mary Elizabeth Ailes

*The Rise of the National Guard*
The Evolution of the American Militia, 1865–1920
Jerry Cooper

*In the Service of the Emperor*
Essays on the Imperial Japanese Army
Edward J. Drea

*You Can't Fight Tanks with Bayonets*
Psychological Warfare against the Japanese Army in the Southwest Pacific
Allison B. Gilmore

*Civilians in the Path of War*
Edited by Mark Grimsley and Clifford J. Rogers

*Soldiers as Citizens*
Former German Officers in the Federal Republic of Germany, 1945–1955
Jay Lockenour

*The Grand Illusion*
The Prussianization of the Chilean Army
William F. Sater and Holger H. Herwig

*The Paraguayan War*
Volume One: Causes and Early Conduct
Thomas L. Whigham

*The Challenge of Change*
Military Institutions and New Realities, 1918–1941
Edited by Harold R. Winton and David R. Mets

www.ingramcontent.com/pod-product-compliance
Lightning Source LLC
Chambersburg PA
CBHW071352300426
44114CB00016B/2039